GeoJournal Library

Volume 131

Series Editor
Barney Warf, University of Kansas, Lawrence, KS, USA

Now accepted for Scopus! Content available on the Scopus site in summer 2021.

This book series serves as a broad platform for scientific contributions in the field of human geography and its sub-disciplines. The series, which published its first volume in 1984, explores theoretical approaches and new perspectives and developments in the field of human geography.

Some topics covered by the series are:

– Economic Geography
– Political Geography
– Cultural Geography
– Historical Geography
– Health and Medical Geography
– Environmental Geography and Sustainable Development
– Legal Geography and Policy
– Urban Geography
– Geospatial Techniques
– Urban Planning and Development
– Land Use Modelling
– and much more

Publishing a broad portfolio of peer-reviewed scientific books, GeoJournal Library invites book proposals for research monographs and edited volumes. The books can range from theoretical approaches to empirical studies and contain interdisciplinary approaches, case studies and best-practice assessments. The books in the series provide a great resource to academics, researchers and practitioners in the field.

Oana-Ramona Ilovan • Iwona Markuszewska
Editors

Preserving and Constructing Place Attachment in Europe

Foreword by Tiziana Banini

 Springer

Editors
Oana-Ramona Ilovan ⓘ
Faculty of Geography and Territorial
Identities and Development Research Centre
Babeş-Bolyai University
Cluj-Napoca, Romania

Iwona Markuszewska ⓘ
Faculty of Geographical and Geological
Sciences
Adam Mickiewicz University in Poznań
Poznan, Poland

This research was supported by the National Science Centre (Narodowe Centrum Nauki) in Poland (2019/33/N/HS4/01670); Narodowym Centrum NaukiNarodowym Centrum Nauki (2019/33/N/HS4/01670).

ISSN 0924-5499　　　　　　　ISSN 2215-0072　(electronic)
GeoJournal Library
ISBN 978-3-031-09777-5　　　ISBN 978-3-031-09775-1　(eBook)
https://doi.org/10.1007/978-3-031-09775-1

This Springer imprint is published by the registered company Springer Nature Switzerland AG
The registered company address is: Gewerbestrasse 11, 6330 Cham, Switzerland

Foreword

Place Attachment and The Power of Geographical Approaches

Dealing with place attachment implies two basic issues, still subject to discussion within the scientific community: the one related to its definition, the other to the methodological aspects. In other words, what is place attachment? And how can it be detected? The first question is due to the confusion between the terms strictly connected to place attachment (sense of place, rootedness, belonging, identity of place, place dependence and place satisfaction) and the consequent need for clarification (Giuliani, 2003; Peng et al., 2020). The second question concerns geography in particular, which has produced a large amount of theoretical studies on place and related concepts, but still, few are the methodological and empirical ones. Above all, it is a question of understanding what the contribution of geography to place attachment can be today, given that since at least 40 years environmental psychology has produced most of the research on this topic, both theoretical and empirical.

Geography began to deal with place, sense of place and related concepts starting from the 1970s , thanks to humanistic geography. Although anticipated by the seminal papers of J.K. Wright (1947) and D. Lowenthal (1961), the works of Tuan (1974), Relph (1976) and other humanistic geographers opened a universe of new reflections to geographic research. Focusing on people's emotional ties with places, conceived as meaningful spaces for subjects and communities, humanistic geographers devoted most of their attention to theoretical aspects, drawing inspiration from M. Heidegger, M. Merleau-Ponty, E. Casey, J. Malpass and other phenomenological thinkers. Marxist and feminist geographers soon accused humanistic geography to recall a nostalgic, closed, universalist, essentialist and male chauvinist vision of the place, proposing an open, hybrid and progressive concept of it, which immediately obtained a generalised positive response. As a result, humanistic geography crossed a relative "exile" during the 1980s (Seamon, 2014). Afterwards, the intuitions of humanist geographers became of fundamental importance for the post-structuralist developments of the whole human geography (Murdoch, 2006). However, the contributions of geographers on place attachment have been limited so far, since they have often spoken of this notion in an implicit way, or as a synonym for "place rootedness" or "place belonging" (Diener & Hagen, 2022).

Thanks also to the contribution of humanistic geography, place attachment (and related concepts) has progressively become a domain of environmental psychology. Many definitions have been given on place attachment from this discipline. Generally speaking, it indicates the positive emotional ties that connect subjects with places, mainly the residential ones, so that Hidalgo and Hernandez (2001, p. 274) define place attachment as "a positive affective bond between an individual and a specific place, the main characteristic of which is the tendency of the individual to maintain closeness to such a place". In this regard, the length of residence, the social relationships in the considered setting and the identification with the neighbourhood, as well as aesthetic and symbolic values, seem to be predictors of place attachment (Altman & Low, 1992; Korpela, 2012). Environmental psychology studies also underline that place attachment is of fundamental importance for psychological balance and good adjustment, for overcoming identity crises and giving people the stability they need in an ever changing world, as well as for experiencing positive emotions by establishing a healthy relationship with places (Scannell & Gifford, 2017).

Although environmental psychology research confirms that people are mostly attached to the local scale, followed by the national one (Lewicka, 2011), the discipline has discussed the issue of place attachment in an era marked by mobility and globalisation. On this point, in the debate between particularists ("places where people live continue to matter as they provide a sense of 'home' in an increasingly turbulent world") and universalists ("the consequence of people's increased mobility is that they can no longer develop thick attachments to places") (Duyvendak, 2011, pp. 9–10), environmental psychology has played a crucial role. In fact, regardless of how much people's practices are based on mobility, some form of place attachment is always present in their lives (Lewicka, 2008). Therefore, place attachment remains a relevant topic of inquiry, given that research in this field highlights how the increased mobility of people, if anything, generates more places to feel attached to, rather than no attachment to any place (Di Masso et al., 2019).

In the light of the relevant scientific literature produced by environmental psychology on place attachment, both at a theoretical and empirical level, what can be the contribution of geography?

Geographic perspective could be prominent precisely because environmental psychology has focused attention on one of the three components of place attachment formalised by Scannell and Gifford (2010), namely *Person*, neglecting the other two (*Process, Place*) (Lewicka, 2011). In particular, psychology has dealt with the affective and emotional dimension of place attachment, as well as on the cognitive and behavioural one (Lewicka, 2008), and devoting attention to individual place experiences has led this discipline to neglect the socio-political implications of such attachments (Sebastien, 2020). On the other hand, planning and decision-making studies focus mainly on the quality of the physical components of the place, overlooking the relational bonds between people and places (Ujang & Zakarija, 2015).

As Oana-Ramona Ilovan and Iwona Markuszewska state in their comprehensive introduction to this volume, "The specificity of studies undertaken by geographers consists of placing the research problem in a spatial context". This means considering the relationship between people and their living environment in terms of collective perceptions, representations, relations and practices "through which people develop meaningful connections with places".

One of the keywords related to place attachment is "experience": from a geographical point of view, there is no experience without a place, that is human experiences are always situated in a spatial context (Cresswell, 2015; Seamon, 2018). This means that, beyond the subjective experiences (direct or mediated by representations), there is a physical referent to which our attachment is related. However, the first definitions given by humanistic geographers, focused on the characteristics of places able to solicit emotions, feelings and aesthetic appreciation, have been replaced over time by the idea, shared at an interdisciplinary level, that place is above all a social construction, material and symbolic at the same time, which affects behaviour and decisions (Manzo & Devine-Wright, 2014; Sebastien, 2020). Considering places in their ever-changing is equally important; therefore, a relevant question from a geographical point of view concerns how the processes of deterritorialisation or reterritorialisation affect or not place attachment. In this perspective, place attachment is an ongoing and multidimensional socio-spatial process.

An interactive relationship exists between people and places: human experiences, values, representations, feelings and emotions transform (abstract) spaces into (meaningful) places, as well as place's features and dynamics contribute to generating place identities, place attachments, rootedness and senses of place. Thus, as people and places are assumed to be ever changing entities, there's no possibility to support the essentialist rhetoric that attributes innate and unchangeable qualities to places, which Massey (1994) assimilated to a conservative and reactionary political position. Similarly, place attachment cannot be conceived in a static, closed and taken-for-granted way, because this would mean presuming a coincidence between places and cultures that cannot be sustained at the time of globalisation and the so-called *mobility turn*. In this regard, the place attachment of migrants and diasporic people, which involves both attachment and movement (Fortier, 2005), offers a universe of significant inquiry, not yet fully addressed in geography. Indeed, such studies would be useful to understand in a metaphorical sense the identities and multiple place attachments that connote the lives of many individuals and groups, as well as to detect the contemporary meaning of other geographical key concepts, such as scale, representation and border (Mendoza & Morén-Alegret, 2013).

Working geographically on place attachment, and related concepts, makes the object/subject relation an issue even more evident for the discipline, due to all the related ontological and epistemological implications. Indeed, geography, unlike other social and humanistic disciplines, has to deal with a material referent, that is the Earth's surface in its multiple articulations and configurations. After a long experience of theoretical approaches centred on Cartesian rationalism, that is, on the presumed objectivity and neutrality of knowledge, geographers have become aware that any of their descriptions of the world can only be partial and incomplete, reflecting the values, priorities and visions of the interpreting subjects. Geography produces metaphorical knowledge, as G. Dematteis already stated in the 1980s (Fall & Minca, 2013), which is anything but politically innocent.

In the context of humanistic geography, Nicholas Entrikin took a similar stance, speaking of a *betweenness of place*, in order to describe "the basic tension that exists between the relatively subjective, existential sense of place and the relatively objective, naturalistic conception of place" (Entrikin, 1991, p. 7). However, only with the *cultural turn* of the early 1980s, territories and places from objective and neutral entities started to be conceived as social constructions, to whose definition narratives, representations, and social practices concur (cf. Banini & Ilovan, 2021). This led many geographers to keep distance from any essentialised vision of territories and places, since "[t]o say that an entity or a fact is constructed is to render it fragile by removing its character as evidence" (Sebastien, 2020, p. 205).

Thanks to the seminal contributions of Massey (2005), Harvey (2006) and other scholars - as anticipated above - an open, porous, hybrid, relational and progressive idea of the place has become pervasive in geography. Place is mainly considered for its connections, flows and transcalar relations. Place is a node of global networks, not necessarily hierarchical, which change over time and, as anthropologist Escobar (2001, p. 169) suggests, operate more as fractal structures than like fixed architectures. Similarly, also place attachment has been conceived in an open, flexible, dynamic and multidimensional way (Diener & Hagen, 2022).

The contribution of geography to place attachment also lies in its methods, because unlike environmental psychology, whose work is mainly based on tests, questionnaires, scales of measurement and rigorous procedural standards, geography uses a range of interpretive approaches: oral histories, interviews, focus groups, as well as visual and participatory methos (i.e., community mapping, narrative mapping and walking interviews) (Smith & Aranha, 2022). As Ilovan and Markuszewska underline in their introduction to this volume, qualitative methods not only "allow for more in-depth and multispectral analysis of the concept of place attachment" but also enable "the co-production of knowledge" between researchers and respondents. In other words, geographic research practices have increasingly been considered as a contextual and contingent process of knowledge construction. Different are also the main aims of the research: if environmental psychology tends to use the information gathered during the surveys to measure the intensity and the typologies of place attachment, geography is mainly interested in analysing the socio-political implications of the different place attachments (e.g. in terms of effective or potential conflicts, and related possible solutions).

A common interest between environmental psychology and geography studies lies in the attention paid to pro-environmental behaviours and participatory practices. Several environmental psychology studies have shown a frequent association between place attachment and the actions that individuals or groups promote for the sustainable use of resources and the protection of the environment (Scannell & Gifford, 2010). Similarly, geography's interest for citizens' participation in decision-making processes has gained relevance during the last decades, in the wake of the growing attention for the social engagement of the discipline. However, still few contributions have examined participatory processes in the light of place attachment, focusing rather on the socio-political dimension of citizen's movements, civic networks and collective action strategies.

Another theme of interest raised by psychology (and also experienced by scholars of other disciplines who have dealt with it) is that place attachment, as well as place identity, often operates outside of conscious awareness (Giuliani, 2003; Korpela, 2012), at least until it is threatened by natural or human events. In this sense, undertaking participatory research-action pathways, working together with residents and actors, could be a tool not only for soliciting place awareness but also for negotiating different interests and needs, so as to reach shared visions and objectives. In other words, place attachment can be built collectively, for the benefit of both social relations and people-place relationships. In this perspective, territorial identity, as well as place attachment, is not so much a reference for "being", as for "becoming" together (Banini, 2017, 2021). Building a collective "place consciousness" (Magnaghi, 2005, p. 79), based on both the awareness of place potentialities and the emotional ties that link people to places, means exactly to open a never-ending dialogue between different actors, aimed at pursuing shared and contextualised goals.

Diener and Hagen (2021), in their introduction to the recent special issue of *Geographical Review* focused on place attachment, assert that place attachment studies would benefit greatly from more explicit contributions by geographers. The same reflection can be found in other recent geographical contributions on the subject (cf. Smith, 2018; Sebastien, 2020), which underline the need for new conceptual frameworks focused on place attachments, for both the scientific advancement and the public engagement of the discipline. Further interdisciplinary dialogue and collaboration, especially between geography and psychology, is also considered necessary (Devine-Wright, 2015).

This volume, edited by Oana-Ramona Ilovan and Iwona Markuszewska, represents a relevant example of the contribution that geography can give to place attachment studies. If the editors' introduction presents an accurate critical review of the interdisciplinary scientific literature on place attachment and related concepts, highlighting the multiple dimensions involved in such a notion, the chapters of the book examine a rich variety of case studies related to many European contexts: from Spain to Romania, from Poland to Portugal, and from Italy to Estonia. In these chapters, the authors deal with place attachment in different spatial contexts (i.e. rural and urban, natural and transboundary, and touristic and residential), using different theoretical frameworks (i.e. phenomenology and social constructivism), perspectives (i.e. regional development, participatory practices, de-industrialisation, urban regeneration processes and social conflict), methods (i.e. semi-structured interviews, in-depth interviews, questionnaires and textual analysis) and subjective experiences (i.e. those of second-home owners, entrepreneurs, gentrifiers, activists, young people, linguistic minorities and metro users), providing a wide range of bibliographic, theoretical and methodological references.

The conclusions of the volume, written by the editors, underline the relevance of place attachment in spatial planning practices, supporting the idea of a "sensitive spatial planning", that is connected "to ordinary people's wishes, needs, concerns, and lives". The editors also highlight the golden threads that run through the chapters of the volume, with particular attention to the breaking, strengthening or (re) construction of the emotional ties between people and places, due to the transformations that cross places and/or the changes of people's lived experiences. Place attachment as a tool for both scientific research advancement and social action is also underlined, as well as further developments on this topic are suggested, for example in the light of the growing relevance of digital experiences as a mediator of the relationship between people and places.

Proposing a collective book on place attachment today is an act of courage and a challenge, as it implies the (re)reading of the key notions of humanistic geography in light of both the interdisciplinary context and the relational, post-structuralist and constructivist turns of geography, while filling the gap in geographic empirical studies on place attachment and related concepts at the same time. Above all, the book shows the variety of perspectives through which place attachment can be understood at the time of mobility, digital communications and environmental emergencies, reflecting traditions, social priorities, narratives and discourses developed in different European territorial and academics contexts, which often differ both from each other and the Anglophone mainstream.

For all this, I am honoured to have been invited to write the foreword to this book, and I wish the editors and all authors the success this challenging collective work deserves.

Faculty of Arts and Humanities   Tiziana Banini
Sapienza University of Rome
Rome, Italy
e-mail: tiziana.banini@uniroma1.it

References

Altman, I., & Low, S. (eds.) (1992). *Place attachment.* Plenum Press.
Banini, T. (2017). Proposing a theoretical framework for local territorial identities: Concepts, questions and pitfalls. *Territorial Identity and Development,* 2(2), 16–23.
Banini, T. (2021). Chapter 1. Towards a methodology for constructing local territorial identities. In Ilovan, O.-R. (ed.), *Territorial Identities in Action* (pp. 13–39). Presa Universitară Clujeană.
Banini T., Ilovan, O.-R. (eds.) (2021). *Representing place and territorial identities in Europe. discourses, images, and practices.* GeoJournal Library, vol. 127. Springer.
Creswell, T. (2015). *Place. An introduction, Second edition.* Wiley.
Devine-Wright, P. (2015). Local attachments and identities: A theoretical and empirical project across disciplinary boundaries. *Progress in Human Geography,* 39(4), 527–530.

Diener, A. C. & Hagen, J. (2022). The power of place in place attachment. *Geographical Review, 112*(1), 1–5.

Di Masso, A., Williams, D. R., Raymond, C. M., Buchecker, M., Degenhardt, B., Devine-Wright, P., Hertzog, A., Lewicka, M., Manzo, L., Shahrad, A., Stedman, R., Verbrugge, L., & von Wirth, T. (2019). Between fixities and flows: Navigating place attachments in an increasingly mobile world. *Journal of Environmental Psychology, 61*, 125–133.

Duyvendak, J. W. (2011). *The politics of home belonging and nostalgia in Western Europe and the United States*. Palgrave Macmillan.

Entrikin, J. N. (1991). *The betweenness of place. Towards a geography of modernity*. Macmillan.

Escobar, A. (2001). Culture sits in Places: Reflections on Globalism and Subaltern Strategies of Localization. *Political Geography, 20*, 139–174.

Fall, J., & Minca, C. (2012). Not a geography of what doesn't exist, but a counter-geography of what does. Rereading Giuseppe Dematteis' "Le Metafore della Terra". *Progress in Human Geography, 37*(4), 542–563.

Fortier, A-M. (2005). Diaspora. In Atkinson D., Jackson P., Sibley D., Washboune N. (Eds.), *Cultural geography. A critical dictionary of key concepts* (pp. 182–187). I.B. Tauris.

Giuliani, M. V. (2003). Theory of attachment and place attachment. In M. Bonnes, T. Lee & M. Bonaiuto (Eds.), *Psychological theories for environmental issues* (pp. 137–170). Ashgate.

Harvey, D. (2006). Space as keyword. In Castree N., & Gregory D. (Eds.), *David Harvey: A critical reader* (pp. 270–293). Blackwell.

Hidalgo, M. C., & Hernández, B. (2001). Place attachment: Conceptual and empirical questions. *Journal of Environmental Psychology, 21*(3), 273–281.

Korpela, K. M. (2012). Place attachment. In Clayton S. (Ed.), *The Oxford handbook of environmental and conservation psychology* (pp. 148–163). Oxford University Press.

Lewicka, M. (2008). Place attachment, place identity, and place memory: Restoring the forgotten city past. *Journal of Environmental Psychology, 28*, 209–231.

Lewicka, M. (2011). Place attachment: How far have we come in the last 40 years? *Journal of Environmental Psychology, 31*(3), 207–230.

Lowenthal, D. (1961). Geography, experience and imagination: Towards a geographical epistemology. *Annals of the Association of American Geographers, 51*, 241–260.

Magnaghi, A. (2005). *The urban village. A charter for democracy and local self-sustainable development*. Zed Books.

Manzo, L., & Devine-Wright, P. (2014). *Place attachment: Advances in theory, methods and applications*. Routledge.

Massey, D. (1994). A global sense of place. In Massey D., *Space, place and gender* (pp. 146–156). University of Minnesota Press.

Massey, D. (2005). *For Space*. London: Sage.

Mendoza, C. & Morén-Alegret R. (2013). Exploring methods and techniques for the analysis of senses of place and migration. *Progress in Human Geography, 37*(6), 762–785.

Murdoch, J. (2006). *Post-structuralist geography. A guide to relational space*. London: Sage.

Peng, J., Strijker, D. &. Wu, Q. (2020). Place identity: How far have we come in exploring its meanings? *Frontiers in Psychology, 11*, 294. https://doi.org/10.3389/fpsyg.2020.00294

Relph, E. (1976). *Place and Placeness*. Pion.

Scannell, L., & Gifford, R. (2010). The relations between natural and civic place attachment and pro-environmental behavior. *Journal of Environmental Psychology, 30*, 289–297.

Scannell, L., & Gifford, R. (2017). The experienced psychological benefits of place attachment. *Journal of Environmental Psychology, 51*, 256–269.

Seamon, D. (2014). Lived Emplacement and the Locality of Being: A Return to Humanistic Geography?. In Aitken S. & Valentine G. (Eds.), *Approaches to Human Geography, Second Edition* (pp. 35–48). Sage.

Seamon, D. (2018). *Life takes place: Phenomenology, lifeworlds, and place making*. Routledge.

Sebastien, L. (2020). The power of place in understanding place attachments and meanings. *Geoforum, 108*, 204–216.

Smith, J. (ed.) (2018). *Explorations in place attachment*. Routledge.

Smith, J. S. & Aranha R. (2022). Cognitive mapping as a method to assess people's attachment to place. *Geographical Review, 112*(1), 6–26.

Tuan, Y.-F. (1974). *Topophilia. A study of environmental perception, attitudes and values*. Englewoods Cliffs.

Ujang, N. & Zakarija K. (2015). Place attachment and the value of place in the life of the users. *Procedia. Social and Behavioral Sciences, 168*, 373–380.

Wright, J. K. (1947). Terrae incognitae: The place of imagination in geography. *Annals of the Association of American Geographers, 37*(1), 1–15.

Contents

Chapter 1
Introduction: Place Attachment – Theory and Practice

Oana-Ramona Ilovan ⓘ **and Iwona Markuszewska** ⓘ

1.1 The Message of This Book

Geographers, anthropologists, environmental psychologists, landscape architects, historians, and sociologists examined place and people's bonds with places. Place attachment underwent many interpretations and intersected varied methodological concepts and practical approaches (Altman & Low, 1992; Lewicka, 2011; Manzo & Devine-Wright, 2014; Kirkness & Tijé-Dra, 2017b; Smith, 2019). In this volume, we emphasise the usefulness for theory and practice (i.e., finding solutions to problems) of exploring people's bonds with places based on unique or shared subjective experiences, in diverse European geographical and cultural contexts. This collective book discusses, through a series of case studies, people's manifold material and symbolic ties to places. It aims to present the geographical approach to place attachment in the specific European context, and to show, at the same time, that it is not possible to argue for a singular research paradigm in this area of inquiry. The included studies and their theoretical frameworks are linked, besides *place attachment*, by the overarching concepts of *place*, of *territorial identity* (or identity of the place) (cf. Banini & Ilovan, 2021b), and of *landscape*. Many of the case studies presented in this book dwell on the relationship between territorial identities

O.-R. Ilovan
Department of Regional Geography and Territorial Planning, Faculty of Geography
and Territorial Identities and Development Research Centre, Babeş-Bolyai University,
Cluj-Napoca, Romania
e-mail: oana.ilovan@ubbcluj.ro

I. Markuszewska (✉)
Department of Environmental Remote Sensing and Soil Science, Faculty of Geographical
and Geological Sciences, Institute of Physical Geography and Environmental Planning,
Adam Mickiewicz University, Poznań, Poland
e-mail: iwona.markuszewska@amu.edu.pl

(symbolic meanings of place, distinctiveness, and identification with place) and place attachment. They include research on processes through which people become attached to places and through which their attachments are changed or lost. Many chapters draw on a phenomenological approach to place attachment: attachment is investigated through individuals' and groups' narratives (cf. Seamon, 2014, p. 14).

This book captures the latest achievements, both theoretical and empirical, of geographers who deal with the most important aspects of place-oriented studies (place identity, distinctiveness of the place, place belonging, and place dependence), in a process of building and maintaining the sense of place. By referencing to existing achievements concerning place-focused studies, our intention is to point out the contribution of geographers in research on place attachment and to emphasise the role of participatory communities in the process of shaping the sense, meaning and identification with places and landscapes. Paying attention to local communities is justified by the fact that they participate at the process of place / landscape planning and management directly or indirectly, consciously or unconsciously, since even non-participation (deliberate or due to decision makers) translates a political will into a spatial choice. During communities' more or less active participation process, bottom-up initiatives are the result of their emotional relations to place. Utilising a diverse spectrum of qualitative and qualitative tools, and applying theoretical geographical thoughts to empirical data, this book offers a European context for a theoretical and methodological overview about place attachment. The findings concerning the relationships between communities and places prove the importance of places and place attachments for the functioning of local societies, which are shaping and (re)transforming the place in harmony with personal, community and social experiences, history and memories, as well as with the physical nature or materiality of place.

1.2   Research on *Place*: The Contributions of Human Geographers

When Seamon and Sowers (2008) wrote *Astronomy has the heaven, history has time and geography has place*, they reiterated unequivocally that *place* is the subject of geographical research. The first conceptual place-oriented contributions belong to humanist geographers (Tuan, 1974, 1977; Relph, 1976), whose conceptual frameworks were further developed by other geographers (for instance, Agnew, 1987; Sack, 1988; Cresswell, 2004; Smith & Cartlidge, 2011). However, as Cresswell (2009) noted, while the word 'place' has been used since geography-oriented studies have been conducted, it was only in the 1970s that it was clarified in Human Geography. In the early 1970s, the branch publications of human geographers presented consolidated knowledge about place, in the context of place having an integral role in the human experience (Markuszewska, 2019). The following should be mentioned: *Topophilia: A Study of Environmental Perception, Attitudes and Values* (1974), *Space and Place: The Perspective of Experience* (1977), both by Yi-Fu Tuan, and *Place and Placelessness* by Edward Relph (1976).

Since then, place has been a central concept in Human Geography, whose complex meanings can be synthetised into the following three: it is *a location or point on the Earth*, it is *an area where territorial identities and sense of place are produced* and it is *a setting (locale) where people act on a daily basis* (Agnew, 1987; Castree, 2009). These meanings have remained stable throughout geographical academic discourse, although one should consider that the first meaning is the oldest (Hartshorne, 1939), and the other two developed starting with the 1970s (Castree, 2009, p. 155). Places are characterised by physical (environmental) and human aspects. Humanistic geographers emphasised the subjectivity of human experience and studied carefully lifeworlds: local experiences, attachments, and sense of place.

Human subjectivity, in the form of feelings about places, the values and meanings attached to places, is as real and impactful as the materiality of places. And place is the locus of daily human experiences. Thus, places are defined by three dimensions, based on human presence in place: the physical, the imaginative, and the affective (Castree, 2009, p. 163). Therefore, the sense of place is multiple in one and the same place, depending on the variety of individuals and groups living in the respective area. Likewise, the identity of the place (or territorial identity, distinctiveness) may vary according to who are the ones constructing the respective discourse. In fact, mainstream and alternative discourses about territorial identity exist for a certain area (cf. Banini & Ilovan, 2021a).

Place and identity of place have been conceptualised in different ways. Place was defined phenomenologically by Seamon, drawing on a tradition developed by Relph (1976): "place can be defined as any environmental locus in and through which individual or group actions, experiences, intentions, and meanings are drawn together spatially" or place is "rather, the indivisible, normally unnoticed phenomenon of person-or-people-experiencing-place" (Seamon, 2014, p. 11). Therefore, place is dynamic and complex, it is a "lived structure" (Seamon, 2014, p. 11). Physical space and people are intertwined, one cannot be defined or exist without the other, one is an integral part of the other. Thus, place is a relevant research concept, defined through human emotions and experiences, besides its materiality. Places are central to self- and collective images and definitions. Place is a meaningful location (cf. Sebastien, 2020), and, in this book, we define *place as that part of space that embodies experiences, values, and emotions*. As such, included contributions showcase the temporal and social rhythms, mundane routines and lived experiences through which space is appropriated and transformed into place.

Places are different (unique) and interconnected. They are not bounded, but open entities, with porous boundaries, and their differences are "both cause and effect of place connections" (Castree, 2009, p. 154). These place differences are objective and subjective. In fact, globalisation thrives exactly on place differences, which endure also because of increasing connections with other places in the world. The local and global worlds are not only connected with increased intensity, but interdependent, they mutually constitute and determine one another; places have changed due to global forces and local responses to these (Agnew, 1989; Massey, 1995; Castree, 2009), resulting the nowadays 'glocal' nature of identity (Castree, 2009, pp. 164–166). Considering the above-mentioned features of place, we propose a relational understanding of place, which is socially constructed. The construction of place involves local, national, and global actors and processes. These are not mutually exclusive, but they melt down to form the distinctiveness of places and people's bonds to them (cf. Massey, 1994; Banini & Ilovan, 2021a, b). This is one common feature of territorial identities, landscapes, and representations of places: their construction in specific to social, economic, and political contexts (Cosgrove, 1985; Rose, 2014). According to their characteristics, two ways of considering places have been identified: essentialist and anti-essentialist. The essentialist way of considering places means that there are places that are supposed to have a *genius loci*, or authenticity, featuring conservative meanings, as opposed to the anti-essentialist, dynamic, open and progressive way of considering places (Relph, 1976; Massey, 1995; Cresswell, 2004; Lewicka et al., 2019); there are also non-places (meaningless locations or "homogenised places of flow") (Lewicka et al., 2019, p. 5).

Seamon identifies place identity as one of the six processes that generate place and place attachment based on people's lived experience in place (Seamon, 2014). Rituals add layers of legitimacy to present regional and local identities. Places are defined individually and collectively through individual's and community's experiences and feelings in those places. Their identity is both validated and contested depending on what groups define it. Place identity is a component of self-identity due to the process of individual's self-identification with place; shared place experiences, memories, meanings and representations can form a community-placed self-identity. This process is often neither peaceful, nor taken for granted, so that collective place identity needs to be negotiated.

Space acquires meaning because of individual's investment in it, but also in the context of a specific cultural background. Space and local community's cultural beliefs, activities and representations interact, they are integral to each other and produce places. Representations are constructed both by the local community and external actors at different spatial scales. As a result, we can have different representations of the same places (e.g., home, neighbourhood, city, etc.) (Mannarini et al., 2006). Both physical features and representations of place influence place attachment through the meanings ascribed to those places (Lewicka, 2008). Referring to representations, place meanings and attachments are influenced by national and ethnic discourses about identity (Lewicka, 2008), and these are present in place memory (with official ideologies transmitted to people in historical time) (Ilovan, 2020). Monuments/objects can reify people's attachment to the imagined communities they feel they belong to; but they can also represent a symbol of oppression, violence, and social injustice. That is why research on people's relationship between past and present, place memory, place identity and place attachment (Lewicka, 2008; Ilovan et al., 2016, 2019) assumes relevant importance. Place has a material component, but different ways of living, feeling, and considering it. Place is territorial, social, cultural and psychological. It is a result of presence and absence that is significant to people in a multitude of ways, which may impact both individual and group well-being.

Despite the great scientific achievements in research on place, a precise limitation of *the spatial dimension of what we call 'a place'* has not been already specified. Therefore, a freely outlined interpretation proposed by Cresswell (2004) fits to this spatial indeterminacy, namely: places range from the corner of a room to the whole planet. Nevertheless, when conducting an empirical investigation and analysing community bonding and community-place relationships, the neighbourhood (intended as a small-size spatial context) is an elected dimension of a place. Spatial boundaries defined in this way are used in research on 'place of residence', or alternatively, a place as a temporary residence in the concept of second homes. However, when we examine the attachment to places in open areas (e.g., large-scale national parks) or 'ordinary' landscapes (e.g., agricultural), the boundaries are usually determined by the mental range of the place which people feel bonded to and rooted in. They can be both large areas and selected specific fragments of space, due to uniqueness and people's emotional identification with them.

Guided by the premises of emotionality, it is assumed that people are connected with a place (as both a material and immaterial entity) by *relationships based on emotional ties* (Relph, 1976), *experience, and on the creation of feeling and thought* (Tuan, 1977). Nonetheless, how do people relate to their human environment and natural setting to make them a 'place'? This is also essential in the process of becoming a place. Cresswell (2009) suggests that space becomes a place when it is used and lived, while experience is at the heart of what place means. He explains that being human means being 'in place', whereas being in place means to be 'attached' or 'rooted'. In addition, the place-making process includes certain characteristics of the respective place, such as: a source of means for survival and physical safety, emotional and psychological support and comfort, feelings of stability and familiarity (Shumaker & Taylor, 1983).

Relph (1976) noted that geographical reality is the place where someone is, and it may be the starting point for shaping people's relationships with the geographical space. Larsen and Johnson (2012) clarified this by saying that Human Geography emphasises place as the centre for meaning and emotional attachment, while place is created as humans respond to the environs. Hence, places are emotions and intangible formations of values linking communities with their physical location in space. A place is alive as long as it evokes emotions and its transformation and reshaping (planned or actually taking place) do not remain indifferent to people. We assume that the relationships that people have with place are reciprocal, which means that both the place affects the community, and the community affects the place.

Then, places are perceived to have *distinctive identities* based on physical, functional, social, cultural (symbolic), and historic meanings. Meanings of place are narratives that are continuously written and actively take part at constructing the identity of places and people. These meanings influence people's relationships with place. They are constructed through experiences in and interactions with place and the entire historical and social context, involving all three dimensions of time: past, present, and future. Local distinctiveness enhances pride and stronger place attachment. Place attachment embeds values and symbols that define the territorial identity of an area, therefore place attachment is a reminder of shared identity and evolution in time.

1.3 Research on Place Attachment: Key Ideas and Contributions

1.3.1 Defining Place Attachment

In general, place attachment is defined as "a set of positive affective bonds" that people develop with their living environment" (Carrus et al., 2014, p. 154), therefore, it consists of an individual psychological process. However, also ambivalent and negative bonds contribute to the construction of place attachment (cf. Manzo, 2005). Thus, place attachment is the *multidimensional process* of building relations with place and its *result*, which is the emotional bond, where place is social (arena and symbol) and physical (natural and built) (Devine-Wright, 2014). Place attachment is also defined as "an outcome of humans' transactions with their habitats" (Carrus et al., 2014, p. 154). It engenders feelings of security, familiarity and homeness. Finally, place attachment can be defined as "a community practice of love", reflecting the connections among the physical, social, and economic potential of place (Thompson Fullilove, 2014, pp. 146–147).

1.3.2 Evolution of Place Attachment Research

Despite the early achievements of geographers (cf. Tuan, 1974, 1977; Relph, 1976; Agnew, 1987), environmental psychologists took up the leading role in place studies about place attachment with the landmark book of Irwin Altman and Setha Low: *Place Attachment* (1992). The respective collective volume was a milestone in researching people's relation with their environment, and it has guided so far much of the research on place identity, sense of place, and place dependence (Manzo & Devine-Wright, 2020). However, place attachment remains a broad concept studied by several sciences due to its multifaceted nature.

Geography, because of its focus on space and place, is one of the sciences that is engaged with place attachment research. The relevance of research on place attachment in Geography relies on the need of understanding the relationships between individuals and communities and their living environment. The way people perceive, represent, and relate to this environment influence their decisions and behaviour, eventually impacting public policies, spatial planning, quality of life and overall well-being. Geographers can research and reveal the social processes through which people develop meaningful connections with places. From this perspective, attachment is not only a psychological process, but also a social practice (Di Masso et al., 2014, p. 81).

Being aware of the fact that place has been a subject matter central to many natural and social sciences, as well as to the humanities, in the first part of this section, we shall refer to the geographical research tradition, then, we point out the intersections between Geography and contributions of other fields, the latter being also relevant for geographical research and theoretical and methodological discourses on place attachment. According to the humanistic approach in Geography, initiated in the late 1960s, which was a reaction to the positivist and mainstream research tradition, place is not a single location and container of activities, but it is a meaningful part of space that people may get attached to emotionally. This 'meaning-based approach' enlarged the theoretical and methodological approaches to the research on place and place attachment (e.g., phenomenology, hermeneutics), therefore the usefulness of qualitative methodology to analyse place meaning.

Place attachment has been researched for various spatial levels and human's life stages, undergoing both positivist and phenomenological approaches. Humanistic Geography, exploring the human's experiences, thoughts, emotions, agency, etc. underlined people's attachment to place and the creation of place identity, as parts of what made people human (cf. Tuan, 1976, 1978) and researched the concept of sense of place in a reaction to geographers' prior insistence on an 'objective' and positivist epistemology in academic Geography. In addition, Human Geography, contesting the Humanistic Geography's tendency to essentialise place, also engaged in a critical way with the concept of power and its role in the production of space and place.

The first decade of the twenty-first century witnessed the flowering of various research horizons concerning place, where environmental psychologists became the predominant group of scholars who dealt with the issue of place attachment. The achievements of these researchers are reflected in the subject matter of the works published in two major journals: *Journal of Environmental Psychology* and *Environment and Behavior*. These journals hosted articles dedicated to place attachment research besides other topics. Among the outstanding and ground-breaking works (encompassing both place-oriented theoretical approaches and empirical analyses involving varied methodology and case studies), the following have made a significant scientific contribution: Proshansky et al. (1983), Brown et al. (2003), Mazumdar and Mazumdar (2004), Manzo (2005), Lewicka (2010), Raymond et al. (2010), Scannell and Gifford (2010a), Anton and Lawrence (2014), Larson et al. (2015), and Brick et al. (2017). We underline that a focus on quantitative methods has been observed. In this research context, qualitative methods and human geographers' achievements were relegated to the background (Smith, 2019).

As Diener and Hagen (2020) noted, while psychologists and sociologists made an outstanding contribution to research on place attachment, the number of publications of human geographers in their leading periodicals (e.g., *Progress in Human Geography, Geographical Review*) was negligible. However, this means neither that geographers were not interested in place-oriented studies, nor that they had no significant achievements in this regard. The critical remarks of Diener and Hagen to the contribution of non-geographers' studies concern, for instance, the selective personal characteristics of the surveyed population, while the geographical context of the place ceased to matter.

The specificity of studies undertaken by geographers consists of placing the research problem in a spatial context. In relation to place-oriented research, there are landscapes or territories that exactly fulfil the role of spatially limited places.

Geographers who conduct research on landscape and/or territories and who analyse people-place relationships value these relations due to the concept of territorial identity (Banini & Ilovan, 2021a). Indeed, place attachment comprehensively captures the human-space relationships, and the contributions of Brown and peers (2003, 2015) are excellent examples in this respect. Landscape and territorial identity, however, have their supremacy in research related to planning and the management of a certain geographical setting. Keeping this in mind, and maintaining the golden thread of this book, which is research on how the personal/common emotional bond to territory and landscape is built, maintained and transformed in a spatial planning context, the selectiveness of the geographical perspective is fully justified. It is useful to underline that according to human geographers, place attachment is a component of territorial identity, besides place identity and identity of place (characteristic features) (Banini, 2021; Banini & Ilovan, 2021b).

Building and strengthening the people's perception of landscape can be found, *inter alia*, in the works of the following: Lee (2003), Stobbelaar and Pedroli (2011), Egoz (2013), Antrop (2013), Loupa-Ramos (2016), and Markuszewska (2019). Noteworthy is also a collective book edited by Tiziana Banini and Oana-Ramona Ilovan (2021a). Other research on landscape identity has analysed the supposed spirit or unique sense of place (*genius loci*) (e.g., Antrop, 2000), assuming that it may contribute to local and national identity. The landscape, with its physical features, cultural uniqueness and place belonging can symbolise a gender group identity (Einhorn, 2000) and a national identity (Nogué & Vicente, 2004; Hagen, 2020). In addition to this, one should emphasise that, in geographical place-focused studies, the essential question is how place changes over time and how practical planning activities can strengthen or undermine the meaning of certain places (Seamon, 2018). This is especially important as current changes of place impact on landscape and environment both at local and regional scales.

Sebastien (2020) points out that research is based on the social aspects of attachment and therefore the spatial dimension of place attachment is not enough discussed, and it is high time to rehabilitate the role of place in place attachment research, especially by showing how attachments are influenced by the physical attributes of place. We also think that the social and physical dimensions of place are integrated, and research should interpret them from a holistic perspective: "The 'social' is not separated from the 'physical', but produces as well as reproduces the matter of place" (Pohl, 2017, p. 32). Social interaction is crucial in the process of mediating the meanings of place. Place is socially constructed and negotiated. Attachment to place and to community can be separated only artificially as research proved that the social dimension of attachment is crucial for attachment to place: "places do not exist apart from human experience and understandings; they are always places-for" (Hufford, 1992, p. 232) and "place, in our general lexicon, refers to space that has been given meaning through personal, group, or cultural processes" (Low & Altman, 1992, p. 5). Place is "a setting of experience" (Rubinstein & Parmelee, 1992, p. 139) and means familiarity. It is "a transactional, contextual, holistic phenomenon" (Williams, 2014, p. 97). Communities are territorial and places cannot be defined outside human presence and activity. Meanings are culturally based, and culture is context specific. Stories narrate territorial identities and attachments for the physical and social structure: "The place may, therefore, be a medium or milieu which embeds and is a repository of a variety of life experiences" (Low & Altman, 1992, p. 10).

In addition to the above-mentioned, place attachment is analysed by geographers as part of the local and regional identity (Paasi, 1986, 2003; Ilovan et al., 2016, 2019; Banini, 2021). From this perspective, it requires ritual enactments that support it as well as the respective territorial identity, engendering a feeling of unity between past and present at the individual and collective levels. Attachment is reinforced through discourses and practices about the identity of the place and its future. Looking back to the past and towards the future are significant dimensions of place attachment. They shape discourses and practices of the present. Identity of the place and appropriation of place (and its distinctiveness/identity) are interrelated and dynamic. Appropriation of place supposes a transformational process for those involved, contributing to their emotional state. Therefore, identity of place or territorial identity is made of many layers and influence the practices through which people appropriate place. At the same time, such appropriation practices impact territorial identity and its continuous construction. Identities and place attachments are cumulative in time, similar to the historical evolution of a territory and personal evolution. The most poignant example of relationship between place identity and place attachment is contained by Feldman's (1996) concept of 'settlement identity' which refers to the fact that people identify with a certain type of settlement or place that they try to find when residential move is underway in order to ensure a sense of continuity through similar residential experiences in the new place.

1.3.3 Measurement of Place Attachment

Research considered the formation of place attachment (the psychological, environmental, economic, cultural, and social processes) and the roles of place attachment in shaping emotional relations with the physical location (Altman & Low, 1992; Manzo & Devine-Wright, 2014; Kirkness & Tijé-Dra, 2017b; Smith, 2019). Out of the factors contributing to the creation of place attachment, the psychological ones were the most researched.

Environmental psychologists contributed extensively to create scales in order to measure place attachment. They studied attachment to residential and non-residential places. Community, neighbourhood, home, and environment were the most frequent topics for research on place attachment. For environmental psychologists, *place attachment is an emotion that can be measured*, and *place is the locus of people's attachment*. One interpretative model of place attachment includes it in the sense of place concept, besides place identity and place dependence. This exemplifies the existence of a wide array of concepts that are used to characterise people-place bonds. Expressions of the bond between people and places are the following: individual, collective, social, physical, affective, cognitive, and behavioural

(Hernández et al., 2014, p. 128). Therefore, quantitative approaches to place attachment research focused on the measurable features of individuals concerning their social and economic situation in various geographical contexts, as well as choices regarding residential length and mobility (cf. Lewicka, 2014).

At present, place attachment research tradition is divided into quantitative approaches (characteristic of Environmental Psychology) and qualitative ones (mainly employed within Human Geography). Qualitative studies on place attachment have increased starting with the 2000s, and used representations of place, as they resulted from interviews and work with visual aids (e.g., images) in order to identify significant themes related to place and place attachment. Places differ on a multitude of features and those differences are reflected in place attachment processes. Attachment is one aspect of place that contributes to its construction, the emotional bond between people and place impacts either of the two. Place meanings are individual or shared, based on tangible and intangible/symbolic elements, and are active parts in the process of creating attachment, therefore, we consider that maintaining a division of research into quantitative and qualitative approaches, the former focusing on individual's attachment and the latter on place meanings, is artificial and could be detrimental to advancing research on place attachment. Agreeing with Lewicka's (2011, pp. 14–15) statement that "quantitative measures, such as various place attachment scales, grasp the differentiation among people with regard to subjective importance and strength of emotional bonds with places, but they are little-suited for measuring what the places mean", we emphasise that qualitative approaches, give a more complex picture of human-place relationships.

In addition, to understand the formation of place attachment, researchers focused on people's feelings, beliefs, attitudes, and behaviours and these were also measured in Environmental Psychology (Lewicka, 2011). Environmental psychologists research the causes that lead to certain meanings people attach to places. On the other hand, Geographers explore these meanings and interpret them to show how identity of place is constructed, and then used to justify people's actions. Often, the narrative about place is inclusive for some and excludes others. To geographers, *place is a meaningful area.* Human Geographers studied the meanings of place and explained them within a certain cultural context, relying on the connection between place meanings and the expression of place attachment (i.e., in the form of those feelings, beliefs, attitudes, and behaviours) (Tuan, 1974; Seamon, 2014).

Different theories and empirical approaches to place attachment led to the development of different methodological frameworks, but much of the analysis and research on place attachment is done from a quantitative research perspective. Such research answers the question "how much?" in a very convenient manner to advantage the possibility of obtaining a large research sample and the easiness of comparison. Quantitative research which focuses on "why?" and "how?" oriented question allows to gain deeper understanding of the emotional bonding with a place (cf. Bondi, 2016). Due to the use of more intensive response methods, we gain a wider perspective on: *Why are people getting attached to certain places? How is one's attachment to place shaped and changed over time? How do people's choices about place (living place / workplace) influence their emotional relation with place?*

How does people's experience affect their perspective of a place? For data collection and analysis, methods commonly used in Human Geography fulfil their task in the field of research on place attachment. We believe that these qualitative methods allow for more in-depth and multispectral analysis of the concept of place attachment because personal emotional connection to place is not easily expressed with numerical instruments.

1.3.4 The Nature of Place Attachment: Dynamic

The dominant perspective to place attachment in research has been that attachment is static, with no or little attention paid to change or to the dynamism of place or of human life course that, in turn, affect place attachment. Recent research made a plea to consider the dynamic nature of place attachment and thus recognise it is socially constructed (Manzo & Devine-Wright, 2014). Place attachment persists over time, it is nurtured, but it is nevertheless subject to change that can either strengthen or disrupt the respective bond (e.g., weak attachment, alienation, or lack of attachment). We are advocating for emphasising in research the dynamic nature of place attachment and the complexity of factors and feelings that contribute to its construction.

First, because *changes in society and in places* influence the dynamics and types of attachments to place that individuals and communities develop. Attachments to place (individual and collectively shared attachments) evolve due to *the evolution of both communities/societies and places*. Making places and communities are continuous processes. The social and physical fabric of place may undergo changes that affect the attachment. Scannell and Gifford (2010b) discuss place attachment as physical and social (i.e., the socially based one and the one based on the physical traits of place), and they distinguish among three psychological processes: affect, cognition and behaviour (or emotion, identity and action). This dynamic nature of the geographical processes makes the concept of place attachment a permanent topic of research, with great potential to influence spatial decisions that impact people's lives.

Places are inhabited and remembered, therefore both experience and memory play a key role in preserving and constructing continuously place attachment. The role of time and place in the creation of attachment is explored through research that is sensitive to the cultural context. As such, place attachment appears as a representation of past, present and future. Therefore, multiple realities coexist in space and time. Territorial identities and attachments are continuously negotiated through practices and rhetorical strategies by people and/or communities that are then shaped themselves by the respective identities of place and attachments. Both territorial identities and attachments are performed and thus their continuation is ensured. The relationship with places is continuously recreated and nurtured through activities in place, as well as through acquiring more knowledge about it and expressing interest in its future (Banini & Ilovan, 2021a).

Second, "place attachment is rarely static" (Seamon, 2014, p. 16) because *affective relationships shift over time*. The dynamics of place attachment is influenced by people's feelings of control over the place where they live. Little control in decisions about their place and when unwanted changes appear is disruptive for place attachment (Devine-Wright, 2014, p. 171). Due to the generative aspects of place, Seamon proposed six place processes for study in order to better understand people's attachment to place. These are: place interaction (e.g., place ballet), place identity, place release, place realisation (e.g., landscape – a palpable presence made of physical and anthropic elements), place creation and place intensification (e.g., practices that strengthen place) (Seamon, 2014, pp. 16–19). All these contribute to people's affective bonds with place and therefore place attachment is defined as the interplay among the above-mentioned place processes (Seamon, 2014, p. 19). Seamon exemplifies the spectrum of emotional engagement with place "that ranges from appreciation, pleasure, and fondness to concern, respect, responsibility, care, and deep love of place" (Seamon, 2014, p. 20). These have been discussed or measured in research on place attachment so far. People's different perceptions of place and choices lead to different types of place attachment for the same location. In addition, it should be emphasised that also attachment to multiple places is possible.

Place attachment was characterised as *'traditional'* (rootedness or inherited attachment and continuity) and *'active'* (choosing where to live and getting involved in actions meant to improve that living environment) (Lewicka, 2014). Hummon (1992) distinguishes between *every day* and *ideological rootedness* as types of place attachment. Traditional attachment or everyday rootedness appears when the place is "inherited" and active attachment (when the place is "discovered") (Lewicka, 2014, p. 55). Active attachment is forged when genealogy (history of family) and the history of place are discovered due to an active interest in the past. Length of residence predicts better traditional attachment and interest in the past predicts better active attachment (cf. Lewicka, 2014, p. 56). When we consider these two types of place attachment (traditional and active), it is necessary to point out that communities of identity and communities of interest can coexist in the same place. The role of leadership as a component of social capital is significant in this process. It strengthens social capital and community place attachment (Mihaylov & Perkins, 2014).

1.3.5   Sources of Place Attachment

Place attachment encompasses the idea of meaningful relations with place, but based on a multitude of sources for such bonding. A valuable contribution to place attachment research belongs to Low, who identifies *six cultural sources of such bonding*. These are "(1) genealogical bonding through history or family, (2) linkage through loss of land or destruction, (3) economic ties through ownership, inheritance, and politics, (4) cosmological bonding through spiritual or mythological relationships, (5) linkage through religious and secular pilgrimage, and participation in celebratory cultural events, and (6) narrative ties through storytelling and place naming" (Low, 1992, p. 9).

Besides this, another source of place attachment is *resistance and activism* (developed during periods of crises) (Mutică & Ilovan, 2022). Activism inspires and gives hope to the residents who want to stay put and even alter the tainted public image of place. Resistance practice can generate collective identity and feelings of belonging to group and place. The role of activism is visible in constructing attachment because crisis means not only danger, but also opportunity. During crisis periods, solidarity and mutual support foster place attachment. Basic spatial rights are reflected in the development of place attachment, of residents' emotional well-being: "the right of presence, of being in a place, of use and action, of appropriation; of modification, and of disposition" (Lynch, 1981; Chawla, 1992, p. 62).

In the same vein, we point out that *memory* plays a significant role in preserving and constructing place attachment. Time and place attachment are connected. The past, our memories and previous social and place attachments shape present place experiences and attachments. Memories are rooted in places and provide people with a feeling of continuity. Memories show the continuity between past and present, in the same place, thus they enable attachment to place. Memories are our anchors to connect places with people in the past. Therefore, places foster a sense of personal and/or collective continuity and of fulfilment and these feelings influence decisions (to stay, to move away, to get involved in caring for the place, etc.). Memory is the 'glue' connecting people to places (Lewicka, 2014, p. 51).

Interpersonal attachment (through feelings of security and comfort, and behaviours such as proximity-seeking) is triggering affective bonding in place and place attachment (Scannell & Gifford, 2014). *Social cohesion* based on friendship, family ties, various local solidarities, shared values and relentless efforts to make home, place, and community, as well as *genius loci* construct place attachment. Stability of housing and the related mutual support networks are a source of place attachment (Manzo & Devine-Wright, 2014). Place attachment is produced by *interacting with knowledge* about family history (genealogy) and with history of the place itself. The sense of groundedness is a result of knowing about the evolution of family, community, and place (Lewicka, 2014). *Existential rootedness to place* or the authenticity of being born and living in a certain place is considered one source of place attachment, revealing strong connections built over long periods, translated into behaviour. *The sense of belonging and appropriation of place* are necessary for the formation of place attachment. *The familiarity of landscape* is a source of place attachment. *Everyday landscapes*, livelihoods and patterns are sources of place attachment, as individuals and communities feel grounded in place. The meaning of landscape in creating place attachment will be discussed in Sect. 1.3.6. To sum up, place attachments differ in terms of sources and aims. However, the interrelatedness of several such sources is usually the explanation for people's bonding to their living environments, involving simultaneously individual and collective processes.

Feelings occur in space and time and thus attachment is dependent on both dimensions. Affiliations to the present are based on associations to the past. The spatial, temporal, and social dimensions are intertwined in the formation of place

Fig. 1.1 Dimensions of
place attachment. (Source:
Own elaboration)

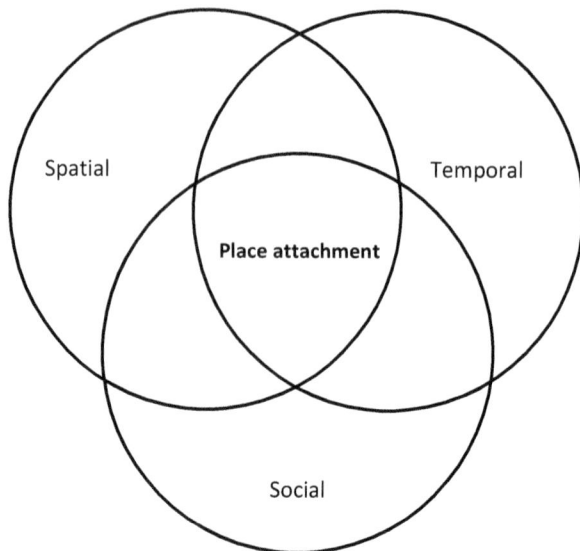

attachment (Fig. 1.1). People value places based on past experiences, present practices, and future promises. Both historical and spatial perspectives are necessary to
understand present territorial identities and attachments. These are context oriented,
a product of the interaction of time, space, and people. Consequently, people are
co-inhabitants of a unique context in time and space, they are performing a specific
place-ballet (i.e., time-space routines) (cf. Seamon, 1980). The place is lived, and
the place-ballet is acquired over time. Memories related to place and time (routines,
events) create belonging to place.

Along the same line, research showed that *mobility* does not have a negative
impact on place attachment, challenging the assumption that mobility may weaken
attachment (Hummon, 1992, p. 276). On the contrary, it can lead to multiple place
attachments, as well as to different types of such attachments (cf. Gustafson, 2014;
Di Masso et al., 2019). Mobility is no longer or always a disruptive factor for place
attachment, but an opportunity to grow roots in new places (Lewicka, 2014, p. 57).
The highly globalised and mobile world we are living in is reflected in people's
choices of attachment, and this are no longer constructed towards one single place,
but these choices diversified and led to multiple place attachments. Forming new
place bonds is more common than before the development of mobility at such a high
rate (i.e., during the last decades). Multiple place attachments may coexist, the new
attachment does not necessarily replace old ones or lost attachments (cf. Scannell &
Gifford, 2014, pp. 28–29), although one attachment may be perceived as central and
the other secondary. At the same time, since human experience is rooted in place,
due to the role of memory in maintaining attachment to place, this bond is not
eroded or disappearing because of a more mobile and globalised world.

Place attachment is not created only through a "mentally enclosed experience",
but also through individual and social activities. For instance, the *practices of*

experiencing place are equally important to this process of producing attachments to places (e.g., meeting points and social networks enable people to develop their roots in place) (cf. Di Masso et al., 2014). Place is conceptualised as a cultural construction where attachment emerges through social action (Pellow, 1992, p. 188). Thus, places are the result of specific articulations of social relations. Research on place experience is fundamental in order to reveal how individuals develop feelings of attachment to place.

Also, *meanings of place* are a source of place attachment. There are multiple dimensions of place meaning and experience and thus the variety of sources for place attachment processes. *Place discourse* is constitutive of attachment to place and of what has been defined as 'settled community'. The social is defined spatially, leading to the inclusion of some groups and the exclusion of other, irrespective of the feeling about space of those people. A positive image of place influences in a positive way self-image and attachment to place. However, meaningful places are not always sources of positive emotions. Negative or mixed emotions associated with place were proven to be also relevant for the process of forming attachment bonds to place, besides the positive ones (Manzo, 2005; Kirkness & Tijé-Dra, 2017b). Finally, territorial stigma and existing prejudices about a place can be and are contested by residents and this is a source of place attachment. This will be discussed in detail in Sect. 1.3.7. Other documented sources of attachment are: attachment to *possessions* (i.e. the bonds to the material environment), attachment to *a certain period of one's life or to certain events* that define who we are. *Symbols and collective values* also engender attachment (Altman & Low, 1992).

The factors influencing emotional investment in place are: long-term residence, social and civic involvement, proximity to local landmarks, life cycle stage, quality of living (i.e. housing), ownership, existence of local friends and family, etc. (Hummon, 1992, pp. 257–258). Thus, these are objective and subjective aspects of the sources that generate place attachment.

Nevertheless, irrespective of their sources, identities and attachments are territorialised. Territorial identities and place attachments are created, maintained, and transformed through material and symbolic practices. The physical environment and social construction contribute together to the creation of the sense of place and attachment to place.

1.3.6 The Meaning of Landscape in the Process of Creating Place Attachment

The contributions of this book are situated among geographical studies, and thus the spatial dimension of a place refers to the environment and the landscape with which people feel an emotional connectedness. The geographical literature is rich in various interpretations of the concept of landscape. For instance, physical geographers stress physical aspects of space, landscape components and relationships between them including the inherent influence of the anthropopressure (Richling & Solon, 2011). Nevertheless, in order to understand the relationship with a place, the physical-geographical perception of landscape must be filtered through a humanistic approach, which includes a non-physical perception of landscape (Brown & Raymond, 2007). Hence, the concept of landscape can summarise its complex interpretation as holistic, the landscape bridges natural and cultural aspects, and links past with present (Antrop, 2005). Defined in this way, the landscape consists not only of a physical reality, but contains mental, social, and cultural elements. This means that a landscape is made of ideas, concepts, principles, words and works. The landscape is also just about anything subject to memory, as experience is filtered through memory, and memory becomes landscape (Palang et al., 2005). Thus, in landscape studies, the focus is on the mutual relationship between people and landscape, as society influences landscapes and community groups are influenced by landscapes.

Landscapes, as the "setting for human experience and activity" (Riley, 1992, p. 13), are places where people learn their way through life, experiencing it through their senses and by means of socialising with the others. The landscape is a shared reference, a palimpsest of place. It is a reference (for meanings, emotions) because people are aware of it. Local landscapes are symbolic extensions of the self; especially in the cases where people participated at creating the landscape, they identify with it more intensely. The extended self includes attachment to our surroundings, which is both functional and emotional (Belk, 1992, p. 38). Landscapes that are built by locals themselves have higher potential for attachment, they are part of the local identity. The familiarity of the landscape is a consequence of frequent use and personal and collective experiences. Thus, affective relationships appear between people and landscapes of everyday life (i.e., ordinary) (Riley, 1992). Place attachment reflects the complexity of human experiences, both individual and collective and the landscape is part of these.

Consequently, those who studied place directed their research also to the concepts of *identity, landscape,* and *representation.* From the late 1980s, cultural geographers proposed the reading of landscapes as texts whose production and meanings could be identified by analysing both landscapes and the contexts of their creation (Duncan & Duncan, 1988). In this approach, the politics of representation drew much of cultural geographers' attention, especially after the publishing of Edward Said's *Orientalism* (1995). It is the setting, but many times, the landscape is seen as an active player due to the symbols of power it is made of. The landscape is "a social and political fact, designed, owned, and maintained by people" (Riley, 1992, p. 31).

The landscape is made of a physical layer (the focus of Landscape Ecology) that contributes to the aesthetics of landscape, and a cultural layer (the cultural landscape as basic concept in Cultural Geography). The cultural landscape is a symbol of group and/or community identity, it is a representation of its practices, beliefs, and knowledge. An integrated approach to landscape means understanding the connections between these layers and the processes that produce the landscape (both physical and cultural processes). Therefore, it has been argued that landscapes, due to their morphological features (first discussed in depth by Sauer, in his work on pre-modern cultural landscapes 1963 [1925]) can showcase cultural differences (Meinig, 1979). The local distinctiveness of the landscape contributes to the creation of territorial identities (or to the identity of the place).

The landscape has been defined either as a physical area or as a social process, where each of the following are integral to the creation of the other: the physical layer, social practices, and landscape representations. That means that landscapes are characterised by material and ideological features (i.e., they represent social relations). Therefore, landscapes can be defined as what they are (cultural products) and by the functions they have in a certain society (as ideological processes and reflections of power relations with impact on social life). In particular, representational practices are important in the production of landscapes and social relations within a society (Cosgrove, 1984; Duncan, 1990).

In addition, landscape research underlined that groups of people, although contributing to the creation of cultural landscapes, do not read them in the same way: different ways of seeing are characteristic of different groups due to features such as class (cf. Cosgrove, 1984; Duncan, 1990) or other unequal power relations based on ethnicity, race, gender, and sexuality (Mitchell, 2003). Landscapes reflect the backgrounds, values, and interests of those who produced them (Rose, 1993), but this does not prevent the appearance of alternative readings of the same landscape.

Moreover, people's reading of landscape and of landscape representations construct the meanings they attribute to places and the bonds they create between them and those places. The landscape is just one feature of place that can be assumed to be a source of attachment. Landscapes influence how places are experienced. People produce landscapes (materially and through representations) and these landscapes shape people and their relations to their living environment, their place identities and place attachments. The relationship among landscape, landscape representations and place attachment, especially related to aesthetics (its visual qualities) has been studied by identifying people's reactions to patterns (i.e., pattern – a certain functional homogeneity of the respective represented places) in a landscape (more patterns means that the better liked will be the respective landscape; also a share of nature and the presence of people lead to better liking the landscape) (Iwanczak & Lewicka, 2020).

Finally, the European Landscape Convention (Council of Europe, 2000) defines landscape as an area whose character resulted from the action and interaction of human and/or natural forces. The Convention pays attention to the overriding role of landscape in creating the European identity, noting in the Preamble: "the landscape contributes to the formation of local cultures and [...] it is a basic component of the European natural and cultural heritage, contributing to human well-being and consolidation of the European identity" (Council of Europe, 2000, p. 1). Overall, the Convention stresses the role of people's perceptions: landscape means "an area, as perceived by people, whose character is the result of the action and interaction of natural and/or human factors" (Council of Europe, 2000, art. 1).

1.3.7 Tainted Places and Place Attachment

Despite common belief and expectations (exploited also in research), place attachment is not based only on the appreciative features of an area. Positive and negative affects are part of place attachment, belonging and exclusion interact in the production of place attachment. Even conflicted emotions about a place (e.g., the residential area), which are quite often, lead to place attachment, not only positive ones. This "shadow side of place attachments" (Manzo & Devine-Wright, 2014, p. 184) still needs further research, although a valuable contribution is represented by the book edited by Kirkness and Tijé-Dra (2017b). They advanced research on the relationship between territorial stigma and place attachment, emphasising the heterogeneity and complexity of experiencing territorial stigma across time and space (i.e., territorial stigma can hinder or enable place attachment). The book edited by Kirkness and Tijé-Dra (2017b) challenges the normative assumptions about place attachments with relevant case studies at the neighbourhood level. Place attachment is viewed through the lens of social and spatial stigma, showing that attachments are not positive affective bonds by default. The tensions between place stigma and place pride are part of living in a neighbourhood with negative reputation. They answered the following questions: *What does the process of constructing place attachment in stigmatised areas consist of? What is the relationship between place attachment and territorial stigma? What are the functions of place attachment in the context of stigma? How are place attachments formed by those having limited power and control over their life and places, like the ones living in poverty?* They showed that negative reputations have long lasting structural consequences and social and physical security enforce place attachment. But where both or either of them are lacking, like in stigmatised places, this does not necessarily erode or lead to a loss of place attachment.

Marginalisation processes lead to this territorial stigma (concept developed by Wacquant, 2007) and the stigma reinforces the marginalisation of the already vulnerable groups (Kirkness & Tijé-Dra, 2017b). However, residents of stigmatised places develop attachments to these. Stigma is internalised by residents, but they still feel attached to place and that they belong to a community that provides them with safeness and stability. Positive, negative and ambivalent feelings may be experienced at the same time regarding one's place of attachment. Such research is still marginal in Geography and in other sciences because more attention has been paid to a quite romanticised perspective upon people's emotional bonds to places, especially to their residences (e.g., home as the prototypical place of attachment) and this has become a normative approach to place attachment study. More attention should be paid, in research, to the "critical counter-narrative to the rhetoric of distress" (Manzo & Devine-Wright, 2014, p. 182).

Then, the territorial impact of the stigmatisation discourse is strong. Territorial stigma justifies state-led development strategies that ignore residents (Husseini de Araújo & Batista da Costa, 2017; Zhang, 2017). There are documented strong entanglements between state government (public administration), developers and territorial stigmatisation (Kirkness & Tijé-Dra, 2017b). Other interests are advanced than those of the people who lose their place (often represented as marginalised area), because of demolition and relocation (i.e., domicide), leaving them with trauma.

In addition, social discrimination is defined also from a spatial perspective, especially in the case of these places that have a negative reputation. Place pride based on 'counter-scripts' was reported as a reaction to defamation of places from outside (Kirkness & Tijé-Dra, 2017b). Familiarity and mutual support networks compensate for stigma and stigmatised places are not so ugly and bad places to live in. Counter narratives of the lived space are created by residents during a symbolic struggle to defend their place against distortions and overgeneralisations. These distortions are part of the symbolic violence perpetrated by the dominant narratives constructed from the outside and which usually support people's displacement (Zhang, 2017).

Moreover, place-based identity is enhanced by stigma and residents' agency is still relevant for territorial development, sense of self-worth, of home, place pride and place attachment (Husseini de Araújo & Batista da Costa, 2017; Kirkness & Tijé-Dra, 2017a). What they are is defined by where they live. Those places matter, they are worth fighting for, employing the most efficient protest and coping strategies against negative impact from outside (e.g., based on sanitising or erasing such places). Residents' resistance movements or their taking a stand have consequences on place attachments and future research should pay more attention to those processes.

To sum up, research so far shows that emancipation from territorial stigma is possible, and that people develop place attachment despite all hardships. They fight back stigmatisation, they contest it by pointing out aspects to be proud of, even the ones that were misrepresented and vilified, and their ability to make life under harsh circumstances is a source of pride. Stigmatised places are claimed by their residents. People have a high adaptive capacity and placemaking continues despite the inflecting of stigma by powerful economic and political interests (Kirkness & Tijé-Dra, 2017b).

1.3.8   Functions of Place Attachment

Among the functions that place attachment serves are those of motivation, security, control, satisfaction, self-confidence, stability, continuity, it provides relaxation related opportunities, and reminders of significant moments and experiences, contributing to the construction of territorial identities (i.e., distinctiveness), group identities and self-identity. Place attachment influences how places are experienced daily, it contributes to the creation of a sense of place and the other way around. Also, through place attachment discourses, territorial identities are communicated to insiders and outsiders.

Most significantly, place attachment fulfils a fundamental human need, that of belonging (Relph, 1976; Raagmaa, 2002). People need "to be grounded in place" (Lewicka, 2014, p. 51). Places of attachment are safe havens, they offer a secure base, perceived as such even if they are not objectively safe, but the feeling of security is a result of stronger attachment. Place attachments are integrated into the self-definitions of individuals and communities, they provide self-esteem, and stability in a changing world (Brown & Perkins, 1992, p. 280). Attachments to place maintain a sense of past, place, and self.

Besides higher levels of life satisfaction, place attachment means better social capital. Place attachment implies solidarity, but is not inherently beneficial if it leads to exclusionary practices. It contributes to citizen empowerment and participation (at individual and community levels) based on shared past (identity, values), present concerns and future goals. Place attachment is a motivator for action (Lewicka, 2005; Mihaylov & Perkins, 2014), within communities and should be considered in policies that target improvement of place and quality of life at various scales. Moreover, the scale of place may influence the type or strength of attachment because attachment is influenced by different factors (i.e. physical setting, social interaction, discourses on territorial identities, mobility, etc.) (Lewicka, 2005, 2008). Identification with place and community leads to acting on their behalf and for their protection and benefit; civic activism promotes social cohesion and well-being.

Finally, there are positive links between place attachment and behaviour or rather behavioural intentions (Scannell & Gifford, 2010b). Place-protective attitudes and behaviours led to defining civic place attachment (cf. Carrus et al., 2014, p. 158). In addition, development policies that are perceived as place enhancing may be supported by those who declare strong place attachment. Place attachment can play a critical role in policy making, especially when policy actions introduce drastic social, economic, and environmental changes. Participatory processes and governance based on inclusiveness could benefit from place attached communities and individuals in order to find best solutions, efficient implementation, and, in general, the needed acceptance and support for change and sustainable development (Lewicka, 2005; Carrus et al., 2014). Moreover, place attached individuals and communities are more resilient when coping with risk (cf. Carrus et al., 2014, p. 158).

1.3.9   Loss of Place Attachment

Natural or human triggered disasters, as well as planning decisions and place development can lead to disruptions in place attachment, therefore, "topophilia, like other love, requires the risk of being hurt" (Hester, 2014, p. 200). Research has showed that "people do not abandon collapsing places" (Thompson Fullilove, 2014, p. 146) due to memories of better periods and hopes for the future. Their emotional engagements defy any practical constraints or unfavourable circumstances. Disruptions of person-place bonds (e.g., continuity with the past, local distinctiveness, and livelihoods) were reported to affect people's overall state (Kirkness & Tijé-Dra, 2017b). But can place attachment be repaired, rebuilt, regenerated? One extreme situation is that of forced mobility, which undermines attachment.

Displacement means starting life from scratch; residents' loss is felt both materially and symbolically. The cost of losing home is usually understated as only economic calculations tend to be considered. Significant ties and networks with the others (family, friends, neighbours, community) are broken. The subsequent root shock is the traumatic stress reaction to the loss of place and attachment to it. People experience feelings of loss, mourning, and grief, following changes to places, when places and attachments are disrupted, destroyed, or lost. These 'soul destroying' effects appear because of place destroying actions and decisions. Displacement is costly emotionally as well as from a social and economic perspective. As place is defined as a geographical location and a social system, a nod in the global system, through displacement, the geographical and social ties are undergoing a rupture (Thompson Fullilove, 2014, pp. 141–142). Displacement means a dissolution of social networks, trust and norms, that is a loss of social capital, which is highly significant for development. This happens especially in property-led development, coupled with social and spatial re-design, through a cleansing of space, of any traces of previous territorial identity and belonging markers. Obsolete places need to be revitalised, but, in fact, the transition from home to sanitised spaces excludes poor and disadvantaged groups. Discourses about the grim present legitimise intervention and the bright future. Territorial problems are meant to be erased by erasing the landscape itself.

1.3.10 Conceptual Frameworks of Place/ Landscape Attachment

Scannell and Gifford (2010a) proposed a tripartite framework of place attachment, the main dimensions of which are: person, psychological process, and place. In this framework, *person* refers to a culture, a group, or to an individual. Analysing this dimension boils down to answering the following questions: *Who is attached?* To what extent is attachment relying on individually and collectively held meanings? The *psychological process* consists of affect, cognition, and behaviour, and it is described by the following question: *How are affect, cognition, and behaviour expressed in attachment?* The third dimension is *place* (both social and physical) as the object of the attachment: *What is the attachment to? What is the nature of this place?*

Raymond et al. (2010) also compiled a three-dimensional model of place attachment. The authors admitted that their model is similar, from a conceptual perspective, to the tripartite model of place attachment by Scannell and Gifford (2010a), but, at the same time, they pointed out important differences. This model consists of the following attributes: personal, community and natural environment. The *personal* attribute refers to place identity (a mixture of feelings about specific physical settings and symbolic connections to place, which define who we are) and place dependence (a functional connection resulting from individual's physical connection to a setting). The *community* context relates to social bonding, which is defined as feelings of belongingness to a group (e.g., friends, family), and as the emotional connections built on shared interests, concerns, and history. The *environmental* attribute refers to nature bonding (e.g., implicit or explicit connection to some the non-human natural environment), created on cognitive representation, emotional response or history.

In turn, the model proposed by human geographers – Diener and Hagen (2020) – emphasises the importance of the geographical setting in understanding the synchrony of *self/community* and *place* that elucidates how activities, individuals, and communities come to be perceived as site-specific and attached to place. These elements (place and self/community) occupy the central position of this model, while the other components, intertwining with each other, represent: nature (materiality/familiarity), social relations (performance/partiality), and meaning (narration/memory). As Diener and Hagen explain, the framework proposed by them depicts the integrative dynamism of place in which place meaning is building through (both conscious and unconscious) actions, experiences, and perceptions of individuals and groups. To put it in other words, the materiality/familiarity of place derives from nature, the performance/partiality of place derives from social relations, and the narration/memory of place derives from meaning.

1.4   Why Place Attachment Again?

A decade ago, Maria Lewicka (2011) asked whether place was still significant to people in the current globalised world, observing how much the world had changed since the 1970s, when the first place-related concepts were constructed. This book is, in a way, the answer to that question and proof that the debate and lively discourse over attachment to place has not ceased, on the contrary, it gains new interest, from scientists, communities, and policymakers. Presenting this book, our intention is to update the concept of place attachment with research on the relationships between people and their localities, and on the emotional bonds to the spatial location and the community in place. Bearing in mind the geographical perception of place in this book, geographers contribute to the achievements of place attachment studies with research reflecting the progress in theoretical and methodological developments.

This book provides a comprehensive case study-based perspective on the topic of place attachment, considering theory, methodology and practice. It points out that processes of building place attachment is increasingly salient topic within Human Geography research, complementing the current research which is dominated by Environmental Psychology. This book considers the following research perspectives: (1) Quantitative and qualitative approaches to researching place attachment during community transformation; (2) Preserving and building place attachment under new social, cultural, and economic challenges; (3) From topophilia to topophobia. From topophobia to topophilia. Local community perception of landscape changes; (4) Feelings of connectedness and loss of place in fragile communities, undergoing disruptive changes; (5) Living together – how multicultural and multinational integrated communities contribute to shaping common place identity and place attachment; (6) Processes of enhancing the sustainability of communities through place attachment; (7) Greening and making a better place. Sustainable development of regenerated landscapes and places; (8) Urban bioregions. Urban/rural regeneration practices, social capital, and activism in creating place attachment; (9) Tangible and intangible resources for sustainable development and (re) connecting people to places.

The European outlook on locally and regionally place-making processes considered geographically spread case studies, located in Austria, Croatia, Estonia, Germany, Ireland, Italy, Poland, Portugal, Romania, Spain, and Sweden. We have made every effort to achieve a holistic and complex overview on how place is preserved and (re)constructed by presenting the cultural background, policy aims and natural values of places. Our book provides rich material and multifaceted discussions on the topic of place attachment. A series of seventeen case studies and a theoretical chapter, besides introduction and conclusions to the book, consider the social, environmental, economic, and political effects of creating, strengthening, and maintaining place attachment. They stand for a variety of approaches (theoretical and methodological) on the topic of place attachment. Each of the seventeen chapters deals with a relevant case study. The strong theoretical framework of the book combines a qualitative methodology with various scales which fills the gap in previous quantitative approaches to place attachment studies. Having seventeen case studies from different regions, the book offers quite comprehensive perspectives about the contemporary research on place attachment: from the local to the regional level, from cultural to natural landscapes, from urban through industrial to rural areas. It provides a convincing scientific approach of the local, regional, national, and global factors constructing and shaping community place attachment in Europe.

Contributions question the place transition and landscape changes in shaping place attachment. This is a key question not only in Europe but also on a global scale, that can inform about the influence and pressures on place transitions, both positive and negative. Europe is highly diverse regionally, as different local and regional circumstances (economic, social, cultural, natural, political, etc.) influence this differentiation. And this, finally, influences how individuals build their bonds with local places, and place attachment. While the presented outcomes and results are locally and regionally significant, they also hold a national and international interest and importance. The methodology follows mainly a qualitative approach, which is complementing to existing quantitative measurement of place attachment.

Through this book, we also argue that qualitative and 'subjective' research methodology is equally valid to study place attachment as the quantitative and 'objective' one, and, in some cases, more appropriate (Sebastien, 2020, p. 208). For instance, micro-scale analysis of the creation and destruction of place attachments shows the multitude of ways through which individuals and communities actively participate in these processes. This research approach challenges the dangerous discourses about the passiveness of the people (i.e., individuals as numbers in statistics or as passive victims or happy beneficiaries of (re)development). We advocate for research where understanding place and place attachment is realised from a participatory perspective, by involving the locals in the research activities. Such methodology helps comprehend and express how their attachments are formed. In this context, we point out also the relevance and usefulness of explorative studies, using qualitative methods with non-representative samples. Qualitative methodology enables the co-production of knowledge, where 'superior' academic data is balanced and talked back to by grassroots understandings and people's situated knowledges. In addition, qualitative methods stimulate deeper levels of reflection for all research participants (researchers and respondents).

Through participatory and collaborative research, and performative practices, residents express opinions, feelings and understandings about place and their bonds to it in their own words (and in their own terms). They create themselves the knowledge and counter narratives that could be useful to generate and implement public policies. Such research not only is beneficial to the society through its products (i.e., alternate forms of knowledge), and through shedding new light on common tropes, but it empowers ordinary people and contributes to capacity building at the local level. These are crucial pre-requisites for sustainable development.

We also underline the power that case studies have in documenting and showcasing good practice examples in the creation of place attachments, as well as the detrimental discourses and practices to this process. The case study approach is necessary and critical for methodological and theoretical clarity and advances in place attachment research.

Starting from an open, dynamic, relational, and participatory concept of place attachment, our book discusses first *place making and place attachment processes through place-based development and community place-driven actions*. Apart from that, the book presents examples of creating *place attachment through nature- and culture-based contexts*. The following part focuses on *sustainable planning and territorial identities enhancing place attachment*. Finally, the book presents and discusses *(re)constructing place attachment: regeneration of (post)industrial areas and urban recovery.*

Finally, this collective book is a contribution to the field of place attachment, the presented research results having also practical importance. Our contribution presents a geographical point of view, which captures different social, natural, economic, and political environments. Not only it is an input from and for geographers, but it could be also a reference for landscape planners, sociologists, psychologists, environmental and political scientists, and for members of community movements.

References

Agnew, J. A. (1987). *Place and politics: The geographical mediation of state and society*. Allen and Unwin.

Agnew, J. (1989). The devaluation of place in social science. In J. Agnew & J. Duncan (Eds.), *The power of place* (pp. 9–30). Allen and Unwin.

Altman, I., & Low, M. S. (Eds.). (1992). *Place attachment*. Plenum Press.

Anton, C. E., & Lawrence, C. (2014). Home is where the heart is: The effect of place of residence on place attachment and community participation. *Journal of Environmental Psychology, 40*, 451–461.

Antrop, M. (2000). Where are the genii loci? In B. Pedroli (Ed.), *Landscape—Our Home, Lebensraum Landschaft. Essays on the culture of the European landscape as a task* (pp. 29–34). Indigo, Zeist, Freies Geistesleben.

Antrop, M. (2005). Why landscapes of the past are important for the future. *Landscape and Urban Planning, 70*, 21–34.

Antrop, M. (2013). A brief history of landscape research. In P. Howard, I. Thompson, & E. Waterton (Eds.), *The Routledge companion to landscape studies* (pp. 12–22). Routledge Taylor & Francis Group.

Banini, T. (2021). Chapter 1. Towards a methodology for constructing local territorial identities. In O.-R. Ilovan (Ed.), *Territorial identities in action* (pp. 13–39). Presa Universitară Clujeană.

Banini, T., & Ilovan, O.-R. (Eds.). (2021a). *Representing place and territorial identities in Europe. Discourses, images, and practices* (GeoJournal Library, Vol. 127). Springer. https://www.springer.com/gp/book/9783030667658

Banini, T., & Ilovan, O.-R. (2021b). Introduction: Dealing with territorial/place identity representations. In T. Banini & O.-R. Ilovan (Eds.), *Representing place/territorial identity in Europe. Discourses, images, and practices* (pp. 1–19). Springer. https://doi.org/10.1007/978-3-030-66766-5_1

Belk, W. R. (1992). Attachment to possessions. In I. Altman & M. S. Low (Eds.), *Place attachment* (pp. 37–62). Plenum Press.

Bondi, L. (2016). The place of emotions in research: From partitioning emotion and reason to the emotional dynamics of research relationships. In J. Davidson, L. Bondi, & M. Smith (Eds.), *Emotional geographies* (pp. 231–246). Routledge Taylor & Francis Group.

Brick, C., Sherman, D. K., & Kim, H. S. (2017). "Green to be seen" and "brown to keep down": Visibility moderates the effect of identity on pro-environmental behaviour. *Journal of Environmental Psychology, 51*, 226–238.

Brown, B. B., & Perkins, D. D. (1992). Disruptions in place attachment. In I. Altman & M. S. Low (Eds.), *Place attachment* (pp. 279–304). Plenum Press.

Brown, G., & Raymond, C. (2007). The relationship between place attachment and landscape values: Toward mapping place attachment. *Applied Geography, 27*, 89–111.

Brown, B., Perkins, D. D., & Brown, G. (2003). Place attachment in a revitalizing neighborhood: Individual and block levels of analysis. *Journal of Environmental Psychology, 23*(3), 259–271.

Brown, G., Raymond, C. M., & Corcoran, J. (2015). Mapping and measuring place attachment. *Applied Geography, 57*, 42–53.

Carrus, G., Scopelliti, M., Fornara, F., Bonnes, M., & Bonaiuto, M. (2014). Place attachment, community identification, and pro-environmental engagement. In C. L. Manzo & P. Devine-Wright (Eds.), *Place attachment. Advances in theory, methods and applications* (pp. 154–164). Routledge.

Castree, N. (2009). Place: Connections and boundaries in an interdependent world. In N. J. Clifford, S. L. Holloway, S. P. Rice, & G. Valentine (Eds.), *Key concepts in geography* (2nd ed., pp. 153–172). Sage.

Chawla, L. (1992). Childhood place attachments. In I. Altman & M. S. Low (Eds.), *Place attachment* (pp. 63–86). Plenum Press.

Cosgrove, D. (1984). *Social formation and symbolic landscape*. Barnes & Noble.

Cosgrove, D. (1985). Prospect, perspective and the evolution of the landscape idea. *Transactions of the Institute of British Geographers, 10*, 45–62.

Council of Europe (2000). The European landscape convention. .

Cresswell, T. (2004). *Place: A short introduction*. Blackwell.

Cresswell, T. (2009). Place. In R. Kitchin & N. Thrift (Eds.), *International encyclopaedia of human geography* (pp. 169–177). Elsevier.

Devine-Wright, P. (2014). Dynamics of place attachment in a climate changed world. In C. L. Manzo & P. Devine-Wright (Eds.), *Place attachment. Advances in theory, methods and applications* (pp. 165–177). Routledge.

Di Masso, A., Dixon, J., & Durrheim, K. (2014). Place attachment as discursive practice. In C. L. Manzo & P. Devine-Wright (Eds.), *Place attachment. Advances in theory, methods and applications* (pp. 75–86). Routledge.

Di Masso, A., Williams, D. R., Raymond, C. M., Buchecker, M., Degenhardt, B., Devine-Wright, P., Hertzogg, A., Lewicka, M., Manzoi, L., Shahrad, A., Stedmank, R., Verbruggel, L., & von Wirth, T. (2019). Between fixities and flows: Navigating place attachments in an increasingly mobile world. *Journal of Environmental Psychology, 61*, 125–133.

Diener, A. C., & Hagen, J. (2020). Geographies of place attachment: A place-based model of materiality, performance, and narration. *Geographical Review*, 1–16. forthcoming.

Duncan, J. (1990). *The city as text: The politics of landscape interpretation in the Kandyan kingdom*. Cambridge University Press.

Duncan, J., & Duncan, N. (1988). (Re)reading the landscape? *Environment and Planning D: Society and Space, 6*, 117–126.

Egoz, S. (2013). Landscape and identity: Beyond a geography of one place. In P. Howard, I. Thompson, & E. Waterton (Eds.), *The Routledge companion of landscape studies* (pp. 272–285). Routledge.

Einhorn, B. (2000). Gender, nation, landscape and identity in narratives of exile and return. *Women's Studies International Forum, 23*(6), 701–713.

Feldman, R. M. (1996). Constancy and change in attachments to types of settlements. *Environment and Behavior, 28*, 419–445.

Gustafson, P. (2014). Place attachment in an age of mobility. In L. C. Manzo & P. Devine-Wright (Eds.), *Place attachment. Advances in theory, methods and applications* (pp. 37–48). Routledge.

Hagen, J. (2020). Places of memory, historic preservation, and place attachment in Nazi Germany. *Geographical Review*, forthcoming.

Hartshorne, R. (1939). *The nature of geography*. Association of American Geographers.

Hernández, B., Hidalgo, M. C., & Ruiz, C. (2014). Theoretical and methodological aspects of research on place attachment. In C. L. Manzo & P. Devine-Wright (Eds.), *Place attachment. Advances in theory, methods and applications* (pp. 125–137). Routledge.

Hester, T. R. (2014). Do not detach! Instructions from and for community design. In C. L. Manzo & P. Devine-Wright (Eds.), *Place attachment. Advances in theory, methods and applications* (pp. 191–206). Routledge.

Hufford, M. (1992). Thresholds to an alternate realm: Mapping the chaseworld in New Jersey's Pine Barrens. In I. Altman & M. S. Low (Eds.), *Place attachment* (pp. 231–252). Plenum Press.

Hummon, M. D. (1992). Community attachment. Local sentiment and sense of place. In I. Altman & M. S. Low (Eds.), *Place attachment* (pp. 253–278). Plenum Press.

Husseini de Araújo, S., & Batista da Costa, E. (2017). From social hell to heaven? The intermingling processes of territorial stigmatisation, agency from below and gentrification in the Varjão, Brazil. In P. Kirkness & A. Tijé-Dra (Eds.), *Negative neighbourhood reputation and place attachment. The production and contestation of territorial stigma* (pp. 158–177). Routledge.

Ilovan, O.-R. (2020). The development discourse during socialist Romania in visual representations of the urban area. *Journal of Urban History*, 1–35. https://doi.org/10.1177/0096144220982957

Ilovan, O.-R., Scridon, I., Havadi-Nagy, K. X., & Huciu, D. (2016). Tracing the military frontier district of Năsăud. Territorial identity and regional development. *Mitteilungen der Österreichischen Geographischen Gesellschaft, 158*, 215–244.

Ilovan, O.-R., Voicu, C.-G., & Colcer, A.-M. (2019). Recovering the past for resilient communities: Territorial identity, cultural landscape and symbolic places in Năsăud Town, Romania. *Europa Regional, 26*(2), 14–28. https://nbnresolving.org/urn:nbn:de:0168-ssoar-66830-6

Iwanczak, B., & Lewicka, M. (2020). Affective map of Warsaw: Testing Alexander's pattern language theory in an urban landscape. *Landscape and Urban Planning, 204*, art. no. 103910. https://doi.org/10.1016/j.landurbplan.2020.103910

Kirkness, P., & Tijé-Dra, A. (2017a). Voices from the quartiers populaires: Belonging to stigmatised French urban neighbourhoods. In P. Kirkness & A. Tijé-Dra (Eds.), *Negative neighbourhood reputation and place attachment. The production and contestation of territorial stigma* (pp. 119–137). Routledge.

Kirkness, P., & Tijé-Dra, A. (Eds.). (2017b). *Negative neighbourhood reputation and place attachment. The production and contestation of territorial stigma*. Routledge.

Larsen, S. C., & Johnson, J. T. (2012). Toward and open sense of place: Phenomenology, affinity, and the question of being. *Annals of the Association of American Geographers, 102*(3), 632–646.

Larson, L. R., Stedman, R. C., Cooper, C. B., & Decker, D. J. (2015). Understanding the multidimensional structure of pro-environmental behavior. *Journal of Environmental Psychology, 43*, 112–124.

Lee, T. (2003). Schema theory and the role of socio-spatial schemata in environmental psychology. In M. Bonnes, T. Lee, & M. Bonaiuto (Eds.), *Psychological theories for environmental issues* (pp. 27–62). Ashgate.

Lewicka, M. (2005). Ways to make people active: The role of place attachment, cultural capital, and neighborhood ties. *Journal of Environmental Psychology, 25*(4), 381–395.

Lewicka, M. (2008). Place attachment, place identity, and place memory: Restoring the forgotten city past. *Journal of Environmental Psychology, 28*(3), 209–231.

Lewicka, M. (2010). What makes neighborhood different from home and city? Effects of place scale on place attachment. *Journal of Environmental Psychology, 30*, 35–51.

Lewicka, M. (2011). Place attachment: How far have we come in the last 40 years? *Journal of Environmental Psychology, 31*(3), 207–230. https://doi.org/10.1016/J.JENVP.2010.10.001

Lewicka, M. (2014). In search of roots: Memory as enabler of place attachment. In C. L. Manzo & P. Devine-Wright (Eds.), *Place attachment. Advances in theory, methods and applications* (pp. 49–60). Routledge.

Lewicka, M., Rowinski, K., Iwanczak, B., Balaj, B., Kula, A. M., Oleksy, T., Prusik, M., Torunczyk-Ruiz, S., & Wnuk, A. (2019). On the essentialism of places: Between conservative and progressive meanings. *Journal of Environmental Psychology, 65*, Art. no. 101318. https://doi.org/10.1016/j.jenvp.2019.101318

Loupa Ramos, I., Bernardo, F., Carvalho, S., & Van Eetvelde, V. (2016). Landscape identity: Implications for policy making. *Land Use Policy, 53*, 36–43.

Low, M. S. (1992). Symbolic ties that bind. In I. Altman & M. S. Low (Eds.), *Place attachment* (pp. 165–185). Plenum Press.

Low, M. S., & Altman, I. (1992). Place attachment. A conceptual inquiry. In I. Altman & M. S. Low (Eds.), *Place attachment* (pp. 1–12). Plenum Press.

Lynch, K. (1981). *A theory of good city form*. M.I.T. Press.

Mannarini, T., Tartaglia, S., Fedi, A., & Greganti, K. (2006). Image of neighborhood, self-image and sense of community. *Journal of Environmental Psychology, 26*(3), 202–214. https://doi.org/10.1016/j.jenvp.2006.07.008

Manzo, L. C. (2005). For better or worse: Exploring multiple dimensions of place meaning. *Journal of Environmental Psychology, 25*, 67–86.

Manzo, C. L., & Devine-Wright, P. (Eds.). (2014). *Place attachment. Advances in theory, methods and applications*. Routledge.

Manzo, L. C., & Devine-Wright, P. (2020). Introduction. In L. C. Manzo & P. Devine-Wright (Eds.), *Place attachment. Advances in theory, methods and applications* (2nd ed., pp. 1–8). Routledge.

Markuszewska, I. (2019). *Emotional landscape: Socio-environmental conflict and place attachment* (Experience from the Wielkopolska Region. Studia I Prace z Geografii No. 70). Bogucki Wydawnictwo Naukowe.

Massey, D. (1994). *Space, place and gender*. Polity Press.

Massey, D. (1995). The conceptualisation of place. In D. Massey & P. Jess (Eds.), *A place in the world?* (pp. 46–79). Oxford University Press.

Mazumdar, S., & Mazumdar, S. (2004). Religion and place attachment: A study of sacred places. *Journal of Environmental Psychology, 24*, 385–397.

Meinig, D. W. (Ed.). (1979). *The interpretation of ordinary landscapes: Geographical essays*. Oxford University Press.

Mihaylov, N., & Perkins, D. D. (2014). Community place attachment and its role in social capital development. In C. L. Manzo & P. Devine-Wright (Eds.), *Place attachment. Advances in theory, methods and applications* (pp. 61–74). Routledge.

Mitchell, D. (2003). Cultural landscapes: Just landscapes or landscapes of justice? *Progress in Human Geography, 27*, 787–796.

Mutică, P., & Ilovan, O.-R. (2022). Advocacy for territorial and people-centered approaches to development in Romania: Place attachment based on industrial heritage, forthcoming.

Nogué, J., & Vicente, J. (2004). Landscape and national identity in Catalonia. *Political Geography, 23*, 113–132.

Paasi, A. (1986). The institutionalization of regions: A theoretical framework for the understanding of the emergence of regions and the constitutions of regional identity. *Fennia, 164*, 105–146.

Paasi, A. (2003). Region and place: Regional identity in question. *Progress in Human Geography, 27*, 475–485.

Palang, H., Helmfrid, S., Antrop, M., & Alumäe, H. (2005). Rural landscapes: Past processes and future strategies. *Landscape and Urban Planning, 70*, 3–8.

Pellow, D. (1992). Spaces that teach: Attachment to the African compound. In I. Altman & M. S. Low (Eds.), *Place attachment* (pp. 187–210). Plenum Press.

Pohl, L. (2017). Imaginary politics of the branded city: Right-wing terrorism as a mediated object of stigmatisation. In P. Kirkness & A. Tijé-Dra (Eds.), *Negative neighbourhood reputation and place attachment. The production and contestation of territorial stigma* (pp. 27–41). Routledge.

Proshansky, H. M., Fabian, A. K., & Kaminoff, R. (1983). Place-identity: Physical world socialization of the self. *Journal of Environmental Psychology, 3*(1), 57–83.

Raagmaa, G. (2002). Regional identity in regional development and planning. *European Planning Studies, 10*(1), 55–76.

Raymond, C. M., Brown, G., & Weber, D. (2010). The measurement of place attachment: Personal, community, and environmental connections. *Journal of Environmental Psychology, 30*, 422–434.

Relph, E. (1976). *Place and placelessness*. Pion.

Richling, A., & Solon, J. (2011). *Ekologia krajobrazu* [Landscape ecology]. Wydawnictwo Naukowe PWN.

Riley, R. (1992). Attachment to the ordinary landscape. In I. Altman & S. Low (Eds.), *Place attachment* (pp. 13–35). Plenum Press.

Rose, G. (1993). *Feminism and geography: The limits of geographical knowledge*. University of Minnesota Press.

Rose, G. (2014). *Visual methodologies. An introduction to researching with visual materials* (3rd ed.). Sage.

Rubinstein, L. R., & Parmelee, A. P. (1992). Attachment to place and the representation of the life course by the elderly. In I. Altman & M. S. Low (Eds.), *Place attachment* (pp. 139–163). Plenum Press.

Sack, R. D. (1988). The consumer's world: Place as context. *Annals of the Association of American Geographers, 78*(4), 642–664.

Said, E. (1995). *Orientalism*. Penguin. (First published 1978).

Sauer, C. (1963). The morphology of landscape [1925]. In J. Leighly (Ed.), *Land and life: A selection of the writings of Carl Ortwin Sauer* (pp. 315–350). University of California Press.

Scannell, L., & Gifford, R. (2010a). Defining place attachment: A tripartite organizing framework. *Journal of Environmental Psychology, 30*, 1–10.

Scannell, L., & Gifford, R. (2010b). The relations between natural and civic place attachment and pro-environmental behavior. *Journal of Environmental Psychology, 30*(3), 289–297. https://doi.org/10.1016/j.jenvp.2010.01.010

Scannell, L., & Gifford, R. (2014). Comparing the theories of interpersonal and place attachment. In C. L. Manzo & P. Devine-Wright (Eds.), *Place attachment. Advances in theory, methods and applications* (pp. 23–36). Routledge.

Seamon, D. (1980). Body-subject, time–space routines, and place-ballets. In A. Buttimer & D. Seamon (Eds.), *The human experience of space and place* (pp. 148–165). St. Martin's Press.

Seamon, D. (2014). Chapter 1. Place attachment and phenomenology. The synergistic dynamism of place. In C. L. Manzo & P. Devine-Wright (Eds.), *Place attachment. Advances in theory, methods and applications* (pp. 11–22). Routledge.

Seamon, D. (2018). *Life takes place: Phenomenology, lifeworlds, and place making.* Routledge.

Seamon, D., & Sowers, J. (2008). *Place and placelessness, Edward Relph.* In P. Hubbard, R. Kitchen, & G. Valentine (Eds.), *Key texts in human geography* (pp. 43–51). Sage.

Sebastien, L. (2020). The power of place in understanding place attachments and meanings. *Geoforum, 108*, 204–216. https://doi.org/10.1016/j.geoforum.2019.11.001

Shumaker, S. A., & Taylor, R. B. (1983). Toward a clarification of people-place relationships: A model of attachment to place. In N. R. Feimer & E. S. Geller (Eds.), *Environmental psychology: Directions and perspectives* (pp. 219–251). Praeger.

Smith, J. S. (Ed.). (2019). *Explorations in place attachment.* Routledge.

Smith, J. S., & Cartlidge, M. R. (2011). Place attachment among retirees in Greensburg, Kansas. *Geographical Review, 101*(4), 536–555.

Stobbelaar, D. J., & Pedroli, B. (2011). Perspectives on landscape identity: A conceptual challenge. *Landscape Research, 36*(3), 321–339.

Thompson Fullilove, M. (2014). "The frayed knot". What happens to place attachment in the context of serial forced displacement? In C. L. Manzo & P. Devine-Wright (Eds.), *Place attachment. Advances in theory, methods and applications* (pp. 141–153). Routledge.

Tuan, Y.-F. (1974). *Topophilia: A study of environmental perceptions, attitudes, and values.* Prentice-Hall.

Tuan, Y.-F. (1976). Humanistic geography. *Annals of the Association of American Geographers, 66*, 266–276.

Tuan, Y.-F. (1977). *Space and place: The perspective to experience.* University of Minnesota Press.

Tuan, Y.-F. (1978). Literature and geography: Implications for geographical research. In D. Ley & M. Samuels (Eds.), *Humanistic geography: Prospects and problems* (pp. 194–206). Croom Helm.

Wacquant, L. (2007). Territorial stigmatization in the age of advanced marginality. *Thesis Eleven, 91*(1), 66–77.

Williams, R.D. (2014). "Beyond the commodity metaphor," revisited: Some methodological reflections on place attachment research. In C. L. Manzo & P. Devine-Wright (Eds.), *Place attachment. Advances in theory, methods and applications* (pp. 89-99). : Routledge.

Zhang, Y. (2017). 'This is my "Wo"'. Making home in Shanghai's Lower Quarter. In P. Kirkness & A. Tijé-Dra (Eds.), *Negative neighbourhood reputation and place attachment. The production and contestation of territorial stigma* (pp. 138–157). Routledge.

Part I
Place Making and Place Attachment Through Place-Based Development and Community Place-Driven Actions

Chapter 2
Between Knowledge and Feelings. How Place Attachment Can Strengthen the Sensitive Planning of Landscapes

Iwona Markuszewska ⓘ

2.1 Introduction

According to the European Landscape Convention (Council of Europe, 2000), all forward-looking actions whose role is to enhance, restore or create landscape refer to planning systems. Due to practical, empirical and legal conditions, landscape planning follows the principles of spatial planning. In order to provide democratic procedures, the planning system should involve community participation and should be based on transparent rules which guarantee social and procedural justice. Above all, however, the democratic principles of planning come from the fact that a landscape serves the community around it. Therefore, the voices of residents should be instrumental in making decisions about changes to the landscape or land use.

Participatory planning is doubtless desirable from the perspective of the social control for the decision-making process. This seems to be particularly important in relation to communities with short-term participatory experiences. This is true, for instance, for the post-socialist countries of Central and Eastern Europe. Nevertheless, as noticed in planning practices in Poland, people criticise the pattern of social participation as they do not enjoy having considerable influence in the decision-making process (Ociepa-Kubicka, 2015; Daniel 2019; Hajduk, 2021). To be more precise, what is expected from participants is that they accept ready-made solutions rather than implement bottom-up initiatives. On the other hand, planning authorities are of the opinion that public voices should be limited because otherwise, spatial planning would have to support selfish individual interests instead of working for the

I. Markuszewska (✉)
Department of Environmental Remote Sensing and Soil Science, Faculty of Geographical and Geological Sciences, Institute of Physical Geography and Environmental Planning, Adam Mickiewicz University, Poznań, Poland
e-mail: iwona.markuszewska@amu.edu.pl

© The Author(s), under exclusive license to Springer Nature Switzerland AG 2022
O.-R. Ilovan, I. Markuszewska (eds.), *Preserving and Constructing Place Attachment in Europe*, GeoJournal Library 131,
https://doi.org/10.1007/978-3-031-09775-1_2

common good. In addition to this, the participation of residents is perceived as an obstacle to the smooth running of procedures for adopting a draft local plan. However, this convention is not limited exclusively to specific countries or traditions in landscape planning. As Fainstein (2009) stressed, the abuse of private interests is common, even in societies with long democratic traditions.

Landscape planning is, in essence, a set of propositions for transforming land use. Due to differences of opinion, members of local communities are usually very unhappy with proposed changes. However, people's attitude depends on how much they are familiar with a place and how emotionally attached they are to a particular material setting. For instance, the literature demonstrates that highly attached people are sceptical and unwilling to accept changes due to potential loss of ties to a place (Markuszewska, 2019). In addition to this, inhabitants may have serious worries, such as the deterioration of environmental quality and human well-being, which consequently may weaken place bonding. Thus, defence of the inviolable status quo can be manifested through place protection actions (Devine-Wright, 2009). Regardless of this, however, I perceive the involvement of the local community as indispensable in the planning process. I have termed this specific socially oriented approach sensitive planning. In the subsequent sections, I will take a detailed look at some reasons for this.

Despite current system consents for public consultation and participation, the procedures of local planning restrict opportunities for citizens to become actively involved in it. Therefore, by presenting the weaknesses of spatial planning procedures in Poland, I have proposed a new approach – sensitive planning – that puts local actors in a strong position in formal proceedings. Sensitive planning emphasises the importance and preservation of those material and non-material characteristics of a landscape that residents consider important from the point of view of the history of a place, the memory of a place, and other cultural and social values that build genii loci, as well as all those values of the natural environment that distinguish a geographical location from others. Having this in mind, sensitive planning is a socially oriented model of landscape planning whose pillars are constructed from the affective values of the local community and sensory detection of the iconic elements of landscape. I argue that including both emotional attachment to a place and sensory perception of a landscape in the planning process can be the antidote to conflicts and, at the same time, can enhance the sense of procedural justice. Most of all, however, sensitive planning keeps a balance between bottom-up initiatives and top-down actions, as well as between tangible and intangible dimensions of landscape transformation.

To this end, the research questions of this chapter are the following: (1) How can place attachment strengthen the sensitive planning of landscapes? and (2) How can sensitive planning be a supportive tool in the conventional modus operandi of landscape planning? In answering these questions, I present a brief outline of social and procedural justice in the process of landscape planning and conceptualise the emotional relationship between community and landscape. After this I present a theoretical framework for the analysis that has been developed by myself for sensitive planning. The next section investigates the empirical implementation of sensitive planning, including its limitations in relation to conventional practices.

2.2   Methodological Anchor

In this chapter, I address the criticisms of planning paradigms that reflect on major planning issues such as participatory planning and procedural justice. The starting point of my research was a review of the formal procedures of spatial planning in Poland and, specifically, a recognition of the role of community members and local leaders in planning policies and procedures. By analysing the participatory planning process (Ustawa z dnia 27 marca 2003 r. o planowaniu i zagospodarowaniu przestrzennym [Act of the 27th of March 2003 on Planning and Spatial Development ...], and participatory observation during 2010–2022), I identified the critical components of procedural justice. At the same time, I proposed a model for shaping and maintaining sensitive relationships between people and landscape. My intention in doing this was to show that the emotional connection to place and the sensitive perception of landscape are undervalued in the planning process. Furthermore, I intended to contribute a different perspective of planning mechanisms to the Polish system. Consequently, I have introduced a concept of people-oriented sensitive planning that can support conventional landscape planning.

2.3   The Spatial Planning System in Poland

In Poland, since the transition from a centrally managed to a market-led economy, citizens' participation in planning has become accepted (Zastawnik, 2015). This was in the early 1990s, when new laws came into effect (Ustawa z dnia 27 marca 2003 r. o planowaniu i zagospodarowaniu przestrzennym [Act of the 27th of March 2003 on Planning and Spatial Development ...]). In addition, the pre-accession process to the European Union was introduced and, after Poland's accession, EU law was adopted. At that time, Ustawa z dnia 3 października 2008 r. o udostępnianiu informacji o środowisku i jego ochronie, udziale społeczeństwa w ochronie środowiska oraz o ocenach oddziaływania na środowisko [Act of the 3rd of October 2008 ...], was passed, inter alia, which ensured citizens' control over the proceedings. This created, at least theoretically, a relatively important role for society and formed a democratic groundwork for including bottom-up initiatives when discussing landscape transformation.

Considering Fig. 2.1, which shows the formal procedures for designing a local zoning plan, social participation is limited to participating in informing meetings and expressing reservations about draft zoning plans (steps marked in red). Nonetheless, according to the provision of the Act of 27 March 2003 on Planning and Spatial Development, it is assumed that public participation in the planning

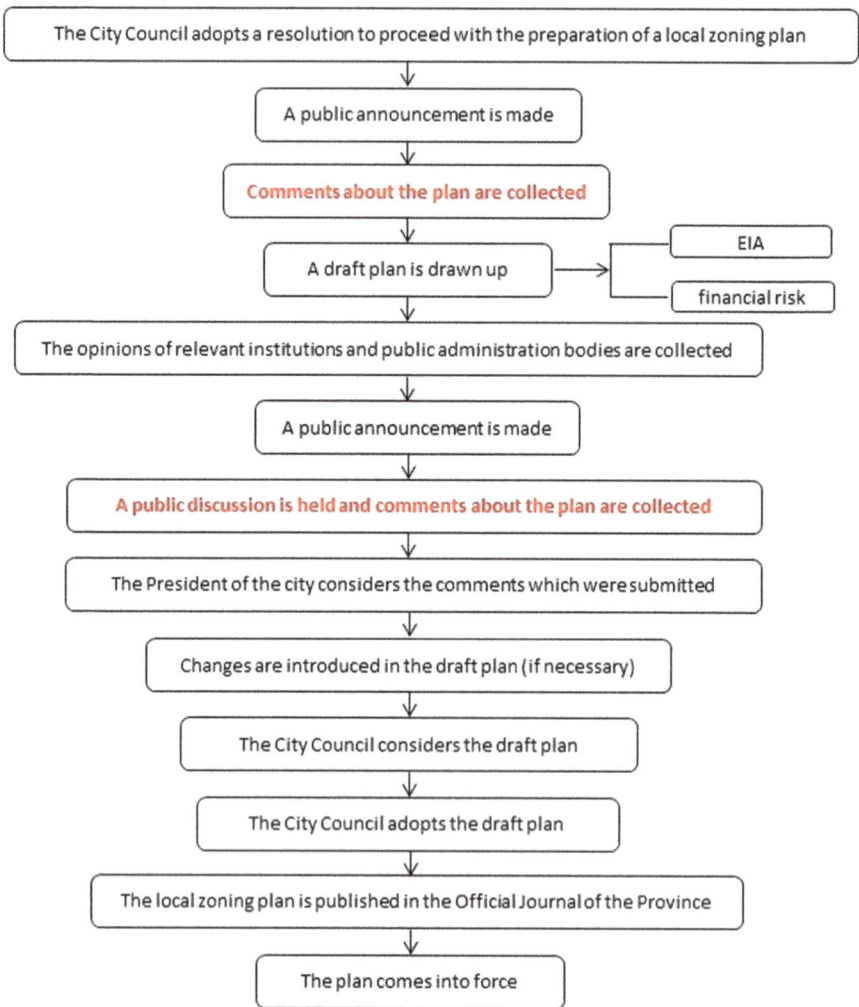

Fig. 2.1 Formal procedures of spatial planning in Poland. (Source: Own compilation based on Ustawa z dnia 27 marca 2003 r. o planowaniu i zagospodarowaniu przestrzennym [Act of the 27th of March 2003 on Planning and Spatial Development])

procedure begins with the announcement that a draft local plan has been created. This information must be made public in an advertisement in the local press and by announcement, as well as in a manner customary for a particular area. The real involvement of citizens in the planning process is, however, to submit propositions for the plan which may not be shorter than 21 days from the date of the official announcement (the first step of public participation). Nonetheless, residents' comments on the local plan are considered as suggestions for preliminary planning arrangements and may be considered or rejected by planning authorities. After the draft plan is made public (with Environmental Impact Assessment – EIA), each citizen can (over at least 14 days) submit comments. At the same time, inhabitants can participate in a public discussion on the provisions contained in the local plan for a particular project (the second step of social participation). Pursuant to the regulations, members of the affected community, non-residents and the representatives of various organisations may actively participate in the discussion. It should be emphasised, however, that the planning authority is not required to justify the inclusion or rejection of the comments submitted to the draft plan, and therefore, it does not have to respond to these comments.

Most of the decision-making manners associated with spatial planning assume that participants have equal access to information regarding the course of the planning process. Nevertheless, research shows that the general public are unfamiliar with the principles of planning and participation in the planning procedure (Ociepa-Kubicka, 2015). Furthermore, the participation of residents only involves commenting on the solutions prepared. The fact that interested parties object to some of the proposals does not mean that the voice of the opposition will be taken into account when continuing work on a draft zoning plan. As Kaczmarek and Wójcicki (2015) note, consultation of public decisions by an authority or administration does not have to include a negotiation or, even more so, the issuing of a settlement. Consultations are, therefore, a way of obtaining opinions, positions, and proposals. In addition, authorities responsible for planning procedures often do not facilitate and do not care for the active participation of residents in the planning process (Daniel, 2019). Thus, decision-making processes are often reasons for conflicts among individuals over different preferences regarding land use. This creates a deep sense of social and procedural injustice.

2.4 Social and Procedural Justice in Landscape Planning

According to Smith (1994), social justice is strictly linked to legal systems, human rights, ethics, and morality. Social justice is a normative concept centred on fairness, equality, equity, rights, and participation (Khechen, 2013). Emani and colleagues (2015) noted that social justice involves creating fair background in which individuals' rights are acknowledged and protected in decision-making procedures.

The contribution of human geographers to theories of social justice refers to the theoretical background and the fundamental elements of this concept (Smith, 1994; Khechen, 2013). Indeed, it is important to understand the evolution of this concept, particularly through David Harvey's concept of social justice (1973), which was developed by other scholars regarding procedural justice (Thibaut & Walker, 1975; Lind & Tyler, 1988), environmental justice (Cutter, 1995), social justice (Smith, 1997), and territorial justice (Smith, 2000).

In terms of planning procedures, social justice refers to procedural fairness, which, according to Tyler (2000), provides people with the opportunity to have a voice in decision-making processes. To be more precise, "[p]eople feel more fairly

treated if they are allowed to participate in the resolution of their problems or conflicts by presenting their suggestions about what should be done" (Tyler, 2000, p. 5).
In general, scholars who deal with procedural justice focus attention on fairness in
individual participation during the planning process and emphasise the expression
of public opinion through the formal procedures of the planning process (Lawrence
et al., 1997). However, Emani and colleagues (2015, p. 2) suggested that "procedural justice is concerned with how decisions are made rather than the outcome of
those decisions". In this way, the decision-making process is perceived as socially
fair, thereby ensuring that the level of public acceptance is enhanced (Mercer-
Mapstone et al., 2018). Following on from this, many researchers espoused increasing the role of residents in the planning process (Stone, 1989; Tauxe, 1995; Healey
& Gilroy, 2016).

It seems, however, that what makes the procedures fair is transparency. How
participants are informed about the subsequent steps of the planning process affects
the credibility and mutual trust of the involved parties. Thus, the role of the informative system is to provide information to the public and to create a chance for effective participation of all those who are affected by the case (Lind & Tyler, 1988;
Solum, 2004). It is worth paying attention to a certain duality concerning the active
participation of society. Some scholars believe that the exclusion of some of the
possible participants from the planning process is procedurally unjust (Emani et al.,
2015). On the other hand, there are those who claim that including everyone is practically impossible (Feinstein, 2009).

In addition, active participation of the members of the local community legiti-
mises fair procedures. Emani et al. (2015, p. 126) emphasise that "[a] fair planning
process must include both legitimate representatives and active participation in
order to ensure that the public's voice will be properly considered". Community
members recognise formal procedures as fair if they can openly express their opinion and have an influence on the final decision and implementation process (Emain
et al., 2015; Markuszewska, 2019). For this reason, the current system of social
participation in the planning process in Poland is not socially focused because discussions and written comments of ready-made propositions, which are commonly
used in public input, are difficult to assess as socially and procedurally fair. Thus,
this traditional attitude to public participation brings counterproductive outcomes
and creates the grounds for mistrust (Innes & Booher, 2004; Markuszewska, 2019).

2.5   The Process of Building Sensitive Bonds
         with the Landscape

The starting point for creating sensitive bonds with the landscape (Fig. 2.2) was my
concurring with the criticism expressed by Maria Lewicka (2011), who stated that
place attachment studies have focused more on the human component (the domain
of psychological research) rather than on those of place and process (the domain of

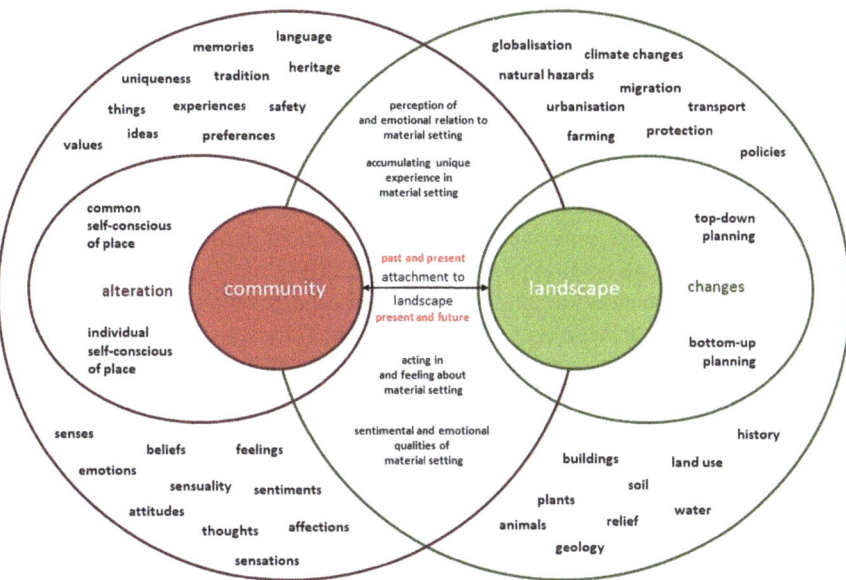

Fig. 2.2 The framework of landscape attachment. (Source: Own elaboration)

geographical study). For this reason, and bearing in mind the arguments of other scholars (e.g., Hummon, 1992; Low, 1992; Riley, 1992; Hay, 1998; Scannell & Gifford, 2010), I assumed that, in the process of placemaking, ties between people and places are essential.

Based on a literature review of the building, maintaining, and changing of human attachment to place and landscape (Tuan, 1974, 1975; Relph, 1976; Proshansky et al., 1983; Sack, 1988; Hay, 1998; Agnew, 1987; Antrop, 2003, 2005; Cresswell, 2004, 2015; Palang et al., 2011), as well as my own experience, I compiled a place-making framework which supports a multi-stage process of creating bonds with a geographical setting. This model highlights the role of community in a place as the essential manifestation of its presence and the role of an active community in collectively shaping, managing, and planning the landscape.

Community attachment has a special meaning in this framework as social involvement and active participation are vital in the process of transforming neighbourhoods and/or landscape planning. Interpersonal relations turned out to be significant in the social place forming process as community attachment can create a positive relation to place and landscape (Carrus et al., 2014). The bonds formed with the community in a place, and the feeling of belonging to a neighbourhood have a powerful meaning in structuring community networks that mandate common/group identities and a sense of community. Social involvement in local initiatives, voluntary actions in grassroots organisations and participation in formal and informal bottom-up initiatives are the key to success in the struggle to protect a place. In turn, human identification with a particular landscape, such as a place of residence, reflects one's identification with the local community (Fornara et al., 2019; Markuszewska, 2019).

However, attachment to landscape is understood more broadly than attachment to a place. While place is frequently understood as the home or neighbourhood, landscape as a spatial geographical setting may include both the immediate locality and the region, which is a geographical unit utilised for spatial planning. For this reason, landscape researchers (including geographers and architects) consider the connection to landscape (a physical location) as essential in creating and maintaining both individual and common identities (Egoz, 2013).

When creating the model of attachment to landscape, my intention was to include holistic and dynamic approaches that interpret people-landscape relationships under the constant influence of changeable policies about landscape planning and human management. Having this in mind, I agree with Lorzing (2001), who proposes that a landscape is a piece of land which is characterised by the joint effects of natural forces and human intervention. I am in accord with Oliveira and his colleagues (2010, p. 802), who put forward the idea of landscapes as follows: "Natural (primary or modified, preserved or degraded, etc.) and cultural (agricultural, industrial, rural, urban, mixed, etc.) landscapes are constituted of spatial fixes, defined as the sum of permanently and temporarily rooted and anchored elements of the natural heritage, population and human-made economic and cultural heritage in a geographical area". In addition to this, a very important presumption is that various natural and cultural processes affect landscape changes. As for the latter, cultural values build bonds between past and present, as well as between present and future. They are essential requirements in creating place and landscape identity, a feeling of belonging that ensures a sense of place, and finally, a sense of community (Swanwick, 2012).

Landscapes consist of natural and non-natural components which are embedded in the history of a certain place (Markuszewska, 2019). As a whole, all landscape components create the character of the local landscape, but only those which are unique and specific may create a symbolic identity-based meaning for the local community. This landscape-oriented perspective encourages people to (unwittingly or intentionally) build emotional bonds to a place that constitute place attachment and strengthen the sense of identifying with the locality. Nevertheless, the historical value of the place is important as well because it determines the meaning of the landscape components and gives a sense of place. In addition, what makes place attachment stronger is human satisfaction with the landscape they live in, as well as having the opportunity to transform it according to their wishes. In contrast, what weakens place identity is dissatisfaction with the place of living, which happens when the landscape loses its natural, cultural, and symbolic meaning.

In addition to what has been assumed, I would like to stress that an inherent aspect of landscape transformation is time. However, change is twofold, and thus concerns both people's changing perceptions of a landscape and the fact that landscapes change dynamically over time. The inter-personal changeability of individuals causes people's perception of the landscape to change. This is influenced by age, requirements, self-awareness, education, and economic status, as well as by other circumstances (Lewicka, 2011). On the other hand, landscape is under constant human intervention and natural processes (Antrop, 2005; Van Eetvelde & Antrop, 2009). Therefore, the question of how landscape changes affect human-landscape relations arises. That is, well-established attachment to a place is influenced by internal and external conditions, and thus, attachment fluctuates from strong to a weakening of the bond with the place / landscape. Nevertheless, the influence of the above-mentioned factors may or may not shift the "place-feeling" between these two extreme states.

In addition, the concept of landscape is shaped by ideology (Olwig, 2002) and is associated with policy regulations. This is important in reshaping attachment to landscape and in creating territorial development and transition, which involves both the dimension of collective identity and belonging (bottom-up) and the policy of spatial planning (top-down). In addition, the elaborated model of landscape attachment (Fig. 2.2) includes the importance of civil engagement in placemaking and local issues, such as conflicts of land use and natural resources (Devine-Wright, 2009; Markuszewska, 2020), a psychological feeling of place possession (Patterson & Williams, 2005; Gaybrail, 2013) and, in the broader context of analysis, global issues such as migration, immigration and climate change (Lewicka, 2011). The presented process of forming attachment to landscape is an attempt to collect various place-related concepts in one framework. Bearing this in mind, I am fully aware that my proposal is not a universal model of landscape attachment and will not solve the issue of the methodology for how to measure place in a complex manner. Nonetheless, my intention is to highlight the importance of building relationships with landscape in the process of making decisions regarding landscape changes.

2.6 The Concept of Sensitive Planning

In formulating the background to the concept of sensitive planning, I assumed that the process of landscape planning should meet the expectations of the community for what constitutes the fairness and justice of formal procedures. Following on from this, it is important to define how to create a fair framework for social and procedural justice in sensitive planning. Without doubt, the needs of the participants at landscape planning must be integrated into the legal rules of proceedings, but not in a way that diminishes the value of those participants, as it currently does. However, contrary to the current procedures, emotional connection with landscape, perception of landscape via a sensitive context and social values should all be recognised.

Sensitive planning is a socially oriented approach to the planning process. It can be an alternative to traditional strategies for actions taken in the field of landscape planning. Acquiring knowledge about a location, becoming familiar with a place, and building emotional bonds with it create mutual relationships between the people in a place and its material dimensions. These are all arguments for focusing the planning process on the local community. Sensitive planning draws attention to the intangible dimensions of a place and manages the space in such a way as to be able to preserve and maintain specific genii loci. This is because, in this context, sensitivity means a crucial perception of a certain geographical location through the senses and emotions; a vital understanding of how people build, shape, maintain and enhance connections to places and relationships with the surrounding environment and with the people in a place.

In addition, sensitive planning draws from sensory interactions with a particular place based on a complex relationship with a physical location and the non-physical context of a place. This is manifested in such actions in a landscape which detect the most preferable for citizens' directions of its transformation in the future. This approach to planning practices concerns the predictability of possible side-effects that cannot be demonstrated in classical simulations of changes, such as predictions resulted from emotional rootedness in a place, as well as sensory and spiritual feelings around a particular space.

This sensitive bond with place, however, can influence specific psychological perceptions of a place and attitudes towards ownership of a public space. Namely, the tamed place/landscape implies a feeling of 'my-ness', as the landscape begins to be perceived from 'my own' perspective. This attitude is a potential source of conflicts in the planning process, in particular in scheduling landscape changes. This sensitive bond with place, however, can be an advantage in indicating directions of potential landscape changes based on preconceptions about 'what is the best thing for this place'? Apart from this, what makes sensitive planning important is 'a sense of place', which boils down to the declaration: 'I know what is good and what is bad for this place'. 'This place', however, not 'my place'. A deep understanding of place stands in contradiction to an egoistic self-centred understanding of place possession as, in fact, 'this place' means 'our place', where 'us' are all those members of the affected community who manifest place-protection behaviour and protect the public interest and the rights of the majority. A compromise solution like this does not necessarily consider a wide range of individual suggestions as propositions accepted by the democratic majority have priority. Thus, these bottom-up, commonly worked out propositions should be taken into account by decision makers in the planning process. Since decisions relating to landscape planning are to serve the benefit of residents, their voice should be vital to the planning process, following the assumption that local people know a place inside out and are able to judge what is best for that place.

The process of building a bond with a place demonstrates how important is the attachment to a certain place for the people, to take responsibility for it in the process of planning changes. This highlights the possible prevention of those changes which would loosen, weaken, or even break the bonds with a landscape. Moreover, sensitive planning puts the emphasis on place rootedness, on the sensory feeling of place. In this meaning, the landscape is not only a physical space, but above all a metaphysical experience of 'being in a place through sensory and spiritual experience'. A full experience of a place means understanding the people who live there. There are also memories and emotions that arise in contact with the landscape. This multi-faceted and comprehensive experience of a place shapes the narrative sensitivity of landscape users and reshapes the meaning of place.

In addition, experience of a place and deep rootedness release and shape the feeling of 'at-homeness' and 'at-placeness'. People who are deeply attached to a landscape are not landscape users – they become an indispensable and authentic part of the landscape. The findings of my pilot study evidenced this. It concerned changes in the landscape that tame this space and adapt it to mass tourism (paper in progress). Opening the landscape to 'external' tourists resulted in the local inhabitants being less enamoured with that place, changing their emotional attitude towards it, which was expressed by the reluctance to be in the landscape as it was no longer familiar to them (personal observation). The results of my observations prove that failing to take into account the residents' expectations is fatal and leads to a loss of relationship with place.

2.7 Sensitive Planning via Conventional Planning

Above, I presented a justification for sensitive planning as an alternative answer to conventional landscape planning. I argued that sensitive planning can avoid conflicts around new land use, which commonly accompanies the landscape planning process. There are numerous challenges in the landscape planning process, bearing in mind the varied and often conflicting wishes of different landscape users, who want fair access to it. Thus, integrating sensitive planning into the formal proceedings and decision-making of landscape planning may enhance social fairness and social trust in authorities.

However, what makes this approach superior is that it privileges the voices of the local community (participants of landscape planning) in the decision-making process. Focusing the proceedings on bottom-up initiatives and propositions follows from the conviction that those who are deeply rooted in a place are the most appropriate authority to identify the most desirable landscape changes. This is not only a confirmation of the sense of place experience as a consequence of living in a certain geographical location for a long time, but most of all a sensitive feeling of place resulting from an emotional relationship with the surrounding space.

Sensitive planning does not negate all the necessary data that landscape (spatial) planning requires (e.g., the natural, economic, and social cultural conditions of the area in question). Undoubtedly, these data are required to understand the possibilities and limitations of landscape development. However, 'sensitive' data gathered from residents provide vital information about the people in a place, such as their needs, and thus these supplementary data find their usefulness in creating local zoning plans. Along with local people, planning authorities can identify strategies for landscape changes by analysing these data.

By involving residents in the planning process, we obtain a much more comprehensive analysis that takes into account many more factors than the traditional approach to planning. It allows for a multi-faceted assessment of the situation. It makes it possible to predict those scenarios of change that are undesirable for the local community and propose reasonable solutions that resolve conflicts through generally acceptable fall-back options. Sensitive planning allows preventive action to be taken much faster than the traditional approach to planning. However, sensitive planning is not free from legal restrictions.

Achieving success in the field of sensitive planning requires the maturity of all those involved in the planning process. I understand 'maturity' to entail making compromises which serve public interests and common social goods. Reaching this goal requires not only the involvement of residents, but also the appropriate approach of planners and decision-makers. Their role is to convince the sceptical members of the community of the credibility of zoning plans. At this point, I would like to refer to the words of Healey and Gilroy (2016, p. 47): "That planning, as an idea and practice, should belong to citizens is a long-standing ideal within the planning tradition". These authors criticise politicians, bureaucrats and technocrats for acting "'for citizens' guided by some superior knowledge of what 'people' want and 'the public interest'" (Healey & Gilroy, 2016, p. 47).

To foster social equity, it is important to shift from an approach based on keeping the community at a distance to an approach emphasising cooperation with and active participation of the local community in landscape planning. Thanks to cooperation among participants a consensus can be reached. This involves the openness of the authorities to suggestions, allowing residents to participate in the joint development of the plan rather than only giving the right to planners and developers to consult on the project, which implies a lack of trust in the residents.

In particular, contrary to the rather passive social participation in the planning process in force in Poland, in sensitive planning, bottom-up proposals are given priority. This means that the draft plan must be approved by the affected community. In addition, priority is given to those investments and activities that preserve the identity of the place and, at the same time, maintain bonds with the landscape, while also calming any concerns residents might have with the quality of the landscape. Sensitive planning emphasises transparency. For this to be possible, the formal procedures of landscape planning should start with outdoor meetings and workshops. Following this, round-table discussions and negotiations should be carried out to further the decision-making process. Unfortunately, the current principles of spatial planning do not provide such an option. Moreover, activities in this area are not supported by landscape audits, whose role is to implement in Poland the provisions of the European Landscape Convention (Majchrowska & Papińska, 2018).

Poland is not alone in having an imperfect landscape planning process, which has been described in this chapter as marginal public participation. This problem was highlighted by other scientists who analysed the specificity of planning procedures. Due to the above, the sensitive approach to planning landscape changes that I have proposed puts emphasis on active social participation. Thus, sensitive planning engages local actors through workshops, debates, and community consultations. This approach can be successfully adopted as a tool to support traditional planning procedures in any democratic planning system.

2.8   Conclusions

To conclude, sensitive planning is socially oriented landscape planning that integrates active participation of local actors from the beginning to the end of formal procedures. The active participation of residents is manifested through workshops, round-table discussions, and negotiations. Sensitive planning uses the feeling of being in a place and emotional ties with it to support locals in being actively involved in bottom-up initiatives. However, bottom-up proposals and initiatives should follow legal, planning, environmental and economic restrictions and should represent most of the participants involved in the process. This is an opportunity to win over local communities and reduce confrontations of bottom-up proposals and come to a consensus by challenging top-down propositions. When constructing the framework of sensitive planning, an assessment of the individual perceptions of a landscape through the experience of a place via visual, sensual, spiritual, and emotional values is considered. It should be emphasised that both tangible and intangible dimensions of landscape play an equal role in the decision-making process. Defined in this way, the framework of sensitive planning can provide social and procedural justice.

References

Agnew, J. A. (1987). *Place and politics: The geographical mediation of state and society*. Allen and Unwin.

Antrop, M. (2003). The role of cultural values in modern landscapes. The Flemishexample. In H. Palang & G. Fry (Eds.), *Landscape interfaces: Cultural heritage in changing landscapes* (pp. 91–108). Kluwer Academic Publishers.

Antrop, M. (2005). Why landscapes of the past are important for the future? *Landscape and Urban Planning, 70*, 21–34.

Carrus, G., Scopelliti, M., Fornara, F., Bonnes, M., & Bonaiuto, M. (2014). Place attachment, community identification, and pro-environmental engagement. In L. C. Manzo & P. Devine Wright (Eds.), *Place attachment. Advances in theory, methods and applications* (pp. 154–164). Routledge.

Council of Europe. (2000). *European Landscape Convention 2000* (European Treaty series – No. 176).

Cresswell, T. (2004). *Place: A short introduction*. Blackwell.

Cresswell, T. (2015). *Place: An introduction* (2nd ed.). Wiley-Blackwell.

Cutter, S. L. (1995). Race, class and environmental justice. *Progress in Human Geography, 19*, 111–122.

Daniel, P. (2019). Udział społeczeństwa w procedurze planistycznej – rzeczywiste uprawnienie czy "przykry" obowiązek organu [Public participation in the planning procedure – A real right or an 'unpleasant' duty of an authority]. *Samorząd Terytorialny, 7–8*, 7–16.

Devine-Wright, P. (2009). Rethinking NIMBYism: The role of place attachment and place identity in explaining place-protective action. *Journal of Community and Applied Social Psychology, 19*, 426–441.

Egoz, S. (2013). Landscape and identity: Beyond a geography of one place. In P. Howard, I. Thompson, & E. Waterton (Eds.), *The Routledge companion of landscape studies* (pp. 272–285). Routledge.

Emami, P., Xu, W., Bjornlund, H., & Johnston, T. (2015). A framework for assessing the procedural justice in integrated resource planning processes. *Sustainable Development and Planning, 193*, 119–130.

Fainstein, S. (2009). Spatial justice and planning. *JSSJ – Justice Spatiale/Spatial Justice, 1*, 1–13.

Fornara, F., Troffa, R., Valera, S., & Vidal, T. (2019). European and natural landscapes as carriers of place identity: A correlational study in Italian and Spanish regions. *Landscape Research, 44*(6), 757–767.

Graybill, J. K. (2013). Mapping an emotional topography of an ecological homeland: The case of Sakhalin Island, Russia. *Emotion, Space and Society, 8*, 39–50.

Hajduk, S. (2021). *Partycypacja społeczna w zarządzaniu przestrzennym w kontekście planistycznym* [Social participation in spatial management in the planning context]. Oficyna Wydawnicza Politechniki Białostockiej.

Harvey, D. (1973). *Social justice and the city*. Edward Arnold.

Hay, R. (1998). Sense of place in developmental context. *Journal of Environmental Psychology, 18*(1), 5–29.

Healey, P., & Gilroy, R. (2016). Towards a people-sensitive planning. In J. Hillier & J. Metzger (Eds.), *Connections: Exploring contemporary planning theory and practice with Patsy Healey* (pp. 47–59). Routledge.

Hummon, D. M. (1992). Community attachment: Local sentiment and sense of place. In I. Altman & S. M. Low (Eds.), *Place attachment* (pp. 253–278). Plenum Press.

Innes, J., & Booher, D. (2004). Reframing public participation: Strategies for the 21st century. *Planning Theory & Practice, 5*(4), 419–439.

Kaczmarek, T., & Wójcicki, M. (2015). Uspołecznienie procesu planowania przestrzennego na przykładzie miasta Poznania [Socialisation of the spatial planning process on the example of the city of Poznań]. *Ruch Prawniczy, Ekonomiczny i Socjologiczny, LXXVII*(1), 219–236.

Khechen, M. (2013). *Social justice: Concepts, principles, tools and challenges* (pp. 1–26). Economic and Social Commission for Western Asia (ESCWA).

Lawrence, R., Daniels, S., & Stankey, G. (1997). Procedural justice and public involvement in natural resource decision making. *Society and Natural Resources, 10*, 577–589.

Lewicka, M. (2011). Place attachment: How far have we come in the last 40 years? *Journal of Environmental Psychology, 31*, 207–230.

Lind, E., & Tyler, T. (1988). *The social psychology of procedural justice*. Plenum Publishing Corporation.

Lorzing, H. (2001). *The nature of landscape: A personal quest*. 010 Publishers.

Low, S. M. (1992). Symbolic ties that bind: Place attachment in the plaza. In I. Altman & S. M. Low (Eds.), *Place attachment* (pp. 165–186). Plenum Press.

Majchrowska, A., & Papińska, E. (2018). Audyt krajobrazowy narzędziem innowacji społecznej [Landscape audit as a tool of social innovation]. *Acta Universitas Lodziensis, 32*, 51–67.

Markuszewska, I. (2019). *Emotional landscape: Socio-environmental conflict and place attachment*. Bogucki Wydawnictwo Naukowe.

Markuszewska, I. (2020). From NIMBY to YIMBY: When a new open cast mine creates land use conflict. In A. Kołodziejczak & L. Kaczmarek (Eds.), *Gospodarowanie gruntami na obszarach wiejskich* (pp. 149–168). Bogucki Wydawnictwo Naukowe.

Mercer-Mapstone, L., Rifkin, W., Louis, W. R., & Moffat, K. (2018). Company-community dialogue builds relationships, fairness, and trust leading to social acceptance of Australian mining developments. *Journal of Cleaner Production, 184*, 671–677.

Ociepa-Kubicka, A. (2015). Udział społeczności w procedurze planowania przestrzennego [Community participation in the spatial planning procedure]. *Inżynieria i Ochrona Środowiska, 18*(4), 471–481.

Oliveira, J., Roca, Z., & Leitão, N. (2010). Territorial identity and development: From topophilia to terraphilia. *Land Use Policy, 27*, 801–814.

Olwig, K. R. (2002). *Landscape, nature and the body politic: From Britain's Renaissance to America's new world.* University of Wisconsin Press.

Palang, H., Alumäe, H., Printsmann, A., Rehema, M., Sepp, K., & Sooväli-Sepping, H. (2011). Social landscape: Ten years of planning 'valuable landscapes' in Estonia. *Land Use Policy, 28*, 19–25.

Patterson, M. E., & Williams, D. R. (2005). Maintaining research traditions on place: Diversity of thought and scientific progress. *Journal of Environmental Psychology, 25*, 361–380.

Proshansky, H. M., Fabian, A. K., & Kaminoff, R. (1983). Place-identity: Physical world socialization of the self. *Journal of Environmental Psychology, 3*(1), 57–83.

Relph, E. (1976). *Place and placelessness.* Pion.

Riley, R. B. (1992). Attachment to the ordinary landscape. In I. Altman & S. M. Low (Eds.), *Place attachment* (pp. 13–35). Plenum Press.

Sack, R. D. (1988). The consumer's world: Place as context. *Annals of the Association of American Geographers, 78*(4), 642–664.

Scannell, L., & Gifford, R. (2010). Defining place attachment: A tripartite organizing framework. *Journal of Environmental Psychology, 30*(1), 1–10.

Smith, D. M. (1994). *Geography and social justice.* Blackwell Publisher.

Smith, D. M. (1997). Back to the good life: Towards an enlarged conception of social justice. *Environment and Planning D: Society and Space, 15*, 19–35.

Smith, D. M. (2000). Moral progress in human geography: Transcending the place of good fortune. *Progress in Human Geography, 24*, 1–18.

Solum, L. (2004). Procedural justice. *Southern California Law Review, 78*, 181–321.

Stone, L. (1989). Cultural crossroads of community participation in development: A case from Nepal. *Human Organization, 48*(3), 203–213.

Swanwick, C. (2012). The assessment of countryside and landscape character in England: An overview. In K. Bishop & A. Phillips (Eds.), *Countryside planning. New approaches to management and conservation* (pp. 109–124). Earthscan.

Tauxe, C. (1995). Marginalizing public participation in local planning: An ethnographic account. *Journal of the American Planning Association, 61*(4), 441–471.

Thibaut, J., & Walker, L. (1975). *Procedural justice.* Lawrence Erlbaum Associates Inc.

Tuan, Y. F. (1974). *Topophilia: A study of environmental perceptions, attitudes, and values.* Prentice-Hall.

Tuan, Y.-F. (1975). Place: An experiential perspective. *Geographical Review, 65*(2), 151–165.

Tyler, T. R. (2000). Social justice: Outcome and procedure. *International Journal of Psychology, 35*(2), 117–125.

Ustawa z dnia 27 marca 2003 r. o planowaniu i zagospodarowaniu przestrzennym, Dz. U. 2003 Nr 80 poz. 717, z późniejszymi zmianami [Act of the 27th of March 2003 on Planning and Spatial Development, Journal of Laws of 2003 No. 80, item 717 as amended]. https://isap.sejm.gov.pl/isap.nsf/DocDetails.xsp?id=WDU20210000741

Ustawa z dnia 3 października 2008 r. o udostępnianiu informacji o środowisku i jego ochronie, udziale społeczeństwa w ochronie środowiska oraz o ocenach oddziaływania na środowisko, Dz. U. 2008 Nr 199 poz. 1227, z późniejszymi zmianami [Act of the 3rd of October 2008 on the Provision of information on the Environment and its Protection, Public Participation in Environmental Protection and on Environmental Impact Assessments, Journal of Laws of 2008 No. 199, item 1227 as amended]. http://isap.sejm.gov.pl/isap.nsf/DocDetails.xsp?id=WDU20081991227

Van Eetvelde, V., & Antrop, M. (2009). Indicators for assessing changing landscape character of cultural landscapes in Flanders (Belgium). *Land Use Policy, 26*, 901–910.

Zastawnik, A. (2015). Spatial planning with public participation. *Technical Transcations Architecture, 1-A*, 165–189.

Chapter 3
The Role of Place Attachment and the Moderating Factors in Shaping the Future Second-Home Usage Pattern: Evidence from the Polish Mountains

Adam Czarnecki (iD), **Aneta Dacko** (iD), **Mariusz Dacko** (iD), and **Manu Rantanen** (iD)

3.1 Introduction

In Europe, second homes have risen in their popularity as a recreation form since the 1950s (Shucksmith, 1983). This tendency has been proven by an increase in the scale of this social phenomenon both statistically (reflected by the number of second homes and their users) (CSO, 2021) and spatially (manifested through the geographical spread of second homes beyond suburban and tourist regions) (Terzić et al., 2020).

From the point of view of local host-communities and their authorities (e.g., regarding local development), not only are the above statistical and spatial scales of the phenomenon important, but so are the number of the owner's/user's visits and, even more significant, the length of stay during a year. The reason is that this implies

A. Czarnecki (✉)
Institute of Rural and Agricultural Development, Polish Academy of Sciences,
Warsaw, Poland
e-mail: aczarnecki@irwirpan.waw.pl

A. Dacko
Department of Agricultural Geodesy, Cadastre and Photogrammetry,
'Hugo Kołłątaj' University of Agriculture in Krakow, Krakow, Poland
e-mail: a.dacko@ur.krakow.pl

M. Dacko
Department of Economics and Food Economy, 'Hugo Kołłątaj' University of Agriculture
in Krakow, Krakow, Poland
e-mail: m.dacko@ur.krakow.pl

M. Rantanen
Ruralia Institute, University of Helsinki, Mikkeli, Finland
e-mail: manu.rantanen@helsinki.fi

a range of aspects and areas of the community life/functioning encompassing the size and structure of spending on local goods and services (Czarnecki, 2018), which is of value for local economies, as well as the need and actual use of locally provided infrastructure and services, which, in turn, pose challenges for the municipal budgets (Slätmo et al., 2019). What is more, the consequence of the number of second homes, users and the visit duration may be indicative when assessing the tourist pressure on local natural resources and landscape (Martínez-Roget et al., 2020) or recognising the encounters and relations with the host-community considered as a basis for social integration (Aronsson, 1993).

Hence it is of interest for the local community to be aware – possibly in advance – of the prevailing planned/future home-usage tendencies as well as of forces and factors that shape them. Given the above, this chapter aims to identify the role of the place attachment concept constituents and of some intervening factors in the owners' future plans for home usage in the well-established tourism region in southern Poland – the Little Beskid mountain range.

3.2 Literature Review

3.2.1 Place Attachment and the Use of Second Homes

Second homes are often inherited (Hiltunen & Rehunen, 2014). Their owners may have roots in the host-community (Flemsæter, 2009) or may have gained previous leisure experience on spot (Giuliani, 1991). Roots and duration of stay at the second home are important predictors of place attachment (Hernández et al., 2007). However, in the light of the research objective the question arises of whether the relationship might be vice-versa that is the place attachment would impact the second-home usage.

Owning a second home means that the owner develops their place attachment to two different locations (primary and the second home). In Norway, it has been found that place attachment, linked to the family roots, influences development of the second-home market (Tjørve et al., 2012). Second-home owners with previous ties and the family members living in their second-home region are less sensitive to the distance than those without such experience. Hence those who have strong place attachment continue using their second homes despite the long distance. This feature also applies to the next generation of users, who seem to maintain the sense of belonging and hence continue using their inherited second homes (Tjørve et al., 2012).

Place attachment is a very broad concept, including a variety of components (Anton & Lawrence, 2014). One of the most important for this study is community attachment. This is the social aspect of the place attachment concept which refers to an emotional connection to the members of a community (Hummon, 1992). Kasarda and Janowitz (1974) measured this from three perspectives: sense of community, interests, and community sentiments (whether the residents feel sorry to leave the community). Their results proved that length of housing duration is an important factor shaping local community attachment. Other factors explaining this in a systemic model are socio-economic position in the society and the individual's life-stage (Matarrita-Cascante et al., 2010). However, it takes time, at least a couple of years for a person to establish relationships with permanent or other seasonal residents and forge links in the second-home destination unless they have roots there. Importantly, community attachment is a key-condition of rural in-migration and intention to stay (Ulrich-Schad et al., 2013). Thus, it is likely that second-home owners who demonstrate a strong attachment to the local community are also more willing to continue the second-home living.

According to Stedman (2006), social connections are more important for permanent residents than for seasonal residents, but seasonal residents who visit their cottages frequently are stronger attached to the region than the locals. The frequent visitors interact with friends and neighbours at the same or at a more intense level than locals (Jennings & Krannich, 2013). Many second-home owners indeed have a strong community attachment, which can be measured by days spent in their second homes, engagement in community's activities, degree of social interaction with the locals and length of residence (Matarrita-Cascante et al., 2010).

3.2.2   Intervening Factors in the Use of Second Homes

Undoubtedly, the owner's certain socio-demographics are decisive for planning the future use of the second home (Pitkänen et al., 2020b). The owner's age and the related stage in the family life cycle are of great importance, since a large part of second-home owners are retirees or people of pre-retirement age (CSO, 2014; Voutilainen et al., 2021). The lives of these people are not restricted by professional duties, so they can plan or actually spend longer periods or at least visit a second home more frequently. What is more, they are often empty-nesters, thus home obligations are also less restrictive. Hence, for people of pre-retirement age, the plans for the future use (after retiring) seem more far-reaching and likely to be put into practice (Adamiak, 2014) contrarily to people of working age, for whom the occupation is usually important, which, in conjunction with the family life cycle (full family, young family with no children yet), may altogether have an impact on the usage plans, making them more limited in time.

However, seeing that the future usage plans may not be shaped by the same factors as changes in the length of stay within a year, it is worth referring to previous studies about the intergenerational comparisons with regard to the future leisure patterns in Finland. Pitkänen et al. (2014) found that representatives of the generation Y (i.e., those born between 1982 and 2005) are eager to spend time in second homes in the future, and hence their second-home usage will continue. Based on the megatrends of population ageing and urbanisation, it has been claimed that time spent in second homes will increase in the future, since older age groups and urban residents use second homes on average more than younger ones and rural residents (Strandell et al., 2020). Contrary to the media speculations on future home-usage by younger generations (Pitkänen et al., 2014), several studies conclude that demand for second homes will continue internationally (Hall & Müller, 2018). In this respect, it is necessary to refer to the instance of the length of ownership, since, naturally, it is expected that, despite their age, occupation and stage of the family life cycle, the new owners' future use will expand, while for the older owners, considering their age and the resulting potential health problems, these plans may be limited, especially if the second home is already more intensely used by their descendants and is thus planned to be passed on (Lagerqvist et al., 2014).

Besides personal and the ownership-related factors, certain attributes of the local context considered both at a micro- (home) and meso-scale (surroundings/settlement/municipality), can be seen as critical for prolonging or shortening the stay. Based on the previous studies, the home-usage tendency is highly dependent upon whether the second home is winterised (Stergiou et al., 2016), particularly important for stays in high-latitude and mountain locations. It is also likely that the home size, equipment, and infrastructure are taken into account when planning the stay. In addition, availability and proximity to product and service providers constitute an important factor in improving the living conditions and facilitating longer stays, not to mention the intention to move to the second home permanently (Sarman & Czarnecki, 2020). In this respect, access to everyday necessities as well as to health-care services is often considered decisive (Overvåg, 2011).

It should be noted that the causative factors of a given home-usage pattern may sometimes be radically altered by sudden and unpredictable events (e.g., natural disasters or pandemics) (Czarnecki et al., 2021). In the short term, the COVID-19 pandemic has had a remarkable effect on the second-home market, as people have sought asylum from rural areas while the international and urban tourism has suffered restrictions. At the same time, remote work at second homes has become more common, also because of digitalisation and changes in working life (Pitkänen et al., 2020a).

However, the importance of the push/pull trade-off between the primary-home and second-home setting characteristics is significantly moderated by relational factors, often reduced to the geographical or time distance between the two locations (Back & Marjavaara, 2017). Second-home owners cover the entire mobility spectrum from short-term (weekend) to long-term/seasonal stays extending beyond summer or winter holidays (Müller, 2002). Shorter distances may be reflected in numerous albeit limited (weekend) stays or one-day visits without staying overnight more equally distributed throughout the year, while the longer distances may result in a small number of relatively long stays, for instance encompassing whole summer holidays. Bearing in mind the time when the survey for this study was carried out (July–November 2020), the influence of such a relational factor was somewhat distorted by the COVID-19 pandemic and the resulting restrictions on mobilities.

3.3   Methodology

3.3.1   Data and Methods

Data on future home-usage patterns along with information relevant for creating the explanatory model were gathered using a questionnaire addressed to second-home owners of holiday, summer homes. The survey was carried out from July to November 2020, in the Little Beskid mountains range (Fig. 3.1), one of the well-established tourism areas in Poland. We used three approaches:

- direct face-to-face interviews with respondents holidaying at their second homes;
- respondents filling in an online questionnaire themselves;
- filling in the questionnaire during a telephone conversation with respondents.

A set of 36 independent variables (Table 3.1) were used for 155 observations to construct the explanatory model of the owners' planned future home-usage patterns. The data were collected from 175 interviewees; however, 20 interviews were excluded from the statistical analysis due to their incompleteness.

The explained variable was the second-home owners' responses to the question about the most likely/realistic scenario for the usage-pattern of their second homes in the short-term (next 3 years). Three main modes of the second-home usage were thus covered:

- status quo/no change (67% observations),
- increase/more intense (23% observations), and
- decrease/less intense (10% observations).

When collecting the data, it must be stressed that the first wave of the COVID-19 pandemic was just coming to an end in Poland: when answering the questions and

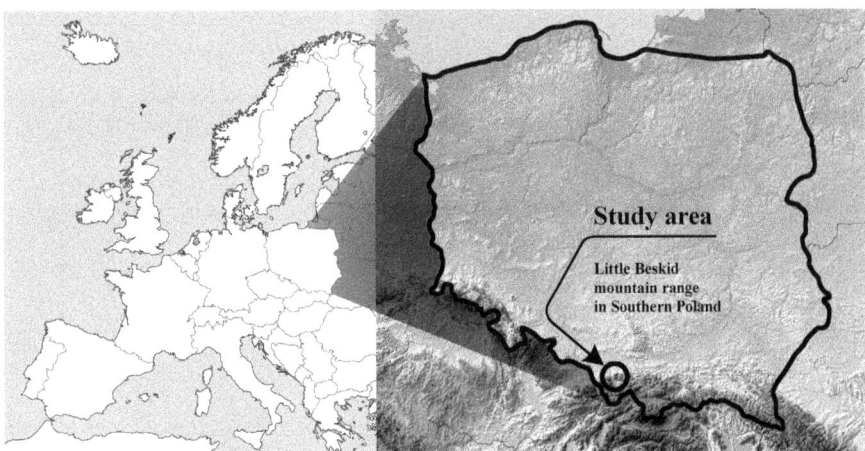

Fig. 3.1   Location of the study area – the Little Beskid mountain range. (Source: Own elaboration)

Table 3.1 Characteristics of the second-home future usage predictors/factors (explanatory variables)

Predictor/factor		Type of variable	Specification of variable (values, categories)
Second-home ownership	Length (years)	ConNum	From 1 year to 46 years
	Way of coming into possession of the second home	CatNom	1 – Inherited or gifted 2 – Purchased 3 – Partly inherited or gifted and partly purchased 4 – Self-built on inherited or gifted plot 5 – Self-built on purchased plot 6 – Other
Second-home location motives	Family and friends in the area	CatNom	0 – No 1 – Yes
	Family roots		
	Place of birth		
	Familiarity with the area		
	Peaceful location and close to nature		
Second home characteristics	Winterised		
Second-home surrounding area characteristics	Shops and services (within 1 km radius)		

Place attachment statements	CatOrd	1 – Strongly disagree
I care about what happens to the area		2 – Disagree
I socialise with local people		3 – Neither agree, nor disagree
I socialise with other second-home owners		4 – Agree
I feel I am a member of the local community		5 – Strongly agree
I feel I am a member of the second-home community		
I am involved in the community activities		
I feel that I can really be myself here		
It is my favourite place to be		
I feel accepted by the local community		
Most people in the community can be trusted		
I have a lot in common with other second-home owners		
I have a lot in common with the local community		
Second-home owners' contribution to local development is appreciated by the locals		
I have lots of family memories		
The natural environment is more important than the local community		
I feel I am responsible for the development of the area		
Distance from primary to second home	ConNum	From 15 min to 240 min
Time distance (minutes)		
Physical distance (kilometres)		From 10 km to 320 km
COVID-19 pandemic	CatNom	0 – No, it will not influence
Opinion about the impact on the future second home-usage		1 – Yes, it will influence

(continued)

Table 3.1 (continued)

Predictor/factor		Type of variable	Specification of variable (values, categories)
Respondent's socio-demographics	Gender	CatNom	0 – Female 1 – Male
	Age (age economic groups)	CatOrd	1 – Working mobile 2 – Working non-mobile 3 – Post-working
	Education	CatNom	1 – Elementary school 2 – Vocational school 3 – High school 4 – University
Respondent's household characteristics	Size (number of household members)	CatOrd	From 1 person to 7 people
	Children (up to 18 years of age)	CatNom	0 – No 1 – Yes
	Net average monthly income	CatOrd	1 – 2000 PLN[a] and less 2 – 2001 to 4000 PLN 3 – 4001 to 6000 PLN 4 – 6001 to 8000 PLN 5 – 8001 to 10,000 PLN 6 – 10,001 to 15,000 PLN 7 – 15,001 PLN and more
Primary residence characteristics	Type	CatNom	1 – House (detached house/semi-detached/terraced house) 0 – Flat/apartment
	Size (floor usage space; sq. m)	ConNum	From 30 sq. m to 200 sq. m

Source: Own elaboration

Abbreviations: *CatNom* categorical nominal, *CatOrd* categorical ordinal, *ConNum* continuous numerical

[a] PLN 1.00 = € 0.22, a mean value, at the archive exchange rate, for July 2020 to November 2020 when the survey was carried out

formulating the most likely future home-usage scenario, 22% of respondents took into consideration the potential influence of COVID-19. During the first wave of the pandemic, the number of new/every-day infections in Poland did not go over 600. The coronavirus then still affected so small number of people that it rather lived on in people's imaginations and in the mass media. To support this view, the related research findings for Poland showed that for most second-home owners their home-usage pattern in 2020, during the first wave of the COVID-19 remained the same as previously (2019). However, for those changing the usage, it was more likely to prolong the stay by moving in, working online, or travelling to work, rather than shortening it (Czarnecki et al., 2021).

In order to develop an explanatory model for the future/planned second-home usage, the classification-tree learning method was chosen. Precisely, the Classification and Regression Tree (C & RT) interactive module available in the Statistica 13 software was employed. In its interactive variant, C & RT constitutes an effective tool for recognising latent relationships within the dataset. It makes possible the inclusion of the expert's knowledge in the process of constructing the model. Such trees can be corrected by truncating and examining alternative predictors and splitting rules.

The following assumptions were made:

- costs of incorrect classifications are equal;
- goodness of fit is assessed using the Gini Index;
- the stop rule is to truncate when a misclassification error occurs;
- each of the end nodes consists of at least five observations;
- the control of the quality of results is performed using a V-fold cross-validation for V = 10.

Taking advantage of the interactive nature of C & RT enabled the authors to influence the model-creating process when several predictors obtained similar values of statistics and they could be used interchangeably. Then, using the expert knowledge, a predictor was selected that better fitted the logical sequence of divisions in the tree structure. Applying the classification rules presented in the graph made it possible to draw conclusions about conditions of changes in the owners' second-home usage tendencies. The percentage of incorrect classifications was 27%, while the standard error was 0.036. Such accuracy was considered acceptable, bearing in mind that the research was not guided by the authors' interest in predicting the future second-home usage pattern, but rather pursuing the research's exploration goals, that is to recognise and examine the determinants of these patterns with particular emphasis on the impact of place attachment (including community attachment and place belonging) supplemented by intervening/moderating explanatory factors such as owner's socio-demographics, length of ownership, travel distances from primary to second home and so on.

The measurement of place attachment was based on the number of statements referring to various aspects of the place attachment concept that is community attachment, rootedness, and place belonging. Each of the statements included in the questionnaire form was answered by the second-home owners surveyed using the Likert scale (from 1 – Strongly disagree to 5 – Strongly agree).

3.3.2   Survey Sample

The majority of the second-home owners surveyed were retirees (of post-working age) (Table 3.2). Empty-nesters, including single-person households, predominated, although relatively often it was a household with one or two sometimes adult children. Respondents with a higher education level prevailed. The owners were relatively affluent: if they were working – as business owners, CEOs, middle-level managers, specialists, white-collar workers – they were well-paid. The owner's primary home was usually located in densely populated regions of southern Poland, in large cities (over 100,000 inhabitants, such Krakow or urban areas in the Upper Silesian conurbation).

Most owners travelled to their second homes for no longer than 120 min, and within this category for almost half the travel time was up to 30 min. Over a third of respondents were considered "new" owners of their second homes, since they had come into possession of their properties up to 10 years before the survey (the average length of ownership was 15 years). The owners demonstrated a variety of ways of coming into the possession of the second home: the most common was purchase, followed by self-built homes on a purchased plot of land. Inherited or gifted homes were slightly less common. The all-year-round (winterised) homes predominated, while, at the same time, most properties ranged from 51 to 100 m^2. Over half of these second homes were in compact settlement units, which to some extent resulted from the settlement pattern typical of southern regions of Poland. Consequently, the majority were within walking distance of the nearest shops and basic services. The homes surveyed were surrounded by other holiday and summer properties rather than by the local people's permanent residences.

3.4   Results

In line with the goal of modelling the reality, by employing the C & RTs (generalisation, simplification, reduction, focus on key-factors), a simple diagram recognising forces shaping the future second-home usage pattern was sought. The model examined therefore consisted of only eight shared and nine end-nodes. The most important explanatory factors come at the top of the graph, splitting the tree into its main branches; then the less important factors appear further down the tree. Relating to the structure of the analysed usage patterns that is "status quo/no change" (67%), "more intensely" (23%) and "less intensely" (10%), five end-nodes (IDs = 38, 39,

Table 3.2 Sample structure

Attribute	Category	Proportion	Attribute	Category	Proportion
Gender	Female	47%	Location of the primary home[c]	Large city	63%
	Male	53%		Medium-sized town	20%
	No data	0%		Small town	7%
Age (age economic groups)[a]	Working mobile	20%		Rural locality	6%
	Working non-mobile	44%		No data	4%
	Post-working	34%	Travel time to the second home	30 min or less	17%
	No data	2%		31–60 min	28%
Household size	1	12%		61–120 min	48%
	2	39%		121 min or more	6%
	3–4	39%		No data	1%
	5 or more	8%	Length of ownership	5 years or less	20%
	No data	2%		6–10 years	17%
Number of children under 18 years of age in the household	0	67%		11–20 years	29%
	1	20%		21–30 years	18%
	2	9%		31–40 years	10%
	3 or more	2%		41 years or more	6%
	No data	2%		No data	0%
Education	Elementary school	2%			
	Vocational school	9%	Way of coming into possession of second home	Inherited or gifted	22%
	High school	31%		Purchased	31%
	University	58%		Partly inherited and partly purchased	2%
	No data	0%		Built on inherited or gifted plot	5%
Main occupation	Business owner	11%		Built on purchased plot	29%
	Specialist and white-collar worker	36%		Other	11%
	Manual worker	4%		No data	0%
	Retired	40%	Second home winterised	Yes	55%
	Other	8%		No	44%
	No data	1%		No data	1%

(continued)

Table 3.2 (continued)

Attribute	Category	Proportion	Attribute	Category	Proportion
Household income	2000 PLN[b] or less	6%	Length of stay at the second home (from March to August 2020)	9 days or less	12%
	2001–4000 PLN	26%		10–29 days	16%
	4001–6000 PLN	19%		30–59 days	27%
	6001–8000 PLN	15%		60–99 days	16%
	8001–10,000 PLN	12%		100 days or more	20%
	10,001–15,000 PLN	6%		No data	10%
			Second home area[d]	Shops and services	79%
	15,001 PLN or more	7%		Homes of permanent residents	46%
	No data	9%		Other second homes	69%

Source: Own elaboration

[a]Working mobile age: 18–44, working non-mobile age: males 45–64, females 45–59, post-working age: males 65+, females 60+

[b]PLN 1.00 = € 0.22, a mean value, at the archive exchange rate, for July 2020 to November 2020 when the survey was carried out

[c]Large city: over 100,000 residents, medium-sized town: from 20,001 to 100,000 residents, small town – up to 20,000 residents, and rural locality: without town privileges

[d]Multiple responses, which altogether may exceed the number of respondents (100%)

43, 44, and 45) grouped on the right-hand branch of the tree indicated possible reasons for demonstrating a "status quo" pattern. They were not "pure" nodes, although the likelihood of this pattern occurring was the greatest in these cases. Two end-nodes contributed to our understanding of the more intense home-usage pattern (IDs = 32 and 42), while another two end-nodes (positioned on the left-hand branch of the tree) made it possible to learn more about the drivers of the less intense pattern (IDs = 33 and 34).

The main factor influencing respondents' planned/future home-usage pattern was the length of ownership of the second home (Fig. 3.2; Node 1). Accordingly, the root node of the tree was split into two branches representing diverse and distinctive structures of the home-usage patterns. The first subset (the entire left-hand branch of the tree) covered the relatively "new" owners who came into possession of the second home in the last 3 years (since the survey was carried out) (Node 30). For this group, the planned usage-intense tendency unsurprisingly predominated, while the other two patterns (usage-extensive/usage-limited and "status quo") remained similarly less common. This apparently homogenous sub-population turned out to be differentiated by applying a relational factor, that is the physical distance from

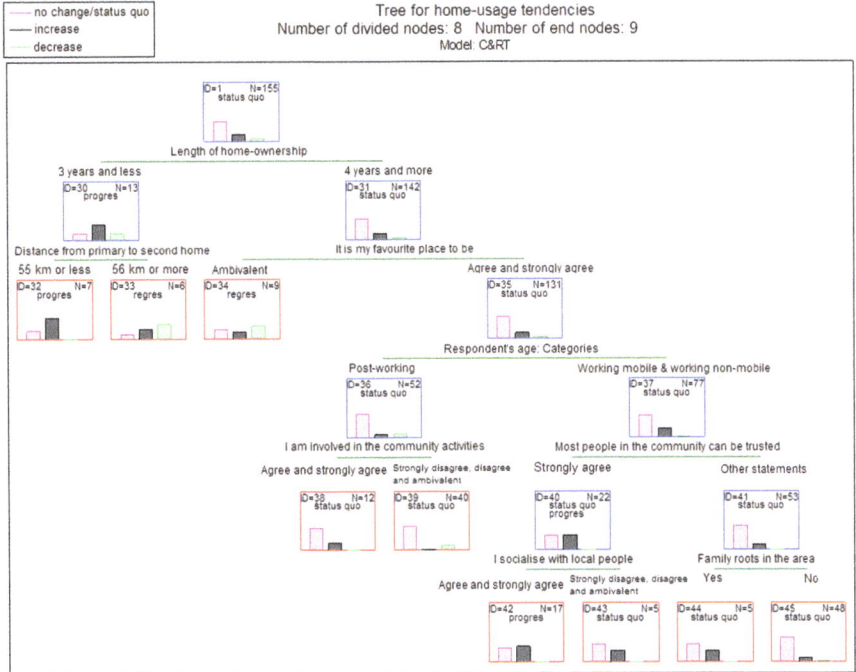

Fig. 3.2 Classification tree for the future/planned home-usage tendencies. (Source: Own elaboration)

primary to second home. Accordingly, "new" owners who travelled shorter distances (up to 55 km) intended to extend their future stay or – less often – did not plan to change the current usage pattern (Node 32). Interestingly, however, usage-extensive tendency was most common for "new owners" who had to travel further (56 km or more) to their cottages (Node 33).

Returning to the tree's main node, its right-hand branch covered all the future/planned home-usage patterns depending upon a length of ownership longer than 3 years, which reflected a diverse range of usage patterns, albeit with a highly differentiated incidence (Node 31). The first explanatory factor for this subset introduced was one of the components of the place attachment/belonging concept, based on the respondent's statement that the second home was his/her favourite place to be. For respondents who supported and strongly supported that opinion, the "status quo" usage-tendency predominated, and the planned decrease in usage was almost not-existent (Node 35). For those who were ambivalent (neither agree, nor disagree) the usage-limited pattern was most common (Node 34). Of those who expressed positive feelings about the second home being their favourite place, another explanatory factor differentiating this sub-population was the respondent's economic age, described by three categories: working mobile, working non-mobile, and post-working. The relatively young owners of working and working mobile age declared they would keep the current usage mode or would demonstrate a more intensive stay (Node 37), while for those of a post-working age the "status quo" usage-pattern predominated with an opposite extensive (usage-limited) mode (Node 36).

In addition, the home-usage by the group of older owners was differentiated by one of the community attachment components – the owner's involvement in community activities; for those who agreed or strongly agreed with that related statement, there was a "status quo" tendency with an incidence of "usage-intensive" pattern (Node 38). At the same time, for those who were not involved in community activities (or were ambivalent about the statement), the same "status quo" pattern was most common, albeit slightly discounted by the usage-limited pattern (Node 39).

On the other hand, the predominant usage-patterns of younger owners were further explained by another community-related variable, that is trust and confidence in local people. For the younger owners, who agreed or strongly agreed with the statement that "most people in the local community can be trusted", the "usage-intensive" and the "status quo" patterns were equally common, while the usage-limited one was non-existent (Node 40). For younger owners who disagreed, strongly disagreed or were ambivalent about this opinion, the tendency to maintain the current usage pattern predominated, while a planned increase in usage was considered less likely (Node 41).

Finally, the two sub-groups of owners who, on one hand, expressed favourable opinions about the local community in terms of trust/confidence and demonstrated contradictory (more pessimistic) views about this issue on the other hand, were differentiated by another community attachment component and family roots, respectively. These were important in understanding that keeping in touch with local permanent residents implies the owner's declarations towards extending the stay at the second home or, to a lesser extent, maintaining the "no change" pattern (Node 42). For owners who did not support this statement, the "status quo" tendency prevailed over the "usage-intensive" pattern (Node 43). In the latter group (those who expressed less favourable opinions about trust in local people), for those who admitted having family roots in the area, the "usage-intensive" pattern was almost equally common as for the predominant "status quo" tendency (Node 44), while for those who had no such roots in the second home location, the "no change" tendency was most common, with only marginal incidence of the two remaining home-usage patterns (Node 45).

3.5 Discussion and Conclusions

Given the scarcity of studies focusing on changes in second-home usage, this research aims at recognising the future tendencies in this respect as well as at explaining them by making use of the place attachment concept and some intervening factors. First, this study proved that most of the surveyed owners (two thirds) planned to maintain the current usage pattern. The tendency was greatly shaped by the length of ownership of the second home especially in conjunction with individual's socio-demographics, namely the owner's age (incorporated in the model as another interrelated albeit less important factor) and his/her life stage as already indicated in previous studies (Pitkänen et al., 2020b).

The findings of a Finnish survey (Pitkänen et al., 2014) proved gradual increase in the home usage with the owner's age reaching its peak after retirement, which supports the results of this study for working mobile and working non-mobile (pre-retired) individuals. However, the tendency switches into the relatively uncommon (a tenth of respondents) "less-intensive" usage if the owner is of advanced age and, specifically, when the related health problems are more likely and affect the potential and actual usages.

On the other hand, "new" owners and, at the same time, those who are relatively young usually made favourable home-usage plans, aiming to use the newly acquired/inherited property most effectively, so this can be reflected in the prevailing "more-intensive" usage tendency (covering a quarter of the owners surveyed), as already proved in some earlier studies (Adamiak, 2014; Voutilainen et al., 2021). Furthermore, the intention to increase future home-usage may result from the owner's view of his/her prospective retirement, which would guarantee more spare time for leisure purposes at the cottage. Then, in this respect, a valuable explanation could be a reference to the evidence-based results in a Finnish study by Strandell et al. (2020), in which they argued that time spent in second homes will increase in future, since older age groups and urban residents already use their secondary residences on average more than younger ones and rural residents. Thus, concerning owner's age, life cycle stage and the related length of second-home ownership, results of this study confirm what Pitkänen et al. (2014) argued about the youngest and oldest age groups: that in terms of home usage, they deviate from the pattern demonstrated by retirees and those who prepare for retirement.

Besides socio-demographic and ownership-related variables, the broadly considered social factor exemplified by place attachment and, as part of it, by community attachment, rootedness and place belonging, was of great importance in explaining home-usage plans. It is worth noting that the stronger the social ties and confidence in the locals, as well as the involvement in host-community activities, the more likely is the planned "more intensive" usage, while the "status quo" tendency is less likely, not to mention sporadic chances of shortening the stay at the cottage. The importance of community attachment in explaining the home-usage trajectories echoes some previous findings in which this social force was seen as a key-predictor of a more general/macro trend – rural in-migration (Ulrich-Schad et al., 2013). In this regard, it is worth noting that second-home owners usually demonstrate strong community attachment (Matarrita-Cascante et al., 2010). Such a causal link is fully supported by the study's findings, which highlight the role of this social factor in forming the home-usage mode. What is more, this research also proved the importance of certain manifestations of community attachment used in some earlier studies as measures of this specific component of place attachment, namely involvement in local activities, socialising with the locals and the length of residence (comparable to length of ownership in this study focusing on second homes) (Matarrita-Cascante et al., 2010).

In addition, another component of the place attachment concept, that is rooted-ness, played a role for a relatively limited group of owners in shaping their home-usage pattern. Despite the owner's family roots in the second-home area turning out to be influential in extending or at least maintaining the current usage mode, it was not possible to verify arguments by Tjørve et al. (2012) about the Norwegian second-home owners' family ties in the host-community diminishing the impact of the relational factor (distance to be travelled) on the home-usage pattern. This was due to the absence of the distance-related variable in the tree branch where the root-edness factor emerged.

Finally, likewise the length of ownership, the relational factor, exemplified by the travel distance to the second home, was confirmed to be a crucial moderating force in distinguishing the opposite "more intensive" and "less intensive" home-usage tendencies among the owners. This objective circumstance was found significant in another Norwegian study (cf. Overvåg, 2009), which proved that distance influ-enced different aspects of the owner's conduct, including the home-usage pattern.

Given that second-home owners may constitute a powerful stakeholder group whose contribution to both local society and the economy is considered significant, it is important to learn more about their plans and intentions towards second-home usage in the mid/long run. Seeing that most second-home owners plan to maintain the current usage tendency and some tend to extend/intensify their stay, this can be seen as a positive and promising sign for the local business sector and, to some extent, for the social fabric of the host communities, while it poses certain chal-lenges for the municipal budgets regarding infrastructure maintenance and service provision, as well as the mitigation of environmental impacts.

In particular for struggling and declining rural communities, hosting the second-home phenomenon could be important in understanding and making use of the rea-sons behind different home-usage patterns. Specifically, the broadly considered social factor including community attachment, community involvement, and rela-tionships, as well as trust in the local residents can be considered as most valuable, since it indicates some aspects that might be still improved and, in light of this study, may be successfully translated into more positive and intensive usage-strategies that more indirectly bring certain positive outcomes for the wider community.

References

Adamiak, C. (2014). *Drugie domy w Borach Tucholskich* [Second homes in the Tuchola Forest]. Wydział Nauk o Ziemi, Uniwersytet Mikołaja Kopernika. Retrieved 2 Jan 2022 from https://repozytorium.umk.pl/bitstream/handle/item/2595/Drugie%20domy%20w%20Borach%20Tucholskich.pdf?sequence=1

Anton, C. E., & Lawrence, C. (2014). Home is where the heart is: The effect of place of residence on place attachment and community participation. *Journal of Environmental Psychology, 40*, 451–461. https://doi.org/10.1016/j.jenvp.2014.10.007

Aronsson, L. (1993). Mötet: en studie i Smögen av turisters, fritidsboendes och bofastas använd-ning av tid och rum [The encounter: A study of tourists', second-home owners' and residents' use of time and space in Smögen]. *Forskningsrapport Samhällsvetenskap, 93*(1), Högskolan i Karlstad, Gruppen för regionalvetenskaplig forskning. University College.

Back, A., & Marjavaara, R. (2017). Mapping an invisible population: The uneven geography of second-home tourism. *Tourism Geographies, 19*(4), 595–611. https://doi.org/10.1080/1461668 8.2017.1331260

CSO. (2014). *Turystyka i wypoczynek w gospodarstwach domowych w 2013 r* [Tourism and leisure in households in 2013]. Central Statistical Office: Warsaw. Retrieved 11 Jan 2022 from https://stat.gov.pl/obszary-tematyczne/kultura-turystyka-sport/turystyka/turystyka-i-wypoczynek-w-gospodarstwach-domowych-w-2013-r-,3,3.html

CSO. (2021). *Local data bank, Central Statistical Office 2006–2020*. Central Statistical Office.

Czarnecki, A. (2018). *Going local? Linking and integrating second-home owners with the community's economy: A comparative study between Finnish and Polish second-home owners.* Peter Lang Publishing.

Czarnecki, A., Dacko, A., & Dacko, M. (2021). Changes in mobility patterns and the switch-ing roles of second homes as a result of the first wave of COVID-19. *Journal of Sustainable Tourism.* https://doi.org/10.1080/09669582.2021.2006201

Flemsæter, F. (2009). The role of home in property enactment on Norwegian smallholdings. *Norsk Geografisk Tidsskrift – Norwegian Journal of Geography, 63,* 204–214. https://doi.org/10.1080/00291950903239030

Giuliani, M. V. (1991). Towards an analysis of mental representations of attachment to the home. *The Journal of Architectural and Planning Research, 8*(2), 133–146.

Hall, C. M., & Müller, D. K. (2018). The future of second homes. In C. M. Hall & D. K. Müller (Eds.), *The Routledge handbook of second home tourism and mobilities* (pp. 355–360). Routledge.

Hernández, B., Hidalgo, M. C., Salazar-Laplace, M. E., & Hess, S. (2007). Place attachment and place identity in natives and non-natives. *Journal of Environmental Psychology, 27*(4), 310–319. https://doi.org/10.1016/j.jenvp.2007.06.003

Hiltunen, M. J., & Rehunen, A. (2014). Second home mobility in Finland: Patterns, practices and relations of leisure oriented mobile lifestyle. *Fennia, 192*(1), 1–22. Retrieved 11 Jan 2022 from https://fennia.journal.fi/article/view/8384

Hummon, D. H. (1992). Community attachment: Local sentiment and sense of place. *Human Behavior & Environment: Advances in Theory & Research, 12,* 253–278.

Jennings, B. M., & Krannich, R. S. (2013). Bonded to whom? Social interactions in a high-amenity rural setting. *Community Development, 44*(1), 3–22. https://doi.org/10.1080/1557533 0.2011.583355

Kasarda, J. D., & Janowitz, M. (1974). Community attachment in mass society. *American Sociological Review, 39*(3), 328–339. https://doi.org/10.2307/2094293

Lagerqvist, M., Nordin, U., & Strandin Pers, A. (2014). The more, the merrier? Experiences of shared usage and generational intersections at second homes in Sweden. *Tourism, Leisure and Global Change, 1,* NPSH-49. Papers from the IGU Conference on New Perspectives on Second Homes, 9–11 June 2014, Skeviks gård, Stockholm, Sweden.

Martínez-Roget, F., Moutela, J. A., & Rodríguez, X. A. (2020). Length of stay and sustainability: Evidence from the Schist Villages Network (SVN) in Portugal. *Sustainability, 12,* 4025. https://doi.org/10.3390/su12104025

Matarrita-Cascante, D., Stedman, R., & Luloff, A. E. (2010). Permanent and seasonal resi-dents' community attachment in natural amenity-rich areas: Exploring the contribu-tion of landscape-related factors. *Environment and Behavior, 42*(2), 197–220. https://doi.org/10.1177/0013916509332383

Müller, D. K. (2002). German second homeowners in Sweden: Some remarks on the Tourism – Migration – Nexus. *Tourisme et Migrations, 18*(1), 67–86. https://doi.org/10.4000/remi.636

Overvåg, K. (2009). *Second homes in Eastern Norway: From marginal land to commodity.* *Doctoral thesis.* Norwegian University of Science and Technology, Faculty of Social Sciences and Technology Management, Department of Geography. Retrieved December 9, 2020, from https://ntnuopen.ntnu.no/ntnu-xmlui/bitstream/handle/11250/265331/311115_FULLTEXT02. pdf?sequence=2&isAllowed=y

Overvåg, K. (2011). Second homes: Migration or circulation? *Norsk Geografisk Tidsskrift – Norwegian Journal of Geography, 65*(3), 154–164. https://doi.org/10.1080/0029195 1.2011.598237

Pitkänen, K., Puhakka, R., Semi, J., & Hall, C. M. (2014). Generation Y and second homes: Continuity and change in Finnish outdoor recreation. *Tourism Review International, 18*(3), 207–221. https://doi.org/10.3727/154427214X14101901317273

Pitkänen, K., Hannonen, O., Toso, S., Gallent, N., Hamiduddin, I., Halseth, G., Hall, C. M., Müller, D. K., Treivish, A., & Nefedova, T. (2020a). Second homes during corona – Safe or unsafe haven and for whom? Reflections from researchers around the world. *Finnish Journal of Tourism Research, 16*(2), 20–39. https://doi.org/10.33351/mt.97559

Pitkänen, K., Lehtimäki, J., & Puhakka, R. (2020b). How do rural second homes affect human health and well-being? Review of potential impacts. *International Journal of Environmental Research and Public Health, 17*, 6748. https://doi.org/10.3390/ijerph17186748

Sarman, I., & Czarnecki, A. (2020). Swiss second-home owners' intentions of changing housing patterns. *Moravian Geographical Reports, 28*(3), 208–222. https://doi.org/10.2478/mgr-2020-0015

Shucksmith, D. M. (1983). Second homes: A framework for policy. *The Town Planning Review, 54*(2), 174–193.

Slätmo, E., Vestergård, L. O., Lidmo, J., & Turunen, E. (2019). *Urban–rural flows from seasonal tourism and second homes: Planning challenges and strategies in the Nordics* (Nordregio Report 2019, 13). Nordregio.

Stedman, R. C. (2006). Understanding place attachment among second home owners. *American Behavioral Scientist, 50*(2), 187–205. https://doi.org/10.1177/0002764206290633

Stergiou, D., Papatheodorou, A., & Tsartas, P. (2016). Second home conversion during the economic crisis: The case of Artemida, Greece. *Social & Cultural Geography, 18*(8), 1129–1151. https://doi.org/10.1080/14649365.2016.1242151

Strandell, A., Pitkänen, K., & Rehunen, A. (2020). Miten kaupungistuminen ja väestön ikääntyminen vaikuttavat vapaa-ajan asumisen suosioon? [How do urbanisation and the population aging affect the popularity of the second-home living?]. *Matkailututkimus, 16*(1), 74–92. https://doi.org/10.33351/mt.88575

Terzić, A., Drobnjaković, M., & Petrevska, B. (2020). Traditional Serbian countryside and second-home tourism perspectives. *European Countryside, 12*(3), 312–332. https://doi.org/10.2478/euco-2020-0018

Tjørve, E., Flognfeldt, T., & Calf Tjørve, K. M. (2012). The effects of distance and belonging on second-home markets. *Tourism Geographies: An International Journal of Tourism Space, Place and Environment, 15*(2), 268–291. https://doi.org/10.1080/14616688.2012.726264

Ulrich-Schad, J. D., Henly, M., & Safford, T. G. (2013). The role of community assessments, place, and the Great Recession in the migration intentions of rural Americans. *Rural Sociology, 78*(3), 371–398. https://doi.org/10.1111/ruso.12016

Voutilainen, O., Korhonen, K., Ovaska, U., & Vihinen, H. (2021). *Mökkibarometri 2021* [Cottage barometer 2021]. Luonnonvara-jabiotaloudentutkimus, 47/2020. Luonnonvarakeskus.

Chapter 4
Place Attached Entrepreneurs as Place-Based Leaders

Grete Kindel (iD)

4.1 Introduction

In a globalising world, it is important that every inhabited place finds its own uniqueness, because "the (re)valorisation and strengthening of the identity of peripheral and lagging rural regions is the key to their competitiveness in the global market" (Roca & de Nazaré Oliveira-Roca, 2007, p. 434). Globalisation is not just an economic phenomenon – it has social, political, environmental, and cultural dimensions that influence the quality of local life (Müller & Korsgaard, 2018). Embeddedness is considered as a local phenomenon that ensures the socio-economic development of rural areas (Fløysand & Sjøholt, 2007, p. 205). The quality of life in particular places is in turn affected by the people who interact with the geographic location: inhabitants, and the public, private and non-profit sector. In the late 1970s, Relph (1976), Tuan (1979), and Proshansky and peers (1983) studied and developed the concept of sense of place, which explains the interaction between humans and place.

Sense of place is a broader phenomenon which describes how place influences people, and which can be subdivided into dimensions like place attachment, place identity, place dependence, *genius loci*, spirit of place, etc. The concept of place refers to the subjective experience of a person in the physical environment (Morgan, 2010, p. 11). Whereas place as a phenomenon is related to personal experience and cognition, it has been difficult for researchers to define, examine and measure it. In a modern world, where people commute between different places, it seems that places have lost their relevance. But as Jones (1992) argued, people need attachment to significant places because without it they feel estrangement or alienation from their environment.

G. Kindel (✉)
School of Economics and Business Administration, University of Tartu, Tartu, Estonia
e-mail: grete.kindel@ut.ee

© The Author(s), under exclusive license to Springer Nature   67
Switzerland AG 2022
O.-R. Ilovan, I. Markuszewska (eds.), *Preserving and Constructing Place Attachment in Europe*, GeoJournal Library 131,
https://doi.org/10.1007/978-3-031-09775-1_4

In my study, the focus is put on place attachment and identity. Manzo and Perkins (2006, p. 347) state that researchers still need to learn more about the place attachment as a process. So far studies have focused on the defining and developing of place attachment (Scannell & Gifford, 2010; Hidalgo & Hernández, 2001; Morgan, 2010) and identity theories (Twigger-Ross & Uzzell, 1996) and fewer papers (Jones, 1992; Manzo & Perkins, 2006) have studied the interaction between place and different human groups, like entrepreneurs. Müller and Korsgaard (2018) suggest supplementing entrepreneurship research with in-depth studies concerning the place embeddedness impact on venture outputs. Entrepreneurs are embedded with places, create, innovate, and develop practical ideas (Hambleton, 2011) which raise regional productivity and competitiveness, enrich local economies (Müller & Korsgaard, 2018), and therefore recreate, renew, and reify the identity of place (McKeever et al., 2015, p. 50).

Based on two case studies from Estonia and 24 in-depth interviews, this paper analyses entrepreneurs as place-based leaders, their attachment and identity in geographic peripheries. In this chapter, I will focus on the following aspects to understand entrepreneurs' interaction with a place:

1. what is the nature of entrepreneurs' attachment with places in peripheries?
2. in which way place attachment and identity influence entrepreneurs' behaviour in place?

The structure of the paper contains a theoretical overview, methods, case studies, results, discussion on general implications and conclusions.

4.2   Conceptual Framework of Place Attachment

Place attachment is a multifaceted and complex phenomenon consisting of human emotional aspects like place bonding, behaviour, cognition, and affection (Chow & Healey, 2008, p. 363). Jorgensen and Stedman (2001, p. 238) define place attachment as "an individual's affective or emotional connection to a spatial setting", where persons "prefer to remain or they feel comfortable, safe, stable and creating memories [...] shared with friends" and family (Hernández et al., 2007, p. 310).

To clarify the mechanism of place attachment, then Scannell and Gifford (2010) developed a tripartite model of place attachment, a framework which helps to understand a bond between a place and individual/group, manifested through affective, cognitive, and behavioural psychological processes. This model contains three dimensions (Fig. 4.1) (Scannell & Gifford, 2010, p. 2):

1. a person is the actor whose attachment is based on individually or collectively held meanings. It answers the questions: (1) who is attached and (2) to what extent is it based on individually and collectively held meanings?

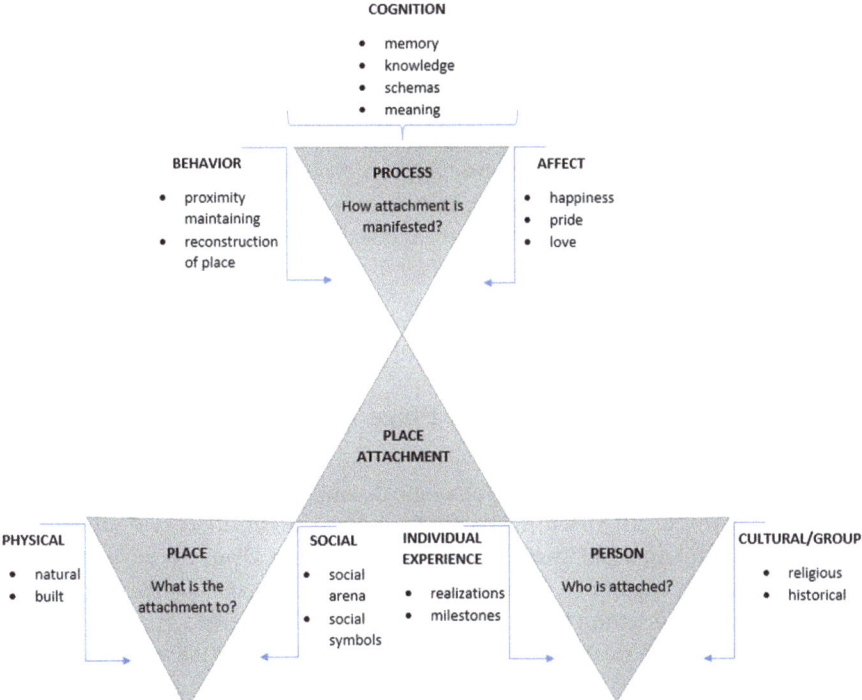

Fig. 4.1 The tripartite model of place attachment. (Source: Author's elaboration based on Scannell and Gifford (2010, p. 2). Reproduced with permission)

2. the psychological process concerns the way that individuals and groups are related to a place. It answers the question: (1) how are affect, cognition, and behaviour manifested in the attachment?
3. place is the object of attachment. It answers the questions: (1) what is the attachment to, and (2) what is the nature of this place?

According to Scannell and Gifford (2010), the affective component reflects emotional connection, and the cognitive component reflects concerns, thoughts, knowledge, and beliefs related to a place. The behavioural component expresses attachment trough actions in a spatial context (Scannell & Gifford, 2010, p. 4).

People's attachment to place increases with age, routine, and the length of residence (Hidalgo & Hernández, 2001; Hernández et al., 2007, p. 317). These are associated with "greater social ties, including the number of local acquaintances, friends and relatives and in turn these social bonds predict local community attitudes and sentiments" (Scannell & Gifford, 2010, p. 5). Scannell and Gifford (2010, p. 5) state that interactions with other people, in particular place influences personal attachment at social group level, that the place represents. Greater attachment creates more interest and a desire to participate (Hidalgo & Hernández, 2001) in local life. Hay (1998, p. 261) found that long-term residents are more embedded with their place and their community, hence time fosters stronger place attachment.

Kibler et al. (2015) explored sub-group levels and studied entrepreneurs' bond with place. They suggest distinguishing emotional ('caring about the place') and instrumental ('using the place') place attachment. The first refers to the entrepreneur's feelings about and affective bond with a place and/or its residents and instrumental attachment refers to entrepreneur's closeness to place (Kibler et al., 2015, p. 26). According to Kibler and peers (2015, p. 6) "strong emotional attachment means that an entrepreneur cares much and identifies strongly with the place and/or its residents". Instrumental place attachment consists of trust, social capital, previous experiences which enable achieving their aims and entrepreneurial activities in the place (Kibler et al., 2015, p. 6).

4.3   Conceptual Framework of Place Identity

Place identity is the emotional, psychological, and symbolic bond with a place (Anton & Lawrence, 2016), which is part of our personal self-identity (Lalli, 1992). According to Jorgensen and Stedman (2001, p. 238) place identity is a combination of an "individual's cognitions, beliefs, perceptions, or thoughts that the self invests in a particular spatial setting". According to Nanzer (2004, p. 364), the "dimensions of personal identity in relation to physical environment" affect the development of place identity.

According to Hernández et al. (2007, p. 311) "place attachment develops before place identity, because a person could be attached to a place but not identify herself/himself with it, whereas another could have a strong personal identity with a place and not high place attachment", at least in the case of non-natives. Place attachment is fostered through our personal place-based experience and over time this bond shapes our personal self-identity and place becomes part of us (Nanzer, 2004). Identification can arise from cognition, affect, behaviour, physical and social environment or individual, group, cultural experience which are related to a particular place (Fig. 4.1). Belonging to a certain place means a significant relationship between a human being and the environment, and this relationship is an act of identification (Manenti, 2011) and "any place can hold meaning to a particular person" (Nanzer, 2004, p. 366).

Peng et al. (2020) created a model to explain the interaction between the process of place and personal identity formation (Fig. 4.2). This model is based on Paasi's (1986) regional identity concept, which includes three shapes: symbolic, institutional, and physical. The symbolic shape (name, history, traditions, etc.) distinguishes place from all other places, and constitutes the frame of reference in which the structures of expectations are grounded and by means of which they are reproduced. The institutional shape (economic, political, legal, educational, cultural, etc.) reproduces places and place consciousness. The physical shape (territory, landscape, buildings, land use, etc.) identifies a territory as a "distinct unit in the spatial structure" (Paasi, 1986, p. 124). Personal identity consists of physical appearance (hair, skin, attire, etc.), behaviour (dialect, skill, traditional practice, etc.), attitude

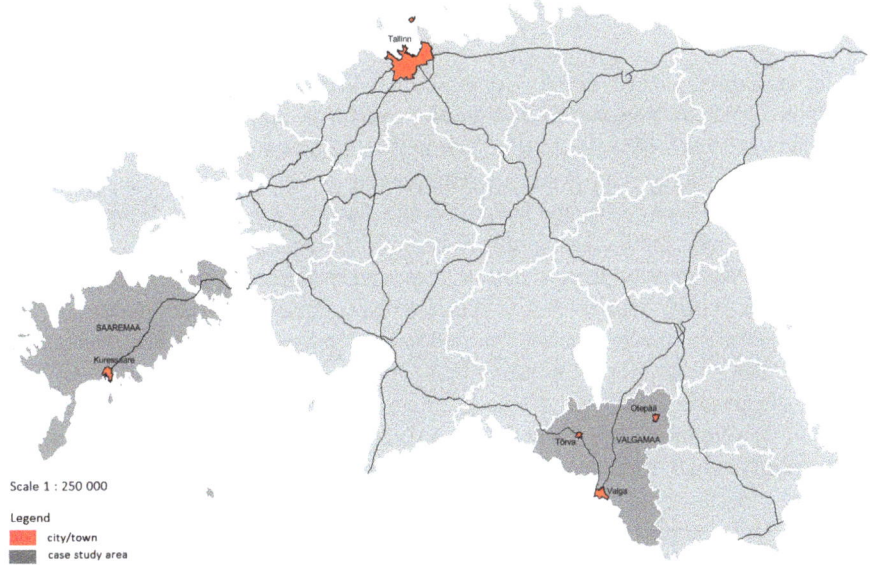

Fig. 4.2 The locations of case study areas in Estonia. (Source: Author's elaboration)

(patriotism, goal, preference, etc.) and mental (nervous system) which is influenced by physical, symbolic, and the institutional shape of place (Raagmaa, 2002). According to Peng and peers (2020, p. 14), a person's social collective and individual identity is influenced by place and the other way around.

Twigger-Ross and Uzzell (1996) present two ways explaining place identity as a phenomenon. The first indicates to a person who identify herself/himself with a place and is subject to the same rules as social identification in social identity theory. For example, if someone lives in London, then they identify themselves as Londoners. This is social identification, and it "expresses membership of people who are defined by location", showing the relationship between the self and environment (Twigger-Ross & Uzzell, 1996, p. 206). The second way is through "place identity which describes the person's socialisation with the physical world if identity processes operating between place and identity are the same as between groups and identity" (Twigger-Ross & Uzzell, 1996, p. 206). Anton and Lawrence (2014) state that the place becomes part of a person's self-identity if it arises from the memories associated with the place and the people who live there. Through memories, people create a meaning to the place and connect it to the self and personal identity (Scannell & Gifford, 2010). It is possible to feel attachment after a single visit of place, but "place identity is more likely to occur after multiple visits" (Genson et al., 2010, p. 23) or long-term emersion in the environment (Nanzer, 2004).

For Twigger-Ross and Uzzell (1996, p. 207), identity is the ambition to develop personal distinctiveness or uniqueness, as a lifestyle and a "specific type of relationship with a person's home environment, which is clearly distinct from any other type of relationship or place".

4.4 Place and Entrepreneurs

So far researchers have mainly focused on entrepreneurs' role in enterprises (Lindgren, 2012; McKergow, 2015) and less on their role outside business. Fortunato and Alter (2015, p. 445) found that "culture, local and state policies, social and physical infrastructure can influence entrepreneurial behaviour", especially if an entrepreneur has been associated with a specific place for a long time. Entrepreneurs not just create jobs and increase profit, but also solve local problems, resolve uncertainty, revive the spirit of the past and/or future, and influence community and place (Fortunato & Alter, 2015, p. 446). Kibler and peers (2015, p. 28) encourage to research the role of place-attached emotions to understand "how entrepreneurs contribute to regional development during their venture's journey".

The spatial context is found significant to the entrepreneurial process, a key driver of development (Müller & Korsgaard, 2018). Korsgaard et al. (2015, p. 9) recommend to study rural entrepreneurship separately from other types of business activities, "because of its particular spatial characteristics". Place attachment encourages please-based entrepreneurs to keep their ventures in one place (Kibler et al., 2015). Fortunato and Alter (2015) suggest that entrepreneurs have a key role in rural places to ensure healthy, vibrant local communities and that the relationships between places and entrepreneurs need to be studied to understand how these influence local development. They propose not to focus on the traditional economic growth that entrepreneurs create, but rather on their contribution to community life (Fortunato & Alter, 2015).

Entrepreneurship provides individuals with higher income and social status and shapes the reputation and identity of place (Lagendijk et al., 2011). Desirable socio-economic well-being depends on which kind of entrepreneurs are leading local identity processes. Places with powerful and positive reputations attract foreign investments, new entrepreneurs, etc. easier and faster (Anholt, 2006), but this requires strong leadership and good cooperation between the community and entrepreneurs, where all contribute to the place. Reputation is valuable and hence it is worth investing into reputable places and communities. The role of image or place identity creation and promotion is carried out by local leaders (entrepreneurs, political and non-political leaders) who have more power or possibilities to design it (Raagmaa, 2002).

Thomas et al. (2008, p. 34) studied the role of sense of place in business activities and noticed that business organisations can be more efficient if they fully realise the place where they are operating, because this knowledge helps them to "make better decisions regarding the location of their business and adjust their activities and behaviour in the community". If an entrepreneur has grown up or lived for a long time in one place, then he or she has developed social relations there (Mackloet et al., 2006; Dahl & Sorenson, 2012). Roots, relations, and experiences in the local community are a base for social capital which in turn is advantageous for one's own enterprise. Entrepreneurial activities are shaped by the social, institutional, economic, and spatial context and this in turn frames the content and result of these activities (Müller & Korsgaard, 2018, p. 224).

The longer an entrepreneur is attached to a particular place, the higher the probability to establish his or her business or remain in the same place (Dahl & Sorenson, 2012). Long-term entrepreneurs use personal and business networks to build and develop community (Mackloet et al., 2006). Fortunato and Alter (2015) suggest paying more attention to relationships between entrepreneurship and community when developing strategies on other topics such as innovation, income, digital revolution, green turn, etc.

4.5   Research Design

My study compares the social phenomena in two rural counties of the Estonian geographical peripheries, using Keddie's (2006) comparative case study methodology. According to Mills and peers (2010, p. 175) the comparative case study helps to "find contrasts, similarities and patterns between different cases; thus, it rests on the combinations of various sources and data". According to Ryan (2009, p. 109), qualitative research and, specifically, face-to-face interviews are suitable to explore emotional and symbolic dimensions of place attachment, "adding depth and richness to our understanding". In my study, I did not measure place attachment, but I studied through interviews the nature of place attachment for entrepreneurs and how it influenced their personal identity and contribution to place. I focused on the in-depth interview method to understand content and relationship between entrepreneurs and place. Guion and collaborators (2011) underlined that the in-depth qualitative interview allows to explore deeply the respondent's feelings and perspectives on a subject, being also appropriate to elicit in-depth information from relatively few interviewees (Guion et al., 2011, p. 1). When preparing an interview plan, I decided to divide it into four parts: storytelling of venture, place attachment, place identity and entrepreneurs contribution to place. The final interview plan consisted of 19 questions and 18 sub-questions, which helped to clarify main questions (Annex 1).

I selected Saare and Valga (Fig. 4.2) counties on the edges of Estonia, equally distant (~ 230 km) from the capital Tallinn. The population in the two counties is almost the same, but territorial characteristics and background are different.

Saare county is located in the West-Estonia and consists of three islands: Saaremaa, Muhu, and Ruhnu. The history of Saaremaa dates to Viking times, including heroic stories of burning down the Swedish old capital Sigtuna in 1187. The Kuressaare district (*Arenburgischer* Kreis in German) was established in 1731 within today's boundaries of Saare county. Today, approximately 33,100 inhabitants live in Saare county on 2937 km^2 (Statistics Estonia, 2016). The county centre and the biggest town is Kuressaare (13,449 inhabitants). After the administrative reform in Estonia in 2017, municipalities on Saare island were amalgamated to one big municipality, whereas Muhu and Ruhnu remained independent.

A ferry trip from Kuivastu to Virtsu takes 20 min (in low season 16 one-way trips a day), a trip by car from Kuressaare to Tallinn takes 4.5 h, and three times a day by plane (40 min). Saaremaa is a popular tourism destination among Estonians and foreigners due to its spas, culture (food, folklore), and nature. The uniqueness of Saaremaa originates from the Soviet era when Saaremaa was a closed border zone until the 1990s.

Valga County is located in South-Estonia with 28,370 inhabitants on 1917 km² (Statistics Estonia, 2016). The historical territorial district Valga Kreis (*Walk* in German) was created in 1783 and most of it is located in Latvia, only the town of Valga and its surrounding area are located in Estonia. In 1920, Valga County, located completely within Estonian borders, was established. Therefore, Valga County is a relatively new administrative district compared with Saare County.

Valgamaa has a border with the Republic of Latvia. The county centre and the biggest town Valga (12,632 inhabitants) constitute a twin-town with Valka in Latvia. Until their separation in 1920, Valga and Valka in northern Latvia formed one united town. As a result of the administrative reform in 2017, 12 villages left to the Tartu County, and 12 municipalities were amalgamated into three: Otepää, Tõrva, and Valga municipalities. Driving from Valga to Tallinn takes 3 h and to Riga 2.5 h. Valgamaa is well known by its nature. Otepää is a famous ski tourism destination but is more connected with Tartu.

After selection of the case studies, I created a list of enterprises in both counties. I used the Estonian enterprises database which included detailed data for the 1991–2015 period. In 2015, there were 103 enterprises active in Saaremaa and 69 in Valgamaa. Out of this, I decided to select the footloose manufacturing and transportation firms because of their largest impact to the local economic environment. The final sample consisted of manufacturing (food, wood, metals, plastics, machinery, etc.) and transportation/logistics companies operating in Saaremaa/Valgamaa in 2005–2015 and with more than 10 employees in 2015. After selection, I kept 41 ventures in Saaremaa and 23 in Valgamaa. The period of 2005–2015 was selected because it also includes the global financial crisis of 2007–2008, which was a critical time for enterprises and determined their viability.

The last step before fieldwork was to draw up an interview plan, which consisted of two sections: general and sense of place questions. Twelve in-depth interviews with entrepreneurs in Saaremaa took place in November 2017 and twelve in Valgamaa in December 2017 and in February 2018. The interviews were held in offices and lasted for 12–150 min. All 22 interviews were recorded and transcribed.

4.6   Results and Discussion

When analysing the enterprise data, I noticed that business activity is higher on Saaremaa. Also, the two counties can be distinguished by the nature of the business environment. Furniture and metal manufacturing are common for Valgamaa, and shipbuilding, electronics, and food manufacturing for Saaremaa. Half of the enterprises from Saaremaa and Valgamaa had foreign owners (in this case local managers were interviewed) and others are domestic ventures. In Valgamaa the enterprises in my sample are owned by locals.

I interviewed twenty-two entrepreneurs. Fifteen of them were men and seven were women. Fifteen interviewees were over 40 years old, and seven interviewees were younger than 40. Eight of the interviewees in Saaremaa were born on the island, one person had roots in Saaremaa and three of the entrepreneurs were new-comers (i.e., they had no previous connection with island). Six interviewees were born in Valgmaa and two were newcomers without any previous connection with the county, while other two were commuters who had ventures in Valgamaa, but their permanent home was in another county. Therefore, half of the interviewees were born and raised in the same area.

4.6.1 Place Attachment of Interviewees in Saaremaa and Valgamaa

Each interviewee from Saaremaa feels attachment at the island level, without speci-fying a particular location. Island communities are usually closed and for newcom-ers blending is complicated, even in the presence of roots. Despite integration failures, newcomers often feel a stronger attachment to Saaremaa than to the place where they were born.

Most of the interviewees from Valgamaa feel attachment to the homeplace (region, town, village) level and not to the county level. Commuters in Valgamaa do not feel any attachment to the county, for them it is the place for their enterprise, but not a place to live. Also, commuters are ready to move their enterprise to another place, if needed.

In both counties, entrepreneurs feel attachment to the physical environment and to the social one (family, relatives, friends, etc.). Nature is the main reason why they still live there. Modern, but private, safe, and silent living environment are keywords in Saaremaa and nature in Valgamaa.

In Saaremaa, entrepreneurs and other leaders work with their children and com-munity to escalate place attachment among inhabitants. The entrepreneurs strive to get young people with their families back to Saaremaa. However, the entrepreneurs in Valgamaa behave in the opposite way, they encourage young people to move away. According to Kibler and peers (2015), interviewees in Saaremaa feel emo-tional and in Valgamaa instrumental attachment:

> Attachment to Saaremaa is stronger than to Valgamaa. When I speak to people from Saaremaa who live outside Saaremaa then they are ready to move back to Saaremaa if they get a job there, 100% no doubt. When I am in Valgamaa, in my birthplace, then people say that if they find a new job somewhere else than in Valgamaa then they move away, no doubt. (E2_S)

In my study, the tripartite model (Fig. 4.1 – Scannell & Gifford, 2010, p. 2) shows the same relation between the entrepreneurs (person) and place (physical and social). In both counties, the dominant place dimension is a physical aspect like nature, pure living environment, etc. In both counties, the social component is in the background, although it is still important. The psychological dimensions are different: the affective component is the most influential in Saaremaa where entrepreneurs are proud of their home island and possess a great desire to return to the island even if it requires more efforts and expenses. Interviewees in Valgamaa, on the opposite, do not feel so much pride and love for their county and are not prone to return to their homeplace. The cognition aspect is common in both counties, as earlier experiences and memory have played a role in increasing entrepreneurs' attachment to place.

4.6.2   Place Identity of the Interviewees in Saaremaa and Valgamaa

Interviewees from Saaremaa call themselves "saarlased", that is, "islanders" – the common name for the people who live in Saaremaa, even if their roots are not related to the island. Even if locals disagree that newcomers can carry the island identity (only those born on the island can be islanders), the interviewees who were newcomers confirmed that they, too, identify themselves as "saarlased". This confirms Scannell and Gifford's (2010) results that attachment is a community process where through culture are created shared historical experiences and values, which are transmitted to subsequent generations. Islands generate stationary people and due to that everyone knows each other, and roots are stronger than in mainland, because of clearly bounded territory. These interviewees told me that if they go outside the island, they always introduce themselves as "saarlased" even if they were born and had lived for decades somewhere else.

To open and describe the role of place identity among the entrepreneurs was easier for "saarlased" than for the interviewees from Valgamaa. Saaremaa people have also their own dialect, which is easily recognisable to other Estonians and distinguishes "saarlased" from other Estonians:

> When I go somewhere then strangers immediately notice that I'm from Saaremaa when I start to speak and tell me: Oh, you are from Saaremaa, you can't pronounce the letter 'õ'. (E4_S)

One important aspect of the common identity in Saaremaa is the seaside nature. Most of the interviewees were sure that many things together create the identity of Saaremaa: the dialect, people, nature, etc. It was conveyed that identity is not time constant, it changes in time, but still there is something which distinguishes Saaremaa from other parts of the world:

> ... identity is like an enterprise you have to work with all the time. It's like marketing. You have to think all the time how I will do this and for whom, is it good enough?! (E3_S)

Valgamaa consists of different subregions and each of them carries its own identity. Thus, for the interviewees it was hard to describe a common Valgamaa identity. For them Valgamaa is just an administrative unit, without a specific identity. Every village and town have their own identity, but there is no common identity at the county level. The fragmented identity dates to the 18th century when Valga County was created and most of its area spread to Latvian territory. Only two parishes out of eleven were on the current Estonian side. The Valgamaa was formed in 1920 from parts of historical Tartu, Viljandi and Võru counties, distinct from their dialect, culture, and traditions. Therefore, present-day Valgamaa is artificially created and mixed by different territories and people. Even though borders were changed in the 1920s, people remained, carrying their own dialect, culture and traditions in the mixed Valgamaa:

> First of all, the administrative division which is the basis of Valga County. ... But I think we don't have anything special here that others don't have. (E2_V)

"Saarlased" are sure they worry more about their reputation than other Estonians, because they are afraid to lose the popularity and mystery that attract outsiders. "Saarlased" work hard to be positively featured in Estonian media and this confirms Twigger-Ross and Uzzell's (1996) findings that identity is evolving if community members desire to maintain their own distinctiveness or uniqueness by creating social, behavioural, physical, etc. features that are clearly distinct from others.

The Valgamaa interviewees described their county as peripheral – on the edge of Estonia. They were worried about the reputation of Valgamaa, which is better than years ago when unemployment was high. Today the environment and infrastructure in the county is better, but economic development is still restrained. Valga people feel living in a periphery, but this does not apply to Tõrva and Otepää. Otepää is a leading ski-tourism destination, while Tõrva is a nice place to live with children:

> We had one media guru who researched our image and later he said that Valgamaa is like the Estonian Siberia. It wounded us and we didn't agree with this statement. (E3_V)

4.6.3   Entrepreneurs' Influence on Place

In both counties the entrepreneurs feel responsible to the place and the community. The incomes and jobs of working-age inhabitants depend on entrepreneurs. As well, the interviewees noticed that development of the local environment and community depends on their contribution. Entrepreneurship provides the individuals living and working in a particular place with an income and social status. According to Lagendijk and peers (2011, p. 164), "entrepreneurship can invest in a place with a particular socioeconomic identity, including a reputation for particular forms of doing business which benefit the area as a whole".

Entrepreneurs in both counties are or have been involved in different community actions, entrepreneurs' clubs or in local politics. Anton and Lawrence (2016) found that place attachment encourages and motivates people to be more involved in civic actions. The interviewees play sports, sing in choirs are part of NGOs, and of the municipality council. Half of the interviewees are or have been involved in local municipality councils or are part of local parties. They participate in local politics to influence the life quality and/or to develop the local business environment.

Entrepreneurs in Saaremaa are dedicated to education issues, they are members of the board of trustees at schools to provide good education for local children and adults. Somehow, they hope to educate future employees and entrepreneurs to their enterprises or for Saaremaa and due to that they contribute to education issues. Also, good education helps to attract young families and top specialists (back) to Saaremaa.

Entrepreneurs in Saaremaa trust their employees more than anywhere else. They are willing to pay more wages to lure back young families. Entrepreneurs and other leaders ensure the *genius loci* of Saaremaa, but it can only happen if educated and experienced "saarlased" return to the island. Good relationships among them are the basis for the positive development of Saaremaa.

In Valgamaa, entrepreneurs also invest in the local living environment and in children. Mostly they support young athletes, local events and improve the school environment, etc. For instance, one enterprise has been supporting first class pupils in the local school for more than 15 years – buying school bags for pupils. Their priority is to ensure the viability of the local village life and community.

In both counties the interviewees mentioned they value cooperation with their competitors. On Saaremaa, entrepreneurs have one common aim – to create an environment where everyone wants to live. Similarly, entrepreneurs in Valgamaa try to support each other but somehow generalise it over South-Estonia, not only Valgamaa. Several entrepreneurs said that if some other enterprise grows and becomes successful, then they will probably abandon Valgamaa.

The entrepreneurs who support sports tend to be related to sports or have employees who are related. For them it is important that sports habits and traditions last in that place. One entrepreneur from Valgamaa said that for him it was important to ensure the viability of places where his employees lived. If they create a likeable living environment and promote good education, then children start to love their home county and are more likely to return in the future. Places with a tainted image, without young families and contemporary facilities force young people and families to leave to find better places. These so-called placeless places are futile also for enterprises. Therefore, entrepreneurs keep their places of operation alive by supporting the local life and living environment:

> I have told several presidents that we need better regional policy. I am not a politician, and I don't want to intervene, but I see and feel that I must support these small villages to maintain our local life and to provide opportunities for people. This is the reason why I support children; they should feel that in their homeplace they also have opportunities. (E4_V)

Fortunato and Alter (2015) have found that embedded entrepreneurs have desire to contribute to the local community, they solve local problems, reducing uncertainty, hold the spirit of the past and/or future. Attachment creates care for a place (Kibler et al. 2015; Anton & Lawrence, 2016) and, thus, it can be said that entrepreneurs in Saaremaa and Valgamaa are informal public leaders – they have a strong sense of commitment to help other community members and to create economic wealth for the community (Shaw & Carter, 2007; Sundin, 2011).

4.7   Conclusion

In this chapter, I studied the nature of entrepreneurs' attachment to places in peripheries. I selected two case study areas (Saare and Valga County) in Estonian peripheries and interviewed 22 entrepreneurs who had ventures in these areas. The results of this study confirmed that entrepreneurs in Saaremaa felt attached to the island and interviewees identified themselves with it, even if they were newcomers. Saaremaa is a unique county in Estonia, inaccessible to people from the mainland, and area with different culture and dialect. In addition, the image of the island wass very good and it attracted returnees, new inhabitants, tourists, investors, etc. In Valgamaa, entrepreneurs were more attached at town and village level, and they lacked a specific common identity, because the history of county territory was fragmented, and different villages or municipalities had merged and subtracted over time. Also the image of Valgamaa was poor, making the county unattractive. It is important to notice thatin both counties community identity had an important role – common values, traditions, norms, culture, etc. help to foster a stronger attachment for children, young people, and newcomers. The interviewees were sure that the identity of a specific place might prove a competitive advantage on the global market and help to attract new inhabitants or bring back those who had already left.

In addition, I studied how engagement influenced entrepreneurs to be place-based leaders. As Manzo and Perkins (2006) stated that place attachment and identity motivated people to care more about their place, the same was verified in the case study areas. Entrepreneurs in Saaremaa and Valgamaa contributed to the local living environment. They supported the local cultural life, improved the local education quality, and participated in local policy. Through these activities, the entrepreneurs strengthened the local place identity and regional development, hoping that a good image was attractive for new inhabitants or new investments. As some interviewees said, they were responsible for the local image and their task was to promote their county in order to grow interest in it.

My study results confirmed that place attached entrepreneurs in peripheral areas wished to contribute to place and local community development and they acted like place-based leaders. In such area, one should pay more attention to entrepreneurs and their bond with place. Entrepreneurs should be encouraged to get more involved in local life and exhibit their impact on the development of the place.

Annex 1: Interview Questions

Story and Place Attachment of Venture

1. Please tell the story of your venture. When was your enterprise founded, by whom, what is your main field of activity, why did you start your venture in Saaremaa/Valgamaa?
2. Why is your company still in Saaremaa/Valgamaa and not elsewhere?

   2.1. Has the idea of moving ever occurred?

3. If you had the opportunity to move your venture elsewhere, would you use this opportunity?

   3.1 If so, where would you prefer to move your venture and why?
   3.2 What circumstances would influence the decision to move?

4. To what extent is your venture dependent on the resources provided by your current location?

Person and Place Attachment

5. How long have you been associated with Saaremaa/Valgamaa?
6. What relation do you have with Saaremaa/Valgamaa?

   6.1 Are your family and relatives from Saaremaa/Valgamaa?

      7.1.1 How do kinship ties affect your relationship with Saaremaa/Valgamaa?

   6.2 What brought you to Saaremaa/Valgamaa?

7. What does Saaremaa/Valgamaa mean to you?

   7.1 Has the meaning change?

      7.1.1 What has caused the change?

8. How much time do you spend in Saaremaa/Valgamaa?

   8.1 How often do you travel outside Saaremaa/Valgamaa?

9. If you had the opportunity to move elsewhere, would you move?

   9.1 What would be the incentive to move?

      9.1.1 How much would leaving your family and relatives affect your decision to move?
      9.1.2 Where would you like to move?

   9.2 What is keeping you here?

Person and Place Identity

10. If you had to introduce yourself, what place would you associate yourself with?
11. Do you identify yourself as saarlane/valgamaallane? Please explain your answer.
12. Do you think Saaremaa/Valgamaa has its own identity?

    12.1 What is it based on?
    12.2 What role does your venture play in the development of Saaremaa/Valgamaa's identity?

13. What advantages/disadvantages does the identity of Saaremaa/Valgamaa have on your venture?
14. How would you describe the current reputation of Saaremaa/Valgamaa? Why do you think so?
15. What do you think, is the sense of community in Saaremaa/Valgamaa strong/weak? Why do you think so?

    15.1 What makes it strong/weak?

Place-Based Leadership

16. Do you feel part of the Saaremaa/Valgamaa community?
17. What is your role as a person in the community of Saaremaa/Valgamaa?

    17.1 What motivates you to take this role?

18. What is the role of your venture in the community of Saaremaa/Valgamaa?

    18.1 What motivates you to take this role?

19. How important is it for you as entrepreneur/manager that Saaremaa/Valgamaa and its inhabitants are doing well?

References

Anholt, S. (2006). The Anholt-GMI City Brands Index: How the world sees the world's cities. *Place Branding and Public Diplomacy, 2*, 18–31. https://doi.org/10.1057/palgrave.pb.5990042

Anton, C. E., & Lawrence, C. (2014). Home is where the heart is: The effect of place of residence on place attachment and community participation. *Journal of Environmental Psychology, 40*, 451–461.

Anton, C. E., & Lawrence, C. (2016). The relationship between place attachment, the theory of planned behaviour and residents' response to place change. *Journal of Environmental Psychology, 47*, 145–154.

Chow, K., & Healey, M. (2008). Place attachment and place identity: First-year undergraduates making the transition from home to university. *Journal of Environmental Psychology, 28*, 362–372.

Dahl, M. S., & Sorenson, O. (2012). Home sweet home: Entrepreneurs' location choices and the performance of their ventures. *Management Science, 58*(6), 1059–1071.

Fløysand, A., & Sjøholt, P. (2007). Rural development and embeddedness: The importance of human relations for industrial restructuring in rural areas. *Sociologia Ruralis, 47*, 205–227.

Fortunato, W. P. M., & Alter, T. (2015). Community entrepreneurship development: An introduction. *Community Development, 46*(5), 444–455.

Genson, J.F.N., Garst, B., & Lambur, M. (2010). Examining the interrelationship of motivation and place attachment in a residential 4-H camping environment, Virginia Polytechnic Institute and State University. https://vtechworks.lib.vt.edu/handle/10919/32238. Accessed 21 Jan 2022

Guion, L., Diehl, D., & McDonald, D. (2011). Conducting an in-depth interview. University of Florida, 1–3. https://doi.org/10.32473/edis-fy393-2011

Hambleton, R. (2011). Place-based leadership in a global era. *Commonwealth Journal of Local Governance*, 8/9, 8–32.

Hay, R. (1998). A rooted sense of place in cross-cultural perspective. *Canadian Geographer/Le Géographe canadien, 42*, 245–266.

Hernández, B., Hidalgo, C. M., Salazar-Laplace, M. E., & Hess, S. (2007). Place attachment and place identity in natives and non-natives. *Journal of Environmental Psychology, 27*, 310–319.

Hidalgo, M. C., & Hernández, B. (2001). Place attachment: Conceptual and empirical questions. *Journal of Environmental Psychology, 21*(3), 273–281. https://doi.org/10.1006/jevp.2001.0221

Jones, K. (1992). Sense of place for Ojai California. *California Geographer, 38*, 79–94.

Jorgensen, B., & Stedman, R. (2001). Sense of place as an attitude: Lakeshore owners attitudes toward their properties. *Journal of Environmental Psychology, 21*(3), 233–248.

Keddie, V. (2006). Case study method. In V. Jupp (Ed.), *The Sage dictionary of social research methods* (pp. 20–21). Sage.

Kibler, E., Fink, M., Lang, R., & Muñoz, P. (2015). Place attachment and social legitimacy: Revisiting the sustainable entrepreneurship journey. *Journal of Business Venturing Insights, 3*, 24–29.

Korsgaard, S., Müller, S., & Tanvig, H. (2015). Rural entrepreneurship or entrepreneurship in the rural – Between place and space. *International Journal of Entrepreneurial Behavior & Research, 21*, 5–26.

Lagendijk, A., Pijpers, R., Ent, G., van Lanen, B., Hendrikx, R., & Maussart, L. (2011). Multiple worlds in a single street: Ethnic entrepreneurship and the construction of a global sense of place. *Space and Polity, 15*(2), 163–181.

Lalli, M. (1992). Urban-related identity: Theory, measurement, and empirical findings. *Journal of Environmental Psychology, 12*(4), 285–303.

Lindgren, M. (2012). The thought economy. In *21st century management. Palgrave studies in European Union politics*. Palgrave Macmillan.

Mackloet, A., Schutjens, V.A.J.M., & Korteweg, P. (2006). Home-based business: Exploring the place attachment of entrepreneurs. In *46th Congress of the European Regional Science Association: "Enlargement, Southern Europe and the Mediterranean", August 30th – September 3rd, 2006, Volos, Greece, European Regional Science Association (ERSA)*. Louvain-la-Neuve. http://hdl.handle.net/10419/118471. Accessed 21 Jan 2022

Manenti, C. (2011). Sustainability and place identity. *Procedia Engineering (International Conference on Green Buildings and Sustainable Cities), 21*, 1104–1109.

Manzo, L., & Perkins, D. (2006). Finding common ground: The importance of place attachment to community participation and planning. *Journal of Planning Literature, 20*(4), 335–350.

McKeever, E., Jack, S., & Anderson, A. (2015). Embedded entrepreneurship in the creative re-construction of place. *Journal of Business Venturing, 30*(1), 50–65.

McKergow, M. (2015). Develop authentic leadership – Be a good host approaching leadership in a new way using the familiar techniques of hosting. *Strategic HR Review, 14*(3), 85–88.

Mills, A., Durepos, G., & Wiebe, E. (2010). Comparative case study. In *Encyclopedia of case study research* (pp. 175–276). Sage.

Morgan, P. (2010). Towards a developmental theory of place attachment. *Journal of Environmental Psychology, 30*, 11–22.

Müller, S., & Korsgaard, S. (2018). Resources and bridging: The role of spatial context in rural entrepreneurship. *Entrepreneurship & Regional Development, 30*(1–2), 224–255.

Nanzer, B. (2004). Measuring sense of place: A scale for Michigan. *Administrative Theory & Praxis, 26*(3), 362–382.

Paasi, A. (1986). The institutionalization of regions: A theoretical framework for understanding the emergence of regions and the constitution of regional identity. *Fennia – International Journal of Geography, 164*(1), 105–146.

Peng, J., Strijker, D., & Wu, Q. (2020). Place identity: How far have we come in exploring its meanings? *Frontiers in Psychology, 11*, 1–19.

Proshansky, H. M., Fabian, A. K., & Kaminoff, R. (1983). Place-identity: Physical world socialization of the self. *Journal of Environmental Psychology, 3*(1), 57–83.

Raagmaa, G. (2002). Regional identity in regional development and planning. *European Planning Studies, 10*(1), 55–76.

Relph, E. (1976). *Place and placelessness*. Pion.

Roca, Z., & de Nazaré Oliveira-Roca, M. (2007). Affirmation of territorial identity: A development policy issue. *Land Use Policy, 24*(2), 434–442.

Ryan, M. (2009). Mixed methodology approach to place attachment and consumption behaviour: A rural town perspective. *Electronic Journal of Business Research Methods, 7*(1), 107–116.

Scannell, L., & Gifford, R. (2010). Defining place attachment: A tripartite organizing framework. *Journal of Environmental Psychology, 30*(1), 1–10.

Shaw, E., & Carter, S. (2007). Social entrepreneurship. *Journal of Small Business and Enterprise Development, 14*(3), 418–434.

Statistiscs Estonia. (2016). *E-database*. Available at https://andmed.stat.ee/en/stat

Sundin, E. (2011). Entrepreneurship and social and community care. *Journal of Enterprising Communities: People and Places in the Global Economy, 5*(3), 212–222.

Thomas, F. D., Gaede, D., Jurin, R. R., & Connolly, S. L. (2008). Understanding the link between business organizations and construction of community sense of place: The place based network model. *Community Development, 39*(3), 33–45.

Tuan, Y. F. (1979). *Landscapes of fear*. Pantheon.

Twigger-Ross, C., & Uzzell, D. (1996). Place and identity processes. *Journal of Environmental Psychology, 16*(3), 205–220.

Chapter 5
Gentrification as Discourse and Practice When Building Territorial Identities and Place Attachment

Ingmar Pastak (iD)

5.1 Introduction

Gentrification, in its simplest definition, is the process of changing residents in a location which is initiated through the development of local residential and commercial properties (Bridge, 2006). It mainly involves a residential turnover towards younger, wealthier, and more active residents. Gentrification has an impact on the lives both of long-term residents (the working class and their descendants) and of those who move into these areas (the 'gentrifiers'), who actually experience the physical, social, and economic processes of upgrading (Pastak, 2021). Local upgrading will change not only how the neighbourhood looks but also the identity of the area, social relations, and the local community's meeting places (Blokland, 2009). Therefore, gentrification can be seen as a place-making process which involves the introduction of new ideas, tastes, and ideologies (i.e., *imaginations, narratives, and discourses*) which, in turn, as a result of this process, changes the area to one which is more attractive and triggers the process of even more new residents moving in.

Previous studies have confirmed the idea that gentrifying neighbourhoods are the locations for community building and that new residents rapidly build up social ties within a neighbourhood (Bridge, 2006; Ocejo, 2011). However, most recent research has been carried out when studying the displacement (or dis-attachment) of local residents because of the pressures of gentrification, and there is limited information available about how new residents create place attachment through their local grassroots place-making processes and their contributions to the local community. Furthermore, the question remains unanswered regarding how the context of

I. Pastak (✉)
Department of Geography, Institute for Ecology and Earth Sciences,
University of Tartu, Tartu, Estonia
e-mail: ingmar.pastak@ut.ee

© The Author(s), under exclusive license to Springer Nature
Switzerland AG 2022
O.-R. Ilovan, I. Markuszewska (eds.), *Preserving and Constructing Place Attachment in Europe*, GeoJournal Library 131,
https://doi.org/10.1007/978-3-031-09775-1_5

gentrification influences their place attachment. Within the present study, I will apply Edward Soja's triangular place epistemology (1996) with the aim to provide an in-depth analysis of how the materiality (involving *context and location*) and representations (involving *imaginations, narratives, and discourses*) meet at the intersection of place-making at home (*place attachment*). This research will be targeted at providing an answer to the following research questions:

1. What makes gentrifiers contribute towards local grassroots place-making?
2. How is the territorial identity of gentrification created?
3. How does it contribute to place attachment?

In order to answer these questions, I apply qualitative methodology and analyse interviews conducted with new residents (the 'gentrifiers'), urban planners, property developers, and local entrepreneurs. Estonia's capital city, Tallinn, has a district named Põhja-Tallinn ('Northern Tallinn') which will be used as the case study for this chapter, providing a good reference point when it comes to gentrifying neighbourhoods which involve the in-migration of a young generation which has its own environmental worldview and lifestyle requirements, eager to change the identity of a former industrial area into a 'hip' and creative neighbourhood.

5.2 Theoretical Overview

Gentrification is traditionally defined as the transformation of working-class inner-city areas into middle-class neighbourhoods, and it refers specifically to the displacement of low-income residents as a result of high-income groups moving to the area (Cocola-Gant, 2019). Although it was initially understood as a property market eviction process driven by the economic mechanisms of pricing out the low-income working class, the concept of displacement by gentrification was further developed. A recent definition of gentrification reads the process rather as a symbolic disconnection from the place itself (Atkinson, 2015), declaring that the definition of displacement should not be defined by physical out-migration but should instead be explained as a phenomenological 'dis-attachment' from a place. If displacement is rather a process of estrangement and can take place without individuals physically having to move out (Davidson, 2009), then gentrification can refer to a disruption in the qualities of a neighbourhood, which are fundamental for perceiving the area as 'home'(Blokland, 2009). Furthermore, the process can be transferred from working class neighbourhoods to middle-class areas, and also from city centres to rural areas (Phillips, 2004; Lees et al., 2016).

Indeed, physical, social, and symbolic changes in a neighbourhood can create feelings of estrangement regarding 'place' (Davidson, 2009). Dis-attachment has been positioned so that it captures long-term residents who are often characterised in gentrification literature as being middle-aged or older, while earning less and often also having obtained a lower level of education (Blasius et al., 2016). For long-term residents, changes that accompany gentrification are often perceived as a form of disruption in the community, felt not as a continuation from previous community encounters and past community networks (Blokland, 2009; Ocejo, 2011). Studies which aimed at unravelling the commercial and retail changes in gentrifying neighbourhoods tended to document the upwards transformation of local entrepreneurship in terms of social class (Zukin, 2008), declaring that new cafeterias, restaurants, and community encounters tended to follow the lifestyles and tastes of the new residents – often referred to as hipsters or bohemian gentrifiers (Hubbard, 2016).

However, gentrification should not be read only as a dis-attaching process. Various studies showed that place attachment and dis-attachment often took place in parallel during the process of gentrification (Paton, 2012; Valli, 2015). The process of building up new community relations and increasing place attachment is noted as something which is to be enjoyed by new residents (the 'gentrifiers'), who are often characterised as childless, under 35 years of age, highly educated, and receiving higher-than-average income (Bridge, 2007). Younger newcomers tend to be more active, eager to make a 'place' and build up new community relations, and local identity. It is expected that they followed people of their own age and those who exhibit the same kind of lifestyle and desires when it comes to their thinking of how a place should be developed (Phillipson, 2007).

Something which is more common to urban areas in historical city centre neighbourhoods is the recent process of place-making, which tends to be built upon the growing eco-narrative that has already gained massive popularity with today's younger generations (Pastak, 2021). This narrative relates to an eco-friendly lifestyle and environmentally friendly ways of thinking, while defining areas in which such lifestyles can be undertaken (one such is an area which is undergoing gentrification, one with private gardens, or which is close to local parks or the sea, along with other environmentally positive qualities). The eco-narrative is represented in such locations in terms of local collective place-making practices, such as eco-renovation (Fig. 5.1), or a DIY culture,[1] and includes performative actions and place-making activities which relate for instance to street food festivals, flea markets, and eco-renovation or organic cosmetics workshops (cf. Pastak & Kährik, 2021) which help to build a strong identity of gentrification.

The identity of a 'place' has attracted many scholars since the cultural turn and Tuan's influential work (1977). Starting from local process and an individual sense of belonging, the perspective regarding identity as a social construction has now been widened to take in larger territorial scales (Banini & Ilovan, 2021). Referred to as territorial identity, the identity of a neighbourhood, a city, or a region can be defined as "a process of social construction, open and dynamic, through which the collectivities settled in a given territory choose the distinctive features of the territory they inhabit or where they act in, shaping shared values, solutions, actions, and future trends" (Banini, 2017, p. 18). This definition is based on place perceptions and feelings of connectedness, common interests, and collective activities instead of physical and political boundaries.

---

[1] Do-It-Yourself refers to building, modifying, refurbishing, or repairing things without the direct aid of external experts or professionals.

Fig. 5.1 The gentrification-aesthetic outlook of the local cafeteria. (Source: The author, 2017)

Table 5.1 Mainfeatures of space according to Soja's trialectical epistemology

	Definition	Main attribute	Examples
Firstspace	Directly-made and empirically-measurable physical contributions to place	Form	Built environment, infrastructure and physical boundaries
Secondspace	Subjective, symbolic, and imagined contributions to a place	Imagination (mental)	Maps, art, planning documents, newspaper representations
Thirdspace	Personal and collective spatial practices and perceptions	Meaning	community activism and resistance, place-making

Source: Own elaboration, based on Soja (1996)

Edward Soja's work offers a taxonomy to the ontological understanding of place perceptions. Soja (1996) argues for the trialectic nature of place, distinguishing three layers of spatiality (Table 5.1).

(i) The 'firstspace' refers to directly-made and empirically-measurable physical contributions to 'place'. This so-called empirical sphere signifies the built environment in the neighbourhood, along with its infrastructure and physical boundaries. Firstspace gives *form* to the place (Moles, 2008).

(ii) The 'secondspace' marks out subjective, symbolic, and imagined contributions to a place. This so-called symbolic sphere for the most part engages individual and collective understanding: the way in which people speak about a place and imagine it to be (Meskell-Brocken, 2020). This includes various publications, media representations, art, maps, and advertisements. Symbolic representations often lay on top of the place-making narratives which have been created in the form of the collective imaginations regarding a place, and the available means of storytelling, serving to influence the discourse regarding the place and its locality (Atkinson, 2015). Secondspace is the conceptualisation of firstspace, which provides the *image* for the place, although the imagination is always ideological and political, and is related to culture. Place-making, as it is activated by architects, urban planners, and property developers, takes place within this sphere (Martin, 2005).

(iii) Finally, the 'thirdspace' consists of personal and collective spatial practices and perceptions. This combines both firstspace and secondspace, the 'real' and imagined space. This sphere can only be reached through personal contribution to and experiences gained from the place. Being well suited with the idea of territorial identity, the home is in this chapter as a place which is not only limited to the boundaries of an apartment or a house, but which also includes how it has been seen within the sense of the neighbourhood (or a city) in which a person lives, engaging local streets and parks, social networks, and activities (Pull & Richard, 2019). Place-making, which includes local activism or local entrepreneurs, tends to develop within this sphere. Thirdspace provides the place with *meaning* but is always open to interpretation, being flexible, vibrant, and controversial.

An example of thirdspace could be a beer shop. As firstspace, it as a geographical area in the neighbourhood but it also declares the condition of the building and its infrastructure. The secondspace view would tend to emphasise it as a place in which goods are bought and sold. It is known that craft breweries in US are often restricted to (post-)industrial districts (Nilsson et al., 2018), and craft beers are often sold in bars which are located within gentrifying neighbourhoods (Zukin, 2008) and this reveals the close relation between form (the firstspace) and the stories and image (the secondspace). The thirdspace view would explain a beer shop as a place in which people come together in order to socialise, gossip, and buy local products.

It has been argued that new residents tend to actively create the 'storyline of gentrification' (Pastak, 2021). Without craft beer we could possibly not talk about hipsters and their role in gentrification. However, it must be presumed that not all residents – and even not all local gentrifiers – prefer craft beer. The question remains regarding why craft beer has received a dominant position in the local image and how this serves to shape the local identity, along with the additional question of whether it has any meaning for the established residents. The available literature has not provided a grounded explanation for how the inner and outer perspectives of a place tend to intersect within the construction of the identity of a place (Meskell-Brocken, 2020). Soja's trinity of space (1996) can be used to understand how place perceptions and their symbolic implications (such as the identity of 'place') are created, and how these contribute to place attachment.

5.3   Methodology

5.3.1   Study Area

Northern Tallinn is one of the eight city districts in Tallinn. The history of the area goes back to the nineteenth century, when wooden housing was built for fishermen and the ports were built up. During the twentieth century, with the development of rail infrastructure, the area became one of the main locations for industrial production. It hosted also housing for industrial workers that date to this period. Later, between the 1950s and 1990s, the area became a hotspot for Soviet industrial production, mainly known through its shipyards and electronics industry (Tammaru et al., 2016).

The image of the neighbourhood has generally been linked to its former working-class residents, its industrial production, and the prevailing poor living conditions. At the end of the Soviet period, Northern Tallinn was affected by the collapse of the manufacturing industry, and many factories were closed. It became a deprived neighbourhood until the 2000s, when this area began to experience a general refurbishment of its housing stock mostly by the initiative of its private owners and a concentration of new developments, all of which took place hand-in-hand with socio-economic uplift, the overall process being referred to as gentrification (Ruoppila & Kährik, 2003).

New residents have significantly higher social status, along with a superior education level and income when compared to the existing long-term residents (Pastak, 2021). A large proportion of the newer residents shows increased levels of cultural consumption in favour of environmentalism and eco-products, such as new and trendy 'authentic' markets with farmer's shops, craft breweries, craft burger restaurants, second-hand clothes and furniture shops, and organic cosmetics brands (Pastak et al., 2019). New residents, who have arrived since the start of the 2000s, have mainly moved into the low-rise pre-Second World War housing stock, which is the main housing type to attract newcomers into the district, along with new buildings which have mainly been built along the seafront in former industrial properties (Pastak & Kährik, 2016).

5.3.2   Research Material and Methods

I have applied qualitative methodology in this study in order to collect and analyse the available information regarding the district and its changes. The data includes twenty-eight semi-structured interviews conducted within a long-time span (i.e. between 2015 and 2022), with new residents (who moved into Northern Tallinn after 2000), urban planners, property developers, and local entrepreneurs. All interviewees have been kept anonymous and pseudonyms have been applied in this chapter in order to guarantee their anonymity. The interview guide consisted mainly of open-ended questions regarding social networks and activities which took place within the neighbourhood, the use of private and public space, the perceptions of neighbourhood development and its residential change, and discussions regarding place-making processes within the private and public sphere.

I used qualitative thematic content analysis to understand the residents' particular experiences, place attachment and mechanisms, and reflections on the role of gentrification for neighbourhood identity and place attachment. In the first stage of the analysis, I arranged the interview data inductively into excerpts, these being the main themes which interviewees used when speaking about the place. In the second stage, I grouped the excerpts several times, with explanations being added along with cause-and-effect relations in order to identify how gentrification influences the new residents' place attachment.

5.4 Results and Discussions

The results of the thematic content analysis show interesting connections when placed within Soja's space trialectics. These provide a level of perspective for the material in general, and the perception-related features of relations to a place specifically, combining it with personal social practices.

5.4.1 What Makes Gentrifiers Contribute Towards Local Grassroots Place-Making?

In the early stages of gentrification, *the poor condition of buildings and poor neighbourhood aesthetics* generate the need to refurbish those buildings and to contribute to neighbourhood development. It shows that these firstspace qualities which are attributed to local housing, along with the condition of streets and public space, have tended to guide locals towards taking action. This statement is not in line with some accounts on place attachment which underline that dissatisfaction with the physical quality of the neighbourhood reduces place attachment (Hummon, 1992). It rather supports recent accounts which consider place attachment to be ambivalent or even that it lays upon negative bonds (Manzo, 2005). My argument here is that these results reveal the complexity of relations within places, which can be better understood via triangular epistemology. When firstplace and secondplace features are distinguished as forming the different but interconnected spheres of belonging, then place attachment can be understood as "situated within the concatenation – the series of interconnected things – of place, belonging, social memory, embodied subjectivity and everyday experiences" (Degnen, 2016, p. 1646), and means that dissatisfaction with physical qualities can lead to activism which eventually increases place attachment (Carrus et al., 2013).

Some interviewees questioned what kind of effect this had on place attachment if once there was less to contribute or such upgrading work could not be undertaken by the residents. For example, it was claimed by Tatjana that:

community activism belongs to a space which is not ready.

She continues by adding:

it looks, when it comes to the new buildings, 'bought,' as a finalised high-cost product in the area, there you can see also more superficial ties with the neighbourhood in question.

The second catalyst concerning specific patterns of place-making in gentrifying neighbourhoods has been *low budget*. It is crucial to underscore that gentrification entails different participants, such as artists, low-income young people, and also those who have their own interests in developing local private property and who are more active when it comes to building and redesigning their properties, whether studios, offices, and apartments.

The gentrification process in Northern Tallinn started around the beginning of the 2000s, and involved many young people and artists who found a cheap location in which to live or perform. These people were often in their early twenties to early thirties, and at the stage of life in which they could still be classed as being professionally inexperienced. Several interviewees expressed how their low-budget earnings influenced their choices when choosing materials with which to refurbish their place and carrying out DIY indoor design work. This revealed that the eco-narrative was not merely a lifestyle choice or part of one's imagination of how a place which involved a home should be designed but also, for some, an unavoidable solution. Jaan, a man in his early thirties who has lived in Northern Tallinn about 8 years explained his and his neighbours' experiences:

There are many people who are living in this area who can be described as enjoying a hipster lifestyle, and who live from payday to payday. Most likely they have used bank loans to be able to buy an apartment. I also have a bank loan. I think that people who buy apartments in older buildings tend to have less money, so they look out for cheaper apartments which they afford to purchase and then they start to think about how they can refurbish the place.

Jaan went on to describe how residents carry out refurbishment work by themselves:

Many people do the refurbishment work themselves. The result is not always fully polished, but rather depends upon what they are capable of. My neighbours also carried out refurbishment work on their own. We helped them out by carrying out some work which they couldn't handle themselves.

At the same time, their place-making activities – from refurbishment work to organising community gatherings – were also influenced by their views on how such work should be carried out and what kind of place identity they were aiming for. The results confirm that the process of gentrifying neighbourhood – mainly due to an influx of *people who hold an environmental world-view* – enabled the eco-narrative to be firmly rooted in local place-making practices. The eco-narrative was well suited to the specific style used in refurbishment work, when such public places (offices, studios, cafeterias, or restaurants, for instance) and individual places (mostly homes) could be visually identified by their 'unsanitised finishings', their air of re-use and re-making (using second-hand materials and second-use furniture, which also promises in its own way to be eco-friendly), and a continuation to use a somewhat 'seedy' industrial style. All this allows residents to carry out their own refurbishment work and to fine-tune the physical appearance of their properties while still on a low budget.

5.4.2 How Is the Territorial Identity of Gentrification Created?

In the second phase of the interviews, respondents were asked about the local buzz, and about stories regarding the gentrification discourse. My aim was to get to know more about the heredity behind the gentrification narrative, and to study how the territorial identity was created in terms of gentrification. This section aims to study the secondspace features of gentrification identity.

Reflections about gentrification as a wider process have drawn mainly on *references from abroad*. Most interviewees considered gentrification not specifically a product of local place-making, instead pointing out similarities to the process which took place in Western European and American cities. Some interviewees also mentioned place-making practices which were undertaken by local property developers, such as the provision of temporary use housing which involved artists and creative businesses in the first phase of the revitalisation of old industrial housing, then aiming to attract more solvent clients. An interview with someone who was responsible for the launch and continuation of place-making activities, in terms of inviting people into a former industrial site which had been abandoned for years, said that:

> in the early days we just took our examples from places in Berlin when it came to learning how to make work this idea of providing creative office space which was located in a run-down building.

Other interviewees described in detail how they searched online for information about ideas when it came to creating eco-friendly refurbishment projects.

Secondly, *the gentrification discourse is re-produced* and supported *by* local urban planners who see gentrification to belong to the global shift in *urban governance and planning agenda*. They find it a useful way in which to redevelop deprived neighbourhoods. The magnitude and consequent effects of gentrification on the refurbishment of a formerly run-down working-class area of the city, and the rapid economic revitalisation of local food and retail outlets, have also created a level of trust amongst planners in terms of gentrification deserving to be handled as an effective strategy.

According to an architect:

> ...urban planning has been weak during the last twenty years. It is believed that the private sector is almighty. [...] It has been observed that the homeless are leaving Northern Tallinn, that the buildings are being refurbished, and that every month a new café or company is opened. Consequently, it must be a good model and no public sector involvement is

required! But, at the same time, this model does not work in the interests of the public space or the community, but in the interests of the property market. The involvement of the creative economy and the 'eco' label in development activities has become fashionable over the last ten years and is used vigorously everywhere.

The extent to which public funds are applied in order to support the local housing upgrade – from schemes for street design to the creation of new streets and publicly-owned buildings – shows that Northern Tallinn has become as priority area for public and private investments. The second way in which city government authorities empower gentrification is to prefer demolition and/or to encourage the appearance of new buildings in gentrifying neighbourhoods (cf. Crookes, 2021). Seaside properties which were typically closed off during the Soviet era, for industrial and port activities or for military purposes, have freely provided an opportunity to be developed into attractive residential and commercial locations. This result is in line with many studies. Similar signals were first documented in late 1980s US cities by David Harvey (1989), who found that entrepreneurialism was, in general, favoured by state-led policies in order to initiate re-investment by local and international corporate developers. Davidson and Lees (2005) confirmed years later that gentrification had been promoted widely throughout the contemporary entrepreneurial ideology concerning urban planning.

Media representations formed a third imaginational praxis within the overall identity of gentrification. The question in the interviews regarding media representations of Northern Tallinn elicited some interesting opinions. Most interviewees admitted that they had seen YouTube videos, travel vlogs, and newspaper stories in the media which were promoting the image of gentrification. They partially enjoy the area's reputation, a Cinderella story: from a run-down neighbourhood to a trendy and – for some – high-end area, a cultural hotspot with so many events and happenings. A large slice of this information and media representations is shared and discussed by residents on the local community Facebook page. There they also make fun of themselves, and about the identity of the hipster. Residents are aware of the gentrifier stereotype and, interestingly, partially feel that this does not describe them personally although they do partially acknowledge some similarities, such as distinguishing their tastes and preferences in terms of food and retail goods, worldviews, and lifestyle. Another interviewee, Maria, in her early twenties, has lived in the area for about 2 years, and she has noticed the impact of the media discourse on local identity:

> It is interesting that in our neighbourhood's Facebook group there are people I do not personally know, but I do know what they're doing, what they're buying, and where they're going. I have noticed that they are ordinary people who are a bit more pro-ecological and that they value a sense of community. However, if you open a newspaper, you will get the impression that all locals are hipsters, wear moustaches, ride bicycles, and eat vegetarian food. I don't feel like a hipster myself. Perhaps I just have hipster tendencies (laughs).

5.4.3 How Does Gentrifiers' Place-Making and the Territorial Identity of Gentrification Contribute to Place Attachment?

Finally, in the third part I ask the question regarding how the firstspace and second-space praxis contributes to place attachment, which I see as particularly belonging to thirdspace. The responses to my questions were somewhat surprising. Many young interviewees had a strong feeling of 'home' despite having lived there for less than 5 years. Peeter, who has lived in the area for 2 years, goes for deep place attachment:

> I have such a feeling of home here that the entire district is my home. I definitely have a more personal relationship with this area; not only with the building and my neighbours, but I also recognise other people who live around here whom I find to be similar to me, who are easy to talk to when you see them for the first time in your life, and with whom you could do something together. Every activity I do binds me to this place and the neighbourhood.

This statement in not in line with the common approach regarding place attachment (Relph, 1976; Tuan, 1977). The classic approach claims place attachment is present and manifested in long-term stewardship – living in the neighbourhood – which draws attention to and hopefully allows people to learn from gentrifying neighbourhoods about establishing feelings of 'home' within a short period of time. The analysis confirms firstly that any kind of spatial practice – or, as it has been termed by one interviewee, a personal 'touch', such as the refurbishment of homes or offices – most likely serves to increase place attachment. Gentrification, in the early stages of neighbourhood development in Tallinn, has taken place so that most of the cleaning of garden areas or greens, smaller areas of refurbishment work, is already carried out by the owner-occupier newcomers themselves. This also includes community participation.

Marko explains that the neighbourhood has perceived itself as contributable:

> Some old buildings are still in ruins here. Northern Tallinn is not yet fully refurbished, and this tends to inspire. I like such a developing environment in which you can have a say in how it will be developed, and that you can actually feel this development taking place. An acquaintance of mine said that Northern Tallinn is bubbling. Everything is changing and that change is not yet complete. And it certainly does have an effect on [local] people who are more open to everything.

This argument interestingly highlights the mutual relations between place and socio-spatial contribution. It is often considered that more attached individuals are more likely to contribute to a place (Carrus et al., 2013). The conversations during the interviews also served to point out the importance of the fact that, when an area is perceived to be a location for community development, it will increase place attachment. This confirms the concept that community activism is crucial as it creates bonds to a place with those residents who are active in its improvement, but that it also creates the symbolism of a community even for those who are not active in its improvement, or who do not frequently participate in community activities. Such symbolism, which refers to Soja's secondspace, also serves to attract new incomers (gentrifiers), who find this way of living in an active community, along with an environmentally positive lifestyle and location, attractive to move into.

5.5 Conclusions

The cultural turn has led to an increased level of understanding of firstspace, in terms of its social production, whereas "the casual flow in the other direction, that is, to how material geographies and spatial practices shape and affect subjectivity, consciousness, rationality, historicality, and sociality" has been underestimated (Soja, 1996, p. 77). In the present chapter, I have discussed how materiality (the context and location) and representations (imaginations, narratives, and discourses) meet in the intersection of place-making at home. The latter is understood not in terms of property being owned but as an entire neighbourhood during the process of gentrification. To conclude, three points are underlined below:

1. Gentrifying neighbourhoods host more active residents and are a good case study source when it comes to observing the intricacies of place attachment.
2. Results confirm that gentrification is not purely a property market process, but it lies deeply within discourses and practices constructing place attachment.
3. Such a form of place attachment has been established due to the interaction of several conducive circumstances: the enabling characteristics of the physical environment (the poor condition of the area's buildings) and those of the residents (the limited resources of newcomers), the internalisation of global gentrification practices and gentrifier lifestyles and, finally, through the approval of the contemporary urban planning approach. These results confirm that place attachment which relates to gentrification is a combination of materiality and imagination, and that gentrification can be defined as a discourse and practice in terms of wisely building regional identities and place attachment.

Based on these main take-aways from my research, I have two recommendations for further research and policy implementation. First, those constraints which are put in place by the dominating urban-rural dichotomy should be eliminated when addressing young people, creatives, and anyone who is involved in activism. The locations which younger generations find attractive tend to change over time. They depend upon the narratives and discourses which spread through the people of their generation. This provides an opportunity to learn from one place in order to address challenges in a second one, regarding the investigation of the urban gentrification process when it comes to being able to offer knowledge of how to build resilient and active communities in rural areas (cf. Phillips, 2004). This knowledge especially tends to acquire a special value within the context of a pandemic in which the urban-rural divide has been reconceptualised by many young people who had more flexible work duties and financial opportunities when they chose to move to the countryside. Secondly, and perhaps most intriguingly, this study shows that personal contributions (a spatial practice both in terms of positive and negative experiences) may rapidly increase place attachment. This supports the argument that place attachment does not require only positive experiences about a specific place, and neither does it require positive perceptions regarding place identity.

Finally, the present study has some limitations. I am aware that the interviewees varied in their ability to express their perceptions and spatial practices: those who were more engaged in place and community, such as active place-makers and community enthusiasts, were more likely to be more communicative, and those less engaged were also more reticent and less communicative This fulfils the aim of the study in terms of attempting to discover how active gentrifiers build their ties with a place, but more attention should be paid to a study of place attachment amongst a wider span of people, those who enjoy different lifestyles, and who are of other age groups.

References

Atkinson, R. (2015). Losing one's place: Narratives of neighbourhood change, market injustice and symbolic displacement. *Housing, Theory and Society, 32*(4), 373–388.

Banini, T. (2017). Proposing a theoretical framework for local territorial identities: Concepts, questions and pitfalls. *Territorial Identity and Development, 2*(2), 16–23.

Banini, T., & Ilovan, O.-R. (2021). Introduction: Dealing with territorial/place identity representations. In T. Banini & O.-R. Ilovan (Eds.), *Representing place and territorial identities in Europe* (pp. 1–19). Springer.

Blasius, J., Friedrichs, J., & Rühl, H. (2016). Pioneers and gentrifiers in the process of gentrification. *International Journal of Housing Policy, 16*(1), 50–69.

Blokland, T. (2009). Celebrating local histories and defining neighbourhood communities: Place-making in a gentrified neighbourhood. *Urban Studies, 46*(8), 1593–1610.

Bridge, G. (2006). It's not just a question of taste: Gentrification, the neighbourhood, and cultural capital. *Environment and Planning A, 38*, 1965–1978.

Bridge, G. (2007). A global gentrifier class? *Environment and Planning A, 39*(1), 32–46.

Carrus, G., Scopelliti, M., Fornara, F., Bonnes, M., & Bonaiuto, M. (2013). Place attachment, community identification, and pro-environmental engagement. In L. C. Manzo & P. Devine-Wright (Eds.), *Place attachment: Advances in theory, methods and applications* (pp. 154–164). Routledge.

Cocola-Gant, A. (2019). Gentrification and displacement urban inequality in cities of late capitalism. In T. Schwanen & R. Van Kempen (Eds.), *Handbook of urban geography* (pp. 297–310). Edward Elgar Publishing.

Crookes, L. (2021). Scripting the 'badlands' of housing market renewal. In P. Kirkness & A. Tijé-Dra (Eds.), *Negative neighbourhood reputation and place attachment* (pp. 81–101). Routledge.

Davidson, M. (2009). Displacement, space and dwelling: Placing gentrification debate. *Ethics, Place and Environment, 12*(2), 219–234.

Davidson, M., & Lees, L. (2005). New-build 'gentrification' and London's riverside renaissance. *Environment and Planning A, 37*(7), 1165–1190.

Degnen, C. (2016). Socialising place attachment: Place, social memory and embodied affordances. *Ageing and Society, 36*(8), 1645–1667.

Harvey, D. (1989). From managerialism to entrepreneurialism: The transformation in urban governance in late capitalism. *Geografiska Annaler, 71B*(1), 3–17.

Hubbard, P. (2016). Hipsters on our high streets: Consuming the gentrification frontier. *Sociological Research Online, 21*(3), 1–6.

Hummon, D. M. (1992). Community attachment: Local sentiment and sense of place. In I. Altman & S. M. Low (Eds.), *Place attachment* (pp. 253–278). Plenum Press.

Lees, L., Shin, H. B., & López Morales, E. (2016). *Planetary gentrification*. Polity Press.

Manzo, L. C. (2005). For better or worse: Exploring multiple dimensions of place meaning. *Journal of Environmental Psychology, 25*, 67–86.

Martin, G. P. (2005). Narratives great and small: Neighbourhood change, place and identity in Notting Hill. *International Journal of Urban and Regional Research, 29*(1), 67–88.

Meskell-Brocken, S. (2020). First, second and third: Exploring Soja's thirdspace theory in relation to everyday arts and culture for young people. In T. Ashley & A. Weedon (Eds.), *Developing a sense of place: The role of the arts in regenerating communities* (pp. 240–254). UCL Press.

Moles, K. (2008). A walk in thirdspace: Place, methods and walking. *Sociological Research Online, 13*(4), 1–9.

Nilsson, I., Reid, N., & Lehnert, M. (2018). Geographic patterns of craft breweries at the intraurban scale. *The Professional Geographer, 70*(1), 114–125.

Ocejo, R. E. (2011). The early gentrifier: Weaving a nostalgia narrative on the Lower East Side. *City and Community, 10*(3), 285–310.

Pastak, I. (2021). *Gentrification and displacement of long-term residents in post-industrial neighbourhoods of Tallinn*. PhD thesis. University of Tartu.

Pastak, I., & Kährik, A. (2016). Impacts of culture-led flagship projects on local communities in the context of post-socialist Tallinn. *Czech Sociological Review, 52*(6), 963–990.

Pastak, I., & Kährik, A. (2021). Symbolic displacement revisited: Place-making narratives in gentrifying neighbourhoods of Tallinn. *International Journal of Urban and Regional Research, 45*(5), 814–834.

Pastak, I., Kindsiko, E., Tammaru, T., Kleinhans, R., & Van Ham, M. (2019). Commercial gentrification in postindustrial neighbourhoods: A dynamic view from an entrepreneur's perspective. *Tijdschrift voor Economische en Sociale Geografie, 110*(5), 588–604.

Paton, K. (2012). Not the only power in town? Challenging binaries and bringing the working class into gentrification research. In G. Bridge, T. Butler, & L. Lees (Eds.), *Mixed communities: Gentrification by stealth?* (pp. 251–270). Policy Press.

Phillips, M. (2004). Other geographies of gentrification. *Progress in Human Geography, 28*(1), 5–30.

Phillipson, C. (2007). The 'elected' and the 'excluded': Sociological perspectives on the experience of place and community in old age. *Ageing and Society, 27*(3), 321–342.

Pull, E., & Åse, R. (2019). Domicide: Displacement and dispossessions in Uppsala, Sweden. *Social and Cultural Geography, 22*(4), 545–564.

Relph, E. (1976). *Place and placelessness*. Pion.

Ruoppila, S., & Kährik, A. (2003). Socio-economic residential differentiation in post-Socialist Tallinn. *Journal of Housing and the Built Environment, 18*(1), 49–73.

Soja, E. W. (1996). *Thirdspace: Journeys to Los Angeles and other real-and-imagined places*. Blackwell.

Tammaru, T., Kindsiko, E., Holvandus, J., Leetmaa, K., Pastak, I., & Väiko, A. (2016). *DIVERCITIES: Dealing with urban diversity – The case of Tallinn, Estonia*. University of Tartu, Faculty of Science and Technology.

Tuan, Y.-F. (1977). Space and place: Humanistic perspective. In S. Gale & G. Olsson (Eds.), *Philosophy in geography. Theory and decision library* (pp. 409–427). Springer.

Valli, C. (2015). A sense of displacement: Long-time residents' feelings of displacement in gentrifying Bushwick, New York. *International Journal of Urban and Regional Research, 39*(6), 1191–1208.

Zukin, S. (2008). Consuming authenticity: From outposts of difference to means of exclusion. *Cultural Studies, 22*(5), 724–748.

Chapter 6
Constructing Place Attachment and Planning the Future of the Neighbourhood. Case Study: Mănăştur, Cluj-Napoca, Romania

Oana-Ramona Ilovan ⓘ and Bianca Sorina Răcăşan ⓘ

6.1 Introduction

Most recently, top-down development and planning prescriptions tend to lose ground in favour of the many local inputs of various stakeholders. These inputs propose including various knowledge, democratising practices, enhancing place awareness for many groups, enabling civic empowerment, bottom-up approaches to development, participation, community building, and fostering sustainable development, constructing or enhancing territorial identities, and place attachment. In this study, we aimed to assess how strong was the relationship between territorial identities and place attachment at the neighbourhood level. To achieve this goal, we had two key objectives. The first objective was to explore how locals used and thought about Mănăştur neighbourhood of Cluj-Napoca City, in Romania, considering how identities, webs of familiarity, and attachments were exhibited in a local newspaper. The second objective was to find out whether local initiatives and practices enhanced people's neighbourhood place attachment.

For this two-fold purpose, we used the case study approach and discourse analysis to process the research material represented by a community-led local newspaper: *Buletin de Mănăştur*. The research questions were the following: How is the

O.-R. Ilovan
Department of Regional Geography and Territorial Planning, Faculty of Geography and Territorial Identities and Development Research Centre, Babeş-Bolyai University, Cluj-Napoca, Romania
e-mail: oana.ilovan@ubbcluj.ro

B. S. Răcăşan (✉)
Department of Human Geography and Tourism, Faculty of Geography and Territorial Identities and Development Research Centre, Babeş-Bolyai University, Cluj-Napoca, Romania
e-mail: bianca.racasan@ubbcluj.ro

© The Author(s), under exclusive license to Springer Nature
Switzerland AG 2022
O.-R. Ilovan, I. Markuszewska (eds.), *Preserving and Constructing Place Attachment in Europe*, GeoJournal Library 131,
https://doi.org/10.1007/978-3-031-09775-1_6

identity of the neighbourhood and place attachment reflected and constructed in the newspaper? How do representations about the neighbourhood and bottom-up civic initiatives impact inhabitants' place attachment? Which are the features of place attachment in Mănăştur? Are research results relevant to inform spatial planning policy decisions?

6.2 Theoretical Background

Place attachment is a multidimensional process that characterises people's bonds with places significant to them; it consists of people-place linkages that answer basic human needs (Tuan, 1974; Relph, 1976; Low and Altman, 1992; Scannell and Gifford, 2010a). The first and most frequent used spatial levels to research people's attachment to places have been the city, the neighbourhood, home and the landscape, through the stages of individuals' course of life (Tuan, 1974, 1980; Relph, 1976; Buttimer and Seamon, 1980; Altman and Low, 1992; Manzo and Devine-Wright, 2014; Kirkness and Tijé-Dra, 2017a, b). In addition, place attachment is a multidimensional concept that "integrates components related to the psychology of the individual (behavioral, cognitive and affective dimensions) and to the specificity of place (scale, natural and cultural objects, the countryside)" (Sebastien, 2020, p. 206). In this conceptual context, the identity of a place and the identification with it (i.e. place identity) are strongly connected and intertwined, because one is a precondition for the other (Lewicka, 2008, p. 221; Lewicka et al., 2019, p. 2; Banini, 2021, p. 214). Moreover, place identity contributes to individual's identity construction process (Mannarini et al., 2006, p. 203). To sum up, research so far illustrates the multidisciplinary foundations of place attachment.

In our research, we used the following as a working definition of place attachment, within the person–process–place (PPP) framework proposed by Scannell and Gifford (2010a, p. 5): "place attachment is a bond between an individual or group and a place that can vary in terms of spatial level, degree of specificity, and social or physical features of the place, and is manifested through affective, cognitive, and behavioral psychological processes". We chose the PPP framework because it is an inclusive and comprehensive one, integrating all dimensions of place attachment and previous strands of research on it; it encompasses the research tradition on place attachment (Scannell and Gifford, 2010a, p. 7).

Likewise, there are other two concepts, besides place attachment, that we used: identity of place and neighbourhood. Identity of place refers to those qualities that distinguish it from another (Mannarini et al., 2006, p. 202). It consists of a place-specific essentialism (e.g., naturalness, historicity, the *genius loci*, and a sense of insidedness) (Lewicka et al., 2019, p. 11). However, place is seen also as an artifact (Lewicka, 2005; Lewicka et al., 2019), undergoing a process of material and symbolic construction (Banini, 2021; Banini and Ilovan, 2021).

We connected this distinctiveness of place with the concept of neighbourhood, due to the choice of our case study. A neighbourhood is a "meaningful urban area with an established identity acknowledged by residents", which is more psychologically relevant than a street block (Mannarini et al., 2006, p. 204). A neighbourhood is a place, it is relational, it undergoes territorial and symbolic shaping (Paasi, 1986), and it can be described, in some cases, as a community, which is defined as "several intertwined dimensions of places: physical environment, relational bonds, symbolic connection, political influence, and cultural heritage" (Mannarini et al., 2006, pp. 203–204).

Neighbourhoods are socially constructed, imagined, and sensed. Therefore, a neighbourhood is a meaningful place, which encompasses both conservative and progressive understandings of place (Lewicka et al., 2019, p. 2), and a progressive sense of place (Massey, 1994). Sense of place is defined through the sub-dimensions of attachment and identity, thus it is a larger construct (Jorgensen and Stedman, 2001). The neighbourhood was defined also as a sub-place of the urban system (Bonnes et al., 1990), to which locals can be symbolically bonded. Both autobiographical and historical continuity are needs satisfied by the neighbourhood when people identify with it (Iwańczak and Lewicka, 2020).

The nature of emotional bonds between people and places is given especially by social interactions in a neighbourhood: "[p]laces are, therefore, repositories and contexts within which interpersonal, community, and cultural relationships occur, and it is to those social relationships, not just to place qua place, to which people are attached" (Low and Altman, 1992, p. 7). Moreover, we worked with a local newspaper as research material and therefore we interpreted place attachment "in the subjective terms of affective and cognitive representations" (Seamon, 2014, p. 12).

6.3   Study Area: The Becoming of Mănăştur Neighbourhood

Mănăştur is one of the twenty neighbourhoods of Cluj-Napoca city. The city has a little more than 300,000 inhabitants, out of which more than 100,000 live in Mănăştur (on an area of about 180 km^2), one of the biggest neighbourhoods of Romania. Its origins are in a village that was urbanised in a forced manner. The place-related implications and definitions of the community's identity started from its location in the proximity and periphery of the powerful city of Cluj. Treated with urban violence during Ceauşescu's regime (similarly to other cities in Romania during forced industrialisation), Mănăştur was first a dormitory neighbourhood, later mainly a working-class one, and constantly adapted to new challenges in 'after 1989' Romania. Its inhabitants originated from the other parts of the city and the rural area.

6.4   Research Material and Methods

We used *Buletin de Mănăştur*, the first printed newspaper of the neighbourhood, as research material. This consists of the printed version of its first seven editions (as the newspaper also has an online version spanning from 2017 to present). According to the editor-in-chief, each of the printed editions (16 pages long) had 5000 copies and was distributed for free to the locals. This was the reason why we chose the printed version: it reached also those people who did not use the internet. These editions are presented in Table 6.1.

For this study, we observed a methodological research proposal for territorial identity at the local scale (Banini, 2021). This consists of studying the construction of territorial identity by "using a series of criteria belonging to multiple survey dimensions: observable and measurable characteristics of the territory, representations, sense of belonging, and local practices" (Banini, 2021, p. 31). All these are presented in the local newspaper. In addition, our research developed within the three-dimensional organising framework proposed by Scannell and Gifford (2010a) to study place attachment: person-place-process. More exactly, we applied the following theoretical and analytical framework to interpret the written text in *Buletin de Mănăştur*: place attachment has three dimensions – *personal* with cultural/group elements (religious and historical shared meanings) and individual elements (experiences, realisations and milestones), *place* as social (social arena and social symbol) and physical (natural and built), and *process*, including affect (happiness, pride, love), cognition (memory, knowledge, schemas, meaning) and behaviour (proximity-maintaining and reconstruction of place) (Scannell and Gifford, 2010a, p. 2). We considered only written text, because of space restrictions and as we assumed that it might have been easier for the newspaper to explicate (not only convey) knowledge and related emotions through words rather than through images.

Table 6.1 *Buletin de Mănăştur* newspaper. Brief description of the research material

Printed editions	Dates	Coordinators
No. 1	May 2017	Arcadia media S.R.L.[a]
No. 2	June–July 2017	Arcadia media S.R.L.
No. 3	September 2017	Colectiv A[b] and Arcadia media S.R.L.
No. 4	October 2017	Colectiv A and Arcadia media S.R.L.
No. 5	November 2017	Colectiv A and Arcadia media S.R.L.
No. 6	May 2018	Arcadia media S.R.L.
No. 7	September 2019	Arcadia media S.R.L.

Source: Own elaboration based on Buletin de Mănăştur, 2017, 2018, 2019
[a] Arcadia Media is a private advertising agency
[b] Colectiv A is a cultural NGO which promotes active culture and contributes to the development of the artistic environment of Cluj-Napoca city, by means of national and international projects. In Mănăştur, Laura Panait, a community facilitator, and Silviu Medeşan, architect, coordinated the activation of the neighbourhood in La Terenuri/At the Playgrounds area, the largest green space in the neighbourhood

Qualitative methodology is the most appropriate to explain the inhabitants' understandings and feelings towards the objects of their attachment (places, people, groups, etc.). We used discourse analysis for excerpts from all printed editions of the newspaper. In *Buletin de Mănăștur,* the neighbourhood is produced by the locals through self-representations and through their opinions, perceptions, judgements about their neighbourhood and through articulating in discourses their bond with it. Thus, we focused on how the neighbourhood was represented and discussed in the local newspaper, either by regular inhabitants themselves or by the journalists reporting on events, people, and places in the area. We did not measure place attachment.

6.5 Results

6.5.1 Identity: Characteristics and Representations of the Neighbourhood

In the first printed edition, the concept of neighbourhood [*cartier* in Romanian] is defined:

CARTIÉR – Part of a city which is different from the others due to its features (geographical, historical, etc.) and which forms an organic unity. (No. 1, p. 1)

It is described as having a heart (a central area) and lungs (its peripheral, green area). One of the oldest settlements in the region (mid-ninth century), first mentioned in documents in 1063, "Kolozsmonostor, meaning 'the abbey of Cluj', and, in the Transylvanian Saxon dialect, Appesdorf or in German Abtsdorf, translated as 'the Abbot's village'" (No. 1, p. 15), it is the "most populated neighbourhood of Cluj: Manhattanshtur, more than 100,000 inhabitants" (No. 1, p. 3). In the past, it was perceived as a tough and fearsome neighbourhood. Now, the residents see Mănăștur as the most beautiful neighbourhood of the city, where they can share a community feeling. The neighbourhood is first experienced through the senses: "the pie from Mănăștur, the smell of schnitzels from upstairs, wine tasting in garages" (No. 3, p. 3).

However, representations of the neighbourhood are diverse and, sometimes, contrasting: it is an ongoing building site or it is peaceful, smelling of spring, lilac and jasmine. All necessary services exist in the neighbourhood, very good public transport access and closeness to city centre. All these were appreciated by residents. Invitations to experience Mănăștur in new ways are addressed: to become active in community life, to improve it and keep it lively.

Buletin de Mănăștur presents the neighbourhood as a socio-cognitive product of its inhabitants whose voices are heard through this local newspaper. It presents the meanings, the assessments, and the emotions that people relate to their residential district.

The residents are named 'mănăştureni', which is a local demonym claimed by the inhabitants. A similar situation does not exist for the other neighbourhoods of the city of Cluj-Napoca (i.e., locals do not take the name of their neighbourhood). This signifies both their belonging to this specific locale and a sense of their symbolic ownership of Mănăştur. The demonym echoes the community. It testifies that their process of collective identity construction is fastened on the neighbourhood.

The reader learns that the neighbourhood is a home at the symbolic level, embodying their sentimental belonging, even for those who no longer live in Mănăştur. The newspaper also discloses elements of youth belonging, familiarity, safety and pride, as these are experienced and expressed by the young themselves, by narrating their practices, activities, and movements in the neighbourhood. *Buletin de Mănăştur* offers an inclusive image of the neighbourhood, with all generations represented. It insists on the significance of the neighbourhood for the three age groups, with activities involving them all. They are described as active participants and confident urban agents in shaping their neighbourhood.

The neighbourhood hosts over 100,000 inhabitants but still the local newspaper includes several representations of the organic connection between them and their living environment: "people connected to the neighbourhood through and umbilical cord" (No. 4, p. 2), or in love with it. An organic identification with Mănăştur is underlined: the neighbourhood and its imagined community is in you, part of you even when you no longer live there. People acknowledge that the neighbourhood or specific places within it are now part of who they are: "you can take the people out of the neighbourhood, but you cannot take the neighbourhood out of the people" (No. 3, p. 1). People feel that they would be different if living somewhere else, because the neighbourhood is part of who they are. In addition, the 'we' and 'they' discourse is meant to emphasise the uniqueness of those living in *Mănăştur*. Thus, the social is defined in spatial terms: "here starts Mănăştur!" Their collective identity is spatially defined.

The neighbourhood is perceived as built environment, social environment, local culture, and personal meanings (cf. Hummon, 1992, p. 261), where territorial identity and attachment are continuously re-created. According to its social dimension, place is defined as a social arena for interactions. The space of Mănăştur is both functional and affective: place attachment is characterised by "the different emotions associated with the place, as well as the type of place identity and place dependence" (Sebastien, 2020, p. 209).

Mănăştur is an essentialist place. This has its specificity, it is different compared to other places, it is unique. One can easily feel part of this place, it draws in with its atmosphere, sense of insidedness and genius loci, the dimensions of historicity and naturalness. This place has a coherent history, and residents would like to stay longer in this place (cf. Lewicka et al., 2019, pp. 8–10). Mănăştur is also an anti-essentialist place due to its public areas (cf. Iwańczak and Lewicka, 2020, p. 2). This is a modern and chaotic place, open to strangers, dynamic, exciting, and lively. It has a complex history, with different cultural influences (Lewicka et al., 2019, p. 8).

Thus, place can be both conservative and progressive (Iwańczak and Lewicka, 2020, p. 3), and Mănăştur is represented as both.

Scannell and Gifford (2010a) define the three psychological aspects or dimensions of place attachment: *affect*, considered the most important of the three, or topophilia (cf. Tuan, 1974) or an emotional investment in the respective place, *cognition*, which includes the knowledge, meanings, beliefs, and memories that locals associate with their neighbourhood, and *behaviour*. Through the representations in the newspaper, residents' knowledge is enriched, and their "symbolic community" is constructed, because "attachment is based on the representations of the past that the setting contains" (Hunter, 1974, quoted in Scannell and Gifford, 2010a, p. 3). Their neighbourhood is familiar, people become attached to it because they know it and its character. And therefore, as a continuation of this, the nature of the place becomes part of inhabitants' sense of self, of their identity or self-definition (Scannell and Gifford, 2010a, p. 3). The representations included in *Buletin de Mănăştur* construct discursively the identity of the people and of their neighbourhood, and, at the same time, influence their understandings and perceptions of places, familiar landscapes, and community events.

Representations of their place of residence rely heavily on the historical and cultural aspects of their neighbourhood. This finding corroborates with the results of Mannarini and peers (2006). Out of these, in the present chapter we discuss the link between distinctiveness given by resistance in historic time, place attachment and pro-active behaviour for improving the neighbourhood environment and social life. The cognitive and emotional dimensions of these representations of the neighbourhood focus on the community rather than on the physical environment.

6.5.2 Sense of Belonging

In this section, we focus on the role of *Buletin de Mănăştur* in constructing attachment to the neighbourhood. *Buletin de Mănăştur* (re)presents the process of bonding to places in a diachronic approach, where the "context is composed of strips of time and space" (Pellow, 1992, p. 190). It highlights the societal processes leading to what Mănăştur is and to what its inhabitants feel about the neighbourhood (places and community) at present.

"Buletin", the first word in the title of the newspaper, is a word in Romanian which has two meanings: (1) short actuality public interest report and (2) ID or official document that attests someone's identity. The newspaper aims to act as an opinion setter, it is itself a construction made of valued representations; it shapes the imaginary of the readers in Mănăştur. Perceptions and representations of Mănăştur and its people have direct impact on the image of this neighbourhood and on how locals relate to it: their sense of pride and a potential strengthening of social relations.

The newspaper leads the reader through the historical, economic, and social construction of Mănăştur. It also sets an agenda for action to solve issues that inhabitants must cope with daily. There are not enough meeting places and lack of community centres where people could socialise and talk about or plan the future of Mănăştur, lack of arranged green and sports area in *La Terenuri/At the Playgrounds* (currently a project for a sports and leisure facility is underway), and much degraded and dirty urban space:

> *Buletin de Mănăştur*, an identity, but also a platform that reflects the life of the community. What you do every day at work, at school, at the clinic, at the shop or at the gym, what you do well (and others like you could do if you identified the model to follow), here, in Buletin, we can present and capitalise on. From here we start together to develop the community and neighbourhood. The stories of Mănăştur come from its history, but they are written day by day, we continuously define the present. (No. 1, p. 1)

Buletin de Mănăştur is a different kind of newspaper, it is meant to reflect people's sense of place. It describes attachment to real places in the neighbourhood, as well as to the symbols of places. It enforces residents' narrative ties by reproducing stories and names of places. *Buletin de Mănăştur* (re)presents the cultural, social, economic, and psychological processes associated with the creation and development of place attachment, as well as its roles in the neighbourhood. It promotes a collectively shared attachment to the neighbourhood, as residents construct and reproduce it themselves in the pages of the newspaper, through discourses about themselves and neighbourhood identity. Representations in the local newspaper provide readers with diverse possibilities for self-identification. Familiar landmarks are presented, voicing residents' sense of home and of local identity. It expresses a certain degree of neighbourhood satisfaction, and the presence of a community, as "a spatial-social context" (Hummon, 1992, p. 255). But it is not only inward-looking, as examples from other neighbourhoods of Romania are sometimes brought in (e.g., in Bucharest).

The editors of the newspaper declared their objectives when first publishing it:

> The neighbourhood is the place where you are displeased because wastepaper is thrown in the street, it is the place where thousands of children go to school, it is the place where the young, trained abroad, can return and succeed, it is the place where people like you and me can get actively involved. And these things, once said and exhibited, give our community a chance to recover, actualise and assume the spirit of Mănăştur. We present the neighbourhood as you (not) know, see it or was seen by those who once lived here. We try to outline it as it appears in the visions of those who believe in this community's future. (No. 1, p. 1)

A selective perspective on past and present in the neighbourhood is offered. The memory of the place and the everchanging present are the two leitmotifs of the newspaper. Thus, *Buletin de Mănăştur* embeds also affective attachment to ideas, memories, preferences, and attitudes. Memories are brought back to locals' attention and reinforce images of the past, as well as attachment.

The first question we answered when researching place attachment using the local newspaper was: How is represented the place dimension of place attachment in Mănăştur neighbourhood and what do people feel, know about it and how do they behave in the represented places? In *Buletin de Mănăştur*, the relationships of the residents with the neighbourhood are the focus of representations. The newspaper encourages self-conscious affiliation to the neighbourhood. It represents people's place attachment as conscious, individual, and collective. The personal experiences of shared life and of their own biography are foregrounded in the newspaper.

The neighbourhood is named home, where the atmosphere is a familiar one, neighbours meet, eat and drink together, talk to friends and admire their children on the stage where they perform when events are organised – an opportunity to ponder on the evolution of the neighbourhood and of the city:

> I have been living in Mănăştur for more than fifteen years and, honestly, I have no idea when it became 'home'. Is it because of the neighbours who greet you even if they don't know you? Is it because of The Playgrounds and the nearby forest? Is it because of the shops where, during vacations, they post on their doors: 'I kiss you'? *[regionalism used for the verb to kiss]* Is it because of the mixture of concrete and greenery? Is it because of the hedgehogs and bats around the apartment buildings? Is it because of the love and family we started here, our children born and raised here, our friends, our volunteering, our involvement in the other's problems, distress, and joy? Eventually the answer does not matter. Now, Mănăştur is home for me and my family. (No. 7, p. 3)

Buletin de Mănăştur reveals inhabitants' representations and constructs these representations, creating meanings for places and experiences. The narrative process is fundamental in place making, as the newspaper (re)presents and, thus, maintains the individually and collectively created and shared meanings. Reading this local newspaper, we understand how the neighbourhood is socially and physically experienced and constructed, and, most importantly, how it is imagined because this shows inhabitants' willingness to stay and get involved in its becoming.

Buletin de Mănăştur exhibits a discourse that empowers the residents, raises awareness concerning their neighbourhood and it is an arena where locals can make their voices heard and actions promoted and seen. The neighbourhood is a social arena because it hosts the co-production (NGOs, associations and residents – especially due to the initiatives and involvement of Colectiv A, which promotes active culture) of many cultural and social events promoting the culture produced in the neighbourhood by all generations (i.e. the Days of Mănăştur within the celebration of the Days of Cluj), such as film projections, dance shows, workshops for children and youth, debates, consultations; NGOs raise inhabitants' awareness, sense of pride, and encourage their individual and common responsibility for their neighbourhood. It shows how the urban tissue is co-created with the residents, strengthening the local community and the feeling of belonging. *Buletin de Mănăştur* is a catalyst for conversations about Mănăştur. The newspaper becomes part of locals' everyday life, it mediates inhabitants' relationship with their neighbourhood. It is constructing territorial identity and place attachment in a bottom-up way, similarly to civic actions.

The newspaper itself becomes an ID card for all those who identify with its discourse. It is symbolic for what it means to be an insider in the neighbourhood, it opened for people an opportunity to appropriate a local image that they can construct themselves, from one newspaper edition to the next. The neighbourhood is materially and socially shaped daily and its symbolic shaping is enabled by the newspaper. The readers read how their neighbourhood is perceived and reproduced by themselves while they experience it in real time. The newspaper contributes to a process of local branding: highlights of local history, heritage, personalities (past and present) are some of the elements presented forging a coherent image of the neighbourhood and, potentially, a coherent sense of place. *Buletin de Mănăştur* includes the signifiers that construct people's representations and sense of place, influencing attachment (affective, cognitive, and behavioural); here patterns of thought and action are legitimised.

The newspaper does not only mirror local identity, but also it is a 'living' proof of how this identity is created highlighting the image of harmonious and desirous neighbourhood (cf. Gunder, 2005). This is not an ideal or perfect urban living in a neighbourhood, but a desirable one.

6.5.3   Local Practices. Past, Present, and Future

Past: Resistance

In the newspaper, the neighbourhood is presented as the descendant of the village which was renowned for its resistance to oppressive actions perpetrated by officials of the nearby Cluj centuries ago. The history of the neighbourhood makes the locals feel as one, as a distinct group, although most of them are newcomers since the time the neighbourhood was built, and their features make the group a highly heterogeneous one. Self-esteem and social status are supported by inhabitants' identification with their neighbourhood. Local identities are contingent, and the portrait is a coherent one, but never fully complete. However, the identity of the neighbourhood is made of people's interest in and fight for a common cause and their care about what happens in the neighbourhood. Nevertheless, not all residents might identify with this identity, as one can distinguish between three categories of inhabitants: (1) those who lived in the rural village of Mănăştur, (2) those brought (from Cluj and many other villages) during the socialist urbanisation, and (3) those who came after the 1990s and especially after the 2000s.

Identity through resistance, in historical time, focused on the survival of their community (the word 'community' appears very often in the newspaper). Three instances are referred to. The first is proof of being part of a long history, feeding pride and the importance of the community. This history meant resistance during conflicts:

> the frequent conflicts for establishing the border between the Abbey of Mănăştur and the city, the fact that there was the Chapter House [Latin, *capitulum*], where they validated Medieval documents of the properties owned by the Transylvanian nobility. (No. 2, p. 1)

The second proof refers to the moment when communists took power over in Romania (1947) and then when Romanians overthrew the communist regime (1989):

> The overtaking of power by the communist regime determined a new mobilisation of the people in Mănăştur: they wanted to boycott the settlement of communism in Mănăştur. 'So far democracy, from here on Mănăştur' – expression that asserts their opposition against communists. (No. 2, p. 3)

Democracy here refers to popular democracy, in fact the Communist dictatorship:

> The demonstrants (university students together with the inhabitants of Mănăştur, about 400) who were coming from Mănăştur, carrying bludgeons and iron bars were arrested. A similar action took place again around the Beer Factory, in December 1989, but then there were victims. (No. 2, p. 3)

"So far democracy, from here on Mănăştur" is the motto of the second, third, fourth and fifth editions of the printed newspaper, underlining the role of their resistance identity. The above-mentioned key events generate meaning for the people. The subtext of the newspaper is that locals share the same attachments and meanings.

This distinctiveness was paramount in constructing the identity discourse and instances of individual and collective memory are represented in the newspaper. Memories of previous periods maintain attachment. Place attachment is a product of different place identities (Lewicka, 2008, p. 214), and in Mănăştur, it is based on the common idea of resistance against adversities for the good of the neighbourhood.

The culture of this neighbourhood has several features reiterated in the newspaper: resistance to communist authorities, rural practices brought to or maintained in the urban area (gardening, talking to neighbours, while sitting on benches in front of the apartment building, which are part of the familiar physical and social settings of the neighbourhood), and civic involvement. A sense of social identity is exemplified as inhabitants are aware of their belonging to the neighbourhood community defined by resistance spirit. The neighbourhood symbolises the group of residents, who describe themselves as tough and courageous, pointing out that the motto of Mănăştur, not only of its rugby team, is "Born to dare":

> The famous inscription 'So far democracy, from here on Mănăştur" emphasises: the courage, pride, and unity of the people of Mănăştur. (No. 2, p. 3)

Buletin de Mănăştur offers a multifaceted representation of the neighbourhood, as well as glimpses into a 'territorial mentality', as "local identities have become a highly influential aspect of everyday life" (Pohl, 2017, p. 27). The newspaper represents Mănăştur as an autonomous entity throughout history, which is a source of pride and place attachment. Strong local identity is a predictor of place attachment (Lewicka, 2008). Place attachment is expressed through sense of community and sense of self-worth.

Present: Civic Actions

Heritage speaks of the community's very old and deep roots in local and regional history (i.e., Transylvanian). It shows authenticity and continuity and, thus, people's rootedness in the neighbourhood (especially in the case of the first two categories mentioned in the previous section), their attachment to Mănăştur is reified by attachment to heritage that reminds them of the past. However, through its discursive production of space, the newspaper is a convincing representation of locals living in the present and of their vitality, as well as work for and participation at events that acknowledge their uniqueness and neighbourhood pride. This newspaper uncovers the emotional geographies of those who contributed to its writing (both journalists and their local 'informers'), the hopes, desires, needs, and concerns of these people. The feeling of sharing the local identity and belonging has a positive impact on civic action (Lewicka, 2005). Also, civic actions are now part of their collective memory. These actions build relationships and identities in a certain place. *Buletin de Mănăștur* is celebrating people and places of the neighbourhood. A constellation of places and social relations construct the meaning and identity of Mănăștur, articulate a sense of community and locals' feelings towards it.

Concerning the behavioural manifestation of place attachment, this has two dimensions: reconstruction of place and proximity-maintaining (Scannell and Gifford, 2010a). Reconstruction of place is ensured by activating and getting involved in the neighbourhood life, regenerating abandoned places through new uses, organising the first community festival, building temporary furniture, the encouragement of selective collecting and recycling, raising awareness about food waste, creating a playscape or alternative playground for several ages, delimiting a place where teenagers can socialise, building new footbridges over the creek, finding a new name for the alley along the creek, engendering participatory processes, etc.:

> Together with the high school pupils in the neighbourhood: we chose a wall nearby Cinema Dacia and we activated it through a participatory process! This year we continue with three walls of garages along the section Cinema Dacia - La Terenuri, more exactly along the alley nearby Calvaria Creek. (No. 6, p. 12)

Pride and place attachment means collaboration for a better neighbourhood:

> If we want to be really proud of Cluj and Mănăștur, then only by cooperating with the authorities and the private sector will we be able to bring positive change. (No. 6, p. 11)

Proximity-maintaining is attained through activities with neighbours and friends, through organising cultural and social activities for all age groups, a flea market, workshops, open-air activities, support for local music culture, volunteering for activities with the children in the neighbourhood, especially during their summer holiday, exploring the neighbourhood and debating current topics about urban changes, and spending quality time in the neighbourhood.

Moreover, place attachment means to encompass a future together in the neighbourhood, to plan and implement sustainable actions:

> Change comes if you start to take care of the place where you live and try to make it more beautiful, if you try in some way to bring your part of good. It is about the feeling of belonging to place, about a try to humanise space. (No. 1, p. 8)

People declare their love for the neighbourhood and cannot see themselves living elsewhere:

> For me it is a big and pleasant neighbourhood! I wouldn't live anywhere else. (No. 6, p. 6)

Commitment to remain appears also due to a territorially rooted lifestyle:

The neighbourhood is OK and I wouldn't like to move anywhere else because I got used here. I like flowers, I have been selling them for twenty years. My parents had this business first and I inherited it. (No. 5, p. 10)

Our children grow, the number of parking lots decreases, there are more cars, but we do not move out from the neighbourhood (yet) and we want to make it again how we like it to be: a more relaxing neighbourhood, where you like to come back … HOME!. (No. 6, p. 11)

The *Days of Mănăştur* activate certain spaces of the neighbourhood, by means of civic and cultural actions. Participation in cultural activities and volunteering strengthen place attachment:

And what with the music and the volunteering for the Days of Mănăştur this neighbourhood got into my soul. (No. 6, p. 14)

I like this community, I like what they organise each year for the Days of Mănăştur … I love this neighbourhood. (No. 3, p. 5)

The newspaper also reveals inhabitants' critical discourses about their lived space, but these are put into a context of care and activism for solving problems and improving quality of life. The local's fight for the right to their neighbourhood by being more aware and taking responsibility for their actions is a leitmotif of the present. *Buletin de Mănăştur* describes individual and collective agencies that awaken the community spirit and shape the neighbourhood, by building meaningful places, especially through entertainment to civic actions. Another achievement is the neighbourhood festival with activities for all ages, promoting local talents and intergenerational cooperation. Also about the current urban situation in the neighbourhood and urban education.

The Community Festival organised by the Group of Civic Initiative for Mănăştur together with the Association Colectiv A, during the Days of Cluj – the first community festival dedicated to a neighbourhood and its needs –activities for all ages, emphasising local talents, urban education, work among generations, the idea of debate concerning the work for our initiative, and on the urbanistic state of the neighbourhood. (No. 6, p. 16)

Considering the group or community dimension, residents are represented as or identify with the idea of being sons and daughters of the old or new Mănăştur. "We, mănăşturenii [the inhabitants of Mănăştur]". In addition, community facilitators were active for a few years, especially from two NGOs: The Group of Civic Initiative for Mănăştur and Colectiv A. Other mentioned groups are the senior citizens, the gardeners, prominent persons (personalities in sports, arts and culture in general, politicians, university professors).

Workshops are organised to enable locals to become aware of and care for their neighbourhood, to learn to represent the community themselves, through text, image, music, and also request public authorities to inform and consult them concerning the neighbourhood:

Innovative workshops for teenagers to raise citizens' awareness from an early age concerning design, architecture and urbanism problems. (No. 4, p. 30)

Fig. 6.1 Welcome to Mănăştur – graffiti on a wall opposite to Cinema Dacia (upper part) and activated garage walls (lower part). (Source: Oana-Ramona Ilovan, 2018)

> ... questioning the use of public space, current needs, but also the perspectives of the citizens living here. (No. 6, p. 12)

People are part of workshops for landscape solutions and graffiti workshops to activate in a participatory manner (involving locals in the process) walls of some garages in a highly used area (Fig. 6.1).

Certain behaviours that improve the quality of place (cleaning, caring for it) are an expression of locals' attachment, especially if manifested in public (park, green areas) or semi-private spaces (e.g., on the hallways of the apartment buildings or in front of them). People are proud of activities such as regular cleaning campaigns in the neighbourhood and nearby forest, as well as in one of the neighbourhood schools. These are considered as milestones of their active involvement in the community, to improve the quality of the built and natural environment. Also mentioned is the local youth's fight to convince authorities that a bus line (19 bus line) important to them should be kept active and extended.

Buletin de Mănăştur (re)presents not only the linear time, but also the meanings and activities included in recurring events (such as The Days of Mănăştur), annual or seasonal rituals enabled by certain celebratory occasions. Through these, residents reattach to their neighbourhood (and especially its places and values are negotiated and shared). These environments attain meaning through such ritual performances, which socially reproduce the neighbourhood.

Place has a dual nature (Iwańczak and Lewicka, 2020, p. 2), and the sources of place attachment and identity accordingly: they are static and dynamic. The main

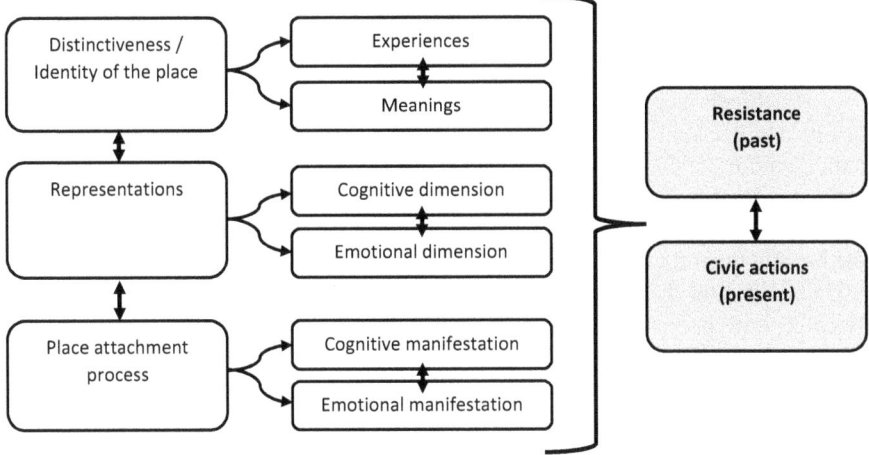

Fig. 6.2 Territorial identity of Mănăştur: the link between identity of place, representations, and place attachment. (Source: Own elaboration)

sources of developing attachment in this neighbourhood are built and immaterial heritage, activities, initiatives, which are central to their identities and self-definition. All these are represented in *Buletin de Mănăştur*. The newspaper also shows that inhabitants' assessment of their neighbourhood is based on subjective experiences in the area, more than on features of the physical setting (cf. also Mannarini et al., 2006, p. 211). The relationship between the immaterial heritage of the past (resistance) and the civic actions of the present, as well as the correlation among local territorial identity, representations of this and people's place attachment, are represented in Fig. 6.2.

Future: Attachment and Planning

The research material results illustrate the physical and civic dimension of place attachment. Future planning actions should consider the central elements to residents' physical and social place attachment because these explain their engagement with pro-environmental behaviour and activities for improving their lives and meaningful places for them. The type of attachment is relevant to the type of behaviour or action it can determine or influence (Scannell and Gifford, 2010b). In Mănăştur, if people value their social and cultural symbols, they will have pro-active behaviour towards them or they will defend them.

We considered that the concept of place attachment clarifies people's personal and collective choices in the urban environment. Spatial planning and urban redevelopment initiatives and actions should acknowledge and carefully treat people's affective, cognitive and behavioural bonds with their neighbourhood, by incorporating, not challenging or destroying these attachments, because places and communities are not disposable in the process of development. Special attention should be paid to initiatives that avoid the dissolution of social networks and place attachment, key factors in the existence of people and of the community. In Mănăştur, place attachment is a key driver of protective actions in the neighbourhood. Such results help decision makers understand key elements motivating people's behaviour, therefore relevant from a societal perspective (i.e., for spatial planning). Residents describe themselves by employing adjectives describing the neighbourhood. They are representing themselves as authentic, tough, and dynamic, interested in and open for affective and practical investment in place.

Understanding the local environment, capitalising on situated knowledge and attachment are necessary for the planning practice. The people, as beneficiaries of neighbourhood improvements should be consulted. Ignoring people's attachments and their right to the neighbourhood, to shape it according to their desires and needs, to "co-determine the social, cultural and physical future of their neighbourhood" (Kirkness and Tijé-Dra, 2017a, b, p. 134) leads to deeply problematic spatial planning decisions (Husseini de Araújo and Batista da Costa, 2017; Zhang, 2017). Attachments are inherently fragile and may be destroyed during redevelopment processes. Therefore, finding the most appropriate spatial planning actions by considering local identities and place attachments is a must. This search for solutions in the case of Mănăştur should involve negotiating place, identity and home in Mănăştur and capitalising on the social capital so significant for spatial planning where the residents' opinions matter for decision-making. Civic involvement is reported in the newspaper to have heightened locals' experiences in the neighbourhood (socialising, cleaning, entertainment activities and raising awareness, sports, etc.) and developed place protective attitudes.

Our results show that for the residents of Mănăştur, place attachment relies both on social and physical features of their neighbourhood, but the former is better represented and advocated for in the local newspaper. In addition, this newspaper underlines the collectively held meanings about the neighbourhood, highlighting attachment to the community. However, place references are frequent in this newspaper and are identified as objects of individual (personal connections to place) and collective attachment (shared symbolic meanings and shared experiences, e.g., spending time together to work or have fun). Sometimes these two levels overlap (e.g. The Days of Mănăştur, La Terenuri).

Places are also meaningful because of the social life activities that they host, not merely/solely for their natural endowments and beauty. Places become symbolic frames of reference for neighbourhood social and cultural life. Mutual support, friendship, and social networks are forged in certain meeting places in Mănăştur. According to the local newspaper, these are *La Terenuri* (a common space for the neighbourhood community), *Cinema Dacia*, some schools, the local library, bars, restaurants, areas in front of the apartment buildings, the little gardens nearby, small shops, the local food market (Fig. 6.3). These are the most common places where people meet, get to know each other, and enjoy living together in the neighbourhood. They narrate how they use the social spaces within the neighbourhood and the identities (personal and collective) that they deploy. In such instances, they perform

Fig. 6.3 In Mănăştur: Cinema Dacia, the local library and urban landscape with apartment buildings in the central area. (Source: Bianca Sorina Răcăşan, 2022)

a spatial identification with their neighbourhood through places and enforce their place bonding and belonging. The community of Mănăştur is depicted as bounded to places in this neighbourhood. The newspaper (re)presents both traditionally and actively attached locals. In *Buletin de Mănăştur* people take a stand concerning various aspects of their neighbourhood (perceived either as good or bad).

Physical and social space overlap in the green area of *La Terenuri*. "La Terenuri. Common Space in Mănăștur" is a community initiative coordinated by Association Colectiv A started in 2012 to raise awareness about the issue of green areas and the need to protect the existing ones. This is also a critique of property-led neighbourhood development in a fierce period of urban capitalism. Defending the neighbourhood from real estate business targeting the green area in *La Terenuri*, people feel they develop or strengthen their place attachment as a result of activism and civic actions. Part of this resistance action is using space in creative and varied ways, and thus appropriating it. It hosts examples of individual and group use of space which acquires meaning within the micro-geography of the neighbourhood (Fig. 6.4). Because the culture of spatial planning is resistant to change, long-term transformation can be achieved through mainstreaming short-term strategies and improvements, through identifying catalysts for change (Medeșan and Panait, 2017; Ilovan et al., 2020).

6.6 Conclusions

Our study, based on the local newspaper, *Buletin de Mănăștur*, as research material, shows that physical-social place attachment is characteristic to the inhabitants of Mănăștur. *Buletin de Mănăștur* (re)presents the diversity and complexity of processes that contribute to the construction of identity of the place and place attachment. First, we argue that Mănăștur is a meaningful environment, invested with positive emotions of love and pride. The overall image of the neighbourhood is a positive one, feeding locals' pride and prospects. Thus, place attachment is positively related to urban reminders, *Buletin de Mănăștur* being one of them.

We did not measure attachment to place, but we did explore how the distinctiveness of the neighbourhood and place attachment were represented in *Buletin de Mănăștur*. We analysed a narrative from the inside about continuity and change, while belonging was constructed. We examined how feelings of attachment to Mănăștur were related to representations of the neighbourhood. More exactly, we realised an in-depth study of urban neighbourhood representations and of their relation to inhabitants' feelings of pride and belonging, as expressed in this mass media source. Representations show the sources of attachment and thus the types of attachment (e.g., physical and social). We pointed out that people are mainly attached to the social symbols of the neighbourhood. The link between resistance identity, place attachment and civic actions is the key finding of our research on Mănăștur neighbourhood.

The final purpose of our study was to offer insights into the relevance of place attachment for spatial planning decisions at the level of one distinctive neighbourhood in Cluj-Napoca: Mănăștur. It is our belief that place-tailored interventions are the answer to specific and localised problems, and, therefore, our research enables such an approach. Planning could benefit of the analysis of people-place bonds in

Fig. 6.4 La Terenuri – Common Space in Mănăştur. (Source: Oana-Romona Ilovan, 2018)

this neighbourhood and understanding of the key features of the construct of place attachment in Mănăştur.

A limitation of our research is that the documented perspective is a partial one, based on a single (although diverse and inclusive) source (i.e., the local newspaper and only the printed editions) to explore representations and inhabitants' place attachment. Then, it may be that the newspaper deliberately focused on positive and comfortable experiences in the neighbourhood. Another limitation consists of the social desirability that may be characterising the published material, but this does not mean that the influence of these discourses is weaker.

However, the relevance of this source is high for the analysis of the relationship between representations of the neighbourhood and locals' perceptions, ideas, knowledge, and feelings about it. We, therefore, can conclude that the local newspaper, in the few printed editions that we analysed, created a coherent image of the neighbourhood that was strongly reflected in inhabitants' feelings about it. *Buletin de Mănăştur* is a good source to see and understand how the neighbourhood as place is perceived and represented by its inhabitants during an ongoing process of constructing attachment to place and community.

Further studies could explore whether the online editions of the respective newspaper and the latest ones bring new insights into the analysis of place attachment. Moreover, future research should study if locals' attachment, perceptions, representations, opinions have an impact on spatial planning decisions. These results could be triangulated with those of a future survey concerning people's place identity, attachment, and identity of the neighbourhood (that is, besides what has resulted from representations and affective, cognitive, and behavioural attachment expressions in the local newspaper).

Acknowledgements We gratefully acknowledge the support offered by Mihai Armanca, the editor-in-chief of the newspaper *Buletin de Mănăştur*. He answered our questions about the newspaper, about the editors' aims and intentions, and he kindly helped us during the process of collecting the research material we needed.

Note All translations from Romanian are by the authors.

References

Altman, I., & Low, M. S. (Eds.). (1992). *Place attachment*. Plenum Press.

Banini, T. (2021). Chapter 1. Towards a methodology for constructing local territorial identities. In O.-R. Ilovan (Ed.), *Territorial identities in action* (pp. 13–39). Presa Universitară Clujeană.

Banini, T., & Ilovan, O.-R. (2021). Introduction: Dealing with territorial/place identity representations. In T. Banini & O.-R. Ilovan (Eds.), *Representing place/territorial identity in Europe. Discourses, images, and practices* (pp. 1–19). Springer. https://doi.org/10.1007/978-3-030-66766-5_1

Bonnes, M., Mannetti, L., Secchiaroli, G., & Tanucci, G. (1990). The city as a multi-place system: An analysis of people-urban environment transactions. *Journal of Environmental Psychology, 10*, 37–65.

Buletin de Mănăştur. (2017, 2018, 2019). 1st to 7th editions. Cluj-Napoca: Arcadia Media S.R.L.

Buttimer, A., & Seamon, D. (Eds.). (1980). *The human experience of space and place*. Croon Helm.

Gunder, M. (2005). The production of desirous space: Mere fantasies of the utopian city? *Planning Theory, 4*(2), 173–199.

Hummon, M. D. (1992). Community attachment. Local sentiment and sense of place. In I. Altman & M. S. Low (Eds.), *Place attachment* (pp. 253–278). Plenum Press.

Husseini de Araújo, S., & Batista da Costa, E. (2017). From social hell to heaven? The intermingling processes of territorial stigmatisation, agency from below and gentrification in the Varjão, Brazil. In P. Kirkness & A. Tijé-Dra (Eds.), *Negative neighbourhood reputation and place attachment. The production and contestation of territorial stigma* (pp. 158–177). Routledge.

Ilovan, O.-R., Medeșan, S., Colcer, A.-M., Adorean, E.-C., Dulamă, M. E., Cîineanu, M.-D., & Benedek, R. (2020). In V. Chiș (Ed.), *Raising civic awareness and involvement through urban regeneration: At the playgrounds, Mănăștur* (Vol. 85, pp. 273–281). 7th Edition of Education Reflection Development International Conference 2019, European Proceedings of Social and Behavioural Sciences. https://doi.org/10.15405/epsbs.2020.06.27

Iwańczak, B., & Lewicka, M. (2020). Affective map of Warsaw: Testing Alexander's pattern language theory in an urban landscape. *Landscape and Urban Planning, 204*, Art. no. 103910. https://doi.org/10.1016/j.landurbplan.2020.103910

Jorgensen, B. S., & Stedman, R. C. (2001). Sense of place as an attitude: Lakeshore owners' attitudes toward their properties. *Journal of Environmental Psychology, 21*, 233–248.

Kirkness, P., & Tijé-Dra, A. (Eds.). (2017a). *Negative neighbourhood reputation and place attachment. The production and contestation of territorial stigma*. Routledge.

Kirkness, P., & Tijé-Dra, A. (2017b). Voices from the quartiers populaires: Belonging to stigmatised French urban neighbourhoods. In P. Kirkness & A. Tijé-Dra (Eds.), *Negative neighbourhood reputation and place attachment. The production and contestation of territorial stigma* (pp. 119–137). Routledge.

Lewicka, M. (2005). Ways to make people active: Role of place attachment, cultural capital and neighborhood ties. *Journal of Environmental Psychology, 4*, 381–395.

Lewicka, M. (2008). Place attachment, place identity, and place memory: Restoring the forgotten city past. *Journal of Environmental Psychology, 28*(3), 209–231. https://doi.org/10.1016/j.jenvp.2008.02.001

Lewicka, M., Rowinski, K., Iwanczak, B., Balaj, B., Kula, A. M., Oleksy, T., Prusik, M., Torunczyk-Ruiz, S., & Wnuk, A. (2019). On the essentialism of places: Between conservative and progressive meanings. *Journal of Environmental Psychology, 65*, Art. no. 101318. https://doi.org/10.1016/j.jenvp.2019.101318

Low, M. S., & Altman, I. (1992). Place attachment. A conceptual inquiry. In I. Altman & M. S. Low (Eds.), *Place attachment* (pp. 1–12). Plenum Press.

Mannarini, T., Tartaglia, S., Fedi, A., & Greganti, K. (2006). Image of neighborhood, self-image and sense of community. *Journal of Environmental Psychology, 26*(3), 202–214. https://doi.org/10.1016/j.jenvp.2006.07.008

Manzo, C. L., & Devine-Wright, P. (Eds.). (2014). *Place attachment. Advances in theory, methods and applications*. Routledge.

Massey, D. (1994). *Space, place and gender*. Polity Press.

Medeșan, S., & Panait, L. (2017). *cARTier. Interventii Periferice [cARTier. Peripheral interventions]*. Idea.

Paasi, A. (1986). The institutionalization of regions: A theoretical framework for understanding the emergence of regions and the constitution of regional identity. *Fennia, 164*(1), 105–146.

Pellow, D. (1992). Spaces that teach. Attachment to the African compound. In I. Altman & M. S. Low (Eds.), *Place attachment* (pp. 187–210). Plenum Press.

Pohl, L. (2017). Imaginary politics of the branded city: Right-wing terrorism as a mediated object of stigmatisation. In P. Kirkness & A. Tijé-Dra (Eds.), *Negative neighbourhood reputation and place attachment. The production and contestation of territorial stigma* (pp. 27–41). Routledge.

Relph, E. (1976). *Place and placelessness*. Pion.

Scannell, L., & Gifford, R. (2010a). Defining place attachment: A tripartite organizing framework. *Journal of Environmental Psychology, 30*, 1–10.

Scannell, L., & Gifford, R. (2010b). The relations between natural and civic place attachment and pro-environmental behavior. *Journal of Environmental Psychology, 30*(3), 289–297. https://doi.org/10.1016/j.jenvp.2010.01.010

Seamon, D. (2014). Chapter 1. Place attachment and phenomenology. The synergistic dynamism of place. In C. L. Manzo & P. Devine-Wright (Eds.), *Place attachment. Advances in theory, methods and applications* (pp. 11–22). Routledge.

Sebastien, L. (2020). The power of place in understanding place attachments and meanings. *Geoforum, 108*, 204–216. https://doi.org/10.1016/j.geoforum.2019.11.001

Tuan, Y. F. (1974). *Topophilia: A study of environmental perception, attitudes, and values*. NJ: Prentice Hall.

Tuan, Y. F. (1980). Rootedness versus sense of place. *Landscape, 4*, 3–8.

Zhang, Y. (2017). 'This is my "Wo"'. Making home in Shanghai's lower quarter. In P. Kirkness & A. Tijé-Dra (Eds.), *Negative neighbourhood reputation and place attachment. The production and contestation of territorial stigma* (pp. 138–157). Routledge.

Part II
Nature- and Culture-Based Place Attachment

Chapter 7
Place Attachment Through Negotiation. How Citizens and Materiality Co-create Urban Spaces in Darmstadt, Germany

Anna-Lisa Müller ⓘ

7.1 Introduction

The argument pursued in this chapter is that both sociality and materiality play a key role in constituting place attachment. When analysing forms of place attachment, it is thus important to consider both the social and the material environment of people's lives. In addition, place attachment is not a stable and fixed entity; rather, it is dynamic, in a constant state of flux, and can only temporarily be fixed. Furthermore, place attachment is negotiated, both between individuals and collectives.

In the following, I will show how citizens and urban materiality engage in a process of co-creating place attachment. The empirical data stem from autoethnographic observation and photographic documentation in the city of Darmstadt, Germany, and show that materiality is both a means to stabilise attachments to particular places and a means to re-frame local belonging and place attachment. This example then is evidence for the broader argument followed in this chapter that place attachment should be understood as dynamic over time and fundamentally intertwined with the material qualities of spaces.

A.-L. Müller (✉)
Institute for Interdisciplinary Research on Conflict and Violence (IKG), Bielefeld University, Bielefeld, Germany
e-mail: anna-lisa.mueller@uni-bielefeld.de

© The Author(s), under exclusive license to Springer Nature Switzerland AG 2022
O.-R. Ilovan, I. Markuszewska (eds.), *Preserving and Constructing Place Attachment in Europe*, GeoJournal Library 131,
https://doi.org/10.1007/978-3-031-09775-1_7

7.2 Theoretical Framework

When analysing the characteristics of place attachment in urban environments, it is key to specify what I understand as urban environment, which I use synonymously with the term city, and how I conceptualise place attachment. This will be the focus of the following.

7.2.1 Cities as Socio-material Assemblages

What is a city? There are at least two answers to this question: an administrative and a social scientific answer. In administrative terms, a city is a human settlement, defined by administrative borders and with a certain number of inhabitants. The quantitative size of the population qualifying a settlement as city varies over time and space. In Germany at the time of writing, a settlement with 100,000 and more inhabitants is termed city ("Großstadt"), making up for the largest administrative unit regarding settlements in the German context (*Stadtentwicklungsbericht Der Bundesregierung 2020*, 2021, p. 8). In social scientific terms, cities are also characterised by their quantitative size of population and, especially, population density, but also by additional qualitative aspects such as heterogeneity of population in terms of social, cultural and demographic background; heterogeneity of economy; and differentiation of society in terms of division of labour, diversity of institutions, and variety in the built environment such as co-existence of residential and commercial areas and areas for recreation and work (for an early and to date formative analysis see Simmel, 1995 [1903]).

In this contribution, I follow the social scientific understanding of a city. More precisely, a city as understood here is characterised as a human settlement that is heterogeneous in social, economic, institutional, and material terms. The latter comprises perceivable physical, both humanly created and other, non-processed things around us (Reichmann & Müller, 2015). It includes technological infrastructure, streets, pavements, benches, squares as well as fences, bushes, trees, but even parked cars (Kurnicki, 2022) and cast away surgical masks. The latter – parked cars and cast away masks – point to the fact that a city is not a fixed, over time and space stable entity. Rather, it is in a constant state of flux and depends on individuals, groups, institutions as well as infrastructures, policies and societies as such to appear as a stable, immobile entity (Farias & Bender, 2009).

To grasp cities as socio-material entities (Müller, 2017), I add a social-constructivist understanding of space to the conceptualisation. Following Löw (2001), I argue that social spaces are constituted in cities as results of people interacting with and relating to the built environment and the people around them. Individuals and groups constitute spaces in a city, and these spaces differ from one another because the people who constitute them differ according to age, gender, biography, lifestyle, etc. This then has also fundamental consequences for the respective emotional bonds they develop with places, that is: for place attachment.

7.2.2 Place Attachment

When discussing place attachment in the context of cities, it is key to consider the heterogeneity of both material-spatial environment and inhabitants. Consequently, we can observe a multitude of forms that place attachment in cities take on.

The concept of 'place attachment' is closely related to the concept of 'belonging' but emphasises the environment in which individuals and groups live. Both concepts share, however, their focus on the emotional and affective dimension of people's relations, either to human or to non-human actors. Place attachment is particularly suited for bringing together the emotional and the spatial dimension of place-related belonging.

Proshansky et al. (1983) stress that an individual's identity is constituted through distinguishing oneself from other, human and non-human actors and relating oneself to places (here understood as "physical settings" – Proshansky et al., 1983, p. 62). Establishing relations to places is then a fundamental part of constituting the self. Place attachment denotes this particular effect that locations have for people's emotional belonging and, ultimately, for their individual and collective identity.

Research on place attachment has been and is done in various disciplines. Early research can be found in phenomenology with its focus on the interrelation of individual behaviour and surrounding environment (for an overview cf. Low & Altman, 1992, pp. 1–2). Research sites were often people's homes as well as sacred places (Low & Altman, 1992, p. 2), serving as examples for people's emotional bonds to particular places (cf. also Fried, 1963). For psychology, Gustafson (2001) has worked out the relevance of locations for emotional attachments, and Pollini (2005) formulated a sociological conceptualisation of the socio-spatial dimensions of place attachment. Researchers have also addressed place attachment with a particular focus on its temporality (Milligan, 1998) and on its relation to living in a diaspora (Deutsch, 2005).

To explain the relation between the different elements entailed in place attachment, Scannell and Gifford (2010, p. 2) developed a concept showing that three different things partake in the constitution of attachment to places: (1) an individual person, (2) the location at which the person is situated, and (3) a psychological process including emotions and behaviour patterns. It is then important to consider who the individual is who establishes a connection to a place and to what extent this connection is based on individual preferences or is embedded in collectively shared values and belongings. The psychological process is closely related to that, as it addresses the forms in which affects and behavioural patterns become manifest in place attachment. The question here is: what kinds of behavioural patterns indicate that a person feels attached to a place? Finally, the characteristics of the particular location to which the person feels attached to need to be identified. Here, it is key to ask for the characteristics of the places to which the person feels particularly attached to, for the kind of bonds s/he establishes and for the key features of these places (e.g., regarding their materiality and spatiality).

For my contribution, I focus on two of these aspects, the social dimension and the location. When analysing place attachment in urban environments, it is key to acknowledge that people can feel attached to very different kinds of places and that these attachments can both be positive and negative (Manzo, 2014). In addition, the temporal and interactional aspects of place attachment are important to be considered. As I argue that place attachment is (1) processual in character, (2) only temporarily stable and (3) the result of an interplay of sociality and materiality, the dynamic character of place attachment must be considered in conceptualising and empirically investigating it.

7.3 Methodology

To empirically strengthen my argument on the dynamic nature of place attachment and on the role that materiality plays for establishing and keeping up attachments to certain places, I use data from recent research in Darmstadt, Germany. This city can be classified as ordinary city (Robinson, 2006): part of a network of regional mid-sized and larger cities, site of numerous medium-sized enterprises, with an average population in terms of age, destination of origin and purchasing power, to name only a few. Thus, Darmstadt is neither a global city such as Frankfurt am Main, nor a declining city such as Recklinghausen. In 2021, I did fieldwork in Darmstadt on several occasions, focusing on the negotiation of society taking place within the city in general and addressing the role of urban public spaces in particular. During the research, one site within the city turned out to be key for these negotiation processes: the Georg-Büchner-Platz. In the following, I first introduce this urban square and then present the methods and data used for the results presented and discussed in the then following sections.

7.3.1 Case Study Georg-Büchner-Platz, Darmstadt

For this contribution, I zoom in into the city of Darmstadt and onto one of its inner-city squares: the Georg-Büchner-Platz. Darmstadt is a mid-sized German city with just under 160,000 inhabitants, located in the federal state of Hessen, in proximity of the metropolis Frankfurt/Main. Comprising different districts with different socio-demographic characteristics, the inner-city area in which the Georg-Büchner-Platz is located is the area where the city's heterogeneous society meets and inter-mingles. Located in front of the biggest local theater, Staatstheater Darmstadt, the square is both a representational and a fundamentally social space. Since 2010, it is in its today's shape, after having seen several different functions and design over the decades commencing in 1804 when it served as botanical garden of the hereditary Grand Duke Ludwig I.

The square is located in downtown Darmstadt, at the southern end of the pedestrian zone (Fig. 7.1). It is slightly sloping. One short side is bordered by the Staatstheater Darmstadt; opposite is, slightly offset, a church, the Kuppelkirche (Fig. 7.2). Apartment buildings are located on the long sides, and there is an underground car park below the square. The square itself is equipped to allow for different uses: benches, a water fountain, a sandbox, exits to the underground car park, stair-like green areas that are interrupted by stone steps, and the area in front of the theater (Fig. 7.3). With its design and equipment, the square offers different ways of using it. Here, I want to highlight three features of the square that are important for my research: the square's non-commercial usage, its role as forecourt of the Staatstheater, and its proximity to the surrounding residential area.

The non-commercial use of the space is a key feature: staying there without consuming anything is possible. Adjacent supermarkets, cafés and restaurants with take-away offers, especially during the months of the Covid-19 pandemic, make it possible to eat and drink on the square, but it is not the condition as it would be in a commercial café.

For the Staatstheater as cultural institution, the square plays a key role both as infrastructure (car parking for visitors in the underground car park) and as forecourt as it is located directly in front of the building of the theater and is architecturally attached to it. In pandemic times, with the prohibition of indoor events and

Fig. 7.1 The location of the Georg-Büchner-Platz in die city of Darmstadt. (Source: Open Street Map 2022 © OpenStreetMap contributors)

Fig. 7.2 The Georg-Büchner-Platz in front of the Staatstheater, located east of the theatre building and in between residential buildings. (Source: Open Street Map 2022 © OpenStreetMap contributors)

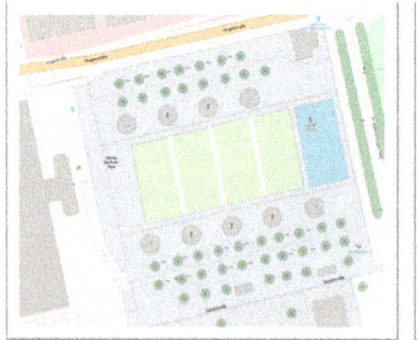

Fig. 7.3 The Georg-Büchner-Platz: spatial design and equipment. (Source: Open Street Map 2022 (© OpenStreetMap contributors) and Anna-Lisa Müller, 2021)

performances, the open space in front of the theatre turned out to be especially valuable as a series of performances was taking place in front of the theater, entitled "Come into the open!"

Third and finally, the square's location within a residential area (Fig. 7.2) has consequences for the people living around the square. For them, the square has other characteristics: it is the reason for disturbed sleep at night when groups of people use the square as a party venue. It provides them with views over urban green outside their window that also prevents others from looking directly into their kitchen or bedroom. And it can be used as an indication of place of residency and navigating tool: "Cycle to Georg-Büchner-Platz, and then turn right in front of the theatre."

With its location in the city-centre of Darmstadt, its characteristic design and the multitude of functions and possible usages connected to it, the Georg-Büchner-Platz turned out to be a highly interesting sight for research on place attachment and social negotiation processes.

7.3.2 Observation, Informal Interviews, Documents

Most part of the fieldwork was conducted between April and July 2021, with occasional additional visits to the city prior and after that date. Thus, data on the Georg-Büchner-Platz and its role within the local civil society stem from the period between May 2018 and November 2021. As the prime phase of fieldwork took place during the Corona-pandemics, I decided for a set of methods that allowed for keeping a physical distance to other people and to ensure safety for both researcher and participants (for a description on how the pandemic affected urban life in Germany, see Müller & Tuitjer, 2022). I used documentary photography, document analysis and auto-ethnography (e.g. Denzin, 2014; Bochner & Ellis, 2016; for a methodological reflection see Holt, 2003).

As I was a temporary citizen of Darmstadt during April and July 2021, as fellow of the Darmstadt-based Schader Foundation (Müller, 2021), I was invited to four informal talks on Darmstadt, among other things on the city's civil society, its cultural institutions including the Staatstheater and on its built environment and spatial design. These talks took place in small groups, in accordance with the regulations to combat the spread of the Covid-19 virus as applicable at the respective time. In addition, informal interviews with inhabitants, commuters working in Darmstadt, and visitors added data to the data set. Furthermore, I selected documents on the Georg-Büchner-Platz, namely reports, brochures, and planning documents, that were publicly available. All written data were analysed using qualitative content analysis; the visual material was used as accompanying material and serves here primarily illustrative purposes.

In the following, I present selected results of my research on the Georg-Büchner-Platz. To do so and to introduce the reader to the scene, I will use vignettes which are a combination of extracts from my fieldnotes and visual impressions, documenting selected social situations that I encountered during my research.

7.4 Results and Discussion

In the following, I will first present vignettes with insights into the field that will set the scene for the then following presentation and discussion of selected results. The results address two dimensions of the key topic of this edited volume: place attachment. As introduced in the theory section, these dimensions are the material-spatial aspect of place attachment and the role of negotiations for producing, preserving, and potentially altering senses of place attachment.

7.4.1   Setting the Scene: Vignettes from Darmstadt

The following vignettes present excerpts from my field notes in Darmstadt. Vignette 1 focusses on the experiences I had on an ordinary weekday. Vignette 2 displays my experiences during an evening when the Staatstheater had a performance on the theatre's terrace.

What these vignettes hint at and what my ethnographic data overall show is that the people who use the site differ in terms of age, gender, form of use and lifestyle. At different times of the day and on different days of the week, they use the location in different ways. There is a juxtaposition of very different uses, and the people who use the space are similar despite their differences as they see something in this place that they consider valuable. It can be the function, it can be the view of the theater, it can be the geographical location or the presence of like-minded people. But it can also be, as in the case of the man brushing his teeth that I portrayed in vignette 1, the emptiness of the square at certain times of the day that makes it appealing to go there.

7.4.2   The Georg-Büchner-Platz: Spatial-Material Square and Social Space

My empirical data from autoethnographic observation and photographic documentation in Darmstadt show that materiality is both a means to stabilise attachments to particular places and a means to re-frame local belonging and place attachment. What is very obvious when analysing the case of the Georg-Büchner-Platz is the importance of the spatial-material design of the square. It allows for access for almost everyone: there are few physical barriers to enter the square and to move around. The stairs are flat, and it is possible to move alongside the square without using stairs, making the place available also for people with wheelchairs, baby buggies or shopping trolleys. As my fieldnotes document, people of very different age and bodily ability are present at the Georg-Büchner-Platz, and with different devices. There are kids playing in the water fountains, bmx-cyclists doing tricks around the sculpture or on benches, elderly people and people with wheeled walking frames passing the square in the shade of the trees or sitting on the benches, but also people in their mid-30s and -40s, dressed in suits, spending their lunch breaks on the stone stairs and consuming take-away food and drinks. Thus, the square's material and spatial characteristics allow for very different usages by very different people.

In addition, the character of the Georg-Büchner-Platz as site with no necessity to consume anything and without a dominant usage makes it a socially accessible site. The lack of a dominant usage is mirrored by the fact that no signs prohibit a particular usage or encourage it. Rather, the material design and spatial setting of the square invites for diverse usages. They are executed at different times of the day and by different people. For instance, when using the site for brushing one's teeth unhinderedly (see vignette 1 – Fig. 7.4) or when using it as place to meet friends over a beer after work. Through their practices of using the square, these people create emotional bonds to it and feel attached to the place.

The data show that the people using the Georg-Büchner-Platz establish senses of place attachment. And these people vary in age, gender, social and economic

It is Tuesday morning, 7:30 am. I have left my flat to enjoy a short walk in what promises to be a sunny day. It is still cool outside. Few people are on the streets. I decide to take the street towards the Georg-Büchner-Platz. It will lead me towards the city centre with its pedestrian precinct, and I hope to find a café that is already open to buy a coffee. As we are in corona times, I have to look for a place that sells coffee to go or offers places to sit outdoors. I pass the Kuppelkirche and turn slightly left to cast a view on the Georg-Büchner-Platz. At the far end, in front of the Staatstheater, I spot the people from the city cleaning who empty the bins and collect litter. Except them, the square is empty.

I proceed down to Luisenplatz and find one coffeeshop offering hot beverages to go. Interesting that all other spots are still closed. As it is a weekday, people are on their way to work. But – and I assume this is also due to corona – the Luisenplatz which is a real hub with its bus and tram stops appears surprisingly quiet. Almost extinct.

Coffee in my hand, I decide to walk back to the Georg-Büchner-Platz. Due to its location on top of a small hill, it is exposed to the sun almost all day round. I imagine myself sitting in the sun, enjoying the sight of the theatre building, sipping my coffee and listening to the birds singing in the trees alongside the square.

When I arrive at the square, it is as I imagined: the square is almost fully sunny, the city cleaning has completed their work, birds are singing. I sit down on one of the stone steps. They feel cold from beneath. I take my scarf to have it a little warmer to sit on. I take a sip of my coffee. Lukewarm by now. I look around. Am I the only person here? Where are the kids playing here in the afternoon? The youngsters spending their nights? Still in bed. Then I spot a person on the righthand side of the place. Oh, I am not the only one here. I take a closer look. It is a man in his 50s, although I can't really say. Next to him there are three big plastic bags, heavily used. He wears a long coat, greyish, brown trousers and has brown-grey hair. He is doing something, but I can't really see what. I take another sip of my coffee and look somewhere else. The theatre has left parts of the coulisse of the current play on the balcony. Due to corona, they have decided to play outdoors, so the coulisse is now part of the theater's appearance throughout the day, even if there is no performance. From the corner of my eye, I see a movement. The man has turned, and now I can see what he does: brushing his teeth. It is a very private scene that I observe. I now figure out that he is most probably a homeless man, taking advantage of the fact that the Georg-Büchner-Platz at this time of the day is not occupied by others. Suddenly I feel a bit bad that I now disturb his privacy. But he doesn't appear to take notice of me. Or he ignores the fact that I am here.

Fig. 7.4 Vignette 1 – observations on a weekday morning. (Source: Anna-Lisa Müller, 2021)

background, biography, and lifestyle. They use the Georg-Büchner-Platz for very different purposes. And interestingly, they all relate to the same site and make use of the same materiality, though at different times, in different ways and for different reasons.

My argument is that this seemingly paradoxical situation of multiple forms of attachment to the same place can be explained when considering seriously the interplay of sociality and materiality that we observe at the Georg-Büchner-Platz. As the square has low barriers both in material-spatial terms and in social terms, it is by design an open and integrative site (Müller & Reichmann, 2020). Its accessibility allows for different usages by different people and thus enables the production of different social spaces at the same location (Lefèbvre, 1991; Löw, 2001). For these spaces, the very materiality of the square such as the benches, the water fountain or the stairs is essential (Reichmann & Müller, 2015). These social spaces exist simultaneously and turn the Georg-Büchner-Platz into a multi-dimensional urban space. And every space that is created – the space of the playing field for kids, of the bathroom for a homeless man, of the students' bar – refers to emotional bonds between the Georg-Büchner-Platz and the respective person or group.

Thus, the Georg-Büchner-Platz is both a spatial-material square and a social space; and it is the very interplay of the sociality *at* and the materiality *of* the Georg-Büchner-Platz that brings about multiple forms of attachments *to* the place.

In the following, I will elaborate on the role that negotiation plays for these modes of place attachments.

7.4.3   Negotiating Place Attachment at the Georg-Büchner-Platz

My empirical data show that materiality in general and the material-spatial design of the Georg-Büchner-Platz in particular is a means to stabilise attachments to particular places and to re-frame local belonging and attachment. Thus, materiality plays a key role for bringing about sociality in Darmstadt. The Georg-Büchner-Platz with its central location in the city of Darmstadt is a good example to show how both attachment to a place and belonging to a society are negotiated in urban public space. As I have discussed above, one of the key characteristics of the Georg-Büchner-Platz is that different people do particular things at the same or at different times of the day and year on the same square. The social spaces they constitute by doing things on the square – playing, having lunch, meeting friends, sunbathing – overlap in spatial terms: they happen at the same geographic location. Often, they also overlap in temporal terms: they take place at the same time (see especially vignette 2 – Fig. 7.5).

Seeing others doing other things on the same site means – at best – to acknowledge this "otherness" as part of an "ourness" (Simmel, 1908). This goes together with understanding that others do the things on the site because they like the site as

It is a sunny evening in Darmstadt. I know that the theatre has started its new programme, entitled "Komm' ins Freie" ("Come outdoors"). And I know that they will play on the terrace of the theatre which is located just opposite the Georg-Büchner-Platz. I am curious how the setting will be: will they have huge curtains to prevent spectators from the square from watching the show? Will there be a huge crowd in front of the terrace behind the barrier who want to watch but not pay for the performance?

I decide to walk from my flat to the square, down the Wilhelminenstraße. It is a warm, sunny evening, allowing for staying outside quite long without freezing. I decide to approach the theatre from the Kuppelkirche and walk alongside the Georg-Büchner-Platz. When I arrive at the north-eastern end of the square, I see that the play has already started. From the square, I can see the rows of chairs with people sitting on them. They look at a spot in front of them. I assume that this would be the stage as I cannot see it myself – and I see it nowhere else. What I as spectator can see, however, is the backstage where the actors wait for their cue. I see staff members running around there, checking the costumes, and cuing the actors.

Today, I feel very comfortable observing the scene and the people around me. Different from other moments, many other people are here as observers, so I am just one of many. However, there are less people than I had expected who watch the play as defaulting audience. Some sit on the square's stairs just in front of the terrace, chat with each other but also pay attention to the play. I see a lot of grey hair there. Others just sit on those stairs that are more in the middle of the square and cast a look every now and then. For example, when the audience applauds. These people seem to be younger. Then suddenly, a man comes on his bike, passing by the theatre between the terrace and the square. This happens rather often. But today it appears a little weird, especially because the man doesn't turn his head at all when passing by the terrace – and the play is in full swing. He turns right after the terrace and is soon gone.

After I've spent about 20 minutes on the square, it becomes rather boring. The scenery doesn't really change, and I also feel a bit bad about only watching and not attending the play as part of the paying audience. I know that cultural institutions such as theatres have a hard time coping with Covid-related restrictions and depend on entrance fees. I decide to leave the place. When I turn my back to the theatre to walk up the hill and towards the Kuppelkirche, I realise that quite a few people have by now gathered on the square. They tend to stay in the half of the square that is farther away from the theatre and gather in little groups. Many seem to be in their mid-20s, some have darker skintone than others, and I see men and women alike. The setting now appears to be rather normal for a sunny evening, an ordinary evening on Darmstadt's Georg-Büchner-Platz, with ordinarily diverse groups of people gathering and spending their time chatting, drinking, taking pictures of one another with their smartphones and, less frequently, eating.

Fig. 7.5 Vignette 2 – observations on an evening during a theatre performance. (Source: Anna-Lisa Müller, 2021)

much as we do: they have the same preference for the same location. Understanding this then means to identify a commonality that we have with others which has the potential to bridge the differences between us.

This is one way how an urban square and emotional attachments related to it can contribute to bringing about social cohesion in a city and in society. The other way in which the square and related place attachment plays a role for society is that it becomes the site where place attachment is negotiated. Negotiation here takes place through practices rather than through direct communication. By using the site simultaneously for different purposes – sunbathing, chatting, reading, playing, arguing – communication occurs through people's bodily presence within a finite realm. Without speaking to each other, the different groups and individuals on the Georg-Büchner-Platz relate to each other, as the homeless man did to me and vice versa (vignette 1 – Fig. 7.4). Through this, social relationships are negotiated, and dominant usages of the site assigned to people, locations and times are stabilised: drinking beer in the middle of the square is a dominant usage at summer evenings; playing with the water fountain might be dominant at sunny summer afternoons, but only for people of a younger age.

As results of these negotiation processes, place attachments are created: kids feel emotionally attached to the Georg-Büchner-Platz as they know it as their site for playing with a water fountain. Adolescents have emotional bonds to the Georg-Büchner-Platz as they understand it as their meeting place on mild summer evenings. Through these place attachments, they establish feelings of belonging to the city and to its community.[1] Belonging to a community and feeling attached to its places then is a prerequisite for feeling empowered to make claims to the society (i.e., claims to belong to it). Thus, negotiating place attachment on an urban square in a city can be one step towards becoming a mature citizen.

What the data from Darmstadt show is that the material-spatial design of a city with its urban squares, such as the Georg-Büchner-Platz, is a facilitator for social interaction and negotiation to take place. Place attachment in cities stems from the constant (re-)negotiatons between individuals and groups in urban space and their interaction with the space's materiality. Thus, place attachment here is processual in character, only temporarily stable and the result of an interplay of sociality and materiality.

---

[1] It is important to note that not everyone in Darmstadt feels attached to the Georg-Büchner-Platz, especially not with its current material-spatial design. During my fieldwork, I was told that the square now lacks niches where people can gather without being observed by others. The former design of the square included such niches, and this was portrayed to me as a key element why the square was so attractive during adolescence, being "the only location where we could be among ourselves in public" (informal interview, Darmstadt 2021).

7.5 Conclusion

The argument pursued in this chapter was that sociality and materiality play a key role in constituting place attachment. Urban squares such as Darmstadt's Georg-Büchner-Platz are examples of sites that are both locations of social interaction and negotiation, as well as places to which people feel attached to and find commonality with strangers through this shared emotional bond to a place. The Georg-Büchner-Platz is an example of multifunctional places that allow for a multitude of usages at different times of the day and for different people and that have low social and physical barriers. With this, they can be facilitators for social cohesion.

These findings have significant policy implications. If the goal is to create environments to which people feel attached to and that facilitate belonging to a community, it is key to allow for such spaces to emerge. The case of the Georg-Büchner-Platz shows that both the material-spatial design of urban squares and its social-political framework are important: low physical and social barriers are the prerequisites for place attachment. This includes to allow for the unforeseen to happen and to have the courage to endure uncertainty and (economic) pressure.

Public spaces like the Georg-Büchner-Platz are sites where people with different backgrounds, biographies and values are simultaneously present and interact with each other through their bodily presence. What people share is their emotional bond to a particular urban square, and this is a commonality that can help overcome differences and animosities and lead to social cohesion. Thus, the material-spatial design of a city and its squares is equally important to societies as are social interaction, communication or shared norms and values.

In this sense, the concept of place attachment helps to shed light on the complex and dynamic lifeworlds of people, taking place at concrete locations in societies in particular moments in time and space. Place attachment is both the result and the starting point of negotiation processes, it is in a constant state of flux and only temporarily stable.

Acknowledgements Many thanks to the OpenStreetMap contributors for providing the maps used in this publication. The license agreements can be found here: www.openstreetmap.org/copyright and here: www.opendatacommons.org/licenses/odbl.

References

Bochner, A. P., & Ellis, C. (2016). *Evocative autoethnography: Writing lives and telling stories*. Left Coast Press.
Bundesministerium des Innern, für Bau und Heimat (Ed.). (2021). *Stadtentwicklungsbericht der Bundesregierung 2020* (p. 156). Bundesministerium des Innern, für Bau und Heimat. https://www.bmi.bund.de/SharedDocs/downloads/DE/veroeffentlichungen/2021/04/stadtentwicklungsbericht-2020.pdf?__blob=publicationFile&v=2
Denzin, N. K. (2014). *Interpretive autoethnography* (2nd ed.). Sage.

Deutsch, N. L. (2005). A second home. In B. J. Hirsch (Ed.), *A place to call home: After-school programs for urban youth* (pp. 41–56). American Psychological Association/Teachers College Press.

Farias, I., & Bender, T. (Eds.). (2009). *Urban assemblages: How actor-network theory changes urban studies*. Routledge Chapman & Hall.

Fried, M. (1963). Grieving for a lost home. In L. J. Duhl (Ed.), *The urban condition. People and policy in the metropolis* (pp. 124–152). Simon & Schuster.

Gustafson, P. (2001). Roots and routes: Exploring the relationship between place attachment and mobility. *Environment and Behavior, 33*(5), 667–686. https://doi.org/10.1177/00139160121973188

Holt, N. L. (2003). Representation, legitimation, and autoethnography: An autoethnographic writing story. *International Journal of Qualitative Methods, 2*(1), 18–28. https://doi.org/10.1177/160940690300200102

Kurnicki, K. (2022). What do cars do when they are parked? Material objects and infrastructuring in social practices. *Mobilities, 17*(1), 37–52. https://doi.org/10.1080/17450101.2021.1981538

Lefêbvre, H. (1991). *The production of space*. Blackwell Publishers.

Löw, M. (2001). *Raumsoziologie*. Suhrkamp.

Low, S. M., & Altman, I. (1992). *Place attachment* (pp. 1–12). Springer. https://doi.org/10.1007/978-1-4684-8753-4_1

Manzo, L. C. (2014). Exploring the shadow side: Place attachment in the context of stigma, displacement, and social housing. In L. C. Manzo & P. Devine-Wright (Eds.), *Place attachment. Advances in theory, methods and applications* (pp. 178–190). Routledge.

Milligan, M. J. (1998). Interactional past and potential: The social construction of place attachment. *Symbolic Interaction, 21*(1), 1–33. https://doi.org/10.1525/si.1998.21.1.1

Müller, A.-L. (2017). Infrastrukturen als Akteure. Die Materialität urbaner Infrastrukturen und ihre Bedeutung für das Soziale. In M. Flitner, J. Lossau, & A.-L. Müller (Eds.), *Infrastrukturen der Stadt* (pp. 125–141). Springer Fachmedien. https://doi.org/10.1007/978-3-658-10424-5_7

Müller, A.-L. (2021). Wissenschaftliche Heimat in der Stiftung. Die neue Schader-Residence in Darmstadt. *Stiftung & Sponsoring, 5*(21), 14–15.

Müller, A.-L., & Reichmann, W. (2020). Architektur und Teilhabe. In S. Meier & K. Schlenker (Eds.), *Teilhabe und Raum. Interdisziplinäre Perspektiven* (pp. 65–82). Barbara Budrich.

Müller, A.-L., & Tuitjer, L. (2022). Rre-vitalising discourses of solidarity: Governing populations in times of uncertainty and crisis. In M. Hellmann, T. Kettunen, S. Salmivaara, & J. Stoneham (Eds.), *Governing human lives and health in pandemic times. Social control policies* (pp. 37–54). Routledge.

Pollini, G. (2005). Elements of a theory of place attachment and socio-territorial belonging. *International Review of Sociology, 15*(3), 497–515. https://doi.org/10.1080/03906700500272483

Proshansky, H. M., Fabian, A. K., & Kaminoff, R. (1983). Place-identity: Physical world socialization of the self. *Journal of Environmental Psychology, 3*, 57–83.

Reichmann, W., & Müller, A.-L. (2015). The secrets of architecture's actions. In *Architecture, materiality and society. Connecting sociology of architecture with science and technology studies* (pp. 2–23). Palgrave Macmillan.

Robinson, J. (2006). *Ordinary cities: Between modernity and development*. Routledge.

Scannell, L., & Gifford, R. (2010). Defining place attachment: A tripartite organizing framework. *Journal of Environmental Psychology, 30*(1), 1–10. https://doi.org/10.1016/j.jenvp.2009.09.006

Simmel, G. (1908). *Soziologie. Untersuchungen über die Form der Vergesellschaftung*. Duncker & Humblot.

Simmel, G. (1995). Die Großstädte und das Geistesleben. In O. Rammstedt (Ed.), *Aufsätze und Abhandlungen 1901—1908. Band I* (Vol. 7, pp. 116–131). Suhrkamp.

Chapter 8
Places of Wander: The Value of Community Attachment for Coastal Tourism

Desiree Farrell ⓘ **and Liam M. Carr** ⓘ

8.1 Introduction

The growth of local-scale tourism, as a valuable and viable element to economic and social diversification, has generated lasting change to the communities within which it develops (Torres-Delgado & Saarinen, 2014). These development pathways are guided both by supply- and demand-side drivers (Richards, 2014a) that reflect a more deeply embedded conflict in the practice of 'place making'. Lew (2017) describes the conceptual difference of *place-making* and *placemaking* as opposite ends of the 'place making continuum' principally as a question of authenticity. Place-making is an organic, bottom-up practice. Place is shaped and reshaped into a form that continues to authentically reflect the community while simultaneously developing into a place for tourism. Conversely, placemaking reflects a top-down, master planned effort to develop tourism. Being a top-down approach, destinations are consciously and unconsciously *rebranded* to appeal to a particular tourist demographic as a principal means of spurring development, even if this means that the community benefitting from tourism are experienced less authentically.

Lew frames the loss of place authenticity as a pragmatic, but not inevitable, outcome from the principally economic motivations of tourism which prioritise *place-making* over *place-making*. At the most extreme, local identity of place may be completely detached from that of the tourist (Lai & Ooi, 2015), although most places will have some mixture of both, falling within the continuum rather than at the end. Lew (2017, p. 456) extends this consideration of place making to "both the

D. Farrell (✉) · L. M. Carr
School of Geography, Archaeology & Irish Studies, National University of Ireland Galway, Galway, Ireland
e-mail: desiree.farrell@nuigalway.ie; liam.m.carr@nuigalway.ie

O.-R. Ilovan, I. Markuszewska (eds.), *Preserving and Constructing Place Attachment in Europe*, GeoJournal Library 131,
https://doi.org/10.1007/978-3-031-09775-1_8

137

tangible and the intangible, many of which are seen in the everyday practices of people who occupy these planned places".

These everyday practices lead to complementary aspects of the place making continuum and authenticity: *place attachment* and *place identity*. Place attachment and place identity are best examined and interpreted phenomenologically, considering subjective representations and objective factors (Seamon, 2014). The concept of place attachment, and the means by which it is studied, represents an inevitable theoretical complexity due to its dynamic and subjective connections to "locales that are at once ecological, built, social, and symbolic environments" (Hummon, 1992, p. 253). As a bond between people and their environs forms, place attachment shapes how individuals identify with and experience the place. At the most basic level, such bonds represent the well-trod concepts of the 'familiar', where place attachment is strong, versus the 'unfamiliar' or 'distant' (Seamon, 2000; Felder, 2021). As a more conceptual space, place attachment represents an oftentimes emotionally strengthened bond between people and their environs as *home*. How a community relates to, defines, and represents their home locale is informed by this attachment, which in turn is a reflection of the organic *place-making* process and leads to a subjectively perceived identity of place (Peng et al., 2020).

Proshansky et al. (1983) state that place identity *is attachment to a place* ascribed by an individual. Others have asserted that place attachment and place identity are separate constructs, with place attachment developing *prior to the formation of place identity* (Hernández et al., 2007; Peng et al., 2020).

Place identity is derived from elements that distinguish it from others and is formed after being established in both spatial and social structures (Paasi, 1991, 2002). Place identity includes individuals' subjective perceptions of geographic space (Peng et al., 2020), as well experiences, beliefs, and values invested in a specific setting (Jorgensen & Stedman, 2001; Hallak et al., 2012). In this way, Knapp (2006) claims that when attempting to understand a place, people's consciousness of that place cannot be overlooked because the identity of a place exists as both material and within the mental sphere.

As it relates to tourism, place identity impacts resident attitudes towards tourism and their willingness to participate (Nunkoo & Gursoy, 2012; Wang & Chen, 2015). How these attitudes are shaped is seen to be based upon whether place identity is being properly and respectfully represented through the lens of tourism. Uzzell (1995) likened these attitudes to expressions of pride of place, while Gu and Ryan (2008) posited that place membership improves self-esteem. These studies, and those conducted in a similar vein, present evidence that residents benefit from a tourism 'product' when it reflects their own sense of place identity.

Yet, such a pathway is not guaranteed. The practice of tourism, particularly as a *placemaking* enterprise that seeks to provide tourist experiences as a 'product' separated from the environs within which it is enjoyed, can lose the support of the community (Smith, 1994). A similar outcome can arise when promises to the community are unfulfilled. Given the strength of attachment, those who promote tourism for a community, be they entrepreneur or government-led initiative, need to develop and keep the trust of a community central to their plans (Nunkoo et al., 2012; Nunkoo & Gursoy, 2016). Such outcomes have been well documented by scholarship surrounding 'sustainable tourism' (McMinn, 1997; Tao & Wall, 2009; Zolfani et al.,

2015) and 'cultural tourism' (Bachleitner & Zins, 1999; MacLeod, 2006), both which would have a vested interest in positive portrayals of place identity that affirms place attachment for tourist and resident alike.

This chapter explores the relationships between place attachment, identity, and practices of place making vis-à-vis *place-making* and *placemaking* through the lens of tourism by presenting the case study of Rathmullan, a rural village in County Donegal, Ireland along the coast of Lough Swilly. In addition to being a popular summer tourist destination for a variety of recreational activities both on and off the water, Rathmullan is a culturally important place in Irish history, having been the point of departure in 1607 by Hugh O'Neill, Rory O'Donnell and roughly 90 others loyal to these Ulster chieftains, who left seeking Spanish reinforcements for their ongoing battles with English forces. This departure, which allowed England to further extend power in Ireland, is known as the Flight of the Earls.

8.2 Along the Way: A Case Study of Rathmullan, Co. Donegal, Ireland

Since Fáilte Ireland launched the Wild Atlantic Way in 2014, a 2500 km coastal touring route on Ireland's west coast, marine and coastal tourism in Ireland has experienced steady growth. An estimated 11.3 million overseas visitors toured Ireland in 2019, resulting in over €5.8 billion in revenue (Fáilte Ireland, 2021). However, growth within the tourism sector, due in part to the success of the Wild Atlantic Way, has created sustainability challenges and introduced development and governance barriers for these local, often rural communities (Kelly et al., 2021). Despite tourism being considered an effective impetus for rural development and regeneration (Sharpley, 2002), there exists a disproportionate distribution of tourism costs and benefits in rural communities along Ireland's west coast.

Using a multimethod approach, we investigated the dynamic relationship between place-making and placemaking in shaping and reshaping place attachment and identity of Rathmullan. Q methodology, substantiated by semi-structured interviews and participatory mapping, revealed the range of values and perceptions of the Wild Atlantic Way and its impact on the Rathmullan community. In doing so, we present a framework that compares community-led *place-making* against branded *placemaking*, and how it is important to balance those tensions in order to nurture and strengthen place attachment and identity.

8.3 Research Design: A Multi-method Approach

A multi-method research design was employed to capture a holistic understanding of community dynamics, perspectives and identities that make up Rathmullan. The work applied a phenomenological perspective, such that both subjective and objective elements would be examined to avoid a "reductive rendition of the wholeness of the relationship" (Seamon, 2014, p. 12).

8.3.1 Part 1: Q Methodology and Identified Community Factors

Conducting Q Methodology

Q methodology (Q) is primarily employed to discern perceptions of individuals on a given topic from the vantage point of self-reference (McKeown & Thomas, 2013). Originally developed for use in psychology (Stephenson, 1935), Q has since been adapted as a mixed methods approach to assess subjectivity in a range of high-bias examinations centred on the human-environmental relationship at the community-level (Ellis et al., 2007; Frantzi et al., 2009; Webler et al., 2009; Carr & Liu, 2016; Farrell et al., 2017). Q applies correlation and factor analysis to reveal human subjectivity, in the process transcending the categorical divide of qualitative/quantitative research (McKeown & Thomas, 2013). Gargan and Brown (1993, pp. 348–349) have stated that the "special contribution of Q-methodology to decision making is that it helps overcome the limitations of the mind in dealing with complexity, and also serves to locate elements of consensus (if they exist) that might otherwise go unnoticed in the emotional turmoil of political debate".

Q is comprised of five elements: Q concourse, the full range of discursive considerations; Q-set, the condensed subsample of the Q concourse; P-set, or the participant pool; Q sort, the ranked output from each individual participant; and analysis. The Q concourse is composed of the full range of considerations relevant to the topic at hand (Farrell et al., 2017). These considerations are often presented as statements, and are generated from various sources including interviews, academic papers, grey literature, websites, and media. Statements are gathered until a 'saturation point' is reached, where the addition of new statements does not add any diversity to the existing set of statements. Once the concourse reaches saturation, the collection of statements is condensed and refined to best represent the themes and opinions gathered using neutral, language (Watts & Stenner, 2005). The resulting Q-set must be robust enough to meet research objectives, while minimising the demands made of the participants (Carr & Liu, 2016). If the Q-set remains too large, it can become unmanageable for participants, while a set too small can exclude key perspectives or values from the discourse.

For this research, a 25-statement Q-set was employed, using a quasi-normal distribution for statements to be sorted in relation to one another based on how strongly the participant agrees with that statement, on a Likert scale of −4 (most disagree) to +4 (most agree). The community of Rathmullan was invited to participate in this research due to their geographical location on the Wild Atlantic Way route, serving as a gateway village for designated Discovery Points on the route itself, as well as their organisation and engagement as a community. The community working group, Rathmullan: The Way Forward, was identified as a community 'gatekeeper', with members contributing to the research objectives while also growing the P-set by recruiting other community members as well as various individuals from within the tourism and hospitality sectors in and around Rathmullan. While 20 individuals participated in some aspects of the research, the final P-set consists of 13 individuals.

Analysing Q Methodology

Q employs correlation and factor analysis that is *by-person*, resulting in a relational analysis of each configuration (Q sort) against every other Q sort (Watts & Stenner, 2005). Factor analysis is performed within a software package designed for analysing Q datasets, in this case Ken-Q Analysis software (Banasick, 2019). Factor groups, which represent the full breadth of perspectives established in the Q-set and then explored through the Q sorts, are identified through calculated eigenvalues. Factors with eigenvalues greater than one were kept, following Addams and Proops (2000), producing a single correlation matrix. This matrix undergoes Varimax rotation to maximise the variance expressed among Q sorts, ideally enriching the interpretive potential of extracted factors. Following rotation, each Q sort is associated with a particular factor through their calculated factor loading that best reflects overall perceptions that are most similar to their own, a process known as 'flagging' (Addams & Proops, 2000). Using weighted averages of defining Q sorts, factor arrays are presented with the rank value of each statement, according to each factor. The factor arrays represent the best estimate Q sort, or idealised sort for each factor, using Factor Scores (F-scores) that relate back to the quasi-normal distribution of Likert scores (Carr, 2019). These, paired with insights from statistically distinguishing statements, are then subjected to interpretation and substantiated using qualitative data from participant interviews. The final analysis and interpretation of Q-methodology represents a unified configuration of each factor group's views on the subject of analysis (i.e., the Wild Atlantic Way).

8.3.2   Part 2: Participatory Mapping of Community Values

Stakeholder participation and mapping can be done with instrumental goals in mind, as a retrospective practice to gain insight into past experiences, or as a means for the co-creation of knowledge (Skarlatidou et al., 2019). Di Gessa et al. (2008, p. 3) have found that "making the map is not the end of the empowerment process but the beginning [and] the community's capacity to use the map for its own benefit must be enhanced". Dragouni and Fouseki (2018) found that a community's willingness to engage with cultural tourism development is linked with high place attachment. Mapping was utilised in the context of this research as an exercise in place-making, community empowerment and values assessment, and as a means of gathering consensus to better understand available options for engaging with tourism as a community.

Workshop participants were provided with a base map of the region, centred on Rathmullan and Lough Swilly. To reduce bias, the base map was purposefully constructed without identifying features (e.g., established tourism locations, national parks), following the 'No-Name' mapping method (Di Gessa et al., 2008). Participant perception and local knowledge was explored through their drawn responses to the following three prompts:

1. Where in your community does the Wild Atlantic Way demonstrate significant value (cultural, ethical, recreational, etc.)?
2. Where do you consider to be the most significant area(s) for tourism in your community?
3. Where do you consider to be the most significant area(s) for the economy in your community?

Individual maps were uniformly colour-coded and then digitally scanned. Areas of consensus were carried through onto a composite map which represented the generalised values of the participants regarding tourism and the Wild Atlantic Way for Rathmullan.

8.4   Results and Discussion

8.4.1   Identified Factors in the Rathmullan Community

From the 13 community stakeholders who participated in the Q sorting phase in this study, four factors were extracted, accounting for 67% of the total study variance (Table 8.1). Each factor represents a distinct perspective of the Wild Atlantic Way and how it impacts the Rathmullan community (Table 8.2).

Factor 1 – Optimists
Factor 1 is defined by the views of three individuals, explaining 20% of the total study variance. Factor 1 is distinguished by beliefs that national policies can help address emerging issues along the Wild Atlantic Way (statement 4: +4), while agreeing with the perception that policy makers do not fully engage with the community regarding tourism (statement 3: +3). Of relevance to this study, Factor 1 members share a blended perspective on the duality of *place-making* and *placemaking* (statement 21: +3; statement 20: +2), where to fully experience what Rathmullan means, it must be lived in. This perception extends to the idea that, for Factor 1, the Wild Atlantic Way has always existed (i.e., *place-making*), but has now been given signs and a name (i.e., *placemaking*). This is further strengthened by their disagreement with statement 25 (F-score: −3): "the Wild Atlantic Way substitutes my community's existing character with one marketed to tourism expectations".

This perception of a blended sense of *place-making* and *placemaking* extends to a nuanced sense of how Factor 1 considers tourism as it relates to Rathmullan. For them, tourism is not just a business (statement 11: +2), yet there is a sense that all tourists are the same (statement 22: +2). At face-value, this position seems contradictory, but it is not the *individualised* view that tourists are the same – in fact it is

Table 8.1 Factor matrix, with factor loadings

Q sort	Factor 1	Factor 2	Factor 3	Factor 4
1	0.072	0.474	0.157	**0.587**
2	**0.807**	−0.233	0.092	0.215
3	0.163	**0.815**	0.206	−0.038
4	0.379	−0.020	**0.742**	0.061
5	**0.775**	0.245	0.185	0.107
6	0.328	−0.344	−0.083	**0.690**
7	0.455	0.254	0.066	**0.506**
8	0.086	−0.035	−0.127	**0.879**
9	0.424	**0.496**	−0.064	0.382
10	**0.737**	0.252	−0.291	0.174
11	−0.258	**0.650**	0.304	0.144
12	−0.175	0.182	**0.707**	−0.140
13	−0.259	−0.695	**0.259**	0.169
% total variance	**20**	**19**	**11**	**17**

Defining Q sorts for each factor are indicated in bold

Table 8.2 Factor arrays and F-scores, by statement

	Statement	Factor Arrays			
		1	2	3	4
1	The Wild Atlantic Way initiative enhances the identity of my community.	0	3	0	0
2	My community has unique local knowledge that should be used to pursue local tourism opportunities.	1	0	-2	4
3	Policy makers do not fully engage with my community with regards to tourism opportunities.	3	2	-3	0
4	National policies can help address emerging issues along the Wild Atlantic Way.	4	2	3	1
5	My community is empowered to be involved in the development of the Wild Atlantic Way.	0	1	3	1
6	I feel empowered by the Wild Atlantic Way to be involved in the experience of visiting tourists.	-2	0	1	-4
7	The Wild Atlantic Way operates separate from my community.	-1	-3	-4	0
8	The success of the Wild Atlantic Way locally is owed to my community's engagement.	1	-1	4	-2
9	My community prioritises satisfaction levels of visiting tourists.	0	1	0	-2
10	My community provides a unique 'non-touristy' experience for visitors.	0	-3	-3	1
11	Tourism is not just a business.	2	-1	0	-2
12	The Wild Atlantic Way has improved my quality of life economically.	-4	2	-1	-3
13	The Wild Atlantic Way has improved my quality of life socially.	-3	1	0	-3
14	The Wild Atlantic Way has improved local environmental conditions.	-1	0	-2	-1
15	My community's cultural heritage is not solely defined by the Wild Atlantic Way.	-1	0	1	2
16	Tourists share in our Irish heritage when they visit my community.	1	-1	2	-1
17	My community's cultural values exist beyond marketed local tourism destinations.	1	1	-1	2
18	The values which define my community offer a unique identity unlike that of other destinations along the Wild Atlantic Way.	-1	-1	2	3
19	The Wild Atlantic Way route itself connects my community to neighbouring communities in new ways.	-2	0	2	1
20	The value of my community can only be fully understood through the process of living in it.	2	-2	1	2
21	The Wild Atlantic Way has always existed. It has just been given a name and signs to help tourists find their way around.	3	3	-1	3
22	My community views all visiting tourists as the same.	2	-2	-1	0
23	Local authorities have met their legal obligations to consult with my community when developing tourism plans.	-2	-2	-2	-1
24	The growth in tourism due to the Wild Atlantic Way can be felt in my community.	0	4	1	0
25	The Wild Atlantic Way substitutes my community's existing character with one marketed to tourist expectations.	-3	-4	0	-1

Source: Own elaboration

the opposite entirely, that Factor 1 members are keenly aware of the range of tourist types and interests and are offering a critique of the community's barriers.

Viewed collectively, Factor 1 members might best be described as optimists who recognise that, for the benefit of their community, the Wild Atlantic Way remains a work in progress. For them, the Wild Atlantic Way has not improved their quality of life socially (statement 13: −3) or economically (statement 12: −4). The success of the Wild Atlantic Way locally is not considered to be fully attributed to the engagement of the community (statement 8: +1; statement 24: 0), and Factor 1 members are indifferent to the idea that the community provides a non-touristy experience for visitors (statement 9: 0).

Donegal's own identity is one of geographical and political isolation within the Republic of Ireland, and this identity has served as a barrier to tourism. One group member describes their county as having been *"cut-off"*, with *"tourists [only] coming as far as Sligo"*. Historically, tourists who did travel to Donegal were primarily from Northern Ireland – especially during the period of conflict from the late 1960s to 1998, between the Republic of Ireland and Northern Ireland (part of the United Kingdom) known as 'The Troubles' – contributing to the generational feeling of isolation. Perhaps this collective memory of tourism as it was, paired with the new promises from Fáilte Ireland of what tourism can be, has contributed to the viewpoints defining Factor 1. This group represents an optimistic attitude of how committing to engagement with tourism can be a means of ensuring Rathmullan's identity becomes increasingly central to its role as a Wild Atlantic Way destination. As summed up by one member, *"community is made up of everybody in the area though of course everyone in the area doesn't participate in the community"*.

Factor 2 – Partners

Factor 2 is made up of three individuals, accounting for 19% of the total study variance. Collectively, Factor 2 members own, or have previously owned, tourism-related businesses which may inform their view about tourism growth and economic benefits (statement 12: +2). Factor 2 members agree with the idea that growth in tourism due to the Wild Atlantic Way can be felt in their community (statement 24: +4). They also are the only group who show strong positive agreement with Statement 1 'The Wild Atlantic Way initiative enhances the identity of my community' (F-score: +3).

Perhaps owing to their business roles, Factor 2 members argue that tourism, due to the Wild Atlantic Way, is a reflection of their own experience (statement 25: −4), suggesting strongly that, to these individuals, organic, locally driven *place-making* is one and the same as the *placemaking*. This perspective is further strengthened by disagreements to statements 7 (F-score: −3) and 10 (F-score: −3), both of which propose distinctive aspects between Rathmullan for locals and Rathmullan for tourists. As summed up by one Factor 2 member, *"People will say that Donegal is very like Kerry, but it couldn't be further from the truth, really. The scenery is very similar, but your cultural experiences will be very different... the actual offerings are very different"*. Factor 2 members emphasise the potential for the Wild Atlantic Way to drive local as well as regional growth, making them advocates of a partnered, inclusive approach to the growth of the tourism sector.

Factor 3 – Creators

Factor 3 includes three individuals who account for 11% of the total study variance. Factor 3 members present a strongly organic, locally driven perspective to the *place-making* versus *placemaking* dynamic that shapes Rathmullan's identity. While Factor 3 members share a similar view to Factor 2 in that Rathmullan and tourism are heavily entwined (statement 7: −4; statement 10: −3), they distinguish themselves by holding a position that it is their efforts that have created Rathmullan as a popular destination along the Wild Atlantic Way (statement 8: +4; statement 18: +2). To Factor 3 members, the Wild Atlantic Way serves as a national initiative (statement 4: +3; statement 21: −1) that empowers localities like Rathmullan to then create a tourist experience that is reflective of their own community (statement 5: +3). How localities pursue this opportunity is ultimately up to themselves, as Factor 3 members sense that policies serve principally as a blueprint rather than a reliable resource (statement 3: −3; statement 23: −2).

The sense of initiative and creation of a tourism *product* – itself a branded version of their own community – is unique within this study. The Wild Atlantic Way route is seen by Factor 3 members as a way to connect villages within the region in new ways (statement 19: +2), allowing for tourists to more fully experience the 'Irishness' in an authentic yet locally curated manner (statement 16: +2; statement 17: −1). Their persistent feeling of empowerment and willingness to engage with the Wild Atlantic Way as an initiative, despite an acute awareness of existing limitations and unreliable support from authorities is perhaps best summed up by one Factor 3 response: *"you have to empower yourselves… otherwise small towns cannot control their own destiny"*.

Factor 4 –Bystanders

Factor 4 (17% of the total study variance) is comprised of four individuals. In contrast to Factor 3, Factor 4 members do not feel empowered by the Wild Atlantic Way to create a tourist version of their community (statement 6: −4; statement 8: −2), despite a belief that what they could offer would be welcome (statement 2: +4). In a way, Factor 4 members feel like bystanders, supportive of what the Wild Atlantic Way can offer Rathmullan (statement 18: +3, statement 21: +3), yet powerless to shaping what that might be (statement 9: −2; statement 11: −2; statement 12: −3; statement 13: −3; statement 24: 0). Their views of the Wild Atlantic Way reflect the practice of *placemaking* that is dissonant to their experience and perspective within their community (statement 15: +2; statement 16: −1; statement 17: +2; statement 20: +2).

8.4.2   Community Consensus

Factor groups are defined by distinguishing statements, yet to more fully contextualise the various positions held within a community like Rathmullan, it is as important to understand where agreement exists. Areas of agreement can build consensus within a community around various issues or concerns (Carr, 2019). In this study, negative views were shared on a sense of insufficient community consultation by authorities (statement 23) and a degradation on the local environment due to the Wild Atlantic Way (statement 14), despite recognising that national policies, properly structured to balance the dynamic between *place-making* and *placemaking*, can bring stability and clarity to future development of the tourism sector (statement 4).

Such stability has the effect of reassuring community members who might be on the fence about their own involvement and *place-making* interactions with tourism, either personally or as a business endeavour. There is a desire for promotion by tourism bodies to match and support the community's engagement with the initiative. Several participants mentioned the need for Rathmullan to be promoted more in order to support local businesses and encourage more opportunity for the community. This suggests that a partnered approach may produce the greatest set of tangible (i.e., economic) and intangible (i.e., social, cultural, recreational) environmental benefits at multiple scales within the region (Fig. 8.1), echoing the work of Bosman and Dredge (2011), who noted that most successful tourist destinations usually exhibit aspects of both *place-making* and *placemaking*.

8.5   Conclusion

One concern of tourism in Ireland, even prior to the establishment of the Wild Atlantic Way, has been the fear of the homogenisation of Ireland into one tourism experience (Kneafsey, 1998). Part of the success of the Wild Atlantic Way has been its *placemaking* ability to promote a consistent tourism product that is broadly appealing to a wide range of tourists. Product recognition consistency generates and maintains tourism demand (Sedmak & Kociper, 2017), yet at the risk of localities losing their unique identities. Communities like Rathmullan have legitimate concerns that the Wild Atlantic Way promotes interchangeability, a critique known as *sameness* (Richards, 2014b; Lew, 2017) that dilutes the *place-making* potential of the community, their cultural foundation, and the tourism offerings that they can generate from these roots. Homogenisation is promoted by international consumption patterns, resulting in efforts at the local or community level to maintain uniqueness (Reisinger, 2009). The more tourists take to the Wild Atlantic Way expecting to view its rugged cliffs, photograph wandering sheep, and settle into a 'traditional' Irish pub for a pint of Guinness (Carr, 2016), the more a community like Rathmullan will feel pressure to prioritise that experience over something more locally authentic. In turn, such a progression may lead to growing dissatisfaction within the community, weakening their sense of place attachment. Or, to put it more simply, members becoming alienated from their way of life, or no longer able to see their *home* (McLeod, 2004). Wherever a community may be at along the place making continuum, when it comes to developing and sustaining its tourism, a sense of attachment and identity is essential.

Place identity, as revealed through this investigation into place attachment, is strengthened by the community-created map representing Rathmullan community values (Fig. 8.1). While a complementary aspect of the research presented here, the

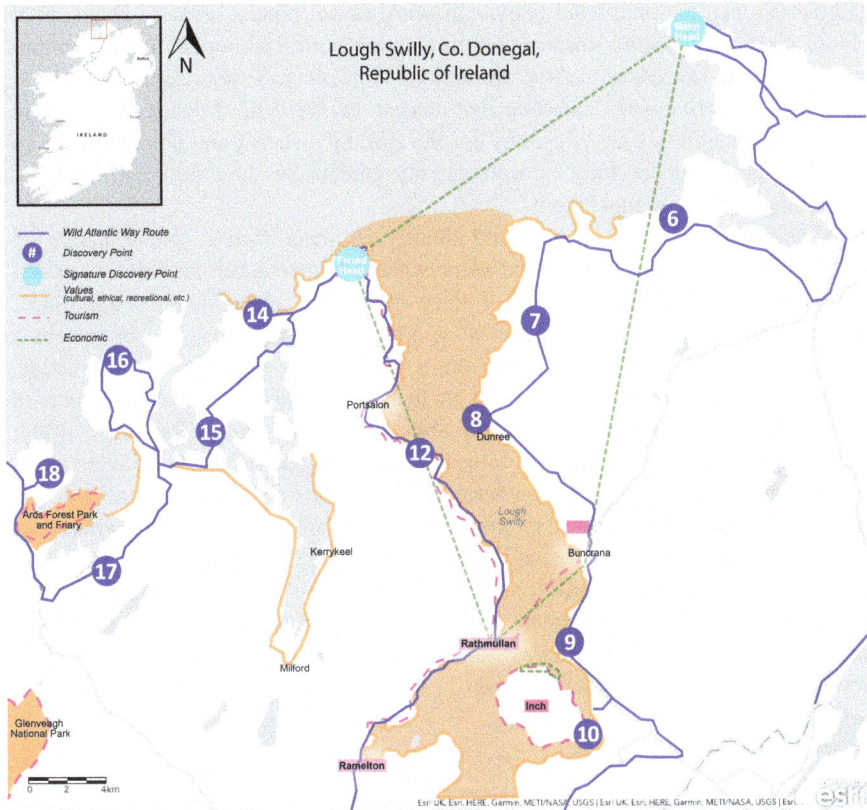

Fig. 8.1 Rathmullan community values and official Wild Atlantic Way route, featuring Discovery and Signature Discovery Points. (Source: Desiree Farrell; base map: ESRI UK)

community values map brings forward intangible cultural, recreational, historical values that align with the practice of *place-making*. With an energetic core group in Rathmullan the Way Forward advancing community-supported tourism opportunities, the village of Rathmullan has created a marketable identity that remains true to their own sense of *home*. As Fig. 8.1 shows, local values align closely (i.e., *place-making*) within the route of the Wild Atlantic Way (i.e., *placemaking*) and its Discovery Points around Lough Swilly. In doing so, Rathmullan becomes a *place-making* destination in its own right while also serving as a *placemaking* gateway to Lough Swilly and the Fanad Peninsula.

Rathmullan sits in an important place along Lough Swilly for tourism. In a number of interrelated ways (i.e., the pink 'economic' and green 'tourism' connections illustrated in Fig. 8.1), the success of the Wild Atlantic Way will depend upon the success of Rathmullan, and vice versa. The Rathmullan community is best positioned to help identify emerging concerns that may harm tourism, be they infrastructural, environmental, economic, or even perceptual. Fáilte Ireland, leveraging its position as a national-level body, can serve as an 'honest broker' (Hawkins & Mann, 2007), facilitating lines of communication with Rathmullan and coordinating appropriate responses to the community's concerns in support of its *placemaking* commitments toward ensuring the success of the Wild Atlantic Way. These mutual responsibilities are necessary for developing a strong and positive sense of place that can be successfully incorporated into tourism, without diluting identity or weakening a sense of attachment.

We argue that place attachment and identity can be utilised to better balance the tensions between *place-making* and *placemaking*. Our research provides an example of how embedded the concepts of place attachment, place identities and place-making are in communities, and how tapping into those linkages can sustain a community's tourism opportunities through collaborative engagement. In practice, this might look like moving away from the homogenisation of tourism locales toward the hybridisation of consumer and community space (Reisinger, 2009; Everett, 2012). While the specific values and perceptions of the Rathmullan community cannot be used to make generalised statements about other locations, this research approach can be used to characterise tourism destinations elsewhere and hopefully encourage the inclusion of local values and knowledge in tourism planning and place making. Additionally, with the tourism industry being heavily impacted by the COVID-19 pandemic, communities have an opportunity to overhaul their approach to tourism engagement and better align their recovery and future development in more sustainable ways.

References

Addams, H., & Proops, J. (Eds.). (2000). *Social discourse and environmental policy: An application of Q methodology*. Edward Elgar Publishing.

Bachleitner, R., & Zins, A. H. (1999). Cultural tourism in rural communities: The residents' perspective. *Journal of Business Research, 44*, 199–209.

Banasick, S. (2019). *Ken-Q analysis (Version 1.0.6) [software]*. Available from https://shawnbanasick.github.io/ken-q-analysis/doi:10.5281/zenodo.1300201

Bosman, C., & Dredge, D. (2011). Histories of placemaking in the Gold Coast City: The neoliberal norm, the state story and the community narrative. In *Urban research program* (Research paper 33 (April)). Griffith University.

Carr, L. M. (2016). Preserving identity along the Wild Atlantic Way. SEMRU Working Paper Series, Whitaker Institute of Innovation and Societal Change, Policy Brief No. 8.

Carr, L. M. (2019). Seeking stakeholder consensus within Ireland's conflicted salmon aquaculture space. *Marine Policy, 99*, 201–212.

Carr, L. M., & Liu, D. Y. (2016). Measuring stakeholder perspectives on environmental and community stability in a tourism-dependent economy. *International Journal of Tourism Research, 18*, 620–632.

Di Gessa, S., Poole, P., & Bending, T. (2008). *Participatory mapping as a tool for empowerment: Experiences and lessons learned from the ILC network* (p. 45). ILC/IFAD.

Dragouni, M., & Fouseki, K. (2018). Drivers of community participation in heritage tourism planning: An empirical investigation. *Journal of Heritage Tourism, 13*(3), 237–256.

Ellis, G., Barry, J., & Robinson, C. (2007). Many ways to say 'no', different ways to say 'yes': Applying Q-methodology to understand public acceptance of wind farm proposals. *Journal of Environmental Planning and Management, 50*, 517–557.

Everett, S. (2012). Production places or consumption spaces? The place-making agency of food tourism in Ireland and Scotland. *Tourism Geographies, 14*(4), 535–554.

Fáilte Ireland. (2021). *Key tourism facts: 2019*. Fáilte Ireland, Dublin. https://www.failteireland. ie/FailteIreland/media/WebsiteStructure/Documents/3_ResearcR_Insights/4_Visitor_Insights/ KeyTourismFacts_2019.pdf?ext=.pdf

Farrell, D., Carr, L., & Fahy, F. (2017). On the subject of typology: How Irish coastal communities' subjectivities reveal intrinsic values towards coastal environments. *Ocean and Coastal Management, 146*, 135–143.

Felder, M. (2021). Familiarity as a practical sense of place. *Sociological Theory, 39*(3), 180–199.

Frantzi, S., Carter, N. T., & Lovett, J. C. (2009). Exploring discourses on international environmental regime effectiveness with Q methodology: A case study of the Mediterranean action plan. *Journal of Environmental Management, 90*, 177–189.

Gargan, J. J., & Brown, S. R. (1993). What is to be done? Anticipating the future and mobilizing prudence. *Policy Sciences, 26*, 347–359.

Gu, H., & Ryan, C. (2008). Place attachment, identity and community impacts of tourism – The case of a Beijing Hutong. *Tourism Management, 29*, 637–647.

Hallak, R., Brown, G., & Lindsay, N. J. (2012). The place identity – Performance relationship among tourism entrepreneurs: A structural equation modelling analysis. *Tourism Management, 33*(1), 143–154.

Hawkins, D. E., & Mann, S. (2007). The World Bank's role in tourism development. *Annals of Tourism Research, 34*(2), 348–363.

Hernández, B., Hidalgo, M. C., Salazar-Laplace, M. E., & Hess, S. (2007). Place attachment and place identity in natives and non-natives. *Journal of Environmental Psychology, 27*, 310–319.

Hummon, D. M. (1992). Community attachment: Local sentiment and sense of place. In I. Altman & S. M. Low (Eds.), *Place attachment. Human behavior and environment (Advances in theory and research)* (Vol. 12, pp. 253–278). Springer.

Jorgensen, B. S., & Stedman, R. C. (2001). Sense of place as an attitude: Lakeshore owners' attitudes toward their properties. *Journal of Environmental Psychology, 21*(3), 233–248.

Kelly, C., McAteer, B., Fahy, F., Carr, L., Norton, D., Farrell, D., Corless, R., Hynes, S., Kyriazi, Z., Marhadour, A., Kalaydjian, R., & Flannery, W. (2021). Blue growth: A transitions approach to developing sustainable pathways. *Journal of Ocean and Coastal Economics, 8*(2), Article 8.

Knapp, W. (2006). Planning in peri-urban regions: On regional identity and organizing capacity. In N. Bertrand & V. Kreibich (Eds.), *Europe's city-regions competitiveness: Growth regulation and peri-urban land management* (pp. 61–84). Uitgeverij Van Gorcum.

Kneafsey, M. (1998). Tourism and place identity: A case-study in rural Ireland. *Irish Geography, 31*(2), 111–123.

Lai, S., & Ooi, C. S. (2015). Branded as a world heritage city: The politics afterwards. *Place Branding and Public Diplomacy, 11*, 276–292.

Lew, A. (2017). Tourism planning and place making: Place-making or placemaking? *Tourism Geographies, 19*(3), 448–466.

MacLeod, D. (2006). Cultural tourism: Aspects of authenticity and commodification. In *Cultural tourism in a changing world: Politics, participation and (re)presentation* (pp. 177–190). Channel View.

McKeown, B., & Thomas, D. (2013). *Q methodology* (2nd ed.). Sage.

McLeod, D. (2004). *Tourism, globalization and cultural change: An island community perspective*. Channel View.

McMinn, S. (1997). The challenge of sustainable tourism. *Environmentalist, 17*, 135–141.

Nunkoo, R., & Gursoy, D. (2012). Residents' support for tourism: An identity perspective. *Annals of Tourism Research, 39*(1), 243–268.

Nunkoo, R., & Gursoy, D. (2016). Rethinking the role of power and trust in tourism planning. *Journal of Hospitality Marketing and Management, 25*(4), 512–522.

Nunkoo, R., Ramkissoon, H., & Gursoy, D. (2012). Public trust in tourism institutions. *Annals of Tourism Research, 39*(3), 1538–1564.

Paasi, A. (1991). Deconstructing regions: Notes on the scales of spatial life. *Environment & Planning A, 23*, 239–256.

Paasi, A. (2002). Regional identities and the challenge of the mobile world. In T. O. Engen (Ed.), *Kulturell Identitet og Regional Utvikling* (pp. 33–48). Høgskolen i Hedmark.

Peng, J., Strijker, D., & Wu, Q. (2020). Place identity: How far have we come in exploring its meanings? *Frontiers in Psychology, 11*, 294.

Proshansky, H. M., Fabian, A. K., & Kaminof, R. (1983). Place identity: Physical world and socialization of the self. *Journal of Environmental Psychology, 3*, 57–83.

Reisinger, Y. (2009). *International tourism: Cultures and behavior*. Butterworth-Heinemann.

Richards, G. (2014a). *Tourism trends: The convergence of culture and tourism*. Academy for Leisure NHTV University of Applied Sciences.

Richards, G. (2014b). Creativity and tourism in the city. *Current Issues in Tourism, 17*(2), 119–144.

Seamon, D. (2000). A way of seeing people and place: Phenomenology in behavior research. In S. Wapner, J. Demick, T. Yamamoto, & H. Minami (Eds.), *Theoretical perspectives in environment-behavior research* (pp. 157–178).

Seamon, D. (2014). Place attachment and phenomenology: The synergistic dynamism of place. In L. C. Manzo & P. Devine-Wright (Eds.), *Place attachment: Advances in theory, methods, and applications* (pp. 11–22). Routledge.

Sedmak, G., & Kociper, T. (2017). The consistency of a tourism product: A new conceptual framework. *European Journal of Tourism Research, 17*, 102–115.

Sharpley, R. (2002). Rural tourism and the challenge of tourism diversification: The case of Cyprus. *Tourism Management, 23*, 233–244.

Skarlatidou, A., Suškevičs, M., Göbel, C., Prūse, B., Tauginienė, L., Mascarenhas, A., Mazzonetto, M., Sheppard, A., Barrett, J., Haklay, M., Baruch, A., Moraitopoulou, E.-A., Austen, K., Baïz, I., Berditchevskaia, A., Berényi, E., Hoyte, S., Kleijssen, L., Kragh, G., … Wyszomirski, P. (2019). The value of stakeholder mapping to enhance co-creation in citizen science initiatives. *Citizen Science: Theory and Practice, 4*(1), 1–10.

Smith, S. L. J. (1994). The tourism product. *Annals of Tourism Research, 21*(3), 582–595.

Stephenson, W. (1935). Correlating persons instead of tests. *Journal of Personality, 4*(1), 17–24.

Tao, T. C. H., & Wall, G. (2009). Tourism as a sustainable livelihood strategy. *Tourism Management, 30*, 90–98.

Torres-Delgado, A., & Saarinen, J. (2014). Using indicators to assess sustainable tourism development: A review. *Tourism Geographies, 16*, 31–47.

Uzzell, D. L. (1995). Conferring a sense of place identity: The role of museums. *The International Journal of Heritage Studies, 1*, 4.

Wang, S., & Chen, J. S. (2015). The influence of place identity on perceived tourism impacts. *Annals of Tourism Research, 52*, 16–28.

Watts, S., & Stenner, P. (2005). Doing Q methodology: Theory, method and interpretation. *Qualitative Research in Psychology, 2*, 67–91.

Webler, T., Danielson, S., & Tuler, S. (2009). *Using Q method to reveal social perspectives in environmental research*. Social and Environmental Research Institute. Available from http://www.seri-us.org/sites/default/files/Qprimer.pdf

Zolfani, S. H., Sedaghat, M., Maknoon, R., & Zavadskas, E. K. (2015). Sustainable tourism: A comprehensive literature review on frameworks and applications. *Economic Research – Ekonomska Istrazivanja, 28*, 1–30.

Chapter 9
Methodology for Identifying Urban Types: A Tool for Assessing Urban Place Attachment

Hugo Castro Noblejas ⓘ, **José M. Orellana Macías** ⓘ, and **Matías F. Mérida Rodríguez** ⓘ

9.1 Introduction and Theoretical Background

The urban typology can be described as the physical lie of the elements and fluxes composing the cities (i.e., land use patterns, population and construction density, infrastructure and equipment or transport and communication networks). It is the result of demographic, socio-economic and politico-cultural processes developed over time and space. The characterisation and morphological assessment of an urban area allows knowing how it works (Banister et al., 1997). These assessments have become more complex due to new techniques of spatial and statistical analysis, as observed in studies both at urban scale (Abrantes et al., 2019), and intra-urban scale (Weston, 2002; Xu et al., 2019).

The first studies that focused on the urban growth types were mainly developed in the United States and in the United Kingdom during the 1960s and 1970s. In these countries, the suburban growth was barely controlled in the surroundings of the cities. Conzen (1960) proposed a morphogenetic methodology, other significant studies were the Buchanan report (2015), and those carried out by Berry in 1974, linking the transport by car, enhanced by the new models of urban growth, with the loss of environmental quality. Research became more sophisticated over time with

H. Castro Noblejas (✉) · M. F. Mérida Rodríguez
Department of Geography, University of Málaga, Malaga, Spain
e-mail: hugocastro@uma.es; mmerida@uma.es

J. M. Orellana Macías
Geological and Mining Institute of Spain, Zaragoza, Spain
e-mail: jm.orellana@igme.es

the aim of characterising the aspects of the expansion zones, the so-called suburban zones. Suburbanisation became the dominant and preferred urban typology. The new unregulated and dispersed growth brought new social and urban problems that were answered with proposals addressed to modernising and redesigning cities (Kasarda, 1978; Baldassare, 1986). In the 1980s, these studies were developed in Northern Europe, which experienced a gradually less compact, sprawl-type urbanism.

In the twenty-first century, research began to focus on the European Mediterranean countries, where scattered urban patterns grew rapidly, partially due to socio-economic phenomena such as the development of touristic areas (Catalán et al., 2008). Overall, the European studies not only have focused on quantifying the urban expansion at a city-region scale, but also on comparing the expansion in cities across the continent (Arribas-Bel et al., 2011; Salvati et al., 2016).

This fast territorial process affects the functionality and morphology of urban spaces, is framed in the current scenario of higher urban mobility, the relocation of social activities, globalisation, increasing homogeneity of cities and the loss of the cultural characteristics (Beatley, 2004). To some authors, these aspects have determined an increasing cultural distancing, and thus, a loss of place attachment (Arefi, 1999). On the contrary, according to other authors, territories have gained a greater relevance in the modern world (Gustafson, 2006). Following this idea, the disappearance of recognisable places revitalises the sense of belonging. The term place attachment describes the sense of belonging to a place (Banini & Ilovan, 2021), and it distinguishes between the satisfaction of social needs provided by the cities, and the symbolic and emotional links developed between people and the place where they live.

In recent decades, the number of studies and scientific papers related to place attachment has grown (Lewicka, 2011). One of the aspects with increasing relevance is the use of tools like Geographic Information Systems (GIS) to develop studies in this field. GIS can be especially used to measure urban aspects (e.g., size of the building, construction density, distances, green areas), so the implementation of GIS to study phenomena related to place attachment has been used by authors at a national scale (Taima & Asami, 2019), as well as at a neighbourhood scale (Hur et al., 2010).

According to Abrantes and peers (2019), three types of approaches to quantitatively delimitate urban units can be mentioned: (a) a classical demographic and econometric perspective based on the bivariate and multivariate analysis of statistical indicators; (b) a more morphological perspective based on GIS, remote sensing and spatial metrics (Bhatta et al., 2010; Pons & Rullán, 2014). These techniques are used to map urban variables and types of land use from which the degree of construction and other socio-economic parameters can be obtained (Herold et al., 2003; Kasanko et al., 2006), as observed in the Urban Atlas European Project; and (c) a multidimensional perspective that links spatial metrics to analyse patterns and lies in association with classical statistical indicators (Galster et al., 2001; Reis et al., 2016). This wide methodological range determines the necessary orientation of the selected variable according to the particular urban characteristics and the spatial scale of the analysis, as well as to the objective of the analysis (Reis et al., 2016).

In any case, it is essential to re-evaluate the methodologies to assess urban areas from functional and abstract perspectives to new perceptive and human approaches. Following this idea, place attachment has started to be estimated by means of Participatory GIS (Public Participation GIS – PPSIG) and mapping methods related to crowdsourcing. This has allowed developing methods to identify place attachment from a spatial point of view (Brown et al., 2015; Maguire & Klinkenberg, 2018; Wang, 2021) both in urban and natural frameworks. Among the conclusions drawn from these studies, of interest for the focus of the present research is the link between the spatial distribution of mapped landscape values (or home area values) and attachment to the mapped place (Brown et al., 2015).

Therefore, the main objective of this chapter is to propose a methodology to identify and categorise urban types based on variables with influence in the landscape and its perception in a coastal Mediterranean area of Spain, mostly residential, as a first step to establish the inclusion of urban landscape units in studies of attachment to lived space. This is especially necessary in rapidly growing urban areas, where traditional types lose prominence in favour of new and disparate ones. This process affects traditional identity and generates new identities based on new landscapes, which, firstly, must be delimited and characterised.

9.2 Materials and Methods

9.2.1 Study Area

The study area comprises the central section of Marbella, a coastal municipality located in Costa del Sol (Málaga), southern Spain (Fig. 9.1). The study area includes the main urban core of the city, which has experienced fast urban growth around the historic centre since mid-twentieth century.

Until the 1950s, this coastal area was eminently rural, based on a traditional agricultural and fishing economic model. After the construction of the first hotels in the 1950s, a new economic model quickly grew, focused on tourism. This change was often promoted by politicians and companies related to Franco's dictatorship, who played a key role in tourism and politics in Costa del Sol (Fernández-Carrión, 2005). The tourism potentiality of the area was based on its coastal nature, a mild climate, an attractive landscape, and an easy international access due to Málaga international airport (García Manrique, 1984). The main consequence of such a disruptive change was the rupture of the traditional social and economic models of the area. The new models were now linked to an urban development characterised by the urban growth that resulted in a real estate boom sometimes associated to political and business corruption (Murray, 2015). The tourism growth brought an uncontrolled urban expansion of the traditional towns (Ferre & Ruíz-Sinoga, 1986), not only ignoring the preservation or creation of green areas within them, but also weakening people's place attachment.

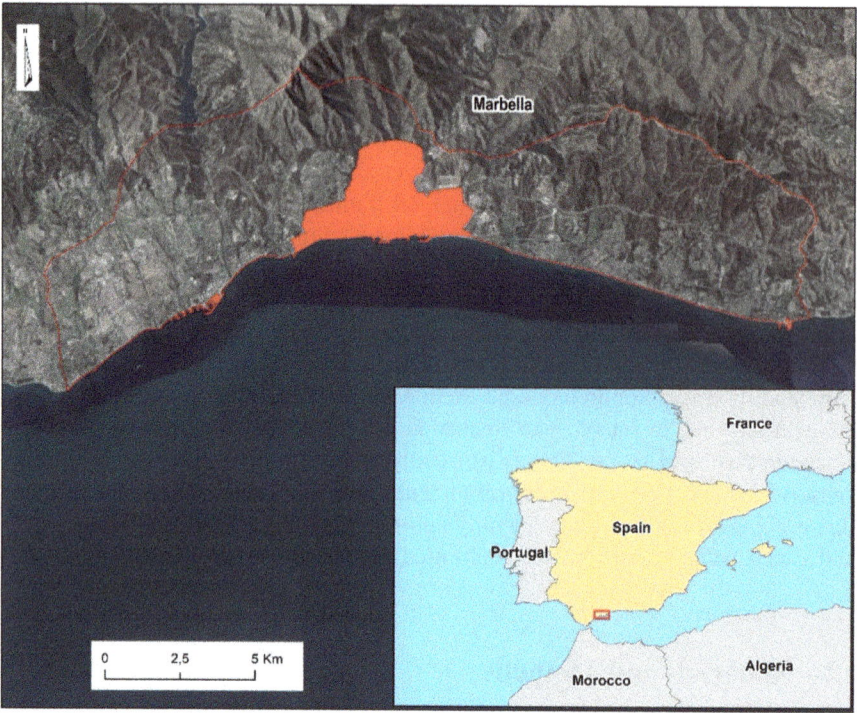

Fig. 9.1 Location of the case study. (Source: Authors' elaboration)

However, although the economic model is similar in all the municipalities, Marbella has a brand as high-class touristic destination. This status is supported by the legacy of the first hotels in the area and the construction of a marina (Puerto Banús) in the 1970s, which became one of the main touristic landmarks to the national and international high-class society. Additionally, a key aspect to maintain this status was the development of a low-density constructive model that includes landscape elements in real estate, mainly golf courses (Villar, 2013). Currently, Marbella is part of Costa del Sol conurbation, developed alongside the coastline as a result of the intense urban growth experienced during the last 60 years. The population has increased from 9921 inhabitants in 1950 to 147,958 in 2021, distributed between the main urban core and several secondary nuclei: San Pedro Alcántara, Nueva Andalucía, and Las Chapas.

9.2.2   Methods

The selected variables for the classification of urban units were the following: (1) the average height of the buildings, (2) the constructive density, considering the ratio between the plot and the built area, (3) the road density, with a weighted analysis of the road hierarchy, (4) the presence of tree and high shrub cover (high cover), and (5) the low shrub and herbaceous cover (low cover). The primary criterion followed to choose the variables, except for variables 4 and 5, is the open access to the data, both in the study area and in other territories where the methodological proposal could be implemented. In the case of vegetation, it has been decided to establish two variables with the aim of allowing distinguishing parks and forests, with a higher biomass index and a greater capacity to cast shadow, and gardens and other equipment, with low size species and without capacity to cast shadows. Variables 4 and 5 have been empirically analysed by remote sensing.

In order to process information on vegetation cover, the most recent aerial orthophotography of the Spanish National Plan for Aerial Orthophotography (PNOA), with a 0.5 m resolution, was used. Although this method has a drawback related to the Red, Green and Blue (RGB) spectrum, where surfaces of different characteristics (vegetable, urban, aquatic) can share colour scheme, we empirically tested this, and it was the most efficient way to calculate vegetation cover due to fast image processing and high resolution. The link of the colours within the visible spectrum with the vegetation elements was based on a supervised procedure, supported by machine learning analysis validated by a point layer sample. Finally, through photointerpretation, we corrected output mistakes, essentially shadows and small buildings, such as roofs, paved areas, and even inland water bodies.

Cluster Analysis

The raw information of the variables, except for the vegetation cover, was available, so some numerical calculations and pre-processes had to be made before performing the analysis. For example, the variable average construction height, information provided by the Spanish Cadastre on the maximum height of the construction units, was decoded in order to convert the information into numerical. From this variable, the constructive density variable was calculated, multiplying the maximum height by the surface of the footprint of the building unit itself (volumetry) and dividing the result by the surface of the plot.

On the other hand, the variable road density was categorised following a hierarchical classification. The wider the road, the greater weight was given since they had more traffic. Unlike streets and avenues, roads act as a perceptive limit for the pedestrian (Lynch, 1960). Once the categorisation was made, the *Line Density* tool in ArcMap 10.3 was applied and the resulting information was transformed into a vector format.

In order to implement a non-supervised classification of the study area according to variables, the percentage of high vegetation cover and low vegetation cover in each cell were calculated separately. To do so, the following steps were taken:

Step 1. Creation of the grid: a 1 ha cell size was considered, which allowed obtaining a representative view of the area perceived by a potential observer in the street. It was created with the ArcGIS *Create Fishnet* tool. The resulting layer is a rectangular grid georeferenced over the reference layer (study area boundaries).

Step 2. The percentage of vegetation per cell was calculated, and the layer's table of attributes was joined with the information of the other variables by using the *Spatial Join* tool in ArcGIS 10.3.

Once we obtained the table of attributes with the information of all the variables for each cell, we performed a multivariate data analysis. The aim was to create a representative number of clusters that gathered cells with similar characteristics to spatially differentiate construction types. We used a grid with 1201 cells with information of the five variables. For the cluster analysis, the validation of the starting data, and its graphical representation, the clusterSim, ggpubr, factoextra, clustertend and cluster libraries of the R code (R Development Core Team, 2016) were used.

The first step was the standardisation of the variables between 0 and 1, following Eq. 9.1.

$$x \text{ } normalised = \frac{x - \min(x)}{\max(x) - \min(x)} \tag{9.1}$$

Where *x normalised* is the standardised value between 0 and 1, whereas *min(x)* and *max(x)* are the minimum and the maximum value of the variable, respectively.

Once the variables had been standardised, we assessed whether data were suitable to be clustered through the Visual Assessment of Cluster Tendency (Fig. 9.2) and the Hopkins index (H = 0′089). This index measures the clustering trend of a dataset based on the probability that those data are uniform. According to the index, values close to 0 show that there are clusters within the data, so it is appropriate to

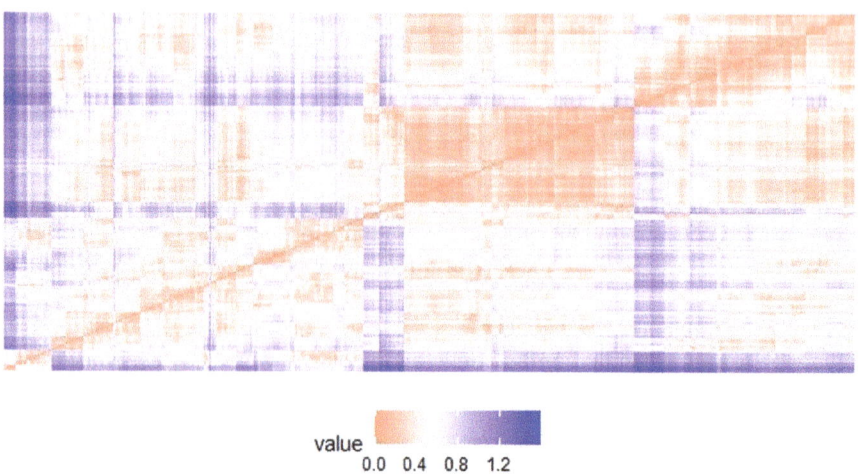

Fig. 9.2 Visual Assessment of cluster Tendency (VAT). (Source: Authors' elaboration)

perform a cluster analysis. Finally, data were examined by a multivariate cluster analysis. The square Euclidean distance was used to measure similarity and the Ward's method was considered to obtain hierarchical associations.

Validation Methods

In this phase, we carried out a two-step validation process of the cluster classification. First, we mapped the results obtained in the cluster analysis, and we verified by photointerpretation that the clusters created by the algorithm made spatial sense in the study area. Subsequently, its statistical robustness was checked by means of the silhouette plot and the Dunn Index in Rstudio.

The consistency of the clustering method was assessed by the cluster silhouette plot (Fig. 9.3). The silhouette plot displays a measure of how close each point in one cluster is to points in the same cluster. The value ranges between 1 and −1, and the closer the score to 1, the more similar are the observations within a cluster, whereas scores lower than 0 indicate that some points may belong to a different cluster. As displayed in Fig. 9.3, the clusters are consistent since all the points are well classified in each cluster. Additionally, despite the complexity and heterogeneity of the data, according to Dunn Index, the clusters are compact (Dunn Index = 0.82). Therefore, they represent the urban types within the study area as distinguishable urban landscape units.

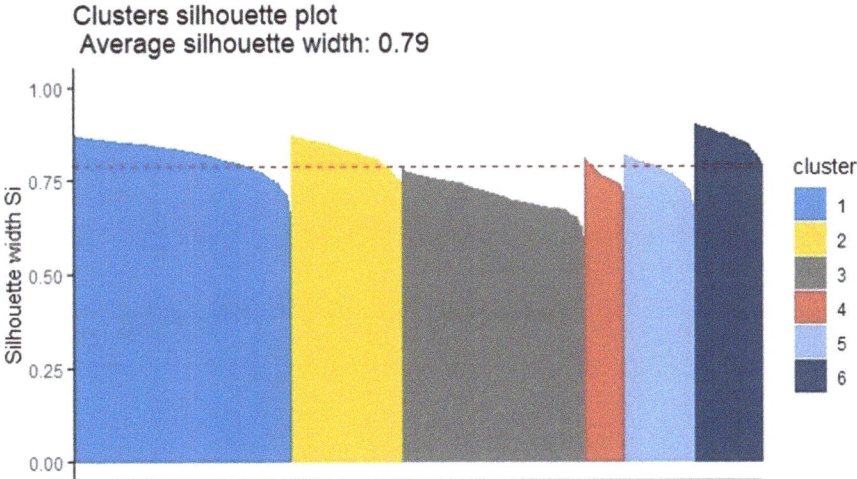

Fig. 9.3 Cluster Silhouette Plot. (Source: Authors' elaboration)

9.3   Results

In this section, the results obtained from the implementation of all the variables are displayed, the statistical robustness of the procedure is tested, and the main characteristics of the clusters are explained. First, the number of cells grouped in each cluster is shown in Table 9.1, followed by their spatial distribution on the map in Fig. 9.4.

Cluster 1 includes areas with moderate vegetation density (both high and low cover), moderate constructive density, low building height and moderate road density. This cluster represents the characteristic urban typology developed in the last decades, with villas, semi-detached houses, and low buildings with private gardens. The road network is dense, mostly dendritic, and tends to communicate with the highway by a single carriageway. Spatially, it may be considered as a second circle around the historic centre, and as it can be observed in Table 9.1, it is the largest cluster.

Cluster 2 includes areas with very low vegetation density, moderate and high constructive density, moderate and low building height, and high road density. Three landscape units can be differentiated within cluster 2, all of them with a high road density: the historic centre, with a complex road network formed by narrow streets, and a high construction density; the seafront of the city, and the industrial site, at the south-eastern part of the study area.

Cluster 3 gathers cells with high proportion of low vegetation cover, and very dense high vegetation cover (above 24% of the cell's surface). This cluster is also characterised by very low construction density, low building height (one-two floors), and low road density. Spatially, cluster 3 is observed in peripheral areas, where villas and semi-detached houses with private gardens and parks are the most common buildings. Cluster 3 also includes public parks and riverbanks.

Cluster 4 represents areas with variable vegetation cover, but with high construction density, moderate and high building height, as well as a high road density. From an urban approach, this cluster includes two types of areas easily differentiated: the

Table 9.1 Basin information of the clusters

Cluster	Number of cells	% of the study area
1	389	32.4
2	127	10.6
3	130	10.8
4	199	16.6
5	155	12.9
6	201	16.7
Total	1201	100

Source: Authors' elaboration

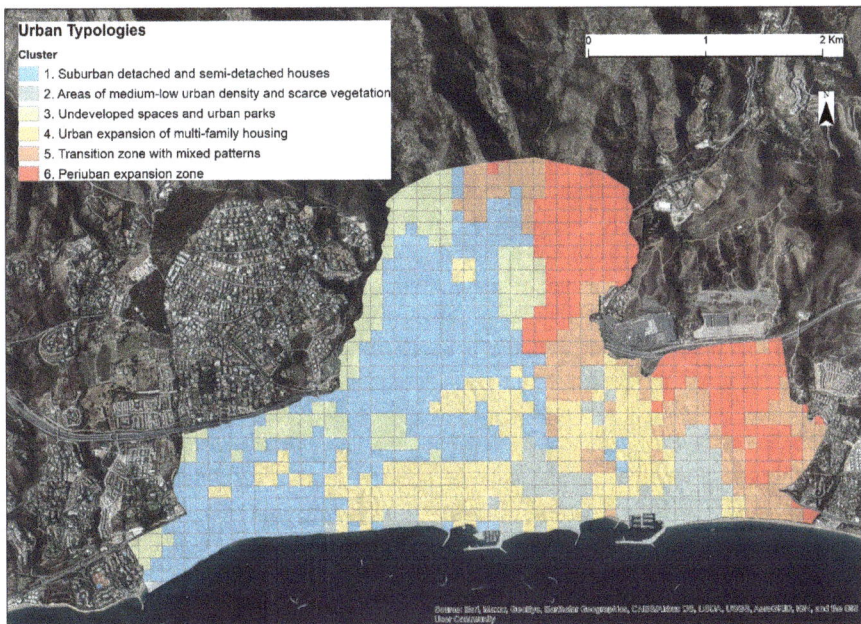

Fig. 9.4 Urban types distinguished within the study area after cluster classification. (Source: Authors' elaboration)

areas with hotels, residential buildings, and office facilities, which follow an open planning model, with gardens, trees and wide pedestrian areas, and working-class neighbourhoods with low building height but high construction density. Cluster 4 covers some of the areas next to the historic centre since they were the first expansion areas of the city a few decades ago.

Cluster 5 represents areas with low vegetation density, low construction density, low building height (one-two floors) and low and moderate road density. This cluster gathers suburban areas already urbanised, formed by scattered residential areas, plots, and, occasionally, industrial, and commercial activities. From a spatial view, cluster 5 is observed along the eastern section of the study area, usually, next to cluster 6.

Finally, cluster 6 includes areas with moderate high vegetation cover and very high low vegetation cover. Construction density is very low or inexistent, whereas height of the buildings is rarely higher than one floor. Road density ranges between very low and moderate, since some cells of the clusters are next to the main highway. Overall, this cluster includes peripheral areas where residential and urban land uses coexist with traditional agricultural activities.

9.4 Discussion

From a methodological point of view, we would like to highlight the specificity of this study to be implemented in Mediterranean areas. It is important to underline this aspect because of the spectral signatures focused on the Mediterranean flora, with perennial arboreal vegetation, abundant scrub land and rare grass areas, besides the private gardens and golf courses. Secondly, because of the characteristics of the urban units in this region, where it is common to find more than 500-year-old historic centres, show the influence of ancient cultures such as Roman or Arabic. Those urban units have disparate urban fabrics that overlap and clearly contrast with modern urban expansions, fundamentally those developed since the mid-twentieth century. On the contrary, we have not considered important industrial activities, nor their potential impact on the landscape since they are not common in the region.

The use of the vegetation cover enriches the analysis of the urban types, especially if it is assessed from a landscape perspective, and it has allowed to delimit six different classes of urban forms. The split of the vegetation cover into two subvariables, high cover (trees) and low cover (shrubs and grass), enables the separation of urban areas with similar public zones, such as golf courses and forest parks, and even nuancing the similarity of the vast suburban area. This differentiation implies the possibility of applying the proposed methodology in planning matters of large study areas, both for zoning and characterisation of the territory and the possibility of diagnosing areas with problems related to landscape value in an initial phase.

Unlike previous procedures provided by Herold and peers (2003) and Kasanko and collaborators (2006), which are based on remote sensing to map urban variables and classify land uses, our methodology implies an alternative method of analysis in those territories where an open access vectorial geodatabase is not available. It is also worthy to mention the methodological proposal by Guyot and peers (2021), which is accurate and robust, but requires up to 17 indicators to perform the categorisation, whereas we provide an easily and quickly replicable method. Furthermore, although the Proximity Band (PB) developed by Araldi and Fusco (2019) is very interesting, it tends to generate excessively detailed spatial units, which are valid for an architectural analysis, but they do not usually represent the real landscape units (Berghauser & Haupt, 2009). A similar issue can be identified from the European Urban Atlas (2018); European Commission (2020), since it excessively split urban units due to a perspective related to land uses instead of landscape characterisation.

In our method, a potential improvement to consider is the analysis of non-urban areas, since some uses and land covers, such as industrial or agricultural, have not been considered. Additionally, the territorial complexity of Marbella, with mixed and uneven urban developments, has hampered its spatial classification in six clusters. This may mean that different urban areas are included into the same cluster, since they share urban characteristics. The upcoming improvements affect cluster 2, where the historic centre is classified together with the industrial park and the seafront. Although they obviously have different landscape and perceptive characteristics, they share similar building heights and road density. In relation to cluster 2, the result may be improved by a better pre-processing of the road network information. Nevertheless, the spatial classification in more clusters would imply problems of statistical robustness, which would affect the replicability of the methodology in other territorial units and would produce an unrealistic fragmentation of the territory. Moreover, the addition of more categories would lead to the loss of synthesis capacity, and it would hamper the interpretation of the results. Fortunately, photointerpretation enables an easy detection of the urban landscape types that are included within a certain cluster, so the territorial interpretation of the technician is strongly recommended.

The methodological proposal is designed considering a series of drawbacks of the basic information. To carry out the remote sensing analysis, the optimal information would have been the images published by Pléiades 1A and Pléiades 1B, with 0.5 m/px resolution, or the images provided by SPOT-6 and SPOT-7, with a resolution of 1.5 m/px. This means multispectral images with greater precision distinguishing the land surfaces and a high resolution. On the other hand, the orthophotography analysis, which considers the visible area of the electromagnetic spectrum, requires the post-edition and correction of the resulting layer, mainly shadows, inland water bodies and other elements and artificial surfaces (e.g., paved roads and roofs) since their spectral colour is similar to the vegetation. The rest of the variables were easier to process, although they required a prior information treatment. For instance, the average height of the buildings cannot automatically distinguish areas where there is a strong difference in height between nearby buildings, whereas the statistical analysis of road density could be improved by differentiating pedestrian streets, regular streets, and roads.

The results of this methodology allow delimiting a series of urban types with distinguishable landscape characteristics. In our opinion, from these urban units it is possible to diagnose the main landscape elements of urban forms that reinforce the identity of the inhabitants with their city and that allow to build friendlier and more welcoming cities (Yang, 2007). This hypothesis can be tested by implementing the proposed method in the elaboration of spatial perception models (Nitavska, 2020). One of the aspects in which further analysis is needed is the importance of urban green spaces, which has already been defined as element that influences the sense of belonging to a place (Bonaiuto et al., 1999). This semi-automated methodological procedure also enables analysing the physical transformations of a given city and the impact on the identity of citizens over time, given that the urban landscape is a complex structure resulting from the interaction between human beings and their environment, which is constantly changing depending on communities, lifestyles and economic model. Its application can be especially interesting in territorial units with a very rapid demographic and urban growth, where the population rooted in the territory loses its identity landscape references, while a large part of the population maintains territorial links with its place of origin, as is the case of the present study area.

9.5 Conclusions

The proposed method allows to classify the main landscape and urban types at an intra-urban scale. The use of vegetation, separated as two variables according to its size, along the physical characteristics of the city, has a key role in classifying urban areas and enables linking urban units to social perceptions (e.g., place attachment), spatial functionality and economic value (e.g., the higher presence of vegetation tends to increase the positive perception of an area, and thus its price increase). In addition, the territorial consistency of the results is statistically supported and spatially coherent with the distribution of the cells among the clusters.

The separation of the vegetation cover according to its size can potentially enable new types of spatial and urban analysis in the framework of urban and territorial planning. Regarding estimation of vegetation, other methods may also be considered, although they currently require higher computational time or are more expensive. The main research line in which we are currently working is based on the implementation of the method in larger territorial units (e.g., regions). Additionally, the use of new variables related to natural and socio-economic characteristics of the area, as well as the incorporation of information related to social perception of the urban areas (e.g., place attachment, sense of belonging, etc.) is also being tested.

The proposed mapping method can be implemented in a spatial analysis research focused on place attachment (Brown et al., 2015), and it can help to delimit and characterise the relationship between urban types and the sense of belonging, particularly in the case of extensive typologies, which have become a new sign of identity of the urban landscape. Additionally, the combination of the method with other quantitative and qualitative scientific techniques can be focused on the population's needs and interests, which may contribute to design urban plans that pay attention to the social functionality of urban areas. In our opinion, this not only would contribute to strengthen ties between residents and the cities where they live, but it would also help to correct intra-urban inequality and the negative connotation of some urban areas. Additionally, it can be useful for the study of the interaction between identity and the urban geographic environment, for comparative studies on the transition from physical to socially cognitive identity.

Acknowledgement This work is part of the project "Paisaje y valor inmobiliario en diversos modelos territoriales de entornos litorales y sublitorales mediterráneos", financed by the Ministry of Sciences, Innovation and Universities (Spain) (PGC2018-097652-B-I00). Main researcher: Matías F. Mérida Rodríguez.

References

Abrantes, P., Rocha, J., Marques da Costa, E., Gomes, E., Morgado, P., & Costa, N. (2019). Modelling urban form: A multidimensional typology of urban occupation for spatial analysis. *Environment and Planning B: Urban Analytics and City Science, 46*(1), 47–65. https://doi.org/10.1177/2F2399808317700140

Araldi, A., & Fusco, G. (2019). From the street to the metropolitan region: Pedestrian perspective in urban fabric analysis. *Environment and Planning B: Urban Analytics and City Science, 46*(7), 1243–1263. https://doi.org/10.1177/2F2399808319832612

Arefi, M. (1999). Non-place and placelessness as narratives of loss: Rethinking the notion of place. *Journal of Urban Design, 4*(2), 179–193. https://doi.org/10.1080/13574809908724445

Arribas-Bel, D., Nijkamp, P., & Scholten, H. (2011). Multidimensional urban sprawl in Europe: A self-organizing map approach. *Computers, Environment and Urban Systems, 35*(4), 263–275. https://doi.org/10.1016/j.compenvurbsys.2010.10.002

Baldassare, M. (1986). *Trouble in paradise: The suburban transformation in America.* Columbia University Press.

Banini, T., & Ilovan, O.-R. (2021). Introduction: Dealing with territorial/place identity representations. In T. Banini & O.-R. Ilovan (Eds.), *Representing place and territorial identities in Europe* (pp. 1–19). Springer.

Banister, D., Watson, S., & Wood, C. (1997). Sustainable cities: transport, energy, and urban form. *Environment and Planning B: planning and design, 24*(1), 125–143.

Beatley, T. (2004). *Native to nowhere: Sustaining home and community in a global age.* Island Press.

Berghauser Pont, M., & Haupt, P. (2009). *Space, density and urban form.* PhD. Technische Universiteit Delft. https://repository.tudelft.nl/islandora/object/uuid:0e8cdd4d-80d0-4c4c-97dc-dbb9e5eee7c2/datastream/OBJ/download. Accessed on 7 July 2021.

Berry, B. J. L. (1974). *Do variations in urban form affect environmental quality?* IIASA Research Memorandum, Laxenburg, Austria. http://pure.iiasa.ac.at/id/eprint/182/1/RM-74-024.pdf. Accessed on 7 July 2021.

Bhatta, B., Saraswati, S., & Bandyopadhyay, D. (2010). Urban sprawl measurement from remote sensing data. *Applied Geography, 30*(4), 731–740. https://doi.org/10.1016/j.apgeog.2010.02.002

Bonaiuto, M., Aiello, A., Perugini, M., Bonnes, M., & Ercolani, A. P. (1999). Multidimensional perception of residential environment quality and neighbourhood attachment in the urban environment. *Journal of Environmental Psychology, 19*(4), 331–352. https://doi.org/10.1006/jevp.1999.0138

Brown, G., Raymond, C. M., & Corcoran, J. (2015). Mapping and measuring place attachment. *Applied Geography, 57*, 42–53. https://doi.org/10.1016/j.apgeog.2014.12.011

Buchanan, C. (2015). *Traffic in towns: A study of the long term problems of traffic in urban areas.* Routledge.

Catalán, B., Saurí, D., & Serra, P. (2008). Urban sprawl in the Mediterranean? Patterns of growth and change in the Barcelona Metropolitan Region 1993–2000. *Landscape and Urban Planning, 85*(3–4), 174–184. https://doi.org/10.1016/j.landurbplan.2007.11.004

Conzen, M. R. G. (1960). Alnwick, Northumberland: A study in town-plan analysis. *Transactions and Papers (Institute of British Geographers), 27*, iii–122.

European Commission. (2020). *Urban atlas 2018.* FUA Delivery Report. Available online https://land.copernicus.eu/local/urban-atlas/urban-atlas-2018?tab=download. Accessed on 8 Apr 2021.

Fernández-Carrión, M. H. (2005). Empresarios del turismo en la Costa del Sol. In *VIII Congreso de la Asociación de Historia Económica*, 13–16 de septiembre de 2005. Universidades de A Coruña, Santiago de Compostela y Vigo, Santiago de Compostela, Spain.

Ferre, E., & Ruíz-Sinoga, J. D. (1986). Algunos aspectos del impacto del turismo en la Costa del Sol Occidental: el caso de Marbella. *Baetica. Estudios de Arte, Geografía e Historia, 9*, 57–73.

Galster, G., Hanson, R., Ratcliffe, M. R., Wolman, H., Coleman, S., & Freihage, J. (2001). Wrestling sprawl to the ground: Defining and measuring an elusive concept. *Housing Policy Debate, 12*(4), 681–717. https://doi.org/10.1080/10511482.2001.9521426

García Manrique, E. (1984). La Costa occidental malagueña. In M. Alcobendas (Ed.), *Málaga, 1* (pp. 229–260). Granada.

Gustafson, P. (2006). Place attachment and mobility. In N. McIntyre, D. Williams, & K. McHugh (Eds.), *Multiple dwelling and tourism: Negotiating place, home and identity* (pp. 17–31). CAB International.

Guyot, M., Araldi, A., Fusco, G., & Thomas, I. (2021). The urban form of Brussels from the street perspective: The role of vegetation in the definition of the urban fabric. *Landscape and Urban Planning, 205*, 103947. https://doi.org/10.1016/j.landurbplan.2020.103947

Herold, M., Goldstein, N. C., & Clarke, K. C. (2003). The spatiotemporal form of urban growth: Measurement, analysis and modeling. *Remote Sensing of Environment, 86*(3), 286–302. https://doi.org/10.1016/S0034-4257(03)00075-0

Hur, M., Nasar, J. L., & Chun, B. (2010). Neighborhood satisfaction, physical and perceived naturalness and openness. *Journal of Environmental Psychology, 30*(1), 52–59. https://doi.org/10.1016/j.jenvp.2009.05.005

Kasanko, M., Barredo, J. I., Lavalle, C., McCormick, N., Demicheli, L., Sagris, V., & Brezger, A. (2006). Are European cities becoming dispersed? A comparative analysis of 15 European urban areas. *Landscape and Urban Planning, 77*(1–2), 111–130. https://doi.org/10.1016/j.landurbplan.2005.02.003

Kasarda, J. D. (1978). Urbanization, community, and the metropolitan problem. In D. Street (Ed.), *Handbook of contemporary urban life* (pp. 27–57). Jossey-Bass Publishers.

Lewicka, M. (2011). Place attachment: How far have we come in the last 40 years? *Journal of Environmental Psychology, 31*(3), 207–230. https://doi.org/10.1016/j.jenvp.2010.10.001

Lynch, K. (1960). *The image of the city* (Vol. 11). MIT Press.

Maguire, B., & Klinkenberg, B. (2018). Visualization of place attachment. *Applied Geography, 99*, 77–88. https://doi.org/10.1016/j.apgeog.2018.07.007

Murray, I. (2015). *Capitalismo y Turismo en España. Del "Milagro Económico" a la "Gran Crisis"*. Alba Sud Editorial. Retrieved from www.albasud.org/publ/docs/68.ca.pdf

Nitavska, N. (2020). The spatial structure of the landscape as one of the elements of the landscape identity. *IOP Conference Series: Materials Science and Engineering, 960*(4), 042001. IOP Publishing. https://doi.org/10.1088/1757-899X/960/4/042001

Pons, A., & Rullan, O. (2014). The expansion of urbanisation in the Balearic Islands (1956–2006). *Journal of Marine and Island Cultures, 3*(2), 78–88. https://doi.org/10.1016/j.imic.2014.11.004

R Development Core Team. (2016). R: A Language and Environment for Statistical Computing. Vienna, Austria: R Foundation for Statistical Computing. https://www.R-project.org/

Reis, J. P., Silva, E. A., & Pinho, P. (2016). Spatial metrics to study urban patterns in growing and shrinking cities. *Urban Geography, 37*(2), 246–271. https://doi.org/10.1080/02723638.2015.1096118

Salvati, L., Venanzoni, G., Serra, P., & Carlucci, M. (2016). Scattered or polycentric? Untangling urban growth in three southern European metropolitan regions through exploratory spatial data analysis. *The Annals of Regional Science, 57*(1), 1–29. https://doi.org/10.1007/s00168-016-0758-5

Taima, M., & Asami, Y. (2019). Estimation of average place attachment level in a region of Japan. *GeoJournal, 84*(5), 1365–1381. https://doi.org/10.1007/s10708-018-9927-7

Villar Lama, A. (2013). La mercantilización del paisaje litoral del mediterráneo andaluz: El caso paradigmático de la Costa del Sol y los campos de golf. *Revista de estudios regionales, 96*, 215–242.

Wang, Y. (2021). Building emotional GIS: A spatial investigation of place attachment for urban historic environments in Edinburgh, Scotland. In R. Madgin & J. Lesh (Eds.), *People-centred methodologies for heritage conservation* (pp. 159–176). Routledge.

Weston, L. M. (2002). A methodology to evaluate neighborhood urban form. *Planning Forum, 8*, 64–77. https://repositories.lib.utexas.edu/bitstream/handle/2152/30374/planningforumv8.pdf?sequence=2#page=68. Accessed on 6 July 2021

Xu, C., Haase, D., Su, M., & Yang, Z. (2019). The impact of urban compactness on energy-related greenhouse gas emissions across EU member states: Population density vs physical compactness. *Applied Energy, 254*, 113671. https://doi.org/10.1016/j.apenergy.2019.113671

Yang, B. E. (2007). The role of landscape architecture in the creation and management of the environment-friendly cities in Korea. *International Journal of Urban Sciences, 11*(2), 156–167. https://doi.org/10.1080/12265934.2007.9693616

Chapter 10
Gender and Age Differences for Perceptual Qualities of a Forest Landscape in Relation to Dramatic Landscape Change Processes: Implications for Connections to Place

Åsa Ode Sang ⓘ, Andrew Butler ⓘ, and Igor Knez ⓘ

10.1 Introduction

The landscape of Sweden is to a large degree characterised by forest covers. Consequently, the forest landscape contributes to a broad range of diverse and important ecosystem services (production of timber, biodiversity, recreation, etc.). The importance of Swedish forest as a vessel for multiple functions and services is emphasised by the equal status engendered to both forest production and biodiversity within the Swedish Forest Act (SFS, 1979, 1993), as well as by the importance that cultural heritage, aesthetic, and social values of forest hold within the Swedish Environmental goals (SEOC, 2009).

Forest landscapes produce numerous and diverse forms of cultural ecosystem services: aesthetic qualities, spiritual experience, recreational possibilities, a sense of identity, and the basis for attachment to place, services that are fundamental for people's well-being. Studies of the use of forest for recreational activities emphasise the importance of the convenience and accessibility provided by local forests, areas requiring minimal travel and enhancing the possibility of frequent visits (Van

Å. O. Sang
Department of Landscape Architecture, Planning and Management, Swedish University of Agricultural Science, Uppsala, Sweden
e-mail: asa.sang@slu.se

A. Butler (✉)
Department of Urban and Rural Development, Swedish University of Agricultural Science, Uppsala, Sweden
e-mail: andrew.butler@slu.se

I. Knez
Department of Social Work and Psychology, University of Gävle, Gävle, Sweden
e-mail: igor.knez@hig.se

O.-R. Ilovan, I. Markuszewska (eds.), *Preserving and Constructing Place Attachment in Europe*, GeoJournal Library 131,
https://doi.org/10.1007/978-3-031-09775-1_10

Herzele & Wiedemann, 2003; Neuvonen et al., 2007). Visits to forests has been shown to contribute to both self-reported as well as measured aspects of well-being (Norman et al., 2010). An underlying driver for several of these cultural ecosystem services is the quality of the forest that we experience through our perception.

While the closeness of an area has been singled out as the most important factor for the use of a forest area, research has also emphasised the importance that access and experiential qualities have over the choice of areas individuals visit (Van Herzele & Wiedemann, 2003; Koppen et al., 2014). With regards to access this comprises both the actual physical accessibility, the extent to which we could walk through the landscape as well as how we are allowed to access the landscape, sometimes referred to as the socio-psychological dimension of accessibility (Koppen et al., 2014). To what degree we feel we have a right to access is determined both by the actual juridical right of access and the sense of feeling welcome. For forest landscapes, the physical access could be hindered by ground cover or density of forest making it difficult to access. In Sweden, public right of access provides freedom to access privately owned forests. However, this freedom can be restricted through, for example, issues arising from natural disasters such as forest fire, which result in signage, roadblocks, etc. reducing the perceived access to the landscape.

Previous studies have highlighted the importance of landscape characteristics for preference (Kaplan & Kaplan, 1989; Nassauer, 1995; Purcell & Lamb, 1998; Ode et al., 2009), place attachment (Stedman, 2003; Davenport & Anderson, 2005), cultural ecosystem service such as recreation, aesthetic experience, and experience of well-being (Lovell et al., 2014; Ode Sang et al., 2016). Experiential classification, such as perceptual categories based on visual experience, has the potential to be an important basis for attachment to the landscape. A framework for analysing visual qualities of landscape was devised by Tveit and peers (2006). In the study presented in this chapter we focus on the following subset from Tveit et al. framework: visual scale (openness), naturalness, stewardship, disturbance, complexity, and coherence, all contributing to the experience of the forest (Gobster, 1999; Sheppard, 2001; Ode & Fry, 2002; Heyman et al., 2011; Hough, 2014; Ode Sang et al., 2016).

Research has highlighted the influence sound has on our perception, and subsequent connection to our surroundings. Natural sounds have been shown to contribute to a positive experience of our environment (Viollon et al., 2002; Hedblom et al., 2014) and decreasing stress (Alvarsson et al., 2010). Recent studies also highlight the importance of natural sounds in the experience and perception of naturalness (Annerstedt et al., 2013; Hedblom et al., 2017).

The forest is a dynamic entity, with changes occurring due to various management operations and natural processes. Contemporary dramatic change to the forest landscape tends to be caused by forest operations such as clear-cutting, causing abrupt transformation of the character and perception of an area. In a forest landscape, dramatic natural events such as forest fire, while infrequent, can completely alter the physical structure of the forest landscape. While there are numerous studies that explored these effects in relation to ecosystem services such as biodiversity (Gustafsson et al., 2019), there are few studies which engage with impact on residents' connections to landscape after such events.

How do these natural occurring events affect individual's perception of the forest, and relation to concepts such as naturalness and stewardship? Does the perception of the area's transformation vary depending on age and gender, as previous studies of landscape experience have suggested (Ode et al., 2009; Svobodova et al., 2012; Sreetheran & Van Den Bosch, 2014; Zoderer et al., 2016; Hedblom et al., 2017)? Several studies on the situations in stable landscapes have shown that women tend to give a higher rating to cultural ecosystem services (Zoderer et al., 2016), to perceptual qualities and preference (Strumse, 1996; Lindemann-Matthies et al., 2010; Svobodova et al., 2012; Filova et al., 2015: Ode Sang et al., 2016), and well-being associated with green areas (Ode Sang et al., 2016), but women also have higher fear level then male respondents in relation to urban green spaces (Sreetheran & Van Den Bosch, 2014). The latter is also observed in fire prone areas (Eriksen, 2015) and underwrites the gendered norms of accepted risk and safety, where males tend to perceive threat to a lesser degree.

Results from a survey by Hedblom et al. (2017) showed that women reported feeling a greater sense of calm when hearing bird song and rustling leaves compared to men. Research in psychology has suggested that women's emotional experiences are much stronger than men's (Harshman & Paivio, 1987) and that women are more emotionally expressive than men (Kring & Gordon, 1998). Greater differences are generally found with stimuli evoking negative emotions (Harshman & Paivio, 1987). It has been suggested that gender differences in emotional reaction are shaped by sociocultural factors, thereby acting as possible mediators for gender differences in emotional response (Grossman & Wood, 1993; Bradley et al., 2001). However, in the words of Brody and Hall (2010, p. 395): "Gender differences in emotional functioning are widely documented, but are often inconsistent across personality, social, cultural, and situational variables, as well as types of emotional processes, quality of emotions, and tasks characteristics."

There is an abundance of research which investigated landscape perception for a given situation (Coeterier, 1996; Lothian, 1999; Tveit, 2009; Sevenant & Antrop, 2010). Studies published on landscape change and its affection on perception and preference of local people tended to focus on either changes in perception of landscape when change occurred over a longer time period (Palmer, 1997; Palmer, 2004) or on the modelling of changes in relation to different policy or climate change scenarios (Dockerty et al., 2001; Sheppard et al., 2013; Ode Sang et al., 2014). Few studies engaged with the impact of dramatic landscape changes, such as forest fire, and its impact for local people and their interaction with the landscape (Toman et al., 2013). In a Swedish context, our own studies revealed the impact of dramatic landscape loss on cognitive and emotional aspects of place-identity and correlated well-being issues (Butler et al., 2018; Knez et al., 2018), the importance of activities for creating and retaining connections to place after a forest fire (Butler et al., 2019, 2021), and the increased impact on those who directly experienced dramatic events (Knez et al., 2021).

In this chapter, we investigate differences in perceptual qualities and changes of those in relation to dramatic and abrupt landscape changes, based on gender and age. Grounded on earlier studies, we hypothesise that:

dramatic natural change has a negative effect on the experience of all perceptual
    categories of landscape;

women and old people would give a higher value to the perceptual categories for the
    landscape;

the negative effect on perceptual qualities in relation to dramatic landscape change
    is stronger for female and old respondents.

This is discussed in relation to how forest landscape could contribute to place
attachment and how this is affected by dramatic changes in the landscape.

10.2 Method

10.2.1 Study Site

The area we address in this study is situated in Bergslagen, in the Southern part of
central Sweden. In a landscape analysis carried out in 2012, the area was classified
as belonging to the character type 'water rich forest landscape' (*Vattenrik skogs-
landskap*). It bridged two separate character areas – 'Nedre Bergslagen' and
'Brukens Skogar' – which are described in broad generic and objective terms as:

> Rolling topography, ranging from 50 to 100 meters above sea level. It contains river valleys
> and small plains that stand out in the forested landscape … Summer houses, wetland, and
> heathland create diversity in the forest area with few key biotopes. Predominantly large-
> scale forest production, distributed among a few large forest owners – Nedre Bergslagen
> (Onsten-Molander, 2016, p. 35; our translation).

In the summer of 2014, this area experienced Sweden's largest wildfire in modern
times (Fig. 10.1). The fire spread over the course of several days and ultimately
affected approximately 14,000 ha of mainly managed forest land. The fire cost the
life of a forest worker and destroyed over 20 houses. It damaged or destroyed
1.4 million cubic meters of timber, three nature reserves and ten habitat protection
areas were affected (Butler et al., 2018; Lidskog & Sjödin, 2018).

The forest fire created a new geography in this landscape. A new boundary
appeared, while elements and aesthetic qualities that formed the basis for the collective and individual identities in the landscape vanished. The loss of landscape elements means that activities and the accessibility they provided were also negatively
impacted.

10.2.2 Sample

In order to investigate issues related to landscape perception and landscape identity,
we conducted a survey consisting of questions concerning landscape related behaviour, experiences, perceptions and attitudes before and after the fire. A postal survey

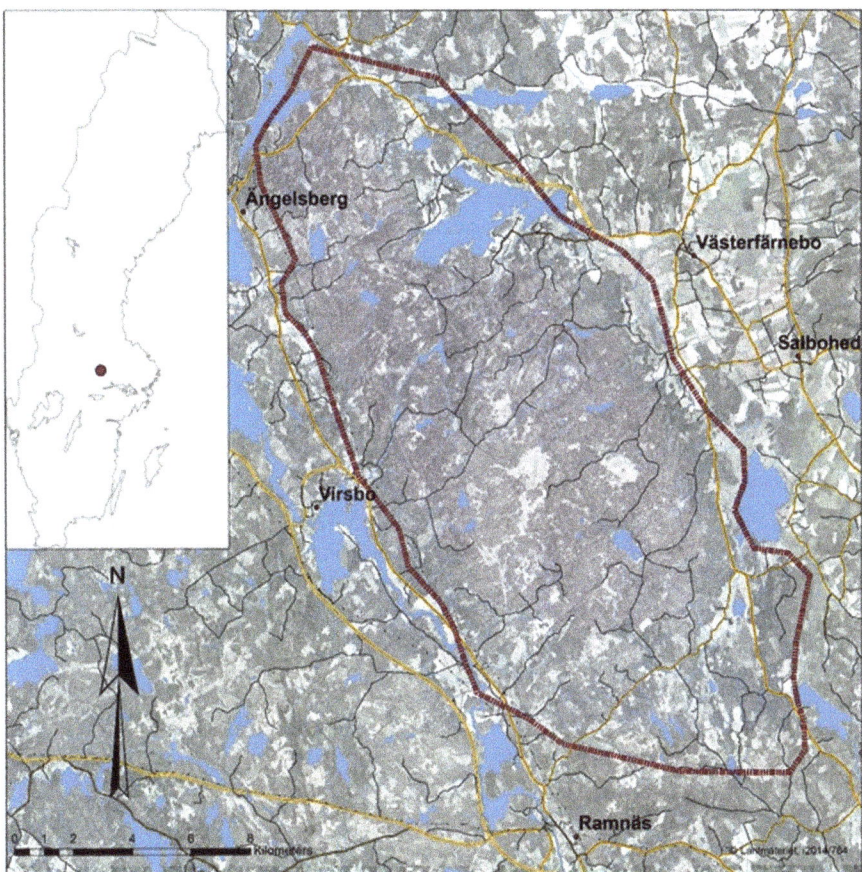

Fig. 10.1 Extent of fire area and location in Sweden. (Source: Own elaboration)

was sent out 1 year after the forest fire to a randomised sub-sample (2264 house-holds) of people living within the post code adjacent to the forest fire area. The postal survey returned 656 replies (29%), including 48.4% female and 51.6% male respondents, distributed across seven age groups: 18–25 (3%), 26–35 (5.6%), 36–45 (10.2%), 46–55 (15%), 56–65 (26.4%), 66–75 (28.9%), and 76–85 (10.9%). We report here only data on the perceptual qualities of landscape before and after the fire related to respondents' gender and age. For these questions, we received 499–512 (76–78%) responses relating to the perceptual quality of landscape before and after the fire.

10.2.3   Measures

The measure of the landscape perceptual quality involved eight dimensions (sub-measures), six of these dimensions covering visual perception based on the framework presented by Tveit et al. (2006), namely naturalness, coherence, complexity; stewardship, disturbance, and scale/openness. These six were complemented with the following non-visual dimensions: accessibility, sound, safety, and overall experience. We asked participants to estimate the perceptual qualities of landscape before and after the fire on a 7-point Likert scale, with 1 equating with completely disagree and 7 with completely agree.

The following complementary statements related to the eight sub-measures were included: naturalness (nature like, species rich, wild), complexity (this was divided into two dimensions – the first involved variation and richness and the second referred to level of organisation; this latter relates closely to the concept of coherence), accessibility (easy accessible, easy to move), scale/openness (easy to get an overview, open, magnificent, small scale, hilly), sound (noise free), safety, overall experience (nice, beautiful, spiritual), stewardship (cared for, rich in historical remains, managed), and disturbance (influenced by humans, with disturbance).

Perceptual qualities were also recognised as significant for driving place meaning and shaping place attachment (Stedman, 2003; Davenport & Anderson, 2005).

10.2.4   Design and Analyses

We used a non-equivalent comparison-group quasi-experimental design (McGuigan, 1990). Compared with a "true experiment" (Liebert & Liebert, 1995), the inferences drawn about the causal relationships between independent and dependent variables may be considered to be weaker.

Independent Variables Three independent variables were included: 2 Gender (females, males) × 2 Age (seven age groups were re-grouped into two: young [26–55 years] and old [56–85 years] respondents, due to rather few persons in Gender by Age cell-combinations; also, the age group of 18–25 years was excluded because this group represented only 3% of respondents) × 2 Time (before, after the fire). An index (mean statistics) was calculated for each of the eight perceptual quality dimensions, in order to include these as within-subject factors (before the fire versus after the fire) in statistical analyses (see below).

Dependent Variables Participants' estimations of the landscape perceptual qualities were used as dependent variable.

Statistical Analyses Mixed analyses of variance (ANOVAs) were preformed, with Gender and Age as between-subject factors and Time as a within-subject factor. Eight analyses were performed, one for each of the eight dimensions (sub-measures) of the landscape perceptual quality. IBM SPSS Statistics 22 software was used for the statistical computations.

10.3   Results

The results are presented in the eight following sections related to the dimensions of the perceptual quality of landscape. Only significant results are reported.

10.3.1   Naturalness

A main effect of Gender, $F(1,495) = 5.18$, $p < .05$ $\eta^2 = .01$, showed that women estimated a higher experience of the nature than men (women $M = 4.06$ $SD = 1.55$ vs. men $M = 3.81$ $SD = 1.44$); thus, independently of age and the fire. In addition, a main effect of Time, $F(1,495) = 834.16$, $p < .001$ $\eta^2 = .63$, showed that all respondents (independently of gender and age) estimated a higher nature experience before than after the fire (before $M = 5.22$ $SD = 1.47$ vs. after $M = 2.65$ $SD = 1.53$).

10.3.2   Complexity

A main effect of Time, $F(1,482) = 506.19$, $p < .001$ $\eta^2 = .51$, showed that all respondents estimated complexity of the landscape as higher before than after the fire (before $M = 4.65$ $SD = 1.53$ vs. after $M = 2.6$ $SD = 1.56$). A within-subject effect showed additionally that, independently of the fire, respondents estimated the site as more varied and rich in variation (dimension 1, see Method section) than well organised (dimension 2), $F(1,475) = 1348.6$, $p < .001$ $\eta^2 = .74$ (dimension 1 $M = 2.58$ $SD = 1.55$ vs. dimension 2 $M = 2.3$ $SD = 1.49$).

10.3.3   Accessibility

A main effect of Gender, $F(1,489) = 6.26$, $p < .01$ $\eta^2 = .01$, showed that women experienced a lower level of accessibility than men (women $M = 3.56$ $SD = 1.71$ vs. men $M = 3.88$ $SD = 1.6$). A main effect of Age, $F(1,489) = 8.29$, $p < .01$ $\eta^2 = .02$, showed that elderly experienced a lower level of accessibility than young respondents (young $M = 3.9$ $SD = 1.55$ vs. old $M = 3.45$ $SD = 1.68$); this was, independent of gender or the effect of the fire. A main effect of Time, $F(1,489) = 323.32$, $p < .001$ $\eta^2 = .4$, showed that all respondents estimated the accessibility as higher before than after the fire (before $M = 4.54$ $SD = 1.47$ vs. after $M = 2.9$ $SD = 1.53$). Finally, an

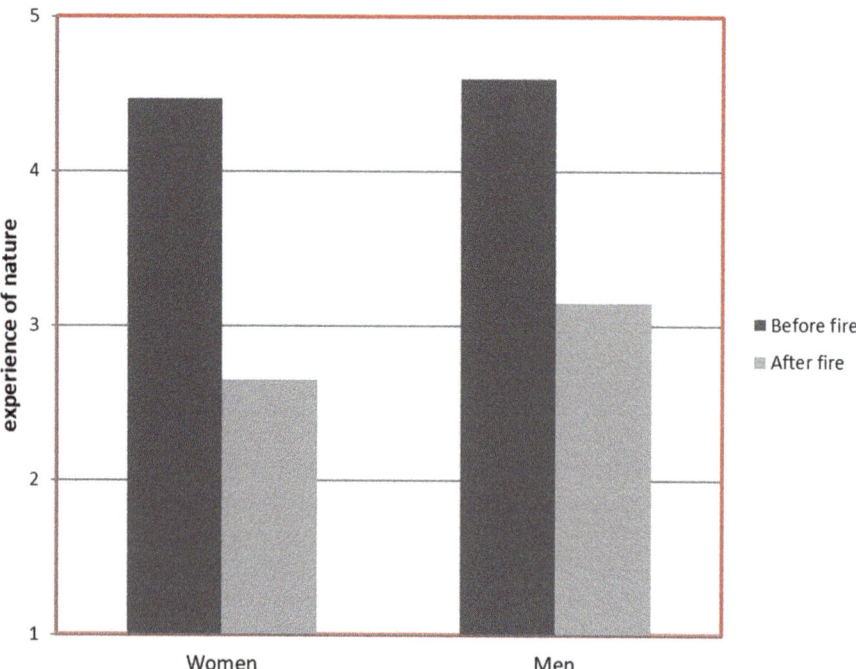

Fig. 10.2 Experience of nature as a function of gender, before and after the fire. (Source: Own elaboration)

interaction effect between Gender and Time, $F(1,489) = 4.25$, $p < .05$ $\eta^2 = .01$, showed that women's experience of lower accessibility was more pronounced after the fire compared to men's (Fig. 10.2).

10.3.4 Openness

A main effect of Age, $F(1,493) = 4.2$, $p < .05$ $\eta^2 = .01$, showed that the elderly experienced less openness than the young (young $M = 4.0$ $SD = 1.2$ vs. old $M = 3.78$ $SD = 1.45$). A main effect of Time, $F(1,493) = 27.23$, $p < .001$ $\eta^2 = .05$, showed that all respondents estimated higher openness before than after the fire (before $M = 4.1$ $SD = 1.33$ vs. after $M = 3.62$ $SD = 1.42$). An interaction effect between Gender and Time, $F(1,493) = 4.86$, $p < .05$ $\eta^2 = .01$, showed that women's compared to men's lower estimations of openness was mostly related to the landscape after the fire (Fig. 10.3). According to Fig. 10.3, a similar interaction effect was shown for the old, $F(1,493) = 10.5$, $p < .001$ $\eta^2 = .02$.

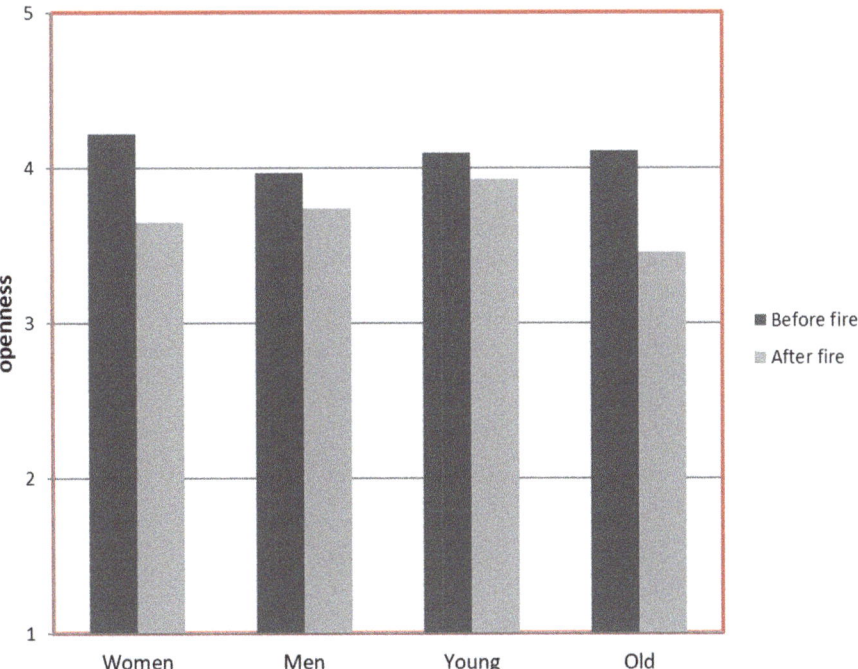

Fig. 10.3 Openness as a function of gender and age, before and after the fire. (Source: Own elaboration)

10.3.5 Sound

A main effect of Time, $F(1,489) = 200.3$, $p < .001$ $\eta^2 = .29$, showed that all respondents experienced the landscape as more noise free before than after the fire (before $M = 5.28$ $SD = 1.8$ vs. after $M = 3.89$ $SD = 1.98$). An interaction effect between Age and Time, $F(1,489) = 11.72$, $p < .001$ $\eta^2 = .02$, showed that the young compared to the old estimated a higher difference in sound perception before and after the fire (Fig. 10.4).

10.3.6 Overall Experience

A main effect of Time, $F(1,512) = 1059.43$, $p < .001$ $\eta^2 = .67$, showed that all respondents estimated higher overall experience before than after the fire (before $M = 5.07$ $SD = 1.47$ vs. after $M = 2.49$ $SD = 1.43$). An interaction effect between Gender and Time, $F(1,512) = 9.25$, $p < .05$ $\eta^2 = .02$, showed that women estimated higher overall experience than men, especially after the fire (Fig. 10.5). Figure 10.5 shows a similar interaction effect for the young respondents, $F(1,512) = 6.2$, $p < .01$ $\eta^2 = .01$.

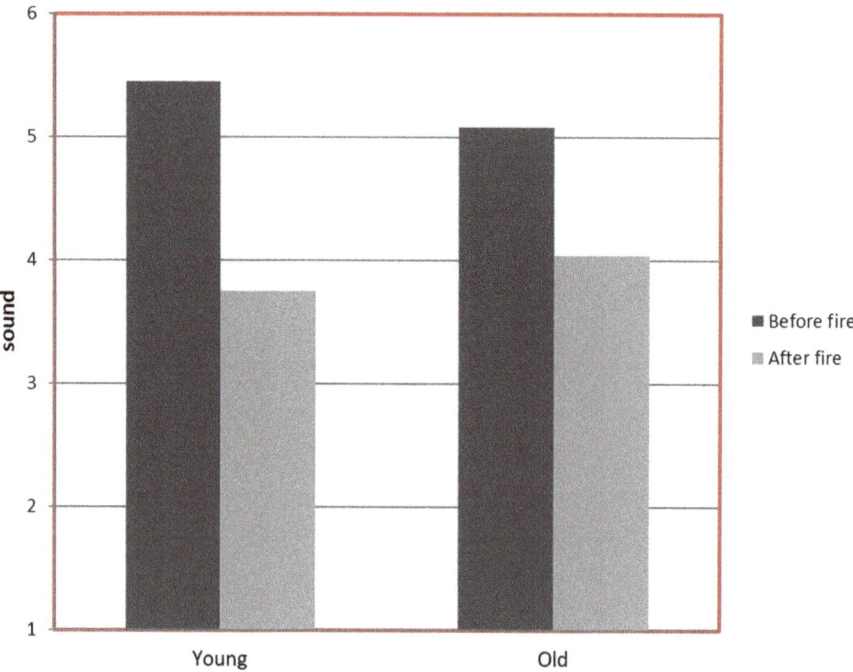

Fig. 10.4 Sound as a function of age, before and after the fire. (Source: Own elaboration)

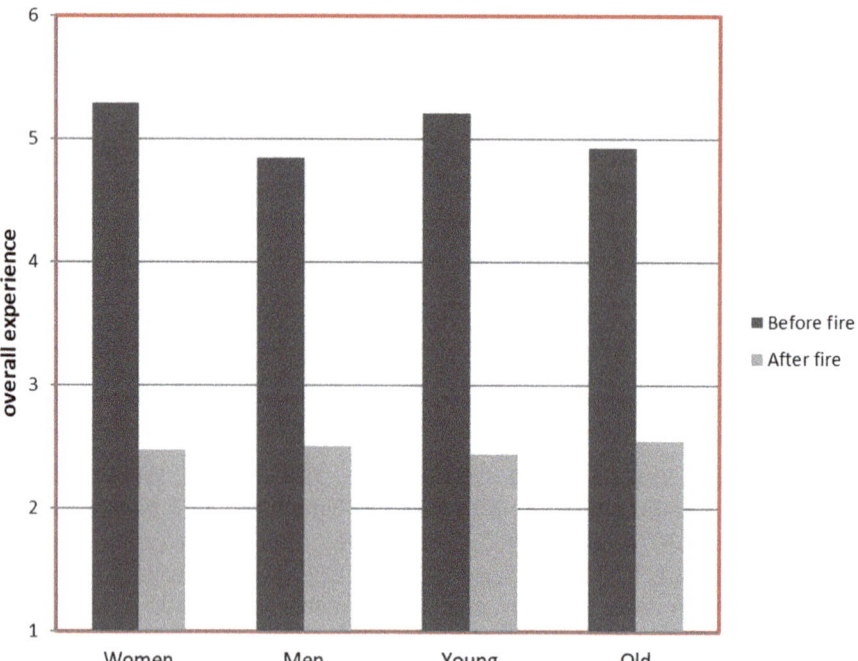

Fig. 10.5 Overall experience as a function of gender and age, before and after the fire. (Source: Own elaboration)

10.3.7   Positive Human Influence

A main effect of Time, $F(1,500) = 210.85$, $p < .001$ $\eta^2 = .3$, showed that all respondents estimated more positive human influence before than after the fire (before $M = 4.11$ $SD = 1.37$ vs. after $M = 3.01$ $SD = 1.43$).

10.3.8   Negative Human Influence

A main effect of Time, $F(1,503) = 311.03$, $p < .001$ $\eta^2 = .38$, showed that all respondents estimated higher negative human influence after than before the fire (before $M = 3.38$ $SD = 1.52$ vs. after $M = 5.03$ $SD = 1.82$). An interaction effect between Gender and Time, $F(1,503) = 12.45$, $p < .001$ $\eta^2 = .02$, showed that women estimated higher negative human influence than men, especially after the fire (Fig. 10.6). Figure 10.6 shows a similar interaction effect for the young respondents, $F(1,503) = 13.44$, $p < .001$ $\eta^2 = .03$.

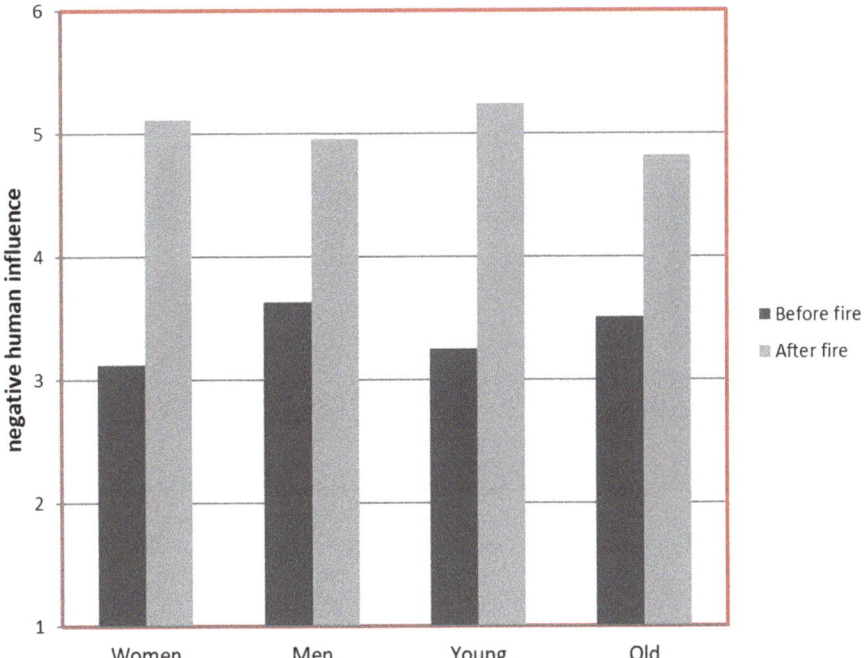

Fig. 10.6 Negative human influence as a function of gender and age, before and after the fire. (Source: Own elaboration)

10.4   Discussion

10.4.1   Perception of Forest Landscapes Before and After a Wildfire

The initial aim of this study was to investigate changes on perceptual qualities of a landscape before and after a fire. Before the fire, the landscape was rated as having a high degree of naturalness (i.e., high rates for nature like, species richness, and sense of wild). It was further characterised as noise free (sound), safe, nice, beautiful, and spiritual (overall experience). It was perceived as being less accessible (easy to access and move), having a degree of complexity (varied and rich in variation), low coherence (well organised), and being of small scale (open, magnificent, hilly, easy to get an overview and small scale). The landscape had a high degree of stewardship (cared for, managed), being rich in historical remains and was perceived as having a low degree of disturbance (negatively influenced by humans). After the forest fire a negative impact was reported on all eight perceptual dimensions of landscape quality (Fig. 10.7), meaning that respondents' perceptions of the landscape were significantly devalued after the fire.

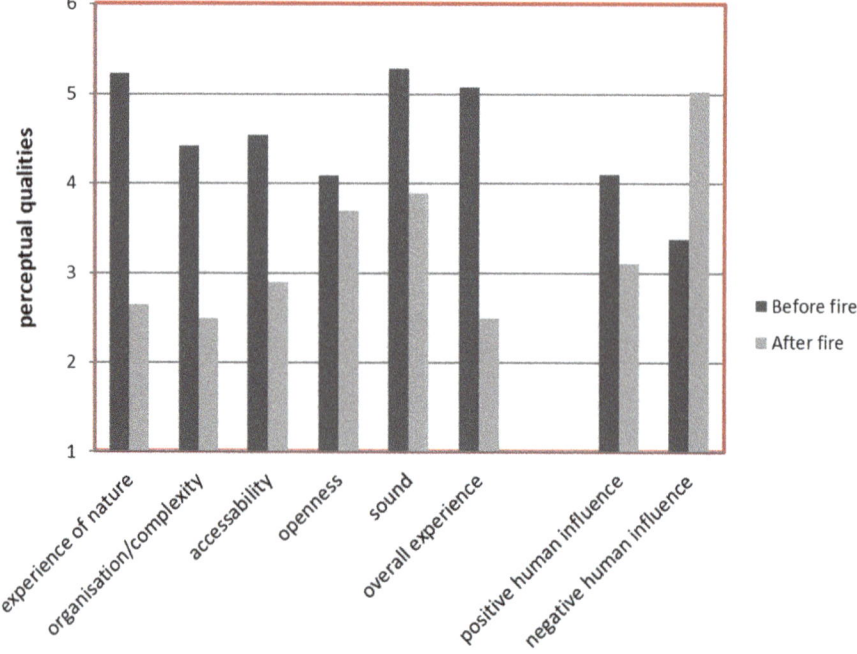

Fig. 10.7 Perceptual qualities (experience of nature; organisation/complexity; accessibility; openness; sound, overall experience; positive influence by humans; negative influence by humans) as a function of time (before and after the fire). (Source: Own elaboration)

This result would suggest that the associated place attachments that are depending on the experience of the landscape would also show a decline. Previous research has highlighted a positive association between one or more perceptual qualities and preference (Herzog & Kutzli, 2002; Ode Sang & Tveit, 2013), aesthetic (Zoderer et al., 2016), recreation (Heyman et al., 2011), and well-being (Lovell et al., 2014).

10.4.2   Gender and Age Differences in Assessing Perceptual Categories for a Landscape Before and After the Forest Fire

The result from our survey showed that in general, before the fire, women experienced the landscape as more nature like, species rich, and wild (naturalness) than men did. This is in line with the results found by Ode Sang et al. (2016).

Compared to men, when women considered the perceptual qualities of the area before and after the fire, they evaluated the landscape as: (1) less easy to access and move (accessibility), (2) less safe, nice, beautiful, and spiritual (overall experience), and (3) more disturbed (negative human influence). We also found that while the assessment of openness, before and after the fire, showed no significant changes for men, this was not the case for women, who registered a perceived loss of openness in relation to this landscape, 1 year after the fire.

The review by Koppen et al. (2014) highlighted the importance of perceived accessibility for the actual use of an area. As women had a stronger perception of the area as less safe, nice, beautiful, spiritual and at the same time more disturbed, this would presumably influence the perceived accessibility and ability to maintain or re-establish attachment. This would mean that there is a decline in the use of the area by women compared to men, when compared to the situation prior to the forest fire. While studies confirmed the link between use and access in an urban context (Koppen et al., 2014), this relationship has been studied to a lesser extent in rural contexts or after dramatic landscape change.

In general, the elderly (56–85 years of age) experienced less accessibility and openness than the young (26–55 years of age) respondents, who estimated a higher difference in landscape sound perception, overall experience (safe, nice, beautiful, and spiritual), and disturbance (negative influence of humans) before and after the fire.

10.4.3   Implications for Place Attachment

Place attachment is a complex and long-term process (Hernández et al., 2007), built on the tripartite of person, process, and place (Scannell & Gifford, 2010). A positive place attachment results in and is at the same time the result of positive perceptions of place (Rollero & De Piccoli, 2010). Non-familiar places, often lack positive perceptions, resulting in spatial anxiety (Fornara et al., 2019). According to our findings, we argue that this does not just relate to new places, but also to familiar places altered beyond recognition, such as through forest fire.

The impact of dramatic landscape change on perceptions of place and consequently place attachment is not consistent across the population; hence, the affected citizens cannot be considered a homogenous group. In this chapter, we have drawn on two variables, age and gender, to attempt to lift the plurality of the impacted population.

The impact reflected in the variable of age and gender differences, can be seen as built on numerous factors including greater likelihood to be rooted in the area (Gustafson, 2001), with length of residency and intensity of engagement in an area recognised as a positive predictors of attachment (Twigger-Ross & Uzzell, 1996). The older residents of the area tend to have developed a stronger connection to a place or landscape, setting down anchors for memories (Knez, 2006). Yet accessibility is also reliant on the ability to physically move around and enjoy the area (Koppen et al., 2014); for the less mobile, obstacles can become significant hindrances and detractors (Suzuki et al., 2021). These factors which may prevent access to a landscape in the short term can be exacerbated over time as the lack of familiarity with place impacts not just on place attachment, but also on perceived safety and security which individuals and groups feel in a place (Sonti et al., 2020). For women, the loss of safe access to a place they have expressed attachment for requires either engaging in an environment they perceive as unsafe or developing connections with other places.

Where individuals do not develop such relationships, they lack emotional connection to place, and consequently tend not be active in improving or maintaining their surroundings (Buchecker et al., 2003; Manzo & Perkins, 2006). This is of heightened significance after forest fires, as engagement in stewardship and decision making has been identified not only for the benefit of the landscape, but also recuperation and regeneration of those impacted by dramatic landscape change (Burns et al., 2008). We must remember that there is no one size fits all, some may be deterred from reconnecting with their landscape through lack of tranquillity, others from hinderance of access or lack of security. Yet, the (re)attachment of individuals and groups to their places and landscapes is essential for the well-being of both individuals and communities.

If we do not address the plurality of the (loss of) attachment, then the landscape increasingly becomes the domain of a certain group who feel more secure and safe in the respective landscape, and who thus inform the discourse of what that landscape can become, defining the practices and activities which dominate in that area.

References

Alvarsson, J. J., Wiens, S., & Nilsson, M. E. (2010). Stress recovery during exposure to nature sound and environmental noise. *International Journal of Environmental Research and Public Health, 7*, 1036–1046.

Annerstedt, M., Jönsson, P., Wallergård, M., Johansson, G., Karlson, B., Grahn, P., Hansen, T. M., & Währborg, P. (2013). Inducing physiological stress recovery with sounds of nature in a virtual reality forest – Results from a pilot study. *Physiology and Behavior, 118*, 240–250.

Bradley, M. M., Codispoti, M., Sabatinelli, D., & Lang, P. J. (2001). Emotion and motivation II: Sex differences in picture processing. *Emotion, 1*, 300.

Brody, L. R., & Hall, J. A. (2010). Gender, emotion, and socialization. In *Handbook of gender research in psychology*. Springer.

Buchecker, M., Hunziker, M., & Kienast, F. (2003). Participatory landscape development: Overcoming social barriers to public involvement. *Landscape and Urban Planning, 64*, 29–46.

Burns, M., Taylor, J., & Hogan, J. (2008). Integrative healing: The importance of community collaboration in postfire recovery and prefire planning. In W. Martin, C. Raish, & B. Kent (Eds.), *Wildfire risk: Human perceptions and management implications*. RFF Press.

Butler, A., Sarlöv-Herlin, I., Knez, I., Ångman, E., Ode Sang, Å., & Åkerskog, A. (2018). Landscape identity, before and after a forest fire. *Landscape Research, 43*(6), 878–889.

Butler, A., Knez, I., Sarlöv-Herlin, I., Åkerskog, A., Sang, Å., & Ångman, E. (2019). Foraging for identity: The relationships between landscape activities and landscape identity after catastrophic landscape change. *Landscape Research, 44*(3), 303–319.

Butler, A., Ångman, E., Ode Sang, Å., Sarlöv-Herlin, I., Åkerskog, A., & Knez, I. (2021). "There will be mushrooms again": Foraging, landscape and forest fire. *Journal of Outdoor Recreation and Tourism, 33*, 100358.

Coeterier, J. F. (1996). Dominant attributes in the perception and evaluation of the Dutch landscape. *Landscape and Urban Planning, 34*, 27–44.

Davenport, M. A., & Anderson, D. H. (2005). Getting from sense of place to place-based management: An interpretive investigation of place meanings and perceptions of landscape change. *Society & Natural Resources, 18*, 625–641.

Dockerty, T., Lovett, A., Appleton, K., & Sunnenberg, G. (2001). *Climate change impacts on landscape: New approaches to visualising rural landscape change*. Jackson Environment Institute, University of East Anglia.

Eriksen, C. (2015). *Gender and wildfire: Landscapes of uncertainty*. Routledge.

Filova, L., Vojar, J., Svobodova, K., & Sklenicka, P. (2015). The effect of landscape type and landscape elements on public visual preferences: Ways to use knowledge in the context of landscape planning. *Journal of Environmental Planning and Management, 58*, 2037–2055.

Fornara, F., Lai, A. E., Bonaiuto, M., & Pazzaglia, F. (2019). Residential place attachment as an adaptive strategy for coping with the reduction of spatial abilities in old age. *Frontiers in Psychology, 10*. Article no. 856.

Gobster, P. H. (1999). An ecological aesthetic for forest landscape management. *Landscape Journal, 18*, 54–64.

Grossman, M., & Wood, W. (1993). Sex differences in intensity of emotional experience: A social role interpretation. *Journal of Personality and Social Psychology, 65*, 1010.

Gustafson, P. (2001). Roots and routes: Exploring the relationship between place attachment and mobility. *Environment and Behavior, 33*, 667–686.

Gustafsson, L., Berglind, M., Granström, A., Grelle, A., Isacsson, G., Kjellander, P., Larsson, S., Lindh, M., Pettersson, L. B., Strengbom, J., Stridh, B., Sävström, T., Thor, G., Wikars, L.-O., & Mikusiński, G. (2019). Rapid ecological response and intensified knowledge accumulation following a north European mega-fire. *Scandinavian Journal of Forest Research, 34*, 234–253.

Harshman, R. A., & Paivio, A. (1987). "Paradoxical" sex differences in self-reported imagery. *Canadian Journal of Psychology/Revue canadienne de psychologie, 41*(3), 287–302.

Hedblom, M., Heyman, E., Antonsson, H., & Gunnarsson, B. (2014). Bird song diversity influences young people's appreciation of urban landscapes. *Urban Forestry & Urban Greening, 13*, 469–474.

Hedblom, M., Knez, I., Gunnarsson, B., & Ode Sang, Å. (2017). Estimations of natural sounds in urban greenery: Potential impact for urban nature preservation. *Royal Society Open Science, 4*, 170037.

Hernández, B., Carmen Hidalgo, M., Salazar-Laplace, M. E., & Hess, S. (2007). Place attachment and place identity in natives and non-natives. *Journal of Environmental Psychology, 27*, 310–319.

Herzog, T. R., & Kutzli, G. E. (2002). Preference and perceived danger in field/forest settings. *Environment and Behavior, 34*, 819–835.

Heyman, E., Gunnarsson, B., Stenseke, M., Henningsson, S., & Tim, G. (2011). Openness as a key-variable for analysis of management trade-offs in urban woodlands. *Urban Forestry & Urban Greening, 10*, 281–293.

Hough, R. L. (2014). Biodiversity and human health: Evidence for causality? *Biodiversity and Conservation, 23*, 267–288.

Kaplan, R., & Kaplan, S. (1989). *The experience of nature*. Cambridge University Press.

Knez, I. (2006). Autobiographical memories for places. *Memory, 14*, 359–377.

Knez, I., Butler, A., Ode Sang, Å., Ångman, E., Sarlöv-Herlin, I., & Åkerskog, A. (2018). Before and after a natural disaster: Disruption in emotion component of place-identity and wellbeing. *Journal of Environmental Psychology, 55*, 11–17.

Knez, I., Willander, J., Butler, A., Ode Sang, Å., Sarlöv-Herlin, I., & Åkerskog, A. (2021). I can still see, hear and smell the fire: Cognitive, emotional and personal consequences of a natural disaster, and the impact of evacuation. *Journal of Environmental Psychology, 74*, 101554.

Koppen, G., Tveit, M. S., Ode Sang, Å., & Dramstad, W. (2014). The challenge of enhancing accessibility to recreational landscapes. *Norsk Geografisk Tidsskrift – Norwegian Journal of Geography, 68*, 145–154.

Kring, A. M., & Gordon, A. H. (1998). Sex differences in emotion: Expression, experience, and physiology. *Journal of Personality and Social Psychology, 74*, 686.

Lidskog, R., & Sjödin, D. (2018). Unintended consequences and risk(y) thinking: The shaping of consequences and responsibilities in relation to environmental disasters. *Sustainability, 10*, 2906.

Liebert, R. M., & Liebert, L. (1995). *Science and behavior. An introduction to methods of psychological research*. Prentice-Hall, Inc.

Lindemann-Matthies, P., Briegel, R., Schüpbach, B., & Junge, X. (2010). Aesthetic preference for a Swiss alpine landscape: The impact of different agricultural land-use with different biodiversity. *Landscape and Urban Planning, 98*, 99–109.

Lothian, A. (1999). Landscape and the philosophy of aesthetics: Is landscape quality inherent in the landscape or in the eye of the beholder? *Landscape and Urban Planning, 44*, 177–198.

Lovell, R., Wheeler, B. W., Higgins, S. L., Irvine, K. N., & Depledge, M. H. (2014). A systematic review of the health and Well-being benefits of biodiverse environments. *Journal of Toxicology and Environmental Health – Part B: Critical Reviews, 17*, 1–20.

Manzo, L. C., & Perkins, D. D. (2006). Finding common ground: The importance of place attachment to community participation and planning. *Journal of Planning Literature, 20*, 335–350.

Mcguigan, F. J. (1990). *Experimental psychology: Methods of research*. Prentice-Hall, Inc.

Nassauer, J. I. (1995). Messy ecosystems, orderly frames. *Landscape Journal, 14*, 161–170.

Neuvonen, M., Sievänen, T., Tönnes, S., & Koskela, T. (2007). Access to green areas and the frequency of visits – A case study in Helsinki. *Urban Forestry and Urban Greening, 6*, 235–247.

Norman, J., Annerstedt, M., Boman, M., & Mattsson, L. (2010). Influence of outdoor recreation on self-rated human health: Comparing three categories of Swedish recreationists. *Scandinavian Journal of Forest Research, 25*, 234–244.

Ode, Å., & Fry, G. (2002). Visual aspects in urban woodland management. *Urban Forestry and Urban Greening, 1*, 15–24.

Ode Sang, Å., & Tveit, M. S. (2013). Perceptions of stewardship in Norwegian agricultural land-scapes. *Land Use Policy, 31*, 557–564.

Ode Sang, Å., Hägerhäll, C., Miller, D., & Donaldson-Selby, G. (2014). The use of visualised land-scapes in order to challenge and develop theory in landscape preference research. In W. Hayek, P. Fricker, & E. Buhmann (Eds.), *Digital landscape architecture* (pp. 362–369). Wichmann.

Ode Sang, Å., Knez, I., Gunnarsson, B., & Hedblom, M. (2016). The effects of naturalness, gender, and age on how urban green space is perceived and used. *Urban Forestry and Urban Greening, 18*, 268–276.

Ode, Å., Fry, G., Tveit, M. S., Messager, P., & Miller, D. (2009). Indicators of perceived natural-ness as drivers of landscape preference. *Journal of Environmental Management, 90*, 375–383.

Onsten-Molander, A. (2016). *Landskapskaraktärsanalys för Västmanlands län* [Landscape char-acter analysis for Västmanlands County]. Länsstyrelsen i Västmanlands län. https://docplayer.se/24543835-Landskapskaraktarsanalys-for-vastmanlands-lan.html. Accessed 17 Feb 2022.

Palmer, J. F. (1997). Stability of landscape perceptions in the face of landscape change. *Landscape and Urban Planning, 37*, 109–113.

Palmer, J. F. (2004). Using spatial metrics to predict scenic perception in a changing landscape: Dennis, Massachusetts. *Landscape and Urban Planning, 69*(2–3), 201–218.

Purcell, A. T., & Lamb, R. J. (1998). Preference and naturalness: An ecological approach. *Landscape and Urban Planning, 42*, 57–66.

Rollero, C., & De Piccoli, N. (2010). Place attachment, identification and environment perception: An empirical study. *Journal of Environmental Psychology, 30*, 198–205.

Scannell, L., & Gifford, R. (2010). Defining place attachment: A tripartite organizing framework. *Journal of Environmental Psychology, 30*, 1–10.

Sevenant, M., & Antrop, M. (2010). The use of latent classes to identify individual differences in the importance of landscape dimensions for aesthetic preference. *Land Use Policy, 27*, 827–842.

Sheppard, S. R. J. (2001). Beyond visual resource management: Emerging theories of an ecologi-cal aesthetic and visible stewardship. In S. R. J. Sheppard & H. W. Harshaw (Eds.), *Forests and landscapes – Linking ecology, sustainability and aesthetics* (IUFRO Researh series, no 6) (pp. 149–173). CABI Publishing.

Sheppard, S. R. J., Shaw, A., Flanders, D., Burch, S., & Schroth, O. (2013). Bringing climate change science to the landscape level: Canadian experiences in using landscape visualisa-tion within participatory processes for community planning. In B. Fu & K. B. Jones (Eds.), *Landscape ecology for sustainable environment and culture* (pp. 121–143). Springer.

Sonti, N. F., Campbell, L. K., Svendsen, E. S., Johnson, M. L., & Novem Auyeung, D. S. (2020). Fear and fascination: Use and perceptions of new York City's forests, wetlands, and landscaped park areas. *Urban Forestry & Urban Greening, 49*, 126601.

Sreetheran, M., & Van Den Bosch, C. (2014). A socio-ecological exploration of fear of crime in urban green spaces – A systematic review. *Urban Forestry and Urban Greening, 13*, 1–18.

Stedman, R. C. (2003). Is it really just a social construction? The contribution of the physical envi-ronment to sense of place. *Society & Natural Resources, 16*, 671–685.

Strumse, E. (1996). Demographic differences in the visual preferences for agrarian landscapes in western Norway. *Journal of Environmental Psychology, 16*, 17–31.

Suzuki, R., Blackwood, J., Webster, N. J., & Shah, S. (2021). Functional limitations and perceived Neighborhood walkability among urban dwelling older adults. *Frontiers. Public Health, 9*, DOI.10.3389/fpubh.2021.675799.

Svobodova, K., Sklenicka, P., Molnarova, K., & Salek, M. (2012). Visual preferences for physical attributes of mining and post-mining landscapes with respect to the sociodemographic charac-teristics of respondents. *Ecological Engineering, 43*, 34–44.

Swedish Environmental Objectives Council (SEOC). (2009). Sweden's environmental objec-tives in brief. *Environmental Objective Council*, Stockholm, Sweden. https://www.government.se/49b75e/contentassets/a13cbca67aef4a12aac9e2792ca494ef/swedens-environmental-objectives%2D%2D-new-perspectives-sou-200983. Accessed 12 Feb 2022.

Swedish Forestry Act (SFS). (1979). *Swedish forestry act* [Online]. http://www.riksdagen.se/sv/Dokument-Lagar/Lagar/Svenskforfattningssamling/Skogsvardslag-1979429_sfs-1979-429/?bet=1979:429. Accessed 12 Feb 2022.

Swedish Forestry Act (SFS). (1993). *Skogsvårdsförordning* [Forest Management Ordinance]. http://www.riksdagen.se/sv/Dokument-Lagar/Lagar/Svenskforfattningssamling/_sfs-1993-1096/. Accessed 12 Feb 2022.

Toman, E., Stidham, M., Mccaffrey, S., & Shindler, B. (2013). *Social science at the wildland-urban Interface: A compendium of research results to create fire-adapted communities.* United States Department of Agriculture Forest Service, Northern Research Station.

Tveit, M. S. (2009). Indicators of visual scale as predictors of landscape preference; a comparison between groups. *Journal of Environmental Management, 90*, 2882–2888.

Tveit, M., Ode, Å., & Fry, G. (2006). Key concepts in a framework for analysing visual landscape character. *Landscape Research, 31*, 229–255.

Twigger-Ross, C., & Uzzell, D. (1996). Place and identity processes. *Journal of Environmental Psychology, 16*, 205–220.

Van Herzele, A., & Wiedemann, T. (2003). A monitoring tool for the provision of accessible and attractive urban green spaces. *Landscape and Urban Planning, 63*, 109–126.

Viollon, S., Lavandier, C., & Drake, C. (2002). Influence of visual setting on sound ratings in an urban environment. *Applied Acoustics, 63*, 493–511.

Zoderer, B. M., Tasser, E., Erb, K. H., Lupo Stanghellini, P. S., & Tappeiner, U. (2016). Identifying and mapping the tourists' perception of cultural ecosystem services: A case study from an alpine region. *Land Use Policy, 56*, 251–261.

Part III
Sustainable Planning and Territorial Identities Enhancing Place Attachment

Chapter 11
Urban and Rural Dynamics Between Economy and Place Attachment. The Case Study of the Region of Sardinia (Italy)

Anna Maria Colavitti ⓘ **and Sergio Serra** ⓘ

11.1 Introduction

The socio-economic changes of the last twenty years have had a great impact not only on production dynamics but also on social ones. In the current context of globalisation, widespread use of technology and predominance of the symbolic and immaterial aspects of products and services, the communities (especially the urban ones, but also the so-called rural communities and, in part, those outside the common schemes of urbanisation) have been exposed to profound changes in the ways of working, consuming, and socialising. One of the several consequences has been an important redefinition of the relationship between the citizen and the territory. Territorial attachment seems to play an essential role in defining place consciousness and thus in establishing civic sense.

Therefore, place attachment can be linked to the practices of citizenship that have a significant influence on how places are produced and how planning tools are designed. In this direction, it is possible to reflect on the relationship between the city and the countryside, which has historically represented a contradictory, as much as unresolved, area of conflict that favours one side or the other.

Historically, the relationship between city and countryside has always been an unbalanced one. On the one hand, the countryside has conditioned the city's possibility of survival; on the other hand, the city, by initiating alternative production mechanisms and innovation processes since the industrial revolution, has made it possible for the countryside to have advantages, but has given the way to large-scale, massive production. In recent times, these relations have been modified, with

A. M. Colavitti (✉) · S. Serra
DICAAR, Department of Civil and Environmental Engineering and Architecture, University of Cagliari, Cagliari, Italy
e-mail: amcolavt@unica.it; sergioserra@unica.it

© The Author(s), under exclusive license to Springer Nature
Switzerland AG 2022
O.-R. Ilovan, I. Markuszewska (eds.), *Preserving and Constructing Place Attachment in Europe*, GeoJournal Library 131,
https://doi.org/10.1007/978-3-031-09775-1_11

the introduction of a new way of considering the urban/rural connection. This is due to some strategic visions that place bioregionalism theories and place attachment at the centre of the reflections and interests of scholars from various backgrounds. The bioregional philosophy has been proposed as an alternative to the perceived failures of state-centred approaches. The management of natural resources on a bioregional scale is a way to improve the connection of communities and their place attachment with the governance of their local environment.

From the point of view of spatial planning and urbanism, the way to interpret this change focuses on adapting planning techniques to improve the tools for managing the territory and the urban-rural landscape and to better regulate the policies linked to them. Our study highlights these changes, illustrating the processes that have led to the most important modifications of the urban/rural relationship inside the planning instruments at local scale. The research aims to analyse the influence of urban and territorial planning on place attachment, in particular if it adopts approaches and strategies aimed at protecting and enhancing place identity and attachment. The final result allows to understand how participation methodologies in the planning tools could contribute to the improvement of place attachment and solve some important critical issues.

11.2   Conceptual Framework

Place attachment is based on the psychological, social, and spatial dimensions of the everyday life of people in their context. Social networks are considered a precondition for place attachment, in which place memory can be threatened by emerging instabilities and uncertainties (Low & Altman, 1992). Citizens can increase their sense of place, influencing public policy in directions of greater social involvement by refining the public decision-making process. Recently, there has been less community involvement in public decision-making processes due to a general difficulty in participating in the decision-making arena, including an absence of public discussion of landscape issues and public projects initiatives. The crisis of politics at the European and perhaps global level affects the state systems eroded by globalisation (Campbell & Hall, 2021) and undermines the construction of the sense of belonging, favouring the measurement of their importance based on gross domestic product (GDP).

In contrast to this view, several studies since the beginning of the 2008 financial crisis have identified the weaknesses of the metrics in use and suggested the need to set up appropriate indicators to capture the changes that mature capitalism has imprinted on post-industrial societies. In fact, GDP does not record such evolutions and merely reports expansion and contraction without illustrating the elements of community well-being or malaise (Stiglitz et al., 2021). On the other hand, these elements can determine a deficit in the organisation of community action and the recomposition of social relationships that have been extinguished by the negative effects of capitalism. How can we reconstruct what has been lost?

Community action is a key component of place attachment because participation in public decision-making that affects a given population's area of interest, demonstrates the existence of place attachment that can be strengthened through citizen engagement activities in the planning process (Falanga, 2022; Hafer & Ran, 2016). However, there is still a lack of relevant literature and research that deals with the relationship between participatory planning and community place attachment.

Assuming that place attachment is the consequence of extensive participatory dynamics and, without going back to Arnstein (1969) who anticipated the levels of citizen participation in the design of social policies, we can imagine that the principles of community place attachment of the last generation are assimilable to the landscape theme (Manzo & Devine Wright, 2014). The importance of the territory to which one belongs and, even more so, the learning of the structural conditions at the basis of the processes, cannot be separated from the relationship between knowledge and experience. At the basis of landscape planning there are paradigms of values that correspond to practices of space use specific to a given community. The theoretical framework related to the landscape values of the community is, occasionally, updated and consolidated at the time of the adaptation of local planning tools that greatly extend the framework of interests and areas of interference in which the community is recognised. In this way, the social capital increases its importance and strengthens the resilience of the community, dealing with desertification and depopulation, which are now a constant condition in many European regions (European Commission, 2018).

11.3 Bridging the Gap Between Town and Country

The countryside has influenced the possibility of the city's survival and, on the other hand, the city, by initiating alternative production mechanisms and innovation processes since the industrial revolution, has guaranteed many advantages to the rural communities. The relationship between urban and rural areas has been historically unbalanced but the processes of globalisation has further accentuated this condition, promoting massive production on a large scale. In the pre-industrial era, the city takes advantage of the resources of the countryside (consumer city), while in the industrial period, the city assumes a dominant role. According to Mumford (1938, p. 3), "Every phase of life in the countryside contributes to the existence of cities".

Building development, since the second post-war period, has driven a progressive and continuous urbanisation of the territory, without any correlation with the quantitative population growth, which has radically changed the rural landscape, in which the interrelation of anthropic and natural factors generates complex and dynamic territorial systems (Agnoletti, 2014; Fanfani, 2006; Poli, 2020). Urban and rural spaces are contexts with almost different characteristics, that cannot in any way be dissociated (Santangelo, 2018). Both are the result of an ongoing process of "social" production of space, whose history dates back to the origin of the agricultural activity that affected deeply the natural landscape (Sereni, 1986). The relationship between territory, resources and populations is a key indicator for interpreting the state of development. City and countryside are traditionally seen as distinct and opposed concepts, as two different and irreconcilable worlds, two modes of social organisation. This is an extremely erroneous image, because agriculture and urban economy are closely linked and, in fact, there is a direct correlation in history between agricultural productivity and urbanisation (Martinotti, 2017).

The spatial organisation and the constitution of places represent a kind of collective and individual practices. Communities, and everyone who is part of them, have the need to establish relationships and a complex identity, composed of a shared identity (of a group as a whole), a particular identity (of a certain group or individual with respect to others) and an individual identity (of the individual or group as dissimilar to all others). We introduce the concept of 'anthropological place' (Augé, 1992), a real and symbolic construction of spaces to which refer all the people who live there. Anthropological places have identity, relational and historical characteristics. Several distinct and individual elements can coexist in the same place, but their mutual relationships and shared identity cannot be neglected. A space that cannot define itself as identity, relational and historical will be defined as a "non-place". Globalisation is a producer of anthropological non-places and does not integrate ancient places into itself, delimiting them and classifying them as places of memory (Augé, 1992).

The processes of globalisation have generated serious imbalances in the relations of production and consumption between the city and the countryside and the emergencies linked to the environmental and climate crisis make it even more necessary to reconsider the socio-economic development strategies for the territory.

This relation of dependence was clearly underlined by Mumford: "Ecologically speaking, the city and countryside are a single unit; if one can do without the other, it is the country, not the city, the farmer, not the burgher" (Mumford, 1938, p. 68). Today, in the post-industrial era, the relevance of environmental processes is clear, both in the countryside and in the urban areas. The recognition of the biological and ecosystem value of soil and its role in the protection of public health has not arrested the phenomenon of land-take, which damages large agricultural areas suitable for food production and destructures the urban form.

The problem does not only affect areas with a high degree of urbanisation or densely populated, but also involves rural areas, which in Europe represent over 80% of the territory and have more than 30% of the total population. In addition, rural areas have the lowest shares of the European population within age groups below 50 years (European Commission, 2018). The economic crisis is most evident in rural areas, especially in those that are marginalised and disadvantaged, leading to a process of abandonment, in addition to depopulation due to a reduced birth rate. The percentage of population at risk of poverty and social exclusion is higher in rural areas than in towns and cities (Eurostat, 2018). The fact that many people still populate these disadvantaged areas is probably explained by a strong sense of place attachment and sense of community, rather than quality of life and job opportunities.

The case study of the Region of Sardinia is useful in order to investigate the influence of place attachment and identity on social and economic dynamics between urban and rural areas, in both historical and contemporary perspectives (Ortu, 2014). Our aim is to outline some strategic visions, based on bioregionalist principles (Fanfani, 2020; Magnaghi, 2020), which focus on the management of natural resources to create a new balance between economy, community, and territory, encouraging sustainable growth and improving local quality of life. In this direction the conservation of agricultural biodiversity is a way to enhance the ecosystem services provisions, ensuring the welfare and an adequate quality of life, and supporting the local agricultural chains. However, at the same time, the "return to the land" could support a regional economy in crisis, promoting local processes of self-determination and contributing to restore a new balance between communities and places, preserving and strengthening local identity and attachment to place.

11.4   Population, Territory, and Economy in the Region of Sardinia

Low population density has historically been a peculiar characteristic of the Sardinian territory and, since the nineteenth century, this has been at the centre of the socio-economic condition of the island. To the same static and underdeveloped economy is partly attributable the tendency to late and limited marriage and the brake on population growth, adopted preventively and voluntarily by the Sardinian population (Corridore, 1902). Since the unification of Italy, the national process of demographic transition also involved Sardinia, where there was a marked demographic growth, until the 1990s. However, this growth was not uniform in all areas of the island. Between the census of 1951 and that of 2011, the percentage of municipalities in demographic decline was about 60%, 228 municipalities out of 377, and more than a third of these (35.5%) recorded a decrease of more than 40%. Hopeless attempts to keep residents in these areas used welfare assistance, following the myth of preserving the inner areas (Sabattini, 2017). In the last decades, Sardinia registered a progressive population decrease: the number of residents amounted to 1,611,621, in December 2019, with a loss of 27,741 inhabitants compared to the 2011 census (ISTAT Permanent Census Data).

The phenomenon of depopulation affects especially some areas of Sardinia, as evidenced by the study "Municipalities in extinction. The scenarios of depopulation in Sardinia", commissioned by the Region of Sardinia in 2013, with the goal of analysing the state of "demographic health" of the Sardinian municipalities. The results are quite worrying, considering that only 148 municipalities out of 377 are in a condition of good demographic health. On the contrary, 101 municipalities are in a critical condition (28.4% of the territory and 24.1% of the regional population) and the remaining 128 municipalities in a very critical or serious condition (26.6% of the territory and 8.5% of the regional population) (Regione Sardegna, 2013).

From a territorial point of view, there is an increase in population in coastal areas and a greater attractiveness of the southern part of the island, while the municipalities that are experiencing depopulation dynamics, usually with a population of less than 3000 inhabitants, are largely located in the mountains or hills. On the contrary, the municipalities in good health are mainly coastal, located in the plains or hills, and have a population of over 3000 inhabitants. In addition, there is a progressive increase in the population's aging, supported by the strong decline in the birth rate, with an average age of the population that increased from 29 years, at the date of the 1951 census, to 44 years in 2011 (Regione Sardegna, 2013).

The 1861 census highlighted the limited presence, almost an absence, of a scattered population: only 6.3% of the Sardinian population lived in isolated houses and farms, characteristic elements of the rural world, while on a national level, it represents on average 32%. Even today, the dispersed habitat constitutes a marginal phenomenon, although the dispersed population increased to 9.5% in 1911 and decreased to 4% in 2001 (Breschi, 2012). In the second half of the twentieth century, the process of population concentration had an intense rate both for the dissolution of the rural economy and for the disordered densification of the settlement pattern of the valley floors, with the formation of peripheral landscapes of "urbanised countryside" (Breschi, 2012).

A limited urban development, consisting mainly of centres of minor relevance, was highlighted in the 1940s by the French geographer Maurice Le Lannou, that described landscapes extensively covered by Mediterranean scrub. The main settlement was Cagliari, the regional capital, a cosmopolitan urban centre connected, with relations of exchange, to the mainland. In addition, Sassari is described as a large rural village with a good supply of urban services and an economy based on agricultural activities. The weakness of urban development is also linked to the lack of internal road system and connections with the mainland, also because of few port facilities along the coasts. The geography of Sardinia is characterised by the presence of the massive central mountains, with territorial areas often totally fragmented by the rivers, making difficult the realisation of a network of road and railway infrastructures, considering the high costs and technical difficulties (La Marmora, 1997; Le Lannou, 1978). Also, the industrial system is very weak, with a low working-class population, structured into small craft enterprises.

In mid-twentieth century, Sardinia was an old rural country characterised by strong isolation that contributed to preserve the archaism of social and economic organisation, customs, languages, and traditions. At that time, tourism had not yet become established in Sardinia and, except for the mining industry, the economic activities were able to preserve ancient landscapes substantially unaltered (Colavitti et al., 2021). Some extensive landscape transformations were introduced during the Fascist period, with the planning of new roads and the realisation of works of reclamation of marshy areas, as well as the creation of rural colonies and a new city (Le Lannou, 1978).

The different environmental and geographical conditions and specificities generate territorial frameworks full of local features and characters, even in the high mountain areas where the population is extremely scarce. Over the centuries, the public interventions to promote the economic development of the island strongly conditioned the territorial distribution of the population and the demographic and settlement dynamics. For example, with agrarian reclamation plans of the years 1920–1938 and with the successive agrarian reform of the years 1952–1956, the recovery of new lands to cultivate determined the consequent internal population redistribution. Even the reclamation works of the second post-war period allowed the eradication of malaria in some plains of the island which remained uninhabited for centuries, enabling the appearance of new settlement developments.

Further initiatives of urban and rural territorial organisation, encouraged by projects for the strengthening of the infrastructural system, allowed the constitution of new communities, on the model of agricultural villages, with the demographic plan of La Nurra and the territorial plan of Sarrabus. The crisis in southern Italy, which also hit Sardinia between 1955 and 1960, contributed to the depopulation of peripheral and mountain territories and the massive transfer of population to the cities. This process was further emphasised by the political attention given to the industrial sector, neglecting the agricultural sector which had been damaged by the excessive fragmentation of land ownership and the backwardness of agricultural techniques and entrepreneurial skills (Clemente, 1964).

The Plan of Rebirth of 1962 launched an important process of industrialisation and modernisation of the Sardinian economic and productive system, which also affected the population dynamics, despite the specific endemic conditions (Colavitti, 2020). The settlement structure of Sardinia had remained substantially unchanged since the unification of Italy until the 1970s. Even the process of modernisation of the social and productive structure did not produce significant changes, with many small urban agglomerations distributed throughout the territory and the growth of some urban centres in coastal areas, with the development of non-agricultural activities. The persistence of the territorial dispersion of settlements suggests a socioeconomic disadvantage, in which the weak development of the tourist industry determines a break in the historical relationship between inland and coastal areas. Coastal settlements, considered more equipped with urban services, have become poles of demographic attraction at the expense of inland areas, whose economies are still based on agriculture and farming (Sabattini, 2017).

11.5   The Rural Areas of Sardinia: Demographic Decline and Economic Development

Sardinia still appears as a low populated territory, characterised by a condition of overall and widespread rurality, and few relevant urban areas (Colavitti et al., 2021). The transformations driven by tourism development, in some parts of the Region, have resulted in the creation of urban poles characterised by an intermediate population density, as for example the north-eastern part of the island. However, there are no real metropolitan cities, although two densely populated areas can be identified in the conurbations of Cagliari and Sassari.

An important part of the territory falls into the category of inner areas (318 municipalities out of a total of 377), which account for over 50% of the regional population. The inner areas are weak and marginal territories, far from the main centres which deliver essential services, but they are rich in important environmental and cultural resources, highly diversified by nature and processes of anthropisation. Within the framework of innovative national policies for development and territorial cohesion, the National Strategy for Inland Areas (SNAI 2014) aims to overcome the marginalisation and demographic decline of inner areas, adopting a place-based approach and multi-level governance to address the needs of territories characterised by significant disadvantages of geographical or demographic nature. The project invests in the promotion and protection of the wealth of the territory and local communities, enhancing their natural and cultural resources, creating new employment circuits and new opportunities, also to counteract demographic decline.

After the Second World War, a remarkably unbalanced redistribution of inhabitants in the territory started, leading to profound changes in the settlement dynamics (Colavitti et al., 2021). The rapid process of urbanisation, in the coastal areas of the island, took place in addition to some modernisation initiatives of the economic system, which further contributed to the depopulation of inland municipalities. Although the Sardinian context is characterised by a very low tendency to change socio-cultural variables, compared to more developed areas, the settlement centres of the coast became poles of demographic attraction against those of the inland areas, with consequent changes in established cultural patterns and pre-existing life (Sabattini, 2017).

The phenomenon of denatality and ageing of the population affects a large part of the regional territory and in particular areas with greater development delays and economic backwardness. Demographic projections suggest the risk of disappearance of several municipalities and the hypothesis of a decline in the Sardinian population of almost 10% over the next thirty years. This risk of disappearance mainly concerns municipalities located in the hills and mountains, with a resident population of less than 1000 inhabitants. The scenario that is predicted, in a close time horizon, concerns settlement patterns of long duration, such as rural villages, which represent a presidium to protect the physical structure of the territory, whose disappearance would result in a serious loss of local identity that will irreversibly change the face of Sardinia.

The factors underlying the dynamics of depopulation are heterogeneous. The emigration of residents, especially young people, in search of job opportunities and services, is one of the main causes of the progressive population aging. Territorial abandonment is stimulated by the inadequacy of services and infrastructure and the reduction of job, income, health, and education opportunities (Bottazzi, 2015). The social and economic changes, consequent to the implementation of the intervention policy started in Sardinia at the beginning of the 1950s, had relevant consequences on the urban structure, which would deserve a more careful and in-depth investigation. The downsizing of the agricultural sector and the development of the service sector have imprinted extensive transformations to the ancient social and economic structure of the island, with the transfer of part of the population employed in primary production activities to the public administration and industry. The loss of the youngest population has led to a further aging of the communities in the internal areas (Colavitti, 2020; Sabattini, 2017).

The economic system of the island is now characterised by the development of the tourism sector, which provides support to manufacturing, crafts and services. Agricultural activity is now showing some slight signs of renewal, after a long period of stagnation and difficulty. The primary sector has a 4% share of the total investment in the region, higher than the Italian average (2.6%), with significant increase in recent years. In 2019, 23.9% of the regional companies operated in agriculture. This is a higher level than the average for the South (19.8%) and the Centre-North (11.5%). However, the high presence of agro-pastoral enterprises is associated with their small size (CRENOS, 2021). Also, pastoralism was affected, in the last twenty years, by deep structural changes that included the establishment of farms, the abandonment of transhumance, the increasingly widespread of permanent settlements in the plains and hills previously cultivated. Therefore, a process of rebirth of farms in the abandoned inner areas took place. Pastoralism represents a sustainable system in a period of environmental crisis to produce material and immaterial goods. The evolution of the agro-pastoral systems of Sardinia, from the fifties of the last century to the current configuration, highlights the local practices of space and resource management, the forms of economic production, as well as the endogenous and exogenous factors that have led to changes and adaptations in the use of agricultural resources and natural pastures. The complementarity between agriculture and pastoralism was also related to the use of common lands, communal and/or encumbered by civic use, in a system of resource management strongly oriented to ensure an internal balance of the local community (Meloni & Farinella, 2015).

11.6   Place identity and Attachment in the Sardinian Landscapes

Sardinia is not excluded from the processes of globalisation and the cycles of the world economy, which are increasing over time the economic dependence of the island on the outside, on global markets, also because of the rupture of the long-term relationship among population, activities, and territory. The landscape is the result of a complex interaction among nature and history, places, and peoples, and represents the main resource on which to base a sustainable and self-resilient economic development. At the same time, the landscape is a fragile resource, subject to conflict between a civilisation, strongly rooted in history and places, and an inevitable process of contamination and influence of imported and allochthonous economic and urban models that determine the progressive erosion of territorial heritage. The Regional Landscape Plan (RLP, 2006) recognised this rupture of the biunivocal community-territory relationship in Sardinia, leading to a crisis of belonging and the inability to 'produce landscape' as a collective and shared living space in continuity with historically consolidated modes. Globalisation determines fast and continuous changes in local territorial systems, historically characterised by the inactivity and permanence of long-lasting landscape units.

In this direction the RLP focuses on identity and cultural values that make up the landscape of Sardinia, a complex and extremely vulnerable asset that is the result of thousands of years of interaction between man and nature. This long-lasting process has led to the integration of the character of places and people's identity, progressively improving place attachment. Identity plays also an essential role for an effective participation (Hafer & Ran, 2016). The landscape protection involves preserving the identity and the memory of its inhabitants both in the coastal areas subject to strong speculative pressures and in the inner areas that are abandoned.

This is a topic that urban planning must necessarily deal with, to implement the principles of the RLP, contributing to create a "map of places", in which to identify the factors of permanence, long duration and conservation, that represent the community's identity, together with the process of change, innovation and development. The study of collective social and cultural identity processes in reference to specific territories is essential in the drafting of a plan. The analysis of the cycles of territorialisation must consider the peculiar cultural identity of each historical society, which is relevant to understand the fundamental values of cities and territories. The risk of overlooking collective socio-cultural identities is that planning could fail, since it must be based on a detailed knowledge of the anthropic component. The investigation of the social model requires the passage from the observation of the existence of a consciousness of belonging to the verification of an identity and of the continuity and temporal rupture in the long term and whether there is a social model tending towards self-preservation and self-reproduction (Carle, 2020).

A first attempt of this innovative approach can be identified in the analytical structure of the RLP. The study of the regional territory is articulated into three main interpretations, from which the elements that make up its identity emerge: environmental, historical-cultural, and settlement. The analysis aimed at identifying the rules to be established so that the values (and disvalues) of each part of the territory are protected from the point of view of what nature (environmental aspect), the sedimentation of history and culture (historical-cultural aspect), the territorial organisation (settlement aspect) have given to the process of landscape construction. As highlighted in the RLP report, the community-territory relationship can be found in the settlement pattern, for example in the small centres and in the dense parcellation of their territories in the well-drained areas of the hills, or in the larger centres and much more widespread territories in the mountains or in the open field landscapes.

Another important relationship that characterises Sardinia concerns the agricultural and pastoral worlds, two different aspects of the economic use of the territorial resources, that is clearly recognisable in the landscape's differences among the plain and the mountain, the fertile areas of plains and hills and the traditional spaces of pastoral nomadism. This relationship was relevant in the past, but it is still present in some parts of Sardinia and represents a key component of place attachment, put at risk by the economic conveniences linked to the phenomena of globalisation.

It is not just a matter of identifying systems of values, but of reconstructing the inhabitants' place attachment, whether in mountain settlements suffering from depopulation or in coastal settlements that are inhabited only for a few months a year. The RLP considered the landscape of Sardinia as the identity of the regional territory, underlining its role as a driver of local development of the communities and as a competitive resource. In recent decades, the relationship between community and territory in Sardinia has been in crisis, in the sensitive areas of the regional territorial heritage, especially in the coastal one. This has compromised the advancement of an innovative 'development model' based on a new pact between community and environment, able to enhance the system of local differences and identity characters.

A strong limitation of the RLP is the particular interest in the coastal strip and the lack of extension, after more than fifteen years, to the inner and rural areas of the island. Rural landscapes have peculiar characteristics in terms of biophysical, geophysical, and historical-cultural connotations, in which agricultural, zootechnical and/or sylvicultural productions are carried out. The landscape value of such areas is also conferred by anthropic elements such as terracing, suburban gardens, the organisation of crops, land reclamation or agrarian reforms. The Regional Landscape Plan can contribute to identify possible virtuous co-evolutions between landscapes inherited from past generations and new investments in the territory, safeguarding the existing relationships between the characteristics of rural settlements and their historical and cultural contexts. On the one hand, the RLP has introduced into the planning system the theme of local identity, as a value to be preserved and strengthened through actions and strategies focused on material and immaterial components. It does not refer directly to place attachment and does not propose to evaluate it in the following phase of local planning. However, it emphasises the importance of participation in identifying the system of identity values on which the landscape projects should be based in local planning. For these reasons, the research on municipal urban plans has only checked for the presence or absence of the concept of place attachment and of measures implicitly aimed at strengthening this component.

The communities' participation in the planning process is necessary both at the regional level of the RLP and at the local level, within the framework of municipal urban plans. Participation makes it possible to highlight, particularly at the local scale, the level of belonging to the territory and identification with the sense of place developed by local populations. One of the biggest difficulties for the planner is to understand the level of place attachment and to investigate the relationship between community and place, that could support the definition of local planning strategies and projects.

Our research has analysed 29 municipal urban plans, which incorporated the guidelines of the RLP, in order to check:

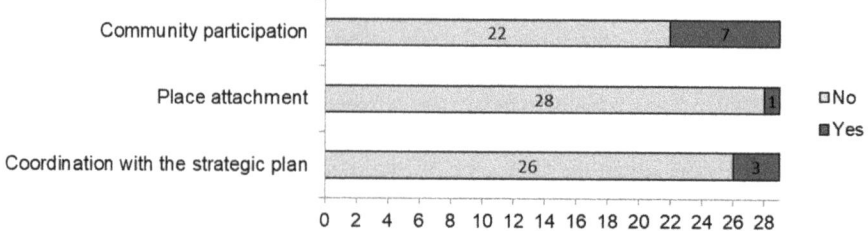

Fig. 11.1 Main results of the analysis of urban local plans already adapted to the RLP. (Source: Authors' elaboration)

- community participation, which refers to the use of participatory methodologies for drafting the plan, with approaches aimed at assessing place attachment (e.g., parish map);
- place attachment (i.e., explicit reference to the concept of place attachment) or the development of analyses, interpretations, and strategies for its enhancement;
- coordination with the strategic plan, based essentially on the outcomes of an intensive participatory activity, the results of which are sometimes used by the urban plan to define the objectives framework and to develop specific projects.

Figure 11.1 shows the results of the analysis, indicating only the number of urban plans in which each of the three components can be identified.

Our research on local plans has shown a serious lack of information and investigation concerning community participation in the planning process. In most of the urban plans currently updated to the Regional Landscape Plan and adopted by local authorities, there are no references to participatory activities that have supported planning choices (76% of plans). Even less consideration is given to place attachment, which is not mentioned in the urban plans. In addition, there is no evidence of indirect analyses of local identity that lead to actions aimed at strengthening communities' attachment to the territory.

In the few cases in which the plan documents refer to local community participation, these practices are represented by public meetings and communication initiatives of decisions and planning choices already adopted. On the other hand, the decision of some municipal administrations (10% of them) to coordinate the urban planning process with the drafting of the strategic plan, which is based more on consultation with the community, can be considered interesting. Spatial planning uses the participatory activities implemented by the strategic planning process to support the definition of strategies and projects.

11.7   Conclusions and Research Perspectives

Place attachment is connected to the relationships among communities, forms of life, traditions, institutions, and the territory (Banini & Ilovan, 2021). Analysing the historical evolution of the territorialisation process that has characterised the context of the Region of Sardinia, a progressive loss of identity and sense of belonging of the community is highlighted, resulting from the breaking of some historical relationships between economy, population, and places. This is one of the most important contemporary issues that also the planning, at different levels, must deal with. There are territories that have lost, in whole or in part, the sense of their evolution and of the continuity of their history (RLP, 2006). The regional landscape planning has an important role in the reconstruction of the unity between the inhabitants and their territory and of the relationship between local societies and space.

The complex production of living space has common features and material cultures that refer to the time and the history of the communities of the historical rural landscapes. The permanence of even the smallest signs of the humanisation of the rural territory, from the old and new landscapes of agriculture and pastoralism to the paths of the hunters in the wooded areas, now depends to the presence of a community that cares for and supports their maintenance. Local landscape projects should ensure the survival of small communities, affected by processes of depopulation and abandonment of many agricultural practices.

The consciousness of belonging is a manifestation of the feeling of attachment to a particular world, a feeling that is part of a collective human behaviour. The place identity has potential for a new model of development, linked to the indissoluble unity of the population and territory. The sense of identity in a given territory is configured over a long historical period, as a combination of identified social models or even as a single social model capable of self-reproduction (Carle, 2020).

The role of place attachment is seen in terms of effectiveness mainly at the landscape scale and not at the local scale because it is a theme that discusses elements and evaluations referable both to the objective and 'material' dimension - it's being a set of physical elements - and to the subjective and 'immaterial' dimension, concerning the values and meanings attributed to it. Its ambivalence, both individual and collective, is a key issue for the territory and the landscape.

Place attachment could motivate community participation in planning. In doing so, it aims to shape the community action. Research results highlight that place attachment is driven not only by physical places, but also by people and communities. Although it is difficult to fit into the different levels of the planning system, the cognitive and affective dimensions of place attachment can act as motivator for community participation in planning and capability resource for local plans, also beyond the municipal boundaries (Moore, 2021).

Place attachment and place identity have not emerged in community planning and development processes due to a lack of interdisciplinary collaboration between psychological disciplines, which focus on individual experiences and meanings, and planners who study place attachment and identity. While looking at place, planners usually used to examine neighbourhood-level dynamics and macro structural forces but do not often look at personal experiences and place attachments. A more holistic and ecological perspective can help overcome this kind of division between research and practice, integrating different approaches to better understand the values of a community and how the meanings of place can be reinforced in the planning process (Manzo & Perkins, 2006).

References

Agnoletti, M. (2014). Rural landscape, nature conservation and culture: Some notes on research trends and management approaches from a (southern) European perspective. *Landscape and Urban Planning, 126*, 66–73.

Arnstein, S. R. (1969). A ladder of citizen participation. *Journal of the American Planning Association, 35*(4), 216–224.

Augé, M. (1992). *Nonluoghi*. Eleuthera.

Banini, T., & Ilovan, O. R. (2021). *Representing place and territorial identities in Europe. Discourses, images, and practices*. Springer.

Bottazzi, G. (2015). Variabili demografiche e sviluppo locale. Considerazioni sullo spopolamento in Sardegna. In B. Meloni (Ed.), *Aree interne e progetti d'area* (pp. 77–88). Rosenberg & Sellier.

Breschi, M. (2012). Il singolare percorso della transizione demografica in Sardegna. In B. M. Breschi (Ed.), *Dinamiche demografiche in Sardegna tra passato e futuro* (pp. 13–32). Forum, Editrice Universitaria Udinese.

Campbell, J. L., & Hall, J. H. (2021). *The world of states*. Cambridge University Press.

Carle, L. (2020). La costruzione sociale del territorio. Antropologia storica e territori. In M. De Marchi & H. K. Zadeh (Eds.), *Territori post-rurali. Genealogie e prospettive* (pp. 77–91). Officina edizioni.

Clemente, F. (1964). *La pianificazione territoriale in Sardegna*. Edizioni Gallizzi.

Colavitti, A. M. (2020). Riflessioni a margine del Laboratorio del Cammino in Sardegna. Ripartire dal territorio contro la deriva dello spopolamento. In L. Lazzarini & S. Marchionni S. (Eds.), *Spazi e corpi in movimento. Fare urbanistica in cammino* (pp. 235–252). Edizioni SdT.

Colavitti, A. M., Ilovan, O. R., Mutică, P., & Serra, S. (2021). Rural areas as actors in the project of regional systems. A comparison between Sardinia and the north-west development region of Romania. *Contesti, 2*(2), 209–234.

Corridore, F. (1902). *Storia documentata della popolazione di Sardegna (1479–1901)*. Carlo Clausen.

CRENOS. (2021). *Economia della Sardegna. 28° Rapporto*. Arkadia Editore.

De Rossi, A. (Ed.). (2018). *Riabitare l'Italia. Le aree interne tra abbandoni e riconquiste*. Donzelli Editore.

European Commission. (2018). *EU rural areas in number*. https://ec.europa.eu/info/strategy/priorities-2019-2024/new-push-european-democracy/long-term-vision-rural-areas/eu-rural-areas-numbers_en. Accessed Feb 2022.

Eurostat (2018). *Living conditions in Europe*. https://ec.europa.eu/eurostat/web/products-eurostat-news/-/edn-20180207-1. Accessed Feb 2022.

Falanga, R. (2022). Understanding place attachment through the lens of urban regeneration. *Insights from Lisbon. Cities, 122*, 1–5.

Fanfani, D. (2006). Il governo del territorio e del paesaggio rurale nello spazio "terzo" periurbano. Il parco agricolo come strumento di politiche e di progetto. *Ri-Vista Ricerche per la progettazione del paesaggio, 6*, 54–59.

Fanfani, D. (2020). Looking forward: Some opportunities and challenges for bioregional planning in current policies and planning framework. In D. Fanfani & A. Matarán Ruiz (Eds.), *Bioregional planning and design: Volume I. perspectives on a transitional century* (pp. 183–191). Springer Nature.

Hafer, J. A., & Ran, B. (2016). Developing a citizen perspective of public participation: Identity construction as citizen motivation to participate. *Administrative Theory & Praxis, 38*(3), 206–222. https://doi.org/10.1080/10841806.2016.1202080

ISTAT, Il Censimento permanente della popolazione in Sardegna. Prima diffusione dei dati definitivi 2018 e 2019. https://www.istat.it/it/files//2021/02/Censimento-permanente-della-popolazione_Sardegna.pdf. Accessed Feb 2022.

La Marmora, A.F. (1997). (translated by M.G. Longhi). *Itinerario dell'Isola di Sardegna*, Nuoro: Illisso. First edition: La Marmora, A.F. (1860). *Itinéraire de l'Ile de Sardaigne, pour faire suite au Voyage en cette contrée*. Turin: Fréres Bocca [first published1860].

Le Lannou, M. (1978). *Pastori e contadini di Sardegna*. Sassari: Ed. La Torre, Sassari [first published 1941].

Low, S. M., & Altman, I. (1992). Place attachment. In I. Altman & S. M. Low (Eds.), *Place attachment. Human behavior and environment* (Vol. 12, pp. 1–12). Springer. https://doi.org/10.1007/978-1-4684-8753-4_1

Magnaghi, A. (2020). *Il principio territoriale*. Bollati Boringhieri.

Manzo, L. C., & Devine Wright, P. (2014). *Place attachment. Advances in theory, methods and applications*. Routledge.

Manzo, L. C., & Perkins, D. (2006). Finding common ground: The importance of place attachment to community participation and planning. *Journal of Planning Literature, 20*(4), 335–350. https://doi.org/10.1177/0885412205286160

Martinotti, G. (2017). In V. Haddock (Ed.), *Sei lezioni sulla città*. Giangiacomo Feltrinelli Editore.

Meloni, B., & Farinella, D. (2015). Il pastoralismo come risorsa per le aree interne. In B. Meloni B. (Ed.), *Aree interne e progetti d'area* (pp. 232–258). Rosenberg & Sellier.

Moore, T. (2021). Planning for place: Place attachment and the founding of rural community land trust. *Journal of Rural Studies, 83*, 21–29.

Mumford, L. (1938). *The culture of cities*. Harcourt Brace Jovanovich Publishers.

Ortu, G. G. (2014). *Ager et urbs. Trame di luogo nella Sardegna medievale e moderna*. Piccola Biblioteca Cuec.

Poli, D. (2020). Il progetto di territorio come pratica sociale. In A. Marson (Ed.), *Urbanistica e pianificazione nella prospettiva territorialista* (pp. 95–106). Quodlibet Studio.

Regione Sardegna. (2013). *Comuni in estinzione Gli scenari dello spopolamento in Sardegna*. http://www.sardegnaprogrammazione.it/documenti/35_84_20140123144714.pdf.   Accessed Feb 2022.

RLP Regional Landscape Plan, Piano Paesaggistico Regionale della Sardegna (2006). https://www.sardegnaterritorio.it/pianificazione/pianopaesaggistico. Accessed Feb 2022.

Sabattini, G. (2017). Il problema dello spopolamento dei Comuni interni. In G. Sabattini (Ed.), *Le città e i territori. Idee per un nuovo assetto dei poteri locali in Sardegna* (pp. 61–74).

Santangelo, M. (2018). Contraposition, juxtaposition, and transposition of the urban and the rural. In E. Gottero (Ed.), *Agrourbanism. Tools for governance and planning of agrarian Landscape*. Springer International Publishing.

Sereni, E. (1986). *Storia del paesaggio agrario italiano*. Roma, Bari: Edizioni Laterza [first published 1961].

SNAI Strategia Nazionale Aree Interne. (2014). *A strategy for inner areas in Italy: definition, objectives, tools and governance*. https://www.agenziacoesione.gov.it/wp-content/uploads/2020/07/MUVAL_31_Aree_interne_ENG.pdf. Accessed Feb 2022.

Stiglitz, J. E., Fitoussi, J. P., & Durand, M. (2021). *Misurare ciò che conta. Al di là del PIL*. Einaudi.

Chapter 12
The Role of Sense of Place in the Recovery of Local Food Systems in Bioregional Contexts. Challenges and Opportunities

David Fanfani ⓘ **and Massimo Rovai** ⓘ

12.1 Introduction: Globalisation and Resurgence of the Food Issue as a Place Making Process

We can consider the Food System – understood as the entire production-consumption process – as a striking example of the process of dis-embedding market laws from society: a process which has been at work for some 150 years. Karl Polanyi (1944) identified and analysed this dis-embedding process and described how the overwhelming commodification and displacement of nature, work and capital were the key drivers of the so-called 'natural', capitalist, and competitive market systems.

In this context, well fed and ignited by an ever-increasing use of fossil energy sources from the nineteenth century onwards, food production and consumption systems have assumed a predominantly globalised structure of networks and flows, thereby drastically weakening food systems based on relations of production and local/regional consumption. This has determined, at least in terms of their 'activity', a fading away and withering of cultural knowledge, societal frameworks and bonds that not only characterised a specific socio-economic context and society but also constituted a dynamic reserve of mutually constructive and supportive identitary relationships between society and territory, between humans and nature in the form of a place-making process (Feagan, 2007) and of a mainly co-evolutionary process (Noorgard, 1994).

D. Fanfani (✉)
Architecture Department, University of Florence, Florence, Italy
e-mail: david.fanfani@unifi.it

M. Rovai
Department of Civil and Industrial Engineering, University of Pisa, Pisa, Italy
e-mail: massimo.rovai@unipi.it

For many years the growing awareness of the social and environmental impact, both local and global, of the processes we have very briefly described – including the current challenge of global warming – has been accompanied by efforts to regenerate/recover and restructure Local Food Systems (LFS). LFS are socio-natural constructs (Marsden, 2004) that can be re-spatialised in accordance with a place-based approach which aims to make the system safer and fairer and to realign human/ecological interaction around the context of place and food. Such outcomes would also assist in mitigating the metabolic rift (Foster, 1999) which negatively impacts the socio-ecological relationship between human settlements and ecosystems within the limits of their reproduction and protection.

From a multi-dimensional and cross-scale perspective (Feagan, 2007), a proactive approach to re-emplacing the Food System (FS) helps reverse the 'thinning out' of local places (Casey, 2001): for instance, the loss of significance previously associated with the fundamental (biological, cultural, social reproductive) relationships that characterised places of life.

From this perspective, LFS and related phenomena can be considered one of the most important fields of study and policy making: LFS can be used to assess the viability of re-localising economies in order to generate community and place recovery, and to foster and facilitate long-term environmental and social resilience.

Feagan (2007) maintains that the reasons for the birth/revival of LFS can be traced back to the theme of reviving the geographical discourse on 'spatiality', and to human geography studies. As LFS re-emerge, there is a 'return' to regional perspectives, albeit in reflexive and critical terms; a result of the interactions between the global factors of structural change and the contingencies and agency of local places. The regional dimension is interpreted as the structuring and mediating context required for fostering enduring social relations.

It is worth noting that this point creates a role for regional involvement in the revitalisation and support of LFS. This role is further reinforced by the introduction of categories such as 'Food-shed' (Hedden, 1929; Kloppenburg et al., 1996), Bioregion (Berg & Dasmann, 1977), Urban Bioregion (Magnaghi, 2014) and City Region Food Systems (Blay-Palmer et al., 2018). All these categories define LFS in terms of regionally-based, self-reliant flows and relations, which in turn foster re-inhabiting practices where 'self-contained' food production-consumption relationships form the basis of new bioregional economies (Scott Cato, 2013) and of social relations based on trust, respect and local knowledge recovery, thereby enhancing a 'social-self' in which food represents a key determinant of identity (KIngsolver, 2003).

This suggests that place and food-related relationships could be used to enable the empowerment and resilience potential of regions and local societies and also to model LFS as catalysts for shedding light on the intrinsically constitutive nature of the relationship between social self and place (Casey, 2001). This in turn suggests the need to better understand the nature and potential relevance of some key elements of such a relation – for instance, place attachment, sense of belonging and community – and how they are variously 'entangled' in this place-making and local identity-building process.

In order to grapple with these research issues and to better model the initial research criteria, Sect. 12.2 of this article briefly addresses some theoretical issues relating to the nature of sense of belonging, place attachment and sense of place – similar concepts – and how they can be framed and related to the regeneration and development of LFS projects and processes. In Sect. 12.3, we describe some case studies in the Tuscany Region (Italy), characterised by joint top-down and bottom-up initiatives which aim to strengthen and recover, at least partially, regionally-shaped and community-based food provision-consumption relationships. We note how the institutional approach and agency of some of these case studies relates to the involvement and engagement of active, local, social partners, and to the creation of both innovative forms of public-private partnership (PPP) and self-organised, self-managed movements.

Section 12.4, provides results, discusses them, and considers the insights and questions which arise from theoretically framing the cases described in Sect. 12.3. We try to evaluate the limits and the potential of LFS initiatives, to assess how effectively they reverse the displacing and dis-empowering effects of the globalised, dis-embedded agri-food production-consumption system. We also propose other possible integrated instruments of territorial policy which could operate in both the spatial dimension and the management and protection of agroecosystems as constitutive elements of the cultural/identity heritage, of the landscape and rural heritage.

The final section highlights the key points of this article and offers suggestions for further research that would deepen our understanding of the mutually constitutive relationship between agri-food systems and the perspective of recovering and unlocking – possibly using innovative methods – resilient LFS to foster bioregions and communities that wish to concretely counter the effects of global warming.

12.2   Theoretical Background

12.2.1   LFS, Place Attachment and Sense of Belonging

Drawing on Trentelman (2009) and Kudryavtsev et al. (2012), we assume that place attachment represents a key component of sense of place. More specifically, exploring the relationship between sense of place and LFS engagement with local inhabitants, Solin (2017) firstly observes how 'place attachment' – defined as the emotional, psychological and physical relationship of sustenance to place – is deeply intertwined with 'place meaning' (i.e. symbolic meanings, namely ecological, cultural and behavioural values) – in developing sense of place and placemaking processes associated with LFS creation and management.

Strongly pro-environment behaviour, sensitivity and knowledge are usually upheld as a starting point for civic engagement in LFS. Solin discovered that land and community proved to be key motivators of this engagement, because they draw on people's 'visceral perception' of food as a unique vehicle for connecting with ecological and place values. Posed in these terms, the relation between people, food and place highlights how deep connection to place is clearly fostered by commitment to LFS. Moreover, once this motivation and connection to place is shared and is the result of common endeavour, LFS can also be conceived as a Common, a way of managing and harnessing local resources that also draws on trust and shared community rules to prevent and address conflicts.

Debucquet et al. (2020) underline how in Community Supported Fishing (CSF) initiatives the sense of belonging to place and to a local community – particularly the cultural and contextual knowledge aspects – strongly hinges upon engagement, volunteering, and socio-cultural commitment. The authors studied a French Community Supported Fishery (CSF), and they noted that participants evaluated their expectations of relational and contextual knowledge exchange about the CSF as extra-market values: 'hedonism' – individual and ethical needs concerning the access to quality and typical food – was the prevalent response. This demonstrates that the relational dimension is positively associated with a sense of belonging which could be further strengthened by a process of relational building up around food and cultural skills (e.g., provision methods and cooking), and that the place-related values it embodies go beyond quality issues.

Debuquet's study demonstrates that sense of place, and place attachment, are both motivators for, and outcomes of, engagement with LFS. This is because increasing knowledge allows original commitment motivations which prompted initial involvement in CSF as LFS to mutually deepen and to increase a relational based and community-oriented sense of belonging. Finally, the community fostering role of LFS also increases a sense of belonging. Rossi and peers (2021) underlines this in their analysis of Alternative Food Networks (AFN) where they consider the value of food as Common, and AFN as the result of a communing process, based on socially shared values of fairness and ecological and social solidarity.

12.2.2   Building Institutions for LFS Governance and Resilience: A Socio-ecological Perspective

Escalera-Reyes (2020) adopts a more direct approach to the organisational and operational dimension of LFS interactions with sense of place issues. He affirms that feelings of collective identification with place (e.g., place attachment and sense of belonging) can be considered as interfaces and their role in establishing socio-ecological systems (SES) – similar to their role in setting up LFS – and in their subsequent evolution and resilience should be analytically scrutinised. Escalera-Reyes assumes place attachment to be the result of a set of bonds with a local environment. These bonds develop gradually, relate to meanings, and can change over time. Feelings of collective identification are grounded in the possibility of unlocking/revealing a sense of belonging (or belongingness) through a 'process of collective identification' that, by means of symbolism and agency, mediated by 'territoriality', transforms place attachment into an anchor of identity. Escalara-Reyes's article highlights the constructive and evolutionary nature of SES, similar to that of LFS, in processes of collective identification where the role and recovery of manifold forms, collective memory and shared inherited knowledge is pivotal in generating innovation and change. To achieve this also requires engagement with political/administrative institutions, so that resilient, self-organised, institutional entities can be established. Although Escalera-Reyes considers place attachment as the precondition for acting in the local context – depending on the situation, 'change-oriented' or 'stability oriented' postures could be adopted (Zwiers et al., 2016) – he underlines the importance of co-evolutionary influence which mutually reinforces sense of belonging and the evolution of the organisational structure to better manage and tap into environmental resources.

12.2.3 Spatialities of the Local Food System: Policy Design, Governance, and Spatial Projects

LFS reframing at the regional/local scale requires that the agri-food chains involved be respatialised, and an entire set of place-based socio-ecological relationships be re-embedded. These processes are not confined to relations of respect, trust and fairness between producers and consumers but also include similar relations between human and non-human worlds, between society and ecology, in accordance with a wider agro-ecological approach (Tornaghi & Dehaene, 2020). Gruenewald (2003) affirms that re-embedding the agri-food chain to meet LFS criteria, entails a combined re-inhabiting and decolonisation process which aims to reverse current settling and exploitative practices among humans and between humans and nature. Furthermore, this vision allows the recovery of a co-evolutionary relationship – inspired by self-reliance development and governance principles – between human settlements and the surrounding territory and towards an LFS system conceived as a collective/community endeavour.

As Feagan (2007) has also pointed out, all this resonates with a well-established tradition in human geography studies of applying the foodshed model (MacKaye, 1920; Hedden, 1929; Kloppenburg et al., 1996) to the recently 'emplaced' nature of suitable LFS. The foodshed model was conceived as the (recovery of) wide-ranging, eco-cultural and circular relationships between a settled community and the surrounding geographical spaces inspired, in general, by fairness, bottom-up, ecological and proximity principles (Kloppenburg et al., 1996). Although they do not refer exclusively to food issues and they encompass a wide set of practices, goals, and voices (Sale, 1985; Aberley, 1999; Evanoff, 2017), the bioregional 'paradigm' and inspiration further increase the focus on place-related food issues encompassed by the foodshed model, especially as they highlight the key relevance of agency for addressing reinhabitation and living-in place recovery concepts and related goals and practices (Berg & Dasmann, 1977).

Given the focus of this article, we should note that some scholars of the biore-gional approach are striving to better reframe a co-evolutionary relationship between urban and rural domains by contouring the features of an 'urban bioregionalism' (Dasmann, 1994; Snyder, 1994), which draws strongly on ecosystem recovery and protection principles but widens the re-inhabiting concept (Thayer, 2003). Starting from individual and small-scale place-based practices and projects, re-inhabiting upscales to an 'urban bioregion' strategic project conceived as a sustainable poly-centric system of medium-sized centres (Atkinson, 1992; Magnaghi, 2014; Fanfani, 2020). In this prospect the 'rural' domain is conceived, echoing the MacKaye leg-acy (MacKaye, 1928), as the 'counter-mould' to jointly enhance the urban form and to host regenerated agro-ecosystem patterns. The objective of these agro-ecosystems is to feed human regional settlements – although their goal is not for self-sufficiency – and to at least address the issue of self-reliance in food provision along with ecosys-tem services for a viable 'City Region Food System' (Blay-Palmer et al., 2018).

The theoretical framework findings provide the best model and focus for the initial research questions relating to the case studies:

Sense of place: pre-condition for or output of LFS?

- Sense of place encompasses place attachment and belongingness. Is it really a precondition (catalyst) which sets off the process for LFS or is it an LFS output? How is it possible to operate when sense of place is lacking or weak?

Relation between LFS resilience/sustainability and sense of place as recovery of relational values and collective memory to cope with innovation.

- What kind of role is played by place attachment in LFS to trigger a process of collective identification and to recover a sense of shared collective memory and belongingness that will, in turn, enhance commitment to, and the resil-ience of, the LFS being studied? Resilience is defined in environmental and social terms and in LFS capacity to support relational values, innovation, and change.

The role of sense of place in broadening and upscaling LFS.

- How do place-focused feelings play out in an LFS initiative to widen and upscale the initiative itself by developing a more structured socio-ecological system (SES) which involves the local community as a whole and goes beyond the original 'niche' dimension? (And, if there is any connection with supra-local market demand looking for labelled produce, how is it managed?)

LFS and empowering policies and self-government for harnessing and reproducing local resources:

- How relevant are place attachment feelings to LFS for framing and supporting locally tailored governance tools for exploiting, enhancing, and promoting local resources (e.g., agro-ecological, farmland). And in what measure do the institutional tools examined favour product innovation and change, and self-organised collective forms of agency and process?

LFS to enhance heritage, place making and stewardship.

- How much of the initiative present in the studied LFS is motivated by hedonism alone and how much also strives to recover and enhance territory heritage values, either material or cognitive, so as to re-embed local development in bioregional terms and foster self-reliance and a place making process?

12.3   Methodology

12.3.1   Selection Criteria of Case Studies

Starting from the observation that food is an important resource/factor for generating a sense of belonging and attachment to places, in this chapter we present some governance models (LFS) that have spread rapidly in Tuscany in recent years. We then evaluate their contribution to generating virtuous relationships between a sense of belonging and attachment to places and enhancement of the territory's heritage with a view to promoting local, equitable and autonomous development in bioregional terms.

The LFS were analysed with reference to both the effectiveness of the governance model as envisaged by the legislation (where there is a reference law) and considering that some experiences included in these models have been monitored by the authors since they were established. In Table 12.1, we report the main features of the cases analysed.

Table 12.1 Key points of the LFS analysed

Type of LFS	Type of organisation	Legislative references	Type of actors involved
Community for Food and Agri-biodiversity	NGO	Yes	Multi-actors
Organic Districts	NGO	Yes	Multi-actors
LFP of Lucca (Piana del Cibo)	NGO	No	Multi-actors
Slow Food Presidia	NGO	No	Multi-actors
Quality & Services	public enterprise	Yes	Public enterprise and municipalities

Source: Authors' elaboration

12.3.2   Case Studies

Community for Food and Agri-biodiversity

This case study refers to the first *Community for Food and Agri-biodiversity (Food Community)* which was established in December 2017 in the area of Garfagnana (Province of Lucca, Tuscany). Since then, other food communities have been established in various places in Tuscany.

Communities for Food and Agri-biodiversity represent a multi-actor, cross-sectoral and network governance mainly between farmers and other private and public subjects committed in some way to food issues and to developing greater awareness of food sovereignty and place attachment issues.[1] These communities are intended to coordinate public and private initiatives that already exist, as well as to promote new projects for the conservation and valorisation of local agro-biodiversity and to overcome the 'niche' dimension of this LFS.

The territory of Garfagnana, enclosed between two mountain ranges (Apuan Alps and the Appennine), is relatively isolated. This has given rise to high levels of biodiversity and to a strong sense of community identity. The Community puts forth actions – and actors, with relative instruments and competences – to foster more resilient, multi-functional farming methods. It also encompasses tourism, culture, education and training, food, and ecosystem services. Specific objectives depend on what local resources are available, and are agreed upon by the members of the Community for Food.

Organic Districts

The *Organic District* (Distretto Biologico) is an innovative territorial governance tool which allows citizens, farmers, institutions, and other actors involved in the agri-food chain to formally agree on a pact for sustainably managing their territory in accordance with the principles of organic farming. So even though the starting point of these districts is their biological supply chains, they adopt a participatory approach to local development, with bottom-up, collaborative relations between public and private actors.

Numerous *Organic Districts* have arisen in Italy since the Italian Association for Organic Agriculture (AIAB) was founded in 1988.[2] In Tuscany, the characteristics of organic districts and their constitutive process were defined in a 2019 regional

---

[1] Italian Law 194/2015, Art. 13, Community of food and biodiversity of agricultural and food interest.

[2] AIAB (Italian Association for Organic Agriculture). In Tuscany, various initiatives have been launched for Organic Districts according to the AIAB disciplinary. Among these we name the Organic Districts of Chianti (constituted), San Gimignano, Montalbano and Fiesole.

law.[3] These districts are mostly municipality based and the process for their establishment is initiated by proposals from local actors. They are identified in territories where agriculture plays a significant role in the local production system and where the importance of local, organic, agricultural production and agri-biodiversity protection meets with the values of territorial identity and landscape of the places.

The Piana del Cibo (LFP of Lucca)

As we have shown, many LFS initiatives have been established to cope with, and overcome, the current unsustainable, unfair, unsafe, and exploitative globalised food system which is characterised by deeply unbalanced producers-providers-consumers power relationships. These initiatives draw on a systemic approach which is enriched by multi-level, cross-sectoral and cross-disciplinary interactions. The concept of collaborative governance has been proved valid. This is defined as a horizontal, interactive approach that gathers myriad actors embodying manifold interests, perspectives and knowledge to develop 'emplaced' coherent Local Food Policies which primarily focus on sustainable diets, socio-economic fairness, food production and availability, food waste management, etc.

In recent years Tuscany and other parts of Italy (Dansero et al., 2019) have participated in Local Food Policy experiences. Here we describe the Piana di Lucca experience. The *Piana del Cibo* (*The Food Plain*) project was set up in 2019 as an institutional unicum involving five municipalities (Lucca, Capannori, Porcari, Altopascio and Villa Basilica). A participatory process was adopted involving about 150 local actors who were called upon to define a charter of principles, a strategy, and a model of collaborative governance with the establishment of a Food Council.

They were guided by the following principles:

- Circularity and food: diversity of organisational models to stimulate virtuous circularity and create conscious, sustainable, equitable, inclusive and resilient food systems;
- Food as knowledge and awareness: knowledge of the local food supply chain as a fundamental information element to guide the food choices of every citizen;
- Food and education: committing the various 'educative agencies' to promoting correct eating habits and food-value awareness among the younger generations;
- Food and inclusion: food as an expression of the cultural identity of communities, peoples and nations, to favour mutual acknowledgement, cultural exchange, social integration, and cohesion;

---

[3] Tuscany Regional Law 151/2019. At the moment the only Organic District established according to the new law is the Organic District of Fiesole, while those of Montalbano (Carmignano and Poggio a Caiano – province of Florence) and Calenzano (province of Florence) are at a rather advanced stage. Other initiatives are underway in Valdera (province of Pisa), Valdichiana and Casentino Valley (province of Arezzo).

- Food and place: local food production is pivotal to reproducing historical and identitary countryside values, promoting tourism, protecting, recuperating and enhancing peri-urban and abandoned rural areas;
- Food as health: healthy eating contributes meaningfully to psycho-physical well-being and to preventing manifold forms of illness.

Slow Food Presidia

Slow Food (SF) is an association that was established in Italy with the aim of promoting good, clean, fair food and since then has gradually spread all over the world.

Among the various projects of central SF is a commitment to the preservation of agricultural biodiversity and to this end the Ark of Taste (Arca del Gusto) was established, to gather the Presidia that belong to the Terra Madre food communities network, and is promoted by the Slow Food Foundation for Biodiversity, a non-profit organisation. *Slow Food Presidia* protect and enhance agricultural and livestock products and some processed foods. They are recognised as particularly meaningful because they significantly link food, places, material culture, traditional skills, and products. For this reason, they represent fundamental expressions and vehicles of attachment to places and a sense of belonging. As such they are based on the organisation of a 'food community' that adopts a valorisation project to promote the economic and social system linked to the product, and also to address fairness, respect for human rights, and equitable revenue issues.

There are 450 *Slow Food Presidia* in more than 50 countries around the world and they involve over thirteen thousand small producers, farmers, and craftsmen. The interesting aspect, from the communicative point of view, is the 'narrating label' that extends the concept of 'quality' beyond the organoleptic and nutritional characteristics to include information on the origin of the product (the territory), the technique of cultivation and/or transformation and the methods of conservation because, in fact, it is the narrative which restores a product's true value.

Quality & Services (Public Owned Enterprise for School Canteens Provision)

Quality & Services is a public limited company (Municipality of Sesto Fiorentino, Campi Bisenzio e Signa, Calenzano, Carmignano and Barberino di Mugello) which operates in the metropolitan area of Florence in the field of collective catering and has as its social object the production and supply of meals for the community, in particular school catering. It prepares about 7,500 meals a day for kindergartens and primary schools.

In 2017, the Administrations involved adopted a new approach, a new philosophy of work: the catering was no longer semi-industrial but a catering of excellence, founded on a 'circular economy' model and on the core principles of slow food: 'good, clean, and fair' that is, socially and environmentally responsible. *Quality &*

Services is oriented towards the sustainability and value of the local territory, the environment, the local gastronomic culture, tasty food, user satisfaction and a strong emphasis on education.

The basic idea is that it is possible to train citizens to be aware of, and oriented towards, the ecological transition, with the starting point being a healthy diet. This is a new model that considers food as a vehicle of both physical well-being and educational-cultural development. *Quality & Services* is a company that dialogues with the local community, users play an active role in a co-production process, making it an integral part of the production process, thus giving rise to a real food community, where this contributes to co-producing what it eats, supporting, and at the same time directing, local production.

12.4 Results and Discussion

12.4.1 Sense of Place: Pre-condition for or Output of the LFS?

Despite the difference of scale and the number of actors involved, in the cases of both *Food Community* and *Slow Food Presidia* a sense of belonging and attachment to places and a desire to defend an endangered agro-biodiversity are the fundamental reasons for their constitution. This also applies, though to a lesser extent, to the experience of *Quality & Service*. Particularly in the case of *Slow Food Presidia,* the awareness of producers (in the first place) and consumers/users/local institutions arises from a strongly felt attachment to places which, in turn, connotes the *SF Presidia* as elements of cultural/identity/symbolic value, highlighting their proactive role. For *Food Community* and *Quality & Services* attachment to places is both a proactive element and an output of the initiative. For the former, enhancing visibility on the market becomes a communication tool that ensures the vitality and resilience of the 'discourse' on belonging and attachment – in terms of sustenance – in the places where these products are produced and consumed. In the case of *Quality & Services* (the company for collective catering), the mission to promote mainly local food best fits with the goal of educating pupils and parents to a conscious citizenship and sense of place, making them aware of the health, fairness and cultural meanings embodied in local food consumption.

Finally, in the cases of *Organic Districts* and *LFP of Lucca,* the sense of belonging and attachment to places are not the main proactive elements in promoting LFS, but they can become an output. In the *Organic Districts,* attachment to place is less marked because the reasons for their establishment mainly arise from respect for the environment and safeguarding the health of citizens/inhabitants: motivations that are valid in any context. The sense of belonging mainly connotes the link between the actors in the *Organic Districts* but it is not necessarily a sense of belonging to the geographical place. In some cases, the actors' desire to guarantee the naturalness of food production and the sustainability of the territory's rural services prevails.

The cross-sector policy of the LFP of Lucca ensures coherent implementation in a range of activities (food safety, relocation of consumption, education, etc.) and strives to stimulate curiosity/interest in researching local products in such a way that local consumers strengthen their sense of belonging and attachment to places. In the Lucca Plain, for instance, there is a difficult situation related to the closure of many small farms and/or the abandonment of agricultural land in peri-urban and hilly areas. Sense of belonging and attachment to the places of consumers are a fundamental strategic lever for underlining the connection between local consumption and a guaranteed income for local farmers whose work contributes to the maintenance of the territory and landscape.

12.4.2   The Relationship Between LFS Resilience/ Sustainability and Sense of Place as a Recovery of Relational Values and a Collective Memory to Cope with Innovation

Food Communities and *Organic District*(s) start by sharing a common territory and its traditions and productive resources. These experiences are strongly oriented in a relational perspective and are fed by contextual, place-based culture. In the case of food communities, the attachment to place is strongly correlated with dimensions of sustenance along with cultural meanings associated with food sovereignty. In these communities the rediscovery and enhancement of cultivation/breeding of varieties/ local breeds often take the form of retro-innovation (Stuiver, 2006), as their products promote more sustainable and resilient systems from the point of view of social, economic, and environmental effects. In the *Organic Districts,* though, attachment to place tends to be oriented towards consumer well-being and adding value in terms of market and territorial marketing. In the case of *Slowfood Presidia*, the regenerative value of place is found in the symbolic/identity component of food and related contextual knowledge but the impact, in terms of relationships and resilience, is limited due to their niche size. The experience of Quality & Services instead seems to reassemble-in-reverse the relationship between the sense of the places, LFS and innovation. An innovation of the whole food provision process to recover cultural identity through the multifaceted meanings assumed by food and to improve the resilience and sustainability of the agri-food local system.

12.4.3   The Role of Sense of Place in Broadening and Upscaling LFS

Food Communities, Organic Districts and Slow Food initiatives usually originated as an aggregation of a limited number of actors (producers, restaurateurs, consumers, etc.) with respect to the subjects who could have potentially adhered to the

LFS. Therefore, at least initially, they are featured as 'niche' LFS and a sense of belonging and attachment to places are levers that need to be used well for communicating within the territory in order to avoid making the impression that these LFS are 'exclusive clubs' that impose strongly ideological 'barriers to entry'.

Conversely, assertive and proactive attitudes can favour the progressive adhesion of other actors and, therefore, an expansion process. In this regard it is worth mentioning the case of a network of biodynamic winemakers in the Piana di Lucca (they are not an *Organic District*). When they started out, there were only a few of them but, thanks to their attitude of openness, persuasion, assistance and collaboration, they managed to expand the number of member companies. But also, for the *Slow Food Presidia* that require a multi-actor community (producers, processors, restaurateurs, retailers, consumers), the sense of belonging and attachment to places must be well developed if the presidium is to expand and maintain its vitality.

With reference to the *LFP of Lucca*, it must be premised that, like the *Food Communities* and *Organic Districts*, the LFP too must have the ability to open to the outside in order to operate. The *LFP of Lucca*, aware of these limits, established values of sustainability, fairness, and solidarity to be implemented through good practices to be followed in a simple way by the actors in order to encourage expansion. This is the case, for example, of a well-balanced and easily accessible network of farmers' markets established on the territory.

In the *Quality & Services* collective catering model, a sense of belonging and attachment to place served to raise awareness of the 'sovereignty' of a fundamental service for the education of the new generations. This has allowed the business to expand into neighbouring municipalities and others further afield – will be added in the future, including recently the Municipality of Florence where about 20,000 meals are delivered daily.

12.4.4   LFS, Empowering Policies and Self-Government for Harnessing and Reproducing Local Resources

All the studied initiatives draw upon and are strongly characterised by a sense of bottom-up, community empowerment, which especially aims to enhance and improve local heritage stewardship and awareness, related to agri-food system use and appraised as a 'common'. An initially shared sense of place, fed by sense of belonging, place attachment and elements of collective memory, represents the support for setting and improving shared responsibilities and place stewardship under the form of local pacts, contracts and mutual commitments, usually within the organisational form of a public-private partnership.

The 'informal' and innovative features of the governance model, adopted by *LFP of Lucca* and by the *Slow Food Presidia* are particularly noteworthy: their inclusive and collaborative approach, totally originated in a bottom-up, self-organised form outside of any institutional framework. The approach of *Food Community* and

Organic Districts is also innovative: public institutions support a community led local development-like approach where public and private parties collaborate to achieve local sustainable development goals. The *Quality & Services* experience returns the service of providing meals for school canteens to public administration, which highlights the appreciative attention that 'public' gives to food as a 'common' and key element of an innovative welfare model.

12.4.5 LFS to Enhance Heritage, Place Making and Stewardship

Through the mediation of territoriality, food issues – embodying emotional and sustenance values – represent an utmost vehicle for place regeneration, both in ecological and landscape (i.e., socio-cultural) terms.

In the *Food Community* case this aspect is particularly remarkable when referring to the territorial agri-biodiversity recovery that has eroded over time (for reasons related to the market, low productivity, reduction in the number of farmers, etc.). Anyway, in this case a critical point to address may be how to conciliate this 'quality turn' in food production with the increased prices of products, mainly related to sustainable farming practices, not always easily accessible for all consumers.

Although the issue of territorial heritage is not pivotal for *LFP of Lucca, Organic Districts* and *Quality & Services*, it is worth noting how these initiatives have generally paved the way for a more general re-embedding of LFS related to local territory – albeit in different ways and with an endogenous and self-reliant perspective. In these experiences 'place resources measures' for (re) production and re-inhabiting can be considered pivotal but the goal of strengthening food sovereignty is also pursued.

Finally, the *Slow Food Presidia,* although it can hardly be considered as pursuing and upscaling place making goals, is pivotal to ensuring the survival and recirculation of local productive models as memories of the past residual with respect to modern agricultural processes. Moreover, they can be also a 'gene pool' which can be tapped to recover farming practices with still suitable and profitable products which are appropriate for bio-regional development and fundamental in creating/ maintaining the sense of place.

12.5   Concluding Remarks

Summarising some key points of the investigation carried out to ascertain the effectiveness of the analysed LFS governance models, the fundamental role of these LFS as a vehicle for a constructive identity relationship between food, inhabitants and place is confirmed. This fosters the two basic components of sense of place: sense of belonging and place attachment (Solin, 2017). There is a mutually supporting relation between sense of place, as a triggering factor of engagement in LFS (Debucquet et al., 2020), 'visceral' perception of food, shared knowledge, ethical motivations, and pro-quality (hedonist) choices. In other words, sense of place can be considered as both a motivator and an outcome of engagement in the food system (Debucquet et al., 2020). Drawing on the cases examined, sense of place emerges as the result of a process of rediscovery of lost collective heritages and of the construction of a progressive collective identification within these heritages (as in the case of the *Slow Food Presidia* or the *Food Communities*). These processes cause sense of place to evolve towards some more structured forms of communication which, in turn, strengthen the identity of the territory and the recently established structured organisational forms (SES) (Escalera-Reyes, 2020). LFS resilience and endurance capabilities are, in turn, affected by the capacity to constantly support the relational dimension between the actors committed to the system, and the capacity to appropriately balance change-oriented and stability-oriented approaches in harnessing local resources and heritage (Zwiers et al., 2016) and enabling different sensibilities.

Furthermore, in the LFS we have described, sense of place becomes a tool for drawing upon a residual and lasting 'gene pool' (Jacobs, 2000) of belongingness and attachment to place, conveyed by a limited set of actors, stakeholders, and activists. A process of memory retrieval and a revived sense of 'commonality' enable this tool to activate the territory's collective endowments. In this context, the food system appears to be an effective lever for enhancing and expanding initiatives, sometimes upscaling them but also triggering place awareness and stewardship which, in turn, reciprocally consolidate place attachment and belongingness.

The experiences we have studied confirm the inductive role played by LFS in terms of place making, and sense of place reconstruction. The policy implications of our findings, however, require further study to help us find effective tools for integrating LFS experiences with territorial planning tools. This is an important issue because the difference between the objectives of territorial planning/design and those of LFS bottom-up initiatives aimed at SES bioregional redevelopment often causes friction.

References

Aberley, D. (1999). Interpreting Bioregionalism: A story from many voices. In M. V. McGinnis (Ed.), *Bioregionalism* (pp. 13–42). Routledge.

Atkinson, A. (1992). The urban bioregion as sustainable development paradigm. *Third World Planning Review, 4*(14), 327–354.

Berg, P., & Dasmann, R. (1977). Reinhabiting California. *The Ecologist, 7*(10), 399–401.

Blay-Palmer, A., Santini, G., Dubbeling, M., Renting, H., Taguchi, M., & Giordano, T. (2018). Validating the city region food system approach: Enacting inclusive, transformational city region food systems. *Sustainability, 10*, 1680. https://doi.org/10.3390/su10051680

Casey, E. S. (2001). Between geography and philosophy: What does it mean to be in the place-world? *Annals of the Association of American Geographers, 91,* 683–693.

Dansero, E., Marino, D., Mazzocchi, G., & Yota, N. (Eds.). (2019). *Lo spazio delle politiche locali del cibo: temi, esperienze e prospettive.* Celid.

Dasmann, R. (1994). Some thought on ecological planning. In I. D. Aberley (Ed.), *Futures by design. The practice of ecological planning* (pp. 36–43). New Society Publisher.

Debucquet, G., Guillotreau, P., Lazuech, G., Salladarré, F., & Troiville, J. (2020). Sense of belonging and commitment to a community-supported fishery. The case of Yeu Island, France. *Review of Agricultural, Food and Environmental Studies, 101*(4), 439–459. https://doi.org/10.1007/s41130-020-00101-3

Escalera-Reyes, J. (2020). Place attachment, feeling of belonging and collective identity in socio-ecological systems: Study case of Pegalajar (Andalusia-Spain). *Sustainability, 12,* 3388. https://doi.org/10.3390/su12083388

Evanoff, R. (2017). Bioregionalism: A brief introduction and overview. *The Aoyama Journal of International Politics, Economics and Communication, 99,* 55–65.

Fanfani, D. (2020). Co-evolutionary recovery of the urban/rural interface. Policies, planning and design issues for the urban bioregion. In D. Fanfani & R. A. Matarán (Eds.), *Bioregional planning and design. Perspective on a transitional century* (pp. 129–150). Springer.

Feagan, R. (2007). The place of food: Mapping out the 'local' in local food systems. *Progress in Human Geography, 31*(1), 23–42.

Foster, J. B. (1999). Marx's theory of metabolic rift: Classical foundations for environmental sociology. *American Journal of Sociology, 105*(2), 366–405.

Gruenewald, D. A. (2003). The best of both worlds: A critical pedagogy of place. *Educational Researcher, 32*(4), 3–12. http://www.pieducators.com/files/Critical-Pedagogy-of-Place.pdf. Accessed 17 Mar 2022.

Hedden, W. (1929). *How great cities are fed.* D.C. Heath and Company.

Jacobs, J. (2000). *The nature of economies.* Random House.

KIngsolver, B. (2003). Foreword. In N. Wirzba (Ed.), *The essential agrarian reader* (pp. ix–xvii). University Press of Kentucky.

Kloppenburg, J., Hendrickson, J., & Stevenson, G. W. (1996). Coming into the foodshed. *Agriculture and Human Values, 13,* 33–42. https://doi.org/10.1007/BF01538225

Kudryavtsev, A., Stedman, R. C., & Krasny, M. E. (2012). Sense of place in environmental education. *Environmental Education Research, 18*(2), 229–250. https://doi.org/10.1080/1350462 2.2011.609615

MacKaye, B. (1920). A plan for cooperation between farmer and consumer. *Monthly Labor Review, 11*(2), 213–233.

MacKaye, B. (1928). *The new exploration. A philosophy of regional planning.* Harcourt Brace & Co.

Magnaghi, A. (2014). *La biorégion urbaine. Petit traité sur le territoire bien commun.* Eterotopia.

Marsden, T. K. (2004). The quest for ecological modernisation: Re-spacing rural development and agri-food studies. *Sociologia Ruralis, 44,* 129–146.

Noorgard, R. B. (1994). *Development betrayed, the end of progress and a coevolutionary revisioning of the future.* Routledge.

Polanyi, K. (1944). *The great transformation. The political and economic origins of our time.* Farrar & Rinehart.

Rossi, A., Coscarello, M., & Biolghini, D. (2021). (Re)commoning food and food systems. The contribution of social innovation from solidarity economy. *Agriculture, 11,* 548. https://doi.org/10.3390/agriculture11060548

Sale, K. (1985). *Dwellers in the land: The bioregional vision.* Sierra Club Book.

Scott Cato, M. (2013). *Bioregional economies. Land, liberty and the pursuit of happiness.* Routledge.

Snyder, G. (1994). Coming to the watershed. In D. Aberley (Ed.), *Futures by design. The practice of ecological planning* (pp. 14–26). New Society Publisher.

Solin, J. (2017). *The place of food systems: Exploring the relationship between sense of place and community food systems engagement*. http://www.susted.com/wordpress/content/the-place-of-food-systems-exploring-the-relationship-between-sense-of-place-and-community-food-systems-engagement_2017_06/. Accessed 10 Jan 2022.

Stuiver, M. (2006). Highlighting the retro side of innovation and its potential for regime change in agriculture. In T. Marsden & J. Murdoch (Eds.), *Between the local and the global, confronting complexity in the contemporary agri-food sector* (Research in Rural Sociology and Development, 12) (pp. 147–173). https://doi.org/10.1016/S1057-1922(06)12007-7

Thayer, R. L. (2003). *LifePlace, bioregional thought and practice*. California University Press.

Tornaghi, C., & Dehaene, M. (2020). The prefigurative power of urban political agroecology: Rethinking the urbanisms of agroecological transitions for food system transformation. *Agroecology and Sustainable Food Systems, 44*(5), 594–610. https://doi.org/10.1080/2168356 5.2019.1680593

Trentelman, C. (2009). Place attachment and community attachment: A primer grounded in the lived experience of a community sociologist. *Society and Natural Resources, 22*, 191–210.

Zwiers, S., Markantoni, M., & Strijker, D. (2016). The role of change- and stability-oriented place attachment in rural community resilience: A case study in south-west Scotland. *Community Development Journal, 53*, 281–300.

Chapter 13
Syrmia – Rethinking the Regional Identity of a (Trans)Border Region: Perception, Self-Identification, and Place Attachment

Srećko Kajić ⓘD, Marin Bogdanić ⓘD, and Borna Fuerst-Bjeliš ⓘD

13.1 Introduction

The region of Syrmia, today split between Croatia and Serbia, is a historical and traditional region with an ancient history, dating back to Roman times. From those times on, the territorial and horonymic continuity (symbolic shape) has been preserved to some extent, despite many political and territorial changes throughout the history of the area. The region of Syrmia has been also established as a political and administrative unit in historical periods, sometimes in its entirety, sometimes divided by borders between different systems. This frequent historical and territorial duality is the most distinctive trait of the region of Syrmia. Presently, the historical and traditional territory of the region of Syrmia is divided, following the collapse of Yugoslavia, between two states: the Republic of Croatia and the Republic of Serbia. Thereby, Syrmia may be considered as a transborder region, encompassing its territorial entirety and actual (as well as historical) divisions.

Standard definitions of the territorial extent and the concept of Syrmia, according to the lexicographic sources (e.g., Miroslav Krleža Institute of Lexicography, 2021), define Syrmia as the territory between the lower courses of the Danube and Sava rivers until their confluence in the east (Serbia), while the western border of the region (in Croatia) is less naturally determined and mostly refers to the Vuka River, based primarily on elements of historical territorial development. Standard definitions of historical and traditional regions do not necessarily correspond to people's perception of the regional concepts and territorial extent. People's perception, regional identity, consciousness, and place attachment depend on many elements of

S. Kajić · M. Bogdanić · B. Fuerst-Bjeliš (✉)
Department of Geography, Faculty of Science, University of Zagreb, Zagreb, Croatia
e-mail: srecko.kajic@student.geog.pmf.hr; marin.bogdanic@student.geog.pmf.hr;
bornafb@geog.pmf.unizg.hr

regional and familial history and experience, narratives, socio-political circumstances, borders – physical or mental, and perspective. Place attachment and place/territorial/regional identity are intertwined and mutually directly dependent, building each other. Place attachment is strong where identity is strong and the other way around, with each of these feelings (and concepts) building on (and from) each other.

The aim of this research is the assessment of the perceptual territorial extent of the region, compared to standard definitions (e.g., encyclopaedic sources), the self-identification of its residents in terms of identification with the region and expressed by place attachment (i.e., intensity and nature of their feelings and bonds with the region). Since the region of Syrmia is a transborder region, currently divided by state border between Croatia and Serbia, one of the aims was to investigate the perception of the persisting unity and commonness of the region and the existence of common practices despite the present state border that divides its traditional and historical territorial and symbolic shape. One of the research questions tackled the feeling of present-day quality of life in the region in terms of perceived secured future perspective (employment, housing). The presumption was that a positive outlook on perspective would strengthen the place attachment and the other way around. Although negative feelings can hinder place (or regional) identity, recent research (Kirkness & Tijé-Dra, 2017) has shown that, on the contrary, negative processes and the reputation of places, even territorial stigmatisation, often lead to the development of deep attachment to the place, which was also confirmed by our research. The methodology used to uncover the answers to the above research questions and aims is based on a mixed-method approach (i.e., questionnaire survey and interviews on both sides – western Croatian and eastern Serbian side of the (trans) border region of Syrmia).

13.2   Theoretical and Conceptual Framework

For a long time, regional identity has been an important category in geographical research, however, its meanings are still vague (Paasi, 2002). The perception of regional identity is fundamentally expressed by the (self-) identification of people with a region, by their regional awareness as a state of mind and by feelings of belonging and attachment to a particular region and to the regional community. The latter is commonly described or conceptualized in versatile ways, but mostly in terms of regional awareness or consciousness, already discussed early in the twentieth century by Hartshorne (1939) and Whittlesey (1954), or in terms of belonging, having affective bonds and attachment to a place or region, termed, and conceptualised lately mostly as place attachment. But relations between these concepts are not simple. Simple is only the fact that concepts of territory, space/place, identity, place attachment and their empirical and theoretical understanding, along with the relations between them, are extremely complex and varied. There is no single or clear relation achieved between them at the moment and it is still under intensive and vivid discussion (Peng et al., 2020). In the last decades, there exists a vast body of literature on place identity in its various terms, conceptions, meanings, and scales.

The term *place* identity was introduced in the 1970s within the interdisciplinary field of environmental psychology as individuals' incorporation of places into the broader concept of *self* (Proshansky, 1976, 1978; Proshansky et al., 1983; Peng et al., 2020). Along with active decades of exploration in other plural disciplines (geography, cultural studies, and other humanities and social sciences), particularly after 2000, the concept significantly developed in versatile ways. Basically, in contrast to the primary one-sided environmental psychology concept of place identity as one constituent part of a broader self-identity, nowadays, under the umbrella of the concept of regional identity, authors mainly differentiate two concepts of place/ regional identity. One is related to that of a place (or a region) itself, and the other to one of the multiple facets of personal identity related to a place/region (Paasi, 2002; Banini & Ilovan, 2021). Personal or social identity/ies, therefore, include several elements, such as gender, class, religion, but also space/place. Since people position themselves simultaneously on multiple identity levels, regions (or generally space/place) are only one element in social formation (Paasi, 2002).

Earlier research in Croatia identified social identity as dimensional and relational, whereas its dimensionality was defined through four conceptual categories: social, cultural, *spatial* and family-gender (Cifrić & Nikodem, 2006, 2007). The latter concept of people's regional identity refers to their self-identification with the region (space/place) and thus may be related to the already discussed concept of regional consciousness in the regional discourse by Hartshorne and Whittlesey, in addition to the other related constructs developed later by environmental psychologists to define and measure persons' relations with places, such as sense of place and place attachment (Shamai, 1991; Altman & Low, 1992; Bauman, 2001; Cross, 2015; Peng et al., 2020), that are of central importance.

Research showed different relations between these concepts. Sometimes place attachment is treated as a synonym of place identity or subsumed within it or as a prerequisite to the identity (Chow & Healey, 2008; Antonsich, 2010; Peng et al., 2020), while in other cases it is, on the contrary, described as a superordinate category to place identity (Kyle et al., 2004). Some authors understood both identity and attachment just as dimensions of sense of place (Jorgensen & Stedman, 2001; Hernández et al., 2007; Chow & Healey, 2008). Shamai (1991), for instance, finds attachment as a phase prior to identification, while Bauman (2001) states that a community's ability to achieve a sense of place and place attachment allows it to reinforce its own identities. There are obvious overlaps and huge differences in understanding, in addition to, as Lewicka (2011) points out, an unclear relation between concepts.

Although differently conceptualised within the complexity of these related concepts, place attachment always concerns the feelings and emotional bonds people have with places, territories or regions, being that rootedness and/or long familial history attachment (narratives). Basic elements of regional identity as defined by Paasi (1986, 2002) and Keating (2000) are cognitive, affective, and instrumental elements. The affective mostly corresponds to the concept of place attachment, which was later rooted in environmental psychology (cf. Altman & Low, 1992) and developed throughout decades as an interdisciplinary topic. According to the extensive research review conducted by Peng et al. (2020, p. 5), place identity obtains its primary foundation in geographical sciences, while place attachment has been a true interdisciplinary hotspot only in the last five years (since 2017).

If there is a lack of some of those elements, either cognitive (embracing territorial and/or symbolic shape), affective one (e.g., weak place attachment or even detachment or alienation), or lack of institutions that sustain and build the region, from whatever reason, the regional identity would be weakened. This might be an important moment in regions affected by considerable population loss, out-migration processes, and negative perceptions of future perspective in the region, as it was showed further in the presented research. The concept of borderlands and border regions are of special importance in this context. Border regions are particularly sensitive to political and territorial changes, which often bring boundary changes and consequently aforementioned negative and marginalising processes which have an impact on positive/negative feelings, perspective, attachment and finally the regional identity issue. Along with the process of deconstruction of borders in a mobile world (Paasi, 2002), there is also a process of re-construction of borders following, for instance, the collapse of former Yugoslavia which displayed the uninterrupted power of socio-political (Paasi, 2021) and mental borders, and in many cases their strengthening. The phenomenon of reaffirmation of boundaries affects emotional bonds and the meaning of place as components of territorial identities.

13.3   The Research Area – Spatial and Temporal Context of Syrmia

The traditional and historical region of Syrmia encompasses the easternmost border area of Croatia with Serbia, along with the Serbian part on the other side. The present state border divide places about two-thirds of Syrmian territory in Serbia, mostly within the local administrative unit *Srem County (Sremski okrug)*, while the Croatian part comprises about one-third of the entire area, primarily encompassed within *Vukovar-Srijem County (Vukovarsko-srijemska županija)* (as defined by Miroslav Krleža Institute of Lexicography, 2021).

The region is named after the Roman city of *Sirmium* (present-day Sremska Mitrovica in Serbia) which was the provincial centre of *Pannonia Sirmiensis*. This was both the first territorial and administrative unit named *Syrmian*. After the Middle Ages (thirteenth and fourteenth century), when the region was split within two medieval royal županijas, *Vuka* (western part) and *Syrmia Županija* (eastern part), the territory of Syrmia was mostly kept in its entirety for centuries (*Sanjak of Syrmia* during the Ottoman rule from sixteenth to eighteenth century; *Syrmia Županija* during the Habsburg rule from eighteenth to twentieth century. and *Syrmia Oblast* within the Kingdom of Serbs, Croats and Slovenes from 1922 to 1929) until the early twentieth century (1929), and division of the territory of the Kingdom of Yugoslavia into banates (*banovina*), which split the Syrmian territorial unit between *Danube Banate* and *Drina* (1929), *Sava* (1931) and *Croatian Banate* (1939). At the end of the Second World War, Syrmia was divided between the then federal states of Croatia and Serbia (i.e., the autonomous province of Voivodina), according to the ethnic basis at the time of the division. The boundaries established then remained, apart from the Croatian War of Independence period, stable to this day (Sekulić, 1997; Fuerst-Bjeliš & Glamuzina, 2021; Miroslav Krleža Institute of Lexicography, 2021).

The two parts of Syrmia have been characterised by different demographic trends (Fig. 13.1). The Croatian part of the region is among the most demographically regressive areas within the country, a fact confirmed by the results of the 2021 census which demonstrate the largest relative decline in population on record. While the total population of Croatia in the intercensal period (2011–2021) declined by 10%, the population of western, Croatian Syrmia, within the frame of Vukovar-Srijem County, declined twice as much – 20%. The turning point in trends was recorded following 1991, when the proceedings of the Croatian War of Independence triggered an avalanche of emigration, especially in the war-torn eastern part of the country. The last three censuses have shown that these trends have taken on even greater proportions and that we can speak of the most demographically fragile area in the country. Conversely, on the other side of the border, in the eastern, Serbian Syrmia, the situation is the opposite, given that the 1990s did not bring significant

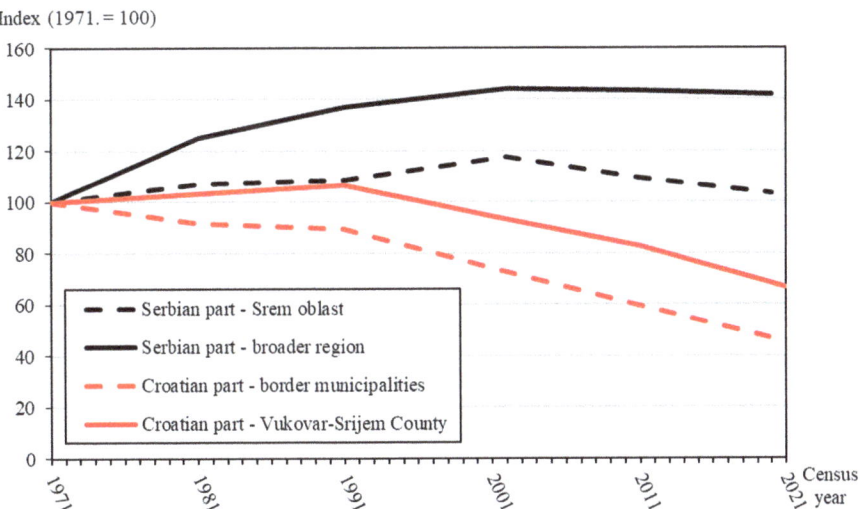

Fig. 13.1 Population trends of Croatian and Serbian parts of Syrmia from 1971 to 2021 (population in 1971 = 100)

*Serbian data for 2020 according to the official population estimate. Croatian Bureau of Statistics, 2022; Statistical Office of the Republic of Serbia, 2021

Source: Authors' elaboration

changes and population growth continued. The line on the top of Fig. 13.1 shows that even though Srem County records a slight decline, the population of the broader Syrmian region, encompassing parts of Novi Sad and Belgrade urban agglomerations on the outer edge of the region, is currently stagnating due to their functional and economic strength that sustains stable demographic trends.

13.4   Methodological Approach

Considering the research aims, a mixed-method approach was used (i.e., both quantitative and qualitative methods including the questionnaire survey and interviews). We conducted a questionnaire survey (N = 795) through early 2020 and the interviews (N = 15) in late 2021. Due to the region's transborder character, along with the timetable of the research during the COVID-19 pandemic, we conducted the research methods online.

We split the questionnaire's results: firstly, between the two countries, and secondly, among people from the Syrmia region, in order to assess the internal perception of the regional identity, and among people from other parts of both respective countries, in order to comparatively analyse the external perception. The questionnaires consisted of both closed and open questions. We obtained more in-depth information by the subsequent semi-structured interviews, again from both sides of the region. Interview inquiries focused on several topics. One was the nature of place attachment, being that of the feeling of rootedness or long historical familial bonds with the region. Furthermore, the sense and strength of regional belonging were explored, along with the perception of unity and commonness of the regional identity of the western (Croatian) and eastern (Serbian) parts of the (trans)border region. The last inquiry also implies the question and perception of possible continuation/or initiation of cross-border cooperation based on the existing place attachment and feeling of mutual regional identity and heritage.

Following data collection, we analysed the respondents' quantitative answers using the method of descriptive statistics in Microsoft Excel, and ArcMap for cartographic visualisations and interpretation of regional self-identification.

Taking into account that perceptual regions cannot be precisely defined due to their nature (Jordan, 1978, cited in Vukosav & Fuerst-Bjeliš, 2015), we based the spatial scope of the study area on the standard definition of the region of Syrmia (cf. Miroslav Krleža Institute of Lexicography, 2021) in both Croatia and Serbia. The boundaries of the research area in Croatia (Fig. 13.2) correspond to those of Vukovar-Srijem County, with the Danube and Sava rivers forming its borders in Serbia. We gathered the data for the research on the local administrative unit (LAU) level (i.e., on the municipal level).

On the territory of the region of Syrmia, there are, therefore, 31 local administrative units in Croatia and 14 in Serbia. Of the Serbian municipalities, 12 are entirely located within the research area, with the better part of the City of Sremska Mitrovica

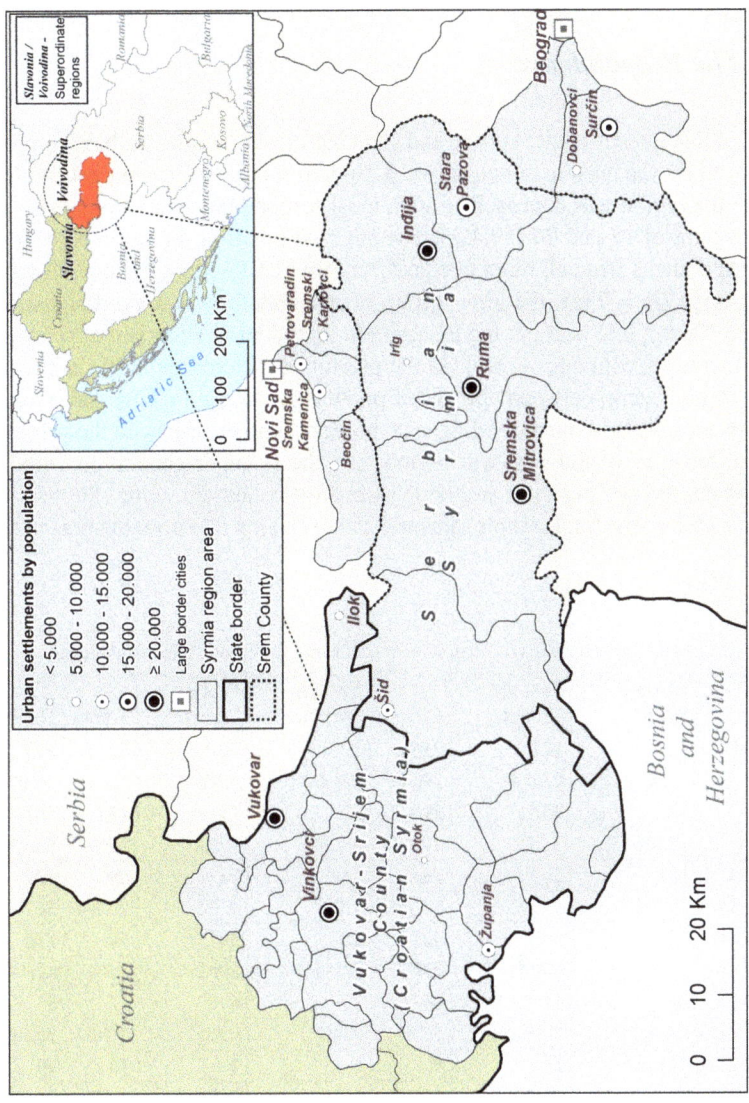

Fig. 13.2 Research area. Western (Croatian) and eastern (Serbian) Syrmia
Source: Authors' elaboration based on GADM, 2018 (GIS shapefiles)

being located in the region. However, only a small part of Bačka Palanka Municipality is found within the research area, which granted its exclusion from the study.

13.5 Results

13.5.1 The Respondents

Due to the online questionnaire survey and snowballing technique, we have applied in the research for the reasons stated above, a random sample of respondents within and outside the region was approached, with most respondents being young people between the ages of 18 and 24 (59.4%). The other near half of the sample (40.6%) included respondents from all other age groups (Table 13.1). Since the overall sample is very large (N = 795), the latter group of respondents has a valid statistical significance. Taking into account the assumption that identification and attachment to a place increases with age, as well as the presumed differences in place attachment that might occur between the older population living in Yugoslavia (and Syrmia in its entirety without a dividing state border), who experienced the war and the political tensions of the post-war period, and the younger generation without this experience, the age group of respondents over 40 years old, with 120 respondents (about 15% of the total sample), ensures the exclusion of a possible bias in the procedure.

Table 13.1 Structural characteristics of respondents according to region/state of residence

Respondents		Western Syrmia	Rest of Croatia	Croatia	Eastern Syrmia	Rest of Serbia	Serbia	Total
By gender	M	65	171	*236*	17	40	*57*	*293*
		8.2%	21.5%	*29.7%*	2.1%	5.0%	*7.2%*	*36.9%*
	F	127	263	*390*	37	75	*112*	*502*
		16.0%	33.1%	*49.1%*	4.7%	9.4%	*14.1%*	*63.1%*
By age	18–24	121	262	*383*	15	74	*89*	*472*
		15.2%	33.0%	*48.2%*	1.9%	9.3%	*11.2%*	*59.4%*
	25–30	12	50	*62*	20	30	*50*	*112*
		1.5%	6.3%	*7.8%*	2.5%	3.8%	*6.3%*	*14.1%*
	31–40	24	44	*68*	11	6	*17*	*85*
		3.0%	5.5%	*8.6%*	1.4%	0.8%	*2.1%*	*10.7%*
	41–50	22	58	*80*	6	4	*10*	*90*
		2.8%	7.3%	*10.1%*	0.8%	0.5%	*1.3%*	*11.3%*
	>50	13	20	*33*	2	1	*3*	*36*
		1.6%	2.5%	*4.2%*	0.3%	0.1%	*0.4%*	*4.5%*
Total		192	434	*626*	54	115	*169*	795
		24,2%	54.6%	*78.7%*	6.8%	14.5%	*21.3%*	100.0%

Source: Authors' research

Nearly two-thirds of all respondents were women, while men made up 37% of respondents. When broken down by place of residence, nearly 80% of respondents were from Croatia, largely due to easier access through the snowballing technique, while the remainder of respondents were from Serbia. In both countries, about one-third of the respondents were from Syrmia, while the rest were from other parts of the respective countries (Table 13.1). Since the mixed-methods approach provides the best data and information, in addition to the questionnaire, we interviewed fifteen residents of Syrmia. In order to obtain a balanced number of responses, we interviewed respondents ranging in age from 19 to 58, with 5 respondents (33%) over the age of 40. Six of the respondents were men and nine were women. Eight of the respondents live in the Croatian part of the region and seven in the Serbian part.

13.5.2 Perception and Identification of the Area

We explored the spatial perception and identification of the region by showing all respondents a map section (taken from Google Maps) showing the area of Syrmia according to its standard definition, as mentioned earlier. We asked them to identify and name the regions (not administrative units, like the county) that they recognised on the map, thus assessing the cognitive and symbolic components of the regional identity.

Having combined the results, for each of the "spatial" groups (Vukovar-Srijem County, rest of Croatia, etc.), we expressed three regional concepts key for this part of our research: Syrmia as the focal region, Slavonia (in Croatia) and Voivodina (in Serbia) as superordinate regions to Syrmia, grouping all other answers into the category "Other" (Fig. 13.3). Since some of the respondents offered more than one answer, the sum of shares in the groups exceeds 100%. In this context, a superordinate region refers to a historical or traditional region of the highest rank within a state. In Croatia, this is Slavonia, which historically encompassed the entire eastern part of Croatia and was one of the "historical lands" of the Croatian state; in Serbia, this is Voivodina, an autonomous region with the highest level of territorial autonomy.

In our analysis of internal perception for the perceptions of respondents in Vukovar-Srijem County, a near 50–50 split between the spatial concepts of Slavonia and Syrmia is visible, while slightly more than one-fifth indicated other concepts, primarily Eastern Croatia. External perception, on the other hand, among respondents from the rest of Croatia, differs markedly. The displayed area was more often recognised as Syrmia (46%) as opposed to Slavonia (26%), along with a significant share of distribution (around 40%) of various other spatial concepts. The survey results from Serbia showed near-total identification and recognition of the region as Syrmia. Voivodina, as a superordinate region, was indicated by only a handful of respondents (4%).

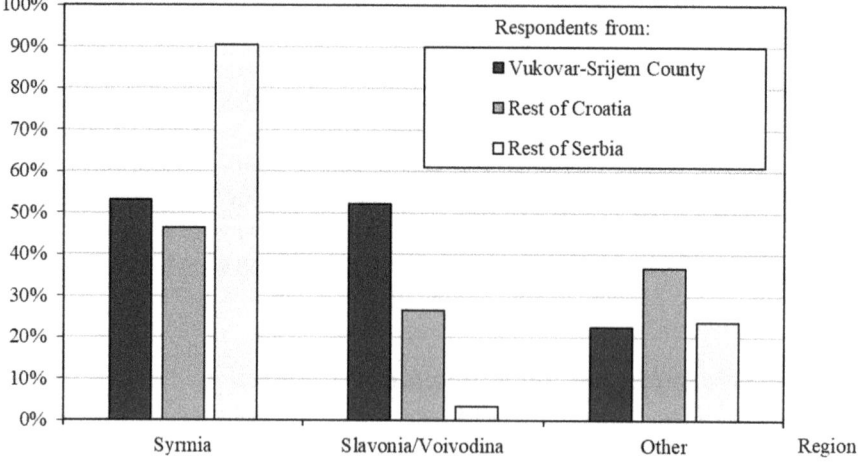

Share of
respondents

Fig. 13.3 Perception/identification of the area of the Croatian and Serbian parts of the traditional region of Syrmia according to respondents from Croatia and Serbia
*in the case of the Croatian part of Syrmia, the second group of columns relates to Slavonia; and Voivodina in the case of the Serbian part of Syrmia
Source: Authors' elaboration

13.5.3   Regional Self-Identification

We researched the regional self-identification of the residents of the Croatian and Serbian parts of Srijem by offering respondents the option of identifying themselves as "Syrmians" or "Slavonians" (in Croatia), or as "Syrmians" or "Voivodinians" (in Serbia). Along with the two options, the respondents had an option to openly iden-tify themselves as they wished; some responses were linked with nationality or other regions (e.g., Dalmatian, Serbian, Rusyn, or Belgradian) and were docu-mented in the "Other" category (Fig. 13.4).

The results showed that a little more than 20% of the respondents in Croatia identified as Syrmians, but the majority (nearly 75%) identified as Slavonians. In Serbia, the situation was diametrically opposite: nearly two-thirds of respondents identified as Syrmians, while only 25% identified as Voivodinians (13% identified themselves as "Other"). Even more indicative is the spatial distribution of results (Fig. 13.5).

In Vukovar-Srijem County, a Syrmian-identified majority is found exclusively along the border with Serbia – in the municipalities of Nijemci, Tovarnik, Lovas, and especially Ilok, 85% of whose population self-identify as Syrmians. Conversely, in the Serbian part, all local administrative units with respondents had a 50% or higher share of Syrmians, apart from parts of larger urban agglomerations of Novi Sad and Belgrade.

Share of respondents

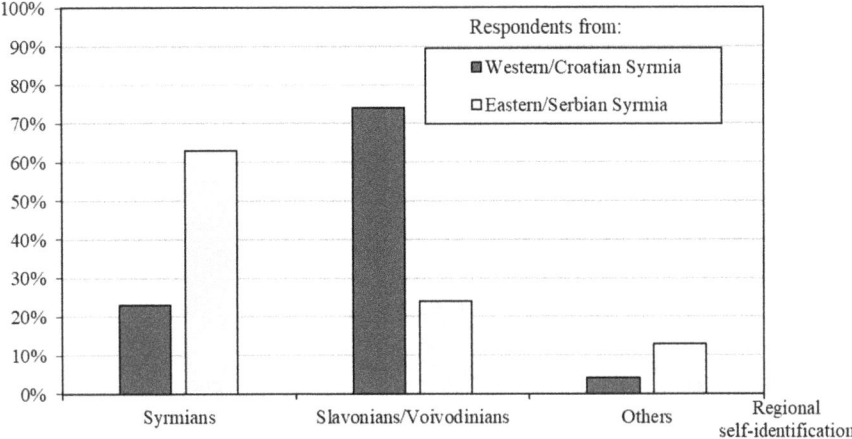

Fig. 13.4 Regional self-identification of respondents from the Croatian and Serbian parts of the traditional region of Syrmia
Source: Authors' elaboration

The question of whether there is a common, transborder Syrmian identity –a perception of the region as a single unit despite the border – showed similar results in both Croatia and Serbia. The perception of a common identity is very expressed and strong, above 50%, and it is above 65% among Croatian respondents (Fig. 13.6).

13.5.4 Primary Level of Territorial Identification

Our research also encompassed the question of the primary level of territorial identity of residents of Syrmia, be it local, regional, or national (Fig. 13.7). Respondents from Croatia nearly uniformly identified, on varying territorial levels, with regional identities being slightly stronger (39%) than local (37%), and one-fourth of respondents identified most strongly with national identity. In Serbia, the results were somewhat differently distributed. Nearly 60% of respondents expressed national identity as that with which they most strongly identified, followed by regional (27%), and local (11%).

13.6 Discussion

The results of the research opened numerous issues related to identity in Syrmia for discussion. Primarily, they related to the perception and identification of the territory of the region, regional self-identification, and the primary level of territorial

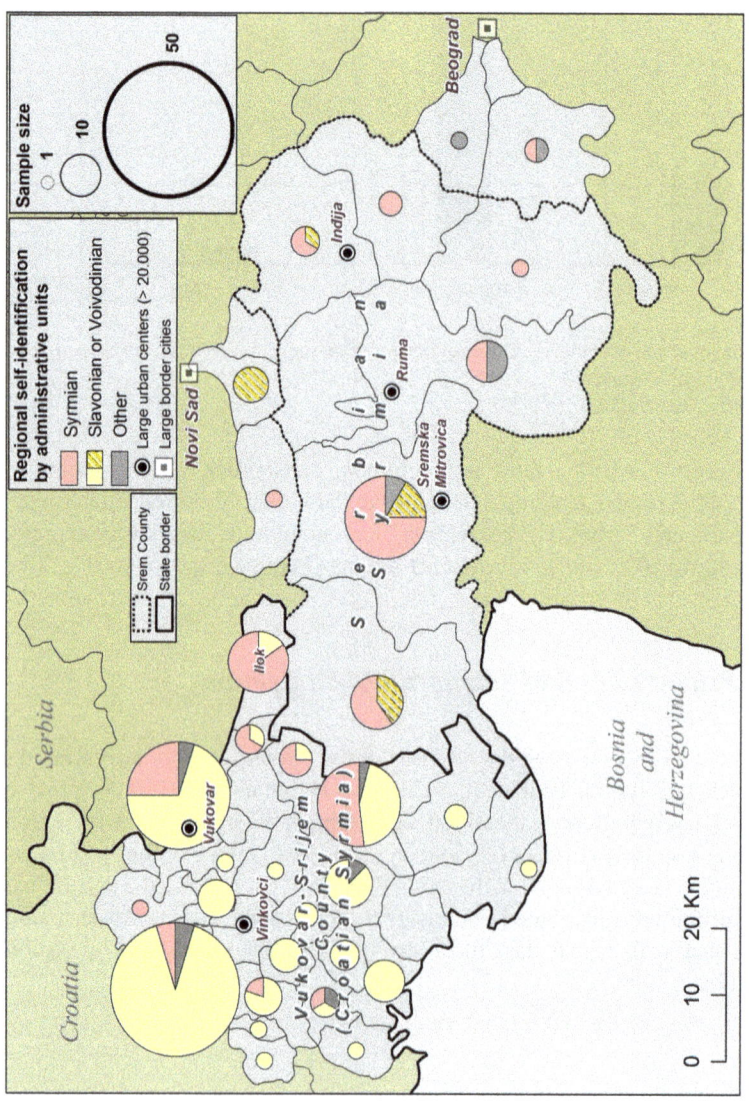

Fig. 13.5 Regional self-identification of respondents from Syrmia, according to LAU
Source: Authors' elaboration based on GADM, 2018 (GIS shapefiles)

Share of respondents

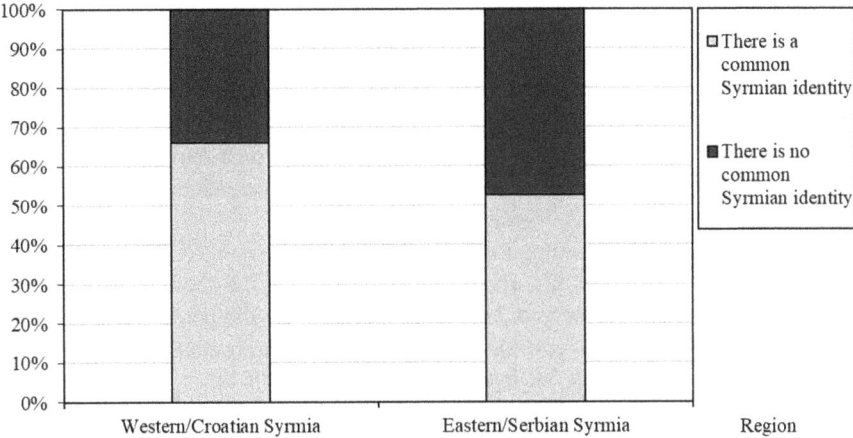

Fig. 13.6 Attitudes of respondents of Syrmia regarding the existence of a common, transborder Syrmian identity
Source: Authors' elaboration

Share of respondents

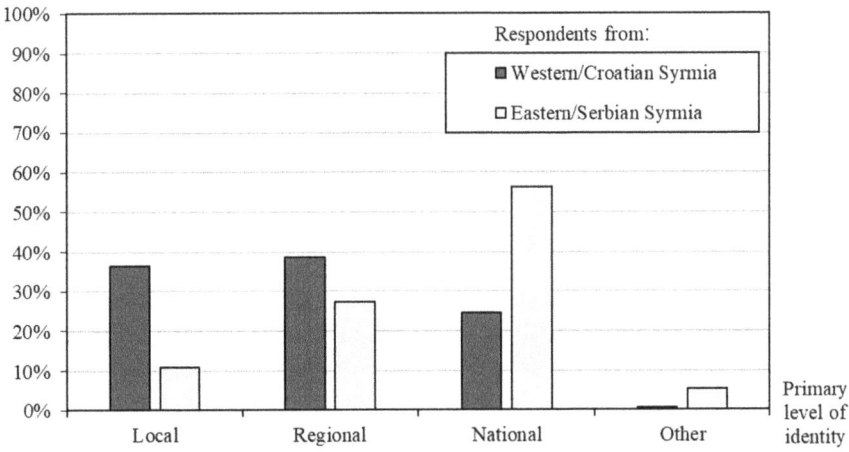

Fig. 13.7 Primary level of territorial identification of respondents in the Croatian and Serbian parts of the traditional region of Syrmia
Source: Authors' elaboration

identification and perception of unity (i.e., of Syrmia as a complete region regardless of the border).

In terms of perception (i.e., recognition and identification of the traditional region of Syrmia), although the internal and external perception of the region was equally strong throughout Croatia, respondents who lived outside Syrmia more strongly differentiated the regional concepts of Slavonia and Syrmia. However, if we compare Croatian respondents from outside Syrmia with Serbian respondents outside Syrmia, we see a clear difference: the Serbian part of the region is almost universally recognized – regarded as Syrmia.

At the same time, Voivodina was only mentioned by a handful of respondents, which is interesting as it is analogous to Slavonia, but in the Serbian part of the region. Differences in perception are significant: the Serbian part of the region is much more recognisable in the external perceptions of residents of Serbia, than the Croatian part of the region is to residents of Croatia.

Although the results regarding internal perceptions of Syrmia (i.e., the conflation of Slavonia and Syrmia), might give the impression that the share of respondents who identify as Slavonian or Syrmian would be equal, we did not find this to be so. Syrmian identity, as far as self-identification goes, is marginalised in favour of Slavonian. Considering this, an interesting comparison of this research could be made with the one conducted by Sarjanović (2014), who, studying regional self-identification in peripheral areas of Slavonia, came to the conclusion that the histori-cal regions of Syrmia and Baranya "are now mostly perceived to be part of a large regional complex in eastern Croatia that is dominated by Slavonia" (Sarjanović, 2014, p. 104). Some of the interviewees hinted at such a relationship – the one in which Slavonia dominates as a spatially superordinate region:

> I consider myself Slavonian because that term encapsulates general cultural differences in relation to other parts of Croatia. (F, 23, Croatia).

Others highlighted the possible national connotations of the regional identities:

> I think that Croats [from Syrmia] tend to self-identify as Slavonians because they perceive the Slavonian identity to emphasise their Croatian identity (M, 44, Croatia).

The latter (stated by a respondent having experience of the Croatian War of Independence along with the post-war politically turbulent period) implicitly points to the obviously existing perception of the transborder nature of Syrmia. Namely, since it is a transborder region, it is also a transnational one, while Slavonia is an unequivocally Croatian regional concept, one of its "historical lands".

Furthermore, Syrmian identity is mostly found along the border and largely dis-sipated further away. Namely, only 5 of 104 respondents from local administrative units that do not border with Serbia considered themselves to be Syrmians (less than 5%). In Serbia, however, the Syrmian identity dominates throughout the region, apart from Novi Sad and Belgrade, which is likely due to their expressed local iden-tity. The survey results' veracity was confirmed by the conducted interviews – most respondents emphasised their Syrmian identity, or dual Syrmian-Voivodinian identity:

> Living in Syrmia since birth, I consider myself both Syrmian and Voivodinian (F, 23, Serbia).

Some respondents even strengthened their regional identity:

Until I enrolled at university [in Novi Sad], I used to feel primarily as a Voivodinian. However, having noted the differences between various parts of the region (regarding accent and mentality), I currently consider myself Syrmian (F, 19, Serbia).

If we compare the spatial reflection of the (majority) Syrmia regional self-identification – the area of the Syrmia perceptual region (as defined in this research) with the borders of the traditional and historical region Syrmia – the differences are obvious. Namely, the Serbian part of the perceptual region, according to documented regional self-identification, encompasses nearly the entire historical region apart from Novi Sad and Belgrade, while, in Croatia, the perceptual region clings exclusively to several municipalities which border Serbia.

Therefore, the results of the perceptions of respondents regarding the existence of a common Syrmian identity, which were, according to survey results, more strongly affirmed in Croatia than in Serbia, are surprising. However, the conducted interviews added another layer to the discussion and yielded several trains of thought regarding the sense (of existence) of a common identity between the two parts of the region (Fig. 13.8). These ideas, as shown by this research, seem to progress in a clockwise manner from the one showing the least amount of commonness (on the left) to the one exhibiting the highest level of sense of common identity (on the right).

Firstly, the state border and the division of Syrmia between the two countries, in addition to all the socio-economic and political consequences that the said division entails (labelled as socio-political reality) strongly curtail the sense of common identity. Most respondents highlight the influence of the border:

I believe the border is quite firm (politically, socially and functionally), granting a minimal connection between the two parts of the region (M, 23, Croatia).

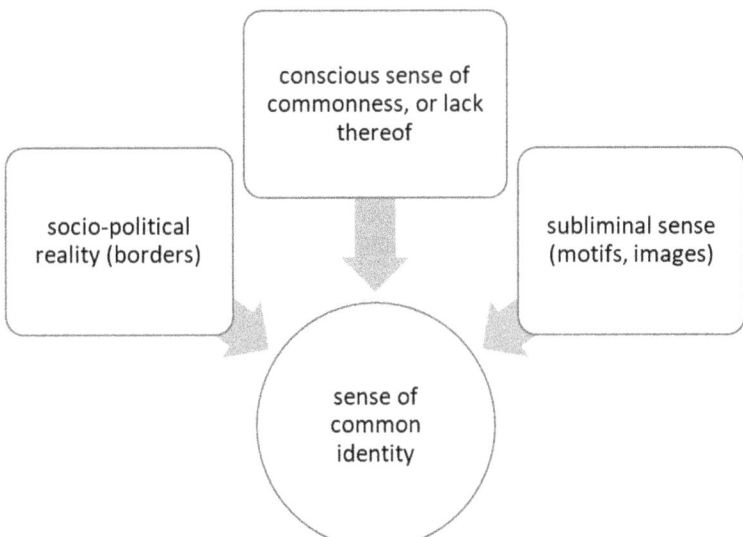

Fig. 13.8 Tripartite model of sense of common identity of a transborder region
Source: Own elaboration

Others, having experienced life in the united region, emphasise the contrast between prior unity and latter national homogenisation impacting sense of commonness:

> [Before the establishment of the state border] Syrmia was very interconnected with people of both nationalities living throughout the region (…) now, the situation is different with many people having migrated from eastern Syrmia to Croatia and vice versa (F, 58, Croatia).

An interesting phenomenon is such a lack of sense of common identity in younger generations to the point of not even knowing about the existence of the other part of the region:

> Honestly, I didn't even know that there was a Croatian part of Syrmia before this interview. So, I personally don't feel any connection (F, 21, Serbia).

The next aspect (labelled as conscious sense of commonness, or lack thereof) encompasses the responses made with a conscious effort to establish whether and to what degree the relationship and commonness exist (or not). The interviewees' responses exhibited a whole spectre of views on common identity. On the positive side, such views included: emphasis of the wholeness of Syrmia as a region, highlighting the cultural and economic connections, as well as shared values, mentality, traditions and customs:

> There clearly is a connection, the intertwining of two nations present in this area for centuries resulted in the formation of a common mentality (F, 23, Serbia).

On the other side, negative outlooks on a shared identity outnumbered the positive ones: refutation of the region's wholeness, the afore-mentioned border and division into two countries, loss of original Syrmian *genre de vie*, different nationalities, languages, religions and script, division of values and identity:

> It is not a single region; after the Croatian War of Independence, identity, values, and traditions were divided into two separate states (F, 46, Croatia).

The final, third aspect, labelled as subliminal sense, proved to be the most unifying one. Unlike the previous aspect, this one deals with a subliminal sense of commonness mirrored in the motifs and images that the inhabitants of the region associate with it. The respondents from both sides of the border had similar motifs of the Syrmia region: its grand rivers, Fruška gora hill and broad plains, common gastronomy and wine-making culture, common traditions, *tamburaši* music, warm hospitality, common dialect, etc. To summarise, although the first two aspects tend to diminish the sense of common identity (to a greater or lesser degree), the third, subliminal aspect exhibits not only the said sense, but also the inhabitants' positive feelings and attachment to the region itself.

The said place attachment was also a prominent leitmotif when we inquired the interviewees about their future perspective regarding the region. Most respondents would prefer to stay in the region, highlighting certain positive aspects of life (calmness, nature, safety, etc.), while emphasising the lack of job opportunities as a primary push factor. Such viewpoints, along with the strong feelings stated through images and motifs, exhibit a refined sense of rootedness, connection and *topophilia* among the inhabitants.

The results of the research regarding the primary territorial identification level with which the respondents mostly identified, made for interesting reading. In Croatia, the three levels of territorial identities were starkly divided, and no level was clearly dominant. The relatively uniform distribution within the research area of Syrmia can be regarded as indicative because it emphasises the fact that there is no strong unifying factor on any level of territorial identification, in contrast to some previous research of other Croatian regions (Marković & Fuerst-Bjeliš, 2015). In Serbia, the results did not vary, and national identity dominated, while regional and local identities were somewhat less expressed by respondents. Although results show that the Syrmian identity (in terms of self-identification) was stronger in Serbia, the regional level of identification was less significantly expressed than among the respondents living in Croatian Syrmia.

It is important to remember that, according to the findings of Pejnović (2009), and Marković and Fuerst-Bjeliš (2015), expressed regional identity is noted in compact communities with stable demographic development, high density of institutions in the area, and common historical-cultural heritage. Despite the common historical and cultural heritage, the region is economically, functionally, and politically separated by the state border (i.e., it cannot be considered compact), with stark differences between its two parts concerning their modern-day demographic, economic and social development within their respective countries. These factors, in addition to a multitude of other ones discussed in this chapter, result in a growing difference in the strength of Syrmian identity. The eastern, Serbian part of the region retains a relatively strong Syrmian identity, unfazed by the superordinated (but often complementary) Voivodinian one, while the western, Croatian part expresses a weakened, spatially restricted Syrmian identity, overshadowed by the broader Slavonian regional identity.

13.7   Conclusion

The process of re-bordering and splitting the region of Syrmia between two states after the collapse of Yugoslavia, accompanied by the consequences of war and political tensions between states, strongly affected the regional identity, perception of unity and place attachment in Syrmia.

When it comes to regional self-identification and subsequently derived proportions of perceptual regions, Syrmian regional identity proved to be strong and almost ubiquitous throughout the Serbian part of the region, except for parts of urban agglomerations of Novi Sad and Beograd. Conversely, Syrmian regional identity in the Croatian part is all but absent in most of the region save for several municipalities near the border with Serbia. Reasons for such results are complex and varied: differing demographic and economic trends (within their countries), differences in area and population in the two parts (a larger part of the region is in Serbia), ambiguousness of the region's boundaries (straightforward in Serbia, vague in Croatia), variable connections to superordinate regions of Slavonia and Voivodina, along with possible national connotations regarding the region in Croatia (contrast between Slavonia as an unequivocally Croatian region and Syrmia as a divided one).

The division of the region resulted in a significant severance of ties (economic, social, functional, etc.) between the two parts of the region, yielding a strong impact on the sense of commonness between the parts. To examine the different facets of this impact, we developed a tripartite model of sense of commonness in transborder regions. According to the model, although the current socio-political reality (split region) impedes any sense of commonness, and the inhabitants' viewpoint on commonness and possible cooperation exhibits an array of differing opinions, both positive and negative, the subliminal sense of commonness persists, with similar images and motifs of the region demonstrating strong feelings and place attachment from both sides of the region.

Apart from the motifs, the inhabitants' outlook on the future also shows the degree of their place attachment. Their cautious positivity and eagerness to stay in the region if the opportunity presents itself (primarily in terms of job security) display a sense of connection and rootedness that exists despite differences in the strength of regional identity. Encouraging is the fact that such an attitude was expressed almost unequivocally by younger generations, demonstrating two important points. First, although place attachment is thought to increase with age, a strong sense of place attachment is evident among the youth, a quality vital to ageing communities and especially in depopulating areas. Second, even in the face of negative demographic and economic trends (particularly in Croatian Syrmia), residents' place attachment remains firm and unyielding. This perspective, shared by residents on both sides of the border, could prove to be a good starting point for stronger cooperation between the two parts of the region. The analysis of the relationship between the place (regional) identity and place attachment thus has shown that they are strongly intertwined, but that their relationship is not (necessarily) directly reciprocal. Indeed, it has been shown that even the negativity of socio-political processes associated with a place or region and even the lack of prospects in the region does not lead to a weakening of place attachment or even to detachment or alienation. Place attachment can be very strong in such places because people value their dwelling place for anchoring a dense network of friendship, kinship, and support (cf. Kirkness & Tijé-Dra, 2017, p. 246).

To sum up, the direct implications of our research point towards the European policy of transborder cooperation whose paradigm could help (re)develop mutual relations among institutions in the region and, most importantly, among inhabitants, as a prerequisite for understanding, cooperation, and friendship. For instance, western, Croatian Syrmia forms a part of the Danube-Drava-Sava Euroregion, together with Hungary and Bosnia and Herzegovina, while Serbia is still not a member. The re-bordering process notwithstanding, our research showed that the place attachment and sense of commonness of the Syrmia region can still be activated in the policy of transborder cooperation. Implementing such policies could reshape the Syrmia region – from the one divided by the border to the one that spans the border.

References

Altman, I., & Low, S. M. (Eds.). (1992). *Place attachment. Human behaviour and environment* (Advances in Theory and Research) (Vol. 12). Springer. https://doi.org/10.1007/978-1-4684-8753-4_1

Antonsich, M. (2010). Meanings of place and aspects of the self: An interdisciplinary and empirical account. *GeoJournal., 75*, 119–132. https://doi.org/10.1007/s10708-009-9290-9

Banini, T., & Ilovan, O.-R. (Eds.). (2021). *Representing place and territorial identities in Europe. Discourses, images and practices* (GeoJournal Library) (Vol. 127). Springer. https://doi.org/10.1007/978-3-030-66766-5

Bauman, Z. (2001). *Community: Seeking safety in an insecure world.* Polity Press/Blackwell Publishing Ltd.

Chow, K., & Healey, M. (2008). Place attachment and place identity: First-year undergraduates making the transition from home to university. *Journal of Environmental Psychology., 28*, 362–372. https://doi.org/10.1016/j.jenvp.2008.02.011

Cifrić, I., & Nikodem, K. (2006). Socijalni identitet u Hrvatskoj [Social Identity in Croatia. Concept and Dimensions of Social Identity]. *Socijalna ekologija, 15*(3), 173–202.

Cifrić, I., & Nikodem, K. (2007). Relacijski identiteti. Socijalni identitet i relacijske dimenzije [Relational Identities: Social Identity and Relational Dimensions]. *Društvena istraživanja, 16*(3 (89)), 331–358. hrcak.srce.hr/18939.

Croatian Bureau of Statistics. (2022). *Census of population, households and Dwellings in 2021.* Zagreb. https://popis2021.hr. Accessed 15 Jan 2022.

Cross, J. E. (2015). Processes of place attachment: An interactional framework. *Symbolic Interaction, 38*, 493–520.

Fuerst-Bjeliš, B., & Glamuzina, N. (2021). *The historical geography of Croatia – Territorial change and cultural landscapes.* Springer. https://doi.org/10.1007/978-3-030-68433-4

GADM. (2018). GADM data. https://gadm.org/data.html. Accessed 10 June 2021.

Hartshorne, R. (1939). *The nature of geography* (Association of American Geographers). Science Press.

Hernández, B., Hidalgo, M. C., Salazar-Laplace, M. E., & Hess, S. (2007). Place attachment and place identity in natives and non-natives. *Journal of Environmental Psychology., 27*, 310–319. https://doi.org/10.1016/j.jenvp.2007.06.003

Jordan, T. (1978). Perceptual regions in Texas. *Geographical Review, 68*, 293–307.

Jorgensen, B. S., & Stedman, R. C. (2001). Sense of place as an attitude: Lakeshore owners' attitudes toward their properties. *Journal of Environmental Psychology., 21*, 233–248. https://doi.org/10.1006/jevp.2001.0226

Keating, M. (2000). *The new regionalism in Western Europe. Territorial restructuring and political change.* Edward Elgar.

Kirkness, P., & Tijé-Dra, A. (Eds.). (2017). *Negative neighbourhood reputation and place attachment. The production and contestation of territorial stigma.* Routledge.

Kyle, G., Graefe, A., Manning, R., & Bacon, J. (2004). Effects of place attachment on users' perceptions of social and environmental conditions in a natural setting. *Journal of Environmental Psychology., 24*, 213–225. https://doi.org/10.1016/j.jenvp.2003.12.006

Lewicka, M. (2011). Place attachment: How far have we come in the last 40 years? *Journal of Environmental Psychology., 31*, 207–230. https://doi.org/10.1016/j.jenvp.2010.10.001

Marković, I., & Fuerst-Bjeliš, B. (2015). Prostorni identitet kao pokretačka snaga razvoja turizma: komparativna analiza regija Bjelovara i Čakovca [Spatial Identity as a Driving Force in Tourism Development: Comparative Analysis of the Bjelovar and Čakovec Regions]. *Hrvatski geografski glasnik, 77*(1), 71–88.

Miroslav Krleža Institute of Lexicography: Srijem [Syrmia]. *Proleksis Encyclopaedia.* https://proleksis.lzmk.hr/46649/. Accessed 22 Feb 2021.

Paasi, A. (1986). The institutionalization of regions: A theoretical framework for understanding the emergence of regions and the constitution of regional identity. *Fennia, 164*, 105–146.

Paasi, A. (2002). Bounded spaces in the mobile world: Deconstructing "regional identity". *Tijdschrift voor Economische en Sociale Geografie, 93*(2), 137–148.

Paasi, A. (2021). Foreword. Place, territory and identities in a fast-changing world. In T. Banini & O.-R. Ilovan (Eds.), *Representing Place and Territorial Identities in Europe. Discourses, Images and Practices* (GeoJournal Library) (Vol. 127). Springer. https://doi.org/10.1007/978-3-030-66766-5

Pejnović, D. (2009). Geografske osnove identiteta Like [The Geographical Foundations of the Lika Identity]. In Ž. Holjevac (Ed.), *Identitet Like: korijeni i razvitak [Lika identity: Roots and Development]* (Vol. 1, pp. 47–84). Institute of Social Sciences Ivo Pilar.

Peng, J., Strijker, D., & Wu, Q. (2020). Place identity: How far have we come in exploring its meanings? *Frontiers in Psychology., 11*, 294. https://doi.org/10.3389/fpsyg.2020.00294

Proshansky, H. M. (1976). *Environmental psychology: people and their physical setting*. Holt, Rinehart and Winston.

Proshansky, H. M. (1978). The city and self-identity. *Environment and Behaviour., 10*, 147–169. https://doi.org/10.1177/0013916578102002

Proshansky, H. M., Fabian, A. K., & Kaminoff, R. (1983). Place identity: Physical world socialization of the self. *Journal of Environmental Psychology, 3*, 57–83. https://doi.org/10.1016/S0272-4944(83)80021-8

Sarjanović, I. (2014). *Slavonija – identitet regije i regionalna samoidentifikacija [Slavonia – identity of the region and regional self-identification]*. Doctoral dissertation. University of Zagreb Faculty of Science, Department of Geography. Zagreb.

Sekulić, A. (1997). *Hrvatski srijemski mjestopisi [Croatian Srijem place names]*. Školska knjiga.

Shamai, S. (1991). Sense of place: An empirical measurement. *Geoforum, 22*, 347–358. https://doi.org/10.1016/0016-7185(91)90017-K

Statistical Office of the Republic of Serbia (2021). *Municipalities and regions in the Republic of Serbia, 2021*. Belgrade. https://www.stat.gov.rs/en-us/publikacije/publication/?p=13352. Accessed 15 Jan 2022

Vukosav, B., & Fuerst-Bjeliš, B. (2015). Media perception of spatial identities: Constructing an imaginative map of Dalmatian interior. *Geoadria, 20*(1), 23–40. https://doi.org/10.15291/geoadria

Whittlesey, D. (1954). The regional concept and the regional method. In P. E. James & C. F. Jones (Eds.), *American geography, inventory and prospect* (pp. 19–68). Syracuse University Press.

Chapter 14
From Place Attachment to Toponymic Attachment: Can Geographical Names Foster Social Cohesion and Regional Development? The Case of South Carinthia (Austria)

Alexis Sancho Reinoso (ID)

14.1 Introduction

Geographical (or place) names are not only witnesses of the past but are also key to an understanding of our present. They are a fundamental part of our cultural landscape, our language, and our identity. In multilingual areas, place names can be a sensitive issue. This is the case in the bilingual part of the Austrian province of Carinthia, where the public use and visibility of Slovene place names have been highly controversial for decades (Pirker, 2011). It was not until 2011 that political agreement to erect 164 bilingual signposts across the region was reached, which contributed decisively to deescalating a historical conflict and normalising the public presence of Slovene names (Hellwig, 2015).

Current initiatives in favour of erecting more bilingual signs in some Carinthian municipalities, most of them with a mainly German-speaking population, can be interpreted as a strong sign of reconciliation after decades of conflict. Less well known are initiatives that foster the preservation of microtoponyms (i.e., names of small-scale territorial features, including field names). In 2010, Slovene field and house names were included in the Austrian National Inventory of UNESCO Intangible Cultural Heritage (Piko-Rustia, 2020). In addition, systematic documentation efforts have led to an increased visibility of certain municipalities in the public space and the publication of a series of bilingual maps. These initiatives might also have contributed to the above-mentioned reconciliation.

This chapter aims to elucidate whether microtoponyms (understood as territorial attachment indicators and identity markers) can contribute to strengthening social

---

A. Sancho Reinoso (✉)
Department of Social and Cultural Anthropology, University of Vienna, Vienna, Austria
e-mail: alexis.sancho.reinoso@univie.ac.at

© The Author(s), under exclusive license to Springer Nature
Switzerland AG 2022
O.-R. Ilovan, I. Markuszewska (eds.), *Preserving and Constructing Place Attachment in Europe*, GeoJournal Library 131,
https://doi.org/10.1007/978-3-031-09775-1_14

and territorial ties and become a driver of regional development. It focuses on south Carinthia, a border area located at a unique crossroads of Germanic, Romanic, and Slavic cultures. There, multilingualism has led to a situation where two different social groups (the monolingual German-speaking majority and the bilingual Slovene-speaking minority) share the places they live, work, take leisure, etc. The region faces the typical challenges of a peripheral rural and mountainous area.

I explore the role geographical names play in the daily lives of the residents, from their personal and subjective perspective, and from a historical, symbolic, and political angle. To achieve this, I have analysed the results of a field survey conducted in south Carinthia between 2016 and 2018 in the framework of the bilateral research project entitled "The Politics and the Poetics of Toponymy, Identity and Place in Multilingual Areas. A Comparative Study of Carinthia (Austria) and the Těšín Area (Czechia)" (see Acknowledgements section).

After a synthetic description of the study area, I present a brief review of contributions from geography and toponymy about place, place attachment and place names as spatial identity features, followed by the methods used to carry out the study. The research results are then presented and interpreted considering the current academic discourse. Finally, the main findings are summarised, and a series of policy recommendations are proposed.

14.2   Presentation of the Case Study Area

The case study is located in the southernmost part of the Austrian province of Carinthia (German: Kärnten; Slovene: Koroška), bordering Italy (Friuli-Venezia-Giulia) and Slovenia (Gorenjska, Savinjska and Koroška). This area stretches from west to east between the municipalities of Feistritz an der Gail/Bistrica na Zilji and Neuhaus/Suha and is shaped by a series of Alpine relief units (notably the Carnic Alps and the Karawanks), two main river valleys (Gail and Drau), and the Basin of Klagenfurt. It is usually divided into three geographical areas: the westernmost Gailtal (Slovene: Zilja), the Rosental (Rož) at the centre, and the easternmost Jauntal (Podjuna) (Fig. 14.1).

This area is heterogeneous in terms of settlement structure and population dynamics. On the one hand, it includes the urban region of Klagenfurt (Celovec in Slovenian) and Villach (Beljak in Slovenian), the two main Carinthian cities. This urban area has a concentration of more than half of the entire population of the province (Amt der Kärntner Landesregierung, 2021b). In contrast, the rest of the area is much less influenced by urban dynamics, particularly the inner mountainous valleys in the southeast, such as the Vellach/Bela Valley, bordering Slovenia. These valleys have a marked rural character and are less well connected to the main communication infrastructure network (Seger, 2019). Tourism is probably the only economic activity that shapes the whole area, although there are important differences in the type and quality of the tourism offer, as well as the target groups.

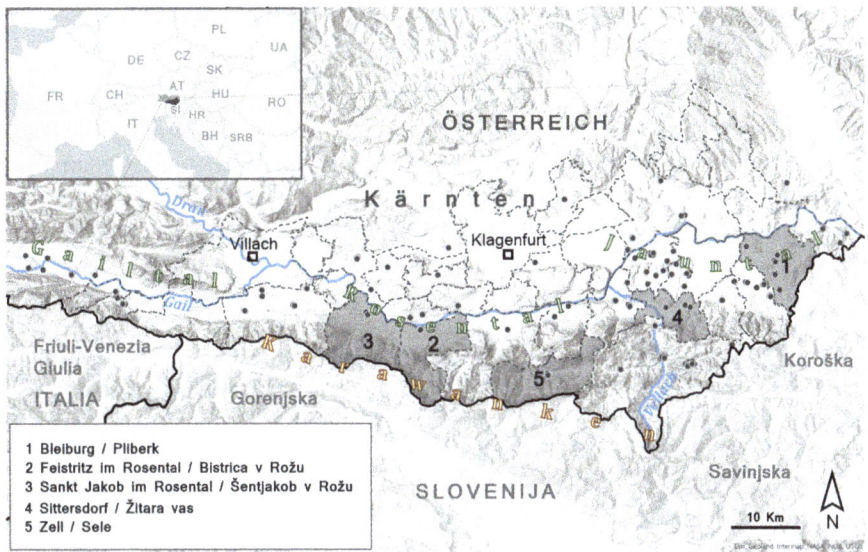

Fig. 14.1 Location and main features of the selected case study area. (Source: Author's elaboration based on ESRI base maps)

This area's bilingual character (German and Slovene) is crucial for this investigation.[1] As mentioned, the so-called 'Carinthian Slovenes' are bilingual and live together with the monolingual German-speaking majority. The Slavonic presence dates back to the sixth century in most parts of the current territory of Austria. Slavonic population was gradually assimilated by the Bavarians, who established themselves after the eighth century (Seger, 2019). While place names of Slavonic roots have remained throughout the Austrian Eastern Alps (Pohl, 2012), the language (which evolved into current Slovene) has been preserved only in south Carinthia. Slovene speakers in Carinthia have gradually declined over the last 150 years. In the most recent census that asked for ethnic affiliation (in 2001), 12,586 respondents declared Slovene as their first language, whereas this figure was more than 85,000 in the 1880 census (Narodni svet Koroški Slovencev, 2021).

Figure 14.1 shows two features of high relevance to this chapter. First, the grey dots indicate the place of residence of the interviewees (see more details in the Research Methods section below). Second, the five municipalities highlighted in dark grey are those selected to showcase the topic of this chapter, namely: the role of microtoponyms in fostering social cohesion and, potentially, regional development. Located in different subregions and shaped by different socio-economic dynamics, these municipalities share a marked bilingual character, which is reflected in past and current attempts to continue to erect bilingual signposts.

---

[1] The case study area corresponds to the bilingual school district declared by federal law (in German: *Minderheiten-Schulgesetz für Kärnten*), according to Art. 7 of the 1955 State Treaty.

14.3   Geographical Names at a Crossroads Between Place Attachment, Identity, and Cultural Heritage

Toponyms lie at the roots of place attachment and space-related identity. The epistemology of place names is intimately related to the phenomenological interpretation of 'place' as "any environmental locus in and through which individual or group actions, experiences, intentions, and meanings are drawn together spatially" (cf. Casey, 2009 and Relph, 1976 in Seamon, 2014, p. 11). Linking places with people creates meaningful locations to which people feel attached (Cresswell, 2004), and this leads to the notion of place attachment. Names are at the core of human existence and have deep emotional and psychological ties (Relph, 1976) or affective bonds (Low & Altman, 1992 in Lewicka, 2014). Place attachment has been interpreted as a compound of different aspects, including "geographical and cultural qualities, (…) degree of personal and social involvement, quality of life, environmental aesthetics, individual and group identity with place" (Seamon, 2014, p. 12). The latter interpretation was highlighted by Williams and Vaske (2003), who identify the two main dimensions of place as identity (i.e. emotional attachment) and dependence (i.e. functional attachment).

Language plays a key role in the process whereby space becomes place. Places need names, otherwise they cannot exist: "naming (…) can draw attention to places and locate them in a wider cultural narrative" (Cresswell, 2004, p. 98). Yi-Fu Tuan (1991) set the foundation of the relationship between language and place making. He argues that place names are not simple arbitrary labels, but that they create places and transform the world into a meaningful and manageable place. As has been argued, place names are one expression of the manifold dimensions of the relationship between humans and the natural world "in making use of natural resources when they reflect natural characteristics, in cultural transformation of the geographical space by shaping it visually and mentally, in identity building with individual members of a cultural group, and with a whole cultural group as labels and in supporting emotional ties" (Jordan, 2012, p. 129). Identity and attachment are therefore vital elements of place names.

Toponymy, the branch of onomastics concerned with the study of toponyms or place names, is situated at a crossroads between history, geography and linguistics, sociology and psychology (Tort & Sancho, 2012). In addition to classic approaches which characterise place names as "windows into the past" (Jordan & Mácha, 2021), the so-called 'critical toponymy' emphasises the cultural and political aspects of naming processes and, significantly, the power relationships behind these processes (Basso, 1996). Consequently, place names are a controversial issue, particularly in multilingual areas. In these places, the "official use of minority names frequently stirs up conflict among the local population" (Jordan, 2012, p. 127). The definitive reasoning behind such a phenomenon is the fact that "a toponym can be a symbol of multiple identities, and the use of two toponyms for one place can be a strong reminder of the multiple place histories and cultural identities which exist for a locale" (Kostanski, 2016, p. 8).

Names of small-scale spatial features, including fields, rivers, forests, mountains, lakes, and many others, are called microtoponyms (Villette & Purves, 2018). In this chapter, field names (or *Flurnamen* in German) are important because they tend to be used in urban settlements (e.g. as street names). Due to their small-scale nature, field names are naturally tied to places, as they denote landscape features and, therefore, have a tremendous power of attachment and identity:

> although many people do not seem to be particularly aware of the historical richness of the place names in their surroundings, they may still feel that the name stock contributes to their link to the land. People who have become acquainted with the etymological contents of names will of course appreciate their historical value to a greater degree. Through the place names of a district small or large, in particular its settlement names, it is possible to read many details of the area's history (Helleland, 2012, p. 102).

Entanglements between place attachment, place identity and microtoponyms are addressed by Kostanski (2016), through what she calls 'toponymic attachment', which is "a positive or negative association individuals and groups make with real or imagined toponyms" (p. 2). Toponymic attachment consists of "develop[ing] an understanding of the relationships between people and toponyms" and of "determin[ing] whether there are underlying factors which assist people and communities in forming attachments to not only the places in which they live, work and relax, but also with the toponyms for those places" (Kostanski, 2016, p. 9). The argument continues: "if humans create an emotional attachment to a place (be it on a small or large scale, in a positive or negative way) then the toponym must, in some form or another, be possible of symbolizing this attachment" (Kostanski, 2016, p. 6). Toponymic attachment naturally leads to 'toponymic identity', which is what "connects a population with their history" (Kostanski, 2016, p. 8). In multilingual areas, perpetuating certain name forms (e.g., in a given majority language) leads to the reinforcement of certain forms of community identity at the expense of others. Toponyms are representations of this community identity (Kostanski, 2016).

The third key element of toponyms is heritage. Place names can play an important role in promoting a territory – for example in tourism marketing through place branding. Signposting and cartography play a key role in this process: "maps and signage can (…) act as a force with which notions of space and definitions of what constitutes a place with worthwhile cultural characteristics are reinforced" (Kostanski, 2016, p. 16). If place names are a cornerstone of place attachment and identity, if they have the capacity to promote the piece of territory they represent, then they constitute cultural elements that can be treated as heritage (i.e., worthy of conservation and commemoration). In the last decade, the United Nations Group of Experts on Geographical Names (UNGEGN) has promoted place names as part of intangible cultural heritage, thereby potentially becoming part of the UNESCO World Heritage List.

Institutional recognition of heritage is arguably a critical development strategy, involving activities, particularly tourism, that might bring benefits to both locals and visitors (Petronela, 2016), and ultimately boosting regional development (Abankina, 2013). On the other hand, becoming part of UNESCO World Heritage might not be a guarantee of (sustainable) development per se, particularly when heritage is managed by national interests, as is the case in some developing countries, instead of being treated as a global richness (Van der Auwera & Schramme, 2014). A recent report from the Council of Europe's Congress of Local and Regional Authorities concludes that:

> policies and actions on cultural heritage allow [cities and regions] to engage with diverse communities within and across borders, to reconcile conflicting narratives and boost the economic strength of their territories to achieve higher living standards. By bringing different stakeholders together, local authorities can contribute to improving sustainable economic development, social inclusion and participatory governance", and that "by adapting and transforming cultural heritage policies (…), local and regional authorities can promote intercultural dialogue and strengthen social cohesion by involving local citizens and improving cooperation with disconnected communities (Toce & Dourou, 2020, p. 29).

One of the main arguments for including place names in the UNESCO World Heritage List is to prevent them from disappearing. This is particularly important when dealing with field names, since contemporary economic restructuring very often leads to rapid disappearance of both the material and non-material dimensions of a cultural landscape, including place names, hitherto preserved through old peasant generations (Piko-Rustia, 2020). When they belong to a minority language, field names are under even more threat of disappearing. In such situations, institutionalisation is a way to preserve them, as is the case in south Carinthia, where Slovene field names were included in the Austrian National Inventory of the UNESCO Intangible Cultural Heritage (Piko-Rustia, 2020).

14.4   Research Methods

This chapter is based on several different methods. The main pillar of the analysis is comprised of semi-structured interviews that were conducted during the research project. The original interview guidelines consisted of 40 questions, addressing such issues as group affiliation, language, and toponyms. Eight questions with special relevance to this chapter were selected (see Table 14.1). During the project, 132 interviews were conducted in total (see Fig. 14.1); 84 of these form the basis of analysis and interpretation in this chapter.

In addition, eight short telephone interviews were conducted with selected representatives from the five municipalities indicated in Fig. 14.1. At least one representative from each municipality was interviewed. These talks took place well after the interviews had been carried out and after the publication of the research project results. They focused on the following three topics: (i) the current municipal policy of bilingual signposting; (ii) local appreciation of further bilingual signposts, particularly street names; and (iii) the potential of field names becoming a regional development factor.

Table 14.1 Interview questions selected for this chapter

Topic	Questions from the guidelines
Tourism development	Does German/Slovene bilingualism make southern Carinthia a more attractive tourism destination?
Signpost perception	How do you/would you perceive bilingual signs in your village/town?
	What do/would these signs in your village/town express?
	Should street name plates also be bilingual?
Signpost appreciation	What do bilingual signposts in Carinthia mean for you?
	When are bilingual signposts appropriate and when not?
Bilingual names in maps	Would you find it appropriate to also reflect Slovene toponyms on tourism/hiking/biking maps?
	Do the official Austrian topographical maps reflect official Slovene toponyms?

Source: Author's elaboration

Another method used for analysis in this chapter was a field survey questionnaire (n = 589) that was also conducted during the research project. The questionnaire covered the same topics as the semi-structured interviews, but it did not reach all population groups in an equal manner, being biased towards well-educated and bilingual respondents. This bias can be identified in the semi-structured interviews too, yet in a much lesser degree (Jordan & Sancho, 2021). Nevertheless, this fact is critical to understand results and discussion, as well as the conclusion sections below. In this chapter, I focus only on one independent variable from the questionnaire (i.e. language spoken at home) and the influence it has on the perception of bilingual signposts (both their presence at local and regional level, as well as their social and cultural significance).

In addition, in order to explore the potential inclusion of place names (as cultural heritage) in regional development strategies, a benchmark analysis of the existing planning tools for regional development that are in force in the case study area (see Table 14.2) was conducted. In this respect, it should be borne in mind that the case study area is divided into three Local Action Groups (LAG) (i.e. associations of local public and private partners managing EU funds, typically from the LEADER programme).

14.5   Results and Discussion

As outlined in the introduction, the findings of this chapter are divided into two themes: first, the extent to which social acceptance of Slovene toponyms indicates an appreciation of place names; and second, why the institutional recognition of field names has not been incorporated into regional development strategies.

Table 14.2 Regional development tools included in the analysis

Planning tool	Period/Date of adoption	Organisation	Included municipalities from the case study area	Source
Regional development strategy	2014–2020	LAG lower Carinthia		Plaimer et al. (2018)
Development strategy	2020	LAG 'surround-ings of Villach'		Primosch (2020)
Regional development strategy	V1.0, July 2021	LAG Hermagor region		Amt der Kärntner Landesregierung (2021a)
Regional development strategy	V1.0, July 2021	Association of Central Carinthian Region		Amt der Kärntner Landesregierung (2021b)
Report on executed LEADER projects	2013–2020	Government of Carinthia	All municipalities	Amt der Kärntner Landesregierung (2020)
Report on best practices from LEADER projects	2000–2013	LAG Nockregion-Oberkärnten	All municipalities	Sacherer (n.d.)

Source: Author's elaboration

14.5.1 Does High Social Acceptance Mean High Appreciation – Or a Negative Toponymic Attachment?

Among the interviewees, there was a distinct positive attitude regarding the presence of bilingual signs (both in Carinthia and in their homeplaces). Results from the field survey questionnaire confirm this overall picture. Nevertheless, there were differences among respondents, mainly based on their language background. There appeared to be a clear divide between bilingual and monolingual respondents. Among the former, practically everyone speaking either Slovene and German or just Slovene at home considered bilingual signs in Carinthia as a "very important" issue and bilingual signs in their home place as "very positive". In contrast, among the latter (i.e. the German-speaking respondents), the degree of support to both issues is tangibly lower. However, it has to be said that positive attitudes are clearly more constructive than explicitly negative ones, which are fairly irrelevant (see Jordan & Sancho, 2021 for further details).

Thus, the results indicate a generalised positive attitude (with the above-indicated nuances) towards the presence of Slovene names on bilingual signs in south Carinthia. Yet, the differences expressed in the questionnaire and particularly in the qualitative field work lead me to argue that a social acceptance of toponyms does not automatically engender social appreciation. I will develop my arguments further by focusing on the role of microtoponyms. Although it has been argued that well-preserved microtoponyms are appreciated by the local population, regardless of their language and cultural background (Piko-Rustia, 2020), the findings from the qualitative data lead me to draw more cautious conclusions. An illustrative example is the on-going process of street naming and the subsequent changes to the address system in certain municipalities, particularly in Sankt Jakob im Rosental/ Šentjakob v Rožu. There, streets are being given names, ostensibly due to urban growth, which make traditional postal addresses (consisting of just the settlement name and the house number) no longer practical. This issue was raised by a significant number of interviewees, who criticised both the nature of new street names:

> In St. Jakob [im Rosental], (…) old field names are being erased from postal addresses and are substituted with invented names such as 'old-sight street', 'cloves street'… They become official names, and with them Slovene-speaking names that structure the locality disappear. (…) something that has evolved across centuries will be now [changed] by unimaginative, mundane names that one can find elsewhere (Interview #32 – 57-year-old male).

> In St. Jakob in Rosental, there is a (…) citizen initiative asking for the conservation of the old place, field and street names. Indeed! This is something valuable! Unlike, I don't know, 'Oak lane' or this kind of stuff… this is… fanciless… and has absolutely neither regional nor cultural value. Disfiguring place names is something I just find cultureless (Interview #39, 54-year-old male).

… as well as the fact that new addresses might become monolingual:

> Our street has a beautiful name, but if I have a completely neutral name such as, I don't know, 'Forest lane', then I write 'Forest lane' and the house number and then 'Sankt Kanzian' [*name of the municipality*] and the postal code. This means that the name of the

village disappears. And St. Kanzian has no bilingual signposts, but Sankt Primus [*Slo: Šentprimož; name of the interviewee's village*] has. This means that my postal address has become only German. It has disappeared [*the bilingual name of the village*]! I don't know whether it was done on purpose or it's just a coincidence (Interview #36, 24-old male; italic text added by author).

When I confronted representatives from the selected municipalities about this issue, a heterogeneous picture emerged. Bleiburg/Pliberk and Zell/Sele are the only municipalities which have adopted bilingual signage for all settlements and a fully bilingual naming policy, which includes street and house name plates. The rest of the municipalities (Sittersdorf/Žitara vas, Feistritz im Rosental/Bistrica v Rožu, and St. Jakob im Rosental/Šentjakob) actively promote bilingual signposting, but they focus exclusively on official town and settlement signage, which *de facto* excludes street names. So far, new street names are being introduced in St. Jakob im Rosental/ Šentjakob v Rožu only, while traditional addresses remain in the others. After having inquired about the reasons for this policy, the mayor of St. Jakob explained that street names are not based on field names "because the municipal council decided on an agreement basis that street names should be monolingual as happens in the rest of Europe", and added that in the municipality, all settlement name plates are already bilingual, as are house name plates. He argued that field names are inevitably disappearing, that they are known only by the peasantry, and that most of them do not have a consolidated written form. Another significant outcome from the interviews is a rather pessimistic vision regarding the role of field names as something that could potentially unite traditionally divided positions about the presence of bilingual names in public spaces:

Field names are as much as important [as the other place names], or even more important, because... I think field names should be of interest for German speakers, (…) because they are part of THEIR homeland. Field names (…) are our direct, almost deep rooted… homeland code. I mean, on signs, on house names and so on. Because they [come] from many generations back in time… and my take on this is that German speakers see them as THEIR treasure and they say: 'yes, this is actually our piece of history, we want to preserve them, because it [the piece] is OURS, precisely ours! (Interview #32 – 57-year-old male).

These kinds of views bring me back to what Kostanski (2016) argues; namely, toponymic attachment can be either positive or negative, and identities can be based on a benign relationship to place names, or on an opposition to them. In spite of a general social acceptance, in practice, only members of the Slovene-speaking minority (in addition to some German-speaking 'sympathisers') show a strong attachment to 'their' names. The majority, though, is not particularly interested in this issue and does not seem to show any particular relationship to Slovene names, including field names. In some cases, it can be stated that most people might still have a sceptical attitude due to the fact that bilingual signposts have been a political and social issue for decades in Carinthia.

On the other hand, conservative attitudes among political representatives, who do not want to test the solidness of the 2011 agreement, can lead to contradictory naming policies. The above-depicted declarations from the representative of St. Jakob are illustrative in this respect. His statements about the lack of consolidated written forms and about field names' inevitable fate are highly controversial. If true, they should be a strong reason to adopt active preservation and promotion policies; which is not the case in most municipalities. In my opinion, these attitudes from both ordinary people and policy makers reflect a lack of a generalised social appreciation of place names. In this case (and following Williams & Vaske, 2003), it seems that 'functional attachment' (based on dependence) exists only if 'emotional attachment' (based on identity) exists.

14.5.2 Does Institutional Recognition of Slovene Field Names Lead to Their Inclusion in Regional Development Strategies?

Just 1 year after Slovenian field names were included in the National Inventory of the UNESCO Intangible Heritage, the cross-border project 'FLU-LED' (Slovenska prosvetna zveza/Slowenischer Kulturverein, 2011), which aimed to preserve and disseminate microtoponyms in local dialectal forms, was initiated among local and regional partners from both sides of the Austrian-Slovenian border. The main outcome of the project was an impressive inventory of names based on documentation gleaned from local knowledge in more than 40 municipalities. FLU-LED is particularly relevant to this chapter for two reasons. First, the project mobilised different generations of the local population: the elderly as local knowledge providers, and the young as a target for education and awareness raising. Second, an array of maps was produced both in digital and paper formats. The base map of the whole region is interactive and is available on the FLU-LED bilingual portal. In addition, a series of bilingual maps (nine as of November 2021) which include field names in both official Slovene and dialectal form has been created. Some of these maps are being used actively by municipal offices for promotion purposes, such as in Finkenstein am Faaker See/Bekštajn ob Baškem jezeru and Feistritz im Rosental/Bistrica v Rožu.

However, more than 10 years after their inclusion on the National Inventory, Slovene microtoponyms are still waiting to receive attention from other public authorities and private actors. After a benchmark analysis of regional development programmes, strategies, and projects (see Research Methods section), it has become evident that microtoponyms are absent from Carinthia's regional development policies. My analysis is based not just on place names, but also on bilingualism in south Carinthia.

In the regional development strategy of Carinthian Central Region (Amt der Kärntner Landesregierung, 2021b), bilingualism is highlighted as one of the main development pillars under the umbrella topic 'liveable space' and, therefore, it is mentioned several times in the document. This represents a further step towards what the previous local development strategy of the Lower Carinthia LAG noted; namely, that bilingualism is an unexploited asset with the potential of becoming a development factor related to the issue of cultural life (Plaimer et al., 2018). A different approach can be identified in the regional development strategy of the 'surroundings of Villach' (Primosch, 2020), which mentions multilingualism (not bilingualism) as an asset related to fostering transboundary relationships (but not in terms of fostering minority languages). Last, in the development strategy of Hermagor district (which affects only one officially bilingual municipality) (Amt der Kärntner Landesregierung, 2021a), nothing can be found on bilingualism; however, it states the need to: (i) consider cultural heritage as a quality of life factor, and (ii) make the border area liveable by preserving regional history and culture. The commonality among all these strategies is that no mention of place names as cultural heritage items to foster economic and/or social development can be found, even though all these tools were developed and adopted well after the inclusion of field names in the National Inventory of Intangible Heritage and the FLU-LED project.

The same trend can be observed in rural development projects that were implemented during the last programming period (2014–2020) within the LEADER programme in Carinthia (Amt der Kärntner Landesregierung, 2020). Some projects are based on cultural exchanges with Italy and Slovenia to foster bi- or multilingualism (e.g., at schools). Other projects currently being carried out are based on bilingualism. Yet, no single initiative based on place names as a cultural asset was identified (neither in past projects nor in current ones). Apart from LEADER, the one other example that should be mentioned is the pan-alpine hiking initiative "Mountaineering Villages", where the municipality of Zell/Sele is involved. It is not by chance that, as the only fully bilingual municipality, Zell/Sele seems to be the only one exploiting its bilingual character for (rural) development purposes.

To sum up, certain commonalities can be identified in both the topics presented. First, if field names are not broadly appreciated, they are not likely to be included in development tools. Second, even though Slovene field names are institutionally recognised at the highest level, they will not necessarily become an asset for socio-economic development. My own experience during both the semi-structured and expert interviews showed that conveying the idea of field names as potentially becoming a regional development asset was not a straightforward task. In practice, the only topic that could be related to this idea was tourism. Most surprisingly, as stated earlier (Jordan & Sancho, 2021), contradictory attitudes towards bilingualism as a tourism asset among Carinthian Slovenes were revealed during the research project fieldwork. The interviews indicated harsh criticism of the authorities for not promoting bilingualism and bilingual names; however, very little seems to be done at an individual level, for example using Slovene names when naming own businesses.

14.6 Concluding Thoughts and Policy Recommendations: Municipal Level Alone Is Not Enough

This chapter aimed to elucidate whether microtoponyms can go beyond territorial attachment and identity markers by contributing to strengthening not only social and territorial ties, but also regional development. The results show evidence that, over the last decade, bilingual place names have received much attention at both the social and political level in south Carinthia. Place names have gained acceptance and have been officially recognised and elevated to Intangible Cultural Heritage status. Nevertheless, social acceptance does not seem to have brought about an overall social appreciation, with both positive and negative toponymic attachment observed. Language seems to be a relevant explanatory factor in this regard: engagement degree with bilingual names is remarkably higher among bilingual (i.e., German and Slovene) speakers. However, and since the interview and (particularly) the questionnaire samples were biased towards certain social groups, a comprehensive picture would be necessary in order to properly calibrate to what extent language (and, particularly bilingualism) shapes place and toponymic attachment.

Even when "most new initiatives for the preservation of field and house names were started by local associations and communities (not academic or central institutions representing the minority)" (Piko-Rustia, 2020, p. 185), I argue that place names are (still) far from forming part of a societal backbone. The persistence of elements that hinder the normalisation of bilingual names, such as simplified postal addresses, illustrates this argument. In bilingual regions with a turbulent past, old wounds might eventually heal, but scars very often remain. Importantly, modern lifestyles tend to obliterate old field names everywhere, meaning that the social appreciation of microtoponyms might be something that does not happen spontaneously at mainstream level, but needs to be actively fostered in order to become a factor of social cohesion.

In spite of the inclusion of bilingual place names in the National Inventory of the UNESCO Intangible Cultural Heritage, public authorities in charge of regional development policies may appreciate the potential of bilingualism, but do not see bilingual place names as an asset to foster regional development in south Carinthia. The FLU-LED project was a unique cross-border action, but is has not become a blueprint for further actors to consider in the arena of rural and regional development.

In a recent communication, the Austrian Board on Geographical Names (AKO) pointed out the challenges that new street names pose, since they *de facto* replace settlement bilingual names in postal addresses. The AKO "hinted explicitly at the value of using field names and/or other traditional local names upon applying new names" (Piko-Rustia et al., 2021, p. 2). In practice, these guidelines are not followed, since the overwhelming number of municipalities just adhere to what was agreed in the 2011 memorandum. This compromise regulates official bilingual signs at the entrance of settlements, but not further elements such as street names. Only Zell/Sele has adopted a fully bilingual signposting policy, which also includes streets, alleys, and square signs. Paradoxically, the interviewed authority from Sankt Jakob im Rosental/ Šentjakob v Rožu highlighted the fact that field names have no written form and therefore cannot be used as street names, while praising the local bilingual map resulting from the FLU-LED project.

This indicates that exclusively bottom-up approaches (i.e., at municipal level) have managed to implement the 2011 consensus in practice, yet they do not seem to be able to fully solve this issue, at least not in a spatially coherent way. In particular, there is no spatial continuity of bilingual signposts in south Carinthia, since each municipality addresses the issue in different degrees. History shows that past attempts to implement top-down approaches (i.e., from the central government) do not work, since they are seen as interference into 'internal issues' by the German-speaking majority. Thus, perhaps it is time for the in-between tier (i.e., the government of Carinthia) to play a key mediator role.

On the other hand, and as the FLU-LED project has shown, it is not just about ensuring the visibility of bilingual names in public spaces. Field names should be promoted in arenas other than official signposting. For instance, they should be included in collaborative cartographic data, notably Open Street Map (OSM). Initiatives using OSM in south Carinthia, such as the network of "Panoramaweg Südalpen" itineraries, would have greater value if they incorporated field names in their maps. For this to happen, however, certain local authorities need to rethink their use of field names and bilingual maps should be developed in a consistent way. This leads us again to the need for supra-municipal cooperation.

Acknowledgements This chapter is based on the results of the research project "The Politics and the Poetics of Toponymy, Identity and Place in Multilingual Areas. A Comparative Study of Carinthia (Austria) and the Těšín Area (Czechia)", funded by the Austrian Science Fund (project number I 2366-G23) and the Czech Grant Agency (project number 16-34841L).

I would like to express my gratitude to Prof. Peter Jordan and particularly to Martina Piko-Rustia, who oriented me in the conception and the development of this chapter.

References

Abankina, T. (2013). Regional development models using cultural heritage resources. *International Journal of Culture, Tourism and Hospitality Research, 7*(1), 3–10. https://doi.org/10.1108/17506181311301318. Accessed 29 Nov 2021.

Amt der Kärntner Landesregierung. (2020). *Unsere Regionen. Dein Projekt. Mein Lebensraum. LEADER als nachhaltiges Instrument der Orts- und Regionalentwicklung in Kärnten.* Amt der Kärntner Landesregierung, Abt. 10 (Land- und Forstwirtschaft, Ländlicher Raum).

Amt der Kärntner Landesregierung. (2021a). *Regionalstrategie Region Hermagor.* Land Kärnten - Abt. 10 Land- und Forstwirtschaft, Ländlicher Raum. https://region-hermagor.at/wp-content/uploads/2DP_Land-Kaernten_Broschuere-Hermagor_Web.x60999.pdf. Accessed 29 Nov 2021.

Amt der Kärntner Landesregierung. (2021b). *Regionalstrategie Region Kärntner Zentralraum.* Amt der Kärntner Landesregierung.

Basso, K. H. (1996). *Wisdom sits in places: Landscape and language among the Western apache.* University of New Mexico Press.

Casey, E. S. (2009). *Getting back into place.* Indiana University Press.

Cresswell, T. (2004). *Place: A short introduction.* Blackwell.

Helleland, B. (2012). Place names and identities. *Names and Identities, 4*(2), 95–116.

Hellwig, V. (2015). Eine konfliktreiche Beziehungsgeschichte. Die Volksgruppenfrage und die Beziehungen zwischen Kärnten und Slowenen. In J. Pirker (Ed.), *Kärnten und Slowenien: Getrennte Wege – Gemeinsame Zukunft* (Vol. 29, pp. 82–91). Nomos/Eurac Research.

Jordan, P. (2012). Place names as ingredients of space-related identity. *Names and Identities, 4*(2), 117–131.

Jordan, P., & Mácha, P. (2021). The wider onomastic scope of the research topic. In P. Jordan, P. Mácha, M. Balode, L. Krtička, U. Obrusnik, P. Pilch, & A. Sancho Reinoso (Eds.), *Place-name politics in multilingual areas. A comparative study of southern Carinthia (Austria) and the Těšín/Cieszyn region (Czechia)* (pp. 13–44). Palgrave Macmillan.

Jordan, P., & Sancho, A. (2021). Questionnaires. In P. Jordan, P. Mácha, M. Balode, L. Krtička, U. Obrusnik, P. Pilch, & A. Sancho Reinoso (Eds.), *Place-name politics in multilingual areas. A comparative study of southern Carinthia (Austria) and the Těšín/Cieszyn region (Czechia)* (pp. 391–400). Palgrave Macmillan.

Kostanski, L. (2016). Toponymic attachment. In C. Hough (Ed.), *The Oxford handbook of names and naming* (pp. 1–18) https://www.oxfordhandbooks.com/view/10.1093/oxfordhb/9780199656431.001.0001/oxfordhb-9780199656431-e-42. Accessed 29 Nov 2021

Lewicka, M. (2014). In search of roots memory as enable of place attachment. In L. Manzo & P. Devine-Wright (Eds.), *Place attachment. Advances in theory, methods, and applications* (pp. 49–60). Routledge.

Low, S. M., & Altman, I. (1992). Place attachment. In I. Altman & S. M. Low (Eds.), *Place attachment* (pp. 1–12). Springer.

Narodni svet Koroški Slovencev. (2021). *Geschichte der Kärntner Slowenen.* http://www.elnet.at/dossier/volkszaehlungen. Accessed 29 Nov 2021.

Petronela, T. (2016). The importance of the intangible cultural heritage in the economy. *Procedia Economics and Finance, 39*, 731–736. https://doi.org/10.1016/S2212-5671(16)30271-4. Accessed 29 Nov 2021.

Piko-Rustia, M. (2020). Evaluation by means of appreciation. Geographical names as (intangible) cultural heritage. *Onomàstica, 6*, 163–189.

Piko-Rustia, M., Olip, N., Apovnik, P., & Domej, T. (2021). *Utilization of communal autonomy for implementing additional bilingual names of populated places and streets in Carinthia (Austria)* (GEGN.2/2021/71/CRP.71; p. 7). UN Group of Experts on Geographical Names.

Pirker, J. (2011). Kärntner Ortstafelstreit – eine "(un)endliche" Geschichte? Juristische und historische Einblicke. In G. Hafner & M. Pandel (Eds.), *Volksgruppenfragen, Kooperation statt Konfrontation* (pp. 127–164). Hermagoras-Mohorjeva.

Plaimer, P., Reiner, V., & Schönherr, I. (2018). *Lokale Entwicklungsstrategie der LAG Regionalkooperation Unterkärnten 2014–2020.* Regionalkooperation Unterkärnten.

Pohl, H.-D. (2012). Zweisprachige Ortstafeln als Zeugen gemeinsamer Geschichte und Kultur. In N. Beclin (Ed.), *Ein Kärnten. Die Lösung* (pp. 123–130). Heyn.

Primosch, I. (2020). *LAG Regional Villach-Umland Entwicklungsstrategie 2020.* Ministerium für ein Lebenswertes Österreich. https://rm-kaernten.at/wp-content/uploads/2018/07/171221-LES_Villach-Umland_14-20_ab-2018.pdf. Accessed 29 Nov 2021

Relph, E. (1976). *Place and placelessness.* Pion.

Sacherer, B. (n.d.). *Best practice projects Kärntens LEADER-Projekte.* LAG Nockregion-Oberkärnten. https://rm-kaernten.at/wp-content/uploads/2018/07/BestProjects_Broschu%CC%88re.pdf. Accessed 29 Nov 2021

Seamon, D. (2014). Place attachment and phenomenology: The synergistic dynamism of place. In L. Manzo & P. Devine-Wright (Eds.), *Place attachment: Advances in theory, methods, and applications* (pp. 11–22). Routledge.

Seger, M. (2019). *Österreich Raum und Gesellschaft.* Naturwissenschaftlicher Verein f. Kärnten.

Slovenska prosvetna zveza/Slowenischer Kulturverein. (2011–2015). *Kulturni portal ledinskih in hišnih imen/Kulturportal der Flur- und Hausnamen (FLU-LED),* 2011–2015, www.flurnamen.at; www.ledinskaimena.si

Toce, B., & Dourou, E. (2020). *Culture without borders: Cultural heritage management for local and regional development* (CG/CUR(2020)15-03; p. 30). Congress of Local and Regional Authorities, Council of Europe. https://rm.coe.int/cg-cur-2020-15-03-en-cultural-heritage/16809f9fbd. Accessed 29 Nov 2021.

Tort, J., & Sancho, A. (2012). Toponyms as 'landscape indicators'. In J. Tort & M. Montagut (Eds.), *Names in daily life. Proceedings of the XXIV ICOS international congress of onomastic sciences* (pp. 1987–2016). Generalitat de Catalunya.

Van der Auwera, S., & Schramme, A. (2014). Cultural heritage policies as a tool for development: Discourse or harmony? *ENCATC Journal of Cultural Management and Policy, 4*(1), 4–8.

Villette, J., & Purves, R. S. (2018). Exploring microtoponyms through linguistic and geographic perspectives. *AGILE 2018* (pp. 1–4). https://agile-online.org/conference_paper/cds/agile_2018/shortpapers/67%20AGILE_2018_Villette_Purves.pdf. Accessed 29 Nov 2021.

Williams, D. R., & Vaske, J. J. (2003). The measurement of place attachment: Validity and generalizability of a psychometric approach. *Forest Science, 49*(6), 830–840.

Yi-Fu Tuan. (1991). Language and the making of place: A narrative-descriptive approach. *Annals of the Association of American Geographers, 81*(4), 684–696. https://doi.org/10.1111/j.1467-8306.1991.tb01715.x

Part IV
(Re)constructing Place Attachment: Regeneration of (Post)industrial Areas and Urban Recovery

Chapter 15
Reclaiming the Face of the City. Can Third-Places Change Place Attachment? Craiova as Case Study

Liliana Popescu (ID), **Cristiana Vîlcea** (ID), **and Amalia Niță** (ID)

15.1   Introduction

Political, economic, and social changes during the last half of the twentieth century have led to the serious decay of many medieval towns throughout Central and Eastern Europe. For the last three decades, the struggle to redefine place meaning and foster place attachment has been a significant burden for many local authorities in this part of Europe, trying to regenerate social and economic activities in the historical parts of the cities, while also reshaping the meaning of place for inhabitants. The historical heartlands of cities are often seen as public social spaces that have been described by Oldenburg and Brissett (1982) as *third places of social interaction*, after home (first places) and place of work (second places), which are appropriated by inhabitants as their own, offering them a sense of distinctiveness.

In this study, we address the significance of revitalisation works for the historical centre (HC) of a post-socialist city to its inhabitants (Craiova, Romania), using a place attachment survey, with the aim to examine the extent to which appropriation of the place and 'aging in place' fosters a positive attachment to place. The chapter begins with discussing the current theoretical framework for place attachment, to provide an understanding of the topic, with particular focus on the definition of the construct, its components and measurement scales. Next, we briefly present the background of the study area, so as to better understand the reasons for its overhaul. Finally, we address the main hypotheses of the study related to residents' place attachment, supported by the results of an online survey. We shall look at three categories of factors related to place attachment: first, predictors such as appropriation of the place and socio-demographic characteristics are correlated with place

L. Popescu · C. Vîlcea (✉) · A. Niță
Geography Department, University of Craiova, Craiova, Romania
e-mail: liliana.popescu@edu.ucv.ro; cristiana.vilcea@edu.ucv.ro; amalia.nita@edu.ucv.ro

© The Author(s), under exclusive license to Springer Nature
Switzerland AG 2022
O.-R. Ilovan, I. Markuszewska (eds.), *Preserving and Constructing Place Attachment in Europe*, GeoJournal Library 131,
https://doi.org/10.1007/978-3-031-09775-1_15

attachment; second, we check for a correlation between people's interest in the history of the place and place attachment and third, depending on the intensity of attachment to the city, we assess how supportive are residents of local strategies aiming to revive the historical part of the city.

15.2   Theoretical Background

It has been theorised that people feel attached to their places of residence and the results of research that focused on perceived residential satisfaction and place attachment during the last two decades proves that this theory is correct (Gustafson, 2001; Bonaiuto et al., 2003; Lewicka, 2005; Hernandez et al., 2007; Devine-Wright, 2011; Lewicka & de Carvalho, 2014). Research on place attachment exists at multiple scales, from residences and neighbourhoods to cities (Bonaiuto et al., 1999, 2003; Hidalgo & Hernandez, 2001; Brown et al., 2003; Hernandez et al., 2007; Lewicka, 2008; Rollero & De Piccoli, 2010; Lewicka & de Carvalho, 2014); still, "much of what we know about place attachments is geared toward dominant experiences of the Global North and from other dominant groups (i.e. people from western, educated, industrialised, rich and democratic societies long considered 'standard subjects' that are actually outliers" (Manzo & Pinto de Carvalho, 2020, p. 117), while this topic has only recently and scarcely received attention in developing countries (Lewicka, 2008; Lewicka & de Carvalho, 2014; Ilovan et al., 2019; Banini & Ilovan, 2021).

Because place attachment has received much attention from various disciplines for almost five decades, there is significant documented information about this topic. Consequently, we begin by reviewing the theoretical development of the construct, then focus on the predictors and measurement scales used to assess place attachment, which will subsequently be applied for the current study.

15.2.1   Place Attachment as a Theoretical Construct

Some of the first researchers of this topic (Relph, 1976; Proshansky et al., 1983) addressed the meanings assigned by people in terms of attachment to various places, the beginning of the new millennium witnessing a surge in studies focusing on the importance of place attachment to built environments (Low, 1992; Gustafson, 2001; Manzo, 2005; Rollero & De Piccoli, 2010) which develops to different intensities within various spatial scales (home, neighbourhood or city) (Hidalgo & Hernandez, 2001).

Place attachment has eclectic origins, with correspondingly diverse philosophies of scientific methodological preferences (Williams, 2014). Since the early works in the field (Relph, 1976), there was a proliferation of concepts and measurement scales for assessing the emotional bonds between humans and places, with almost as many approaches and combinations of different elements (Hernandez et al., 2021), place attachment being considered either as a one-dimensional concept (Hernandez et al., 2007; Rollero & De Piccoli, 2010; Devine-Wright, 2011) or a multi-dimensional construct (Williams & Vaske, 2003; Raymond et al., 2010; Lewicka, 2011; Low & Altman, 2012; Casakin et al., 2021), which includes place dependence (Williams & Vaske, 2003) and place identity (Kyle et al., 2005; Vaske & Kobrin, 2010; Williams, 2014; Maguire & Klinkenberg, 2018). The former dimension is related to functional attachment, while the latter stems from the emotional attachment. This is because place attachment is an "interdisciplinary boundary object", research on this issue "forming and benefitting from a diverse and multidisciplinary inquiry" (Williams & Miller, 2021, p. 13). External and internal drivers determine place changes that characterise the place attachment which is expressed through community participation (Falanga, 2022).

Place attachment, broadly defined as *the bonding of people to places* (Williams & Roggenbuck, 1989; Bonaiuto et al., 1999; Brown et al., 2003; Giuliani, 2003; Manzo, 2003; Low & Altman, 2012)*,* is "a complex and multifaceted concept that has many inseparable, integral, and mutually defining features, qualities, or properties" (Low & Altman, 2012, p. 4) that stem from feelings and emotions (Rollero & De Piccoli, 2010).

In general, there are two uses of the term *place attachment* (Williams, 2014): place equals locus of attachment, when referring to the emotional intensity/ strength of attachment, and centre of meaning (when aiming at the broader psychological processes of attachment). Place attachment primarily stems from the affective bonding that usually people develop with their environmental settings (Low & Altman, 2012), not merely because they are physical entities, but because they relate to the meanings of a particular place, and also form relationships with various persons, which create new experiences for that particular place (Riley, 1992), which is perceived subjectively by each individual (Hummon, 1992). It is exactly this type of experiences which "people find important and meaningful that often lead to significant bonds with the places in which these experiences occur, experience and place thus becoming intertwined" (Manzo, 2005, p. 70).

15.2.2 *Predictors of Place Attachment*

Seen as an emotional bond that arises following the interactions with the physical environment, place attachment develops over a short time (Casakin et al., 2015), with various intensities, considering where the place is located, its size, the amount of contact residents have with it, and not least its (threaten) integrity (Anton & Lawrence, 2014). Length of residence (Lewicka, 2011; Lewicka & de Carvalho, 2014; Casakin et al., 2015), age (i.e., old people are more attached than the young), income and education, as well as gender (Hidalgo & Hernandez, 2001; Anton & Lawrence, 2014) are some of the well-known demographic factors closely related to place attachment. However, only the socio-demographic characteristics are not enough to account for place attachment, since "place attachment is interdependent with other aspects of place—for example, geographical and cultural qualities, relative rootedness in place, degree of personal and social involvement, quality of life, environmental aesthetics, individual and group identity with place" (Seamon, 2014, p. 31).

Among the predictors of place attachment, recent studies point to a complex concept borrowed from social sciences, that of appropriation of space (Brunson et al., 2001; Benages-Albert et al., 2015), defined as psychological processes by which "people claim ownership of, actively use, and ultimately create meaning in and become attached to the physical environment" (Rioux et al., 2017, p. 61). In this context, spending time in a particular place is not sufficient to create psychological attachment, but it certainly provides the proper ground for appropriation, "by which space is transformed into place, resulting in place attachment" (Rioux et al., 2017, p. 66). Other studies point to the fact that awareness, amount of knowledge and interest in the history of the residence city augments place attachment (Lewicka, 2008).

15.2.3 Measurement Scales for Place Attachment

Place attachment has three recognised major components (Low, 1992; Low & Altman, 2012; Sthelecka et al., 2017; Manzo & Devine-Wright, 2021): the affective component (emotional reaction), which is primarily measured (Hidalgo & Hernandez, 2001), the cognitive component (i.e., knowledge, meanings, and memories of a place – *place identity*) and the behavioural one (*place dependence*). Due to various conceptual models related to place attachment, there is a lack of uniformity in the operationalisation of the concepts and the evaluation procedures (Hernandez et al., 2021), "the terminological and conceptual ambiguity and empirical operationalization" (Hidalgo, 2013, p. 251) representing the main hinderance.

Research has demonstrated that there are numerous methods that have been used during the last decades to measure place attachment, starting from various theoretical or epistemological approaches (Williams & Roggenbuck, 1989; Hidalgo & Hernandez, 2001; Bonaiuto et al., 2003; Williams & Vaske, 2003; Raymond et al., 2010; Seamon, 2014; Brown et al., 2015; Manzo & Pinto de Carvalho, 2020). Some authors promote quantitative approaches, others call for qualitative ones or endorse a mixed method approach (Hernandez et al., 2021).

The quantitative procedures for evaluating place attachment as one-dimensional construct generally involve the use of questionnaires (the degree of attachment is assessed using Likert scales), targeting items that focus either on place dependence or place identity as components of place attachment and/or on behaviour and social bonding (Kyle et al., 2005). Among the early works, the scale proposed by Bonaiuto and peers (1999) aimed to assess the extent to which residents felt attached to their neighbourhood, based on their feelings, the desire to keep their current residence and the relevance for the identity of researched residents. A decade later, this scale was validated by confirmatory factorial analysis for the use in research design dealing with residential attachment (Fornara et al., 2010).

Another instrument focusing on place attachment as a one-dimensional concept was developed by Hidalgo and Hernandez (2001) and Hernandez et al. (2007), incorporating aspects related to the affective component (the extent to which inhabitants are satisfied with their residence location, the extent they feel attached to the place/ neighbourhood, whether they want to return to that place).

Lately, researchers have been paying attention to how social and cultural processes influence the meaning of places and relationships to places (Manzo, 2005), since they are "repositories and contexts within which interpersonal, community, and cultural relationships occur, and it is to those social relationships, not just to place qua place, to which people are attached" (Low & Altman, 2012, p. 7). In general, it is the experience people have in space that transforms it "into a culturally meaningful and shared symbol, that is, place" (Low, 1992, p. 166).

15.3 Study Area

Craiova is one of the largest Romanian cities (approximately 300,000 inhabitants), with a history of 500 years, being the de facto administrative centre of Oltenia province for the last centuries.

The historical part of the city covers an area of 380 ha (5% of the city area), with a central location, most of the buildings dating to the end of the nineteenth -beginning of the twentieth century. There were mainly dwellings and shops, but also hotels, administrative, cultural, and financial institutions. As in most Easter European countries, the communist era meant an intensive urban development and renewal, with a disregard toward the safeguarding of heritage properties. At the beginning of the new millennium, this was a rather heterogeneous area from a cultural, social, and economic point of view, inheriting a network of many poor dwellings, as well as trading, administrative, and cultural buildings that faced different political regimes and economic development or decay. Moreover, the historical centre faced a serious image problem, being perceived as an ugly, dirty, and decaying area, with no major attraction points, and with a rather high crime rate (GEA, 2009).

To address the decline of the area, local authorities began a major revitalisation project, focused on physical as well as economic regeneration, aiming at bringing back business to the central area by adapting the buildings for new functions, while preserving and enhancing its historical values. The project was approved by the local administration in 2010, works began in the autumn of 2013 and ended in the summer of 2015. It focused on the ancient heartland of the city, including numerous monument buildings, with clearly defined architectural styles and characteristics, since the aim was to rebuild or maintain the tradition and atmosphere of the old urban settlements, while updating their use for the current period. Authorities encouraged a mix-use concept – a combination of services and tourist functions, trade and work, while diminishing the residential function. Thus emerged an attractive space for various social and cultural activities and events, which became one of the main attraction areas of the city, including restaurants, cafés, hotels, and expensive boutiques, as well as a large pedestrian area.

15.4   Research Hypotheses

Considering the literature review on the topic, we focused the specific hypotheses on the predictors of place attachment – residence time, age, appropriation, interest and knowledge in place history, as well as attitude toward change. We predicted that:

Hypothesis 1. There is a positive correlation between place attachment and residence time, age, education, and place appropriation;

Hypothesis 2. Place attachment stems from people's interest in the history of the place and its preservation;

Hypothesis 3. Residents with stronger attachment to the city will be more supportive of planning strategies to preserve and revive the historical city centre.

15.5   Methodology

15.5.1   Instruments and Data Collection

Although there are numerous methods for measuring place attachment, we did not find any standardised scale; however, the literature review yielded possible survey questions that were previously used for measuring place attachment. These prospective items were reviewed and discussed with two other researchers and then pretested (for length, item comprehensibility and relevance) with ten respondents with different background. The survey covered three different sections. The first part of the questionnaire aimed to assess place attachment – general as well as social attachment to the city, using five place attachment statements rated on a 5-point Likert scale taken from previous studies (Bonaiuto et al., 1999; Hernandez et al., 2007; Casakin et al., 2021), namely the extent to which the respondents enjoy living in a place, whether they feel attached to it or not, as well as items such as: "I would regret moving to another city", which triggers a distancing situation for the respondent and is conducive of place attachment (Hidalgo & Hernandez, 2001). All five items referring to the degree of individual attachment to the city were loaded into one factor, with the help of which we determined attachment to the city.

Part two of the survey included seven questions concerning appropriation of space and interest in the history of the place itself, which is directly related to place attachment (Lewicka & de Carvalho, 2014), while the last section covered sociodemographic factors predicting place attachment.

The online survey was described as a research theme undertaken by the Geography Department of the University of Craiova, being posted on its web page; to obtain a representative sample and minimise as much as possible bias towards a specific group over others, it was distributed and shared online using social media, but also advertised in one of the main newspapers of the city. Data were collected during the first 2 weeks of June 2021.

15.5.2   Data Processing

All data collected in 585 valid questionnaires were statistically processed to find out if there was a correlation between the socio-demographic factors like the length of residence, age, gender, income (Fowler Jr, 2014), appropriation and perception of space that could demonstrate the intensity of place attachment.

Data was processed using the functions in data analysis from Excel to compute the values of standard deviation (SD), mean and p-value for the variables within each hypothesis. The correlation between the variables in all hypotheses (Heumann et al., 2016; Frost, 2019, 2020) was performed with the same software.

15.6   Results

The general socio-demographic statistics (Table 15.1) indicate that 78% of the respondents had been living for more than 20 years in the city, therefore they have witnessed all transformations that the city and the city centre, in particular, faced.

In accordance with Hypothesis 1, the most consistent predictor was appropriation of the space, highly attached people spending generally 1–4 h/per visit, with a much higher frequency (twice a week or several times a week). Age is clearly a good predictor for place attachment, as the most attached people are those aged 44 and over (65%), while almost half of the less attached people are less than 34 years old. Interestingly, 'middle ages' cohorts have fairly equal shares for both the strongly and less attached people (a third of respondents). As Table 15.2 shows, a

Table 15.1 Respondents' demographic characteristics

Age (years)		Gender		Length of residence (years)		Income	
Under 23	12%	Women	64.4%	Less than 5	7%	≤ minimum wage	6%
24–33	17%	Men	35.6%	5–10	6%	Min. – Average wage	27%
34–43	33%			11–20	8%	≥ average wage	47%
44–55	28%			More than 20	78%	No response	20%
Over 55	10%						

Source: Authors' elaboration

Table 15.2 Correlation matrix

	Age	Visits frequency	Time spent	Length of residence
Age*	1			
Visits frequency**	0.734	1		
Time spent***	−0.719	−0.366	1	
Length of residence****	−0.475	−0.798	−0.268	1

Source: Authors' elaboration
$R^2 = 0.503$
* SD = 29.5; p-value = 0.290
** SD = 20.9; p-value = 0.270
*** SD = 133.6
**** SD = 12.02

Table 15.3 Correlation matrix between place attachment and expressed interest in the history of the place and its preservation

	Interested in the history of the HC	Important to preserve the heritage
Interested in the history of the HC·*	1	
Important to preserve the heritage**	0.894	1

Source: Authors' elaboration
$R^2 = 0.969$
* SD = 53.5; p-value = 0.015
** SD = 67.7; p-value = 0.523

good positive correlation was noted between age and the frequency of visits, but although strong, a negative correlation exists (0.89, p < .01) between age and the time spent in the HC for different activities (Table 15.2). The same negative correlation is observed between the frequency of visits and length of residence (−0.798).

Hypothesis 2 postulated that place attachment positively relates to the interest residents have in the history of the place and perceived importance of its preservation. To test this hypothesis, we performed the correlation analysis taking into account the locals who resulted to have a strong attachment to the city and HC in particular. In terms of attachment, there is a strong positive correlation between the interest of the locals in the history of the historical centre and the fact that they consider important the preservation of the existing elements of heritage (Table 15.3).

In line with Hypothesis 3, a strong value of correlation was observed between residents' attachment and their declared support for future planning strategies which imply changing the current use of historical buildings (0.93) with effect on the aspect of the HC, which most of the respondents declared as being important for them (0.97) (Table 15.4). Most people understand the economic and social importance brought by the type of building use, change being seen as necessary to increase the value of the area, but with the preservation of the historical aspect. Also, those with strong attachment view the historical centre as a symbol of the entire community heritage (0.92).

Table 15.4 Correlation matrix between attachment and support of planning strategies

	HC as the symbol of the community heritage	Agree to change the urban land use of the buildings in the HC	The view/aspect of the HC is important
HC as the symbol of the community heritage*	1		
Agree to change the urban land use of the buildings in the HC**	0.926	1	
The view/aspect of the HC is important***	0.972	0.934	1

Source: Authors' elaboration
$R^2 = 0.992$
* SD = 48.9; p-value = 0.738
** SD = 45.3; p-value = 0.220
*** SD = 59.8; p-value = 0.982

15.7 Discussions

In this chapter, we tested three hypotheses targeting place attachment (content and predictors), considering as case study one of the largest cities in Romania. The results support the basic facts already known in literature on place attachment, namely that long time older residents become more attached to the landscape of the city centre and more interested in the city history, and that a stronger attachment means a greater support for local policies focusing on preservation and regeneration of historic areas.

Place attachment was assessed using the emotional bonds people develop with the place, focusing among other things, on their desire and difficulty to move to another city, as well as on what type of attachment people feel to the city (Hidalgo & Hernandez, 2001) (general attachment – *I would regret moving out,* social attachment – *I would miss my family/ friends/ neighbours in particular; I would miss the people in general,* or physical attachment - *I would miss the places*).

Almost a quarter of the interviewees would like to move to another city and another quarter neither agree nor disagree, while more than a third is not fond of this idea. Only 14% would find it easy to move to another city, while for almost half of them would be difficult and very difficult to move (25% and 21%, respectively). Those that would not like to move are generally 33–43 years old (40% of them), followed by the 44–54 age group (30%), women, and have been living in Craiova for more than 20 years. They visit the historical part of the city at least once a week (60%) and spend there up to 4 h/visit, considering it has a positive influence in their daily life (85% of the respondents).

Social attachment is the highest among the respondents, followed by physical attachment. The question *If you were to move to another city, what would you miss the most?* yielded the predicted responses: friends and neighbours in particular (70%), and people in general (24%). More than a quarter of them would miss the activities carried on in this city and about 40% would miss the places they visit (these respondents have the highest share for spending more than 4 h per visit in the historical centre and the most frequent visits).

For the first hypothesis, residence time did not yield quite the expected outcome, as people living in the city for more than 20 years account for the biggest share for both the highly attached and less attached residents. What is more, the majority of those living in the city for less than 5 years is much more attached to the city (50%), while those less attached account for less than 10%. This may be due to the fact that they are generally young (56% are less than 23 years old, while only 16% are over 44 years old), most probably students or recent graduates who moved to the city from the rural area or small towns in the region, Craiova being the most important university centre in this part of the country and the most influential city of the region, with a dynamic economic, social and cultural life (during the last decade, Craiova has always been ranked among the top ten Romanian cities according to the cultural vitality index (Voicu & Dragomir, 2017).

Hypothesis 2 focused on place attachment depending on the declared interest in city history and perceived importance of the preservation of the built heritage, with a stronger correlation between place attachment and interest in city history. However, no matter the degree of attachment, almost all respondents consider that it is important to preserve the built heritage of the city, a fact which may be partially explained by the higher share of people with a higher education degree, but also by the fact that most residents take pride in the historical part of the city and are proud of being part of the city, considering that heritage buildings are very important for the city image, the area having unique and attractive architectural elements (Popescu et al., 2020).

More than three quarters of the respondents are interested in the history of the city and the historical centre, irrespective of gender, and only 5% do not take interest in it. Age is the only significant factor that considerably influences the interest in the history of the place; the highest interest was declared by the 44–54 years old group (91%), followed by the 34–43 years old category (60%), while the lowest interest was declared for the youngest. Contrary to what we expected, the residence period does not significantly influence the interest in the history of the place. It is true that the vast majority of those who declared their interest had been living in the city for more than 20 years (80%), but a similar share (70%) of those who are not interested had been living for the same amount of time. What is more, 72% of those living in Craiova for less than 5 years declared their interest in the history of the place, which is "a means through which a newcomer may feel part of the place's history and thus develop emotional bonds with the (new) place" (Lewicka & de Carvalho, 2014, p. 54).

With respect to the changes envisaged by the local authorities and the revitalisation project, the answers are no longer so clear cut, as the share of those that neither agree nor disagree is the highest (23%) compared to all the other questions, and only 67% of the surveyed sample agree with changes in the use type of the buildings (mainly from residential and commercial to HoReCa, commercial and cultural use). Most of those that agree to changes are 34–54 years old (41%), have been living in the city for more than 20 years (79%) and visit this part of the city at least once a week for one up to four hours.

These findings are of interest for both policy makers and local authorities, who need to understand people's connection to spaces that have turned into places. Understanding how place attachment impacts residents' perception of city landscape changes might help manage conflicts and, moreover, gain better support for the programmes envisaged by local management.

15.8 Conclusions

This chapter is an insight into place attachment within a Romanian city and into how different sociodemographic characteristics of residents influence their valuation and relation among different aspects of place attachment. Various predictors of place attachment, such as residence time, age, appropriation, interest, and knowledge in the history of the place, attitude toward change, were considered when conducting the study.

The first hypothesis proposed a relationship between place attachment and residence time, age, and appropriation of the place. All of them were supported with a strong correlation between the socio-demographic variables (age and length of residence) and the frequency the respondents visit the historical centre for various activities, correlated with the amount of time spent during their visits. Most of the citizens declared spending between one and four hours (71%) while meeting their friends or during leisure activities.

The second hypothesis postulated that people interested in the history of the city and historical centre also agree that it is important to preserve the heritage elements that represent place history. The more knowledge people have about the local history, the more attached to the place they become, as they feel to know it better, to be part of the city they live in. The preservation and renovation of old buildings creates connections between people and history. Again, the results of the study point to the fact that the relationship among interest in city history, importance of heritage preservation and place attachment is strong.

The third hypothesis targeted the support people are willing to offer local authorities in future planning strategies, if these include not only renovation, but also transformation regarding the use of buildings. The citizens who declared low support were concerned about possible traffic or certain activity restrictions.

Considering the results above, the three hypotheses demonstrated that individuals living in the city for more than 20 years are highly attached but also the percentage of those living in the city for less than 5 years is high in terms of city attachment (50%). A large share of respondents is concerned about the preservation of the urban built heritage in the historical centre considering that those architectural elements are unique, attractive and contribute to the positive perception of the city. Specifically, with respect to the revitalisation projects of the historical centre, an important share of respondents agrees with changes in the functionality and use of buildings. Thereby they embrace the change and new roles of the historical centre that may play an important part in the revitalisation process of the urban space.

However, this study shows that the valuation of the different aspects of place attachment changes is not independent of the individuals' socio-demographic characteristics. Various categories of respondents in terms of age, income, length of residence understand the relation between persons and urban places differently. While older generations see urban places, namely the city centre as an economic space, younger generations consider it more as a leisure and social urban space.

These results align with findings of previous studies on the effect that age and residence time have on place attachment, along with interest in history of the place, emotional involvement and support for regeneration policies aimed at preserving places people feel attached to. Planning needs to appraise the diversity of place attachment; thus, these results should be considered for planning strategies targeted toward the preservation and revival of historical city centres, as place attachment may be an essential element when reclaiming the face of the city.

References

Anton, C. E., & Lawrence, C. (2014). Home is where the heart is: The effect of place of residence on place attachment and community participation. *Journal of Environmental Psychology, 40*, 451–461. https://doi.org/10.1016/j.jenvp.2014.10.007

Banini, T., & Ilovan, O. R. (2021). *Representing place and territorial identities in Europe* (Discourses, images, and practices). Springer. https://doi.org/10.1007/978-3-030-66766-5

Benages-Albert, M., Di Masso, A., Porcel, S., Pol, E., & Vall-Casas, P. (2015). Revisiting the appropriation of space in metropolitan river corridors. *Journal of Environmental Psychology, 42*, 1–15. https://doi.org/10.1016/j.jenvp.2015.01.002

Bonaiuto, M., Aiello, A., Perugini, M., Bonnes, M., & Ercolani, A. P. (1999). Multidimensional perception of residential environment quality and Neighbourhood attachment in the urban environment. *Journal of Environmental Psychology, 19*(4), 331–352. https://doi.org/10.1006/jevp.1999.0138

Bonaiuto, M., Fornara, F., & Bonnes, M. (2003). Indexes of perceived residential environment quality and neighbourhood attachment in urban environments: A confirmation study on the city of Rome. *Landscape and Urban Planning, 65*(1–2), 41–52. https://doi.org/10.1016/S0169-2046(02)00236-0

Brown, B., Perkins, D. D., & Brown, G. (2003). Place attachment in a revitalizing neighborhood: Individual and block levels of analysis. *Journal of Environmental Psychology, 23*(3), 259–271. https://doi.org/10.1016/S0272-4944(02)00117-2

Brown, G., Raymond, C., & Corcoran, J. (2015). Mapping and measuring place attachment. *Applied Geography, 57*, 42–53. https://doi.org/10.1016/j.apgeog.2014.12.011

Brunson, L., Kuo, F. E., & Sullivan, W. C. (2001). Resident appropriation of defensible space in public housing: Implications for safety and community. *Environment and Behavior*. https://doi.org/10.1177/00139160121973160

Casakin, H., Hernandez, B., & Ruiz, C. (2015). Place attachment and place identity in Israeli cities: The influence of city size. *Cities, 42*(B), 224–230. https://doi.org/10.1016/j.cities.2014.07.007

Casakin, H., Ruiz, C., & Hernandez, B. (2021). Place attachment and the neighborhood: A case study of Israel. *Social Indicators Research, 155*(1), 315–333. https://doi.org/10.1007/s11205-020-02603-5

Devine-Wright, P. (2011). Place attachment and public acceptance of renewable energy: A tidal energy case study. *Journal of Environmental Psychology, 31*(4), 336–343. https://doi.org/10.1016/j.jenvp.2011.07.001

Falanga, R. (2022). Understanding place attachment through the lens of urban regeneration. Insights from Lisbon. *Cities, 122*, 103590. https://doi.org/10.1016/j.cities.2022.103590

Fornara, F., Bonaiuto, M., & Bonnes, M. (2010). Cross-validation of abbreviated perceived residential environment quality (PREQ) and neighborhood attachment (NA) indicators. *Environment and Behavior, 42*. https://doi.org/10.1177/0013916508330998

Fowler, F. J., Jr. (2014). *Survey research methods* (5th ed.). SAGE.

Frost, J. (2019). *Introduction to statistics: An intuitive guide for analyzing data and unlocking discoveries*. Statistics By Jim Publishing.

Frost, J. (2020). *Hypothesis testing: An intuitive guide for making data driven decisions* (1st ed.). Statistics By Jim Publishing.

Giuliani, M. V. (2003). Theory of attachment and place attachment. In *Psychological theories for environmental issues* (1st ed., pp. 137–170). Routledge.

Gustafson, P. (2001). Roots and routes: Exploring the relationship between place attachment and mobility. *Environment and Behavior, 33*(5), 667–686. https://doi.org/10.1177/00139160121973188

Hernandez, B., Hidalgo, M. C., Salazar-Laplace, M. E., & Hess, S. (2007). Place attachment and place identity in natives and non-natives. *Journal of Environmental Psychology, 27*(4), 310–319. https://doi.org/10.1016/j.jenvp.2007.06.003

Hernandez, B., Hidalgo, M. C., & Ruiz, C. (2021). Theoretical and methodological aspects of research on place attachment. In *Place attachment: Advances in theory, methods and applications* (2nd ed.). Routledge.

Heumann, C., Schomaker, M., & Shalabh. (2016). *Introduction to statistics and data analysis*. Springer. https://doi.org/10.1007/978-3-319-46162-5

Hidalgo, M. C. (2013). Operationalization of place attachment: A consensus proposal. *Estudios de Psicología, 34*(3), 251–259. https://doi.org/10.1174/021093913808295190

Hidalgo, M. C., & Hernandez, B. (2001). Place attachment: Conceptual and empirical questions. *Journal of Environmental Psychology, 21*(3), 273–281. https://doi.org/10.1006/jevp.2001.0221

Hummon, D. (1992). Community attachment: Local sentiment and sense of place. In I. Altman & S. M. Low (Eds.), *Place attachment* (Vol. 12, pp. 253–277). Springer. https://doi.org/10.1007/978-1-4684-8753-4_12

Ilovan, O.-R., Voicu, C.-G., & Colcer, A.-M. (2019). Recovering the past for resilient communities: Territorial identity, cultural landscape and symbolic places in Năsăud town, Romania. *Europa Regional, 26.2018*(2), 14.

Kyle, G., Graefe, A., & Manning, R. (2005). Testing the dimensionality of place attachment in recreational settings. *Environment and Behavior, 37*(2), 153–177. https://doi.org/10.1177/0013916504269654

Lewicka, M. (2005). Ways to make people active: The role of place attachment, cultural capital, and neighborhood ties. *Journal of Environmental Psychology, 25*(4), 381–395. https://doi.org/10.1016/j.jenvp.2005.10.004

Lewicka, M. (2008). Place attachment, place identity, and place memory: Restoring the forgotten city past. *Journal of Environmental Psychology, 28*(3), 209–231. https://doi.org/10.1016/j.jenvp.2008.02.001

Lewicka, M. (2011). Place attachment: How far have we come in the last 40 years? *Journal of Environmental Psychology, 31*(3), 207–230. https://doi.org/10.1016/j.jenvp.2010.10.001

Lewicka, M., & de Carvalho, L. P. (2014). In search of roots: Memory as enabler of place attachment. In *Place attachment: Advances in theory, methods and applications* (1st ed., pp. 49–60). Routledge.

Low, S. M. (1992). Symbolic ties that bind. In *Place attachment. Human behaviour and environment (Advances in theorey and research)* (Vol. 12, pp. 165–185). Springer. https://doi.org/10.1007/978-1-4684-8753-4_8

Low, S. M., & Altman, I. (2012). Place attachment: A conceptual inquiry. In I. Altman & S. M. Low (Eds.), *Place attachment* (2nd ed.). Springer.

Maguire, B., & Klinkenberg, B. (2018). Visualization of place attachment. *Applied Geography, 99*, 77–88. https://doi.org/10.1016/j.apgeog.2018.07.007

Manzo, L. C. (2003). Beyond house and haven: Toward a revisioning of emotional relationships with places. *Journal of Environmental Psychology, 23*(1), 47–61. https://doi.org/10.1016/S0272-4944(02)00074-9

Manzo, L. C. (2005). For better or worse: Exploring multiple dimensions of place meaning. *Journal of Environmental Psychology, 25*(1), 67–86. https://doi.org/10.1016/j.jenvp.2005.01.002

Manzo, L. C., & Devine-Wright, P. (2021). *Place attachment. Advances in theory, methods and applications* (2nd ed.). Routledge.

Manzo, L. C., & Pinto de Carvalho, L. (2020). *The role of qualitative approaches to place attachment research* (Place attachment. Advances in theory, methods and applications) (2nd ed., pp. 111–126). Routledge. https://doi.org/10.4324/9780429274442-7

Oldenburg, R., & Brissett, D. (1982). The third place. *Qualitative Sociology, 5*, 265–284. https://doi.org/10.1007/BF00986754

Popescu, L., Nita, A., & Iordache, C. (2020). Place identity, urban tourism and heritage interpretation: A case study of Craiova, Romania. *Journal of Balkan and Near Eastern Studies, 22*(4), 494–505. https://doi.org/10.1080/19448953.2020.1775401

Proshansky, H. M., Fabian, A. K., & Kaminoff, R. (1983). Place-identity: Physical world socialization of the self. *Journal of Environmental Psychology, 3*(1), 57–83. https://doi.org/10.1016/S0272-4944(83)80021-8

Raymond, C. M., Brown, G., & Weber, D. (2010). The measurement of place attachment: Personal, community, and environmental connections. *Journal of Environmental Psychology, 30*(4), 422–434. https://doi.org/10.1016/j.jenvp.2010.08.002

Relph, E. (1976). *Place and placelessness*. Pion.

Riley, R. B. (1992). Attachment to the ordinary landscape. In I. Altman & S. M. Low (Eds.), *Place attachment* (pp. 13–35). Springer. https://doi.org/10.1007/978-1-4684-8753-4_2

Rioux, L., Scrima, F., & Werner, C. M. (2017). Space appropriation and place attachment: University students create places. *Journal of Environmental Psychology, 50*, 60–68. https://doi.org/10.1016/j.jenvp.2017.02.003

Rollero, C., & De Piccoli, N. (2010). Does place attachment affect social Well-being? *European Review of Applied Psychology, 60*(4), 233–238. https://doi.org/10.1016/j.erap.2010.05.001

Seamon, D. (2014). Place attachment and phenomenology: The synergistic dynamism of place. In L. C. Manzo & P. Devine-Wright (Eds.), *Place attachment: Advances in theory, methods and applications* (pp. 11–22). Routledge.

Sthelecka, M., Boley, B. B., & Woosnam, K. M. (2017). Place attachment and empowerment: Do residents need to be attached to be empowered? *Annals of Tourism Research, 66*, 61–73. https://doi.org/10.1016/j.annals.2017.06.002

GEA. (2009). Study regarding the identification of strategic objectives for the revitalization of Craiova historical centre (in Romanian), *GEA Strategy and Consulting*, 1.0, https://primariacraiova.ro/pozearticole/userfiles/files/01/16748.pdf

Vaske, J. J., & Kobrin, K. C. (2010). Place attachment and environmentally responsible behavior. *The Journal of Environmental Education, 32*(4), 16–21. https://doi.org/10.1080/00958960109598658

Voicu, S., & Dragomir, A. (2017). *Romania's cultural vitality index*. Pro Universitaria Publish House.

Williams, D. R. (2014). 'Beyond the commodity metaphor', revisited. In L. C. Manzo & P. Devine-Wright (Eds.), *Place attachment: Advances in theory, methods and applications*. Routledge.

Williams, D. R., & Miller, B. A. (2021). Metatheoretical moments in place attachment research: Seeking clarity in diversity. In L. C. Manzo & P. Devine-Wright (Eds.), *Place attachment: Advances in theory, methods and applications* (2nd ed.). Routledge.

Williams, D. R., & Roggenbuck, J. W. (1989). Measuring place attachment: Some preliminary results. Paper presented at *Leisure research symposium, San Antonio*, 7, https://www.fs.fed.us/rm/value/docs/nrpa89.pdf

Williams, D. R., & Vaske, J. J. (2003). The measurement of place attachment: Validity and generalizability of a psychometric approach. *Forest Science, 49*(6), 830–840. https://doi.org/10.1093/forestscience/49.6.830

Chapter 16
Rediscovering the Space Beyond Our Doorstep. Place Attachment and Participatory Regeneration Within Urban Courtyards in Poland

Magdalena Miśkowiec ⓘ

16.1 Introduction

The urban regeneration process provides for the renewal and transformation of certain degraded areas. One type of these areas is the semi-public spaces that exist locally in our neighbourhoods. Considering that these spaces are used daily by members of local communities, regeneration should consider not only the existing problems and needs but also the emotional ties of the inhabitants within these places. Many authors have pointed out that a key tool in conducting urban regeneration is the participatory process (Atkinson, 1999; Maginn, 2007; Dargan, 2009; Ferilli et al., 2016). In these studies, a lot of attention is paid to the techniques and tools used and their effectiveness in achieving empowerment, trust, and inclusion, but much less attention is paid to fostering a participatory approach in addressing a community's emotional relationship with a place (Manzo & Perkins, 2006). According to Brown et al. (2003), it seems that learning about the factors that influence place attachment, and the sense of community is an important step toward achieving satisfactory outcomes from revitalization efforts.

Most studies regarding place attachment and urban regeneration connection have been conducted at the neighbourhood level (Brown et al., 2003; Livingston et al., 2010; Strzelecka et al., 2010) and set in the context of popular public spaces, plazas, parks, and green spaces. However, few studies have considered the specificity of small spaces that directly relate to the living space of the local neighbourhood community. This type of space can be referred to as semi-public, which on the one hand does not exclude access for the external user, but on the other hand it is primarily

M. Miśkowiec (✉)
Department of Regional Development, Institute of Geography and Spatial Management,
Faculty of Geography and Geology, Jagiellonian University, Kraków, Poland
e-mail: magda.miskowiec@doctoral.uj.edu.pl

© The Author(s), under exclusive license to Springer Nature
Switzerland AG 2022
O.-R. Ilovan, I. Markuszewska (eds.), *Preserving and Constructing Place Attachment in Europe*, GeoJournal Library 131,
https://doi.org/10.1007/978-3-031-09775-1_16

dedicated to the residents of the closest surrounding area (Dymnicka, 2013). One type of such space is the urban courtyard. These are close to residential areas and primarily serve a transit function, but also provide an area for rest, leisure, and social interaction (Raszka et al., 2014). Since courtyard areas are fragments of green space, they have an important environmental function to improve the local microclimate and biodiversity, which should not be forgotten during the regeneration process (Zamani et al., 2018). In the era of the COVID-19 pandemic, small green spaces in urban centres proved to be the only springboard for local communities in the face of social isolation and the prohibition of movement (Kleinschroth & Kowarik, 2020; Peters & Halleran, 2020). At the same time, with the perceived changes caused by the climate-ecological crisis, courtyard spaces are beginning to be considered important areas for mitigation and adaptation interventions in cities (Taleghani et al., 2014; Sim, 2019).

Therefore, the dynamics of recent experiences prompt an even deeper reflection on the potential of semi-public spaces in the context of urban transformation. The courtyard, being an area of daily interactions with which some residents are connected throughout their lives, is perceived as a unique place in terms of the memories and experiences that some people identify with their home or family (Pellow, 1992). On the other hand, regarding deprived neighbourhoods, because the courtyard area is partially isolated, it may become neglected or even perceived as a dangerous area hosting inappropriate social behaviour (Jałowiecki & Łukowski, 2007). Overall, increasing place attachment in deprived areas has been identified as relevant in providing stability and encouraging residents to engage actively in collective actions of change (Livingston et al., 2010).

Taking these arguments into account, meaningful regeneration of urban courtyard areas can play an important role in co-creating a friendly, ecological, engaging neighbourhood space focused on neighbourly ties, respect for nature and providing a sense of attachment to the place one wants to live in. Thus, the presented chapter will address its attention towards focusing on the importance of place attachment within the participatory regeneration process of urban courtyards. Specifically, the purpose is to analyse the key mechanisms of participatory processes that address the concept of place attachment to semi-public spaces among local community members.

16.2   Place Attachment and Community Participation in Small-Scale Regeneration

This chapter examines community place attachment to an urban courtyard identified as a regenerated area and how this attachment can be addressed or rebuilt through participatory processes. According to Manzo and Devine-Wright (2013), place attachment can be understood as an emotional bond that forms between people and their physical surroundings. This concept can be understood by considering its two dimensions: place identity and place dependence (Williams & Vaske, 2003). Residents may feel a sense of identity with a neighbourhood space because of individual beliefs, preferences, and behavioural tendencies that are important to that environment (Proshansky, 1978). On the other hand, place dependence corresponds to the opportunities that a given environment provides for needs related to goals and activities (Stokols & Shumaker, 1981). Taking both dimensions into account seems important when conducting urban processes aimed at changing the existing function of a degraded area with the simultaneous engagement of the local community (Brown et al., 2003; Manzo & Perkins, 2006; Zhang et al., 2018), and enhancement of community development (Plunkett et al., 2018).

Place attachment can be considered at the level of a single resident's individual beliefs, as well as collectively for the larger neighbourhood community. Much research showed that the positive effects of place attachment include the feeling of having a higher quality of life (Tartaglia, 2012), an enhancement of the sense of self-esteem, ownership, pride, and respect (Low & Altman, 1992; Mitchell et al., 1993), improved neighbourhood ties (Lewicka, 2005), and, eventually, social involvement and collective action (Mesch & Manor, 1998; Mihaylov & Perkins, 2014). Moreover, higher levels of place attachment have been shown to have positive effects on pro-environmental behaviours and activities (Bonaiuto et al., 2002; Scannell & Gifford, 2010; Song & Soopramanien, 2019). Beside these positive effects, the authors also point to the negative effects of place attachment in the form of firm opposition by attached residents to attempts to establish new developments in the existing area (Devine-Wright & Howes, 2010), or the formation of inner-conflicts caused by the influx of new residents into the community (Fried, 2000). In the case of degraded areas, according to Bowles and Gintis (2002), it is important to remember that residents' emotional attachment to place may be dictated by a lack of alternative life choices or opportunities. Additionally, the conditions of a degraded area characterised by housing distress may only mask the strong place attachment of the local community, who does not want to leave (Brown et al., 2003). Considering both the positive and negative contexts of this concept seems crucial in the face of global processes of change, such as climate change and the global COVID-19 pandemic, which have disrupted existing interactions and bonds with significant places (Manzo & Devine-Wright, 2020).

For decision-making processes that relate to making changes to a given urban space, participation is most often used. In regeneration processes that result in projects for the renewal of degraded areas, community participation serves as a tool to identify conditions and address local social, spatial, economic, and environmental inequalities, in direct collaboration with disadvantaged communities. This chapter has limited the analyses to the participatory regeneration of urban courtyards as an example of semi-public and small-scale urban areas. Since the study considered policy-making processes, community participation refers to mostly formal activities. The direct group of participants is the residents from the closest residential area to the urban courtyards.

According to other research, when residents identify and feel attached to their daily environment, they are more willing to protect it, take care of it, and participate in its change. Thus, this positive effect can bring more empowerment and willingness to change in order to improve the quality of life among residents (Minkler & Wallerstein, 2003). Many authors point to the importance of neighbourhood ties in creating a link between place attachment and community participation (Putnam, 2000; Perkins & Long, 2002). When considering the link between place attachment and civic activity, one important factor turns out to be the reference to the history of the place of residence and roots (Lewicka, 2005; Stefaniak et al., 2017), which may contribute to strengthening the sense of community and feeling of pride among residents (Forrest & Kearns, 2001). Additionally, using collective community action as a means of co-production in urban development enhances locals' empowerment (Albrechts, 2013; Rosen & Painter, 2019). It also appears important that participatory approaches can have an impact on rebuilding levels of trust, which, in the case of communities living in deprived areas, can translate into subsequent engagement in collective action (Purdue, 2001). Therefore, the following question can be asked: if place attachment is valuable for achieving positive regeneration outcomes, what mechanisms of community participation can contribute to it being addressed?

16.3 Methodology

The research presented in this chapter refers to the qualitative analysis of the mechanisms of participatory urban regeneration within urban courtyard areas, considering the concept of place attachment among local community members. The research area consists of 16 urban courtyards in six selected Polish cities (Kraków, Gdańsk, Bytom, Olsztyn, Gorzów Wielkopolski, and Kalisz). The case studies are located in cities with a population between 100,000 and 780,000 citizens, representing large cities in Poland. Between 2017 and 2020, the selected courtyards were considered within the regeneration policy processes led by municipal authorities. All case studies were designated in urban policies called Revitalisation Programmes as a part of regenerated areas characterised by a high degree of spatial degradation and with significant accumulation of social, economic, and environmental problems (Urban Regeneration Act, 2015). For the final analysis, those case studies were selected in which residents' participation was a compulsory tool in the projects. Apart from Gorzów Wielkopolski, in the remaining cities, the projects involved external social organisations or private companies as operators conducting the participation process.

In terms of methods, a qualitative approach was used in which a total of 50 in-depth interviews were conducted for all case studies, starting at the end of 2019 and continuing until the beginning of 2021. Interviews were conducted with local community leaders, residents, representatives of NGOs and cultural institutions, municipal officials, participatory process practitioners and academia experts. Additionally, passive participation and observation were used during several participatory meetings and workshops conducted in Krakow. Fieldwork and observation were also conducted in all case studies. The following results analyse those mechanisms of the participatory process that proved to be valuable in addressing and (re)building place attachment among those living close to urban courtyards. The order in which the results are described follows the traditional phases of the participatory process provided in the literature: (1) getting information to and from the public, (2) planning and design, and (3) implementation (Creighton, 2005).

16.4 Results

16.4.1 Local Leaders to Initiate a Change

The first key element of the participation process to invite neighbours into the co-creation of courtyard spaces was to identify and activate local leaders. First, it was important to find people who were active in the community and who formed the grassroots of these areas. In most cases, putting up a poster to promote a neighbourhood meeting was not enough to attract residents about the courtyard initiative. In this case, the door-to-door method turned out to be beneficial when participatory practitioners or local leaders visited apartments with information and an invitation to join the activities. In addition, the possibilities of communicating with residents via social media were used by creating a special Facebook group for each project. During the project, it very often turned out that it was the residents themselves who took charge of the online media, using it later to communicate with their neighbours on current issues. Thanks to the combination of both methods, it was possible to identify local leaders, people interested in the activities, and vulnerable people for whom some support might be needed (elderly, disabled people). According to an NGO representative, this is an excellent method to encourage residents who show some initiative but have not yet had a chance to act and to become local leaders of their neighbourhood. Thanks to the use of this technique, the organisers took the first step towards creating a basis for relations, building trust and, at the same time, getting to know the social structure of the neighbourhood community:

> For us, for example, the first moment is very important, just going from door to door. So, we just go into each tenement house, into each yard, introduce ourselves, knock on each door, talk to each resident. When we do this door-to-door part, we get to know the residents and they get to know us a little bit, we find out a little bit about who we can work with (NGO representative, Kalisz).

16.4.2 (Re)building the Sense of Community

During the next stage of participation, which was aimed at preparing residents for co-design, the important tools and techniques proved to be those that ultimately strengthened the sense of community. In the case of Krakow, organising research walks turned out to be a great way to collectively observe and understand the current functioning of the courtyard area. Residents were treated as experts who knew the area best and were able to skilfully point out its shortcomings and potentials. At this stage, followed by the residents acting as guides through their courtyard, it was possible to notice which of its elements were particularly relevant for the community. On the other hand, places that arouse negative emotions or controversy were immediately indicated, along with the residents' intention to reorganise them. Then, during the workshop meetings, initial ideas, dreams, and visions of how the inhabitants would like to use their courtyard areas were identified together.

In Kalisz, before the common design stage, the so-called *Courtyard Table* was implemented, meaning a meeting of neighbours during which they become acquainted with the history of the surrounding houses, pre-war photos were shown and interesting stories of tenants from the past were told. By reaching back to the roots and interesting historical threads of the area, the process of awakening a sense of uniqueness about one's place of residence begins. An equally interesting initiative in Gdansk was the involvement of the Association of Story Tellers of the Dolne Miasto in the participation process. This association organises cyclical sightseeing tours led by guides who are passionate about local history. The tour aimed to integrate the local community around discovering and presenting the history, everyday life, and future of the Dolne Miasto, as well as the values of the district based on its inhabitants' memories and fates. The knowledge of passionate guides, who often turned out to be residents of the district, was used during participatory workshops and local walks.

Some projects used the potential of art as an excellent transmitter of interpersonal emotions. In Kalisz, the *Courtyard Artist* stage is an artistic event usually taking place in the form of a theatrical performance for children. It is a stage where the prevailing neighbourhood atmosphere and existing relationships were recognised with art and improvisation elements, and possible conflicts were addressed. Artists and facilitators thus gained an insight into the existing social situation and the conflicts in the neighbourhood and could flexibly implement the necessary facilitation, participation, or mediation methods according to the diagnosis:

> After the performance, we ask children and adults what the courtyard culture is, how they understand it. So, the children say to be helpful to each other, to be good to each other. Then, we ask: and when an elderly lady, a neighbour, walks by carrying heavy bags, what then do we have to do? (NGO representative, Kalisz).

The residents emphasised that initiatives that fostered a sense of uniqueness and pride in one's neighbourhood proved to be extremely conducive from their perspective in building neighbourhood bonds. For example, in Olsztyn, each group of residents chose a unique name for their transformed courtyard, including *Zaułek Optymistów (Optimist's Alley) and Nasze Podwórko (Our Courtyard)*. It turned out that including the mechanisms involving artistic activities into the participation process had a major impact on community bonding. In the courtyard of the Centrum D housing estate in Krakow, the residents developed the idea of erecting a sculpture celebrating the work of the artist Marian Kruczek, a resident of this estate from years ago. In Biskupia Górka in Gdańsk, ceramic works made by the residents were displayed in the form of an art installation on the building's façade and in the garden. In Kalisz, as part of artistic activities, children left drawings wishing their neighbours "a nice day" and stuck them on the staircase. On the boards installed in the courtyard, the residents wrote information about the implementation of gardening works, and the children had a field to express their artistic skills. These types of initiatives allow inhabitants to search for and then manifest the values, perspectives, and emotions shared by the neighbourhood community. As a result, the residents' perception of the community may begin to change, and the area itself becomes a more friendly and unique place on a local scale.

16.4.3   Community Members as the Agents of Change

As regeneration brings renewal to a space, the participatory process also has the incredible potential to open a dialogue among residents on how to deal with change and how to prepare for it. At the initial meetings, the residents are very often excellent observers of the ongoing spatial, social, and environmental changes in their place of residence. Some of the most frequently raised problems in all the selected case studies were the perceived environmental changes manifested in the degradation of greenery by parked cars, the problematic rainwater drainage, lack of shade, chaotic collection of municipal waste, and air pollution. Thus, the emerging need to introduce ecological, mitigating, and adaptive solutions to urban areas had an important role in courtyard-related projects. The stage of co-creating in the form of lectures and design workshops made it possible to match appropriate climatic and ecological solutions to the specific conditions of individual spaces. In the cases of Gdańsk (Dolne Miasto, Biskupia Górka) and Olsztyn, local scientists from nearby universities, students, and experts in nature-based solutions were invited to cooperate. In Kalisz, this stage involved the *Courtyard Garden*, where the residents were invited to implement their ideas in the courtyard area. Additionally, the residents became acquainted with the basic principles of urban gardening, including the species of plants to be planted, and frequency of watering and pruning. The results of the joint meetings were the creation of rain gardens and community gardens, the installation of rainwater containers, the removal of several parking spaces to provide room for new plants, and the reorganisation of waste collection (Fig. 16.1).

The direct involvement of the residents as co-designers and co-implementers of the final results proved to be very important in the implementation of changes. In the case of selected courtyards in Bytom, Gdansk (Nowy Port, Dolne Miasto), Olsztyn, and Kalisz, it was assumed that the residents themselves would be responsible for collective actions. It turned out that when the residents took over responsibility for the organisation and implementation of courtyard actions, certain empowerment was released into the community. This was associated with a sense of empowerment among the residents through the achieved results. In the end, it was the residents themselves who were responsible for maintaining the effects of the project by cleaning, watering, and taking care of the greenery. The interviewees

Fig. 16.1 Neighbours collective work in the courtyard at Dolne Miasto district in Gdańsk. (Source: Fundacja Gdańska, 2019)

mentioned that collective actions built a sense of pride from the results they achieved. Neighbourhood cooperation is also a step towards rebuilding sensitivity to other people living close by at a time when we are often driven by individual choices and needs:

> Nowadays people are very focused on themselves and don't notice others. Therefore, I think that making people more sensitive to other people so that they pay attention to what is happening next to them will work to the benefit of all of us (local leader, Olsztyn).

> If neighbours work together on this place, they will take care of, because it is their work, it is their sweat, it is their time, their effort, and at this point, they become the hosts and it seems that this is very good because taking care of such a space gives it a good chance of survival. The point is that it will be continued because these residents will come out, they will integrate, they will get to know each other while working together, and it seems that creating such small communities, in other words - integrating such small communities, is much more beneficial than doing all the work for someone, so we give a rod, we don't give a fish (NGO representative, Gdańsk).

In the interviews with residents, strong emphasis was placed on the value of changing the environment, particularly in the case of courtyard areas which were originally characterised by a very high level of degradation. As the residents themselves emphasised, the positive change in their immediate surroundings provided a seed of hope for change on a larger scale. Some residents became encouraged to look for new opportunities to finance more projects and other forms of involvement in neighbourhood life, thus strengthening local leadership:

> The biggest advantage was that we changed our surroundings ourselves and brought them to a usable condition, so to speak, that just leaving the staircase I don't see those garages, that mud, but somehow it makes me feel uplifted. I open the window and see that it is green, that something is happening as if I didn't live in Bytom (local leader, Bytom).

In the case of Bytom, the residents are raising money to buy flowers, plant seeds, and obtain the necessary gardening equipment. Residents who do not have the money take on gardening jobs instead. According to the local leader, this is an opportunity for some people to get out of the house, interact with others and enjoy nature. For those struggling with addiction problems or poor financial situations, it is a helpful activity to fight exclusion, restoring a sense of being needed by others in the community. The theme of neighbourhood support came up in the interviews, where neighbours not only got to know each other but also noticed and helped each other. Some neighbourhood interactions were established or renewed, and ideally, some level of trust, mutual concern, and a sense of safety was achieved:

> To return to this neighbourly help, once, one tenement house had one big family, believe me, I've lived here in this tenement house since I was born, and neighbourly help was the order of the day. You didn't lock the door to your apartment, you didn't lock your apartment at all. Now, look at all these blocks of flats, these new housing estates. Those people didn't know each other until now. Integration, going out to people and trying to integrate them, but also getting to know each other, to encourage them to act together(NGO representative, Gdańsk).

From the perspective of the experience of the recent COVID-19 pandemic, it appears that during times of social isolation, neighbourhood communities that had strong emotional ties and knew each other well were better able to cope with the situation. In terms of neighbourhood support, residents immediately knew who needed help, including their shopping to be done, or meals to be shared with them. The potential of strong neighbourhood ties in the case of difficult and unforeseen situations was reflected in the immediate grassroots mobilisation where residents themselves organise mutual assistance without the need to involve NGOs. The online neighbourhood groups on Facebook created during the project served as an excellent communicator during the lockdown, where residents were able to post information about material needs, organise collective sewing of masks, and communicate via social media.

The celebration of the effects of the courtyard's transformation turned out to be an important stage in completing the whole process of participation. In each yard, it looked a little different, with neighbourhood meeting events being combined with artistic, educational, or culinary functions. In Kalisz, *The Courtyard Concert* was introduced, where residents were invited to a musical event held in the courtyard area with the participation of musicians from the Kalisz Philharmonic. During the concert, the inhabitants could admire a photographic exhibition of pictures taken during the project, which they could later take away as souvenirs. In the case of courtyards in Gdańsk and Olsztyn, it was the organisation of a neighbourhood barbecue; in the case of Kraków, people came together to plant new plants, and in the case of Gorzów Wielkopolski they had a picnic. Celebration allows residents to experience and enjoy the results together. It is important not to omit this element, so that the residents can have fun in a relaxed atmosphere while feeling that they had a significant role and real impact on the local environment.

16.5   Discussion and Conclusion

This chapter presented an analysis of effective methods and techniques as mechanisms of participatory regeneration processes that have a beneficial influence on community place attachment. It turns out that in those projects in which the emotional attachment of the residents to the courtyard area was addressed, the effects of the regeneration were ultimately perceived as preferable.

First, at the information stage, the most important thing was to address community leadership. The most effective method was direct contact with the residents via the door-to-door method and contact with local NGOs, cultural centres, and the district council. These direct methods were combined with the use of online communication via Facebook to search for grassroots manifestations of residents' activity in their closest environment. All this allowed the initiators of the project to find and engage local leaders as not only the pioneers of change but above all as active partners in the decision-making process.

The significant role of women as local leaders was evident in the study. This is in line with other studies which claimed that women were more likely to be involved in a local community group than men; thus, gender is a significant predictor of community leadership (Wilson & Musick, 1997; Ziersch et al., 2011). Very often, female interviewees mentioned the motivation to create a supportive environment for their children as the primary reason for engaging in participatory activities in their community. Thus, most courtyard-related projects responded to the needs of mothers with children, including the creation of a local playground with a recreation zone. Therefore, a considerable number of methods implemented at the planning and design stage were directly dedicated to children and their mothers (art workshops, theatre performances, circus shows). The potential of women's leadership as frequent users of the space and very attentive observers of neighbourhood life also turned into an opportunity to reach out to and gain the trust of a larger group of residents.

At the planning and design stage, the most important participatory methods, and techniques from the perspective of fostering an emotional connection with the courtyards were those that directly reinforced the sense of community. Learning about the local history of the place through archival photographs and research walks allowed residents to see the evolution of the area over time. Through contact with the past, residents can rediscover the uniqueness of their place of residence. Artistic activities co-created directly with the residents are a beneficial way of evoking such values as vulnerability, trust, respect, and awareness towards collective responsibility. Moreover, implementing the role of art as a tool for participation allowed some residents, who were used to social exclusion, to encounter this form of activity for the first time and to have a different point of view. The effects of artistic interventions in the form of sculptures, mosaics, murals, and all non-material activities draw attention to the potential of often forgotten, atypical areas for art, such as urban courtyards, which are important from the perspective of the everyday functioning of local communities.

The last important element is the implementation of developed design ideas and then the collective production (co-production) of the project. Bovaird et al. (2015) define such actions as collective co-production where the inputs are collectively supplied, and the benefits may be enjoyed by the entire community. The results of the interviews indicate that those projects that introduced collective actions were more positively regarded by the interviewees. Although the area is indicated as being degraded and problematic, the residents were able to achieve positive results of renewal by their own efforts. This awareness stimulates a sense of agency and empowerment by which communities gain mastery over their affairs. However, sometimes, despite collective action, a single event is not enough to stimulate empowerment. In some social processes, a longer-term perspective is needed for the gradual withdrawal of an external animating organisation to provide support in solving residents' problems which they are still unable to cope with on their own. Adopting a transdisciplinary approach by involving artists, scientists, students, urban gardeners, community organisation workers, and facilitators allowed to find different ways to address the values that influenced the neighbourhood's relationship with the local place of residence.

Recent experiences with natural disasters and the COVID-19 pandemic have put local communities to the test. Stay-at-home orders and physical distancing requirements have made it impossible to meet with each other. Also, unpredictable weather conditions, such as torrential downpours and hot days, have hindered people's ability to be outside. Findings indicate that in those courtyards where neighbourhood ties were stronger, there was a natural and grassroots mobilisation of neighbourhood self-help. The immediate lessons from these experiences point to the incredible potential that comes from emotional ties to place and community in helping people to cope with uncertainty and change. The research scope is limited regarding the selected interviewees who were involved in the participatory process, without the insight of those who did not participate. The study is based on limited case studies that are selected examples of courtyard-related initiatives. The suggestion for the future research seems to be to frame the context of coping with change as part of a participatory regeneration policy to enhance the quality of life of urban residents with particular attention directed toward health and environmental values.

Acknowledgement This research was supported by the National Science Centre (Narodowe Centrum Nauki) in Poland, [grant no. 2019/33/N/HS4/01670].

References

Albrechts, L. (2013). Reframing strategic spatial planning by using a coproduction perspective. *Planning Theory, 12*(1), 46–63.

Atkinson, R. (1999). Discourses of partnership and empowerment in contemporary British urban regeneration. *Urban Studies, 36*(1), 59–72.

Bonaiuto, M., Carrus, G., Martorella, H., & Bonnes, M. (2002). Local identity processes and environmental attitudes in land use changes: The case of natural protected areas. *Journal of Economic Psychology, 23*(5), 631–653.

Bovaird, T., Van Ryzin, G. G., Loeffler, E., & Parrado, S. (2015). Activating citizens to participate in collective co-production of public services. *Journal of Social Policy, 44*(1), 1–23.

Bowles, S., & Gintis, H. (2002). Social capital and community governance. *The Economic Journal, 112*, F419–F436.

Brown, B., Perkins, D. D., & Brown, G. (2003). Place attachment in a revitalizing neighborhood: Individual and block levels of analysis. *Journal of Environmental Psychology, 23*(3), 259–271.

Creighton, J. L. (2005). *The public participation handbook: Making better decisions through citizen involvement.* Wiley.

Dargan, L. (2009). Participation and local urban regeneration: The case of the New Deal for Communities (NDC) in the UK. *Regional Studies, 43*(2), 305–317.

Devine-Wright, P., & Howes, Y. (2010). Disruption to place attachment and the protection of restorative environments: A wind energy case study. *Journal of Environmental Psychology, 30*, 271–280.

Dymnicka, M., (2013) *Przestrzeń publiczna a przemiany miasta* [Public space and city transformations]. Wydawnictwo Naukowe Scholar Sp. z oo. [Scientific Publisher Scholar Sp.zoo.].

Ferilli, G., Sacco, P. L., & Blessi, G. T. (2016). Beyond the rhetoric of participation: New challenges and prospects for inclusive urban regeneration. *City, Culture and Society, 7*(2), 95–100.

Forrest, R., & Kearns, A. (2001). Social cohesion, social capital and the neighbourhood. *Urban Studies, 38*(12), 2125–2143.

Fried, M. (2000). Continuities and discontinuities of place. *Journal of Environmental Psychology, 20,193e205.*

Jałowiecki, B., Łukowski, W. (eds.). 2007. *Gettoizacja polskiej przestrzeni miejskiej* [Ghettoisation of Polish urban space]. Wydawnictwo Naukowe Scholar.

Kleinschroth, F., & Kowarik, I. (2020). COVID-19 crisis demonstrates the urgent need for urban greenspaces. *Frontiers in Ecology and the Environment, 18*(6), 318.

Lewicka, M. (2005). Place attachment: How far have we come in the last 40 years? *Journal of Environmental Psychology, 2011*(31), 207–230.

Livingston, M., Bailey, N., & Kearns, A. (2010). Neighbourhood attachment in deprived areas: Evidence from the north of England. *Journal of Housing and the Built Environment, 25*(4), 409–427.

Low, S. M., & Altman, I. (1992). Place attachment: A conceptual inquiry. In I. Altman & S. M. Low (Eds.), *Place attachment* (pp. 1–12). Plenum Press.

Maginn, P. J. (2007). Towards more effective community participation in urban regeneration: The potential of collaborative planning and applied ethnography. *Qualitative Research, 7*(1), 25–43.

Manzo, L. C., & Devine-Wright, P. (2013). *Place attachment: Advances in theory, methods and applications.* Routledge.

Manzo, L. C., & Devine-Wright, P. (2020). *Place attachment: Advances in theory, methods and applications* (2nd ed.). Routledge.

Manzo, L. C., & Perkins, D. D. (2006). Finding common ground: The importance of place attachment to community participation and planning. *Journal of Planning Literature, 20*(4), 335–350.

Mesch, G. S., & Manor, O. (1998). Social ties, environmental perception, and local attachment. *Environment and Behavior, 30*(4), 504–519.

Mihaylov, M., & Perkins, D. D. (2014). *Community place attachment and its role in social capital development.* InPlace attachment: Advances in theory, methods and applications, 61.

Minkler, M., & Wallerstein, N. (2003). *Community based participatory research for health.* Jossey-Bass.

Mitchell, M. Y., Force, J. E., Carroll, M. S., & McLaughlin, W. J. (1993). Forest places of the heart: Incorporating special spaces into public management. *Journal of Forestry, 91*(4), 32–37.

Pellow, D. (1992). Spaces that teach. In *Place attachment* (pp. 187–210). Springer.

Perkins, D. D., & Long, D. A. (2002). Neighborhood sense of community and social capital. In *Psychological sense of community* (pp. 291–318). Springer, Boston, MA.

Peters, T., & Halleran, A. (2020). How our homes impact our health: Using a COVID-19 informed approach to examine urban apartment housing. *Archnet-IJAR: International Journal of Architectural Research.*

Plunkett, D., Phillips, R., & Ucar Kocaoglu, B. (2018). Place attachment and community development. *Journal of Community Practice, 26*(4), 471–482.

Proshansky, H. M. (1978). The city and self-identity. *Environment and Behaviour, 10*, 147–169.

Putnam, R. D. (2000). *Bowling alone: The collapse and revival of American community.* Simon and schuster.

Purdue, D. (2001). Neighbourhood governance: Leadership, trust and social capital. *Urban Studies, 38*, 2211–2224.

Raszka, B., Zienkiewicz, A., Kalbarczyk, R., & Kalbarczyk, E. (2014). Revitalization of Urban courtyards in Wrocław (southwestern Poland). *Polish Journal of Natural Sciences, 29*(3), 225–237.

Rosen, J., & Painter, G. (2019). From citizen control to co-production: Moving beyond a linear conception of citizen participation. *Journal of the American Planning Association, 85*(3), 335–347.

Scannell, L., & Gifford, R. (2010). The relations between natural and civic place attachment and pro-environmental behavior. *Journal of Environmental Psychology, 30*(3), 289–297.

Song, Z., & Soopramanien, D. (2019). Types of place attachment and pro-environmental behaviors of urban residents in Beijing. *Cities, 84*, 112–120.

Sim, D. (2019). *Soft city: Building density for everyday life.* Island Press.

Stefaniak, A., Bilewicz, M., & Lewicka, M. (2017). The merits of teaching local history: Increased place attachment enhances civic engagement and social trust. *Journal of Environmental Psychology, 51*, 217–225.

Stokols, D., & Shumaker, S. A. (1981). *People in places: A transactional view of settings* (pp. 441–488). Concept Publishing Company.

Strzelecka, M., Sorensen, J., & Wicks, B. E. (2010). The role of place attachment in revitalization of neighborhood parks in East St. Louis. *Loisir et Société/Society and Leisure, 33*(2), 251–272.

Taleghani, M., Tenpierik, M., van den Dobbelsteen, A., & Sailor, D. J. (2014). Heat in courtyards: A validated and calibrated parametric study of heat mitigation strategies for urban courtyards in the Netherlands. *Solar Energy, 103*, 108–124.

Tartaglia, S. (2012). Different predictors of quality of life in urban environments. *Social Indicators Research, 113*(3), 1045e1053.

Ustawa o rewitalizacji z dnia 9 października 2015 r. [Act of the Regeneration from 9 October 2015]. (n.d.). Official Journal Dz. U. from http://isap.sejm.gov.pl/DetailsServlet?id=WDU20150001777. Accessed 11 Nov 2021.

Williams, D. R., & Vaske, J. J. (2003). The measurement of place attachment: Validity and generalizability of a psychometric approach. *Forest Science, 49*(6), 830–840.

Wilson, J., & Musick, M. (1997). Who cares – Toward an integrated theory of volunteer work. *American Sociological Review, 62*, 694–713.

Zamani, Z., Heidari, S., & Hanachi, P. (2018). Reviewing the thermal and microclimatic function of courtyards. *Renewable and Sustainable Energy Reviews, 93*, 580–595.

Zhang, H., Matsuoka, R. H., & Huang, Y. J. (2018). How do community planning features affect the place relationship of residents? An investigation of place attachment, social interaction, and community participation. *Sustainability, 10*(8), 2726.

Ziersch, A., Osborne, K., & Baum, F. (2011). Local community group participation: Who participates and what aspects of neighbourhood matter? *Urban Policy and Research, 29*(4), 381–399.

Chapter 17
Reshaping Territorial Identities and Creating Place Attachment Through Transport Infrastructure. Case Studies: The Metros in Almada, Lisbon and Porto

Emanuel-Cristian Adorean ⓘ, **Oana-Ramona Ilovan** ⓘ, and **Iwona Markuszewska** ⓘ

17.1 Introduction

Transport authorities struggle to find the best mobility solutions to new challenges produced by societal phenomena, such as urbanisation, demographic shift, social exclusion, lack of equity in accessibility, pandemics and other health and ecological issues. Besides creating new cityscapes, the introduction of new transport infrastructure changes the urban tissue, impacting territorial identities and place attachments.

Assuming that urban transformations may affect not only the territory where they occur, but also the society itself through new place experiences, the aim of this research is to assess to what extant the introduction of metro systems reshaped the territorial identities and place attachment patterns in three cities of Portugal (i.e., Almada, Lisbon, and Porto), and in their metropolitan areas (Almada is part of the

E.-C. Adorean
Interdisciplinary Centre of Social Sciences, Faculty of Social & Human Sciences, New University of Lisbon, Colégio Almada Negreiros, Lisbon, Portugal
e-mail: adorean.ec@campus.fcsh.unl.pt

O.-R. Ilovan (✉)
Department of Regional Geography and Territorial Planning, Faculty of Geography and Territorial Identities and Development Research Centre, Babeş-Bolyai University, Cluj-Napoca, Romania
e-mail: oana.ilovan@ubbcluj.ro

I. Markuszewska
Department of Environmental Remote Sensing and Soil Science, Faculty of Geographical and Geological Sciences, Institute of Physical Geography and Environmental Planning, Adam Mickiewicz University, Poznań, Poland
e-mail: iwona.markuszewska@amu.edu.pl

© The Author(s), under exclusive license to Springer Nature
Switzerland AG 2022
O.-R. Ilovan, I. Markuszewska (eds.), *Preserving and Constructing Place Attachment in Europe*, GeoJournal Library 131,
https://doi.org/10.1007/978-3-031-09775-1_17

Lisbon Metropolitan Area). The objectives of our research were (i) to contribute to understanding better the territorialisation of the transport infrastructure, (ii) to identify the defining elements of the Portuguese metro systems by analysing their representations in mass media, and (iii) to examine the process of creating users' place attachment to metro places and the metro systems themselves.

Besides introduction, this chapter consists of four parts. In the first one, the theoretical background is presented. In the second, the methodology is explained. Further on, in the results part, the case studies are presented and discussed. In the last part, the conclusions are drawn.

17.2 Theoretical Background

This part includes two sections on the state of the art concerning (1) development, use and impact of the metro in urban areas and (2) how mobility influences people's relation to places.

17.2.1 The Metro: Development, Use and Impact

The need for modern and efficient mass transportation is an elementary condition for people to be able to commute and has become a priority for national and local authorities (Adolphson & Fröidh, 2019; Sipetic et al., 2019). In fact, contemporary cities are defined not only by the historic and modern sites they provide their inhabitants and visitors with, but also by the efficiency, safety, reliability, and aesthetic of their transport systems.

However, there is still no clear or common vision among transport experts, policymakers, and planners about the role of mobility to make cities more liveable (Mohan, 2008). Metro systems are usually perceived to mitigate sprawl and foster density, at the same time reducing residents' reliance on cars due to improved access to affordable transportation. Most metro systems are relatively recent; big cities do not necessarily have larger metro systems, and these spur some decentralisation while shaping greater mass transit use (Gonzalez-Navarro & Turner, 2016). Metros also contribute to gentrification, because the more affluent reduce their commutes by moving in areas near stations.

As stated by Sipetic and peers (2019), a metro system is an image of the society that the urban environment belongs to. It can depict the quality of the collaboration among experts, ruling officials, and public. The territory and the new transport infrastructure adjust to various stakeholders' behaviours, practices, and representations and the appropriation of the transport system plays an essential role in territorial dynamics. This appropriation is a collective construction process involving multiple interactions among several categories of stakeholders that take part at the territorialisation of the metro systems: political and economic actors, and metro users (Delaplace, 2017). Focusing on the location of stations, Facchinetti-Mannone

(2019) suggested various ways of appropriation depending on the centrality degree of the metro stations, on local actors' mobilisation, and on the geographical and historical context of the metro network implementation, resulting in highly diversified territorial dynamics. Moreover, appropriation is a long-term process which begins before the implementation of the new transport infrastructure and goes on even after the trivialisation of its uses (de Vaujany, 2003; Facchinetti-Mannone, 2019).

In a pilot study including volunteers who accepted to provide narrative descriptions on their trips by bus, metro, and train, conducted by the University of California in the Los Angeles metropolitan area, and focused on how the public transport experience shapes users' perceptions, it was found that participants focused exclusively on dysfunctionalities, such as buildings architecture, quality of facilities, services, and street furniture (Fink & Taylor, 2010). However, users' perceptions regarding the impact of a new transport system may vary according to the date this was introduced within the urban area. For instance, a study about the impact of a new public transport route on travel behaviour, physical activity, and health, conducted in Cambridgeshire, United Kingdom, emphasised that there was a certain difference among the old users' perceptions of the public transport system, who most often had higher expectations, and those of non-regular users, who were more prone to assess the introduction of the transport line as positive (Jones et al., 2013). In another research considering the everyday practices of public transport users in two cities in Croatia, results showed differences in passengers' transport systems appropriation according not only to their demographic characteristics, but also as a direct result of the urban area where the transport systems were located (Tomic et al., 2015).

These complex relations among transport, territory, and society make heavy the assessment of transport infrastructure according to economic and spatial changes, with most researchers focusing on understanding the process of territorial changes (Facchinetti-Mannone, 2019). Nevertheless, research was conducted to assess territorial appropriation and users' perceptions of the introduction or the existence of transport systems (Facchinetti-Mannone, 2019; Fink & Taylor, 2010; Jones et al., 2013; Mancheva, 2015; Tomic et al., 2015).

17.2.2 Mobility and People's Relation to Places

Our theoretical approach considers three interconnected concepts: territorial/place identity, representations, and place attachment. Concerning the first, *identity of place* as part of one's identity derives from living in a place (Proshansky, 1978, p. 15; Peng et al., 2020), and *identity of the place* means shared representations and shared connotations attributed to places (Banini, 2021; Banini & Ilovan, 2021, p. 5). Representations build images of places and create identities for the places they refer to. These identities are territorialised (they are symbolically constructed) and appropriated during the process of creating representations and also of performing certain practices associated with those places (Lorimer, 2005; Banini & Ilovan, 2021, pp. 5–6). Therefore, a territory is a dynamic spatial entity, including practices associated to a sense of belonging (Banini, 2021, p. 15).

A key related concept of territorial identity is attachment. Place attachment is part of the territorial/place identity construction process (Banini, 2021, p. 29). Image and place attachment are interconnected social constructs (Silva et al., 2018). People's territorialised bond builds up on representations and discourses (Banini, 2021, p. 22), and the main representations of places have a positive and strong correlation with place attachment, can predict behaviour and strengthen a community's territorial resilience (Stylidis, 2020, pp. 12–16).

Based on this theoretical foundation and in an increasingly mobile world, reflected in the mobilities turn in the Social Sciences (since the early 2000s), the understanding and analysis of place attachment is more and more linked to mobility practices, including regular daily travel, especially in the continuous development and modernisation of the urban area (Di Masso et al., 2019, pp. 2–3). Thus, our research falls into this mobility-related place attachment framework (Di Masso et al., 2019, p. 11) and challenges the 'sedentarist' approach to place attachment. Mobility influences people's relation to places (Banini, 2021, p. 16), but not necessarily weakens it; on the contrary, mobility can sometimes strengthen place attachment (Lewicka, 2014).

Considering the definition of place attachment as the bonding of people to various places and scales (Altman & Low, 1992; Lewicka, 2011; Manzo & Devine-Wright, 2014), we chose the metro as a visited type of place that represents daily mobility in the city, and where one can exemplify and discuss the concepts of place identity, sense of place, place dependence, and place attachment. This is possible due to its features that foreground the metro more as a distinctive and authentic place (than a non-place) and its functional nature within inhabitants' mobility experiences. Thus, we considered the sense of place theory, which is based on perceptions and emotions related to a place, and was developed, among others, by Relph (1976), who claimed that a sense of place depends on social relationships created in a particular place rather than on physical attachment to a place.

It is assumed that sense of place depends on the length or depth of experience within a particular place (Tuan, 1990). This concept of place dependence was developed, among others, by Stokols and Shumaker (1981). Place dependence is defined as a positive bond between individuals and their surrounding environment. Additionally, the sense of dependence is very close to place satisfaction (Shumaker & Taylor, 1983). This concept of sense of place expresses human-environmental interactions, and according to Stedman (2002), a sense of place can be considered as symbolic satisfaction with a spatial setting. Moreover, sense of place is dynamic and polysemic (Massey and Jess, 1995; Banini & Ilovan, 2021).

17.3   Methodology

The case studies selected for this research were the metro systems of Almada, Lisbon and Porto. The methodology included field work and Internet mining for data collection, and GIS techniques, imagery interpretation, media content analysis, and discourse analysis for the processing of the collected data. GIS techniques were used to produce current location maps for the three metro systems under analysis, and to carry out spatial analyses. Further, the visual imagery interpretation was used to analyse the changes within the territory produced by the three metro networks. Finally, the subjective geography of the three metro systems is rendered through two sources: newspaper articles and inhabitants' reactions to the respective newspaper articles, as well as their opinions on social media about the metro systems. The image and the text discourses, having as referent the three metro systems, were the signifiers that we analysed, because image and language are 'mediators' in the process of people's representing places using their knowledge, ideas, and feelings (Raffestin, 2012; Rose, 2016). Therefore, we conducted quantitative media content analysis and discourse analysis. Then, we realised a place attachment analysis based on social media comments. To sum up, the focus was on representations of the metro systems, then on users' opinions, perceptions, and feelings about the metros.

The period for the published articles we used for content and discourse analyses was from June 2015 to November 2021, with 116 selected articles, in Portuguese, approaching different topics for each of the three case studies. The articles were published at different times within the reference period and addressed a distinct topic (we selected them as such in order to avoid repetition) (Table 17.1). The articles were grouped in ten classes according to their content, namely (i) Accessibility, (ii) COVID-related aspects, (iii) Development projects, (iv)

Table 17.1 Media content sample characterisation

Metro systems	No. of selected articles	Newspapers	Publication period
Almada metro	30 articles	Almada Notícias Almadense Correio da Manhã Expresso Impala Jornal de Notícias Jornal Semmais MTS - metro Transportes do Sul Nascer do sol	July 2017 – November 2021
Lisbon metro	41 articles	Diário de Notícias DN Life Jornal de Negócios Jornal de Notícias Mensagem de Lisboa Metropolitano de Lisboa SIC Notícias	June 2015 – November 2021
Porto metro	45 articles	Diário de Notícias Dinheiro vivo Jornal de Notícias Metro do Porto Observador Público	September 2015 – November 2021

Economic aspects, (v) Environment, (vi) Image of territory, (vii) (Inter)operabil-
ity, (viii) Safety and security, (ix) Social aspects, and (x) Other categories. To
assess what class each article belonged to, we used a top 3 scale, with the most
relevant category receiving 3 points. The word frequency counting was performed
by using a word frequency counter platform: Write Words – Word Frequency
Counter (http://www.writewords.org.uk/), which allows to count the frequency
usage of each word in a certain text.

As for content analysis of the social media, we studied both statements that
showed the initiation of the process of place making, and those that indicated deep
manifestations of place identity and place attachment. We focused on activities that
were related to place making, place satisfaction, creating sense of place, place
belonging, and place identity. Qualitative methodology was appropriate and used
for analysing the users' expression of any emotional and visceral experience of
places and events connected to the metro. The data was selected from fan-pages of
Lisbon and Porto Metros. In the case of Almada Metro this assessment was not possible since it did not have social media pages.

17.4   Results and Discussion

This part includes five sections. It is structured based on the three steps proposed by
Banini for a methodology to research local identities (2021, p. 30): first, the territorial
features are narrated (i.e., development of the metro systems in Almada, Lisbon and
Porto), second, representations are identified, interpreted and discussed (i.e., visual
imagery and the appropriation of the metro systems; quantitative media content analysis of newspaper articles about the Portuguese metro systems; discourse analysis and
(re)presenting the metro systems in mass media narratives), and, third, local opinions
on the place or the bonds between locals and territory (i.e. the metro systems) are
analysed (i.e., place attachment analysis based on social media comments).

17.4.1   Development of the Metro Systems in Almada, Lisbon and Porto

In this first section, we present the spatial identity of the three metro systems as
revealed in their material building and development.

Almada Metro (Metro Transportes Do Sul – MTS)

Metro Transportes do Sul (MTS) is a light surface metro made up of three lines:
Line 1 Cacilhas – Corroios, Line 2 Corroios – Pragal and Line 3 Cacilhas –
University, with a total of 14 km and 19 stations, connecting Almada and Seixal
municipalities on the south bank of the Tagus River (Fig. 17.1).

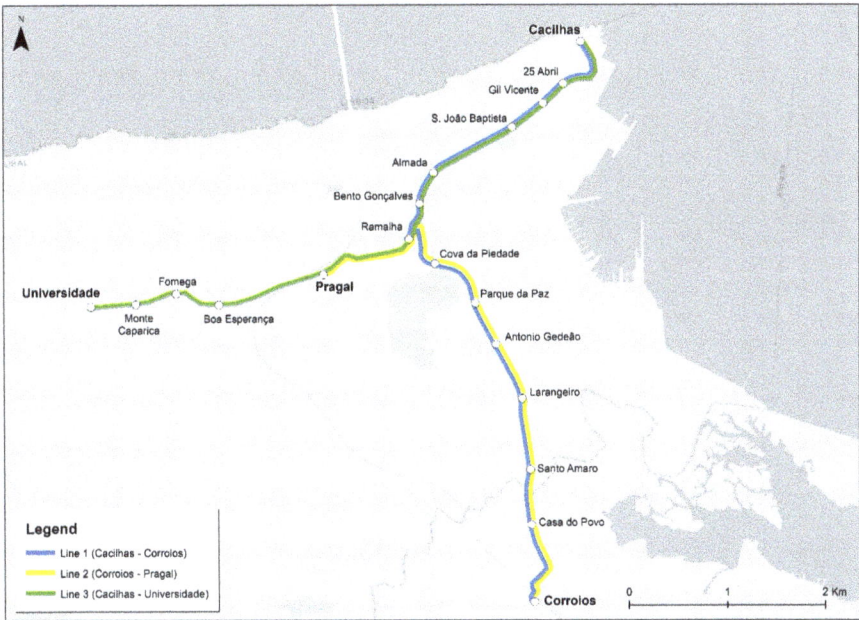

Fig. 17.1 Almada Metro in 2022. (Source: Own elaboration)

The initial project was developed in 1995; work began again in 2002, after a new protocol signed in 1999. The opening of all three lines was realised in 2007–2008 (present network), while a second and a third extension phases currently develop, which foresee the extension through the municipality of Seixal; the connection to Moita and Barreiro are still planned, but they have been suspended since 2008 (MTS, 2022).

Lisbon Metro (Metropolitano de Lisboa)

Lisbon Metro is a rapid transit system in Lisbon, serving partially the municipalities of Odivelas and Amadora in the homonymous counties. At present, it comprises four lines (Fig. 17.2), 56 metro stations, 44.5 km of network extension and 333 carriages. Additionally, it possesses 735 access channels, 281 ticketing vending machines, 234 mechanical stairs, 108 elevators, 69 semi-automatic ticketing vending machines and 202 commercial spaces (Metropolitano de Lisboa, 2022).

The Metropolitano de Lisboa company was set up in January 1948 and its main objective was the technical and economic study of an underground collective transport system. Construction work began in 1955 and, in December 1959, it was inaugurated, consisting of a Y-shaped line with two sections: Sete Rios (Jardim Zoológico)-Rotunda (currently Marquês de Pombal) and Entre Campos-Rotunda (Marquês de Pombal). Metropolitano de Lisboa became a determining factor in the development of Lisbon, outlining urban extension lines, and acting as the main

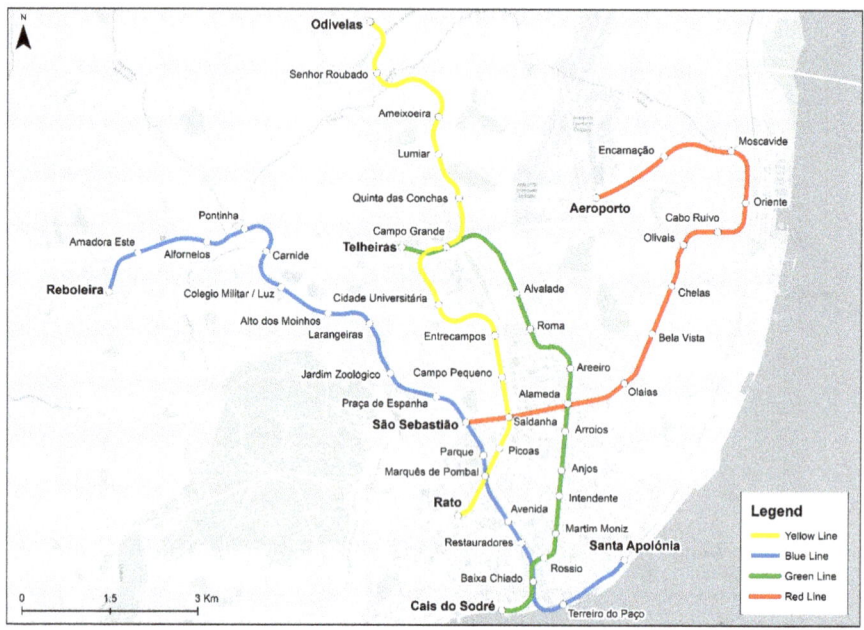

Fig. 17.2 Lisbon Metro in 2022. (Source: Own elaboration)

engine of the urban transport system, due to its speed, frequency and safety. From this point on, the expansion of the metro included four distinct phases.

The first expansion phase (1960–1990) was carried out in several stages. In 1963, the Restauradores/Rossio section started operating. Almost a decade later, in 1972, the Rossio/Anjos/Alvalade section was completed, while in 1988, two new extensions opened, namely Sete Rios (Jardim Zoológico)-Colégio Militar/Luz and Entre Campos-Cidade Universitária.

The second extension phase (1990–1998) included new sections: Cidade Universitária-Campo Grande and Alvalade-Campo Grande in 1993, Colégio Militar-Pontinha, and Marquês de Pombal-Rato in 1997 and Rossio-Baixa/Chiado-Cais do Sodré early in 1998.

The third extension phase was characterised by the Expo '98 world class event and the introduction of the Red Line. It was of great importance, not only for the urban structure, but also because it was a privileged access route, through Oriente station, to Expo '98. Additionally, this period included the extension of the Green Line from Rossio to Cais do Sodré and of the Blue Line from Restauradores to Baixa/Chiado.

The fourth extension phase (2000-present) represents the introduction of new sections, namely Campo Grande-Telheiras on the Green Line in 2002, Campo Grande-Odivelas section on the Yellow Line and Pontinha-Amadora Este on the Blue Line in 2004, Baixa/Chiado-Santa Apolónia on the Blue Line in 2007, Alameda-São Sebastião on the Red Line in 2009, Oriente-Aeroporto in 2012, and

Amadora Este-Reboleira on the Blue Line, in 2016, opened for operation. In addition, work has already begun on transforming the Green Line into a circular one by adding two more stations, namely Estrela and Santos.

Porto Metro (Metro Do Porto)

Porto Metro, one of the largest European light rail networks, has induced positive impact on the social, economic, and environmental layers. Its network consists of 6 lines, summing up 67 km of network, and a transportation capacity of about 9000 people per hour on each line, serving seven counties, namely Gondomar, Maia, Matosinhos, Porto, Póvoa de Varzim, Vila do Conde, and Vila Nova de Gaia.

Porto Metro includes six lines, namely: Line A (Blue) Senhor de Matosinhos-Estádio do Dragão (Porto), Line B (Red) Póvoa de Varzim-Estádio do Dragão (Porto), Line C (Green) ISMAI (Maia)-Campanhã (Porto), Line D (Yellow) São João Hospital-Santo Ovídio (Vila Nova de Gaia), Line E (Violet) Airport (Maia)-Estádio do Dragão (Porto), and Line F (Orange) Senhora da Hora (Matosinhos)-Fânzeres (Gondomar) (Fig. 17.3).

Porto Metro was constructed between 2002 and 2011. Line A, connecting Senhor de Matosinhos to Trindade, was inaugurated in 2002, being extended to Estádio do Dragão two years later, due to the organisation of the European Football Championship which took place in Portugal that year. In 2005, the following were opened: the first section of Line B, connecting Pedras Rubras to Estádio do Dragão, Line C between Maia and Porto, and Line D Vila Nova de Gaia-Porto. In 2006, there were completed the main section of Line B to Póvoa de Varzim, the segment between Forum Maia and ISMAI of Line C, and the segment between Pólo Universitário and São João Hospital of Line D.

In 2007, Line E, connecting the city centre of Porto to Francisco Sá Carneiro Airport, was implemented, while in 2011 the last line (Line F), which connects Estádio do Dragão and Fânzeres in Gondomar, opened. In addition, Line G (Pink) is already under construction, and will connect São Bento to Casa da Música (Metro do Porto, 2022).

17.4.2 Visual Imagery and the Appropriation of the Metro Systems

Visual imagery interpretation is based on the data we collected through field trips and from the social media of the metro systems. Firstly, the introduction of new metro systems has resulted in changes within the urban tissue, such as the appearance of new cityscapes, more visible in the case of surface metro lines (Almada and partially Porto), not invalidating the new urban landscapes generated by underground systems, although their impact is less visible.

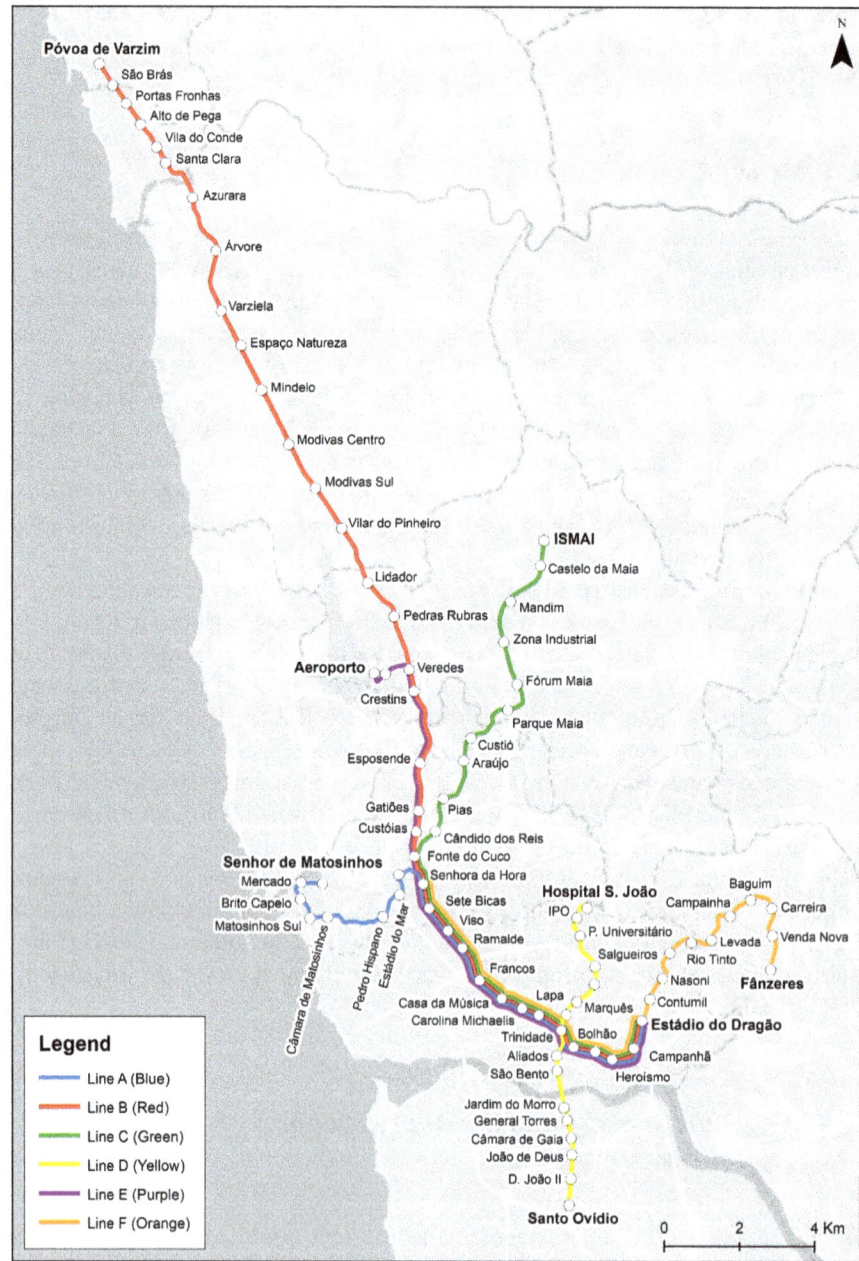

Fig. 17.3 Porto Metro in 2022. (Source: Own elaboration)

On the other hand, the introduction of new metro systems leads to new jobs, not only at the metro facilities, but also by incentivising economic development through the polarisation of new investments, specifically in the case of lines crossing underdeveloped and

Fig. 17.4 Different types of activities at the Almada Metro (upper part) and Lisbon Metro (centre and lower parts). (Source: Cristian Emanuel Adorean, February 2022)

peripheral suburban areas. It may also attract new residents, as the metro systems are considered the most efficient transport means within the urban context. However, it involves temporary circulation restrictions and traffic cuts during the construction or repair phases of lines or stations, and may influence the existing public transport services, including timetables, frequencies, and trajectories.

In addition, more mass transit will impact the modal share, and implicitly will conduct to the decrease of private vehicles use, thus contributing to the decarbonisation of the urban transport systems and leading to more equitable accessibility. Furthermore, metro introduction results in new green and public spaces (Fig. 17.4), thus allowing the achievement of more liveable, safe, healthy, and sustainable cities.

Concerning the appropriation of metro systems, it is important to stress out that despite usual transport practices, such as buying tickets, validating the card or the ticket, waiting for the metro, listening to music, using the phone, having a conversation with a travelling companion, walking through the station, having a coffee, or eating, in the pictures available on the social media networks of Lisbon and Porto metro systems, very frequently occur other types of activities, inside the metro stations or at their surface interfaces: concerts, academic activities, painting or photography exhibitions, protests, solidarity or civic campaigns or other sociocultural actions.

In this process of representing the metro, its identity is constructed. Representations of the identity of the metro as a place of mobility can be identified. This identity takes form from a process of socially constructing representations (Banini & Ilovan, 2021, p. 2). In this identity construction process, the places hosted by the metro are signifier spaces (Banini & Ilovan, 2021, p. 4, citing Vallega, 2003). These representations also influence and create place attachment. They reinforce each other.

The metro space, its identity and place attachment construction processes can be understood through the fixity-flow framework (Di Masso et al., 2019). The metro system is constructed as a web of secure, familiar, and meaningful places due to its stations hosting new and enriching activities and experiences. The 'route' (mobility) and the 'root' (fixity) make up a whole rich mobile experience in the metro system. The administration of the metro aims at effacing the state of placelessness that such a mobility environment may easily acquire, offering its users opportunities to experience the metro and thus cognitively and emotionally relate to it. All these activities allow the consolidation of space representations, by all those interacting with the metro facilities. This is important because most of the people who participate at these activities do so voluntarily. Through this, the metro is embedded within a local sense of belonging, continuously re-articulated.

17.4.3   Quantitative Analysis of Newspaper Articles About the Portuguese Metro Systems

Based on the occurrence of the words used in the newspaper articles and the relations between the identified topics and their meanings, the quantitative media content analysis aimed to classify the representations produced due to the existence of the metro. Representations are constructed based on perceived material and immaterial features of a place (Rose, 2016). The representations identified during this quantitative analysis constituted the subject of an in-depth qualitative analysis, presented in the next sub-section, and aimed at understanding the logic that structured the representations, considering the contextual elements previously highlighted.

The Portuguese Metro Systems in Newspaper Articles: Most Frequent Topics About People and Places

Concerning the dimension of articles, they were rather short, as the average was 166 words (Almada Metro – 179 words, Lisbon Metro – 169 words, and Porto Metro – 149 words). Overall, the word 'territory' was used only seven times within the entire sample (Almada – 1, Lisbon – 2, Porto – 4), while the word 'place' was used 23 times (Almada Metro – 6, Lisbon Metro – 4, Porto Metro – 13), and the word 'attachment' was not mentioned at all.

Considering the various roles people have as individual or collective within the place attachment creation process, it is worth highlighting the formats it embraces in the sample. Our attention is focused on those relating to social bonding. Thus, in the case of Almada Metro, the most used words to refer to the people were 'user' (27 mentions), 'people' (11), 'customer/client' (11), 'passenger' (10), 'family' (8), 'children' (7), 'man' (6), 'citizen' (2), 'human' (2), 'worker' (2) and 'community' (1). Nevertheless, in the articles approaching Lisbon Metro, the most frequent ones were 'passenger' and 'user' (22 mentions each), 'people' (16), 'customer/client' (12), 'children' (10), 'family' (3) and 'community' (2). The articles about Porto Metro mentioned more the terms 'user' (36 mentions), 'customer/client' (25), 'people' (15), 'passenger' (13), 'citizen' (6), 'human' and 'woman' (4 each), 'children', 'community' and 'man' (3 each), and 'family' (2).

In the case of Almada Metro, *the most common themes* were related to aspects regarding the metropolitan intermobility, thus words such as 'transport' (57 mentions), 'metro' (53), 'Lisbon' (36), 'MTS' (36), 'Almada' (35) 'municipalities' (20) and 'metropolitan' (18) were used more. The topics related to the monthly passes, as well as payment methods and timetables resulted in a quite high number of the following words: 'passes' (34 mentions), 'card' (32), 'viva' (30), 'users' (27), 'operators' (26), 'lines' (22), 'tickets' (21), and 'validation' (13). Moreover, the extension and service improvements determined the frequent use of specific terms, such as 'area' (17), 'public' (16), 'service' (16), 'extension' (15), 'surface' (15), and 'network' (10). In contrast, in the case of Lisbon Metro the most frequent word was 'Lisbon' (155 frequencies), while the word 'stations' (133) came second, followed by 'metro' (126) and 'lines' (101). This ranking (Fig. 17.5) is particularly relevant, considering that metro stations are of great importance for place attachment creation, as explained in the next section.

The Portuguese Metro Systems in Newspaper Articles: Contribution of the (Re)Presented Topics to Place Attachment Creation

For Almada Metro (Fig. 17.6), the evolution of the discourse that may impact the place attachment creation showed a positive trend between July 2017 and December 2018, and starting from March 2021, with the most relevant topics centred on mobility week events, toys and cloths collection campaigns, transport digitalisation, development projects, metro extension, urban changes, rehabilitation, fighting phonic pollution and natural disasters awareness campaigns. Nevertheless, the topics that (may) obstruct the place attachment creation are more frequent from April 2019, and they are usually related to accidents involving passengers or car drivers, and COVID-19 measures and restrictions.

Lisbon Metro is the most favoured in terms of positive discourses able to lead to creation of place attachment and territorial identity (Fig. 17.7), perhaps because of its longer history, the architectural features of the metro stations, or simply because of the image that the metro and the stations have been fortifying over time. Hence, it has the highest number of newspaper articles with themes that may have a positive impact on the place attachment creation or strengthening, and they are spread over time. These topics are focused on rehabilitation, repair or maintenance work allowing the improvement not only of the metro's functionality, territorial image, but also of its territorial image through new infrastructure and facilities for disabled people,

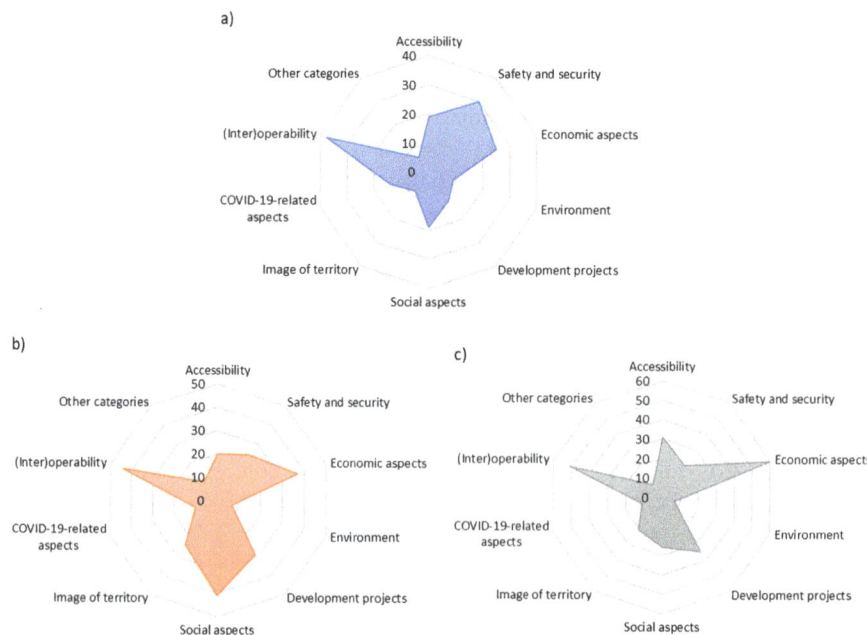

Fig. 17.5 Hierarchy of topics for (**a**) Almada Metro, (**b**) Lisbon Metro and (**c**) Porto Metro. (Source: Own elaboration)

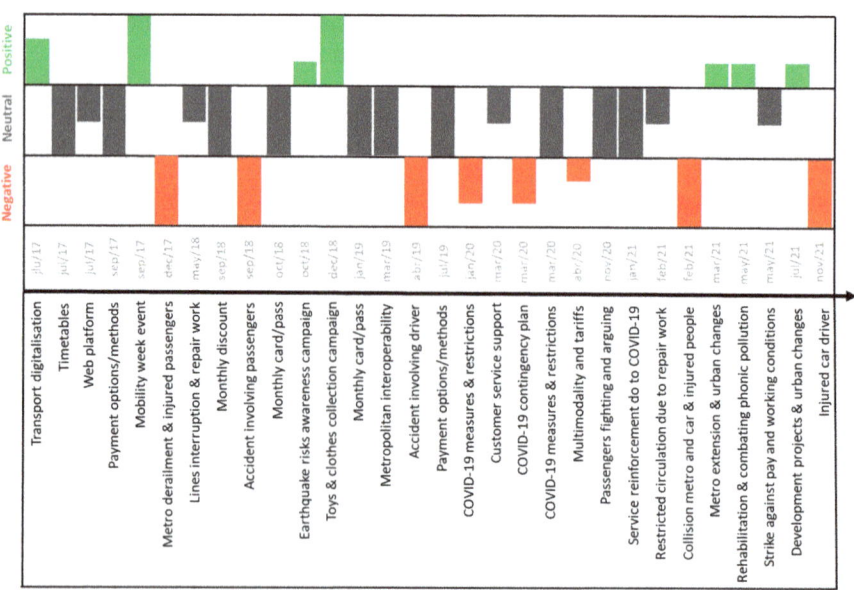

Fig. 17.6 Almada Metro in newspaper articles. Contribution of the (re)presented topics to place attachment creation. (Source: Own elaboration)

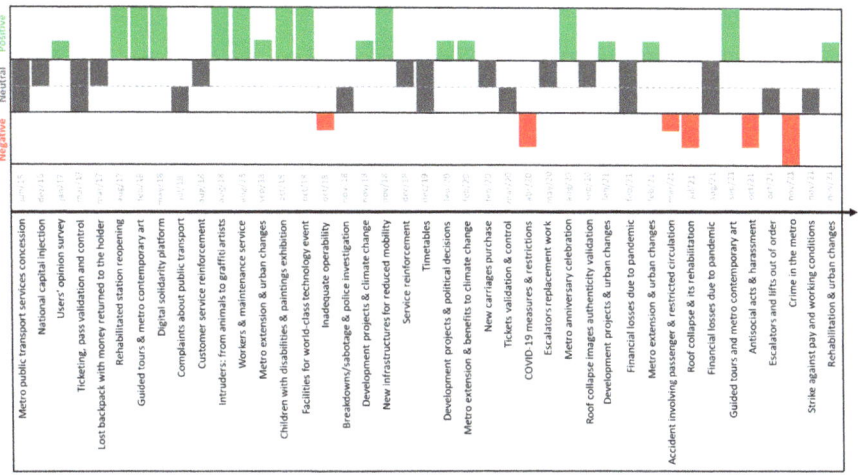

Fig. 17.7 Lisbon Metro in newspaper articles. Contribution of the (re)presented topics to place attachment creation. (Source: Own elaboration)

guided tours highlighting the hosted contemporary art, exhibitions of paintings created by children with disabilities, or social and charity campaigns, including digital solidarity platform creation, facilities for world-class events or metro anniversary celebrations.

However, the themes with a negative impact on the image of the metro and on its territorial identity, especially present beginning with April 2020, refer to inadequate operability because of technical issues, COVID-19 measures and restrictions, accidents involving passengers, and isolated crime cases.

The discourse on Porto Metro reflects the presence of negative aspects between September 2015 and December 2019, focusing on topics such as strike against the concession, accidents involving passengers or drivers, and circulation restrictions (Fig. 17.8). However, the positive aspects, specifically present from September 2019 on, refer to the study and preparations for the metro extension, metro rehabilitation and repair work, social activities such as concerts or image projections of health professionals, in the stations, as a tribute to those that have been fighting against the pandemic.

The discursive construction of the metro in the newspapers is realised through textual representations, while these are connected to and influence people's perceptions, opinions, emotions and enable the construction of their attachment to the metro places. In this case, the power of constructing the metro as a place belongs to mass media – informing people, but also influencing public opinion.

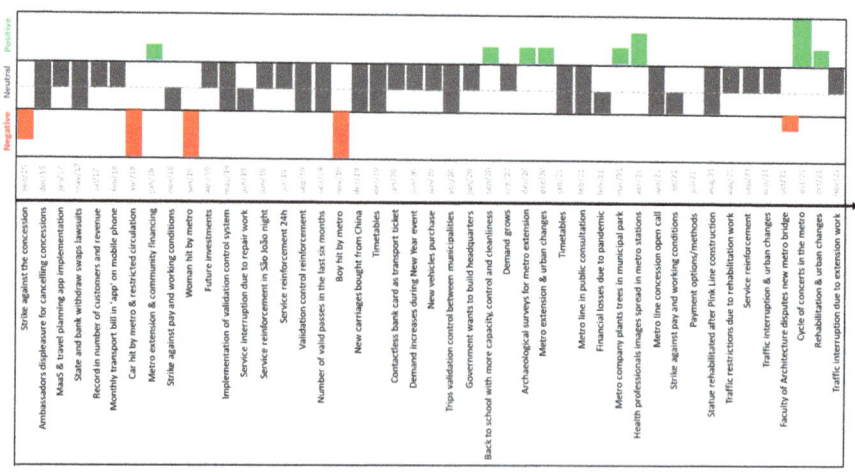

Fig. 17.8 Porto Metro in newspaper articles. Contribution of the (re)presented topics to place attachment creation. (Source: Own elaboration)

17.4.4   Discourse Analysis: (re)Presenting the Metro Systems in Mass Media Narratives

In this section, we present a critical investigation of the representations of the metro in the mass media narratives constructed in the same newspaper articles.

Ever since their first usage, despite their transport function, administrations of metro systems have paid attention to provide their stations and interfaces with artwork which, to a certain extent, minimises the negative effects of the underground environment, humanises and makes spaces attractive. These activities create a sense of place making, giving meaning to a placeless space, and building an emotional bond between metro users and their transport system.

Workers play an essential role in the metro systems since the correct functioning of the involved entities depends on them. By 2020, the three Portuguese metro systems were the places creating a feeling of homeness for almost 2000 people, at least due to spending so much time in the metro places and taking care of them: Almada Metro – 127 employees, Lisbon Metro – 1513 employees, Porto Metro – 332 employees (INE, 2021). The workforce is not limited to day work, as there are 'hidden' employees who carry out maintenance or repair services during the night, and are represented as an efficient and well-coordinated team:

> When the gates close, the curtain falls for passengers and a new show begins in the metro galleries that will last until just before the reopening […]. It's like an orchestra, everyone knows what to do […], a reality completely unknown to users, but with different music: machines working, unhooking, cutting, welding, pounding the rails ... a deafening, almost unbearable melody. (Diário de Notícias, 2018a)

However, sometimes metro stations are places of antisocial behaviour, such as robberies and fights or strikes (Impala, 2020; Observador, 2015).

Aiming at increasing the number of passengers, metro companies use to launch specific campaigns, providing benefits to the existing and potential users, such as 'Pass by Pass campaign' or 25% discount on the price of passes (MTS, 2018a, c). In addition to their main function, the metro systems often have other roles that can reinforce their identity within the urban ecosystem, such as guided tours exploring the hosted contemporary art, exhibitions of paintings and photography, solidarity and charity activities, or awareness raising campaigns that promote citizens' and users' safety and security, among others (i.e., the national exercise 'The Earth Trembles') (MTS, 2018d). For instance, during the 2018 winter holidays, Almada Metro stations were points for the collection of goods that were offered to those in need (MTS, 2018b). Likewise, Lisbon Metro assumed its commitment to promote a corporate strategy in the field of social responsibility and citizenship by lunching the REDE – Rebirth, Raise, Dedicate and Involve – platform, which aimed to connect those in need with those who wanted to help (Diário de Notícias, 2018b).

Also with the aim of increasing the attractiveness of the metros, public transport companies support international events. For instance, Almada Metro supported the 'European Mobility Week', that aimed at disseminating:

> more efficient and healthy ways of living in and enjoying cities, creating moments of reflection and debate on measures that promote more sustainable urban mobility habits and new ways of planning the cities that are friendlier to people and environment. (MTS, 2017)

Furthermore, "Music at the End of the Tunnel" emerged to promote mental health, and included 18 concerts in six underground stations (three stations in Porto and the other in Lisbon), where people were invited:

> to set aside some time of their day to enjoy live music, stop their routine and connect with art and culture. (Metro do Porto, 2021a)

Part of the same category, the painting and portrait exhibitions in metro stations, despite their temporary nature, can increase the attractiveness level of the stations. Within this context:

> "Drawing with you" was the name of a "special exhibition of the children under treatment at the IPO - Portuguese Oncology Institute, inaugurated in the north lobby of the Praça de Espanha station […]" (DN Life, 2018) while, more recently, "110 Portraits of a Struggle" was the "photographic exhibition […] in five Porto Metro stations […], as a tribute to those who, for over a year, have been fighting relentlessly against the COVID-19 pandemic". (Metro do Porto, 2021b)

According to Helena Taborda, spokeswoman of the Lisbon Metro, through guided tours organised on a regular basis, the Metro is able:

> "to spread art in a very specific way, more than what the person who daily passes by the station sees, but sometimes does not look at it with the eyes to see […]". During the guided visits are explained "the reason for a certain artwork, the reason for a certain theme of the station, so that people can look at the stations in a different way." (Diário de Notícias, 2021)

In the case of Lisbon Metro, assuming the identity of a museum is argued for (preserving and exhibiting heritage, and constructing identity):

the most visited museum of contemporary art in Lisbon, because it is open 365 days a year and has about half a million passengers per day, so about half a million visitors. (Diário de Notícias, 2018c)

Thus, the metro is a space of flow, with fixed aspects of experiencing place created in its metro stations.

17.4.5 Place Attachment Analysis Based on Social Media Comments

This section explores the users' perceptions of and feelings about the Lisbon and Porto metros, meanings and values associated with the metro, through their comments on the social media networks.

The feeling of satisfaction is the one making certain places 'ours'. In the analysed case studies, most of the comments were related to dissatisfaction regarding travel frequencies, delay times, inoperability of existing facilities within the stations/interfaces, lack of air conditioning in the summer and, during the pandemic, inappropriate use of mask by people. Nevertheless, there were also positive aspects. The best way to demonstrate the users' feeling of belonging to the metro stations and their interfaces was by expressing their satisfaction with their appearance and functionality of the metro systems:

> Great work in the Porto metropolitan area, good project, for all, I am very happy with our Porto Metro. (M.M., 2017, Porto Metro)

The cognitive and affective image of the metro is built on features of its places and how people experience them. Improved physical and social infrastructure leads to improved experiences and users' stronger functional and emotional bonding with the metro places:

> Thank you for your improvements day by day and for serving us since 1959, with quality, safety, and a good modernisation at European level; thank you for your 62 years of evolution travelling under the Portuguese capital, thank you Lisbon Metro ... (M.A.R.G., 2021, Lisbon Metro)

Among comments, there are those that indicate building a relationship with the place by pointing to favourite stations or metro lines, and by taking selfies in front of the favourite metro stations. In addition, stations that bring people to home are treated with affection:

> The most beautiful station is Baixa –Chiado. (N.P., 2018, Lisbon Metro)

> [...] everyone to the bridge for the selfie with the metro!. (M.C., 2021, Porto Metro)

> [My favourite metro line is] the Green Line because it is the one that takes me closer to home.... (C.R., 2020, Lisbon Metro)

[My favourite is] the Blue Line, because we have time to see all the stations very calmly while we wait for the metro. (F.P., 2020, Lisbon Metro)

Next station, Olivais. The station that likes to know where you are going to. (S.M.T., 2021, Lisbon Metro)

The importance of the metros in the users' daily lives, and thus in creating and strengthening their place attachment, is expressed through feelings of curiosity and/or satisfaction about the expansion of networks, the operation of the stations, of carriages, and through interest in working for the Metro companies:

Good afternoon my friends from Porto Metro, I would like to know if the Vila do Conde station is operational. (H.C., 2017, Porto Metro)

When will MOVE be back? We really need a 24-hour metro at the weekend. (R.J.K., 2019, Porto Metro)

The (future) circular line goes around the centre of Lisbon, right? From Campo Grande to Cais do Sodré?. (A.M.C., 2021, Lisbon Metro)

Good morning, when does the exit to Álvares Cabral in Rato (station) open? (C.S., 2021, Lisbon Metro)

(The station) is beautiful, it's worth the wait. (M.F.S., 2021, Lisbon Metro)

Is the Green Line metro station in Arroios already open and operational? (P.S.S., 2021, Lisbon Metro)

I would like to work in the Porto Metro, how can I apply for a job? (W.L., 2021, Porto Metro)

Why only up to 25 years old? How about giving opportunity (to work for the Metro) to people above that age? (R.F., 2021, Porto Metro)

The metro as public space is shaped by a certain mobility pattern that re-configures the "micro-geographies of everyday life" (Cresswell, 2011, p. 551). Another aspect that defines and consolidates the feeling of place attachment among metro users is the association of the metro's evolution with events in the users' and employees' lives:

Here in Cais do Sodré I worked for the company E. Pinto Bastos until 1962. I am feeling nostalgic and have many good memories. (A.A., 2017, Lisbon Metro)

Time flies. I went to the inauguration. Beautiful times. (H.P., Lisbon Metro, 2018)

The metro system is part of the city's identity and of the urban daily routine, exemplifying the fluid and fixed aspects of urban life and influencing the dynamics of place attachment:

(This is) the station where I take the metro from every day. (A.S.P., 2019, Lisbon Metro)

I have been using that line for 10 years. It opened to the public at 10 AM and on that day I passed through São Sebastião at 7:30 PM in the afternoon after work, I used the line and the journey was much quicker. (G.D., 2019, Lisbon Metro)

The beautiful Olaias station. I have passed through it so many times .... (T.F., 2020, Lisbon Metro)

I've been with you since the first day. (I.C., 2021, Porto Metro)

I have followed the construction of the Lisbon Metro since its beginning and was its collaborator for 41 years. Greetings to the entire Metro Family. (M.P., 2021, Lisbon Metro)

Users' place attachment is fortified during diverse activities organised in the metro, through its interfaces, stations, and carriages. In addition, the sense of belonging to the metro stations and interfaces is highlighted also by the users' concern with the aesthetics of the facilities, often expressed through suggestions for improving the aesthetics of interfaces, stations and carriages or expanding networks:

I don't want to see graffiti inside the stations. (V.V., 2017, Lisbon Metro)

Since you have ordered new carriages, you might give them a nicer 'pillowcase', and some more visible led flags. (G.F., 2021, Lisbon Metro)

Long awaited good news. Do the same to all lines and add more frequencies, and people will thank you. (P.S.S., 2020, Lisbon Metro)

I have seen them (the employees) cleaning a simple carriage in between two stations. That is great. (S.P.C., 2020, Lisbon Metro)

It would be good to expand the lines through Gaia to Boavista. (F.C., 2017, Porto Metro)

Movement is integral to the identity of the metro, and other meaningful connections are realised, establishing a continuity in inhabitants' experiences across space during a day. Movement is integrated with social and cultural experiences that take away the disruptive effect of this transport means:

We all love to sit back and relax, listen to music, read a book or watch a series during the 50 minutes journey by metro. (C.A., 2019, Porto Metro)

[In the metro] it's great for reading books. (S.P.C., 2019, Lisbon Metro)

Additionally, the cultural and social practices associated with the mobility ones, characteristic of the metro, shape people's lived experiences, the organisation of social, cultural, academic, and civic events seems to have a crucial role within the place attachment creation process. It is highlighted through users' interest in the events, confirmation of participation, acknowledgements for the organisation of the events, memories of experiences that took place in the metro during the events, or even dissatisfaction for having missed activities of certain events because of information lack:

Why is there no music at the Casa da Música [Music House] station? (M.C., 2016, Porto Metro)

Well organised, congratulations, I was there. (C.C., 2020, Porto Metro)

(During the academic parties) metro all night long! How I miss it! (M.C., 2020, Porto Metro)

I did not receive any information (about the event) […]. After all I follow you here and receive the newsletters. (R.B.N., 2018, Porto Metro)

The metro is more than an in-between place (i.e., between home and work); it becomes a place in itself, one of the city's territorial anchors (more than a space of physical travel experienced through corporeal mobility), to which people may feel attached or not. The metro becomes a personally meaningful place:

Thank you, Metro do Porto! I'll be there (at the Italian Film Festival event). (L.P., 2018)

Users' representations of place and place attachment influence how a place is perceived (and the other way around), as well as community attitudes and intentional behaviour (i.e., support or lack of it for certain actions benefitting users). These are valuable to policies and spatial planning decisions.

The analysed material shows the continuous dynamic of territorial identity and place attachment. The metro space is remade both through material action and discourse (written text and images within and about the metro system). From inhabitants' reactions in mass media and on social media, concerning the metro system, we understand their ideas, imaginations, and beliefs, which together create their image of the metro system. This image is correlated with the representations in the analysed mass media articles.

17.5   Conclusions

We explored the practices through which the bond between people and place was created within three Portuguese metro systems in the cities of Almada, Lisbon and Porto and their metropolitan areas. We presented *the territorial identities of the metro systems* and a preliminary explanation of *the users' place attachment*, through a period in their evolution, as processes, because both identity and attachment are dynamic constructs. The metros were perceived as a familiar (due to frequent use) realm of mobility. Users liked and were interested in metro activities besides mobility. Place attachment appeared because the metro was attractive due to both its social and physical environments. Objective features and their representations created place identity, which influenced people's attachment to the place.

Our contribution to place-oriented research focused on the creation of place meaning, sense of place and place identity by metro owners and users. Our research emphasised the processual nature of place attachment, where the metro-related places brought new physical elements and more fluid experiences into the fixity of life. Analysing peoples' relations with transport infrastructure, we highlighted the activities which transformed non-places into 'domesticated' spaces.

It is assumed that people do not have emotional bonds with places like this. However, the process of making metro homeness is important, as the metro is an integral part of everyday life for many thousands of residents, both passengers and workers. In a way, people using the metro are dependent on it. Although it is not an always positive emotionally marked relationship, rather resulting from the necessity of everyday commuting, making metro places more pleasant enables people to strengthen their sense of identification with and taking responsibility for them. At the same time, strong place attachment influences people's representations and make them feel safe, despite any risks. The dynamic process of constructing representations of place maintains and reinforces territorial identity and place attachment.

Note All translations from Portuguese were realised by Cristian Emanuel Adorean.

References

Adolphson, M., & Fröidh, O. (2019). Impact on urban form by the localization of railway stations: Evidence from Sweden. *Cities, 95*, 102362.

Altman, I., & Low, M. S. (Eds.). (1992). *Place attachment*. Plenum Press.

Banini, T. (2021). Chapter 1. Towards a methodology for constructing local territorial identities. In O.-R. Ilovan (Ed.), *Territorial identities in action* (pp. 13–39). Presa Universitară Clujeană.

Banini, T., & Ilovan, O.-R. (2021). Introduction: Dealing with territorial/place identity representations. In T. Banini & O.-R. Ilovan (Eds.), *Representing place/territorial identity in Europe. Discourses, images, and practices* (pp. 1–19). Springer. https://doi.org/10.1007/978-3-030-66766-5_1

Bertolini, L., Curtis, C., & Renne, J. (2012). Station area projects in Europe and beyond: Towards transit-oriented development? *Built Environment, 38*(1), 31–50.

Cresswell, T. (2011). Mobilities I: Catching up. *Progress in Human Geography, 35*, 550–558.

de Vaujany, F. X. (2003). Les figures de la gestion du changement sociotechnique. *Sociologie du Travail, 45*, 515–536.

Delaplace, M. (2017). Assessing ex ante the wider effects of high-speed rail services in cities. The lessons drawn from a service innovation-based analysis. *European Review of Service Economics and Management, 3*, 105–131.

Di Masso, A., Williams, D. R., Raymond, C. M., Buchecker, M., Degenhardt, B., Devine-Wright, P., Hertzogg, A., Lewicka, M., Manzoi, L., Shahrad, A., Stedmank, R., Verbruggel, L., & von Wirth, T. (2019). Between fixities and flows: Navigating place attachments in an increasingly mobile world. *Journal of Environmental Psychology, 61*, 125–133.

Diário de Notícias. (2018a). À noite, uma orquestra de toupeiras cuida do metro [At night, an orchestra of 'moles' takes care of the metro]. https://www.dn.pt/edicao-do-dia/12-ago-2018/a--noite-uma-orquestra-de-toupeiras-cuida-do-metro-9590504.html. Accessed 10 Jan 2022.

Diário de Notícias. (2018b). Metro de Lisboa lança plataforma digital de solidariedade [Lisbon Metro launches digital solidarity platform]. https://www.dn.pt/portugal/metro-de-lisboa-lanca-plataforma-rede-para-ajudar-quem-mais-precisa-9303489.html. Accessed on 10 Jan 2022.

Diário de Notícias. (2018c). Um passeio em que o Metro é o destino e não o transporte [A walk where the Metro is the destination and not the transport]. https://www.dn.pt/portugal/um-passeio-em-que-o-metro-e-o-destino-e-nao-o-transporte-9138370.html. Accessed on 10 Jan 2022.

Diário de Notícias. (2021). Metro regressa às visitas guiadas para explicar às pessoas a sua arte [Metro returns to guided tours to explain its art to people]. https://www.dn.pt/local/metro-regressa-as-visitas-guiadas-para-explicar-as-pessoas-a-sua-arte-14156373.html. Accessed 10 Jan 2022.

DN Life (2018). Crianças do IPO pintam como gente grande no Metro de Lisboa [*IPO children paint like adults in Lisbon Metro*]. https://life.dn.pt/criancas-do-ipo-pintam-metro-lisboa/saude/345272/. Accessed 10 Jan 2022.

Facchinetti-Mannone, V. (2019). A methodological approach to analyze the territorial appropriation of high-speed rail from interactions between actions and representations of local actors. *European Planning Studies, 27*(3), 461–482.

Fink, C. N. Y., & Taylor, B. D. (2010). *Zen in the art of travel behavior: Using visual ethnography to understand the transit experience*. University of California Transportation Centre, Final Report.

Gonzalez-Navarro, M. & Turner, M.A. (2016). Subways and Urban Growth: Evidence from Earth. http://individual.utoronto.ca/marcog/attachment/Subways.pdf. Accessed on 22 Nov 2021.

Impala. (2020). Almada. Persegue ladrão que o assaltou no metro e atropela-o [Almada. Chases thief who robbed him in the metro and runs him over]. https://www.impala.pt/noticias/almada-persegue-ladrao-assaltou-metro-atropela/. Accessed 10 Jan 2022.

Jones, C. H. D., Cohn, S., & Ogilvie, D. (2013). Making sense of a new transport system: An ethnographic study of the Cambridgeshire guided busway. *PLoS One, 8*(7), e69254.

Lewicka, M. (2011). Place attachment: How far have we come in the last 40 years? *Journal of Environmental Psychology, 31*(3), 207–230. https://doi.org/10.1016/J.JENVP.2010.10.001

Lewicka, M. (2014). In search of roots. Memory as enabler of place attachment. In L. C. Manzo & P. Devine-Wright (Eds.), *Place attachment. Advances in theory, methods and applications* (pp. 49–59). Routledge.

Lorimer, H. (2005). Cultural geography: The busyness of being 'more-than-representational. *Progress in Human Geography, 29*(1), 83–94.

Mancheva, M.E. (2015). *Hidden transcripts on public transportation: A meta-methodological exploration of visual ethnography in qualitative transportation research*. Master thesis in sustainable development, University of Uppsala, Department of Earth Sciences. http://uu.diva-portal.org/smash/get/diva2:843370/FULLTEXT01.pdf. Accessed on 22 Nov 2021.

Manzo, C. L., & Devine-Wright, P. (Eds.). (2014). *Place attachment. Advances in theory, methods and applications*. Routledge.

Massey, D., & Jess, P. (Eds.). (1995). *A place in the world? Places, cultures and globalization*. Oxford University Press.

Metro do Porto. (2021a). Metro do Porto recebe ciclo de concertos [Porto Metro hosts a series of concerts]. https://viva-porto.pt/metro-do-porto-recebe-ciclo-de-concertos/. Accessed 10 Jan 2022.

Metro do Porto. (2021b). Rostos de profissionais do São João espalhados pelas estações do Metro do Porto [Faces of São João professionals spread throughout Metro do Porto stations]. https://viva-porto.pt/rostos-profissionais-sao-joao-espalhados-pelas-estacoes-metro-porto/. Accessed on 10 January 2022.

Metro do Porto. (2022). Official webpage. https://www.metrodoporto.pt/. Accessed 10 Jan 2022.

Metro Transportes do Sul – MTS. (2017). MTS apoia a Semana Europeia da Mobilidade 2017 em Almada [MTS supports 2017 European Mobility Week in Almada]. https://www.mts.pt/mts-apoia-semana-europeia-da-mobilidade-2017-em-almada/. Accessed 10 Jan 2022.

Metro Transportes do Sul – MTS. (2018a). Alargamento do desconto de 25% [Extending the 25% discount] https://www.mts.pt/4_18escola-tp/. Accessed 10 Jan 2022.

Metro Transportes do Sul – MTS. (2018b). Campanha de Natal MTS [MTS Christmas Campaign]. https://www.mts.pt/campanha-de-natal-mts/. Accessed 10 Jan 2022.

Metro Transportes do Sul – MTS. (2018c). Campanha Passe a Passe [pass by pass campaign]. https://www.mts.pt/campanha-passe-passe/. Accessed 10 Jan 2022.

Metro Transportes do Sul – MTS. (2018d). Exercício Público a Terra Treme, Sensibilização para o Sismo Sísmico [Earthquake Awareness Public Exercise]. https://www.mts.pt/exercicio-publico-a-terra-treme-sensibilizacao-para-o-sismo-sismico/. Aaccessed 10 Jan 2022.

Metro Transportes do Sul – MTS. (2022). Official webpage. https://www.mts.pt/. Accessed 10 Jan 2022.

Metropolitano de Lisboa (2022). Official Webpage. https://www.metrolisboa.pt/. Accessed on 10 January 2022.

Mohan, D. (2008). Mythologies, metro rail systems and future urban transport. *Economic and Political Weekly, 43*(4), 41–53.

National Statistics Institute (INE). (2021). People working in metropolitan transport – Mainland Portugal. https://www.pordata.pt/Portugal/Pessoal+ao+servi%C3%A7o+no+transporte+metropolitano+++Continente-3092. Accessed on 22 Nov 2021.

Observador. (2015). STCP/Metro do Porto. Mais de 500 pessoas num cordão humano contra a concessão [STCP/Porto Metro. Over 500 people in a human cordon against the concession]. https://observador.pt/2015/09/01/stcpmetro-do-porto-500-pessoas-num-cordao-humano-concessao/. Accessed 10 Jan 2022.

Paulsson, A. (2020). The city that the metro system built: Urban transformations and modalities of integrated planning in Stockholm. *Urban Studies, 57*(14), 2936–2955.

Paulsson, A., & Isaksson, K. (2019). Networked authority and regionalised governance: Public transport, a hierarchy of documents and the anti-hierarchy of authorship. *Environment and Planning C: Politics and Space, 37*(6), 985–1004.

Peng, J., Strijker, D., & Wu, Q. (2020). Place identity: How far have we come in exploring its meanings? *Frontiers in Psychology, 11*, 294. https://doi.org/10.3389/fpsyg.2020.00294

Proshansky, H. M. (1978). The City and self-identity. *Environment and Behaviour, 10*(2), 147–169. https://doi.org/10.1177/0013916578102002

Raffestin, C. (2012). Space, territory, and territoriality. *Environment and Planning D: Space and Society, 30*, 121–141.

Relph, E. (1976). *Place and Placelessness*. Pion.

Rose, G. (2016). *Visual methodologies. An introduction to researching with visual materials* (4th ed.). London.

Shumaker, S. A., & Taylor, R. B. (1983). Toward a clarification of people-place relationships: A model of attachment to place. In N. R. Feimer & E. S. Geller (Eds.), *Environmental psychology: Directions and perspectives* (pp. 219–251). Praeger.

Silva, C., Kastenholz, E., & Abrantes, J. L. (2018). Linking mountain image with place-attachment. *Journal of Spatial and Organizational Dynamics, 6*(2), 140–152.

Sipetic, N., Savić, M., & Furundžić, D. (2019). The invisible metro system: The case study of the Belgrade metro system planning. *Tunnelling and Underground Space Technology, 83*(4), 485–497.

Stedman, R. C. (2002). Towards a social psychology of place: Predicting behaviour from place-based cognitions, attitude and identity. *Environment and Behaviour, 34*, 561–581.

Stokols, D., & Shumaker, S. A. (1981). People in places: Transactional view of settings. In J. H. Harvey (Ed.), *Cognition, social behaviour and the environment* (pp. 441–488). Lawrence Erlbaum, Hillsdale.

Stylidis, D. (2020). Using destination image and place attachment to explore support for tourism development: The case of tourism versus non-tourism employees in EILAT. *Journal of Hospitality and Tourism Research, 44*(6), 951–973.

Tomic, V., Relja, R., & Popovic, T. (2015). Ethnography of urban public transport: A tale of two cities in Croatia. *Anthropological Notebooks, 21*(1), 37–59.

Tuan, Y.-F. (1990). *Topophilia: A study of environmental perception, attitudes and values*. Columbia University Press.

Chapter 18
Sustainable Brownfield Regeneration in Baia Mare, Romania. Constructing Place Attachment Through Co-creation and Co-development

Kinga Xénia Havadi-Nagy ⓘ and **Tihamér-Levente Sebestyén** ⓘ

18.1 Introduction

The number of brownfields in a city is considered a benchmark for urban welfare and sustainable land management (Neill & Schlappa, 2016). Hence, nowadays many European urban authorities are called to deploy sustainable land-use management strategies for the derelict areas left as a legacy by decades of poorly integrated and unsystematic land use policies doubled by unsustainable development plans (Neill & Schlappa, 2016; Ferber et al., 2006).

The restructuring of Europe's industry resulted not only in deteriorated, or even contaminated wastelands, but also in broken communities failed by the authorities. Thus "the processes of finding a new future and perhaps a new identity for such land and communities must go hand in hand if regeneration is to be legitimate and truly sustainable" (Ferber et al., 2006, p. 103). Therefore, brownfield remediation actions must refocus from a predominantly "site-based" approach, to a mostly "people-based" endeavour, implementing stakeholders' inclusive strategies (Ferber et al., 2006).

Even socially or environmentally stigmatised and derelict places, like brownfields, can enjoy, maintain, or gain place attachment. Residents of neighbourhoods

K. X. Havadi-Nagy (✉)
Department of Regional Geography and Territorial Planning, Faculty of Geography, Babeş-Bolyai University, Cluj-Napoca, Romania
e-mail: kinga.havadi@ubbcluj.ro

T.-L. Sebestyén
Hungarian Department of Geography, Babeş-Bolyai University, Cluj-Napoca, Romania

Green Energy Innovative Biomass Cluster, Sfântu Gheorghe, Romania
e-mail: tihamer.sebestyen@ubbcluj.ro

© The Author(s), under exclusive license to Springer Nature
Switzerland AG 2022
O.-R. Ilovan, I. Markuszewska (eds.), *Preserving and Constructing Place Attachment in Europe*, GeoJournal Library 131,
https://doi.org/10.1007/978-3-031-09775-1_18

with negative place reputation often remain in tension between submission and resistance to territorial stigma (Kirkness & Tijé-Dra, 2021). Similar is the situation in case of areas of industrial decline, where despite socioeconomic deprivation and material devastation, neighbourhoods can become invested with significance and community identity (Mah, 2009). However, most of the decayed areas are either ignored or constitute an eyesore in the place identity of the community, but once their reputation is improved, brownfields can be converted also on soft reuses, meaning green areas providing different types of Ecosystem Services. Rehabilitating brownfields can trigger a wide range of opportunities to ameliorate urban quality of life, creating economic possibilities, improving urban competitiveness, and mitigating urban sprawl (Schlappa & Ferber, 2016). All these prospects could favour the initiation of a place attachment process or to reinforce the existent bond to place and community.

Baia Mare municipality, located in north-western part of the country, was Romania's mining capital. The city's industrial past in the mining and metallurgical sector caused severe socio-economic consequences and left a legacy of approximately 627 ha of land highly contaminated with heavy metals within the municipal boundaries (Verga, 2020c). Currently the city is facing a wide range of challenges, which include economic decline, population decrease, and environmental contamination (Verga, 2020b). The main urban challenge is to re-incorporate its polluted brownfields into the productive urban circles, which represent a risk to the citizens and the environment; nonetheless, it could also be a key asset to tackle the sustainable development of Baia Mare and its metropolitan area (Verga, 2020b).

A major driver of brownfield regeneration is the economic profitability of individual plots (Ferber et al., 2006), but in Baia Mare most brownfields are currently unprofitable with high reclamation costs and low land value. In this context, thanks to the European Regional Development Fund co-financing, the Urban Innovative Actions' project "Smart Post-Industrial Regenerative Ecosystem's" (SPIRE) phytoremediation strategy provides a low-cost, nature-based solution to clean-up contaminated soils and to repurpose them for new socio-economic functions. The initiative starts a phytoremediation process on five pilot sites, eventually aiming to lay the ground and facilitate the premises for their upscaling to potential development sites and even self-developing sites in the mid- and long-run, respectively. In its endeavour, the SPIRE project partnership applies the principle of subsidiarity, thereby encouraging and facilitating citizens' inclusion and active participation in the co-design of short- and long-term landscaping plans and development strategies for the recovered sites (Verga, 2020c).

Basically, a dysfunctional physical and spatial environment with a disagreeable place ambience and disinterested or alienated people should be metamorphosed through sustainable brownfield regeneration actions into revitalised and safe community public spaces with a distinguished enjoyable place ambience, engaged community and strong place attachment (Seamon, 2014). Working into the direction of changing the identity of the city from "the mining capital of Romania", to a green and sustainable community, place attachment induced by participative approaches may contribute to the desired rebranding of the city, and the formation and maintenance of the new strived for identity.

In this context, the aim of our study is to analyse the applied co-creation and co-development tools and to assess their way of initiating and constructing place attachment during territorial development challenges. The scope of this analysis is to evaluate how these measures succeed to improve the image of these environmentally "tainted urban spaces" (Kirkness & Tijé-Dra, 2021), host opportunities to co-create uses and functions facilitating community building environments and chances.

18.2   Concepts, Resources, and Methodology

18.2.1   Definitions and Concepts

The SPIRE project adopted the currently prevailing definition of *brownfields*, meaning "sites that: have been affected by the former uses of the site and surrounding land, are derelict and underused, may have real or perceived contamination problems, [...], and require intervention to bring them back to beneficial use" (Ferber et al., 2006, p. 3).

Sustainable brownfield regeneration is commonly regarded as "the management, the rehabilitation and return to beneficial use of the brownfield land resource base in such a manner as to ensure the attainment and continue satisfaction of human needs for present and future generations in environmentally non degrading, economically viable, institutionally robust and social acceptable ways" (Verga, 2020b, p. 12).

The economic viability is a decisive factor for brownfield regeneration. Sites with high recovery and development costs, and insignificant market values, as those of Baia Mare, challenge the administrations of several cities (Ferber et al., 2006), as their recovery is not economically profitable on the short run. Possible solution for these sites offer the so called *"gentle" remediation options (GRO)*, low input remediation measures, defined as "risk management strategies/technologies that result in a net gain (or at least no gross reduction) in soil function as well as risk management" (Cundy et al., 2015, p. 102). The SPIRE project applies *phytoextraction*: "removal of metal(loid)s or organics from soils by accumulation in the harvestable biomass of plants" (Cundy et al., 2015, p. 103). Though phytoextraction is the first link in the more complex process of *phytomanagement*, a comprehensive outline and management strategy which, besides risk management, focuses on substantial economic, environmental, and societal benefits in the area's layout, and includes GROs in the integrated site development plans and actions (Cundy et al., 2016; Bardos et al., 2020).

Phytomanagement has a strong social component, which involves *citizen partici-pation and citizen decision-making,* meaning processes that enable citizens to have a say in the matter of brownfields regeneration and reuse. Hereby are two major points important: (1) the ability of citizens to voice their opinions and, (2) the significance of those ideas, needs and suggestions as well as the way they are considered by the decision-making powers (Ferber et al., 2006). In this context former publications like Klusáček (2018), Moosavie and Browne (2021) and Tendero and Plottu (2019) highlight that the involvement of the local population of different age groups, community groups, experts in urban planning and landscape design, researchers, and representatives of local NGOs in the co-creation process, is essential. The co-creation approach guarantees the success in the transformation of a brownfield site (Kabisch, 2019), on the condition that even though not all the ideas formulated during the co-design and co-creation process are adopted, the local decision-makers should keep in mind to assure various amenities and functions in order to rich broader acceptance and a higher rate of use.

Community engagement, collaboration with and through groups of people to discuss topics which impact the social well-being of the affected citizens (Itten et al., 2020), has a particular relevance for brownfields, as it would enhance the sustainability of regeneration projects (Ferber et al., 2006). This is pursued by implementing co-creation and co-production measures. *Co-creation* means involving the citizens at the co-design level, "citizens and professionals sharing power and responsibility to work together in equal, reciprocal, and caring relationships" (Itten et al., 2020, p. 22). Co-creation can therefore be regarded as a procedure which intends to enhance the social legitimacy of decision-making by: (1) creating access for new target groups; (2) including and empowering citizens; (3) enhancing the involvement of various stakeholders; (4) facilitating more intense cooperation and achieving agreements on key questions (Itten et al., 2020). *Co-production* refers to the next level, meaning the active involvement of the citizens in the implementation of the established measures (Itten et al., 2020). Both require an institutional framework and communication infrastructure along an operation which considers stakeholders as equal partners and involves them equitable (Itten et al., 2020).

Place attachment is a complex and multifaceted phenomenon that includes various aspects of people-place/environment links, whereas emotion and feeling are decisive for the notion (Altman & Low, 1992; Seamon, 2014). Place attachment engages an intense mutual interaction of feelings and emotions, knowledge and convictions, as well as perceptions and behaviours (Altman & Low, 1992). It comprises "culturally shared affective meanings and activities associated with place that derive from socio-political, historical, and cultural sources" (Altman & Low, 1992, p. 9), decisive elements of successful participative development approach. In our research area, we have a situation of establishing preconditions and facilitating actions to endorse the place attachment process not only to ordinary landscapes (Riley, 1992), but to stigmatised, derelict and contaminated plots, mostly ignored both by the vicinity and authorities.

18.2.2   Research Material

For our study, we assessed the following materials related to the co-creation and co-production actions of the project: two surveys (results of online questionnaires), two virtual interactive workshops (video material and resumes in shape of power point presentations), five thematic webinars (video material), press releases and media coverage, interviews with SPIRE staff in national and regional radio and TV informative broadcast (video and audio material), as well as project deliverables (text reports). Materials were made public by SPIRE on various online channels (e.g., official website, video watcher channel, social media account).

18.2.3   Methods

In our study we deliberate upon the place attachment process triggered and facilitated by the co-creation and co-production SPIRE actions. We do not intend to measure place attachment, but we consider these co-creation tools as instruments to initiate a place attachment process. For our assessment, we apply the six interconnected processes, identified by Seamon (2014), which support or erode the lived structures and dynamics of a certain place, and enhance or diminish the sort and intensity of emotional bonds with the place (Seamon, 2014). These are: place interaction, place identity, place creation, place intensification, place realisation, and place release. *Place Interaction* refers to regular actions, behaviours, situations, and events, through which citizens connect with the place in their everyday lives and the place gains activity and a sense of environmental presence. *Place Identity* relates to the process whereby people consider the place they live in as a relevant part of their world. Through place interaction the people engage with the place and relate their individual and collective identity with the identity of that place. Involving individuals who care for the place in the *Place Creation* process could result in the most appropriate design and a trigger force for an incipient or strengthened place attachment. Similarly, *Place Intensification* relates to place attachment in that users are more likely to be fond of a place including spatial and material elements and qualities that foster user needs as well as the ambience and character of the place (Seamon, 2014, p. 18). *Place realisation* means the distinctive place ambience generated by the environmental ensemble of the place, coupled with that place's human activities and significances. Committed people draw on their engagement to the place and their "empathetic knowledge of the place to envision and make favourable changes in policy and design so that place interaction, identity and realization are enhanced in positive ways" (Seamon, 2014, p. 18). These circumstances could facilitate *Place Release* processes, which involve "an environmental serendipity of unexpected encounters and events" (Seamon, 2014, p. 17), positive experiences, situations, and surprises related to the place, fuelling its uniqueness and place loyalty (Seamon, 2014, p. 17).

We examined the materials resulted from the above-mentioned activities of SPIRE, identifying the practices of co-creation and co-production they implemented, the target groups, how they handled the challenges, and in which way these actions and instruments create a relationship to the pilot sites, how participants share affective meanings by getting involved into activities, co-developing, and applying sustainable practices.

For the assessment of the inclusive collaborative approach and the methods and tools used by the SPIRE project, we rely on the work of Itten et al. (2020), which provides a comprehensive list of co-creation practices and their definitions: deliberative workshops, collective data collection, visualisation, online tools, living labs, collective inspiration tools, design thinking, storytelling, and schools as embassies.

The co-author is member of the SPIRE consortium. This enabled access to materials not yet published and a deeper insight into the participative approach mechanism the SPIRE applies.

18.3 Results and Discussions

18.3.1 State of Play in Baia Mare and the SPIRE Approach

Baia Mare is a medium-sized town, with a population of approximately 145,000 and comprising a metropolitan area with over 230,000 residents. It is the administrative centre of the Maramureș county (NUTS3) and is currently transitioning from its intensive mining past towards a new sustainable urban development model.

The SPIRE Report "Desk analysis, Research repository & Awareness appraisal" names two main dynamics existing in the evolution of the local urban system: the continuous demographic decline coupled with a progressive aging of the population, and the transition towards a new industrial and economic model after the cease of mining activities (Verga, 2020c). The city struggles with the revitalisation of the local economy and entrepreneurship and is challenged by the remediation and regeneration of the large number of contaminated brownfields.

This field research provided an appraisal of citizens' and stakeholders' perceptions and awareness with respect to socio-economic, socio-cultural, and environmental issues at local level (Verga, 2020c). SPIRE adjusted the aims and scopes of their project to these results, particularly the measures, tools and approaches to specific topics, and their agenda tackle the main challenges expressed in the survey (e.g., labour market, socio-cultural life, environment, and public space domains).

From an *economic* point of view, the SPIRE survey foregrounded two main aspects. Firstly, the sample of population revealed rather weak socio-economic features. Secondly, it disclosed incoherence between demanded and available skills, and an averagely unattractive remuneration, the main causes for outmigration

(Verga, 2020c). In response, the co-designed mentoring and support programme for innovative, youth-led start-ups in the biomass upcycling sector implemented by SPIRE mitigates the lack of entrepreneurship and aims at triggering and stimulating innovative and appealing employment opportunities in the city (Verga, 2020c). Further on the phytoremediation of contaminated soils and the upcycling of the biomass into cascading value streams to produce materials and energy is beneficial for local economy (Verga, 2020c).

From a *socio-cultural* point of view, the field research revealed three key aspects. First, a rather dense network of neighbourhood relations, yet mostly based on loose contacts and superficial acquaintanceship. Second, both indoor and outdoor public places are not the major gathering sites for the local community, as they favour the private places. Finally, respondents reported a lack of cultural and recreation spaces at neighbourhood level (Verga, 2020c).

Attachments to one's town or neighbourhood are significant motivations for people to be more present in those places, to interact with the neighbours, to voice their opinion about vicinity problems and ideas for solutions to protect or improve the community and the public space of their actions (Mihaylov & Perkins, 2014). SPIRE aims to involve all social components in the design of the spaces they live in, ultimately targeting to enhance and/or develop citizens' sense of ownership of public spaces and stimulating a more caring attitude towards the public environment.

The registered lack of community spirit could be an impediment for the participation in co-development activities. However, SPIRE tries to mitigate this risk with a constant dialogical effort with the population, to build a trust relationship with the community and to achieve a broad citizens' involvement engagement (Verga, 2020a).

From an *environmental* point of view, the major problem of Baia Mare, the heavy-metal pollution of soils, does not seem to be a significant concern for the citizenry. The survey registered a general dissatisfaction of the population with the quality, maintenance, and cleanliness of Baia Mare natural spaces, especially because of municipal waste pollution. This seems to be perceived as the worst environmental problem at local level and appears to significantly undermine the willingness of citizens to make use of green spaces (Verga, 2020c).

The survey also showed an increasing awareness about the impacts of individual behaviour on the environment and on the need to take concrete actions, yet this is counterbalanced by a still large resistance to behavioural change (Verga, 2020c). In this respect, SPIRE has the potential and ambition to make a significant impact on citizens' awareness levels concerning environmental issues. The backbone of this effort are the SPIRE participatory and co-creation activities as well as the iLEU (immaterial Local Environmental Utility), as incentive and reward system for eco-friendly behaviour (Verga, 2020c). Further on, SPIRE leverages on the growing environmental sensibility of the younger generations, offers educational activities, so that they could later act as sustainability ambassadors also among less receptive groups (Verga, 2020a) (Fig. 18.1).

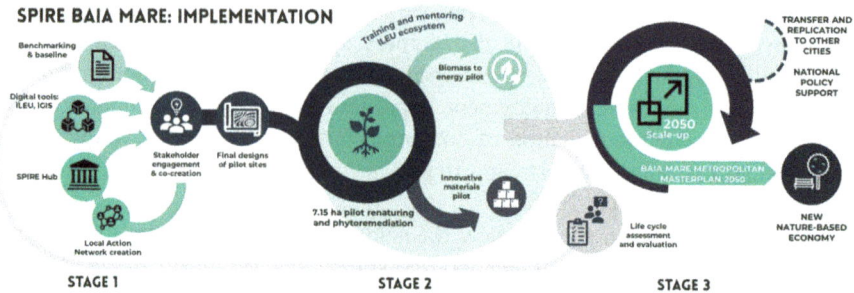

Fig. 18.1 SPIRE Implementation stages and workflow. (Source: Leopa, 2020; Published with permission)

18.3.2 Co-creation and Place Attachment

The complex SPIRE project has high ambitions: enabling a structural environmental, urban anthropic and economic change. The aim is to transform heavy metal pollution from a serious obstacle to local recovery, to an incentive to experiment new approaches to sustainable urban renewal. The precondition to this is a paradigm shift from the locally prevailing attitude of downplaying the seriousness of heavy metal pollution impact and considering green infrastructure as a public good provided by state authorities, to the reformative approach of Nature-Based Solutions (NBS) and green infrastructure as common goods: co-developed, co-monitored, economically reused in local ecosystems (Leopa, 2020).

Brownfield regeneration undertakings contribute to large scale sustainable redevelopment of derelict urban areas, but also face major challenge owing to the complexity of the matter (Ferber et al., 2006). Some of the key aspects relate to the great range of actors partaking at the process. That is why problem-oriented approaches for brownfields need to be inclusive and consider the variety of stakeholders' perspectives as well as the diversity of their values (Ferber et al., 2006). The people living nearby are afflicted with the contaminated mining legacy, but could be also the direct beneficiaries of regeneration processes. These persons are thus significant stakeholders and can actively contribute to the development of customized regeneration strategies (Ferber et al., 2006) for the sites in their vicinity.

With the involvement of various experts collaborating with local municipalities and citizens, as well as the development and application of digital tools and circular-economy business models, but mostly because of its pilot character and as the playground for a scale-up, sustainable development and recovery plan for Baia Mare and its metropolitan area, we can consider the initiative as a *living lab,* all its tools, measures and actions showing experimental features.

The community-building co-development instruments and actions applied in the SPIRE project are goal-oriented and have specific target groups. *Five thematic webinars* addressing the core foci of the project were conducted during October 2020–February 2021. The target group of these learning and knowledge dissemination webinars, were the project partner institutions and organisations of the SPIRE consortium. The goal of the events was to give insight in all the components of the endeavour to all the involved collaborators, but also to develop a certain level of fondness for the spaces and communities they work with, in order to be committed to the aims of the project.

A successful co-creation process addresses topics that are already a concern within a community (Itten et al., 2020) and attachment is generally stronger for places of good environmental quality (Scannell & Grifford, 2014). Therefore, to motivate the community to engage in the co-creation process, SPIRE firstly addressed the general dissatisfaction of the population on the quality, maintenance, and cleanliness of Baia Mare natural spaces (Verga, 2020c). Co-developing and co-creating the places together with the community members according to the own needs might enhance the willingness to spend time there. The implemented attractive functions and infrastructures increase the willingness of participation at community activities, what strengthens place attachment at the neighbourhood level (Scannell & Grifford, 2014), and a sense of ownership. The co-creative actions of SPIRE follow these principles, but they had to recalibrate their collaborative activities due to the challenges participatory practices faced by the restrictions (i.e., social distancing) imposed to counteract the spread of the Corona-19 virus. Trust is a main ingredient of successful participatory approaches. Building trust and facilitating social cooperation in the virtual space was a challenge the SPIRE members took up firstly by seeking advice from experts in re-thinking participation and co-creation in times of social distancing, and secondly by applying several on-line tools and trying to implement a mixed formula of co-creation activities (Fig. 18.2).

The deliberative phase of the citizens inclusive co-design process of the five pilot sites started in November 2020. *Deliberative workshops* as co-creation tools facilitate opportunities for previously identified representatives of the stakeholders, who meet to learn about the subject, the aims and scopes, as well as the common concerns (Itten et al., 2020). Two digital workshops took place at the beginning of the SPIRE project, giving voice to the youth and to the affected communities as well as to the general public. Interactive online tools and collaborative exercises were

Fig. 18.2 SPIRE co-development actions: (**a**) Plantathlon action; (**b**) workshop in the SpireHUB Makerspace. (Source: Tihamér-Levente Sebestyèn, 2021)

applied in this first and important phase of data collection, needs and desire identification and assessment of feasible solutions for the use of the community public spaces. The events aimed to feel the pulse of the community, to involve and to build a community, as the development plans should be elaborated for, with and by the community. The SPIRE co-creation endeavour also serves the purpose to establish and activate the existing local citizen networks, since the community should be involved in the co-development of the Strategic Development Plan of Baia Mare 2050. According to the collected ideas, the citizens of the area want a change, require an intervention and a positive turn in the image of the neighbourhood.

The workshops applied *online co-creation tools*. These facilitate a setting for attendees where they can propose and co-develop various scenarios and can support favourite alternatives by reviewing the advantages and disadvantages of the issue at stake, assisted also by experts. They also serve as a further means of communication and engagement, increase the flow of and access to information which can enhance awareness and lead to well-founded choices (Itten et al., 2020).

Storytelling as co-creation tool is almost omnipresent, even if not intentionally applied by the coordinators, but naturally occurring in the co-design process, as actors inherently narrate and relate to personal experiences in the process of identifying needs, drafting ideas, and exploring possibilities. Narratives inspired from past events or describing future scenarios are "understandable, relatable, and can help listeners engage in the motivations expressed in the stories" (Itten et al., 2020, p. 74).

"Your ideas and creativity is needed to co-create a safe and healthy environment in 5 community public spaces" – was the open call for participation in *two surveys* conducted in 2020. The questionnaires were developed as a basic consultancy level of participation and starting point for further actions. The data collected in the first general survey was the basis of a second one, with customized questionnaires for each site, focused on concrete measures and functions according to the specificities, the neighbourhood profile, and the target groups of each area. The revitalisation measures and functions to create safe and healthy public spaces for the community were selected also in compliance with the restrictions imposed by the contamination and phytoremediation activities.

The main problems identified for the pilot sites reflect the perception of the brownfields as wastelands, derelict, polluted by waste, stigmatized as dangerous and with severe safety issues, not attractive at all, and with access problems. According to De Valck et al. (2019), the main challenge when redeveloping a brownfield site is to remediate the problems that kept it vacant, such as contamination, stigmatisation, or socio-economic stagnation in the community, all valid for the Baia Mare sites. The SPIRE project creates and facilitates instruments to reconnect people to these places in their strive to regenerate landscapes and explore development opportunities. These measures lay the ground for positively experienced bonds, but which evolve gradually over the years from the behavioural, emotional, and cognitive attachments between individuals and/or communities and their socio-physical environment (Mihaylov & Perkins, 2014).

The surveys revealed the desire of the people for green spaces, leisure areas, outdoor sport activities, socializing places, educational functions, permanent or temporary events, parks and playgrounds which would improve the well-being and life quality of the community. These sites and the activities must be appealing for the people to be eager to spend time and get to know the community. The areas are large enough to implement various functions addressing the needs of users of different age groups or interests. Functions adjusted to the needs and desires of the neighbourhood, events and activities could connect the people, raise the individual and collective self-worth and self-pride. Some respondents voice even the possibility of co-management of the spaces by various interested target groups, which would be a further step in the appropriation of the former abandoned and stigmatized territories, proving fondness and devotion to the places.

Visual imagery is an impactful tool to translate both abstract and concrete ideas (Itten et al., 2020). Visualisation in the SPIRE project is applied in fore- and back casting, anticipatory thinking, and visioning, both by conventional, but also by interactive multimedia elements. The use of visual imagery is stipulated also in the selection process of the applications for the start-up mentoring programme. Namely in the second round of selection, the citizens vote six out of ten projects based upon the three minutes short video which the contestants prepare to facilitate envisioning their ideas (Papina, 2021). For each pilot site exist drone recordings of the current state of the areas. Images are significant in establishing a relationship with a place, further on forecasting and anticipatory thinking can generate affective and cognitive ties to the sites, fuelled by anticipation.

Collective inspiration methods are creative processes that can transform, evoke, and motivate ideas and goals worth to pursue (Itten et al., 2020) through spontaneous or coordinated interactions among the stakeholders. The SPIRE Plantathlon actions host collective inspirational moments. The open air one-day event in each pilot site targets the participants to on-site co-creation workshop activities aimed at spreading knowledge on phytoremediation and the potential applications of vegetal biomass (Tanase, 2021), and focused on interactions to spark emotional and cognitive bonds towards the areas (Fig. 18.3).

The *schools* involved in the SPIRE project assume the position of *embassies* of the projects aims and ambitions. They function as host sites for the implementation of sustainable environmental behaviour and examples for the application of renewable energy technologies, as one of the schools' heating installations will be supplied with the biomass produced on the pilot areas. Lectures, project week activities, workshops, frequent interaction with the SPIRE staff challenge school students to formulate own ideas for the sustainable management of decontaminated brownfields and the design and functionalities of the community spaces. They would be one of the main beneficiaries of the rehabilitated green areas and they can contribute to their creation. At the same time, they receive knowledge about sustainability and training in environmentally friendly behaviour, which they can pass over to others and be multipliers. On long-term, the intense involvement in the SPIRE project's actions could contribute to a lasting place attachment, which exhibits strong ties, due to its origin in childhood events and memories.

Fig. 18.3 Phases of co-creation and visualisation of the co-created public green space on one of the pilot sites. (Source: Papina, 2021; Published with permission)

The *iLEU* is a local digital currency. The co-production tool addresses the entire Baia Mare community. Through iLEU, SPIRE aims at raising public awareness and incentivising individuals and businesses to enact more sustainable (Verga, 2020c). On one hand the cautious interaction with the environment could strengthen the relation and enhance the feeling of responsibility for the place. On the other hand, network building and cooperation among various private and public actors facilitated by the iLEU might contribute to build and strengthen the community on city level as well, upscaling the place attachment from neighbourhood to city.

The project applies *Geographic Information Systems (GIS)* for the vegetation monitoring, which provides a complete overview of the intervention area, giving important clues on the vegetation quality and quantity. Besides visualising the momentary ground situation, it also facilitates simulations of impact of replication in further areas. The technical tool is used also for education, gamification, visualisation, assessment and measuring of project key performance indicators (Verga, 2020b). This digital tool can serve for *collective data collection* (Itten et al., 2020) and facilitates the joint interpretation of the evolution and intermediary results of the phytoremediation process.

The purpose of *design thinking* is to comprehend people's needs and creatively outline a proposition to tackle them. The procedure follows a series of sequences: (1) gathering the requests of the people, (2) creating solutions, and (3) testing or experimenting with what works (Itten et al., 2020). Design thinking is an often present in the different phases of the co-creation and co-production process conducted by SPIRE. The deliberative workshops, as well as the questionnaire-based surveys are opportunities to collect ideas from the stakeholders, to identify their needs and to commonly draft possible solutions.

Design thinking is the backbone of *the start-up mentoring programme*, where ideas are developed, tested, experienced with, and implemented. The mentoring programme for innovators, young start-uppers and professionals in green, sustainable and smart transformation products and services is the main element which facilitates the strong co-production aspect of SPIRE. Guided by experts and professionals, the three winner projects use the facilities provided by the SpireHub maker space to create a prototype and scale-up the business idea. SPIRE tackled the scanty entrepreneurial spirit and related shortcomings assessed at the beginning of the project by emphasising the potential gains and benefits of the mentoring programme through a careful outreach and awareness-raising effort. They targeted especially the local youth using schools and community leaders as proxies (Verga, 2020a), but also used media presence. Besides these measures, they also enlarged the catchment area of the contenders.

In spite of the well-developed integrative management plan and the inclusive design of the project, SPIRE faces rather unfavourable socio-cultural conditions for the cooperation of the neighbourhoods. To mitigate this situation, SPIRE conducts a strong dissemination, knowledge transmission and awareness rising campaign addressing to the public by online media, radio and TV programmes, its YouTube channel, social media presence, the dedicated website and off- and online WOM

Table 18.1 Co-creation and co-development tools applied in the SPIRE actions and the induced place attachment processes

SPIRE action	Applied co-creation and co-development tools (Itten et al., 2020)	Place processes (Seamon, 2014)
SPIRE project	living lab	interaction, intensification, creation, realisation, identity, release
Thematic webinars	deliberative workshops, visualisation, online interactive tools	creation, realisation
Onsite and online interactive workshops	deliberative workshops, collective data collection, visualisation, online interactive tools, storytelling, design thinking, collective inspiration tools	interaction, intensification, creation
Surveys	collective data collection	interaction, intensification, creation
iGIS	collective data collection, visualisation	interaction, creation
iLEU	living lab, design thinking	creation, release
Plantathlon	collective data collection, visualisation, collective inspiration tools, storytelling	interaction, intensification, release, identity
SpireHub and Start-up mentoring programme	design thinking, visualisation	interaction, creation, realisation
Schools as embassies	schools as embassies, collective data collection, visualisation, collective inspiration tools, storytelling, living lab, design thinking	interaction, creation, identity, release

Source: Authors' elaboration

(Word of Mouth). Despite the unfavourable background, we notice a goal-oriented application of a variety of inclusive co-creation and co-development tools in the process of sustainable brownfield regeneration (Table 18.1).

18.4 Conclusions

The SPIRE actions of interdisciplinary participative planning and governance implement inclusive knowledge co-production processes enabled through local inter-institutional partnerships and partnerships with the private and NGOs sectors. Desired impacts of these innovative actions refer, on one hand, to the citizens, resulting empowered citizens, with new skills and knowledge in participatory planning processes, as well as to community stewardship for gently regenerated areas, and to a greater array of people embracing the opportunity to use and to be pleased by the green environment resulted with their own contribution (Leopa, 2020). On the other hand, the impacts of the project focus on institutions and authorities, meaning practitioners and policy stakeholders involved in NBS projects, improved governance openness and capacity in relation to urban challenges, particularly brownfield regeneration (Leopa, 2020).

The innovative way of working with the community in reclaiming brownfields as public good and productive green infrastructure (Verga, 2020b) faced some inconveniences because of the lack of legal frameworks and bureaucratic delays. The currently ongoing participative actions of the project have suffered setbacks due to the restraints to supress the COVID-19 pandemic. A survey applied to the involved communities, after the completion of the project, could provide insight into the effectiveness of the participative development tools in the process of creating place attachment.

Looking at the interconnected place processes of Seamon (2014), we observe, that when SPIRE started its participative development activities, the feelings of the neighbourhood towards the five pilot sites of brownfield regeneration were rather disinterest and minimal cognitive awareness or superficial fondness, meaning a lack of place attachment. The participative actions of SPIRE started to destigmatise the polluted and derelict areas, whereat they intensified the interaction with the places and among community members. The cultural, educational, and recreational functions and amenities to be implemented in the community green spaces reflect the needs and desires of the vicinities and create a specific ambience that is appreciated by the local people. These conditions stimulate the fondness to the place, and an intensified on-site presence favours not only new forms of social and cultural development, but also facilitate place release processes.

Co-creating the space strengthens place loyalty, enhances the emotional bond to the areas, but also to the co-working community members. The established and experienced societal relationships could initiate the feeling of place attachment to the public green spaces which provide liveable, healthy and safe environments. Further on, the areas revigorated together could turn into significant elements of the neighbourhoods' identity and the joint achievement of committed citizens could strengthen their self-esteem and pride. Moreover, the fulfilment of contributing to a successful endeavour of improving the quality of urban environment might motivate the people to embrace the possibility of co-developing a long-term strategy for the metropolitan area, and to scale-up place attachment as well.

Acknowledgements The assessed project: "SPIRE – Smart Post-Industrial Regenerative Ecosystem", ID: UIA04-138, is currently on-going and co-financed by Urban Innovative Actions conducted by Municipality of Baia Mare with Urbasofia and other project partners.

The authors thank the SPIRE-coordinators for access to their material.

References

Altman, I., & Low, S. M. (1992). Place Attachment. A conceptual inquiry. In I. Altman & S. M. Low (Eds.), *Place attachment* (pp. 1–12). Plenum Press.

Bardos, P., Spencer, K. L., Ward, R. D., Maco, B. H., & Cundy, A. B. (2020). Integrated and sustainable management of post-industrial coasts. *Frontiers in Environmental Science, 8*, Art. 86. https://doi.org/10.3389/fenvs.2020.00086, https://www.frontiersin.org/article/10.3389/fenvs.2020.00086

Cundy, A., Bardos, P., Puschenreiter, M., Witters, N., Mench, M., Bert, V., Friesl-Hanl, W., Müller, I., Weyens, N., & Vangronsveld, J. (2015). Developing effective decision support for the application of "Gentle" remediation options: The GREENLAND project. *Remediation Journal, 25*, 101–114. https://doi.org/10.1002/rem.21435

Cundy, A. B., Bardos, R. P., Puschenreiter, M., Mench, M., Bert, V., Friesl-Hanl, W., Müller, I., Li, X. N., Weyens, N., Witters, N., & Vangronsveld, J. (2016). Brownfields to green fields: Realising wider benefits from practical contaminant phytomanagement strategies. *Journal of Environmental Management, 15, 184*(Pt 1), 67–77. https://doi.org/10.1016/j.jenvman.2016.03.028

De Valck, J., Beames, A., Liekens, I., Bettens, M., Seuntjens, P., & Broekx, S. (2019). Valuing urban ecosystem services in sustainable brownfield redevelopment. *Ecosystem Services, 35*, 139–149. https://doi.org/10.1016/j.ecoser.2018.12.006

Ferber, U., Grimski, D., Millar, K., & Nathanall, P. (2006). *Sustainable brownfield regeneration: CABERNET network report.* University of Nottingham.

Itten, A. V., Fionnguala, S.-B. F., Sundaram, A., Hoppe, T., & Devine-Wright, P. (2020). *State-of-the-art report for co-creation approaches and practices with a special focus on the sustainable heating transition: Shifft work package 2 deliverable 2.1.1.* https://doi.org/10.13140/RG.2.2.22835.17440

Kabisch, N. (2019). Transformation of urban brownfields through co-creation: The multi-functional Lene-Voigt Park in Leipzig as a case in point. *Urban Transform, 1*, Art. 2. https://doi.org/10.1186/s42854-019-0002-6

Kirkness, P., & Tijé-Dra, A. (2021). Tainted urban spaces at the intersection of urban planning, politics of identity and urban capitalism. In P. Kirkness & A. Tijé-Dra (Eds.), *Negative neighbourhood reputation and place attachment the production and contestation of Territorial stigma* (pp. 252–256). Routledge.

Klusáček, P. (2018). Good governance as a strategic choice in brownfield regeneration: Regional dynamics from the Czech Republic. *Land Use Policy, 73*, 29–39. https://doi.org/10.1016/j.landusepol.2018.01.007

Leopa, S. (2020). *Project deliverable D.4.3.2. Standards and key performance indicators report.* D4.3.2-Standards-and-Key-Performance-Indicators.pdf (spire.city)

Mah, A. (2009). Devastation but also home: Place attachment in areas of industrial decline. *Home Cultures, 6*(3), 287–310. https://doi.org/10.2752/174063109X12462745321462

Mihaylov, N., & Perkins, D. D. (2014). Community place attachment and its role in social capital development. In L. C. Manzo & P. Devine-Wright (Eds.), *Place attachment. Advances in theory, methods and applications* (pp. 61–74). Routledge.

Moosavi, S., & Browne, G. (2021). Advancing the adaptive, participatory and transdisciplinary decision-making framework: The case of a coastal brownfield transformation. *Cities, 111*. https://doi.org/10.1016/j.cities.2021.103106

Neill, W. J. V., & Schlappa, H. (2016). *Future directions for the European shrinking city.* Routledge.

Papina, C. (2021). *SPIRE. Project deliverable: D.6.1.2. Report on co-design workshops with the SPIRE Local Action Network* (unpublished).

Riley, R. B. (1992). Attachment to the ordinary landscape. In I. Altman & S. M. Low (Eds.), *Place attachment. 2. Chapter* (pp. 13–36). Plenum Press.

Scannell, L., & Grifford, R. (2014). Comparing the theories of interpersonal and place attachment. In L. C. Manzo & P. Devine-Wright (Eds.), *Place attachment. Advances in theory, methods and applications* (pp. 23–36). Routledge.

Schlappa, H., & Ferber, U. (2016). Managing brownfield land in stagnant land markets'. In H. Schlappa & W. B. V. Neill (Eds.), *Future directions for the European shrinking city.* Routledge.

Seamon, D. (2014). Place attachment and phenomenology. Thy synergetic dynamism of place. In L. C. Manzo & P. Devine-Wright (Eds.), *Place attachment. Advances in theory, methods and applications* (pp. 11–22). Routledge.

Tanase, A. (2021). *SPIRE. Project deliverable: D.6.5.1. Report on community involvement in preparation, seeding, and planting* (unpublished).

Tendero, M., & Plottu, B. (2019). A participatory decision support system for contaminated brownfield redevelopment: A case study from France. *Journal of Environmental Planning and Management, 62*(10), 1736–1760. https://doi.org/10.1080/09640568.2018.1512476

Verga, P. L. (2020a). *Project deliverable D.4.1.2. Awareness and openness Report*.2020-06-23 – URBASOFIA_PV _ D.4.1.2 • Awareness & Openness Report (spire.city)

Verga, P. L. (2020b). *Project deliverable D.4.3.1. State of the Art Innovation Landscape Report*. 2020-04-30 – D.4.3.1 • State of Art and Innovation Landscape report_FINAL (spire.city)

Verga, P. L. (2020c). *Project deliverable D.4.3.3. State of play in Baia Mare. Desk analysis, Research repository & Awareness appraisal*. 2020-06-22 – URBASOFIA_PV _ D.4.3.3 • Desk analysis, research repository and awareness appraisal_FINAL_v2 (spire.city)

Chapter 19
Restoring Place Attachment in a Ruined Post-industrial Landscape: Change, Sense of Community and Aesthetics in Barreiro, Portugal

Eduardo Brito-Henriques (iD) and **Pablo Costa** (iD)

19.1 Introduction: On Change, Place Attachment and Creativity

In geographical thought, place has traditionally been associated with permanence and stability. Tuan (1977) underlined this fact by distinguishing space and place on the basis of the contrast between movement and pause: "if we think of space as that which allows movement, then place is pause" (p. 6); from his perspective, place was "essentially a static concept" (p. 179), suggestive of stability and security while space denoted "openness, freedom, and threat" (p. 6).

It was common among humanist geographers to insist on this association of place with the durable, constant and stable (e.g. Relph, 1976; Seamon, 1979). This shaped how place attachment was theorised for a long time. Place attachment refers to the emotional bonds that connect people to places (Riley, 1992; Stedman, 2003; Gottwald et al., 2022) through feelings of rootedness, belongingness and familiarity (Raymond et al., 2010), and which are expressed as identification, dependency and satisfaction (Gottwald et al., 2022). Place attachment is a component of the sense of place, a broader concept related to "people's subjective perceptions of their environments and their more or less conscious feelings about those environments" (Hummon, 1992, p. 262), which constitutes a more "complex psychosocial

E. Brito-Henriques (✉)
Centre of Geographical Studies, Institute of Geography and Spatial Planning, University of Lisbon, Lisbon, Portugal

Associated Laboratory TERRA, Lisbon, Portugal
e-mail: eduardo@edu.ulisboa.pt

P. Costa
Lisbon School of Architecture, University of Lisbon, Lisbon, Portugal
e-mail: pablo.costa@campus.ul.pt

structure that organizes self-referent cognitions, emotions and behavioral commitment" (Jorgensen & Stedman, 2001, p. 237). Change, both by means of mobility and the transformation of places, was taken as a factor that destroyed the sense of place and weakened place attachment. According to Tuan (1977, p. 179), "[i]f we see the world as process, constantly changing, we should not be able to develop any sense of place". Environmental psychology, on the other hand, has shown how the period of residence in a place is one of the strongest predictors of emotional attachment to that place, and a condition for the formation of a strong sense of place (Hummon, 1992; Hay, 1998; Nielsen-Pincus et al., 2010; Lewicka, 2011), while other studies have pointed to environmental changes being the cause of psychological suffering (Korjonen-Kuusipuro & Meriläinen-Hyvärinen, 2016; Askland & Bunn, 2018).

However, over the last decades, theory has progressed to acknowledge the relational, mobile and 'open' condition of place (Cresswell, 2015), impacting the approach to place attachment (Williams & Miller, 2021). Globalisation, increased mobilities and the whole range of transformations brought to cities by the restructuring of late capitalism, namely de-industrialisation, ruination, speculative bubbles, homelessness, gentrification, etc., have highlighted the need for a re-theorisation of place attachment no longer conceived in terms of fixed, durable places, but more in the sense of mobile forms of being-in-the-world with a focus on transitory and mutating landscapes (Gustafson, 2009; Lewicka, 2011).

It is against this background that the present study is framed. In this chapter, place attachment is explored in Barreiro, a former industrial city of the suburban belt of Lisbon, Portugal. Since Zukin (1991), it has become common to regard the spaces generated by de-industrialisation like one of the "shifting landscapes" (p. 29) that best epitomises the liminality and fluidity of contemporary urbanisation. Barreiro is an excellent example of this, with the particularity that it is not located in a country with an industrial past and a tradition of working-class culture as in the UK, the USA, Germany and the territories of the former Soviet Union, upon which most of the studies on the impacts of de-industrialisation on the material, social and cultural transformation of places have focused (Edensor, 2005; Mah, 2012; Storm, 2014; DeSilvey, 2017). Barreiro is located in a peripheral Southern European country, where for decades it was almost an exceptional 'industrialisation island'.

Thus, the main aim of this chapter is to discuss the extent to which de-industrialisation erases, erodes or merely redefines the sense of place and the intensity and type of emotional ties that bind people to their environment. The few available ethnographic studies on industrial ruination have already highlighted the heterogeneity and ambiguity of emotions, memories and interpretations elicited by ruination in communities (Mah, 2012; Meier, 2012; Storm, 2014; Emery, 2019), which alone is justification for the discussion to continue.

Secondarily, this chapter seeks to explore the links between industrial ruination, sense of place, creativity and placemaking. On the one hand, several scholars have suggested that ruined spaces stimulate imagination and creativity owing to their sensuous qualities and low social control (Edensor, 2005; Foster, 2014), encourage counter-narratives of history and place that amplify "our ability to act and influence the world" (Eshel, 2010, p. 133), emancipate alternative forms of curating the materialities of memory to those canonised in heritage (DeSilvey, 2017), as well as having become these same spaces the actual source of artistic inspiration and art objects (Apel, 2015). On the other hand, a complementary line of arguments defends the agential power of arts in placemaking and extols their potential in recreating counter-hegemonic and restorative senses of place in ruined, marginalised, and stigmatised landscapes (Puleo, 2014; Harles, 2018; Habibi, 2020). These links will also be examined in the following pages by exploring the case of Barreiro, where several artist and creative industry studios, festivals and cultural associations have emerged and multiplied over recent years (Carmo et al., 2019).

19.2 Case Study and Methodology

The post-industrial landscape of Barreiro has been the object of our research since 2017 through a lengthy ethnographic work which, over the course of these years, has involved multi-method, such as archival research, contemporary archaeology in modern ruins, photo-elicitation with residents, collection of life stories, and hundreds of hours of field observation and interviews with different types of local actors. This work enabled us to become fully immersed in the local context, and therefore much of this knowledge is likely to filter into the reflections and interpretation of reality advanced in this text. However, the facts and arguments presented and developed below are essentially the result of a series of in-depth interviews with actors from Barreiro's creative ecosystem in early 2022.

A total of eleven participants were interviewed whose professional paths had crossed Barreiro at some point, and who had established a strong relationship either with the city or with artistic collectives and/or institutions in the territory. Of these interviewees, seven were male and four were female, eight had been born in Barreiro and the remaining three in different locations (Seixal, Luanda and London). Two of the interviewees had lived in Barreiro only during the period of the artwork and were no longer established in the city. Finally, an effort was made to recruit people from different age groups: three were aged between 20 and 30 years, two between 31 and 40 years, four between 41 and 50 years, and two between 51 and 60 syears. Recruitment contact was made using social-media tools (Facebook and Instagram) and the interviews were held remotely (Zoom platform).

Barreiro is an old industrial city on the outskirts of Lisbon, located on the southern bank of the Tagus estuary, which is around 6 km away as the crow flies and may be reached in 20 min by ferry, but around 40 km by road, as there is no direct bridge, making it is necessary to go around the bay.

The city underwent intense development following the arrival of the railway in 1859, while also developing and expanding its cork industry and consolidating itself as one of the main points of connection between the south and the rest of the country. However, the establishment of the Companhia União Fabril—CUF (1908) industrial complex was responsible for the city's surge of progress in the early twentieth century, which reached its peak in the late 1950s when it became the largest industrial group in the Iberian Peninsula. At the time, CUF occupied almost half of the entire territory of Barreiro's city and its employees, in excess of 11,000, represented almost a third of its entire resident population (Camarão et al., 2008); its diversified production ranged from the extraction of oil from olive pomace for making soap and jute spinning to pioneering processes in the country, such as the manufacture of compound fertilisers and phosphoric acid by submerged combustion. Under a 'paternalistic' strategy, which was common to the large industrial complexes of the time, CUF went beyond the merely productive and economic logic, creating an important network of collective facilities, service provision and social support on such a local scale that the prosperity of the city became dependent on the success of the company (Leal da Silva et al., 2004; Carmo et al., 2019).

Thus, nationalisation of CUF in the second half of the 1970s and the industrial crisis stemming from the Fordist production model led to the company's dismantlement (Leal da Silva et al., 2004). Despite several restructuring efforts and the drafting of survival plans, the company was disbanded and closed many of its production units with low or no economic viability. Hence, a scenario of utter destruction and deprivation was created (Figs. 19.1 and 19.2), while at the same time considerable attention was being given to the toxic environment produced there because of contaminated soils during the decades of the industry's functioning (Fig. 19.3). In 2015,

Fig. 19.1 Barreiro overview: popular housing and industrial ruins. (Photo by Eduardo Brito-Henriques, 2017)

Fig. 19.2   Barreiro overview: post-industrial wastelands. (Photo by Eduardo Brito-Henriques, 2017)

Fig. 19.3   Toxic wastelands in Barreiro. (Photo by Eduardo Brito-Henriques, 2022)

the city accounted for around 195 ha of ruined spaces and vacant land, representing approximately one third of the city's area (Brito-Henriques et al., 2018). The difficulty in reconverting these immense spaces, whether due to their environmental liabilities or the complex financial-political effort typical of peripheral cities, inhibits the involvement of major private investors, resulting in a lack of job creation, ageing population, and the loss of inhabitants. The drastic shrinkage of the population has been recorded in successive censuses, indicating a fall in the population of the municipality of Barreiro from 88,052 inhabitants in 1981 to 78,359 inhabitants in 2021.

Conversely, the city has seen the flourishing and consolidation of a creative and multicultural scene in recent years (Carmo et al., 2019; Matos et al., 2019). Cultural associations and artistic collectives such as ADAO and OUT.RA have used the image of abandonment and exclusion to promote a more 'underground' culture through their projects, just as PADA Studios uses Barreiro's post-industrial landscape to garner new international residents (Figs. 19.4 and 19.5).

Fig. 19.4 New sites of the artistic scene in Barreiro: ADAO association. (Photo by Eduardo Brito-Henriques, 2022)

Fig. 19.5 Creative industries and arts in Barreiro: PADA Studios. (Photo by Eduardo Brito-Henriques, 2022)

19.3   At-Homeness and Sense of Community in Post-industrial Barreiro

In the statements collected from members of Barreiro's creative ecosystem, there was no indication of an annulment or weakening of affective ties with the place. On the contrary, several interviewees exteriorised a deep feeling of at-homeness, explicitly associating Barreiro with home, but even when they did not expressly refer to 'feeling at home'—as several did—this was implied in the way they associated Barreiro with easiness, familiarity, and security.

Almost all the interviewed artists and creatives had spent periods of their biographies in other places for study or work purposes, including being away from Portugal. For those born in Barreiro the option to return was a topic raised by many of them, with far more affective than rational explanations. Terms alluding to 'desire', 'will' and 'need', suggesting carnality and instinctiveness, were frequently used to explain what had motivated this decision, which was almost always connected to subjective perceptions of well-being due to the proximity and conviviality with significant people or familiarity with the community and place. In literature, these types of feelings, ranging from rootedness, attraction and closeness, are usually described as manifestations of place attachment (Seamon, 1979).

Even the artists with no former ties to the place and who were not enrooted there by family memories expressed empathy and emotional affinity. Emma[1] (25–30 years), an English sculptress who became acquainted with Barreiro through an artistic residence at PADA (a private organisation providing exhibition spaces, studios, and artistic residences in Barreiro since 2018) referred to the city as "just my perfect little place" (interview recorded on 11/01/22). Ana, a visual artist connected to PADA, claimed in her interview that:

> when they leave, all the artists feel a special affection for Barreiro. In fact, there are several artists already living in Barreiro. They decided to come here and ended up living in Barreiro. There are Scots, Spanish, American, English… from various countries. It's interesting because they come from very different countries and did not know each other beforehand, and then they come here, meet at PADA, begin working and each one creates a very interesting bond with Barreiro, because Barreiro is a very unique city (Ana, 30–35 years of age, visual artist, interview recorded on 04/01/22).

A crucial element in the formation of this emotional bond with the place appears to lie in the sense of community, translated into a felling of belonging and the experience of inclusion in a community that shares interests and helps each other. In addition to a perception of co-presence and density given by the recognition of other peers, brought to light in practically all the interviews, the idea of a local culture conducive to creative activity as a differentiating element of the place also emerged at times:

> Barreiro has a relaxed feel and an artistic vein that fosters creativity. […] I identify with that. Three or four friends get together, make an association and create a rock festival, or a skate association… they get together and do things (Filipa, 45–50 years of age, cultural director, interview recorded on 20/01/2022).

> It is not a very big city, and everybody knows each other. It's common for someone to know someone who knows someone else… it's a network. […] And then, here in Barreiro, a lot of people are doing the same things. There's the music scene which is very strong: bands, etc. It's a city with people who want to do things (João, 40–45 years of age, visual arts teacher and visual and performing artist, interview recorded on 22/01/2022).

> This is how I see Barreiro: a space for creation, where people who want to create are given a warm welcome. A natural creativity reserve. […] This is where I find people to help me in my projects, […] I can easily get hold of people who can help me and there is always a positive response. People help each other. It is a characteristic that belongs very much to us. […] Nowadays it is a common thing, the hubs, coworking, etc., but I think that in Barreiro it is an organic thing (Martim, 50–55 years of age, designer and collective leader, interview recorded on 27/01/2022).

The statements eloquently highlighted the importance of social capital. The recurrence of the theme of 'associativism' in the interviews, the self-identification of various interviewees as members of 'collectives', and the proliferation of allusions to 'networks', 'ties' and 'partnerships' in the descriptions of their creative work are indications of this relevance. This social capital, in which they invest, fosters a sense

---

[1] The names of the interviewees have been changed to safeguard their anonymity.

of community. Many of the functional relationships and strategic alliances between artists, curators, mediators and audiences are intertwined by webs of affection, giving the social capital an emotional layer. In the accounts there were several references to artists' associations and collectives stemming from groups of friends, and vice-versa, friendships that had developed from artistic partnerships. The bohemian environment, characterised by bars and parties, was another topic that emerged as a *locus* of social capital, namely among the interviewees with a longer-standing integration in Barreiro.

The interviews show that this sense of community, vital for the creation of feelings of identification and belonging to the place (Riley, 1992; Ruggeri, 2021), is not limited to the community of practice of artists and creatives. It overflows beyond this sphere, merging into a notion of community of place that embraces an imagined totality, consisting of all those who live in Barreiro. When asked to talk about what people are like and to describe the local way of life, the interviewees positively highlighted the fact that 'everyone' knows each other and that there is a spirit of solidarity and mutual help:

> The people are nice. Once I was assembling an installation in one of those abandoned industrial spaces. When I went to assemble the part, I found that I needed to weld some parts together. It was a large part and I ended up putting it in a trolley I had to push around the industrial park. So, I went to the workshops near Sotinco [a paint factory for civil construction], a few car workshops, to get some electricity to weld… and the people were great. They gave us electricity, helped us with the welding, offered us a drink, … well, they were fantastic. It's the kind of thing that you would also see in the suburb where I grew up. People don't have much, but they share everything (Daniel, 40–45 years of age, artist, interview recorded on 11/01/22).

> In Barreiro you find that sense of community, of knowing people. You see the same person twice in a place, and after a while you already know each other. You feel you are part of a place. That's what I feel here in Barreiro. In the space of three years of living here, we are from Barreiro (Ana, 30–35 years of age, visual artist, interview recorded on 04/01/22).

These were the kinds of accounts that emerged in the interviews, complemented by more practical and mundane accounts of a simple and quiet life, marked by the authenticity and sluggishness of small towns. Several of the interviewees referred to the advantage of basic things and everyday services being within walking distance, allowing them more quality time for what they enjoy doing and to be with family and friends. Many of these ideas reproduce what Hummon (1992) referred to as "small-town ideology", and therefore cannot be seen as specific to Barreiro's sense of place. Partially mythologised ideas of small-town identity as easy-going, neighbourly and friendly, as opposed to large, stereotyped cities as places of rough and impersonal treatment, where people are uncaring and materialistic, is a resource used by small-town dwellers to maintain high levels of community satisfaction and counter feelings of subalternity and marginalisation (Hummon, 1992). In the case of Barreiro, this identity of place, constructed on the narrative of a 'village-like' city, indeed barely coherent with the memory of industrial Barreiro, may very well generate an even stronger adherence by acting as a buffer against the psychosocial trauma of de-industrialisation and urban shrinkage.

19.4   Materialities, Atmospheres and Aesthetics in Post-industrial Barreiro

In the processes of people's emotional attachment to places the physical character-istics of the environment and its constituent materialities are not negligible (Gustafson, 2001; Stedman, 2003; Raymond et al., 2010). Space matters not only for the memories it evokes and the personal and social meanings with which it is imbued, but also for its material affordances and affective capacities (Griffero, 2014). Different spaces, due to their materiality and atmosphere, are likely to pro-duce positive or negative affectivities of variable intensity, and some are particularly capable of creating emotionally significant environmental socialisations mediated by aesthetics (Gandy, 2017).

The collected accounts suggest that de-industrialisation in Barreiro has created new affective predispositions and opportunities for bodily, performative, aesthetic and emotional relationships of people with the environment that are not fatally marked by negativity. One might assume that the ruinous landscape of a shrinking city devastated by de-industrialisation would dominate Barreiro's sense of place and that this would be mostly associated with negative feelings of repulsion, sadness and resentment. However, this is not what was found.

De-industrialisation emerged in several interviews associated with 'openness' and a certain sense of 'unveiling', a kind of fresh view beyond the factory walls and the veils of smoke. References to the Tagus River were framed by this context, emerging in the interviews as a *locus* of environmental socialisation of particular emotional significance, asserting itself as a central element in the sense of place. Almost all the interviewees spoke of the river front as the 'pearl' of Barreiro and how important and rewarding their experiences in this space had been, recounting walks or bike rides, fishing activities and rowing training. A younger interviewee mentioned how he used to meet friends on the pontoon over the river near the ferries to sunbathe, 'chill out' listening to the swell, and discuss ideas and plan projects between dives into the water, aware that this would have been an impossible experi-ence in his parents' time (Nuno, 20–25 years of age, urban artist and association activist, interview recorded on 02/02/2022). Several expressed gratitude that the relationship with the river had improved in recent years, since the pollution problem had been overcome, or that the demolition of the old factories and the walls fencing their yards had opened new possibilities for mobility and an embodied relationship with space:

> The walls of the industrial city began to disappear, they were literally knocked down and this gave rise to other flows. In the old days you couldn't go from the old Barreiro to Lavradio without having to cross properties and pass through two gates. It felt like you were entering another territory that was not your own; another city. That doesn't exist anymore. You can cross it easily and that perception has gone. […] This riverside relationship is only possible now…, the mere fact that you can walk along it without obstacles is incredible. I don't know how many kilometres of coastline Barreiro has, but […] this is incredible. This is what makes Barreiro special: this relationship with the river (Bernardo, 30–35 years of age, photographer, curator and cultural programmer, interview recorded on 05/01/22).

Not only the river, but urban nature in general was also a highly common theme in the interviews. Listening to the accounts, one is left with the feeling of an ongoing discovery and an effort to reimagine Barreiro as a re-naturalised place, where, somewhat miraculously, encounters and conviviality with other biologies have become possible. Some of our interviewees regretted the industrial and polluted city 'stigma' that still weighs down on Barreiro, and the need to "project an image of Barreiro connected to the environment so that we can eliminate that persistent stigma" (Gonçalo, 45–50 years of age, member of a visual and performing artists collective, interview recorded on 22/01/2022). Ideas of post-industrial rewilding could be detected in allusions to the clams that have begun to reappear in the river and to the novel ecologies emerging in the ruins, which some confessed to being one of the things "that most inspires me" (Carlos, 30–35 years of age, sound artist, interview recorded on 06/01/2022) and "that I like most of all and find intriguing" (Nuno, 20–25 years of age, urban artist and association activist, interview recorded on 02/02/2022). Carlos explained that in this association of ruins and vegetation "there is a degree of nostalgia" because it is related to abandonment and giving up—"it is almost as if we let nature take it over"—, but at the same time it transmits a "positive vibe" as an oracle of a "cleaner" future (06/01/2022). The concepts of 'washing' and 'regeneration' run through his creative work. Carlos told us about his project with sounds, recorded in abandoned factories and in Barreiro's wastewater treatment plant, to confront the 'old industry' that dirtied the water, and had been defeated, and the 'new industry' responsible for the opposite process of "reconverting pollution into water", triumphant in the sound of its functioning (06/01/2022).

The presence of ruins, abandoned industrial hangars and wastelands, produced by the demolition of factories, also proved to be emotionally impressive for the interviewed artists and creatives. An empathetic analysis of the collected accounts reveals that the emotional intersections with those spaces are fundamentally aesthetic, and this explains why negative feelings related to collective memory are not conveyed. By referring to the emotions as being generated in an aesthetic experience of space, we mean that they are based on a poetic form of perception that prioritises sensations, while at the same time involving perceptive judgments shaped by aesthetic values cultivated in the artistic *habitus*.

In fact, all the interviewees were attracted to those post-industrial environments, recognising material affordances in them that enhance creative work and are inspirational. The sense of spaciousness, present not only in the open spaces but also in the built structures, where the large spans and ceiling heights produce special architectural atmospheres, was a highlighted quality in several interviews. The spaciousness of the vacant industrial hangars combined with their isolation render a sense of freedom, giving those spaces functional qualities that foster creative work. Several interviewees referred to the experience of sonic freedom to use noisy machines to prepare their works or to experiment with music and performance out of hours, such as Laura:

> I ended up opening the dance school in the industrial area because it offered me better rental conditions in terms of price. I rented a warehouse and got set to work. One thing I really liked about the space was that it didn't have the typical architecture of a dance school. It was

a raw warehouse, and I really liked that idea of industrialisation, the high ceilings with the beams showing through. Because there are many schools in Germany that are actually designed this way and I always liked that. There's a lot of natural light and a lot of space. [...] And because it was a secluded area where the sound wouldn't interfere with the people around there; even during the day with loud sounds, it wouldn't bother anyone (Laura, 40–45 years of age, dancer and choreographer, interview recorded on 22/01/2022).

In addition to spaciousness, the aesthetic experience of post-industrial spaces is characterised by an indefiniteness, strangeness and semblance of disconformity and dissonance produced by destruction, which is coded in what Trigg (2006) refers to as "post-sublime". Things that outside the artistic *habitus* might be perceived as ugly, horrible or depressing, are received positively by the aesthetic experience of artists on a range of exaltation to pleasurable awe and wonder. The imperfections of the destruction itself, which never completely erases the past and is never absolute or definitive, as well as the possibilities of encounters with new and unexpected ontologies, such as those produced in toxicity, were mentioned by some of the interviewees within the scope of this register:

That environment in Barreiro, of destruction... destruction in inverted commas, right? Of abandonment; that environment is very interesting for us, for everybody, but more for us artists, who always see enormous quality in it. It awakens some curiosity in me, because I work a lot with the reinterpretation of objects and with techniques that are related to destruction. I did a series of drawings with gunpowder... things that destroy paper while they also leave a mark. Things related to that rebirth from destruction or finding meaning in destruction (Daniel, 40–45 years of age, plastic artist, interview recorded on 11/01/22).

There were a lot of purples and greens. I started making a collection of photographs at the beginning... and I've got some type of trashy archive, if you will [laughing]. And the combination of all these materials which had casually been abandoned or, you know, had exploded into the land... the way organic matter takes over and transforms these synthetic materials into new kinds of textures, it's really striking. [...] So, I started digging for soil. And I realised that in the purple soil there were also sodium crystals, and they were bright yellow. And I started to mix this soil with a kind of glue and fiberglass to transform it into a material. One of my works has kind of tiles made of these different sands, different earths, different colours (Emma, 25–30 years, sculptress, interview recorded on 11/01/22).

Finally, a reflection on how the interviewed artists and creatives positioned themselves as actors of change on the spectrum stretching from continuity to rupture, and on the role of their work in place attachment. In all the accounts, the perception of being in a place in transition, a 'liminal zone' in the time space, described by Bernardo as "a kind of threshold" (05/01/2022) and referred to by Ana as "on the verge of something happening" (04/01/2022) was evident, as were their dominant feelings of expectation, enthusiasm, and optimism in relation to this condition and the future. Their self-awareness as transformation agents of the place was also perceptible, both through the social dynamics they introduce and through the artistic objects and events they create. In their conversations with us, several assumed and emphasised the agential power of their work in placemaking, by intervening in the materiality of the space, in the production or manipulation of new affective atmospheres, and then by the reception and impact on the community, in particular the effect it can have on perceptions and representations of place. At this level, the way they evaluate their role and the work they create appears to move more in the direction of a restoration or reactivation of place attachment, creating new affectivities and identification motives with the place, than towards a remaking of the sense of place. Ideas on 'reuse' and 'reinterpretation' of the legacies of place were common in the interviewees' descriptions of their creative work, which suggests more of a mediation between past and future than a rupture.

19.5   Final Discussion and Conclusions

From the case-study of Barreiro, the first conclusion that may be drawn is that places devastated by de-industrialisation, with extensive "ruined post-industrial landscape scars" (Storm, 2014), are not condemned to their sense of place fading away or to detached or alienated communities, contrary to that implied by the classical theory associating spatial change with placelessness (Relph, 1976; Seamon, 1979; Brown & Perkins, 1992), and that advanced in some studies on de-industrialisation (Fullilove, 2021). The evidence collected among the community of artists and creatives of Barreiro was by all accounts suggestive of a strong place attachment. On the scales of sense of place proposed by Shamai (1991), the collected accounts point to the highest rankings, corresponding to what this author designated as "involvement in a place". The correlation between the intensity of place attachment and the strength of the sense of community shared by members of Barreiro's creative ecosystem, within which there is significant investment in social capital, was also clear. This fact suggests that social capital is an important factor in the development of feelings of belonging and satisfaction with the place, thus recommending that policy measures geared towards conserving or restoring place attachment should bear in mind the need to invest in this social resource.

The collected data also challenges findings from previous studies that noted feelings of grief, nostalgia, resentment, and pessimism associated with de-industrialisation (Mah, 2012; Meier, 2012; Storm, 2014). However, several reasons may explain this discrepancy. According to Brown and Perkins (1992), after critical events, there is first a "stressful period of disruption" in which place attachment breaks down and then, a "post-disruption phase" in which new place attachments are constituted, and it is possible that Barreiro is currently in this phase. On the other hand, the sense of place is not homogeneous within a community, with variations being noted according to class, between generations and sub-cultures, and even on a personal level on the basis of "lived memories" (Mah, 2012); therefore, subjective perceptions of the environment of other groups of people in Barreiro, as well as the feelings generated in relation to those perceptions, may well be different. Thus, the argument advanced herein is simply that even places stigmatised by toxic legacies and ravaged by de-industrialisation can generate positivity in specific sub-groups within their communities and be beneficiaries of visions that challenge hegemonic fatalistic narratives of decay, highlighting that of artists and creatives as one of such that may embody this alternative.

Finally, throughout these pages, it has become clear that "place attachment is an embodied relationship to the world" (Williams & Miller, 2021, p. 22), and also how the aesthetic experience can engender new phenomenologies of devastated spaces capable of restoring place attachments in them. This fact appears to confirm the potential of arts and creativity for placemaking. Moreover, the analysed case of Barreiro shows that use of the aesthetic experience in restorative acts of place attachment does not have to entail an impoverishing aestheticisation of the sense of place, as is the case of the culture-led redevelopment projects conducted under the paradigm of 'creative cities', which mainly invest in what Cohendet et al. (2010) have referred to as the 'upperground' of creativity, or in artistic programmes produced under a cloak of apparent irreverence that follow the canon of ruinporn (Apel, 2015). The case of Barreiro clearly illustrates an alternative situation to which placemaking, and the design of restorative place attachment policies should be particularly sensitive: the value of the 'underground' layer of creativity (nonconformist artists, subversive creative practitioners, alternative collectives, etc.) in generating counter-hegemonic senses of place with enormous potential for the enhancement and emancipation of devastated, marginalised and stigmatised spaces.

Acknowledgments This research was funded by Portuguese national funds through the FCT—Fundação para a Ciência e Tecnologia, I.P., under the Project grants UIDB/00295/2020 and UIDP/00295/2020.

References

Apel, D. (2015). *Beautiful terrible ruins: Detroit and the anxiety of decline.* Rutgers University Press.

Askland, H. H., & Bunn, M. (2018). Lived experiences of environmental change: Solastalgia, power and place. *Emotion, Space and Society, 27,* 16–22. https://doi.org/10.1016/j.emospa.2018.02.003

Brito-Henriques, E., Morgado, P., & Cruz, D. (2018). Morfologia da cidade perfurada: padrões espaciais de ruínas e terrenos vacantes em cidades portuguesas [Morphology of the perforated city: Spatial patterns of ruins and vacant land in Portuguese cities]. *Finisterra-Revista Portuguesa de Geografia, 53*(108), 111–133. https://doi.org/10.18055/Finis12160

Brown, B. B., & Perkins, D. D. (1992). Disruptions in place attachment. In I. Altman & S. M. Low (Eds.), *Place attachment* (pp. 279–304). Plenum Press.

Camarão, A., Pereira, A. S., & Leal da Silva, J. (2008). *A Fábrica: 100 anos de CUF no Barreiro [The factory: 100 years of CUF in Barreiro].* Editora Bizâncio.

Carmo, A., Matos, F., & Pereira, S. (2019). Regeneração urbana através da cultura e das artes: o caso do Barreiro [Urban regeneration through culture and the arts: The case of Barreiro]. *Forum Sociológico, 35,* 61–70. https://doi.org/10.4000/sociologico.8670

Cohendet, P., Grandadam, D., & Simon, L. (2010). The anatomy of the creative city. *Industry and Innovation, 17*(1), 91–111. https://doi.org/10.1080/13662710903573869

Cresswell, T. (2015). *Place: An introduction* (2nd ed.). Wiley.

DeSilvey, C. (2017). *Curated decay. Heritage beyond saving.* University of Minnesota Press.

Edensor, T. (2005). *Industrial ruins: Spaces, aesthetics and materiality.* Berg.

Emery, J. (2019). Geographies of deindustrialization and the working-class: Industrial ruination, legacies, and affect. *Geography Compass, 13*(2), 14. https://doi.org/10.1111/gec3.12417

Eshel, A. (2010). Layered time: Ruins as shattered past, ruins as hope in Israeli and German landscapes and literature. In J. Hell & A. Schönle (Eds.), *Ruins of Modernity* (pp. 133–150). Duke University Press.

Foster, J. (2014). Hiding in plain view: Vacancy and prospect in Paris' Petite Ceinture. *Cities, 40*(B), 124–132. https://doi.org/10.1016/j.cities.2013.09.002

Fullilove, M. T. (2021). Revisiting "The Frayed Knot": What happens to place attachment in the context of serial forced displacement? In L. C. Manzo & P. Devine-Wright (Eds.), *Place attachment: Advances in theory, methods and applications* (2nd ed., pp. 173–192). Routledge.

Gandy, M. (2017). Urban atmospheres. *Cultural Geographies, 24*(3), 353–374. https://doi.org/10.1177/1474474017712995

Gottwald, S., Albert, C., & Fagerholm, N. (2022). Combining sense of place theory with the ecosystem services concept: Empirical insights and reflections from a participatory mapping study. *Landscape Ecology, 37*(2), 633–655. https://doi.org/10.1007/s10980-021-01362-z

Griffero, T. (2014). *Atmospheres: Aesthetics of emotional spaces*. Ashgate.

Gustafson, P. (2001). Meanings of place: Everyday experience and theoretical conceptualizations. *Journal of Environmental Psychology, 21*(1), 5–16. https://doi.org/10.1006/jevp.2000.0185

Gustafson, P. (2009). More cosmopolitan, no less local. *European Societies, 11*(1), 25–47. https://doi.org/10.1080/14616690802209689

Habibi, Z. (2020). Whose cultural memory? Disruptive tactics by the creative collectives in George Town, Malaysia. In X. Gu, M. K. Lim, & J. O'Connor (Eds.), *Re-imagining creative cities in twenty-first century Asia* (pp. 113–128). Palgrave Macmillan.

Harles, M. (2018). Creative place-making: Contemporary art practice and urbanization in Dhaka. *Visual Ethnography, 7*(2), 61–79. https://doi.org/10.12835/ve2018.1-0113

Hay, R. (1998). Sense of place in developmental context. *Journal of Environmental Psychology, 18*(1), 5–29. https://doi.org/10.1006/jevp.1997.0060

Hummon, D. M. (1992). Community attachment: Local sentiment and sense of place. In I. Altman & S. M. Low (Eds.), *Place attachment* (pp. 253–278). Plenum Press.

Jorgensen, B. S., & Stedman, R. C. (2001). Sense of place as an attitude: Lakeshore owners attitudes toward their properties. *Journal of Environmental Psychology, 21*(3), 233–248. https://doi.org/10.1006/jevp.2001.0226

Korjonen-Kuusipuro, K., & Meriläinen-Hyvärinen, A. (2016). Living with the loss: Emotional ties to place in the Vuoksi and Talvivaara regions in Finland. *Emotion, Space and Society, 20*, 27–34.

Leal da Silva, J., Gomes, G., & Cruz, I. (2004). Sobre o complexo industrial da C.U.F. no Barreiro [About the CUF industrial park in Barreiro]. In J. M. B. D. Brito, M. Heitor, & M. F. Rollo (Eds.), *Momentos de inovação e engenharia em Portugal no século XX* (pp. 233–244). D. Quixote.

Lewicka, M. (2011). Place attachment: How far have we come in the last 40 years? *Journal of Environmental Psychology, 31*(3), 207–230. https://doi.org/10.1016/j.jenvp.2010.10.001

Mah, A. (2012). *Industrial ruination, community, and place: Landscapes and legacies of urban decline*. University of Toronto Press.

Matos, F., Carmo, A., Pereira, S., & Pinto, A. (2019). Arte urbana no Barreiro Pós-industrial [Urban art in post-industrial Barreiro]. In P. Costa, R. V. Lopes, & J. Bassani (Eds.), *BRR 2018: Quando a periferia se torna trendy* (pp. 190–203). DINÂMIA'CET-IUL, Instituto Universitário de Lisboa.

Meier, L. (2012). Encounters with haunted industrial workplaces and emotions of loss: Class-related senses of place within the memories of metalworkers. *Cultural Geographies, 20*(4), 467–483. https://doi.org/10.1177/1474474012469003

Nielsen-Pincus, M., Hall, T., Force, J. E., & Wulfhorst, J. D. (2010). Sociodemographic effects on place bonding. *Journal of Environmental Psychology, 30*(4), 443–454. https://doi.org/10.1016/j.jenvp.2010.01.007

Puleo, T. (2014). Art-making as place-making following disaster. *Progress in Human Geography, 38*(4), 568–580. https://doi.org/10.1177/0309132513512543

Raymond, C. M., Brown, G., & Weber, D. (2010). The measurement of place attachment: Personal, community, and environmental connections. *Journal of Environmental Psychology, 30*(4), 422–434. https://doi.org/10.1016/j.jenvp.2010.08.002

Relph, E. T. (1976). *Place and placelessness*. Pion.

Riley, R. B. (1992). Attachment to the ordinary landscape. In I. Altman & S. M. Low (Eds.), *Place attachment* (pp. 13–35). Plenum Press.

Ruggeri, D. (2021). The agency of place attachment in the contemporary co-production of community landscapes. In L. C. Manzo & P. Devine-Wright (Eds.), *Place attachment: Advances in theory, methods and applications* (2nd ed., pp. 243–260). Routledge.

Seamon, D. (1979). *A geography of the lifeworld: Movement, rest and encounter*. Croom Helm.

Shamai, S. (1991). Sense of place: An empirical measurement. *Geoforum, 22*(3), 347–358. https://doi.org/10.1016/0016-7185(91)90017-K

Stedman, R. C. (2003). Is it really just a social construction? The contribution of the physical environment to sense of place. *Society & Natural Resources, 16*(8), 671–685. https://doi.org/10.1080/08941920309189

Storm, A. (2014). *Post-industrial landscape scars*. Palgrave Macmillan.

Trigg, D. (2006). *The aesthetics of decay: Nothingness, nostalgia, and the absence of reason*. Peter Lang.

Tuan, Y.-F. (1977). *Space and place: The perspective of experience*. University of Minnesota Press.

Williams, D. R., & Miller, B. A. (2021). Metatheoretical moments in place attachment research: Seeking clarity in diversity. In L. C. Manzo & P. Devine-Wright (Eds.), *Place attachment: Advances in theory, methods and applications* (2nd ed., pp. 13–28). Routledge.

Zukin, S. (1991). *Landscapes of power: From Detroit to Disney World*. University of California Press.

Chapter 20
Conclusions: Reshaping Place Attachment Research

Iwona Markuszewska ⓘ **and Oana-Ramona Ilovan** ⓘ

The conclusions include three parts. First, we argue in favour of place attachment for development, public policy, and spatial planning. In the second part, we summarise the contributions of this collective book to place attachment research. In the last part, we draft a future research agenda on place attachment.

20.1 Relevance of Place Attachment for Development, Public Policy, and Spatial Planning

This book brings to the study of place attachment increased attention to participative planning and community engagement in creating, reshaping, and enhancing emotional bonds with places. For this reason, a lot of space was devoted to the importance of policy and decision-making processes that involve people who are strongly attached to the places they live in.

To show the policy implications of place attachment research, one must discuss the connection between definitions of *development* and *policy*: more exactly, public policies reflect the ideology that governs development at a certain moment, in a

I. Markuszewska
Department of Environmental Remote Sensing and Soil Science, Faculty of Geographical and Geological Sciences, Institute of Physical Geography and Environmental Planning, Adam Mickiewicz University, Poznań, Poland
e-mail: iwona.markuszewska@amu.edu.pl

O.-R. Ilovan (✉)
Department of Regional Geography and Territorial Planning, Faculty of Geography and Territorial Identities and Development Research Centre, Babeş-Bolyai University, Cluj-Napoca, Romania
e-mail: oana.ilovan@ubbcluj.ro

© The Author(s), under exclusive license to Springer Nature
Switzerland AG 2022
O.-R. Ilovan, I. Markuszewska (eds.), *Preserving and Constructing Place Attachment in Europe*, GeoJournal Library 131,
https://doi.org/10.1007/978-3-031-09775-1_20

particular place. One significant idea is that in order to create policies that are sensitive towards places, people and their place attachments, one has to acknowledge the necessity of giving up the 'one size fits all' approach and the quantitative dimension of development as the only basis for policy prescriptions or the only indicator of progress.

Place attachments are based on place meanings (Markuszewska, 2019; Banini, 2021; Banini & Ilovan, 2021a; Ilovan, 2021c) and one factor impacting this meaning is the process of development. Representations and feelings about places are shaped also according to local development processes, which are affected by power relationships and are delineated by particular ideologies across time. Disadvantaged and vulnerable groups and communities tend to be impacted more by spatial development decisions and are at risk of displacement (usually class-led displacement) and of losing their place attachments (Manzo, 2014; Kirkness & Tijé-Dra, 2017b). Place attachments are connected to values, therefore places have power over people. Place attachments may control people's intentions and decisions concerning place, even determining them to choose preserving attachments and place values against any economic benefits that suppose sacrificing them (cf. Hester, 2014). This means that the value of place to inhabitants is higher than for those having economic or other kinds of practical interests (usually exhibited through discourses that legitimate change and development) and this can lead to residents' resistance to change. In fact, public policies and development rhetoric may activate place attachment processes. The discourses in the policy arena and in mass media are many times conflicting with inhabitants' lived experiences of place and their sources of place attachment (Markuszewska, 2021). Consequently, the normative socio-political discourse about development is challenged by people's complex place attachments and experiences in place.

Active place attachment can influence considerably people's acceptance levels of public decisions that affect their livelihoods and places. Therefore, it is high time participatory and sensitive planning takes place, especially to downplay power imbalances between residents and official decision-makers, but also to democratise decision making practices and to include the voices, desires and needs of all interested parties. Participatory and grassroots approaches to development processes should be based on explicit territorial identities and place attachments, emphasising in public debates their role as resources for development, for social capital and in constructing more meaningful and resilient communities and futures.

Previous research showed that discourses of economic and political powerful stakeholders in the process of development tend to delegitimise residents' place attachment with a view to successfully put their objectives into practice (e.g., residential displacement triggered by gentrification and urban regeneration – cf. Kirkness & Tijé-Dra, 2017b). The frequent paternalist attitude of policy makers tends to legitimise development projects that disadvantage poor and marginal social groups, despite insisting otherwise. The entrepreneurial outlook of the state challenges its social purpose. A spatial ideology is created during the normative shaping of urban and rural areas with state-led economic and political discourses about development and well-being. Those outside the norm run the risk of being stigmatised and their places are hierarchised from a social, economic, and spatial point of view. Therefore, the danger that mainstream or normative discourses pose to budding grassroots initiatives and practices that foster place making and place attachments, especially in the case of disadvantaged areas and communities that are morally condemned, stained, or stigmatised. For instance, real-estate market-driven stigmatisation of places polarises groups into winners and losers of development, fuelling spatial and economic disparities, and aggravating inequalities between the wealthy and the poor.

Research underlined the tensions between state logic and the role of the local leadership in protecting place against place destroying development initiatives. During a process of fetishizing space (i.e., the city or the rural area are seen as the human body which must be cured of unhealthy issues), which is part of the redevelopment discourse (Zhang, 2017), resistance and agency from below are crucial in safeguarding place and place attachment (Husseini de Araújo & Batista da Costa, 2017; Mutică & Ilovan, 2022). Especially when neglect and confrontation are the attitudes of the state, rather than support for local voices. Actions, dialogue, and negotiation are needed to find the most appropriate solutions agreed by residents, if not consensus. Ordinary people are capable local development agents, driven by their attachment to and interest in place (Markuszewska, 2020). Thus, the usefulness of the concept of *place attachment* within the neoliberal ideology and discourses on local development to help make a difference in people's lives.

First, when envisioning development, one should consider that place attachment is a value and resource in itself, but at present it seems to be part of the counter hegemonic discourse about societal development and well-being, advocating for a different type of value system (including practices of place-making and community building from below) than the one driven at present by economic growth. In general, agency from below fosters social justice. Considering this, grassroots development is a viable alternative to top-down solutions and their implementation and this fits into neoliberalism, the present paradigm for development policies. Neoliberal approaches advocate for less state intervention and therefore they could accommodate grassroots development supported by the involvement of the civil society and where the economic growth is coupled with social benefits. Within this framework, local communities are activated by NGOs (as service providers) to achieve development on their own terms and feel empowered.

Secondly, again in this context of envisioning development, awareness should be raised that at the local, regional, and national levels, global processes translate into different outcomes, which are highly context specific (Castree, 2009). Thus, globalisation does not mean homogenisation and sameness, because of the heterogeneity of responses at lower spatial scales and due to the diversity of people and cultures, triggering context-specific perspectives on development. More decision-making opportunities concerning development and the challenging of the existent power relations have improved availability at the local scale, and especially for marginalised people and communities; this is why the local is privileged in place attachment studies. However, one should be aware that the local is also featuring divisions, exclusion, and conflict; it is the scale where a multitude of stakeholders push their agendas and a common vision for development is difficult and, sometimes, impossible to achieve. Nevertheless, the benefits of participation and co-operation within the local scale and across scales should not be downplayed. Such participatory processes, based on functional and symbolic ties to people, resources and services within a place, enable place attachment, the use of locals' implicit knowledge and place literacy, they also enable newcomers to get involved and become native to the places they moved in, by developing their emotional, cognitive, and behavioural bonds. They feed people's interest to establish roots and anchor emotionally in place, and to develop a sense of place ownership, a sense of community, and local pride. Place attachment is enforced by liking one's community, by belonging to a group.

Thirdly, non-transparent decision-making is a plague of the society, benefitting those in power and impacting, usually in a negative way, the powerless and the voiceless. The resistance of the latter should be capitalised on by participatory approaches to local development. But this supposes a devolution of power, democratising decision-making and supporting agency from below, which, practice has proved, can be attained by residents' actions and resistance, and by public pressure upon the state and the powerful.

Fourthly, development is a function of power, expressed through both mainstream and alternative social, economic, and cultural practices and approaches that very across space and time. Place attachment proposes a human-centric perspective to development, but care for people's place attachments means also care for places and a focus on sustainability, local understandings of the human-environment bonds and locally based livelihoods.

Finally, one can acknowledge that place attachment research so far has not made visible impact on *public policy*. But what is the policy relevance of this research? The place attachment concept is useful because it brings insights into people's responses to global and local processes and into their relationship with place. Human understandings and choices can be explicated through place attachment, a process that should be more recognised by practitioners due to its high impact on inhabitants' responses to change and on their ability to adapt to change. Research on place attachment enables policy makers to understand people's responses to a variety of challenges (e.g., environmental changes, social and economic ones). Place attachment is relevant for processes concerning local development, social and political activism and resistance, human rights, environmental protection, etc. Contributions of place attachment research to policy-making could inform actions that encourage place-protective behaviours, community involvement, integration of new residents, active and authentic participation at spatial planning, etc.

Ideally, place attachment research should inform and shape public policies on local development; it can showcase diagnoses of and suggestions for (alternative) solutions to local problems. However, it is difficult for academic output to make its way to the policy arena. But even under such circumstances, there is a need to make place attachment research results so far visible through future applied research; even if the relevance of research for policy formulation and intervention is judged from a political point of view.

Researchers' better engagement with policy processes could help the embedding of place attachment research results in the wider and mainstream public debates about development, while still aware of ethical concerns regarding the fact that with such policy engagement the academia may re-enforce the *status quo* and reproduce the existing power relations. Nevertheless, action from within the policy making arena is more impactful (because it tends to have faster results) than criticising from the margins. Considering all this, one of the goals of this book was to collect evidence about place attachment processes at the European level that could be used as arguments in emphasising the relevance of place attachments for 'evidence-based policies'. Policy making decisions could benefit from and should consider results of the scholarly work.

However, policy engagement with place attachment research is just one way of making such research relevant. Other ways include theoretical advancement, raising awareness, empowering individuals and communities, familiarising university students and other researchers with a humanistic perspective on why place matters in a broader societal milieu, etc.

Still, *the development discourse is reflected in public policies and spatial planning*, among other areas that have a material and symbolic impact on place. Place attachments should inform place making. Ignoring them means creating artificial areas, not places. Shared values are embedded in people's livelihoods and daily patterns and life rituals, especially collective ones, create place pride and rootedness. Spatial planning should be sensitive and strive to encourage these. It should also encourage place attachments based on values that promote inclusion, irrespective of race, class, gender, ethnicity, religion, age, health, etc.

Sensitive planning means reconnecting planning to ordinary people's wishes, needs, concerns, and lives. Community attachment, as expressed through involvement in activities benefitting the community, should be capitalised on by spatial planning which is sensitive to the people. Sensitive spatial planning is a proof of the commitment to place of all stakeholders. It means that spatial planners attach more importance to the people than to practical interests that disadvantage the human being and the humanistic approach to development. In addition, such spatial planning goals offer opportunities to develop engaged scholarship, activist methodologies, and research led by those ordinary people themselves.

Moreover, sensitive spatial planning measures are the result of authentic integration of all voices within place and are not tailored to accommodate only hegemonic discourses. The planning process has the role to empower residents to decide where they reject or contribute to change, whether they are moved elsewhere or not. If change is not perceived as answering their needs and wishes, people should be given opportunities to make place how they see fit (Harvey, 1996, p. 325).

Sensitive spatial planning (e.g., the shape of the settings for human activities is critical – cf. Hester, 2014) could be useful in this process of enabling place attachments that unite rather than introduce divisions among individuals and groups. On the contrary, insensitive spatial planning can harm people and places to a great extent. Therefore, this collective volume may also be read as an advocacy for more sensitive perspectives in the theory and practice of place attachment.

20.2   Place Attachment: Where Are We Coming From?

As researchers, we, the editors, represent different geographical fields: Human Geography and Landscape Geography, which makes different how we perceive and measure the 'place'. The contribution of Human Geographers is strongly marked with research on territorial identities (cf. Ilovan, 2020, 2021a, b; Banini & Ilovan, 2021a). On the other hand, the perception of landscape geographers is usually analysed through the lens of people's relations with landscapes (cf. Antrop & Van Eetvelde, 2017; Markuszewska, 2019). To cooperate for this book, we decided to invite researchers who have a geographical perspective on place-making, on building and (re)shaping the emotional relationship with the place. This was because the geographical dimension of space is always shaped and changed by communities in place (i.e., settled communities). Nonetheless, the geographers' contributions are complemented by the findings of academics dealing with the social context of a place (such as sociologists), as well as scholars researching the spatial context of a place and landscape (such as architects and planners). Our aim as editors of this collective volume was to present the achievements in place-oriented studies which are beyond the investigation conducted by environmental psychologists. However, this is not to oppose the achievements of researchers who represent this discipline, but rather to focus on studies from Geography, which also analyse human attachment to the place and landscape. To recognise the merit of environmental psychologists is to draw on methodological approaches developed by them, which found practical application in studies outside the field of Environmental Psychology.

This book complements the present achievements on attachment to place and landscape, and at the same time, it contributes to the discussion and search for answers to the questions: *How is place attachment created?, Why?, What for?* In particular, in searching for the answers to questions that relate to the process of creating and transforming peoples' relations with the place and the landscape, such as the following: *How is the sense of place created and reshaped over time?, How is place identity manifested?, What makes people feel satisfied with being in a certain place?, What causes people to lose ties with place?*, and *How do people form relations with non-places?*

There was an interest in how ties with physical spaces are formed (both positive and negative), including the process of adaptation and making places in abandoned areas (non-places). For this reason, the chapters present different stages of the sense of place: from the beginning of creating attachment to place and landscape through different phases and types of attachments manifested by the inhabitants of the analysed case studies to the example where sense of place has been broken. This overlaps a series of geographical locations of the study areas, their regional and local specificity shaped by the interaction with centrifugal (local) and centripetal (global) factors. Places defined and determined in this way were examined as potential and real locations with which the local communities build, establish, maintain, reshape, and break off emotional bonds. Eventually, the findings have been grouped into four parts: I) Place making and place attachment through place-based development and community place-driven actions, II) Nature- and culture-based place attachment,

III) Sustainable planning and territorial identities enhancing place attachment, and IV) (Re)constructing place attachment: regeneration of (post)industrial areas and urban recovery.

Due to the variety of research approaches used, this book contains both theoretical explorations on building attachment to place and landscape, as well as empirical findings based on in-depth analyses of attachment to place. These studies present a whole range of research methods classified as quantitative and qualitative, but very diverse, taking into account the specificity of the studied context and people's relationship with place, territory and / or landscape. Research results present a comprehensive geographical view of place and landscape as geographical locations and environments of human life. To put it in other words, findings highlight the physical dimension of space and people-place relations, as well as the social perception of the place and community relations in that place. These issues, however, are not separated from each other, because they are intertwined, as place has always both a physical and a non-material dimension. The subtle division reflects the main points of interest of different geographical disciplines; however, their juxtaposition makes them complement each other.

Despite discussions on the sequence of successive processes and states of building relationships with a place (i.e., place dependence, place identity), which in effect lead to building a strong bond with the place (place attachment), undoubtedly, a significant contribution of the authors of individual chapters is testing known and developing new methodological approaches to assess the degree of attachment to place, the causes that build and modify it, as well as factors that strengthen the sense of place and those that destroy this relationship. Apart from this, the authors employed research designs that show a holistic understanding of the concept of place attachment. Moreover, unlike existing research on place attachment, the authors emphasise the role of the participatory community in the process of place making rather than of the individual's perceptions of place. In other words, in the existing body of research on place attachment, the degree/strength of attachment is most often analysed, and moreover, particular attention is paid to the individual perception of place. It can be assumed that the results of these studies answer the question: *How strong is place attachment?* In the chapters presented in this book, the researchers highlight the factors (spatial, planning, social, economic, natural, and human) that influence the strength of place attachment. So, these contributions contain the answer to: *What determines place attachment?* Furthermore, many authors refer to the context of emotional attachment to place. To capture this emotionality, they employ a research approach based on qualitative data analysis. For instance, in-depth interviews provide more sensitive information than that obtained from structured surveys (Ilovan & Doroftei, 2017).

The book starts with an introduction authored by *Oana-Ramona Ilovan and Iwona Markuszewska.* The editors define key features of the concept of place attachment – the emotional bond between people and places. The introduction presented the multi-dimensional aspects of the idea of *place bonding*, including the most important concepts, such as: *place identity, place belonging, place dependence* and it explains the relations among them in a process of building and maintaining the *sense of place*. This part of the book focuses on the role of human geographers and the achievement of Human Geography in place-oriented studies, including qualitative research, which is complementary to the existing body of work conducted mainly by environmental psychologists, who considered especially the quantitative measurement of place attachment. This part juxtaposes the achievements of both scientific fields, and in this way, proves their complementarity in place-oriented studies. In addition, different contributions to place attachment research are discussed; these present a multifaceted and integrated view of how place attachment can be interpreted, measured, and implemented into practice. In addition, the introduction discusses critically the concepts of *place attachment* and *landscape*. One of the golden threads linking these two notions is the topic of *territorial development and transition*, which involves both the dimension of individual/collective place identity and belonging (bottom-up) and the policy of territorial planning and place-making (top-down). The introduction also emphasised the value of the book by presenting its scientific and societal relevance.

The first part, *Place making and place attachment through place-based development and community place-driven actions*, focused on the process of building attachment to places, territories, and landscapes. For instance, specific local conditions of places and subjective features of local actors were the most significant aspects of this place making process. The findings emphasised the meanings of local actors (e.g., leaders or stakeholders) and of the grassroots actions they initiated, which encouraged the community to become involved in place building and protecting activities. Owners of second homes were newcomers, who, through family dependence and neighbour bonding, felt a deep rootedness with temporally inhabited places. Entrepreneurs were leaders – animators who engaged the local population in peripheral areas through activities that inspire a feeling of locality. Young newcomers in gentrified communities created and rebuilt place attachment.

However, this part opened with a theoretical chapter, authored by *Iwona Markuszewska*, who raised the issue of the importance of community participation in place making processes and in building emotional attachment to landscape. Participatory planning and community involvement are given priority in sensitive planning. Having this in mind, *Markuszewska* asked how place attachment strengthened the sensitive planning of landscape. The theoretical framework of landscape sensitive planning was based on the guidelines of social and procedural justice. In this way, *Markuszewska* referred to the contribution of human geographers to discussing the fundamental rights of equality and fairness, as well as to people's having a voice in decision-making processes. Through the process of shaping emotional relations between people and landscape, she explained that positive attitudes could strengthen, and at the same time, encourage local communities for active involvement in landscape governance. Is such idealistic concept likely to be implemented in practice? Yes, if taking into account a mature approach of all those involved in the planning process.

In the second chapter, *Adam Czarnecki, Aneta Dacko, Mariusz Dacko* and *Manu Rantanen* enquired whether the duration of stay at second homes was enough to create deep bonds with temporary locations, and who was more attached to place:

seasonal or permanent residents. The authors analysed the attachment to second homes through the lens of two models: the community attachment (Kasarda & Janowitz, 1974; Hummon, 1992), and, on the other hand, the socio-economic position, and the life-stage (Matarrita-Cascante et al., 2010). The data was collected from second-home owners in the well-established tourism region of the Silesian Beskids in Poland. A classification and regression tree was employed as the analytical method. The findings highlighted those aspects of place making which were crucial in creating the sense of belonging (homeowners declared that the second home was a favourite place for them), in strengthening social bonding (involvement of 'old' homeowners in community activities and 'young' owners' declaration of trust to local community), as well as, in engendering the feeling of family dependence (in relation to second homes that were inherited). *Czarnecki* and *peers* proved that the attachment to second place expressed by the owners of second-homes was very strong, sometimes even stronger than the attachment expressed by members of the local community.

In the next chapter, based on two case studies from Estonia – the geographical peripheries of Saare and Valga counties –, *Grete Kindel* analysed the interaction between place and entrepreneurs. More precisely, she investigated the nature of place attachment for entrepreneurs (as place-based leaders) and answered the question on how their personal identity contributed to place making behaviours (cf. Manzo & Perkins, 2006; Müller & Korsgaard, 2018). *Kindel* emphasised the relevance of qualitative research for the investigation of emotional relations with place. Following Ryan (2009), she assumed that qualitative research methods (such as face-to-face interviews) enabled a researcher to pick up the nuances of people's emotional and symbolic relations with places. By using this approach, her study confirmed the significant role of highly attached entrepreneurs in local development. Her findings showed that the feeling of being a part of local place helped create trust within the community and take care of what is crucial for the local place.

In the next chapter, *Ingmar Pastak* questioned how gentrification influenced place attachment. He noted that the previously conducted investigations focused on displacement (or dis-attachment) of residents when analysing a gentrification context (cf. Blokland, 2009; Ocejo, 2011). In contrast to this, *Pastak* analysed the process of building attachment to places among new residents through place-making activities and involvement in bottom-up initiatives. To explain gentrifies' contribution towards local grassroots place-making and place attachment, the author used Edward Soja's (1996) triangular place epistemology. In particular, using qualitative thematic content analysis, *Pastak* examined the relations between materiality and representations to make place at home. He tested this theoretical assumption in Põhja-Tallinn district (Estonia's capital city). Results confirmed the research hypothesis, and additionally, proved that gentrification was deeply connected to discourses and practices constructing place attachment. Gentrification and place-making practices fostered the construction of territorial identities and place attachments. He contributed with insights into how gentrifying processes triggered reuses, revitalisation, and the transformation of space into meaningful places, and engendered more sustainable practices and eventually livelihoods.

In the last chapter of this part, *Oana-Ramona Ilovan and Bianca Sorina Răcăşan* discussed how a shared sense of belonging to a neighbourhood with a certain territorial identity, informed by shared narratives and representations, impacted the creation of individuals' place attachment. Due to the choice of their case study (Mănăştur neighbourhood of Cluj-Napoca City, Romania), *Ilovan* and *Răcăşan* adopted the concepts of territorial identity (cf. Paasi, 1986; Banini, 2021) and neighbourhood (cf. Mannarini et al., 2006) to analyse progressive understandings of sense of place (Massey, 1994; Jorgensen & Stedman, 2001). *Ilovan* and *Răcăşan* assumed that place attachment (following the framework of Scannell & Gifford, 2010) was based on place meanings (Sebastien, 2020; Banini, 2021; Banini & Ilovan, 2021b), and it was produced by experiences and engaging with those meanings, as well as with the material environment and the other humans in place. Discourse analysis of a community-led local newspaper – *Buletin de Mănăştur* – provided data on how representations about the neighbourhood and bottom-up civic initiatives impacted inhabitants' place attachment. The achievement of this contribution is the model of Mănăştur, which presents the relationship between identity of place, representations, and place attachment. The research showed that creative socialising in places enabled people reconnect spatially and socially. *Ilovan* and *Răcăşan* proved that social and cultural activities and territorial identities were connected, and additionally that civic mindedness was a result of explicit place attachment and of awareness about territorial identity.

The second part of the book deals with issues of nature- and culture-based place attachment. The problem raised in the contributed chapters referred to significant characteristics of the creation of attachment to place during the beginning stage of place making. Moreover, the authors analysed actions which stimulated residents to build and develop emotional bonds with the place they lived in (territory or landscape), as well as, with the people who lived (permanently or temporarily) in that location. However, the last chapter in this section described a situation and factors that led to breaking the emotional ties with place/landscape.

In the first chapter of the second part, *Anna-Lisa Müller* discussed place attachment in the context of cities. She followed the social scientific understanding of a city (cf. Simmel, 1995; Löw, 2001), where social spaces resulted from human interaction with the material environment. Based on the place attachment concept of Scannell and Gifford (2010), *Müller* focused on the dynamism of the social dimension and the materiality of place, as she argued that place attachment was unstable and stemmed from constant (re-)negotiatons between individuals and groups in urban space. In addition, *Müller* considered both positive and negative feelings for people's attachment to places (cf. Manzo, 2014). The inner-city square of Georg-Büchner-Platz in Darmstadt (Germany) served its usefulness in detecting the role that materiality played for establishing and keeping up attachments to certain places. The research (supported by autoethnographic observation and photographic documentation) showed the role of materiality to both stabilise and re-frame belonging and place attachment. At the same time, *Müller's* research proved that place attachment was dynamic and changing over time, and additionally, linked with the material context of a particular place.

In the second chapter, *Desiree Farrell* and *Liam M. Carr* took a deeper look at the process of making place in a touristic destination. With the conceptual support of Lew (2017), the authors analysed the relevance of the concepts of *place-making* (bottom-up) and *placemaking* (top-down) for (re)shaping place attachment and place identity. The authors questioned if the local identity of place might be detached from that of the tourist (cf. Lai & Ooi, 2015). Using a multimethod approach (Q methodology, semi-structured interviews, and participatory mapping), they tested the hypothesis among the inhabitants of Rathmullan, a village on the coast of Lough Swilly (Ireland). The study showed how much tourism development and opportunities depended on the involvement of the locals from tourism-oriented communities. The authors emphasised the dependence of tourism on external circumstances (i.e., including the COVID-19 pandemic). Thus, according to *Farrel* and *Carr*, the role of communities in tourism engagement was crucial to create more sustainable relations with places, and to take on responsibilities for places, which was necessary in order to develop a strong and positive sense of place and to strengthen the sense of attachment.

To estimate place attachment, in the third chapter, *Hugo Castro Noblejas, José M. Orellana Macías,* and *Matías F. Mérida Rodríguez* proposed to use Participatory GIS (Public Participation GIS – PPSIG) and mapping methods. Although this is not the first time when this methodological approach was used (cf. Brown et al., 2015; Maguire & Klinkenberg, 2018; Wang, 2021), the novelty was to test its usefulness in the urban area (in Marbella in Costa del Sol, Spain). Based on urban area classification, the authors proved the usefulness of this method in spatial analysis focusing on place attachment. They considered this method helpful in the delimitation and measurement of relationships among urban types, sense of belonging and the identity of the urban landscape. In addition to this, the authors noted that the combination of this method with other quantitative and qualitative scientific techniques might expand the research in other fields of interests, such as: the residents' needs and demands and the social functionality of urban spaces. In the opinion of *Noblejas* and *peers*, this could strengthen the bonds between people and places, as well as encourage the local communities to actively participate at planning processes.

The last chapter of this part analyses how sudden and catastrophic changes impact people's attachment to landscape. *Åsa Ode Sang, Andrew Butler* and *Igor Knez* examined the impact of forest fire on individuals' connections to their everyday landscape. The study investigated relationships between the perception of a forest landscape and connection to place, before and after a large forest fire. The survey data (based on a Likert scale) were collected from residents living within the forest fire area of Bergslagen (Sweden). Based on Tveit and peers' research (2006), the authors measured the visual qualities of the landscape (naturalness, coherence, complexity, stewardship, disturbance, and visual scale/openness), which were important in gathering people's opinions about their experiences with the forest (Sheppard, 2001; Ode Sang et al., 2016). *Ode Sang* and *peers* detected that both age and gender impacted the perception of the landscape and the relation to the landscape. The authors revealed that the everyday landscape had become a non-familiar place for the residents, triggering loss of attachment and spatial anxiety.

The chapters included in the third part, *Sustainable planning and territorial identities enhancing place attachment*, emphasised the role of the local community's active participation in decision-making processes about the planning and governance of territories. The findings proved that a strong feeling of being attached to a certain place/territory motivated people to be more aware of it and encouraged them to take responsibility for the place. In addition, ethnographic issues were analysed in relation to the meaning of national identity in shaping place attachment.

Assuming that territorial attachment plays a crucial role in defining place consciousness and establishing civic sense (Arnstein, 1969; Banini & Ilovan, 2021b), in the first chapter, *Anna Maria Colavitti* and *Sergio Serra* considered the influence of citizenship practices on how places were created and how planning tools were designed. They discussed the process of reshaping the relationships between city and countryside inside the planning instruments at local scale in the Region of Sardinia (Italy). The selected case study illustrated the communities' progressive loss of identity and sense of belonging. Through the analysis of the Regional Landscape Plans (RLP), the authors explained how participation methodologies in the planning tools could strengthen the sense of place attachment and could contribute to solve critical issues. *Colavitti* and *Serra* argued that regional landscape planning could be vital in reconstructing the unity between inhabitants and their territory and the relationship between local societies and places. Thus, knowledge about the influence of territorial planning on place attachment was essential to assess the usefulness of adaptation strategies for enhancing place identity and place attachment.

In the second chapter, *David Fanfani* and *Massimo Rovai* discussed the regeneration and restructuring of Local Food Systems (LFS) – a governance model, which is a socio-natural construct (Marsden, 2004) – and the symbolic meaning of safety pending in between place and food (cf. Casey, 2001). As the authors explained, LFS had developed as a necessity to stop the negative influences of global changes on local conditions through closing the production-consumption chains at the regional level (bioregion). In this context, LFS could strengthen the sense of value of what was local, and (re)build the lost sense of place and place belonging. The investigation carried out in Toscana, Italy, confirmed the role of LFS in constructing relationships among food, inhabitants and place, in particular in terms of collective attachment to place through the engagement of stakeholders and activists in place making actions and reconstruction of the sense of place. *Fanfani* and *Rovai* noticed that future research on policy implications was needed to find effective tools to integrate LFS experiences with territorial planning tools, as differences between the objectives of territorial planning and those of LFS bottom-up initiatives appeared often.

The chapter of *Srećko Kajić, Marin Bogdanić* and *Borna Fuerst-Bjeliš* provided an in-depth analysis of the regional concepts of identity and attachment in the transborder region of Syrmia, which, since the collapse of Yugoslavia was divided between Croatia and Serbia. The authors built their research on the assumption that a strong place/regional identity enhanced place attachment. The differences between place identity and regional identity (cf. Paasi, 2002) were the starting point of their study. In particular, the authors analysed the strength of residents' attachment to this region, expressed mostly by self-identification. Their findings showed that the division had a significant impact on the sense of commonness between the parts. *Kajić* and *peers* identified a strong sense of place attachment among the youth, and that was vital to ageing communities and especially in areas losing population. The authors' achievement in the discourse on place attachment was to elaborate a tripartite model of the sense of commonness in transborder regions. The authors pointed out that the place attachment and sense of commonness in the region of Syrmia could be capitalised on through the policy of transborder cooperation.

A quite different perspective on place attachment was presented in the fourth chapter, with the contribution of *Alexis Sancho Reinoso*. He analysed how microtoponyms constructed attachment in a bilingual region. For *Reinoso*, microtoponyms were indicators of attachment to place and markers of place identity. He researched the role of geographical names in the daily lives of residents in the south of Carinthia (Austria), a region bordering Italy and Slovenia. In this region, the monolingual German-speaking majority live together with the bilingual Slovene-speaking minority. *Reinoso* considered that toponymic attachment – relationships between people and toponyms (cf. Kostanski, 2016) – was based on language, whose role was to transform space into place and make sense of the place to which people felt attached to (Tuan, 1991; Cresswell, 2004). However, his results underlined that only the Slovene-speaking minority showed strong attachment to 'their' toponyms. The author insisted on enhancing the visibility of bilingual names in public spaces by including them into collaborative cartographic data and creating bilingual maps. Nevertheless, such promotion was the prerogative of the local authorities who, unfortunately, did not see bilingual place names as an asset to foster regional development in the south of Carinthia.

The last part of the book, *(Re)constructing place attachment: regeneration of (post)industrial areas and urban recovery*, deals with two topics: (a) the (re)construction of place attachment in post-industrial areas and (b) the run-down urban districts. Its chapters deal with a different view of the shared public places in towns and cities.

In the first chapter, *Liliana Popescu, Cristiana Vîlcea* and *Amalia Niţă* noted the problem of decay of many medieval towns throughout Central and Eastern Europe. The authors discussed the recovery of derelict urban areas in relation to redefining place meaning and fostering attachment to places like these. *Popescu* and *peers* followed Oldenburg and Brissett (1982) (who named the public-available spaces of cities as the third places of social interaction), to analyse social interactions within open public spaces (community attachment to public spaces attachment – cf. Hidalgo & Hernandez, 2001). The authors analysed the significance of revitalisation for the historical centre of the post-socialist city Craiova (Romania), and measured how residents' different socio-demographic variables influenced their attachment to the respective area. Their results confirmed that attachment to public places was born through spending time there for recreational and social purposes. Likewise, knowledge about the history of the city centre and the renovation of old buildings created connections among people, history, and place. A certain manifestation of psychological attachment, or even 'possessing' a common space, was represented by residents' reluctance to the implementation of changes regarding the use of buildings.

Continuing the topic of renewal and transformation of urban areas, in the next chapter, *Magdalena Miśkowiec's* contribution presented the process of becoming familiar with the semi-public spaces that existed within neighbourhoods. This study differs from the existing studies that examined social ties in public spaces rather than the lived space of the local neighbourhood community. *Miśkowiec* argued that the sense of community was an important factor in rebuilding and recovering emotional bonds with places. Following other scholars (for instance, Ferilli et al., 2016), she acknowledged the participatory process as vital in urban regeneration. In her research, she presented the techniques and tools useful in achieving collective production (co-production) of places, which inputs were collectively supplied, and the benefits enjoyed by the entire community (cf. also Bovaird et al., 2015). She analysed the participatory regeneration processes of urban courtyards in six selected Polish cities (Kraków, Gdańsk, Bytom, Olsztyn, Gorzów Wielkopolski, and Kalisz). Her findings showed the significant role of women as local leaders. Residents' involvement in artistic activities was beneficial for creating bonds with place and for awareness raising towards collective responsibility to the place. The introduced collective actions were positively regarded by the members of the local community, especially during the COVID-19 pandemic period.

The study of *Emanuel-Cristian Adorean, Oana-Ramona Ilovan* and *Iwona Markuszewska* contributes to better understanding how urban transportation impacts society through place experience and to what extent mobility shapes the emotional relations between metro systems and metro users. Place making processes within the metro systems were analysed in three cities of Portugal (Almada, Lisbon, and Porto), and in their metropolitan areas (Almada is part of the Lisbon Metropolitan Area). The authors argued that the metro system constructed the image of the urban area (cf. Sipetic et al., 2019), that representations and place attachment are social constructs (cf. Silva et al., 2018), and that mobility influences people's relation to places (cf. Di Masso et al., 2019; Banini, 2021). The multifaceted qualitative analyses were useful to identify the territorial identity features of the metro systems, the sense of place, and aspects of place dependence. The results of *Adorean* and *peers* showed that the metro was perceived as attractive due to both its social and physical environments. In addition, the contribution of these authors discussed the process of making non-places familiar. They proved that metro users were able to construct emotional relations with the metro beyond its mobility function.

In the fourth chapter, the research aim of *Kinga Xénia Havadi-Nagy* and *Tihamér-Levente Sebestyén* was to consider the available co-creation and co-development tools and instruments (which are vital in participatory planning) to assess the initiation of creating attachment to place. To do this, *Havadi-Nagy* and *Sebestyén* applied to their case study the six interconnected processes of place making (Seamon, 2014) that enhance or diminish the intensity of emotional bonds with place. The authors questioned how certain local actions succeeded to recover the image of degraded areas (called 'tainted urban spaces' by Kirkness & Tijé-Dra, 2017a). Attempts to build bonds with places through place interaction, place identity, place creation, place intensification, place realisation, and place release were examined for the brownfield wasteland in Baia Mare city (Romania). The authors analysed the innovative ways (e.g., deliberative (digital) workshops, storytelling, design thinking, a start-up mentoring programme) of cooperating with the residents that enabled community involvement and authentic engagement in participatory planning processes. All those actions improved community skills and knowledge about participatory planning processes to regenerate brownfields. Additionally, this research showed that participatory planning might rebrand the post-industrial degraded city image into a place that facilitated place renovation processes.

The last chapter discussed place attachment in Barreiro, a former industrial city on the outskirts of Lisbon (Portugal). *Eduardo Brito-Henriques* and *Pablo Costa* analysed the process of creating sense of place (cf. Shamai, 1991). Focusing on a community of artists and creatives (who were deeply involved in place making activities in this post-industrial city), the authors analysed the attachment to abandoned places. The findings of *Brito-Henriques* and *Costa* showed that post-industrial, devastated places displayed their sense of place, which contradicted the classical theory of placelessness (cf. Relph, 1976; Brown & Perkins, 1992). The signs of livening up and recovery of these abandoned places in recent years appeared due to cultural associations and artistic collectives that changed the image of that post-industrial area. The authors confirmed that the intensity of place attachment was correlated with the sense of community, which was translated into a feeling of belonging and common experience. Their findings suggested that social capital was an important factor in the development of feelings of belonging and satisfaction with the place. In addition, *Brito-Henriques* and *Costa* drew our attention to the potential of arts and social creativity for place making actions of devastated, marginalised, and stigmatised places.

The presented findings indicate that what matters in the globalised world is what occurs locally, because this is the *here and now* where *our* place is being made. This is the *here and now* where bonds, relationships, emotions are created, built, strengthened, weakened, which finally (re)shape and transform *our* place. This is the process of scooping up a piece of the world for ourselves, appropriating our local space, which helps us to be anchored in a particular dimension of time and space, and to identify with it. This process makes us part of a place and, at the same time, we create its entirety. This process of building our own identity means that our relationship with place is marked by tenderness and sensitivity, as *our* place is unique to us and proves our existence. Space becomes a material setting for emotional rootedness. A fragile existence linked with the emotional relationship with place that connects the past with the present, the present with the future. In this way, we create places and landscapes, and, at the same time, we are a part of the places and landscapes that have been created by us.

As evidenced by the research results presented in this book, the approach of geographers goes beyond individual/personal relations with the place, and is analysed through the collective community perception of space. Furthermore, the study on place attachment aims to analyse all states of place making and relations with geographical locations, rather than to measure how strong the attachment to place is. In other words, shaping attachment to place is a process that is achieved through cooperative effort and commitment of local community members, as well as through other actively involved local actors. Researchers emphasise the importance of bottom-up actions that make residents feel a part of a certain territory. The findings have confirmed that participatory planning is a key success factor in maintaining positive attitudes towards places and taking responsibility for places.

Place attachment is inconstant and changeable. Certainly, forged relationships and ties with a place, territory or landscape evoke in people satisfaction with being in that geographical location. However, as results have shown, a change in the *status quo* of place reshapes this emotional bond. This is how topophilia could turn into topophobia with all the negative, even hostile feelings that arise from being in a particular location. Other authors support the view that places with a bad reputation, abandoned post-industrial areas, so-called non-places, under favourable conditions can lead to the development of deep attachment to place (cf. Kirkness & Tijé-Dra, 2017b).

20.3   Place Attachment – Where Are We Heading To?

Place attachments are fundamental to experiencing and understanding everyday life. Research on place attachment is bound to continue as long as people live in and interact with place. This book testifies that the inquiry in place attachment is still an expanding field. The concepts related to place attachment are as many as interpretations of place. This is because each place is unique, each place is inhabited by different individuals and groups whose behaviours, attitudes and meanings differ in building a relationship with the place. Therefore, it is impossible to create universal patterns of place attachment.

This book supports the above-mentioned ideas and presents a European perspective. Even though the research assumptions and hypotheses were tested on a local scale, the conclusions that flow from these analyses have a general relevance. That is, regardless of geographic location and considering local factors influencing the process of building relationships with place, the residents' needs towards their place of residence are practically similar everywhere. As a result, the need for attachment to a place, a kind of psychological ownership of the space in which people live, work, travel and rest, and with which they are associated on a daily basis, is an integral part of their identity. Economic, social, cultural, geo-political and legislative differences play a minor role. And additional to this, the need for attachment to place through tradition, history and memory of the place, as well as, through building social ties with residents who share a common space is equally strong everywhere. The only difference among the analysed case studies is the rate of progressive merging with the place.

The results of the studies presented in this book highlight some important reflections from the point of view of future research on place attachment. A new research agenda for place attachment should include at least the paths mentioned below. On the one hand, the strongly stressed need for further research on the process of *recovering and transforming non-places into emotionally valued places*. Despite their bad reputation, post-industrial areas, degraded lands, wasteland, and transport infrastructure are important operational and functional parts of the urban structure, and, contrary to appearances, the inhabitants identify themselves with and look for ways to appropriate. Findings confirmed that residents are not indifferent to these spaces, as it turns out that these unwanted and uninhabited places are important in their consciousness, and they relate to them emotionally. Having this in mind, *in depth research on non-places* (such as airports, railway stations, shopping malls, urban brownfields, etc.) should be extended in the context of shaping attachment processes to these places.

On the other hand, losing the emotional connection with place has been discussed. Losing the connection with place has different reasons; most often such a situation results from the impact of sudden hazards or from long-lasting factors (both natural and human) in the local context. As for the latter, the issue of *solastalgia* – the distress, which is caused by environmental change (Albrecht et al., 2007) has been subjected to numerous studies (Higginbotham et al., 2007; McManus et al., 2014; Warsini et al., 2014); however, it has not been comprehensively analysed. Bearing in mind the consequences of solastalgia (including emotional and existential anxiety), conducting qualitative research is advisable here.

Then, more attention should be paid to participatory mapping as a measurement method for different scales of people's emotional relations to place. This is particularly important for community participation in planning land use and landscape changes. So far, GIS found its usefulness for the study of place making and sense of place as well as for other valuable aspects of place (Brown et al., 2020; Jeffrey & Aranha, 2020). However, the full spectrum of geographic systems has not been used so far in analysing place attachment.

More research is needed on *the negative and ambivalent relationships that people have with their places of residence*, as research so far revealed instances when such bonds are a source for stronger place attachment than for negative loss-related reactions (Kirkness & Tijé-Dra, 2017b). Such studies could shed more light on how place attachment is developed, what factors and experiences contribute to forming this bond to place.

A new challenge for those studying place attachment appeared in the context *of highly mobile societies and increasing interconnectedness between people and places* (Castree, 2009). As a result, place attachment research must consider the implications of a world made of places characterised by flows and networks rather than by stability and bounded communities. So, what is the impact of geographical mobility on place attachment? Both corporeal and mediated mobilities (i.e., by means of the information and communication technology) emphasise the ubiquitous nature of mobility nowadays (Di Masso et al., 2019) and underline the necessity of researching its impact on place attachment construction (i.e., local rootedness and ties) and understandings of place (e.g., 'place as roots' according to the traditional understandings of place attachment versus 'place as routes', where the focus is on the individual's choices and identity, depending on social class and lifestyle)

(Gustafson, 2014). Thus, place attachment was characterised as inward- and outward-looking. For instance, migration research could inform extensively place attachment studies exploring the impact of mobility on bonding and belonging.

In addition to the above-mentioned themes, *the digital experience* requires more attention as it is a quite new and increasingly powerful factor influencing people's experience with place. This should be further researched considering how technology impacts place attachment. *Does the Internet provide a sense of place and attachment to real-world places? Does it enable the creation of a sense of identity in the cyberspace? Do places and mobility need new interpretations in the virtual reality, and how should they be explored in connection to real-life settings and feelings of belonging?*

Moreover, the new research agenda should be *more inclusive from a social point of view*, bringing to the central stage also the experiences and *attachments of the marginalised and the vulnerable*, in the framework of socio-spatial justice (Harvey, 1973, 2008; Soja, 2010). More research, having a critical perspective on power imbalances within society are needed in order to inform more sensitive public policies and support social justice, where the focus is on the humans and their attachments to place.

Within this context, further research should consider *the relationship between gender and place attachment*, as gendered spaces and gendered representations of place may impact people's understandings, emotions, and perceptions of the places they feel attached to (Rose, 2014). Some of the research questions to be explored could be the following: *How do people form bonds to gendered public and private places? What is the role of those gendered representations and meanings of place in the creation of people's place attachment? Are there differences in attachment to place between men and women that are based on gendered representations of the respective areas?*

Perhaps the proposal to examine the *emotional relationship of homeless to urban space* (and its specific non-places) sounds controversial. However, this topic has not been studied yet in the literature on place-oriented studies. Due to the social context of the phenomenon of homelessness, it would be extremely important to know the opinions of these socially discriminated people about their creation of places in public and non-public spaces and about their emotional perception of different places in the urban space.

Finally, *methodological development* can still boost research on place attachments and can enable the appearance of new perspectives on how place and people influence each other (e.g., located story-telling, innovative participatory approaches and methods, walking practices and go-along interviews as outdoor-based methods, and participant-led methods, that provide researchers with descriptions of place meanings and attachments, and immersive experiences for the researcher – cf. Rishbeth, 2014). Also, methodology related questions arise: *How do certain methods enable or constrain place attachment research? What is the researcher's role and position in relation to different methods that contribute to place attachment research?*

Therefore, a geographical perspective on place attachment is relevant and necessary for the theoretical and methodological contributions to advance place attachment scholarship. Interdisciplinary and multidisciplinary research has proved so far the diverse and plural perspectives on place and attachment to place. Considering this, we also argue in favour of supporting *the interdisciplinarity of place attachment research* because the study of human feelings and beliefs about places has been approached in relevant ways by many sciences (Geography, Psychology, Sociology, Anthropology, Architecture, History, etc.). Complex and interdisciplinary theoretical approaches are inevitable because places arise from locales that are simultaneously natural, symbolic, and social environments (Hummon, 1992, p. 253). Relationships between place and identity construction processes has been researched mostly by Geography and Social and Environmental Psychology. Geographers are trained to pay more attention to place, while psychologists to the attachment. *Interdisciplinary research involving Geography and Psychology* is necessary to put into balance the two components of place attachment in terms of answers that should inform spatial planning and public policies focusing on place, community, and individual.

At the same time, place attachment provides especially human geographers with a fertile ground to research experiences, values, meanings, representations, perceptions, and interpretations, in historical and contemporary context. These are also explored by other humanities (as Human Geography itself was conceptualised as such – Cosgrove, 1989, p. 121), and therefore interdisciplinary research on place attachment involving Human Geography and other humanities could open new perspectives.

Nevertheless, one inherent limitation of any research, and of this collective book implicitly, is that it offers only partial perspectives on the construction of place attachments. Further research, as suggested in the possible agenda described above, will address this limitation.

References

Albrecht, G., Sartore, G. M., Connor, L., Higginbotham, N., Freeman, S., Kelly, B., Stain, H., Tonna, A., & Pollard, G. (2007). Solastalgia: The distress caused by environmental change. *Australasian Psychiatry, 15*, 95–98.

Antrop, M., & Van Eetvelde, V. (2017). *Landscape perspectives: The holistic nature of landscape* (Landscape Series, 23) (p. Springer). https://link.springer.com/book/10.1007/978-94-024-1183-6

Arnstein, S. R. (1969). A ladder of citizen participation. *Journal of the American Planning Association, 35*(4), 216–224.

Banini, T. (2021). Chapter 1. Towards a methodology for constructing local territorial identities. In O.-R. Ilovan (Ed.), *Territorial identities in action* (pp. 13–39). Presa Universitară Clujeană.

Banini, T., & Ilovan, O.-R. (Eds.). (2021a). *Representing place and territorial identities in Europe. Discourses, images, and practices* (GeoJournal Library, vol. 127). Springer. https://www.springer.com/gp/book/9783030667658

Banini, T., & Ilovan, O.-R. (2021b). Introduction: Dealing with territorial/place identity representations. In T. Banini & O.-R. Ilovan (Eds.), *Representing place/territorial identity in Europe. Discourses, images, and practices* (pp. 1–19). Springer. https://doi.org/10.1007/978-3-030-66766-5_1

Blokland, T. (2009). Celebrating local histories and defining neighbourhood communities: Place-Making in a gentrified neighbourhood. *Urban Studies, 46*(8), 1593–1610.

Bovaird, T., Van Ryzin, G. G., Loeffler, E., & Parrado, S. (2015). Activating citizens to participate in collective co-production of public services. *Journal of Social Policy, 44*(1), 1–23.

Brown, B. B., & Perkins, D. D. (1992). Disruptions in place attachment. In I. Altman & S. M. Low (Eds.), *Place attachment* (pp. 279–304). Plenum Press.

Brown, G., Raymond, C. M., & Corcoran, J. (2015). Mapping and measuring place attachment. *Applied Geography, 57*, 42–53. https://doi.org/10.1016/j.apgeog.2014.12.011

Brown, G., Reed, P., & Raymond, C. M. (2020). Mapping place values: 10 lessons from two decades of public participation GIS empirical research. *Applied Geography, 116*, 102156.

Casey, E. S. (2001). Between geography and philosophy: What does it mean to be in the place-world? *Annals of the Association of American Geographers, 91*, 683–693.

Castree, N. (2009). Place: Connections and boundaries in an interdependent world. In N. J. Clifford, S. L. Holloway, S. P. Rice, & G. Valentine (Eds.), *Key concepts in geography* (2nd ed., pp. 153–172). Sage.

Cosgrove, D. (1989). Geography is everywhere: Culture and symbolism in human landscapes. In D. Gregory & R. Walford (Eds.), *Horizons in Human Geography* (pp. 118–135). Macmillan.

Cresswell, T. (2004). *Place: A short introduction*. Blackwell.

Di Masso, A., Williams, D. R., Raymond, C. M., Buchecker, M., Degenhardt, B., Devine-Wright, P., Hertzogg, A., Lewicka, M., Manzoi, L., Shahrad, A., Stedmank, R., Verbruggel, L., & von Wirth, T. (2019). Between fixities and flows: Navigating place attachments in an increasingly mobile world. *Journal of Environmental Psychology, 61*, 125–133.

Ferilli, G., Sacco, P. L., & Blessi, G. T. (2016). Beyond the rhetoric of participation: New challenges and prospects for inclusive urban regeneration. *City, Culture and Society, 7*(2), 95–100.

Gustafson, P. (2014). Place attachment in an age of mobility. In L. C. Manzo & P. Devine-Wright (Eds.), *Place attachment. Advances in theory, methods and applications* (pp. 37–48). Routledge.

Harvey, D. (1973). *Social Justice and the City*. Edward Arnold.

Harvey, D. (1996). *Justice, nature and the geography of difference*. Blackwell.

Harvey, D. (2008). The right to the city. *New Left Review, 53*, 23–40.

Hester, T. R. (2014). Do not Detach! Instructions from and for community design. In C. L. Manzo & P. Devine-Wright (Eds.), *Place attachment. Advances in theory, methods and applications* (pp. 191–206). Routledge.

Hidalgo, M. C., & Hernandez, B. (2001). Place attachment: Conceptual and empirical questions. *Journal of Environmental Psychology, 21*(3), 273–281.

Higginbotham, N., Connor, L., Albrecht, G., Freeman, S., & Agho, K. (2007). Validation of an environmental distress scale. *EcoHealth, 3*, 245–254.

Hummon, D. H. (1992). Community attachment: Local sentiment and sense of place. *Human Behavior & Environment: Advances in Theory & Research, 12*, 253–278.

Husseini de Araújo, S., & Batista da Costa, E. (2017). From social Hell to Heaven? The intermingling processes of territorial stigmatisation, agency from below and gentrification in the Varjão, Brazil. In P. Kirkness & A. Tijé-Dra (Eds.), *Negative neighbourhood reputation and place attachment. The production and contestation of territorial stigma* (pp. 158–177). Routledge.

Ilovan, O.-R. (2020). The development discourse during Socialist Romania in visual representations of the urban area. *Journal of Urban History*, 1–35. https://doi.org/10.1177/0096144220982957

Ilovan, O.-R. (2021a). Visual discourse and urban spatial identity in picture postcards during Socialist Romania (1948–1989). In T. Banini & O.-R. Ilovan (Eds.), *Representing place and territorial identities in Europe – Discourses, images, and practices* (GeoJournal Library, vol. 127) (pp. 127–142). Springer. https://doi.org/10.1007/978-3-030-66766-5_9

Ilovan, O.-R. (2021b). Visual discourse on territorial development and political identities in socialist Romania, in comics for pioneers. *Finisterra, LVI*(116), 19–48. https://doi.org/10.18055/Finis21752

Ilovan, O.-R. (Ed.). (2021c). *Territorial identities in action*. Presa Universitară Clujeană.

Ilovan, O.-R., & Doroftei, I. (Eds.). (2017). *Qualitative research in regional geography: A methodological approach*. Presa Universitară Clujeană.

Jeffrey, S. S., & Aranha, R. (2020). Cognitive mapping as a method to assess peoples' attachment to place. *Geographical Review, 112*, 1–21.

Jorgensen, B. S., & Stedman, R. C. (2001). Sense of place as an attitude: Lakeshore owners' attitudes toward their properties. *Journal of Environmental Psychology, 21*, 233–248.

Kasarda, J. D., & Janowitz, M. (1974). Community attachment in mass society. *American Sociological Review, 39*(3), 328–339.

Kirkness, P., & Tijé-Dra, A. (2017a). Conclusion: Tainted urban spaces at the intersection of urban planning, politics of identity and urban capitalism. In P. Kirkness & A. Tijé-Dra (Eds.), *Negative neighbourhood reputation and place attachment the production and contestation of territorial stigma* (pp. 252–256). Routledge.

Kirkness, P., & Tijé-Dra, A. (Eds.). (2017b). *Negative neighbourhood reputation and place attachment. The production and contestation of territorial stigma*. Routledge.

Kostanski, L. (2016). Toponymic attachment. In C. Hough (Ed.), *The Oxford handbook of names and naming* (pp. 1–18). Oxford University Press. https://www.oxfordhandbooks.com/view/10.1093/oxfordhb/9780199656431.001.0001/oxfordhb-9780199656431-e-42. Accessed 22 Mar 2022

Lai, S., & Ooi, C. S. (2015). Branded as a world heritage city: The politics afterwards. *Place Branding and Public Diplomacy, 11*, 276–292.

Lew, A. (2017). Tourism planning and place making: Place-making or placemaking? *Tourism Geographies, 19*(3), 448–466.

Löw, M. (2001). *Raumsoziologie*. Suhrkamp.

Maguire, B., & Klinkenberg, B. (2018). Visualization of place attachment. *Applied Geography, 99*, 77–88.

Mannarini, T., Tartaglia, S., Fedi, A., & Greganti, K. (2006). Image of neighborhood, self-image and sense of community. *Journal of Environmental Psychology, 26*(3), 202–214. https://doi.org/10.1016/j.jenvp.2006.07.008

Manzo, L. C. (2014). Exploring the shadow side: Place attachment in the context of stigma, displacement, and social housing. In L. C. Manzo & P. Devine-Wright (Eds.), *Place attachment. Advances in theory, methods and applications* (pp. 178–190). Routledge.

Manzo, L. C., & Perkins, D. D. (2006). Finding common ground: The importance of place attachment to community participation and planning. *Journal of Planning Literature, 20*(4), 335–350.

Markuszewska, I. (2019). *Emotional landscape: Socio-environmental conflict and place attachment. Experience from the Wielkopolska Region* (Studia I Prace z Geografii No. 70). Bogucki Wydawnictwo Naukowe.

Markuszewska, I. (2020). From NIMBY to YIMBY: When a new open cast mine creates land use conflict. In A. Kołodziejczak & L. Kaczmarek (Eds.), *Gospodarowanie gruntami na obszarach wiejskich [Land management in rural areas]* (pp. 149–168). Bogucki Wydawnictwo Naukowe.

Markuszewska, I. (2021). 'Old trees cannot be replanted': When energy investment meets farmers' resistance. *Journal of Settlements and Spatial Planning, 8*, 5–13.

Marsden, T. K. (2004). The quest for ecological modernisation: Re-spacing rural development and agri-food studies. *Sociologia Ruralis, 44*, 129–146.

Massey, D. (1994). *Space, place and gender*. Polity Press.

Matarrita-Cascante, D., Stedman, R., & Luloff, A. E. (2010). Permanent and seasonal residents' community attachment in natural amenity-rich areas: Exploring the contribution of landscape-related factors. *Environment and Behavior, 42*(2), 197–220.

McManus, P., Albrecht, G., & Graham, R. (2014). Psychoterratic geographies of the Upper Hunter region, Australia. *Geoforum, 51*, 58–65.

Müller, S., & Korsgaard, S. (2018). Resources and bridging: The role of spatial context in rural entrepreneurship. *Entrepreneurship & Regional Development, 30*(1–2), 224–255.

Mutică, P., & Ilovan, O.-R. (2022). *Advocacy for territorial and people-centered approaches to development in Romania: Place attachment based on industrial heritage*, forthcoming.

Ocejo, R. E. (2011). The early gentrifier: Weaving a nostalgia narrative on the Lower East Side. *City and Community, 10*(3), 285–310.

Ode Sang, Å., Knez, I., Gunnarsson, B., & Hedblom, M. (2016). The effects of naturalness, gender, and age on how urban green space is perceived and used. *Urban Forestry and Urban Greening, 18*, 268–276.

Oldenburg, R., & Brissett, D. (1982). The third place. *Qualitative Sociology, 5*, 265–284.

Paasi, A. (1986). The institutionalization of regions: A theoretical framework for understanding the emergence of regions and the constitution of regional identity. *Fennia, 164*(1), 105–146.

Paasi, A. (2002). Bounded spaces in the mobile world: Deconstructing "regional identity". *Tijdschrift voor Economische en Sociale Geografie, 93*(2), 137–148.

Relph, E. T. (1976). *Place and placelessness*. Pion.

Rishbeth, C. (2014). Articulating transnational attachments through on-site narratives. In C. L. Manzo & P. Devine-Wright (Eds.), *Place attachment. Advances in theory, methods and applications* (pp. 100–111). Routledge.

Rose, G. (2014). *Visual methodologies. An introduction to researching with visual materials* (3rd ed.). Sage.

Ryan, M. (2009). Mixed methodology approach to place attachment and consumption behaviour: A rural town perspective. *Electronic Journal of Business Research Methods, 7*(1), 107–116.

Scannell, L., & Gifford, R. (2010). Defining place attachment: A tripartite organizing framework. *Journal of Environmental Psychology, 30*(1), 1–10. https://doi.org/10.1016/j.jenvp.2009.09.006

Seamon, D. (2014). Place attachment and phenomenology. Thy synergetic dynamism of place. In L. C. Manzo & P. Devine-Wright (Eds.), *Place attachment. Advances in theory, methods and applications* (pp. 11–22). Routledge.

Sebastien, L. (2020). The power of place in understanding place attachments and meanings. *Geoforum, 108*, 204–216. https://doi.org/10.1016/j.geoforum.2019.11.001

Shamai, S. (1991). Sense of place: An empirical measurement. *Geoforum, 22*(3), 347–358. https://doi.org/10.1016/0016-7185(91)90017-K

Sheppard, S. R. J. (2001). Beyond visual resource management: Emerging theories of an ecological aesthetic and visible Stewardship. In S. R. J. Sheppard & H. W. Harshaw (Eds.), *Forests and landscapes – Linking ecology, sustainability and aesthetics (IUFRO Researh Series, No 6)* (pp. 149–173). CABI Publishing.

Silva, C., Kastenholz, E., & Abrantes, J. L. (2018). Linking mountain image with place-attachment. *Journal of Spatial and Organizational Dynamics, 6*(2), 140–152.

Simmel, G. (1995). Die Großstädte und das Geistesleben. In O. Rammstedt (Ed.), *Aufsätze und Abhandlungen 1901—1908. Band I* (Vol. 7, pp. 116–131). Suhrkamp.

Sipetic, N., Savić, M., & Furundžić, D. (2019). The invisible metro system: The case study of the Belgrade metro system planning. *Tunnelling and Underground Space Technology, 83*(4), 485–497.

Soja, E. W. (1996). *Thirdspace: Journeys to Los Angeles and other real-and-imagined places*. Blackwell.

Soja, E. W. (2010). *Seeking spatial justice*. University of Minnesota Press.

Tuan, Y.-F. (1991). Language and the making of place: A narrative–descriptive approach. *Annals of the Association of American Geographers, 81*(4), 684–696.

Tveit, M., Ode, Å., & Fry, G. (2006). Key concepts in a framework for analysing visual landscape character. *Landscape Research, 31*, 229–255.

Wang, Y. (2021). Building emotional GIS: A spatial investigation of place attachment for urban historic environments in Edinburgh, Scotland. In R. Madgin & J. Lesh (Eds.), *People-centred methodologies for heritage conservation* (pp. 159–176). Routledge.

Warsini, S., Mills, J., & Usher, K. (2014). Solastalgia: Living with the environmental damage caused by natural disasters. *Prehospital and Disaster Medicine, 29*(1), 87–90.

Zhang, Y. (2017). 'This is my "Wo"'. Making home in Shanghai's Lower Quarter. In P. Kirkness & A. Tijé-Dra (Eds.), *Negative neighbourhood reputation and place attachment. The production and contestation of territorial stigma* (pp. 138–157). Routledge.

Index

Milton Keynes UK
Ingram Content Group UK Ltd.
UKHW021818131023
430521UK00002B/3